D0198572

AMERICAN
SHOGUN

AMERICAN SHOGUN

GENERAL MACARTHUR, EMPEROR HIROHITO AND THE DRAMA OF MODERN JAPAN

ROBERT HARVEY

THE OVERLOOK PRESS

WOODSTOCK & NEW YORK

For my Mother

First published in the United States in 2006 by
The Overlook Press, Peter Mayer Publishers, Inc.
Woodstock & New York

WOODSTOCK:
One Overlook Drive
Woodstock, NY 12498
www.overlookpress.com
[for individual orders, bulk and special sales, contact our Woodstock office]

NEW YORK:
141 Wooster Street
New York, NY 10012

PHOTO CREDITS:
1, 3, 4, 5, 6, 7, 10, 11, 13, 15, 16, 17, 20, 21, 22, 23, 26, 27, 29: Bettmann/Corbis;
2, 9: Hulton-Deutsch Collection/Corbis; 8, 12, 14, 18, 19, 24, 25, 28: CORBIS
Used with permission

The paper used in this book meets the requirements for paper permanence as described in the ANSI Z39.48-1992 standard.

Cataloging-in-Publication Data is available from the Library of Congress

Book design and type formatting by Bernard Schleifer
Manufactured in the United States of America
ISBN 1-58567-682-9
1 3 5 7 9 10 8 6 4 2

CONTENTS

PREFACE

I OWE A GREAT DEBT TO MANY WHO HAVE HELPED ME WITH MY TRAVELING and research in Japan, the Philippines, Burma, Thailand, Singapore and the United States. They include Andrew and Cherry Williams, Simon Scott-Plummer, David Warren, David and Sheila Atterton, Lady Pilcher and Raymond Eyre. I am also particularly grateful to the Japanese Embassy in London, the Foreign Press Institute in Tokyo, the Press Department of the Japanese Foreign Ministry, the Foreign Ministry, the Self-Defence Agency, the Ministry of International Trade and Industry, the Japanese Employers Association and the Hiroshima Peace Memorial Museum. In the United States I owe special thanks to the MacArthur Memorial Archive in Norfolk, Virginia, and to Raymond Seitz, former U.S. ambassador in London. I also owe a huge debt to Jonathan Fenby for his invaluable advice about China.

I owe special thanks to my agent, Gillon Aitken, for his unflagging encouragement and advice, to my superbly professional editors Peter Mayer and Roland Philipps, and to my tolerant, always cheerful and painstaking assistant, Jenny Thomas, who catches almost all of my errors, and her historian husband Geoffrey for alerting me to new research on MacArthur. I also owe my warmest thanks to my mother and sister Antonella, and her husband, Sharif Abdullah al-Hussein for their support during the writing of this book. Finally, most of all I would like to thank my wife Jane and son Oliver, who put up with it all.

A bibliography of main sources is included at the end. Certain books stand out as having provided clear signposts to the direction of my research, although responsibility for my judgments and errors is, of course, entirely my own. On the American side they include Douglas MacArthur's own *Reminiscences*; Arnold Brackman's highly readable *The Other Nuremberg*;

Michael Schaller's brilliant analysis in *The American Occupation of Japan*; William Manchester's readable and microscopic examination of MacArthur's life, *American Caesar*; and Geoffrey Perret's fine military biography, *Old Soldiers Never Die*.

On the Japanese side, deserving special mention are Tashiaki Kawahara's *Hirohito and His Times*; the Pacific War Research Society's *Japan's Longest Day*; John Dower's *Embracing Defeat*, a magisterial, even-handed and fascinating study of the American occupation of Japan; Herbert Bix's *Hirohito and the Making of Modern Japan*, a well-crafted and well-researched indictment of the Emperor; Karol van Wolferen's *The Enigma of Japanese Power*; and Meirion and Susie Harries's *Soldiers of the Sun*. The many other scholars I owe a debt to are listed in the bibliography.

Introduction

THE RELATIONSHIP BETWEEN THE UNITED STATES AND THE REST OF THE world has never perhaps been so complex or pressing than today. It is commonplace among many to think of America as the new "hegemon," "megapower" or global superpower. It is often forgotten that the United States was born in opposition to empire and for more than a century was largely self-contained, pursuing its global economic interests but with only a brief imperialist flurry in the early 1900s, possessing an army which ranked just sixteenth in the world as late as 1930.

But there was an exception. The extraordinary political, military and economic duel between the United States and its principal Pacific rival, Japan, that spanned most of the first half of the twentieth century provides a penetratingly illuminating insight into America's ability to relate to other countries with entirely different religions, cultures, ethnic makeups and political systems as well as much older histories.

This book is a narrative history of that duel across the Pacific as told through the personal stories of the two principal protagonists on either side, Emperor Hirohito of Japan and General Douglas MacArthur. Both were remarkable men. The diffident, uncharismatic, apparently obtuse Hirohito survived as god-ruler of the Japanese for some six decades through internal strife, war, defeat, occupation and economic victory. Hirohito came to rule over a minor power, which within two decades presided over the greatest empire in Asian history, then became a vassal state of America's and then a quarter of a century later reemerged as the world's second strongest economy after the United States.

The domineering MacArthur was a First World War hero who became America's most powerful soldier during the Great Depression, experienced humiliation and crushing defeat in the Philippines, followed by victory over

Japan and proconsular rule as virtually a one-man dictator for six years, wielding more power over a subject people than any American has in history. MacArthur's career spanned a quite astonishing tranche of American history: his father was a hero of the American Civil War while MacArthur himself died dispensing advice to Lyndon B. Johnson about the Vietnam War. During the last three decades of his life the American army grew from being a minor player to the most powerful military machine the world has ever seen, the United States itself from being an isolationist dabbler in world affairs to its sole superpower.

It is obvious enough that MacArthur's experience of handling the American occupation of Japan contains immense lessons for the American occupations of Iraq and Afghanistan and for American intervention abroad generally. The skill with which this remarkable man worked alongside and through existing Japanese institutions should have been an object lesson for the American authorities in Iraq. Similarly his many mistakes and his often overreaching hubris also deserves intense study. But there are also more complex lessons to be derived form the interplay between one of the newest cultures in the world and one of the oldest, a republican democracy and an absolute monarchy with an unbroken line of succession stretching back 2,000 years. Japan was the first country to which America attempted to export democracy and political and economic freedom with, as this book relates, decidedly mixed results.

The relationship between the most powerful Pacific powers, who today are the world's two largest economies, also deserves renewed attention as Japan emerges from decades-long stagnation and begins to reassert itself economically and politically both in Asia and overseas. Japan has for long acted as a kind of American catspaw in stabilizing and balancing the inherently unstable rising economies of East Asia. Today Japan seems to be striving for a more independent role, hopefully eschewing its old nationalism for a more mature approach to the continuing peace of the region.

But it is not only as a forerunner to today's events that I considered the duel across the Pacific worth revisiting. These two extraordinary men take on a still larger dimension as we examine recent historical research. We have learned more than ever before about the creation of modern Japan, the origins of Japanese militarism, as well as the extent of Hirohito's culpability in the decision to go to war; and about MacArthur's near-takeover of Washington during the 1932 Bonus March, his strategy for winning the Pacific War, one of the most brilliant ever devised in military history, his dispute with Truman over the dropping of the atomic bombs on Hiroshima and Nagasaki and—perhaps most interesting of all—his hopes of over-throwing the communist regime in China during the Korean War. His battle of wits with Hirohito reached its apogee when, as American Shogun, he attempted to rebuild Japan along American lines, while the supposedly powerless Emperor and his advisers subtly frustrated him and rallied the Japanese people around a reinvented nationalism, then based on economic power. This book seeks to provide a new perspective on all these events.

The need to cover both lives and events in each country inevitably leads to some overlapping and interruptions of the narrative, but I have tried to keep these to a minimum. The reader must be the judge whether I have succeeded. There have of course been many biographies of MacArthur and many of Hirohito but none, so far as I am aware, that attempted to weave the story into a single whole, as told from both sides, as surely it should. With America currently engaging with very different cultures and international challenges, now seems to be the right moment to revisit the Manichean struggle between the most powerful country in the West and the most powerful in the East and the two extraordinary men that personified it.

Author's Note

THE TERM SHOGUN MEANS "ARMY LEADER" (*SHO* MEANS LEADER, *GUN* means army). It is most familiar to Westerners through the novels of James Clavell, loosely based on the exploits of an English adventurer who reached Japan in the seventeenth century.

The first shallow penetration of Japan had been achieved by Portuguese Jesuits in the sixteenth century. They were followed by the crew of the Dutch ship *Liefde*, only a fifth of whose crew of 100 had survived the punishing journey, who landed at Bungo Harbour on April 12, 1600. William Adams, a huge Englishman, was the strongest among them. He came to the notice of Ieyasu Tokugawa, soon to become Shogun—military ruler—of all Japan, who instructed Adams to teach him Western astronomy, mathematics and geography as well as his trades of shipbuilding and piloting. Adams was honored with the title of *hatamoto* (flag-bearer), a new name, Anjin Sama (Mr. Pilot) and an extensive country estate. When the first British ship, the *Clove*, arrived three years later, the crew were astonished to find their fellow Englishman attired in Japanese robes, serving the Shogun.

Two hundred and fifty years later Ieyasu's distant descendants had a rude awakening with the arrival of a squadron of four "black ships," two of them steamships, commanded by the American Commodore Matthew Perry. Perry, a tough-minded, plainspeaking 60-year-old, had been authorized by President Fillmore in 1853 to act as he chose: "any departure from usage or any error of judgment will be viewed with indulgence." His assignment was to open up trade with Japan, end the practice of treating stranded foreign crews there harshly, and generally assert American naval might.

He arrived, scorned minor emissaries, and handed over a letter demanding port facilities and other concessions to a senior official, before sailing up Yedo (Tokyo) Bay to within sight of the city, implicitly threatening to bombard it and interrupt food and other supplies, almost all of which came by sea. The Shogun's minister acknowledged helplessly "everyone has pointed out that we are without a navy and our coasts are undefended . . . our policy shall be to avoid any definite answer to their request, while at the same time maintaining a peaceful demeanor." Perry sailed away having made his point.

Perry returned even more threateningly in February 1854 with seven ships, and forced the Japanese to sign the Treaty of Kanagawa, which for the first time opened the ports of Hakodate and Shimoda to the Americans for supplies and trade and provided for some consular relations.

No one could have guessed that the salutary shock of Perry's arrival, which triggered revolutionary change in Japan in the shape of the Meiji Restoration, would be echoed less than a century of Japanese economic development and military imperialism later by American conquest and the imposition of an American Shogun, Douglas MacArthur, to rule over the Mikado and this proudest of peoples.

PROLOGUE

O N SEPTEMBER 27, 1945, THERE OCCURRED ONE OF THE MOST extraordinary meetings in human history, that between the conquering MacArthur and the defeated Japanese god-emperor, Hirohito, just two and a half weeks after the latter surrendered following the only use ever of atomic bombs in war. On both sides the meeting was laden with a symbolism which each man and their staff had carefully prepared for: it was a public relations duel of the keenest kind, and one which the Americans left feeling they had won and the Japanese they had lost, while the reverse was probably true. Hirohito was by then fairly certain from all sources that he would be allowed to continue in office; he was perhaps unaware, though, that MacArthur was his foremost champion, or he would have been less nervous.

MacArthur, perhaps the foremost practitioner to date of public relations in American military history, was preparing both to humiliate the Emperor publicly for the consumption of his watching American audience back home, while displaying an almost excessive private sympathy for the predicament of this nominally absolute ruler of a conquered nation. The result was a curious clash of interests that would have been comical, if it were not so momentous, in this meeting between conqueror and conquered, Shogun and Emperor, barbarian and divinity.

MacArthur had predicted, to those that urged him to summon the Emperor, that the mountain would eventually come to him. To order Hirohito to visit, he explained, "would be to outrage the feelings of the Japanese people and to make a martyr of the Emperor in their eyes. No, I shall wait, and in time the Emperor will voluntarily come to see me. In this case the patience of the East rather than the haste of the West will best serve our purpose."

On a preliminary visit, Imperial Grand Chamberlain Fujita had been kept waiting in the lobby—an unpardonable insult to the Japanese, who are punctual beyond belief. He had been ushered into MacArthur's presence and made a speech of ludicrous formality. The palace official, it seemed, could not lower himself actually to ask for an invitation for the Emperor. The foreign minister, Shigeru Yoshida, had to perform the demeaning task later.

Days afterward, the imperial Daimler and four other cars set out at 10 A.M. in a small motorcade with just two motorcycle outriders. According to one Japanese observer, the Emperor was "wearing an extraordinarily somber expression." The Emperor's cortege emerged through the palace gates, across the moat and climbed up the hill beside it; the traffic lights turned red at the Toranomon crossroad, and the Emperor's car stopped— something unheard of in pre-occupation days, when the traffic was halted 30 minutes before his car's departure and all vehicles would be cleared from his route.

Hirohito was wearing a morning coat, striped trousers and a top hat. At the embassy compound, he was not greeted by the supreme commander at the entrance, another piece of unpardonable lèse-majéste to the Japanese. MacArthur, for his part, felt he was bestowing "every honor due to a sovereign": he had gone so far as to keep the meeting wholly secret in advance; there would be no crowds or press photographers to record the humiliation of his adversary.

As Hirohito got out of his car in the embassy compound, he looked bewildered under the gaze of the unsmiling Americans waiting for him. General Bonner Fellers suddenly stepped forward smiling with his hand extended and said, "Welcome, sir." The Emperor was ushered upstairs; his retinue of nine palace officials, including his senior adviser, the Lord Privy Seal, Marquis Koichi Kido, were kept waiting anxiously downstairs. Major Faubion Bowers, MacArthur's aide and interpreter, described Hirohito as looking "frightened to death. As I took his top hat, I noticed his hands were trembling. On meeting MacArthur on the threshold of the drawing room, he bowed low, very low, a servant's bow."

The general was unsmiling and shook his hand formally. An army photographer took three photographs of the two men, one of which was unusable. MacArthur was wearing the standard dress of the occupation forces—a tan army shirt and trousers, with no tie. He stood casually, his legs slightly apart, his hands on his hips. The Emperor, a head shorter, looked as though he could barely hold himself upright against a stress-induced weakness of the legs: in one photograph his legs are straight and his body bearing up; in the other, they are slightly parted, one in front of the other, as though about to give way.

The Japanese press and its readers were to be shocked by MacArthur's studied insolence; he should have been wearing at least full general's uniform in front of the Emperor. It was inconceivable that the American could have been unaware of the impact the photograph and his manner of dress would have. A whole variety of messages were implicit: this was conqueror and conquered. This was a deliberate humiliation of a "divine" emperor: if the institution was to be preserved, it was also to be stripped of pompousness, prostration and deference: it was to be democratized with a vengeance. Above all, MacArthur's pose had been prepared for public opinion at home: his grim insolence was calculated to impress those Americans who had been appalled that the Emperor was not to be prosecuted, and even preserved in office.

New World informality rubbed up against Old World manners and royal modesty, and while there could be no doubt who was dominant physically, to Japanese minds it was Hirohito that towered over MacArthur. Unassuming, modest, in formal dress as a mark of respect toward this merely mortal commoner *gaijin*—the contemptuous Japanese word for foreigner—the Emperor shone in his countrymen's eyes beside his ill-mannered, tieless, jacketless, slovenly hands-on-hips guest. To Americans, still seething with anger against the Japanese atrocities of the war, the master of public relations that was MacArthur had the contemptuous, casual look of a ruler standing beside a colonial subject, a jailer beside a man on trial for his life—which at that meeting Hirohito feared he was. The symbolizm of the two stances was poignant to both sides.

Then they talked, with only Hirohito's personal interpreter present. The Emperor, whose hands were still trembling, did not raise the cup of coffee he had been offered, but accepted a cigarette from MacArthur. For a man who had been accustomed to complete obeisance from anyone he had ever met, including the most powerful in the land, to have to impress and even defer to a foreigner and a commoner must have been an extraordinary experience. Only fragments of the conversation, which was never revealed in full, survive.

It is said that Hirohito was still slightly nervous of being arrested after the detention of his former prime minister, Hideki Tojo, days earlier, and that his advisers were even frightened that he might be poisoned—which may also explain his attitude to the coffee. Yet it seems unlikely that his advisers can have been so ill-informed about American behavior as to believe that either event, even if probable, would take place in front of MacArthur himself. Hirohito's nervousness may have stemmed instead from the message he now sought to impart. MacArthur takes up the story:

> I met him cordially, and recalled that I had at one time been received by his father at the close of the Russo-Japanese war. He was nervous and the stress of the past months showed plainly. I dismissed everyone but his own interpreter, and we sat down before an open fire at one end of the long reception hall. I offered him an American cigarette, which he took with thanks. I noticed how his hands shook as I lighted it for him. I tried to make it as easy for him as I could, but I knew how deep and dreadful must be the agony of his humiliation.
>
> I had an uneasy feeling he might plead his own cause against indictment as a war criminal . . . But my fears were groundless. What he said was this: "I come to you, General MacArthur, to offer myself to the judgment of the powers you represent as the one to bear sole responsibility for every political and military decision made and action taken by my people in the conduct of war." A tremendous impression swept me. This courageous assumption of a responsibility implicit with death, a responsibility clearly belied by facts of which I was fully aware, moved me to the very marrow of my bones. He was an Emperor by inherent birth, but in that instant, I knew I faced the First Gentleman of Japan in his own right.
>
> When he left, I started to tell my wife how he looked, but she stopped me with her rippling laugh, saying, "Oh, I saw him. Arthur [MacArthur's young son] and I were peeking behind the red curtains." It's a funny world, but delightful, no matter how you figure it.

The offer was probably sincere, and certainly courageous—he could not have been sure the Americans would have rejected it. Yet its real purpose must have been to underline to the Americans that if he was to be spared immunity from prosecution—as his advisers had every reason to believe that he would be—the grounds for convicting his subordinates were flimsy indeed. As he had assumed responsibility, he must be prosecuted or pardoned, and his subordinates likewise. The Americans perhaps deliberately turned a blind eye to this gambit.

The general and the Emperor chatted slightly less tensely about other matters. MacArthur is said to have praised Hirohito for his role in ending the war. "The peace party did not prevail until the bombing of Hiroshima created a situation which could be dramatized" the Emperor replied. When asked why he could not prevent the war in the first place, Hirohito is said to have replied—with remarkable obstinacy in the circumstances—"It wasn't clear to me that our course was unjustified. Even now I am not sure how historians will allocate responsibility for the war." MacArthur's terse summing up of the meeting omits any account of whether he imposed conditions on the Emperor at this most favorable opportunity to do so: in particular, whether he required the Emperor to renounce his divinity, which occurred only months later, dressed up, as both sides preferred, as an initiative of the Japanese themselves.

The meeting ended on a much warmer note than it began: the two men appeared cordial as they emerged, and MacArthur even accompanied Hirohito to his car. However, he did not shake the Emperor's hand as he departed, and turned on his heels before the imperial cars left. Hirohito was seen to be very cheerful and relieved on the return journey. He had been publicly humiliated, but personally rehabilitated; he, the institution he embodied, and the system he presided over were all to be spared. MacArthur has the last word:

> The Emperor called on me often after that, our conversations ranging over most of the problems of the world. I always explained carefully the underlying reasons for the occupation policy, and I found he had a more thorough grasp of the democratic concept than almost any Japanese with whom I talked. He played a major role in the spiritual regeneration of Japan, and his loyal co-operation and influence had much to do with the success of the occupation.

PART I
WORLDS APART

1 : THE LITTLE ADJUTANT

IT IS ALMOST IMPOSSIBLE TO CONCEIVE OF MEN GROWING TO MANHOOD IN AS different cultures, backgrounds, circumstances, experiences, or with such completely opposing personalities as the two who met on that fateful September day. They were divided by race, nationality, religion, age, the centuries of their birth, class, family history, the character of their parents, schooling, upbringing, wealth, state of health, interests, sporting prowess, intellectual attainment, appearance and height. One was the representative of the oldest monarchy on earth, a supposedly unbroken 2,000-year-old line descended directly from the sun goddess, Amaterasu Omikami, and thus a living god, reigning over an ancient, crowded land, just emerging from a kind of military dictatorship. The other was the son of a middle-class American military family with pretensions to high birth from one of the youngest countries on the planet, just a century old when he was born, an anti-feudal land of vigor, and restless expansion. They had one thing in particular in common: a martinet-like stiffness, the product of a military upbringing in the one and of a fierce royal upbringing in the other.

Douglas MacArthur's clear, decisive, penetrating eyes first opened on January 26, 1880, at the dusty frontier outpost of Little Rock, Arkansas, in the spartan wooden-planked Arsenal barracks. Later MacArthur was to attempt to stretch his lineage even further than Hirohito, citing the ancient Scottish adage: "there is nothing older except the hills, MacArthurs and the devil." He jumped seamlessly to the "tradition of the family . . . link with the heroic lords of King Arthur and the Knights of the Round Table" and then fast-forwarded again to the fourteenth century when the MacArthur branch of the Campbell Clan, allied to Robert the Bruce, fought the Argyll Branch to a standstill until the reign of James I of Scotland a century later when, after the defeat of their chieftain in 1427, they retired to the shores of Loch Awe near Glasgow.

Nearly 400 years later, in 1825 a widow of the clan set sail for the new country of America taking with her her 11-year-old son Arthur, grandfather of Douglas. Thus, in American lineage, MacArthur was not of Revolutionary stock, still less a founding father: rather he was solid third-generation post-Revolutionary American, and one may surmise from a fairly humble branch of the Highland clan from the fact that he does not specify which. Clearly, though, there was some money. Settling in Chicope Falls, Massachusetts, Arthur attended a reputable school, Wesleyan, before moving to New York, where he was called to the bar in 1840.

Arthur was soon climbing the social hierarchy of his adopted country at a formidable rate. He married well, Aurelia, daughter of Sarah Barney Belchior, whose descendants were to include the aristocratic Franklin Roosevelt and Winston Churchill, through the latter's American mother. They had a son, Arthur Junior, and at the age of 35, like so many ambitious, hopeful Americans, they traveled westward, to Milwaukee, where within two years he had become city attorney and, three years after that, was elected as a Democrat to become lieutenant-governor of the state of Wisconsin—only for the governor on his ticket to be convicted of fraud. Arthur stepped into his place—for just five days, before the defeated Republican candidate was proclaimed the winner.

The setback was temporary. In 1867 he was elected judge of the Second Judicial Circuit, the most important in the state, coming to the attention of President Andrew Johnson, who made him leader of the American delegation to the 1868 Grand Exposition in Paris. In 1870, at the age of 56, Johnson appointed MacArthur associate justice of the Supreme Court of the District of Columbia. He won a reputation for being stern but fair, and for doing good works, sitting on several charitable boards during his 18 years in office. On retiring his intellectual powers were undimmed: he wrote ten books, including one on Mary Queen of Scots, illustrating an unexpected romantic streak in this pillar of rectitude. He died at the age of 82 while on holiday in Atlantic City.

From middling beginnings, Arthur MacArthur had elevated his family to second rank in the land, as a minor politician and respected civic dignitary. A large, impressively bearded figure to his young grandson, he appeared to rub shoulders with the highest in the land at his comfortable home in Washington, then a small provincial town, and made a striking impression, no doubt seeding the boy's interest in politics and power. He had the huge intellect and unexpected sense of humor that were to emerge later in Douglas.

But it was his parents who were responsible for the dominant strain in Douglas's life. Arthur MacArthur Junior showed the same penetrating intellectual curiosity as his lawyerly father. But he was also a tearaway. Short, with a mischievous rough-diamond face and tousled, thick long hair, he showed an immediate fascination with military life as civil war approached to rip America asunder. When war broke out he was just 16; he sought to volunteer for the Union side. His father instead sent him to the local military academy, where he performed well and was recommended for the United States Military Academy.

A friend of his father, Senator Doolittle of Wisconsin, took him to see the President in person to seek his patronage. Abraham Lincoln, tall and magisterial, promised to recommend the short, sturdy youngster for a vacancy the following year. But he would not wait. At the age of 17 he was given the post of first lieutenant and adjutant of the 24th Wisconsin Volunteer Infantry, soon to become a legend in the fighting. When he arrived, his voice nervous and still only breaking, his new commanding officer exclaimed, "I'll write the governor and ask him to send me a man for an adjutant, instead of a boy." He was immediately labeled "the little adjutant."

Determined to prove himself, the teenager plunged into his first battle in October 1862 at Perryville. There he impressed General Philip Sheridan so much that he was promoted to captain. At Murereesboro in Tennessee a bloody three-day battle began in the raw chill of New Year's Day. There the boy captain came into his own. As his son later described the action:

> Fourteen times that day the Wisconsin regiment changed front until, at the end, it was facing directly toward the rear of its original line of battle—and, strange as it may seem, occupying its original breastworks in the opposite direction. The carnage was merciless. The regiment lost nearly 40 percent of its strength. General Sill was killed. Every mounted officer of the 24th was down except the adjutant. In effect, he became its commander. He was everywhere, rallying the ranks, reorganizing the companies, holding on with tooth and nail. The indomitable Sheridan was roaring in his ears, "Pivot, Arthur, pivot! Roll with the punch! He must not turn you!" And when Sheridan rode up that night he patted the lad and with a grin, when he saw the 24th in its original rifle pits facing the other way, said, "Arthur, my boy, congratulations. You haven't lost a foot of ground."

After a bout of typhoid, the little adjutant was back in action at the famous Battle of Missionary Ridge, overlooking Chattanooga (later of choo-choo fame for its sprawling railway yards). The 46,000-strong Confederate Army held the ridge in that grey November of 1863, while the

59,000-strong Union army under General Ulysses Grant was running out of supplies in the valley below. The 24th Wisconsin was ordered to take rifle positions at the bottom of the ridge, a steep, jagged mountain pitted with boulders and gullies rising to 1,000 feet. When this difficult task was achieved under withering fire from above, there seemed nothing to do but retreat.

Instead, without being ordered—a gesture by General Sheridan may have been misinterpreted—and with the 18-year-old adjutant at their head accompanying the color sergeant and two corporals, the 18,000-strong army climbed upward under that grimmest of military disadvantages—ascending a hill under heavy fire from a superior force. Grant turned furiously to his aides, and asked who had ordered the men on this suicidal mission.

No one knew. Arthur climbed onward toward the enemy until he was able at last to plant the colors on the crest of the ridge before collapsing as the Union army routed the Confederates to take the hill.

His fellow officers elected him major. This achievement at Missionary Ridge was no flash-in-the-pan. At Kennesaw Mountain he took part in another suicidal armed attack against an entrenched enemy line on a hill, and was shot through the arm and chest; but his heart was saved by a thick leather wallet. Marching through Georgia the teenager fought in no fewer than 13 battles over a four-month period. He was now appointed colonel—at 19 the youngest officer of that rank in the entire Union army. When he attempted to cast his ballot in the 1864 presidential election, he was challenged as being too young—and his entire regiment refused to vote in sympathy.

In November 1864 he fought heroically in another desperate struggle, the Battle of Franklin. As Arthur and his adjutant were having supper, the Confederates suddenly broke through near their position at the weak center of the Union lines. Arthur's horse was shot from under him and he was wounded in the shoulder and chest.

After recovering from his wounds, Arthur encountered an adversary of an altogether more formidable kind in New Orleans, when two ladies insisted on seeing the general he had just been visiting. As his son retold it:

> The stillness of the dingy office was broken by the voice of the older woman. "I will at once come to the point. We must have the temporary use of transport facilities to move our cotton. Your country has no wish to

antagonize the British to the point of joining the South in the war, and consequently allows blockade running. It would accordingly not regard with dissatisfaction the use of your wagons. In return, here is two hundred and fifty thousand dollars in gold certificates. And, if you need other inducements." she added with a smile, "this young lady will supply them." And with a bow they walked out, leaving the young lady's address on the desk.

My father said his knees were knocking together as they had never done in battle. But the general's voice was crisp and clear as he turned to him and dictated the following dispatch:

"To the President of the United States:

"I have just been offered two hundred and fifty thousand dollars and the most beautiful woman I have ever seen to betray my trust. I am depositing the money with the Treasury of the United States and request immediate relief from this command. They are getting close to my price."

MacArthur resumed his journey to rejoin his regiment and lead it in triumph back to Milwaukee, having lost two thirds of its officers and men. In 1865, the teenage colonel was again a civilian attempting to study law. He could not settle down, and within months had joined the regular army, first as a lowly second lieutenant, then being quickly promoted to full lieutenant and to captain.

He was sent out to the most romantic of outposts in the most romantic of times in America's formative legend—the taming of the Wild West. He fought the native Americans at Utah and Wyoming and variously encountered Jesse James, Wild Bill Hickock and Buffalo Bill. He stood guard at the Union Pacific Railroad as it moved to link up with the Central Pacific line coming from the West Coast. He witnessed the great drought of the 1870s, which sent thousands of cowboys into the range in search of a living and in struggle against one another.

At the age of 29 in 1874 on a visit to New Orleans, he met his match at a Mardi Gras ball. Mary Pinkney (Pinky) Harding was just 22, strikingly sensuous-looking in photographs from that time, with a beautiful complexion, a full mouth and a pretty, extremely determined chin: but her two dominant features were wide, penetrating eyes beneath level eyebrows and a proud prominent nose that stopped her just short of being beautiful. She was of second-tier southern origin, the daughter of a rich Virginian cotton merchant, and of a far more distinguished background than Arthur: her ancestors dated back to the Jamestown settlement, had fought with Washington and Andrew Jackson, and her brothers had fought in the

Confederate army under General Robert Lee. She had spent most of the Civil War unaffected at the family's summer home in North Carolina.

The Yankee war hero unsurprisingly was strongly disapproved of as a northern upstart by these southern aristocrats. When they were married a year later at her family's mansion, Riveredge, in Norfolk, Virginia, the brothers stayed away. Three children followed swiftly: Arthur III, Malcolm and, on January 26, 1880, Douglas. Malcolm died of measles at the age of five in 1883.

The following year Captain MacArthur was ordered to march the nearly 300 miles from Fort Washington to Fort Selden, 60 miles from El Paso, to fight Geronimo's marauders. Little Douglas's first memories were of the march, and the following three years were, for the two little boys and their friend William Hughes, son of the company's first lieutenant, pure heaven, being treated as mascots by the two officers and 46 soldiers in this quasi-desert outpost.

When Douglas was six the family moved to comparative civilization at Fort Leavenworth, Kansas. Young Douglas now attended regular school, where he yearned still for the freedom of the west. His father was an impressive figure: the heroic "boy colonel" was now a ripe 41, and still only a captain who had served dutifully although without distinction in remote outposts, such was the backlog of appointments in the federal army. He had grown a small mustache, put on weight and gravitas through his years of minor command and was soon to wear a pince-nez, which gave him a remarkable resemblance to the later President Theodore Roosevelt. His mind was as keen as ever, however, even in the wilds, and he devoured books on history and constitutional matters, as well as the classics, by the shelf-full (he was eventually to leave 4,000 volumes to his son).

His 34-year-old wife, Pinky, made a vivid impression to a contemporary woman as a vivacious young southern aristocrat of proud bearing: "in my picture of her there is a lot of white muslin dress swishing around and a blaze of white New Mexican sunlight, and in the midst of it this slender, vital creature that I have never forgotten." His eldest son Arthur was a tall, good-looking 10-year-old while the short, seven-year-old Douglas was still wearing girl's clothes, as was fashionable in many households at the time. Both were lively outdoor children, but were already acquiring some of the military bearing of their father and the southern hauteur of their mother.

In 1889 recognition came at last to Arthur MacArthur, after some string-pulling by his father, now a distinguished retired judge in Washington:

he was promoted to major and appointed assistant adjutant-general. He had been commended as "beyond doubt the most distinguished Captain in the Army of the United States for gallantry and good conduct in war. He is a student, a master of his profession, has legal ability which fits him for the position, is exceptional in habit, temperate at all times, yet modest withall."

Arthur served there with distinction and Pinky had at last come into her own. But the nine-year-old Douglas was unimpressed. Three years later Arthur joined the National Academy at Annapolis. A year later the major was ordered to command the garrison at Fort Sam Houston, Texas, a considerable one, and the delighted Douglas's school grades immediately improved at the West Texas Military Academy. He now also excelled on the sportsfield, becoming quarterback of the football team, and tennis champion of the school. The next four years, between the ages of 13 and 16, were "without doubt the happiest of my life," Douglas recalled.

In 1896 his father was ordered to St Paul, Minnesota, to command the Department of the Dakotas. Douglas lived with his mother at the Plankinton House hotel, trotting to school every day two miles away, while his father joined him every weekend. There was forged the inseparable bond between strong-willed mother and son that was to characterize this extraordinary man throughout much of his adult life.

When the time arrived for exams to enter West Point, his mother comforted him with her unusual mixture of solicitude and steely resolve: "Doug, you'll win if you don't lose your nerve. You must believe in yourself, my son, or no one else will believe in you. Be self-confident, self-reliant, and even if you don't make it, you will know you have done your best. Now, go to it." He performed splendidly. His marks were 99.3 against the next man's 77.9. He scored 700 points out of a possible 750.

Douglas suffered from spinal curvature, which disqualified him from the academy—and was to be one of the few things the young MacArthur had in common with the still unborn Emperor of Japan. With the help of a local physician, the young American overcame this through careful, regular exercise. The youngster, brought up in skirts and long hair until the age of seven, had now matured into a tall, muscular, slim young man. His face, characterized in boyhood by huge, questioning, melancholy, dreamy eyes, had now hardened into good-looking, chiseled, strong features. He had inherited his mother's, not his father's, looks—the broad, firm mouth, the dominant, hawk-like nose, above all the strong eyes beneath the level brows, not as haughty as his mother's. His dark hair, faraway eyes and slightly amused expression coupled with teenage uncertainty contrived to give him a slightly raffish look, and he didn't impress the girls with his natural shyness: in particular he was spurned by the daughter of Senator John Lendrum Mitchell. He wrote a wistful poem:

> Fair Western girl with life awhirl
> Of love and fancy free
> 'Tis thee I love
>   All things above
> Why wilt thou not love me?

2 : WEST POINT

OUGLAS'S SUCCESSFUL ENTRANCE TO WEST POINT WAS TO MARK THE first turning point in his life: a second event the same month—June 1898—was to be equally decisive in kindling a lifelong fascination with the Far East. At the age of 53, after a career of youthful success and adult frustration, Arthur MacArthur at last was given a major command, and was on track for the very highest positions in the American army. With the declaration of war against Spain, the now Lieutenant-Colonel MacArthur had fully expected to be posted to take part in the projected invasion of Cuba; instead he was appointed brigadier-general at the head of nearly 5,000 volunteers spearheading General Wesley Merritt's 11,000-strong expeditionary force to wrest the Philippines from Spain.

It was to be the beginning of a nearly half-century family association with the islands. His eighteen-year-old son sought to enlist in the Philippines as his father had in the Civil War, but the latter insisted he attend West Point to prepare himself for fighting "of a magnitude far beyond this." The impact of his father's promotion on the youth can be readily imagined. Already proud, slightly aloof, dreaming of greatness, extremely sensitive, thoughtful and determined, it seemed that real stature had at last come in sight for the family. For the intensely ambitious Pinky, it was no more than long overdue.

With Arthur's departure for his new command, she continued to care for Douglas. A year later, in June 1899, the two of them arrived at the U.S. Military Academy at West Point in its scenic setting under thickly forested hills overlooking the Hudson River where, some 120 years earlier, the defection of its commander Benedict Arnold to the British had so nearly resulted in its capture by the British and America's defeat in the War of Independence. A little further down, Craney's Hotel overlooked the river. Mrs. MacArthur decided to take up residence there to be close to her son. This was not all that unusual—Franklin Roosevelt at Harvard had the same experience—particularly with her husband serving overseas. But it repeated the pattern of maternal influence, even domination, that was to characterize MacArthur for the next 36 years.

He was now to undergo the first real ordeal of his life. As a "plebe"— new boy—he was given quarters in "Beast's Barracks" for his first few weeks as a cadet and subjected to the time-honored practice of "hazing"—bullying. Senior cadets made him recite his father's Civil War record over and over again; he was made to "brace"—stand immobile for an hour; he was forced to "eagle"—practice interminable knee bends over broken glass at the risk of injury when he grew tired. Afterward, in his tent, according to observers he was hysterical and his legs thrashed spasmodically on the floor, but he was determined that no one but his closest classmates should know about this. He was spared even worse traditional tortures, such as being plunged into hot steam, being forced to run a gauntlet as icy water was thrown upon him, or being made to slide naked on a splintered wooden board.

A fellow plebe died under these initiation rites, and a congressional inquiry was called. Douglas was called upon to testify. This plunged him into the serious moral dilemma of choosing between the two iron rules of his mother—"never lie, never tattle." MacArthur told the story later:

> Under questioning I fully explained all the circumstances, but refused to divulge the names of the upper classmen involved. My father and mother had taught me those two immutable principles—never to lie, never to tattle. But here was a desperate situation for me. If the court insisted and ordered me to reveal the names, and I refused to obey the order, it would in all likelihood mean my dismissal and the end of all my hopes and dreams. It would be so easy and expedient to yield, to tell, and who would blame me?
>
> Although more than sixty years have come and gone since then, I can still feel the beads of sweat on my brow, still feel my knees giving way under me and that dreadful nausea that I had felt once before when faced with my competitive examination at the city hall in Milwaukee. I did my best to fend off the question, to dodge the issue, but I was no match for the shrewd old heads who sat in judgment. And then the order came, short, peremptory, unequivocal. At the end I grew weak and pleaded for mercy: that my whole life's hope

lay in being an officer; that always I had been with the colors; that my father, then on the battleline 10,000 miles away, was their comrade-in-arms of the Civil and Indian wars; that I would do anything in the way of punishment, but not to strip me of my uniform. And then—I could not go on—I heard the old soldier who presided say, "Court is recessed. Take him to his quarters."

Questioned by Congressman Edmund H. Driggs of New York, he showed remarkable maturity, poise and capacity for evasion for a 20-year-old:

> DRIGGS: Did you expect when you came to West Point to be treated in this manner?
> MACARTHUR: Not exactly in that manner; no, sir.
> DRIGGS: Did you not consider it cruel at that time?
> MACARTHUR: I was perhaps surprised to some extent.
> DRIGGS: I wish you would answer my question; did you or did you not consider it cruel at that time?
> MACARTHUR: I would like to have you define cruel.
> DRIGGS: All right, sir. Disposed to inflict suffering; indifference in the presence of suffering; hard-hearted; inflicting pain mentally or suffering; causing suffering.
> MACARTHUR: I should say perhaps it was cruel, then.
> Driggs: You have qualified your answer. Was it or was it not cruel?
> MACARTHUR: Yes, sir.

But at a recess in court he had received his instructions from his mother:

> Do you know that your soul is of my soul such a part
> That you seem to be fibre and core of my heart?
> None other can pain me as you, son, can do;
> None other can please me or praise me as you.
> Remember the world will be quick with its blame
> If shadow or shame ever darken your name.
> Like mother, like son, is saying so true
> The world will judge largely of mother by you.
> Be this then your task, if task it shall be
> To force this proud world to do homage to me.
> Be sure it will say, when its verdict you've won
> She reaps as she sowed: "This man is her son!"

MacArthur later claimed he never revealed the names of his tormentors: in fact he gave the names of those who had already graduated or confessed. It was an artful compromise, paving the way for the emergence of the shrewd pragmatist underneath the unbending man of iron. No one could take him to task for not having been frank, but he had secured the admiration of his contemporaries. He was asked by a senior, Arthur Hyde, to be his roommate—or, in the unfortunate West Point jargon, his "wife"— which was unusual for a plebe and conferred considerable privilege.

The incident established not just his cool calculation and ability to bend the truth when he wanted to, but his courage. Like his father at the Battle of Missionary Ridge, it displayed a certain insubordination: for a man whose whole life was to be the army, it was unusual that from the first obedience was not the highest military virtue. MacArthur would never blindly obey, he would question orders then make his own judgment: a stickler for other people obeying orders, he no doubt reconciled this apparent contradiction through his own self-belief.

Whatever his later achievements, it was soon to be evident that in one area MacArthur was timid, backward, even childish in his emotional life, before settling down, at last, in his late fifties. Clearly the intensity of his relationship with this socially ambitious, demanding, bossy and above all self-serving and obsessed tough southern matriarch was a key to understanding his character, as also to the relentless channeling of his energies away from personal pleasure and ordinary satisfaction into military duty and vainglory (a characteristic he shared with his mother). It wasn't that MacArthur's women found it hard to compete with the formidable Pinky, never far from his side; it was that MacArthur's first loyalty was to her rather than to them.

After this first formative experience, Douglas came of age as an impressive and promising young man. At five foot eleven he was above average height for the time, weighing 133 pounds—lean, trim, athletic, of proud bearing. Contemporaries described him as "without doubt the handsomest cadet that ever came into the academy, six-foot tall, and slender, with a fine body and dark flashing eyes"; "a typical West Pointer" who had a ruddy, out-of-doors complexion; "brave as a lion and smart as hell and blessed with style." Less flatteringly he was "presumably arrogant from the age of eight."

He was also studious. He would sometimes work all night, covering his windows with blinds, and study until dawn. He often openly wondered whether he could ever become as great as his father, whom he regarded with "affection and pride." Photographs at the time show that quite quickly his former callow good looks had been replaced with a steely gaze of hauteur and command and an upturned chin that seems almost comical in one so young, compared with the more relaxed faces of his classmates.

Within a year, as he gained his self-confidence at West Point, it became clear he was a born leader and conscious of it, becoming pretty bumptious in the eyes of one of his classmates, displaying athletic prowess, high intelligence as well as his penchant for hard work. He was reprimanded for "swinging arms excessively and marching to the front at parade"; but was usually impeccably dressed "like a clothing store dummy, with his red sash just so and his trousers creased to knife-edge." Drilling plebes, he was described by a superior as "the finest drill master I have ever seen." Although an indifferent basketball player, and only manager of the football team, he excelled at riding and shooting.

He was to graduate with a mark of 98 percent, first in his class of 94, the highest ever recorded at West Point with the exception of General Robert E. Lee of Civil War fame. He scored 100 percent in law, history and English. After serving as a senior corporal in his first year, senior first sergeant in his second, he went out as first captain as Lee had. He was voted cadet most likely to succeed.

He was not all angelic. He was said to have been behind two mischievous exploits with the reveille gun, on one occasion having it hoisted onto the roof of the West Point Academic Building, on another moving it to point at the superintendent's front door. MacArthur himself had fond memories of extracurricular activities, in particular.

That awful moment when a tactical officer caught me on Flirtation Walk publicly kissing a girl, and instead of reporting me for unbecoming conduct, just grinned and said, "Congratulations, Mister MacArthur."

And the day we went to the horseshow in New York, when my roommate, Charles Severson, and "Dotty" Laurson, the Cadet Captain of "E" Company, and myself slipped away and swaggered into Rector's on Broadway, shook hands with "Diamond Jim" Brady, and called for nine martinis. The astounded bartender asked, "Where are the other six?" and "Dotty," striking a Napoleonic posture, bellowed out, pointing to the six waiting glasses, "Their spirits are here." And then we swanked out to a burlesque show. We loved it!

And that day in classroom when the first section was studying the space-time relationship later formulated by Einstein as his Theory of Relativity. The text was complex and, being unable to comprehend it, I committed the pages to memory. When I was called upon to recite, I solemnly reeled off almost word for word what the book said. Our instructor, Colonel Feiberger, looked at me somewhat quizzically and asked, "Do you understand this theory?" It was a bad moment for me, but I did not hesitate in replying, "No, sir." You could have heard a pin drop. I braced myself and waited. And then the slow words of the professor, "Neither do I, Mister MacArthur. Section dismissed." I still do not understand the theory.

He was soon attracting "drags," as girls were called, and he was said to have proposed to eight by the end of his stay at West Point. His mother took each to tea to disillusion them by saying that he was wedded to his career. Most evenings he would meet her for a walk or tea.

It was unclear at this point, given his upbringing in remote military posts, the monastic and Spartan life he had led at West Point, whether he was cut out to be anything other than a soldier. He showed no great verve or imagination in other fields—but then he had never been required to.

Moreover the toughness and segregation of life at West Point seemed intended to breed men quite apart from the normal run of civilian life, an insensitive clutch of militarists. As Winston Churchill observed when he visited West Point, cadets were allowed "far less liberty than in any public schools in our country" under the much criticized British system—and this at the age of up to 24 and 25. MacArthur emerged with flying colors from his military cloister into a world he really knew very little about. When he graduated the words of Secretary of State Elihu Root rang in his ears: "Before you leave the Army, according to all precedents in our history, you will be engaged in another war. It is bound to come, and will come. Prepare your country for that war."

PART II
DAWN OF THE RISING SUN

3 : THE HEIAN PERIOD

JUST AS MACARTHUR CAME OF AGE, AND WAS STILL IN HIS FIRST YEAR AT West Point, on April 29, 1901, a boy was born to the fabulous privilege of an absolute imperial court in circumstances that could hardly have been less like the outpost simplicity in which Douglas had come into the world 21 years before. His own name was Michinomiya. He was to be far better known by his public name of Hirohito, and later Showa. It is not known whether the promising West Point graduate even registered this fact, although it was announced in American newspapers of the time. He certainly could not have known that his fate was to be intimately bound up with that of this sickly, pampered infant.

In November 1867, as Arthur MacArthur was readjusting to life after the end of the American Civil War, there occurred the watershed that is commonly accepted as the starting point of Japan's modern history. The event that is as significant to modern Japan as the English and American Civil Wars, the French and Russian Revolutions, or the unifications of Germany and Italy, was the deposition of the country's 250-year-old military dictatorship, the Tokugawa Shogunate, and the restoration of the Emperor to formal power. It is commonly viewed as the moment when feudal Japan gave way to modern Japan.

It was not a revolution by Japan's disaffected, emerging middle class—the position in many other countries—but a reversion to power of the most anachronistic class of all in Japan—the increasingly downtrodden and redundant class of samurai, warriors hailing back to the Middle Ages. It has been deemed an aristocratic revolution, yet the samurai were less aristocratic in the sense of representing the country's traditional landowning class than a privileged caste defining itself in terms of ancient status and special privileges.

The fact that this rather quixotic class was behind Japan's transformation into a modern state has defined the peculiar direction of the country's development this century. It is rather as if the fox-hunting squirearchy of England, the grandees of the old Confederate South in America, or the landowning gentry of Russia had taken up the banner of social revolution and modernization. To understand how Japan's most anachronistic class seized power in 1867, precipitating a brief but bloody civil war that put into place a tradition that has endured through victory and defeat for a century and a quarter, it is necessary to provide a brief sketch of Japanese society on the eve of universal manhood suffrage in Britain and on the morrow of the American Civil War.

Japan's creation myths bear setting out. In the beginning was the Plain of High Heaven, on which dwelt the gods, among them Izanagi and Izanami, who between them gave birth to the islands of Japan. Izanami died, while Izanagi, as she was washing her eyes and nose, gave birth to three children, the gods of Sun, Moon and Storm. The Goddess of the Sun was Amaterasu Omikami, who was appointed to rule the Plain of High Heaven. Her brother Susanowo-no-Mikoto, His Swift Impetuous Male Augustness, was furious. He also lusted after his sister. When he made advances he was thrown out of her rooms.

He retaliated by throwing excrement over the dining room where she was celebrating the ceremony of the first fruits. He broke down the divisions of the rice fields, and finally—the ultimate insult—flung a rotting piebald horse which he "had flayed with a backward flaying" into her chamber through a hole in the roof. Amaterasu fled into a cave and the world was plunged into darkness.

The gods, appalled, assembled outside the cave and erected a sacred tree into which they placed a jewel in the upper branches and a mirror in the middle ones. They then summoned Ama-no-Uzume, the Heavenly Alarming Female, who performed a wild dance. As Kojiki, the scribe of this period, recounts:

> Her Augustness the Heavenly Alarming Female, hanging the heavenly clubmoss of Mount Kagu as a sash, making the heavenly spindle-tree her head-dress and binding the leaves of bamboo grass in a posy for her hands, laid a tub before the door of the heavenly rock dwelling and stamped till she made it resound. Doing as if possessed by a deity and pulling out the nipples of her breasts, she pushed her skirt-string beneath her private parts. Then the Plain of High Heaven shook and the eight hundred deities laughed together.

Amaterasu, hearing the commotion, emerged from the cave slightly, caught sight of her reflection and, fearing she was to be supplanted by the brilliant beauty in the mirror, came out further, to be seized by the gods and returned to shine in the heavens. Susanowo was expelled from heaven, ending up in the Land of Darkness; there he killed a monster and found a sword in one of its tails. This he presented to Amaterasu.

In keeping with Japan's notion that there is no good or evil, the villainous Susanowo is still admired. Amaterasu's great-great-great-grandson became the first Emperor of Japan after bitter fighting ended with his establishing a palace in Yamato, south of Kyoto, in 660 BC. Thus Japan was founded by a ruler descended from the gods whose heirs were to continue supposedly in unbroken succession to govern Japan to this day. His subjects were the descendants of the god Susanowo, placing the Japanese above all races in being directly descended from the gods. Such was the Creation Myth.

For the best part of two millennia Japan has been aggressively reclusive. A collection of mountainous islands off the coast of Asia, plagued by earthquakes and volcanic eruptions, it was populated originally by colonists from mainland Asia, probably Korea, who displaced the native Ainu people. For centuries an expanding population dwelt on this rough, inhospitable land, a combination which engendered intense poverty. Although national unity proved difficult to impose upon a disparate and remote territory, a regionally based social structure existed: medieval warlords, who alone had the right to bear arms, presided over a destitute and wretched peasantry.

Japan's relations with the outside world were characterized by intense suspicion and insularity punctuated by occasional intervals of outward-looking curiosity. Underlying the hierarchical nature of Japan's feudalism lay the Shinto religion, a primitive cult of multiple deities which glorified war, sacrifice and suicide, revolved around respect for the God-Emperor, and lacked any underlying humanistic tradition. Japan acquired some ethical grounding, however, with the spread of Buddhism, Confucianism and, eventually, of Christianity from mainland Asia. The rather authoritarian countenance of Japanese society was leavened by a purist tradition of arts and aesthetics dating from the Heian period of the eighth to the twelfth centuries. This was Japan's golden age, taking its name from the capital, now Kyoto, under the Fujiwara dynasty.

They ruled according to a fantastic system of government, "marriage politics." The Emperor's brides were chosen exclusively from among Fujiwara girls. The head of the family was almost always the father-in-law or grand-father (or sometimes both) of the reigning sovereign. By the tenth century the Fujiwaras had the Emperor entirely in their grasp. He came to the throne as a youth and was married to a Fujiwara girl; their son would become crown prince. The Emperor was forced to abdicate, usually at the age of about thirty. The son would inherit and the cycle would start again.

The greatest Fujiwara, Michinaga, saw no fewer than four of his daughters married to emperors, who in turn produced three more emper-ors. By the end of his life, Michinaga was the father-in-law of two emper-ors, grandfather of a third, grandfather and great-grandfather of a fourth, grandfather and father-in-law of a fifth. Ivan Morris comments: "The emperors themselves, all-powerful as they might be in theory, were of course not consulted about these matrimonial arrangements; else one imag-ines that at least some of them would have boggled at the fate, a common one during this period, of having to marry their aunts."

Another remarkable feature of politics during the Heian period was that death by no means diminished a man's power. Take the case of the Fujiwaras' great rival:

> Michizane's death in exile was far from being the end of the career; in fact his greatest success came after. In the years following his demise there was a series of catastrophes in the capital—droughts, floods and fires; his chief Fujiwara adversary and the crown prince both died prematurely. All this was attributed to the curse of Michizane's angry ghost, and efforts were made to placate him. The documents relating to his exile were burnt, while the minister himself—now twenty years under the sod—was restored to his former post and promoted to the Senior Second Rank. Even this was not enough to appease the ghost, and seventy years later Michizane was elevated to the supreme post of prime minister.

Heian society, like that of Japan ever since, was obsessed with rank and status. There were ten court ranks, the first three divided into senior and junior, the others into upper and lower. There were some thirty ranks alto-gether, apart from the four reserved for princes of the royal blood.

The main division was between the Third and Fourth Ranks. Those who belonged to the top three ranks were known as Kugyo (High Court Nobles) and acquired all the most valuable privileges. Members of the Fifth Rank and above were appointed by the Emperor. Those beneath were appointed by the Great Council of State, and lacked many important privileges, such as appearing in the Imperial Audience Chamber. Strikingly, court rank determined both one's post in the government and one's wealth; in China and imperial Rome the reverse was true. Entry into the rank hierarchy was decided exclusively by one's family connections.

Members of the first five ranks were paid from special grants of rice land (the source of just about all wealth during this period), ranging from about 200 acres for the Senior First Rank (Prime Minister) to about twenty acres for the Junior Fifth Rank (Minor Counselor). Their children could go to university and were admitted into the rank system when they came of age. Anyone of the fifth rank or above could wear ceremonial dress, could attend the Imperial Audience Chamber, and had special allowances of silk and cloth. Guards and messengers were assigned to him, as well as "Sustenance Households," groups of peasant households, ranging from about 4,000 for the prime minister to about 900 for a member of the Third Rank, which paid him their feudal dues.

The codes and imperial edicts rigorously set out the standard of living appropriate to each rank—the height of one's gatepost, the type of one's carriage, the number of one's outriders. Costume was rigidly defined by rank, "down to the type of fan one could hold: 25 folds for the first three ranks, 23 for the fourth and fifth, 12 for the sixth and below."

Even Emperor Ichijo's pet cat was given the theoretical privilege of wearing the headdress (*koburi*) appropriate to the Fifth Rank and above, and was known by the title of Myobu, which applied to ladies of medium rank.

Small wonder that Morris concludes that if a visitor from England in the eleventh century were deposited in the city of Heian, "He would have been confronted with a world totally different from anything he knew, a world which culturally was many centuries in advance of his own and which in customs, beliefs and social organization was more alien than anything that Gulliver discovered on his travels. For Japan one thousand years ago had developed in a pattern that was almost totally unrelated to the experience of the West."

In the strictly deferential nature of country society, and in the several centers of authority, lay the origins of two distinguishing characteristics of modern Japan: the subservience of Japanese workers at the bottom, and the dispersal of authority at the top. The institution of Emperor, deified under the Shinto religion, provided the national focus for a country that was, to all intents and purposes, a federation of independent baronial states. The Emperor, for all the reverence surrounding his status, was largely impotent, confined to the religious capital of Heina (modern Kyoto) while shoguns ruled in his name. At times, the Emperor's influence was more marginal still, and power even more diffused. Unlike China's emperors, frequently overthrown in the course of history, the Japanese imperial dynasty remained unbroken through two millennia because it remained "above the clouds"—without real power.

4 : THE SHOGUNATE

VASTLY TO OVERSIMPLIFY A LONG AND CONVOLUTED PERIOD OF HISTORY, Heian Japan was succeeded in the thirteenth century by an age of embattled regional warlords, still professing theoretical allegiance to the Emperor, until the advent, in the sixteenth century, of the shoguns—ruthless military dictators. Under these, society was absolutely stratified, under a ruling caste of warriors, whose style of houses, neighborhoods and incomes were graded according to rank. The Confucian educational system known as *shûshigaku* taught that a person's fate and fortune were determined by his birth. No one could, nor should try to, alter his inherited station in life.

Shogunal Japan thus gave the appearance of extreme backwardness in its rigorous notion of hierarchy and refusal to admit outside influences or to modernize. However it was, in some respects, more advanced than the even more hierarchical "imperial Japan" which succeeded it. Yet one of the rare visitors before 1867 would have witnessed scenes that had more in common with the medieval pageantry of Europe than a modern society.

The history of Japan between 1600 and 1850 was a tale of two cities, the nominal capital, Kyoto, and the real capital, Edo (the modern Tokyo) some 200 miles to the north. The main road between the two, the Tokaido, was a bustling highway. Along this the princes of Japan, the *daimyo*, traveled in palanquins, ornate covered seats carried by bearers before which ordinary mortals prostrated themselves in total abjection or risked death. The *daimyo* were invariably accompanied by large bands of retainers and samurai, with their two swords, short skirts and butterfly shoulders, and their hair grown long and twisted tightly into a tail protruding forward like a giant proboscis over otherwise bald skulls. The road was also frequented by pilgrims visiting Kyoto's temples, as well as a mass of commercial traders, actors and working laborers who needed permission to cross the roadblocks set up as a control mechanism by the Shogunate.

It took a week to travel between Edo and Kyoto. The contrast between the two could hardly have been more pronounced. Kyoto was a sprawling, wealthy city on a wide plain between two mountain ridges. It straddled a river feeding a network of canals (which were not extensive enough to make it the Venice of Japan; Florence is a better comparison). The ubiquitous simplicity of Japanese wooden houses extended across the plain in a fine gridlock of streets and buildings; beyond, particularly on the eastern side but also huddled beneath the western ridge, were some of the most evocative temples and shrines in Japan. It was a city where the creative energies of artists under the patronage of a formal and indolent aristocracy were engaged in producing some of the world's most stylized art.

The *ukiyo*, the floating world, had come into being, "a world of fugitive pleasures of theaters and restaurants, wrestling booths and houses of assignation, with their permanent population of actors, dancers, singers, story-tellers, jesters, courtesans, bath girls and itinerant purveyors, among whom mingled the profligate sons of rich merchants, dissolute samurai and naughty apprentices. . . ." In the floating world, money dominated: the merchant lorded it over the warrior. Prostitutes, doctors, writers and painters predominated over imperial servants and police.

Of course, behind this exotic scene was a hard-working, thriving city where extremes of wealth and poverty prevailed. But there could be no greater contrast than that between the pure Confucianist ethic of aristocratic Kyoto and the licentious unstuffiness of bourgeois Edo. The samurai class retained its contempt for the lowest of Japan's four traditional classes—the warriors, the peasants, the artisans and the merchants; yet in practice, as the moneyed economy flourished, it was not long before many samurai and even the great *daimyo* princes were indebted to the merchants.

Edo was thus a nouveau riche city par excellence, a huge sprawl of modern wooden housing where the conventions and extreme formalities that governed Kyoto and the countryside no longer existed. Japan, under the tough-minded absolutism of the Tokugawa shogun, had moved from a kind of feudalism (in the Marxist sense of the word) to the bourgeois age; what no one could have predicted was that the country would—in a limited but important sense—return to a sort of feudalism with the Meiji restoration.

The shogunate, the precursor to MacArthur's domination of Hirohito, was a ruthless military dictatorship, but it never crushed the feudal magnates it had subdued. As time passed, the shogun had lived increasingly in

Edo, within a still larger moated and walled compound than the one in Kyoto; at the time of the move, 1590, Edo was a small castle town which, by 1750, had expanded into a city of more than a million people. While the hereditary shogun gradually lost power to his advisers, as the Emperor had in an earlier epoch, the system maintained a rigid control. In one sense that succeeded: the shogun unified the country through the crudest of methods, compelling the noblemen to submit to his demands through a calculated policy of deliberately impoverishing them, through taxes and other methods, and by hostage-taking: their wives and children were compelled to live in Edo, where the *daimyo* were obliged to visit them every other year. In addition, the nobles had to perform military service and force their retainers to do so.

Thus the Tokugawa shogunate, through its 250-year tenure, reined in the power of the feudal princes, which up to then had been dominant in Japan, without destroying them. A rather unique tension came into being. One of the country's chief characteristics was its mountainous nature, which permitted it to be carved up into a series of autonomous *daimyo* fiefdoms. Those fiefdoms were incapable of mounting a challenge to the administration in Edo because of the latter's strong-arm methods. The shogun was the undisputed master of the land, and capable occasionally of replacing insubordinate princes with his own nominees; but provided the feudal lords behaved themselves, they were allowed to run their virtually self-governing princedoms. This pattern of autonomy by competing great houses ultimately held in check by ferociously feudal rule from the center was to become a distinguishing feature even of twentieth-century Japanese society.

Beneath the *daimyo* were the local worthies, the samurai, a class of warriors comprising fully 10 percent of the population, utterly superior in outlook and increasingly impoverished economically. Their official status could not be grander: they were permitted to wear swords and lord them over commoners who did not show the proper respect. Yet after the centralization of authority around the shogun, the wars between rival *daimyo* that were the samurais' main raison d'être dwindled away; their masters were increasingly squeezed by the taxes of the central government; and many were displaced for showing insubordination to the shogunate. The samurai were traditionally debarred from making money for a living and the class as a whole became poorer and poorer, some 400,000 of them becoming dispossessed *ronin*, wandering the country in search of a lord to serve. They could earn a living only by becoming intellectuals and bureaucrats, professions which were not dishonorable for their caste.

While the shogun thus consciously whittled away at the authority of the old feudal lords and samurai, he proved unable to rein in the growing power of the merchant classes: by the end of the eighteenth century, some 200 merchant houses of enormous wealth had emerged. In the early seventeenth century Mitsui came into being as a high-interest lender, then broke out by setting up a chain of shops 100 years later. Increasingly, the new rich became the lenders and paymasters of the old classes, struggling to keep up under the squeeze imposed by the shogunate.

5 : Aristocratic Revolution

It was astonishing that the whole house of cards, built upon shifting ground, lasted as long as it did. By 1850 the new urban classes had not only antagonized the samurai, but had piled huge new burdens upon the broken backs of the peasantry. The seething ferment of despair that existed among the lower orders in both town and country (four fifths of Japan's 30 million people lived in the countryside) was the most unsettling factor. Like a Japanese volcano, it erupted with increasingly unpredictable, unchanneled frenzy throughout the last years of the shoguns, as economic development came to be based on the growing exploitation of the masses. Few at the top of one of the world's most hierarchical societies showed any concern for this human misery; but many understood the threat that it posed unless static Tokugawa society reformed itself.

The lot of the peasantry around the middle of the last century was one of almost unbelievable misery, tending what has been described as "the most exacting crop in the world" and dominated by the most ferocious system of servitude ever devised which itself was defined by what may be Japan's most significant cultural characteristic: collectivism. The point has been made by Karl Wittfoegel, author of the classic study *Oriental Despotism* among others, that oriental despotism was forged by the need of Eastern societies (and, indeed, one Western one, Inca Peru) to create absolutist, collectivist social systems to manage crops dependent upon community efforts at irrigation. Of few countries is this truer than Japan, a harsh mountain land where rice could only be grown through intensive and backbreaking shared labor. At the beginning of this century, Robertson Scott published a terrifyingly vivid glimpse of the squalor and drudgery involved in that most picturesque of activities, the planting and harvesting of wind-rippled green paddy fields: "Following the turning over of the stubble under water comes the clod-smashing and harrowing by quadrupedal or bipedal labor. It is not only a matter of staggering about and doing heavy work in sludge. The sludge is not clean dirt and water but dirty dirt and water, for it has been heavily dosed with manure, and the farmer is not fastidious as to the source from which he obtains it. And the sludge ordinarily contains leeches. Therefore the cultivator must work in sodden clinging cotton and leg coverings."

After this the rice was planted, transplanted, weeded four times, harvested, threshed, winnowed and polished, the latter taking anything between 200 and 1,000 blows of the mallet, depending upon the quality required. All of these things took an intensive team effort, none more so than the leveling of the ground necessary to grow the rice—which must be absolutely even, or part of the crop will be dry and part saturated by water—the building of low banks of water around the paddy fields, and the irrigation of the field to keep up water lost through evaporation, leakage or recycling.

The system that kept the peasantry on the rice paddies before 1867 was among the most elaborately and fiercely repressive that the world had ever seen. There were at least four levels of oppression: the hierarchy within the family; the hierarchy within the village; the hierarchy of economic dependence, usually between landlord and tenant; and the hierarchy of central government over local community. When all are considered together, the mysteries of Japanese politeness and deference become easier to understand, while it becomes remarkable not that the Japanese peasantry labored so long under conditions of such extreme misery, but that it did so often manage to raise the standard of revolt.

For Japan's samurai, the notion of noblesse oblige, of kindness and concern for one's social inferiors, were utterly alien. Within the family, wives showed absolute respect to their husband, children to parents, particularly the father, younger brothers to elder brothers, girls to boys. Even grown-up children continued to respect their fathers, while parents could break up the marriage of children as old as 40. Elder brothers had total control of younger ones until the latter set up their own households—if they did: many lingered on as unpaid servants of their older brother's family. Women walked behind their husbands and were lower in status—even if they were permitted to perform actions like going shopping, which was prohibited in most other Asian societies.

Marriages were arranged by families and were very rarely the product of spontaneous attraction between people. Subject to the iron rules of deference, families were probably more internally democratic than seems apparent: as in any family, stronger characters dominated weaker ones, and so on. Indeed, the Japanese obsession with consensus building, and with the whole family agreeing upon and supporting a decision—what a Westerner might call collective responsibility, which now governs the largest economic concentrations—has its origins in the rules governing family life. Nevertheless the system was fundamentally patriarchal and authoritarian.

The next unit of control was the village. Each village had a headman, elders, and "delegates," as well as being divided into arguably the most important nucleus of Japanese life—a system of "five man groups." The headman was charged by the central government with keeping accurate records of the village census, levying the rice tax on the village, spending on public works, adjudicating disputes, keeping order and repressing violence. He was a kind of combination of mayor and sheriff. He was assisted by his deputies, three or four from the most prominent families in the village. The delegates were the spokesmen of ordinary villagers to the authorities—a kind of parish council.

The five-man group, to which every peasant family belonged, was a special Japanese refinement. The group was a collective entity each of whose members was regarded as responsible for the misdeeds of another: thus it was in the interest of each member of the group to ensure that his fellows behaved themselves. As every family member was not judged as a separate individual, so every family was judged as part of his group, which was judged as part of the village collective. Individuals had no existence outside the group.

The formal body that drew up the rules affecting the village and administered punishment was the village assembly: the principal punishment consisted of ostracism, *mura hachibu*, where the offender's family is ignored by his fellow villagers except for the purposes of helping fight a fire or attending a funeral. This punishment could be given out for disclosing village secrets, or for generally being obstreperous. Worse still, villagers could be banished altogether for such crimes as stealing, harboring criminals and committing arson: to be turned into an outcast, in a society extolling mutual interdependence, where a person's worth was defined by membership of a group, was a pretty awesome fate. Not only could the members of the offender's five-man group also be punished for his crime, but so could his neighbors and the three families directly across the street.

The real power in the village lay in the hands of the *miyaza* or Shrine Association, containing its oldest and wealthiest families, which chose the headman and the elders and was largely self-perpetuating.

Finally, the young people of each village were regimented through "age groups," which teenagers joined until they were married or reached their early thirties. The groups were run by the older members, and the male groups had authority over the female groups, even, by some accounts, having full sexual access to them, which neither the girls nor their parents could deny. The age groups could ostracize erring members or, in a particularly Orwellian twist, gather outside an offender's home and shout a list of his or her family's misdeeds, along with ritual abuse.

A further level of control was economic: by some estimates there were more tenants than private owners at this period in Japan's history. Although under the Confucianist ideal the landlord was obliged to provide benevolence and protection to his tenants, in practice their dependence on his good temper was virtually total, usually magnified by debts to him; beneath these two were the *genin*, "low persons," a kind of landless laborer (it should be remembered that all these classes stood below the samurai who had the right to behead any of them if he wished).

The fourth bond of subjection was that of the village itself to the local feudal lord, through the samurai, who himself was subject to the Tokugawa shogun. In practice, provided a village paid its dues, it was permitted virtual self-government. Yet certain general laws applied to the peasantry as a whole. As Japanese historian Harumi Befu wrote:

> First, the state manifestly existed for the benefit of the ruling class, and therefore other classes, including the peasants, existed to support the ruling class. Hence the oppressive measures to keep the peasants at the bare subsistence level, taking away every bit of surplus they produced. Second, the peasants were considered by nature stupid, needing detailed regulations for conduct. Third, the society was conceived of in absolutely static terms in which the peasantry had a definite position defined by the ruling elite: hence the numerous regulations aimed at maintaining and emphasizing the status relation of the peasants to other classes, especially to the ruling class. Fourth . . . to the Tokugawa administration, law and

morals were both bound up with the concept of government. Hence the moralistic admonitions intermingled with legal codes and the moralistic tone of legal codes.

A deeply conservative government of hereditary military oligarchs imposing iron and forcible central control upon the country's traditional feudal fiefdoms; a static and miserable peasantry; a thriving and uncontrollable urban melting pot: these were the three principal characteristics of Tokugawa Japan by the early nineteenth century. It was a remarkable achievement for one family to hold sway over such a country for two and a half centuries, particularly as it derived its legitimacy through force, not heredity or popular acceptance. When the end came, it did so because the forces opposed to the status quo had reached a critical mass.

Three principal factors were involved: the misery of the peasantry and the urban proletariat toward the rapacious exactions of the ruling elite and the merchant class had grown so great that fierce uprisings, brutally put down, had become endemic. The shogun's policy of excluding the outside world was no longer practicable—indeed, seemed likely to lead the country toward the kind of colonization by the Western powers already under way elsewhere in Asia; and the dispossessed samurai class and the further flung feudal chieftains—the "outer lords" as opposed to the "inner lords" (who were largely Tokugawa trusties)—saw their chance of revenge against hated central oppression.

The growing revolt of the peasantry against Tokugawa Japan was caused by the willful exploitation of the new capitalist classes, to which the ruling classes were increasingly indebted, passing on an ever greater proportion of their costs and taxes to those below. In addition, rice prices suffered from feverish speculation as the economy grew more complicated. A feudal lord, in order to pay some of his debts, would halve the pay of his farmers, who would insist in turn on greater yields for less pay from the peasants. There were also spectacular crop failures. A single famine in mid-century caused a million deaths among the population. It became common practice for peasant families to put their male children out of doors to die, while girls were commonly sold to the brothels of Edo and Osaka.

In the first hundred years of Tokugawa rule the countryside had been relatively settled: there were only 157 outbreaks of rural unrest throughout the period. Over the next fifty years to 1753 there were 176 cases. For the remaining century of the shogunate, there were some six uprisings every year. The uprisings usually took the form of a mass gathering by a mob and march on the house of the feudal lord, while buildings belonging to the wealthy were sacked. Sometimes the demands of the rioters were granted, sometimes they were brutally dispersed by the soldiers. Almost always the peasant leaders were hideously treated, being decapitated, crucified, boiled in oil or banished.

In the cities, there was simple class-based unrest as the paddy-poor took out their ire on the homes of the rich. In the last 150 years of Tokugawa rule, there were more than 200 urban riots, some 35 of them during the last ten years of the shogun's rule. The most serious riot was headed by a former policeman, Heihachiro Oshio, at Osaka in 1837, who led thousands of townspeople and peasants on a several-day looting spree, which some 30 samurai joined, using primitive guns and hand grenades. When the riot was put down amid considerable bloodshed, Oshio committed suicide. The growing levels of discontent displayed by these riots caused many members of the ruling class to conclude that the static dictatorship of the shoguns could not continue forever.

The discontent of the samurai was less evident, but no less acute. Stranded on fixed incomes, many had lost their feudal lords and become leaderless outlaws who were forbidden by caste from making their own living. It was permissible for the younger children of merchants to marry into the samurai, and thus gain status while injecting capital into this noble, pauperized class. But most samurai formed a huge reserve—perhaps as many as two million—of disenchanted people desperately trying to earn a living from the jobs in government many were forced to take up. The authorities were all too conscious of the dangers they presented: in the cities, the town heads (nanushi) kept a constant watch on their activities. By the mid–nineteenth century the position of the samurai was quite desperate.

The loaded gun pointed at the head of the shogunate was a new Japanese nationalism bred of the evident failure of the government's policy of excluding all outsiders and their goods from the country. As early as 1816, the eighth shogun had relaxed the ban on some imports; yet most trade remained forbidden and Christianity banned. British, American and Russian ships frequently appeared in Japanese waters, were given supplies and then were sent on their way.

During the first half of the nineteenth century, though, overseas interest in Japan increased. The Russians, who had colonized Siberia, looked to Japan for supplies. The British, having defeated China in the Opium Wars of 1842 and been given a lease over Hong Kong, were looking to Japan for trading possibilities. As the contest between the two imperial powers developed, the Russians in 1852 decided to send four ships under Admiral Putyatin all the way from Europe to Japan to secure a privileged commercial treaty. When the Russian flotilla arrived at the southernmost port of Nagasaki in 1853, they were astonished to learn that an American squadron under Commodore Matthew Perry, Douglas MacArthur's direct precursor, despatched by the American government to force the country open to trade, had already arrived in Edo Bay.

The importance of Perry's arrival on Japan's history should not be overstated. The system was largely dying from within. Yet the visit of the four "black ships"—two driven by steam—in Edo Bay (later Tokyo Bay), represented the arrival of messengers of death for the ancien régime. The steamships were symbols of a world whose progress had bypassed that of Japan. They also underscored the vulnerability of Edo itself. The city's food supplies came by sea from the north and the west: Japan, that mountainous nation of semi-autonomous fiefdoms, depended upon the sea for an enormous amount of its essential transport.

Perry was a tough-minded sailor in his late fifties who understood that the Japanese were impressed by power rather than conciliation. An unfortunate incident had occurred in 1846 when Commodore Biddle had made the first American approach to Japan, trying to be conciliatory. Biddle was jostled by a Japanese seaman and accepted an apology; a Japanese diplomat later told an American senator that they did not fear American vengeance after that, as an American commander had failed to punish an ordinary seaman who had treated him disrespectfully.

Perry was determined to have none of that: he treated the emissaries sent by the Japanese to his ship with contempt, insisting on leaving a letter from his President that amounted to an ultimatum demanding the opening of trade relations, and promising to return a year later with a large fleet of ships. Perry had been assured by his American masters that "any departure from usage, or any error of judgment he may commit will be viewed with indulgence." After delivering his missive, the Commodore sailed up the bay, ignoring Japanese warnings, to a position from which it was clear that he could shell the outlying parts of the city; then he departed in grand manner.

A month later Admiral Putyatin's less impressive force arrived and, being much less tough-minded, was kept kicking its heels in Nagasaki for three months. The two visits convinced the Japanese that their policy of total isolation was no longer workable. The Americans had come because of the need for access to supplies for ships employed in the lucrative trade with China; in addition, the Americans were irked with the dismal reception accorded their shipwrecked crews in Japan, who endured months of ill-treatment before being repatriated. The United States, with the opening up of California and the Gold Rush of 1849, had become a Pacific-oriented nation.

Underlying this was the feeling that Japan, an isolated and backward country, was ripe for the commercial picking. An unedifying scramble was under way among three major powers—America, Britain and Russia—two of which were about to go to war with each other in the Crimea. Within a matter of months, Japan realized the utter helplessness that its policy of isolation had led to: it was a nation undefended, without a navy, as ready for absorption by the colonial powers as China had been. For once the cliché about an ostrich sticking its head in the sand as its defense against outside danger had been apposite.

The government's response to the Perry mission was a fevered, frantic attempt to rearm. Gun batteries were erected along the shoreline near Edo, defenses were put up. But when Perry arrived as promised with seven ships in 1854, he delivered his ultimatum: either the Japanese accept his terms, or military operations would begin. Already intimidated by the return of the Russians to Nagasaki a month earlier, Japan surrendered in March 1854, and signed the treaty of Kanagawa, opening up the ports of Hakodate and Shimoda for supplies and trade. The Japanese drew consolation from the fact that these ports were far from Kyoto and Edo. The following October a British contingent under Admiral Sterling arrived in Nagasaki and extracted agreement to call there and at Hakodate.

A month later the tireless and luckless Admiral Putyatin had sailed into Osaka bay, close to the imperial capital at Kyoto, causing consternation among the Japanese. After sailing out, Putyatin's ship, the *Diana*, was badly damaged in a giant whirlpool caused by an earthquake, and eventually sank. The Japanese interpreted this as an indication of the wrath of the gods against their concessions to the barbarians. But Putyatin and his men were rescued and treated with courtesy, and negotiations between Japan and its powerful northern neighbor were soon concluded with partition of the Kurile Islands and the large, mainly uninhabited, island of Sakhalin, which were satisfactory to both sides. Moreover, the Russians were given landing rights at Shimoda, Nagasaki and Hakodate.

By the end of 1855 a formal treaty had been signed with Holland, and the following year America's Townsend Harris became the first resident foreign diplomat in Japan as American consul, using his position to extract privileged terms for the Americans, while playing on Japanese fears of the British—the major naval power in the Far East. He sought an audience with the shogun himself and in December 1857, bearing a presidential letter, he became one of the first outsiders to be brought into the presence of the ruler, the somewhat mannered Iesada Tokugawa, who told him that "he was pleased with the letter sent with the Ambassador for a far distant country, and likewise pleased with his discourse. Intercourse shall be continued forever."

The shogun's decision was in reality dictated by his chief counselor, Masuhiro Abe, who was nothing if not a realist. "Everyone has pointed out that we are without a navy," he told the shogun, arguing that there was no alternative but to make as few concessions as possible from an extremely weak hand. Masuhiro's successor as chief counselor was Naosuke Ii, *daimyo* of Hikone, who was even more aware of the frailty of Japan's position. In 1858 he agreed to the so-called "unequal treaties" by which Edo and other ports were opened up to foreigners, imports were taxed at a low level and nationals from the 18 countries signing the treaty were exempted from Japanese law. The treaties were very close to being a colonial diktat and one, moreover, carried out in the name of a virtually powerless shogun, in defiance of the openly stated wishes of the Emperor, around whom outraged Japanese nationalists had begun to congregate. The treaties caused an outcry and the beginning of a campaign whose rallying cry was, "Revere the Emperor! Expel the barbarians!"—which was later to become the slogan of the Meiji Restoration. Naosuke Ii responded with savage repression.

6 : THE MEIJI EMPEROR

IN JANUARY 1860, AS THE CHIEF MINISTER'S PALANQUIN TRUNDLED DOWN the steep hill alongside the moat that surrounded the stubby walls of the shogun's castle in Edo and turned to enter the Sakurada Gate in deep snow, Ii was attacked by a group of nationalist fanatics and stabbed to death. It was the first of the nationalist assassinations that were to plague Japanese politics for the best part of the next 100 years.

With Ii's death, the shogun and his regime were on the ropes, and they knew it. By 1862 they had been forced to abandon the rule that compelled the *daimyo* to spend every other year in Edo; the family hostage system was also ended. Meanwhile the Choshu clan of "outside" lords had begun a full-scale insurrection in the west, enlisting peasants and townsmen as warriors, violating the old caste system which decreed that samurai alone could bear arms.

The insurrection formally began when Emperor Komei in Kyoto, growing ever bolder as he was chivvied by aristocratic admirers into pushing the crumbling Tokugawa regime over the brink, abruptly issued an edict to the shogun telling him to expel foreigners from Japan the following year. The shogun assured the foreign community that the edict would not be enforced; but fanatics began to attack outsiders with increasing impunity, fired by the knowledge that they were carrying out their divine Emperor's will. In Yokohama and Edo, some foreigners were stabbed to death.

In September 1862, a prominent Englishman, Mr. Richardson, was attacked for unexplained reasons as he traveled the Tokaido road between Edo and Kyoto. The culprits were retainers from Satsuma, which was also in nearly open rebellion against the shogun. The British responded with fury, sending a squadron to bombard, and virtually flatten, the capital of the Satsuma clan at Kagashima. In June 1863, the deadline for the expulsion of "the barbarians" arrived, and Choshu shore guns on the Shimonoseki Straits opened fire upon American, French and Dutch ships, the Americans and the French firing back. In September 1864, the imperialist powers finally lost their patience and a combined British, Dutch, French and American fleet destroyed the Choshu batteries, reopening the Straits. The American public broadly supported this, as the Japanese had fired first.

Yet even the colonial powers were aware that Japan was falling apart. Large parts of the country were effectively under independent rule from the center; the shogun held sway only around Edo, and the loss of tributes paid to him by the rebellious parts of the country was further squeezing an economy already in serious financial difficulties. The British minister, Sir Harry Parkes, carefully watched the direction of events and initiated contacts with the ignorant, rebellious young extremists from the provinces—in marked contrast to the French, who remained closely tied to the shogun.

In 1866 the young shogun Iemochi died, and his guardian, Keiki Tokugawa, came to power. The same year the previously rival armies of Satsuma and Choshu concluded a secret alliance in which the Tosa and Hizen clans also joined. Even part of the merchant class, notably the Mitsui family, sensing which way the wind was blowing, joined forces with these aristocratic backwoodsmen. The Emperor Komei himself was believed to have given this pact his backing. A year later he too was dead and his 15-year-old son, Mutsuhito, the Meiji emperor, had succeeded to his status of mystical divinity within that vastly modest palace in Kyoto as spiritual ruler of the Japanese. He now embodied the hopes of many of his fellow country-men anxious to rid the nation of its crumbling military dictatorship.

In November 1867, matters came to a head. Two armies of the Satsuma and Choshu clans moved into Kyoto, in preparation for an attack on the shogun's palace there, Nijo Castle. Learning of their approach, shogun Keiki also formally received an ultimatum from the head of the Tosa Clan demanding that he restore "the governing powers into the hands of the sovereign and so lay a foundation on which Japan may take her stand as the equal of all other countries."

Keiki fled his palace at night to Osaka, to escape the attack he believed to be imminent. There his loyalists persuaded him that they had sufficient strength to launch a counteroffensive to "rescue" the Emperor from the cap-ital's new masters. In January 1868, the shogun's armies advanced on Kyoto, but were stopped at the towns of Toba and Fushimi. A pitched battle ensued; on the second day, a large part of the shogun's army went over to the Emperor, and the following day the shogun's remaining forces were routed. Keiki took a boat from Osaka to Edo where, with good grace, he bowed to the inevitable and decided that Edo Castle, despite its formidable defenses, should be surrendered; only in Ueno, in the eastern sector of the city, was there some resistance to what were no longer rebel, but imperial forces.

Many clans loyal to the Tokugawa, however, fought on. At Wakamatsu and then at Hokkaido, fighting continued until well into the following year. Keiki himself was spared, perhaps because he had tried to dampen down futile resistance, and was received by the Emperor in 1902.

The final chapter in Japan's Tale of Two Cities was about to be writ-ten: in the autumn of 1868 the youth who had inherited Japan paid a for-mal visit to Edo, the shogun's capital. It was a brilliant, last display of the old Japan. This is how a contemporary observer described it; as the Ho-o-ren or "phoenix car" approached:

> This is a black lacquered palanquin, about six foot square and with a dome-shaped roof; the front is closed only by curtains, and in the center of each side is a latticed window, through which it was possible to see that it

held no one. The Mikado is supposed to travel in it, but has really a more comfortable palanquin . . . the bearers of the car which is carried high upon their shoulders and on a frame which raises it six feet from the ground were . . . all dressed in bright yellow silk . . . There were fully 60 of them immediately surrounding the Ho-o-ren, and the effect of the group, with the brilliant sun lighting up the sheen of the silk and the glitter of the lacquer, was very gorgeous and indescribably strange, comparable to nothing ever seen in any other part of the world.

And now a great silence fell upon the people. As far as the eye could see on either side, the roadsides were densely packed with the crouching populace, in their ordinary position when any official of rank passes by . . . as the phoenix car . . . with its halo of glittering attendants came on . . . the people without order or signal turned their faces to the earth . . . no man moved or spoke for a space, and all seemed to hold their breath for very awe, as the mysterious presence, on whom few are privileged to look and live, was passing by.

The following spring the court moved permanently to the shogun's Castle there, which became the new Imperial Palace. Edo was renamed Tokyo (Eastern Capital). The spiritual ruler of Japan was also now to be its temporal ruler.

All official power in Japan was henceforth to be wielded solely in his name. While this had been nominally true in the past, no observer of Japan had any illusion that the Emperor had possessed real political authority of any kind under the shogunate. The new order was to be modeled on the basis of other constitutional monarchies investigated by the Japanese in the rest of the world.

The decisions of the government would be referred to him, and he sat in on its discussions, even if he usually took no active part. While late twentieth-century writers frequently tried to compare the position of the Emperor during the crucial years leading up to the Pacific War with the previously purely spiritual authority he had in the centuries before the Meiji Restoration, the argument is specious. The Emperor's position after the restoration was entirely different to that before. He was now the formal pinnacle of power; the senior ministers reported to him; he appointed the prime minister and oversaw key decisions, he presided in person over all the great activities of state. The contemplative hermit of Kyoto was no more.

None of this is to suggest that he became Japan's dictator, personally responsible for the decisions affecting Japan up to 1945; even the shogun had, after a time, become the creature of his advisers. In fact the Emperor's power was something entirely new: he stood at the apex of an absolutist system of respect, and was supposed to wield the powers of a European monarch (the Japanese believed this essential to success in the modern world, without knowing exactly what those powers were); yet he was hedged about with the kind of entourage and overmighty advisers that had been a feature of Japanese politics since time immemorial. To some extent the character of the new central authority of the state was to be shaped by the personality of the Emperor himself. Spiritual and temporal power in Japan had converged in a youth barely past puberty who possessed the aura of a god and the authority of a king, running Japan from the single capital of Tokyo.

The Meiji Emperor was a squat, astonishingly energetic young man with pouting lips and a sullen expression, like a bulldog's, who was betrayed by a receding lower chin. His thick black hair combined with his precocious maturity to give him a ferocious look that, as he grew older, inspired affection rather than fear. His taste for court cronies and concubines grew with time, but he never lapsed into dissolution. The Emperor Hirohito's grandfather had been born in 1852, named Mutsuhito, and was to perform a far larger political role than any of his forebears for centuries. Such few eyewitness accounts as have been handed down say he was gruff, occasionally kindly, with a strong constitution.

These were the men who had taken over a backward, isolated country on the further fringes of the civilized world in the second half of the century. There was nothing to suggest power or success about Japan at the time. It was an irrelevance, a string of inhospitable islands at the very end of the earth off the coast of Asia, useful as a staging post for the pickings of the Asian mainland by the colonial powers. The only reason that Japan had not been colonized, probably, was that the major powers—Britain, America and Russia—thought it hardly worth the effort. There could have been little in the early days of the Meiji reign to reassure those who had seized power that Japan was destined for more than a fairly low form of international life.

Within a matter of months, the men who had freed the country from the grip of a crushing and oppressive military dictatorship found themselves embattled on at least three fronts: internationally, they discovered that Japan was far weaker than they had feared. Japan was as naked a nation as it was possible to be. One of the chief motives behind the restoration had been to "expel the barbarian." The new rulers quickly realized that the only way of doing so was to become stronger than he, and this could only be achieved through copying his secrets and his methods. The idea of excluding him was hopelessly outdated, and a passport to becoming his servant, just as China, which for centuries had believed its culture to be superior to any other, was being mercilessly despoiled by the colonizers' military and organizational superiority.

The second front was economic: the country was facing financial ruin, and only the most radical of initiatives would permit it to escape the clutches of a parasitic bureaucratic class, with its mercantilist retainers, squeezing the lifeblood from its hard-pressed rural producers. Thirdly, the very class which had propelled the new regime to power—the warriors, the samurai—was one of the biggest drains on state finances. The country's new rulers had to find some way of redeploying the expectations of the samurai that their time had come again: they could no longer be supported by the state as non-producers. Only two solutions seemed possible—the destruction of privilege so that the samurai might make money just like everyone else, which would create intense resentment among those that failed; and the deflection of their warrior energies abroad.

The Emperor was now at the heart of the political culture. Prior to the Meiji Restoration the office had been passive and mystical. The few foreigners with experience of Japan under the shogun hardly ever heard the Emperor mentioned; the Emperor had performed certain ritual functions at the heart of a stagnant aristocratic court at Kyoto. In order to stage the coup, the "outside lords" who came to power after 1867 looked to turn the Emperor into a more active monarch, endowed not just with divinity but with supreme political authority.

The "above-the-clouds" figure in Kyoto was at first transformed into a modern prototype of the new peripatetic unifier of the nation as a whole. In 1872 the Emperor embarked upon the first of six "Great Circuits" across his country: ships, horses, palanquins and his own two feet carried him from one end of his domains to another, up steep mountain paths and across major rivers. Kaoru Inoue, one of his chief advisers, argued that "[t]he Emperor's visiting all parts of Japan not only infects the people of the Empire with virtue, but also offers the opportunity of displaying direct imperial rule in the flesh," thus strengthening the imprint of monarchical government. The young Emperor Mutsuhito was accessible, stayed in peoples' houses and inns, and was the subject of obeisance and veneration by thousands of subjects eager to see him in person. Perhaps the founders of Meiji Japan intended initially to make him the kind of constitutional monarch they had observed in Britain—loved, respected, but ultimately merely the pinnacle of a system which was firmly in the grasp of government, politicians and people. Not until Hirohito's travels after the Second World War was a Japanese emperor to be so human, so close to his subjects.

As the Emperor grew into adulthood it became clear, moreover, that he at least was unlikely to be purely a puppet of his senior advisers. The extent to which Mutsuhito was involved in day-to-day decisions is a closely guarded secret in the obsessively protective Japanese court even now. Formally he had no authority to intervene in decision-making. He merely approved the decisions of his council, which was later transformed into his cabinet. But as he outlasted his senior advisers, his views counted for more and more. Nor was Mutsuhito a withdrawn or quiet personality. He made clear his passionate interest in two areas of policy: education was a consuming field of concern; the other was war, where it is doubtful that major decisions could have taken place against the express disagreement of the Emperor.

Mutsuhito presided over two major wars: the first Sino-Japanese War and the Russo-Japanese war. As real fighting broke out in September 1894, the imperial headquarters moved south to the port of embarkation for the troops, Hiroshima, "to oversee the imperial affair of war." For eight months the Meiji Emperor was reported as living the life of his troops, experiencing "imperial simplicity" (shisso), living in a small room, sitting on a three-legged stool, wearing out his clothes. "Unheeding of the inconvenience, the Emperor works day and night at military offices, rises at six, retires at midnight and even when resting listens to his aides experienced on military matters." The Emperor gave more than 800,000 cigarettes to the troops, as well as 7,000 gallons of sake.

Almost exactly a decade later, in the Russo-Japanese conflict of 1904–5, the war leader reemerged into prominence. Instead of leading a life of privation, this time the Emperor was credited with most of the decisions affecting war and peace; he also wrote no fewer than 7,526 poems on the subject, during the year and a half of war (mercifully—not least for him—only four lines long). These included such classics as, "When I think of those in battle, I have no heart for the flowers," as well as, "Crush the enemy for the sake of the nation, but never forget to have mercy"—a sentiment Tolstoy criticized as self-contradictory in a celebrated literary duel with the Japanese writer Tokutomi Roka. Although based in Tokyo throughout the war, the Emperor left to celebrate victory at Japan's most sacred shrine of Ise.

It was not just in the field of education and war that the Emperor departed from his much more usual "above the clouds" status to deal with earthly matters. After a violent outbreak of Socialist rioting, which in 1911 resulted in several executions, the crown was responsible for a grant of 1.5 million yen for drugs and medicines for the very poor in order to convey the message that, in the words of the official announcement, "as economic conditions change, the hearts of the people are steadfast." Not just in donations to the poor, but in exhortations to hard work, good manners, simple living and strenuous effort did the Emperor actively exhort his people to overcome hardship without recourse to extremism.

Emperor-worship was also proselytized intensively as part of the nationalist creed that ushered Japan into the twentieth century. The extent to which respect for the Emperor was inculcated, not just as a matter of political culture, but as a deep-seated obligation upon ordinary Japanese, cannot be exaggerated. The Japanese system of *on*, "obligations passively incurred" with which, like original sin in the Christian religion, every Japanese is born, related not just to one's very reason for existence, but to one's parents, one's older brother or sister, one's teachers and one's work, as well as society, symbolized by the Emperor.

Of these *ko-on*, obligation toward the Emperor, was the highest of all, and no man could begin to repay it in full. Duty to the Emperor far eclipsed that to Japan as a country, or to the government. While historically such obligations had always existed, Meiji Japan laid special stress upon them, because the Emperor was the sole source of its legitimacy. Japan had up until then been a divided country whose allegiance to its lords was central. A set of national values in respect of overseas threats had been virtually nonexistent: very few Japanese were even aware of an outside world. Even the uppermost members of the ruling class who traveled to Europe in the late nineteenth century obtained only a crude idea of its society. Barely anything was known about the United States and its history. Its intrusion fueled nationalist sentiment, while the growing severity of taxation helped to erode the feeling of loyalty to one's feudal lord. Thus the Meiji Restoration capitalized upon an always latent loyalty to a "divine Emperor," transforming it into the very lifeblood of twentieth-century Japanese nationalism.

In the 1880s the Meiji Emperor, after his initial descent to earthly status, visiting his people and sharing the experiences of his soldiers, began to rise again "above the clouds," becoming more and more remote. This may in fact have reflected his own autocratic, tough personality as he aged. Almost certainly, though, it was also part of an attempt by the Meiji authorities to return him to his god-like role now that their rule was consolidated. Once again he was to act as symbol for the nation rather than its ruler. The more self-confident the Meiji oligarchs became, the less important the Emperor was to buttressing their status and the more important he became as a symbol of national unity in whose name they chose to act.

The cult of the Emperor was hyped as never before. The Emperor became the distant father of his people. More than 70 of the 100 major imperial edicts of the reign had been published before 1880. He appeared only at grand functions like diplomatic receptions and troop maneuvers. When he traveled through the countryside now, the roads were closed and swept clean. People were fined for wearing disrespectful clothing and indulging in undignified, old-fashioned acts of prostration when he passed. He no longer visited the houses of ordinary mortals, but supped in imperial residences and military bases. He met only local notables.

The bureaucracy around the throne grew tighter. The Imperial Household Ministry, the Kunaisho, became remarkably powerful. Two men dominated the ministry in the later Meiji period: Hisamoto Hijikata, who was minister from 1887 to 1898, and Mitsuaki Tanaka, who ran it from 1898 to 1909. The two men considered themselves the most powerful ministers in the land. Yet in practice the greater power was wielded by Hirobumi Ito, Japan's effective and tough-minded autocratic leader, who was close to Hijikata; and Aritomo Yamagata, the country's effective military strongman, who was a friend of Tanaka. The Emperor himself was closer to Ito, and had some sympathy for his attempts to create a constitutional, even genuinely parliamentary structure for the regime.

By contrast Yamagata was a military autocrat who was slavishly loyal to the imperial system and fought by every means available to propagate its all-powerful status among the Japanese people. Like many ordinary people, Yamagata, the creator of the modern Japanese army, worshipped daily at the shrine of the Emperor. It was Yamagata who was responsible for the growing distance of subjects to Emperor, having been impressed by the way the Russian Czar was kept remote and mysterious from his people—hardly a fortunate comparison, as events turned out.

Yamagata was to be the most powerful man in Japan for years to come, the creator of its military machine and an autocrat of unbending sternness. He was from the first uncharismatic and unappealing in the extreme. Thin and stiff, he was deeply reserved, and troubled by ill-health in his stomach and bowels. Born of samurai stock, he had the characteristic Japanese hatred of the foreigner. When a British vessel raided a village for fuel and water, Yamagata wrote: "The ugly English barbarians behaved with extreme disorder and uncontrollable couthness . . . When we unsheath our swords and kill them, they . . . will be thrown into the deep sea like bits of seaweed." He was brave, and was badly scarred in his forearm when he was appointed to command a Choshu fort attacked by French ships.

As a young man Yamagata was a member of the Kikeitai, "shock troops"—an entirely new concept which consisted of groups of samurai forming the nucleus for a military force of commoners. The idea was that the ancient privileged caste of samurai were too few to resist the foreigners making military incursions into Japan: thus the ancient privileges of the caste had to be shared with commoners—under samurai control, of course. This concept was to be the foundation of Yamagata's subsequent vision of a national conscript army run at the top by Choshu samurai, but soldiered by conscripted commoners.

Yamagata, who in the late Meiji period was often effectively running the country, had the same attitude toward the bureaucracy, which he considered more important than mere politicians. He obtained an imperial ordinance which referred with utter contempt to the parties. His idea was of a detached bureaucracy serving the Emperor while alongside it the non-political armed forces in his service served the nation's interests abroad. Beneath both was Parliament and the political authority, which served only to act as a sometimes tiresome obstacle to government, but one necessary to ensuring the allegiance of the people. It barely occurred to him that the army might some day vie with the bureaucracy for the Emperor's ear. The soldiers would surely obey injunctions to loyalty.

The model for Japan's army was Germany's. The army was advised by a German staff officer, Major Jacob Meckel, to set up a general staff along German lines, whose head reported directly to the commander-in-chief, the Emperor. The war minister also had direct access to the throne, but his principal role was to reconcile the needs of the military with the demands of civilian government. Yamagata underlined the importance of the chief of staff's function by actually resigning as war minister to assume the job in 1878. Military men had a disproportionate influence on government until 1898, holding a majority of cabinet posts until then, and only just under half thereafter.

An imperial ordinance of 1900 decreed that the ministers of war and the navy had to be drawn from generals and admirals on the active service list. Thus cabinets could be brought down if either service withdrew its minister—which was to become of increasing importance during the heyday of Japanese militarism. The navy was given its own general staff in 1891, and direct access to the Emperor after the Sino-Japanese war. From the first, the army was more interested in territorial expansion, the navy in keeping the sea-lanes open for trade which was now seen as necessary to building up Japanese prosperity and global dominance: it became the "moderate" wing of the armed forces.

Yamagata built up the army with quite remarkable speed. By 1895 it comprised some 240,000 men in the field, half of them reserves (conscripts were required to spend seven years with the reserve after completing military service). The core consisted of 78,000 men, equipped with modern arms and professionally trained. Officers were drilled in strategic planning, intelligence work, mobilization, communications and supply. The navy by that time had a still very modest—by the standards of other navies—28 steamships, totalling 57,000 tons in weight. Yet Japanese shipyards were by then beginning to build major warships, rapid-firing guns and torpedoes, in an accelerated program of expansion under the genius of Admiral Heihachiro Togo, as a priority of the imperial government.

7 : THE PLUTOCRATS

THE JAPANESE GOVERNMENT OF 1868, FACED WITH A PRIMITIVE AGRICULtural economy, a reasonably wealthy merchant class and virtually no industry at all, adopted a radical approach to the Japanese economy. It did something quite new, an example that was to be taken up first by the Soviet Union in the 1920s and 1930s, and then by most other developing economies. The model for crash industrialization under state direction was not in fact established by Josef Stalin but by someone who is not a household name at all: Masayoshi Matsukata, a wily bureaucrat who was responsible for the formation of the great Japanese companies that today bestride the world. Matsukata came from a lower samurai family in Satsuma, becoming a provincial governor immediately after the Restoration, with the task of obtaining funds to support the industrialization of Japan.

In 1871 he moved to work in Ito's private office on local tax reform. A visit he made shortly afterward to France impressed him with the dirigiste methods of government finance there. In 1881 he became minister of finance at a time of dire financial difficulty caused by two problems, the massive printing of money immediately after the Restoration, partly to finance the cost of putting down the Satsuma rebellion, and the assault on Japan's home market by foreign companies now that tariffs had been removed. Matsukata formulated the policy of state incubation of Japan's new industries, before selling them off to private buyers.

This interventionism stemmed largely from necessity: the country's merchant class was deeply reluctant to invest. The merchants, nurtured in the sheltered autarchy of Tokugawa Japan, were remarkably conservative, their house rules warning them not to diversify into new lines, not to depart from traditional procedures and not to be disrespectful to the ancestors who had set up the business. In addition, very few merchants supplied foreign buyers or knew anything about machinery. Apart from the wealth of the merchant class, there was virtually no capital available for the new industrialization. Matsukata's ruthless solution was the land tax, which squeezed the peasantry to devastating effect. Again, this was precisely the model fastened upon by Stalin and most developing countries: milking the agricultural sector to provide capital for industry. Another rationale was that the surplus population in the countryside would then flock to the cities to make up the new industrial workforce.

In a third respect, Stalin was to follow the example of Japan. The classic "natural" process of industrialization was for light consumer industries such as textiles to come into being to satisfy local demand for such things as clothes; as they grew and spread, heavy industries providing the machinery for them were created. The Japanese started with heavy industry, partly because they were setting up a wholly new industrial model, partly because the first priority was to set up Japan's war machine. Engineering works, furnaces, arsenals, foundries and shipyards were already being built up at Satsuma and Choshu from the mid-nineteenth century: when the "outside lords" took power, they insisted on the national expansion of major chemical industries, sulphuric acid works, glass and cement factories.

One feature to be absent from Stalin's Russia was the supreme intelligence of the Meiji oligarchs in realizing that, as they had no technological base of their own, they had to learn their methods and techniques wholesale from the West. There was no false pride in Japan, of the kind that led China for centuries to reject the modernizing influence of Western technology. Arsenals sprang up in Nagasaki under Dutch supervision; the French managed the Yokusaka shipyard, arsenal and ironworks; and the English administered other shipyards. As light industries such as textiles began to grow up in the 1870s and 1880s, the English managed the Kagoshima spinning mill; the French, the Tomioka and Fukuoka plants; and the Swiss and Italians, the Maebashi filatures. Bright young Japanese were soon able to absorb the new skills as they took over factory management from the foreigners.

Four giant combines established positions of immense financial and industrial prominence during this period: Mitsui, Mitsubishi (which grabbed up the major shipyards), Sumitomo and Yasuda, which branched into banking and commerce. The lesser groups were largely formed by *daimyo* of previous centuries. Known as the *zaibatsu*, these giant oligopolies were to create an entirely new direction for economic development, skewing the Japanese model into something quite unique, one spawning a powerful business class resembling the semi-independent princedoms of the past which was to challenge government for dominance not just of the Japanese market economy but of the international marketplace.

As noted, the peculiar nature of the *zaibatsu* was shaped by the shortage of capital for industrialization. Because the capital was not put up by a variety of private investors, but by the government, the *zaibatsu* were shaped rather like big government departments, with a pyramid peaking at the summit. The enterprises were usually family-run at the very top, with differing systems of control. Just beneath the families were holding companies which had direct financial control of the numerous member companies. The holding companies managed a network of subsidiaries, interlocking directorates, stockholdings, margin guarantees and loans from the banks that each of the big four had subsumed to itself.

The Mitsuis, a family of bankers and traders going back to the sixteenth century, were the most powerful. The eleven branches of the Mitsui family were represented on a family council which was presided over by the eldest son. The family had a huge base of retainers selected and carefully trained for their complete loyalty. The Mitsui helped to finance the Meiji Restoration, and many have suggested that the company was in some respects the maker of the coup, rather than its chief economic beneficiary. Certainly Mitsui was richly rewarded: the major family companies—Mitsui

Gomei, the Mitsui Bank, Mitsui Bussan and Mitsui Kozan—vastly expanded their holdings from just commerce, banking and mining into textiles, shipping, warehousing, sugar, metals and machinery. By 1937 the company had a staggering market value for the time of $470 million and controlled an empire worth several billions.

Mitsubishi's fortune was largely founded on shipping; it was controlled by the two Iwasaki families, whose elder sons alternated in the post of chief policymaker. By 1944 Mitsubishi had control over a quarter of Japanese shipping and shipbuilding—an immense business; a third of electrical equipment; half of flour milling; nearly two thirds of the production of sheet glass; a third of sugar production; and around 15 percent of coal and metal production, warehousing, bank loans and cotton textiles.

Sumitomo was almost entirely owned and run by the head of the family and specialized in mining and equipment; by 1945 the company had investments of some $100 million in more than 120 companies and 30 industries. Yasuda specialized in banking and had assets of only $35 million by the same time, with direct ownership of around $110 million worth of subsidiaries; yet through its stockholdings the financial giant controlled assets of at least $10 billion. Banking was a major growth area for all the *zaibatsu* during the depression, when they swallowed up struggling small banks. In 1939 the seven big private banks held nearly 60 percent of the total assets and deposits of all banks; four of the seven were Mitsui, Mitsubishi, Sumitomo and Yasuda.

The *zaibatsu* existed alongside an economy of tiny firms and family-based component suppliers, which were entirely dependent upon them and enjoyed no security of contract comparable to that of employees of the big companies. This made them all the more prominent: there was no strong backbone of middle-sized business in Japan. The economic dominance of this handful of companies straddling commerce, industry and banking had enormous benefits in terms of economies of scale, long-term planning, the ability to raise capital, to switch between a failing sector and a newly prosperous one, to cushion company employees from the effect of recession, and to crush competition and suppress trade unionism wherever necessary. Equally, the disadvantages of this system for those outside the *zaibatsu* are readily apparent.

There is a great controversy as to whether the *zaibatsu* houses continued to benefit from government favors and direction and whether they were the creatures of the state or its masters. The straightforward explanation seems the best: government was fully involved in the nineteenth century, both in terms of capital and subsidy. It showered favors upon its privileged supporters in the financial and industrial elite.

It is hard to appreciate adequately the suffering of the workforce as Japan underwent its first, accelerated industrial revolution in a society in which they had no political voice and enjoyed little sympathy from the class that ran them. The peasant class felt the squeeze in two ways; first, there was great agrarian distress as a result of the steep tax increases: no fewer than 368,000 peasants left the land for nonpayment of taxes between 1883 and 1890. The number of tenants in seven prefectures increased from 34 percent in 1883 to 42 percent in 1887. Miserably destitute peasants, unable to make a living from the land, trekked to seek work in textile factories, cement works and foundries: when a new factory was set up, its agents went to scour the countryside, often picking upon particular localities that held some connection with the boss, to find workers to labor in conditions no better than those of eighteenth-century Britain.

Workers had no contracts and were expected to work whenever required at any time of the day or night for wages so low that long hours were essential to survival. They were generally housed in dingy dormitories. Many returned to the countryside, only to find there was nothing there to provide them with a livelihood. Many who persisted in their jobs quickly became ill and died of TB and other diseases. Housing conditions were unsanitary and overcrowded, the food poor, the pay low. Many women in the textile industries fared no better.

Between 1870 and 1923, Japan's economy grew at a rate of around 2.5 percent a year, which probably made it the fastest growing in the world. Growth was in spurts, with short, sharp recessions registered in 1890, 1900–01, and 1907–08. Growth was very largely engineered by government spending, which tripled between 1890 and 1900, then more than doubled again from 183 million yen to 338 million yen in 1910. Defense spending multiplied seven times. With the expansion of heavy industry beginning to get under way through government sponsorship, the ratio of those in industrial employment rose from 31 percent in 1890 to 44 percent in 1915. Most industry, however, was now light industry, with textiles accounting for a third of manufacturing output and half of exports up to 1914. Half of all family labor consisted of women textile workers. By 1912, 44 percent of GNP was still derived from agriculture. The country remained a long way behind the United States economically.

The number of industrial workers had increased more than fifteen-fold between 1888 and 1909—but the figure is less startling when one considers there were only 136,000 industrial workers to begin with, and only 2.5 million in 1909 (there were eight million by 1935). The cities were being transformed: the proportion of the population living in cities of more than 50,000 inhabitants nearly doubled over the same period, from 7 percent to 14 percent. Tokyo's population virtually doubled; Osaka's rose to 1.5 million. As the number of workers grew, so did the first stirrings of industrial militancy. By 1907 strikes were becoming commonplace. They were met, as might be expected, with the threat of dire repression, coupled with a conscience on the part of some Meiji leaders that growing inequality was a problem that would have to be addressed.

As far back as 1901, Yamagata's minister of home affairs, Sumatsu Kencho, was drawing up a package of suppressive measures. The Public Peace Police Act of 1900 had been introduced to ban the Social Democratic party on the day it was founded. In 1905 social dissent in the cities reached new dimensions, albeit over a patriotic issue: the Treaty of Portsmouth, widely regarded as a sellout after the Japanese victory over Russia, was the subject of angry rioting in Hibiya. The following year there were violent demonstrations against rises in tram fares, and in 1907 strikes mushroomed, starting at the Ashio Copper Mine, spreading to the Koike coal mines, the Uraga docks and the Horonai mines. Again the Public Peace Police Act was invoked.

It is not hard to see that these provisions could be invoked against virtually any attempt to form a trade union. As a result the Chinsen Ki, the Period of Submersion, began during which, because unions could not legally be formed, demonstrations usually took violent form, with company property being destroyed and burnt. At the Ashio Copper Mine in 1909, 12,000 miners ran riot, burning housing, throwing bombs and smashing lamps; the riot was finally suppressed by three infantry companies from the Takasaki Regiment headquarters. In 1911 a celebrated tramway strike on New Year's Day in Tokyo resulted in most of the strikers' demands being met, but the imprisonment of 47 of their leaders.

Unsurprisingly, in this climate, the repression led to the formation of an underground socialist movement. The suppressed Social Democratic Party reemerged as the Japan Socialist Party, permitted to organize by the enlightened Saionji government in 1906. However rivals and more extreme offshoots also came into being: Denjiro Kotoku led an anarchist wing, while Sen Katayama led the first Communist Party. The low boiling point of the autocracy toward these new groups was demonstrated by the High Treason Trial of 1910–1911, when Kotoku and eleven other socialists were condemned to death for allegedly plotting against the Emperor. It was clear, on later evidence, that the charges were a complete fabrication, and used as the pretext for a general crackdown on the labor movement. Katayama left the country in disillusion in 1914.

Yamagata formulated a crushingly authoritarian decree in 1910 that marked the formal banning of socialism in Japan. The various remedies suggested by Yamagata included "excluding individualism," promoting "healthy thought" and "expanding vocational education to eliminate the educated unemployed idlers." Yamagata's ideologues argued that "to prevent socialism becoming anarchism as the common flu turns to pneumonia," as well as "individualism, internationalism . . . husbands addressing their wives with the horrific 'san,'" and the light Japanese cuisine being overwhelmed by heavy Western food, the country must return to traditional ancestral values.

8 : Outward Bound

BY THE LAST DECADE OF THE NINETEENTH CENTURY, THE MEANS HAD been forged for one of the world's most backward nations to embark upon a period of sustained military expansion—at about the time when the rest of the world's industrial powers were beginning to doubt the virtues of imperialism.

There were four main motives. The first was defensive. Up to 1868 Japan lay like some prostrate hedgehog before the major imperial powers. The "defense" adopted by the shogun had been to curl up in a prickly ball, expel all foreign influences and pretend that the outside world did not exist. The arrival of predatory American, Russian, British and French warships destroyed any illusion that Japan could resist the major powers militarily; its only protection now was its lack of resources, which made it an unattractive prize.

The second was economic: it took only a short experience of industrialization in the second half of the nineteenth century for Japan to realize that it lacked the necessary ingredients—raw materials and markets—to service its industrial base. Marxist historians have long argued that Western imperialism derived from the need of countries sated with capital to find new outlets by exporting to dependencies overseas. For Japan, the security of its supplies of raw materials and its overseas trade became a simple matter of national economic survival. Once Japan industrialized, it had to safeguard essential imports and markets in a hostile world where both were threatened by predators. That the world was unfriendly, no Japanese doubted: the colonial powers were not going to permit Japan free trade in Asia, which they dominated, without a struggle.

Third, there was a curious mixture of ideological, racial and anti-colonial reasoning which was not entirely without moral force as well as logic. Japan saw itself as an Asian country, albeit one vastly superior to the rest; the Japanese viewed the depredations imposed upon Asia by the colonial powers—America, Russia and Britain—with deep distrust. It was to become their mission to liberate the continent from those powers and impose an authentically Asian form of dependence upon them—one to be based on their concept of filial loyalty, the benevolent subordination of countries to their "father," Japan. This version failed to appreciate that many Asians might consider the relationship of total subordination that children have to their father and subjects to the Emperor in Japan as not the ideal substitute for Western colonialism—indeed, possibly a worse alternative; but Japan's version of "co-prosperity" was certainly an authentically Asian solution.

Fourth, and less forgivably, there was a feeling in Japan that, as a nation which in the space of two generations aspired to become one of the world's great powers, an empire was its due, just as it was that of any major industrial power. The great empty spaces of Manchuria and other parts of Asia beckoned. Japan, to be counted alongside the great European powers and America, had to fight its way to its own sphere of influence, or it would inevitably be squeezed out.

Japanese policy was thus buttressed by a formidable logic, although one that was perhaps out of step with world history. The Japanese statesmen who traveled to Europe failed to appreciate the growing influence of public opinion in the democracies, which had sparked a decline in imperial interest, while anticolonialist movements were breaking out throughout their possessions, increasing the costs of remaining there. Japan was like an young man eager to stake out his own "territory," just as other nations began to outgrow the concept altogether. Japan's national immaturity, while far from being entirely surprising, was to combine with its political underdevelopment to unleash the tragedy of the Pacific War. Unlike the case with German aggression, there was nothing unreasonable or even megalomaniacal about Japan's quest for overseas possessions.

This becomes obvious when looking at the arguments put forward by Yamagata and circulated on at least two occasions. In 1888 he argued that, with the completion of the Trans-Siberian Railway in Russia and the Pacific Railway in Canada, a major clash would ensue between Britain and Russia. He believed the Russians would invade Korea which then, as throughout history, was the Asian bridgehead to Japan. "It is our policy to maintain Korea as an independent nation without ties to China and to keep Korea free of occupation by one of the great nations of Europe." Alongside this fear, Yamagata believed that China, like Japan, might undergo a process of modernization and, from a position of dominating Korea, threaten his country. It was important, therefore, that Japan had the military strength to exert its own claims as Russia, Britain and China struggled for dominance of the region.

Two years later, Yamagata argued that Japan's real frontiers "of interest" extended beyond the country's shoreline. "If we wish to maintain the nation's independence and to rank among the great powers, it is necessary to step forward and defend our line of interest, to be always in a favorable position, and not satisfied to defend only the line of sovereignty. Our line of interest is really in Korea." He extended this notion to arguing that Japan, rather than any of its rivals, must become dominant in East Asia and "ride the wave of victory" there.

Yamagata's theory was set out even more explicitly by Colonel Ogawa Matashi, who was to become his chief of staff, in 1877. He argued that there was a clear possibility that one of the Western powers which had already largely subdued the Middle Kingdom would launch a direct attack upon it, thus threatening Japan's independence. The only possible retaliation was to strike into China on two fronts—a land offensive against Peking from the north and a siege of Shanghai from the sea. The objective would not be to seize China but to trade these two for an "independent" Manchuria, which would in effect become a Japanese protectorate; to create a similar protectorate over southern China; and to take over Taiwan and northern China. Thus, just two decades after the Meiji Restoration, senior army officers were entertaining ideas of a large empire in Asia in order—as they saw it—to forestall the designs of other empires upon the region.

The first flashpoint was Korea, as it had been in 1873. As Japan's closest neighbor on the Asian mainland, separated only by the small Korean

Straits, it had always been a bone of contention between China and Japan. Initially, Korea and Japan had been allies because they had both been hit by the system imposed by China on anyone who traded with that alarmingly decadent country. After the Meiji Restoration, Japan promptly sought to impose its own commercial terms on Korea and, when rebuffed, shrank from war in 1873.

Only two years later Korean shore batteries opened up on Japanese ships—probably as a result of provocation by the latter—and Japan's fleet set sail, demanding that Korea's ports cede preferential trading rights. The intimidated Koreans granted these, and the Chinese retaliated by seeking preferential trading agreements between Korea and the West, as a subtle ruse to secure Western support should Japan invade Korea. In Korea itself views were increasingly polarized between those who favored the status quo, who were pro-Chinese, and pro-Japanese modernizers. In 1884 a coup was carried out by the latter in Seoul, with the help of the Japanese legation. Only Hirobumi Ito's cool head in promptly denying that the Japanese government had been involved avoided hostilities. The uprising was suppressed.

Ten years later, when Japan was much more self-assured militarily, a new spark was found. The Koreans asked for Chinese help in suppressing a group of armed insurgents. The Japanese promptly countered by sending their own forces and demanding that the Korean government undergo a thoroughgoing reform. The Koreans and Chinese indignantly rejected this, and on August 1, 1894, war was declared.

It was characterized by a string of successes that sent popular pride to the rafters. The Japanese quickly surrounded and took Seoul; by mid-September they had taken Pyongyang in the north. A month later Japanese armies had moved into southern Manchuria, north of Korea, and then into the Liaotung Peninsula, taking Port Arthur, the capital, by the end of November. The successes were so overwhelming, and supposedly under the Emperor's personal direction from his headquarters at Hiroshima, that the Japanese public became convinced that it was only a matter of time before the country took its proper status at the front rank of nations. Ostensibly, Japan secured a satisfactory peace agreement as well at Shimonoseki in April. Korea was freed from its vassal status to China and concluded a close alliance with Japan. The Liaotung Peninsula and Taiwan were ceded.

Having spectacularly won the war, Japan proceeded as quickly to lose the peace. In America there remained considerable sympathy for the fellow Pacific anticolonial power. But the major colonial powers—Britain, Germany and France—were alarmed by the speed of the Japanese victory. In addition, the palsied weakness of imperial China, which the major powers had preferred to administer through the "treaty port system," rather than invade, was exposed. On April 11, 1895, the Russians pressed France and Germany to join in the "triple intervention," which demanded that the Liaotang Peninsula be returned to China, for fear that there would otherwise be a "constant threat" from Japan to Peking. The Russian foreign minister, Sergei Witte, feared that otherwise there was a strong possibility that "the Mikado might beat the Chinese empire and Russia would need hundreds of thousands of troops for the defence of her possessions."

Faced by this ultimatum from three great powers, the Japanese had no alternative but to leave. The Russians also brought intense pressure to bear to reassert Korea's independence in fact as well as in name. The Japanese were again forced to agree. The first expedition to the Asian mainland had thus ended with military victory and diplomatic defeat at the hands of the imperial powers—a combination calculated to leave Japan with both an appetite for further intervention and a lasting resentment against the colonial powers.

The Korean campaign had deeply affected the recent attempts to set up a modern constitutional government in Japan; the opposition had no choice but to join in the popular patriotic battle cries at the time. The army's and the navy's successes meanwhile had become the stuff of legend: in particular, the heroic march on Weihaiwei in nightmare conditions after a landing from Port Arthur became the first of Japan's modern military myths. The journals of an unknown second lieutenant were devoured eagerly by a Japanese public which had never savored military success before. "As far as one could see, snow covered the Shantung Peninsula. It was biting cold. Beards hung like icicles, frozen from the chin. To combat frostbite, all extremities had wool protective covers. But the cold iced even our bone marrow. The horses were too cold to continue. We walked . . . In this way we marched for several days." Weihaiwei was seized after three weeks of these grim conditions. A legend had been born, that of Japanese endurance and invincibility.

One further feature of Japan's first overseas military intervention deserves mention. As already observed, Japanese policy was understandable in the context of the struggle for domination in Asia after the country had emerged from isolation. Yet the Japanese had acted in Korea, as they were to act on later occasions, on the flimsiest of legal pretexts—that Chinese troops had been brought in to crush a local rebellion. There was no legal justification for what they did other than that they considered

Korea to be fully within their sphere of intervention, necessary to keeping out their rivals and to forming the beginnings of an enormous integrated economic zone to furnish Japan's needs. It is hard to see any real difference between the justification of this war and that of any other of Japan's colonial wars in terms of national security.

The opportunity for Japan to revenge itself on Russia was not long in coming. The Russians started to overreach themselves, moving forces into the Liaotang Peninsula to the west of Korea: the reality that China was now under their guns prompted a desperate scramble between Russia, Germany and France effectively to divide the country. Russian interests clashed directly with those of Japan: they proposed to build a railway line across Manchuria linking Vladivostok to the Trans-Siberian Railway, with a spur running south to Port Arthur. The Liaotung Peninsula was granted to Russia under a 25-year lease just a few years after Japan had been expelled from its military conquest of the region. Russia now effectively controlled Manchuria, which was of immense strategic importance to Japan. Russia did not actually dominate Korea, viewed by Japanese defense planners as "a dagger aimed at the heart of Japan" and, increasingly, as a strategic extension of Japanese territory. But the Japanese feared that such domination might follow.

After the humiliation of 1895, which had been based on a prickly mixture of diplomatic overconfidence and inexperience, Japan's statesmen sensibly responded to this bullying by the Russians by seeking alliances with the other imperial powers. It quickly found a friend. Britain and the United States had both responded with caution to the greed displayed on the Chinese mainland by Russia, France and Germany. Chary of a major continental involvement, the British in particular prepared to lend support to the American idea of the "Open Door": the new partition of China would be recognized, in effect, provided that Britain and the United States were given free access to the region for trade.

But the British were profoundly uneasy about the expansion of czarist power in the area, and feared that Russian control over Manchuria would exclude British commercial interests. By 1902, the Japanese had taken advantage of this unease. In September, at Britain's initiative, the 1902 Anglo-Japanese alliance was signed, under which the British effectively promised the Japanese that they would not join any anti-Japanese coalition of the kind that had occurred with the Triple Intervention of 1895. The British had learned their lesson. This provided a massive relief for Japan, which had spent the previous seven years doubling the size of its armed forces for what it regarded as an inevitable clash with Russia as well as to build up its power for projection into Asia and to safeguard its economic interests. It meant that it no longer need fear conflict with the most powerful naval force in the region.

War with Russia approached with the inevitability of an irresistible force meeting an immovable object. By 1902, the Japanese army had defined Korea as an essential foreign interest. "For the long-range policy of our country," said a memorandum of the general staff, it was essential that Korea became "part of the Japanese empire." The Russians, far from being content with their gains further north, made it clear that they intended to contest this. As far back as October 1895, the Japanese minister in Korea was implicated in an attempted coup in Seoul in which the country's queen, who hated the Japanese, was murdered. The king escaped to take refuge in the Russian legation.

Hirobumi Ito attempted to limit the danger of open war by agreeing, in effect, to respect Korea's neutrality with Russia. General Yamagata was dispatched to witness the coronation of Czar Nicholas II and reached an agreement by which Korea was placed under an informal joint protectorate of the two nations, which were permitted to maintain armies in the country. The next few years saw frenzied attempts by the Japanese to set up economic ties to advance their interests in Korea. There is evidence that, as the century ended, Russia was getting less interested in its competition with Japan in Korea and more concerned with its rivalry with Britain in China.

In 1900, the Boxer Rebellion broke out across China, primarily aimed against Western economic interests, which prompted a British-led intervention to suppress it and the imposition of crushing indemnities. The Japanese cooperated with the British, while at the same time preparing to utilize it in their own imperial interest from their base at Formosa to make a salient into Fukien Province, a "southern option" for expansion which excited many Japanese military and business leaders. At the last moment, the initiative was called off for fear of offending Japan's ally, Britain.

The Boxer rising had another effect as well: the Russians moved in large number of troops to defend their interests in Manchuria when these came under attack. For Yamagata, among others, this was tantamount to a declaration of war. It was clear, he argued, that Russia was undertaking a "primitive occupation" of Manchuria; China's partition was "inevitable." The Japanese prime minister in 1901, Taro Katsura, argued that Russia "will inevitably extend into Korea and will not end until there is no room left for us." His foreign minister claimed, "If Manchuria becomes the property of Russia, Korea itself cannot remain independent. It is a matter of life and death for Japan." Although over the next three years the Japanese energetically sought the withdrawal of Russian troops from Manchuria by diplomatic means, there was no real progress. Japan had already decided to launch a war against Russia by early 1903. In December, the cabinet reviewed the issue and in early February the following year land and sea forces landed on Korea to launch a massive attack against the Russian forces.

Japan's navy bombarded and quickly bottled up the Russian Far Eastern fleet in Port Arthur, while Japanese forces attacked the city from the land as well. A major offensive was staged in April against Liaotung, spearheading the campaigns against Russian ports in Manchuria. Contrary to Japanese war mythology which asserted that the move was decisive, the offensive was successful only in preventing the Russian navy from posing the kind of danger to the Japanese navy that might have crippled the war effort. The first battles stretched out into the kind of prolonged and bitter trench warfare that the world was to see much more of in the First World War. The Battle of Liaotung took two months to win, but Port Arthur fell only after a year.

In March 1905, the Japanese and Russian forces engaged in the Battle of Mukden, where 250,000 Japanese engaged 350,000 Russians with no decisive result. The Russian Baltic Fleet, which had sailed halfway round the world in order to lift the blockade on Port Arthur, arrived in Tsushima Straits in May, to be attacked by the Japanese fleet under Admiral Heihachiro Togo in one of the most decisive naval engagements of modern times. The victory that had eluded Japan on land was won at sea. The Japanese were already seriously worried about the huge casualty rate and enormous cost of the war; but the Russians, for whom the war had never been much more than a sideshow, blinked first and took advantage of an American offer of mediation to attend the Portsmouth Peace Conference of August, 1905.

There the Russians made major concessions. Japan was given complete freedom of action in Korea, as well as the Liaotang lease and control of the spur railroad from the Chinese Eastern Railway at Harbin down to Port Arthur. In Manchuria the Japanese secured the total expulsion of Russia and won significant concessions for themselves from China, which formally had possession of the country; but this stopped short of exclusive control.

Japan had thus now fought its biggest war in Asia as an ambitious and powerful country and won, although not overwhelmingly, against one of the major colonial powers. It had initiated the fighting but its casus belli—to prevent Russian domination of Manchuria and the Korean peninsula—was one which had aroused sympathy in Britain and America. Japan was viewed as a "plucky little country" which had taken on the Russian bear. Russia's behavior in China had been sufficiently bullying to give Japan the benefit of the doubt. The outcome of the war was in effect to add another colony, Korea, to the one already occupied, Formosa, and to whet Japan's appetite for further gains in Manchuria. Internationally, Japan's alliance with Britain and the general distaste for Russia had earned the country a considerable measure of support: outsiders saw Japan's motives as partially anticolonial, not colonial and bullying in themselves.

Domestically, the huge number of casualties had turned the cult of war shrines into a frenzy, propagated and financed by the state, while jingoism reached new peaks of fervor and anger after the "disappointing" terms of the Portsmouth Peace Treaty. While the war was under way, party politics had virtually ceased: from being an oligarchy dominated by Ito, Japan had become a virtual military dictatorship dominated by Yamagata and his protégé Katsura. Ito himself was dispatched afterward to the important but subordinate post of Japanese resident-general in Korea. Departing with a staff of around 70, a police force of just 250 and two detachments of soldiers, he descended on Korea's "Emperor" in 1807 and forced his abdication. An insurrection broke out which was ruthlessly suppressed, and provided Japan with the excuse formally to annex the country. In October 1909 Ito paid a visit to Harbin and was assassinated by a Korean nationalist. So ended the life of the most influential Meiji figure of them all—a Bismarck considered too soft by his contemporaries in government. By August, 1910, Korea had been formally absorbed into Japan. In Manchuria, Japanese business, at the government's and army's prodding, began a concerted assault on the region's natural resources which quickly offended both the Americans and the British, who were wedded to the "Open Door" policy.

Japan had now reached a dangerous pass in its international behavior. The Meiji Restoration had succeeded in forging a strong national army and navy, as well as a belief that to survive internationally the country must expand. Both the Sino-Japanese war of 1895 and the Russo-Japanese war of 1905–06 had been wars started by the Japanese, each of which had yielded a colony: Formosa first, Korea second. The army was now arguing that the conquest of Manchuria was necessary for the country's security, while business leaders also pressed for its annexation.

The navy, which as we have seen was independent of the army and also directly responsible to the Emperor, had entirely different views. It believed that, for a group of islands like Japan, territorial conquest was much less important than domination of sea lanes and felt that war with the country's main naval rivals, the United States and Britain, was inevitable. Indeed, for a moment after the Russo-Japanese war there was serious friction between Japan and Theodore Roosevelt's America.

American policy toward Japan's decision to press forward in a more aggressive overseas policy seemed calculated to goad and arouse suspicion. Ever since the arrival of Perry's Black Ships, the United States had been a potentially hostile power challenging the Japanese for control of the Pacific. The decision by Presidents McKinley and Roosevelt effectively to annex the Philippines in the early 1900s was viewed with immense alarm in Japan as an attempt to outflank Japan in the western Pacific and penetrate China through its "Open Door" policy, which aggressively promoted American trade interests and, much worse, to probe into Manchuria, which Japan effectively regarded as a subordinate province. The introduction of curbs on Japanese mass migration into California was a further direct provocation, and moreover convinced the Japanese that it must look to China as a potential area for settlement for Japan's overcrowded islands— except that the Americans seemed to be trying to close that off too and incorporate it into their sphere of influence.

Japan's vigorous pursuit of its alliance with Britain which had culminated in the 1902 Anglo-Japanese naval alliance was also cunningly contrived to outflank the Americans: for Japan was determined to achieve naval equality with the Americans, which would be possible if Britain remained neutral, although it could not hope to take on both Anglo-Saxon powers at once. For their part the British were only too glad to secure Japanese support to counter Russian expansionism in east Asia, to be able to wield leverage over the Japanese, and to promote its own interests independently of America.

The Japanese had embarked on the construction of two battle fleets consisting of 12 big ships altogether in the early 1900s, the "eight-four plan." In 1907 Admiral Fukudomi wrote, "The Imperial navy made the United States its sole strategic enemy." With the Japanese and American fleets roughly equal in size, the latter were at a disadvantage owing to the limited cruising range of their warships from the eastern Pacific; moreover the Philippines, where there was no big American naval base, could not easily be defended even then against major Japanese attack.

In 1906–07 President Roosevelt clumsily wielded his "big stick" by staging a "world tour" by the American fleet. He soon realized that he had overreached himself, and America tried out a more moderate policy of rapprochement with Japan, signing the Root-Takahira and Taft-Katsura agreements which confirmed Japan's stake in both Korea and southern Manchuria. In 1910 Japan annexed Korea.

Thus there were three separate directions in which Japan's newfound imperial destiny was spurring the country to further conflict: the temptation to move into Manchuria; the temptation to move into Fukuoka in southern China; and the temptation to take on the "Open Door" powers which had free access to trade in China. As Meiji Japan entered the first decade of the twentieth century in a raucous cacophony of jingoistic nationalism, it was impossible to predict that a brief flurry of enlightenment—which would come to be seen as a period of decadence and weakness by later generations—would soon effectively bottle up the forces of Japanese militarism and imperialism for almost two decades.

9 : "AFFLUENT AND HUMANE"

ON APRIL 29, 1901, A BOY WAS BORN TO PRINCESS SADAKO, THE WIFE of Crown Prince Yoshihito, Emperor Meiji's son, after less than a year of marriage. The boy was called Hirohito, *Hiro* meaning affluent, after an ancient Chinese text which suggested that if a country was affluent, the people would be at peace. *Hito* was the customary imperial name, meaning humane or generous. The infant was, in addition, given the princely name of Michinomiya. Prince Yoshihito wrote the first name in pen and ink, while the imperial household minister wrote the second; they were ceremonially laid on the baby's pillow, while the names were announced at three shrines in the palace gardens. Hirohito was weaned by his mother and wet nurse at the Crown Prince's palace.

Seventy days after the birth, the baby was sent away to be raised by another family, as was the cold custom in the imperial family and among the higher aristocracy. It was believed that a child might be in danger from the rivalries of the principal ladies in the household; toddlers anyway got in the way of court proceedings, and the existence of adult ways and courtesans was not good for an infant's character. General Iwao Oyama, a distinguished officer, was asked to take in the boy. He refused. The responsibility would be too great, and he would be expected to commit suicide if the child fell ill and died.

Count Sumiyoshi Kawamura, a venerable former navy minister, was approached next. He accepted. On July 7 the baby was brought to his villa in Azubu, two miles away from the Crown Prince's residence, and accommodated in a specially built pavilion in the garden. A wet nurse and a doctor and nurse from the imperial palace were in attendance, while the general's wife and daughter were also constantly present. A courtier, Osanaga Kanroji, who wrote an account of Hirohito's early years, bears testimony to the 70-year-old's devotion to his charge. The old man decided to instil in the child "a dauntless spirit to withstand all hardships" and to remove "traces of arrogance and egotism." He arranged for an English governess to give the boy "an independent spirit, a sympathetic heart and a sentiment of gratitude." Little more than a year later the boy was joined by a younger brother, Prince Chichibu.

When Hirohito was not yet four years old, Kawamura died, and his widow petitioned to be relieved of her heavy responsibility. The two princes were transferred to a building in the gardens of the Crown Prince's palace. Less than two years later a special kindergarten was set up nearby. It consisted of three rooms in the classical Japanese style with tatami mats and sliding panels that could be removed to open up a large space. Cotton cushions were tied around the pillars to prevent accidents. Five children, all a year older than the little Prince, so as to advance his development, were selected to be his companions.

Hirohito was a prematurely grave, excessively clumsy child. Kanroji recalled, "He looked formal and serious in his youth, neither smiling nor laughing. He did not appear to take any joy in either exercise or play." He was awkward. "The young Prince Hirohito was not particularly well-coordinated. It even took him a long time to do up the buttons on his Western-style clothes. It was most irritating to stand by and watch him, and one wanted to reach out and help. But one could only stand there patiently, and the more one stared at him, the more he fumbled. We have the expression 'twice more than others,' but for His Majesty, it was 'three times more.'"

The boy suffered from increasingly obvious minor disabilities: he was very nearsighted, which being made to concentrate on distant objects for hours at a time—thought to be a remedy—did nothing to improve. He walked with a shuffle and had a slightly curved spine, which gave him a stoop: sitting in a specially designed chair failed to cure this. He was small and weak, yet usually well disposed to his playmates, sometimes taking the blame for them—as he could not be punished—while on occasion acting the boss and insisting on taking the role of commander-in-chief in childhood war games. He was cosseted and pampered to protect him from physical harm, his aides picking him up when he fell and catching him on one occasion when he jumped from a wall. Two years later, he was sent to the Peers' School, which existed for the highest rank of Japanese aristocratic children.

The principal of the school was General Maresuke Nogi, formerly commander of the Third Army in the Russo-Japanese war, who had taken 203-Meter Hill, a Russian stronghold viewed as unassailable, with the loss of his two sons in battle. Nogi was a personification of everything that was worst and best about Japan's aristocratic warrior tradition. He is said to have been the main influence on Hirohito's early life: certainly the Emperor was to retain a long affection for Nogi, although it can be doubted that in later years, Hirohito, with his wider experience, took the general's purist militarism all that seriously. During the siege of Port Arthur, Nogi had not just presided over the bitterest struggle in the war; he had insisted upon the highest standards of discipline and humanity from his troops, severely punishing any transgression against civilian life and property. He showed that given the right leadership, the Japanese were capable of civilized conduct in war—something seriously called into question half a century later.

The grizzled old warrior was personally approached by the Emperor to become the school's head, in order to transform it from a playground for rich children into a suitable stable for an Emperor. The general himself lived in a small two-story wooden building, and was prey to that tiresome disease of some of the very rich or very important: stinginess, a trait he inculcated into Hirohito as the downside to his modesty. Nogi, as might have been expected, paid special attention to his charge: every day after class the principal would see his imperial pupil off home, straightening his cap, adjusting his salute, giving him a lecture. Once a week the boy received special instruction from the headmaster. In addition, Nogi would often attend Hirohito's classrooms, making him thoroughly nervous.

During five years at the Peers' School, however, the prince gradually overcame his early disabilities. He was forced to undertake rigorous physical training, including cold showers, and to perform athletics and fencing, as well as to become a relatively good swimmer—a sport he enjoyed later. He also became a moderately proficient golfer. The general also had an unconcealed bias against the pleasures of life, which rubbed off on Hirohito, who was never to overindulge himself sensually, as his grandfather and father had, but to prefer retiring, solitary activities.

Hirohito's overdependence upon Nogi stemmed from his virtual lack of family life, apart from that of dedicated attendants; this was quite usual in Japan's aristocratic circles. His grandfather, the Emperor, was distantly genial toward him, smiling at him when the occasion permitted and occasionally encouraging him in his sporting activities. Although gruff and fierce in appearance, the Emperor was reputed to indulge in a small army of concubines, as well as having a penchant for poetry and good claret. He alternated between being a jolly old soul and a severe one.

His son, Yoshihito, was a weak-willed type who from an early age had showed signs of mental instability. Mutsuhito treated his son with formality and distance: he was clearly a major disappointment to his father. Crown Prince Yoshihito was an absentee father: as he reached maturity, he spent as little time in Tokyo as possible, fleeing its severe winters, scarcely seeing Hirohito. He was also an insatiable drunk and womanizer, carrying his father's tastes to extremes. On a memorable occasion Hirohito, at the tender age of four, was plied with sake by his father until he fell over in a stupor. The young prince claimed later that he never touched alcohol from that day. Certainly he never became a womanizer—breaking with the aristocratic tradition of his family.

In 1906, the powerfully built 53-year-old Emperor Mutsuhito, who resisted routine medical checkups and turned down any thorough ones, began to suffer from diabetes and kidney failure. He refused proper examinations or treatment, and continued with the same diet as his condition steadily deteriorated for six years. On July 12, 1912, while attending graduation day at Tokyo Imperial University, the Emperor suddenly complained of feeling tired and short of breath. He underwent his first intensive examination, which revealed that he was suffering from uremic poisoning—which was fatal in those days.

A second opinion was sought from two specialists from the University of Tokyo: as they were not allowed to examine the Emperor without a formal court title, they were officially appointed "Imperial aides" at an emergency ceremony. They were not permitted to give him any kind of injection, however, as his body was divine. When news of the Emperor's illness got out, crowds assembled in front of the palace to pray. The tramcars outside slowed down and blankets were muffled around the rails to reduce the noise. Theaters closed their doors. On July 30 he died.

The death of the Emperor was accompanied by two remarkable rites of passage, each of which symbolized different aspects of the Meiji transformation—and showed its limitations. The first was the funeral itself, an astounding pastiche of ancient and modern Japan. The ceremony began at eight o'clock on the night of September 13, 1912. Temple bells tolled 108 times, cannon boomed in the distance and the processional dirge sounded as the Emperor's cortege emerged from the imperial palace into the eerie torchlight of a Tokyo night. Hundreds of thousands took to the streets to watch the procession of 20,000 go past.

The carriage itself was immense, attended by mourners in traditional court dress. Following them came attendants with bows and halberds, fans and staffs, imperial princes, the palace staff, the *genro*, members of the government, senior civil servants and noblemen, many divesting themselves of drab top hats and tails to revert to traditional pre-Restoration splendor, and members of the two houses of the Diet in tails "like river loach after goldfish, or penguins after golden pheasants," as one observer remarked.

Two hours later the procession reached Aoyama parade ground where, watched by assembled ambassadors and dignitaries, trumpets were sounded and the new Emperor Taisho, Prime Minister Saionji and Imperial Household Minister Watanabe, spoke briefly. The coffin was then laid out on the funeral train for Kyoto, leaving at two in the morning along a line where subjects bowed and prostrated themselves as it passed. When the train reached Kyoto after 340 miles the following afternoon, the body was taken to the imperial tomb at Momoyama.

Six weeks after the Meiji Emperor's death—itself a traumatic event for Hirohito—Nogi appeared after a long absence abroad at the residence of his imperial pupil, his beard untidy, his appearance unkempt, his eyes dull and sunken. He gave the boy two books on the duties of the throne and lectured him, as usual: "Please remember that my physical presence is not necessary for me to be with you in your work. I shall always be watching you and your welfare will always be my concern. Work hard, for your sake, and the sake of Japan."

Just before the funeral cortege left the imperial palace, General Maresuke Nogi and his wife Shizuko, the Emperor's most trusted military aide and guardian to his grandson, Hirohito, seated themselves in front of the imperial portrait in their modest home less than a mile from the funeral site at Aoyama.

The general, it is believed, stabbed her in the heart with a short sword, perhaps because she could not go through with the act of ritual suicide. Then he cut a horizontal gash in his abdomen and tried to sever his head, leaving it partly attached.

They left notes which spoke of "following the lord"—an ancient feudal practice called *Junshi*, to guard the Emperor on his journey through the after-life, which had been outlawed as far back as 1663. Nogi's note also spoke of his shame at having lost the imperial colors during fighting in the Satsuma rebellion of 1877. A possible unspoken motive was the loss of Nogi's two sons in the Russo-Japanese war, after which the general is said to have asked the Emperor for permission to kill himself, but was refused; with the Emperor dead, he had been delivered from his obligation to stay alive.

The suicides caused major controversy, overshadowing the funeral itself. On the one hand, admiration was expressed that the traditional ways of Japan had not come to an end with its passage to modernity. On the other, a dozen other people promptly followed the general's example and committed suicide. People argued that the old, savage Japan should not be glorified in this way. As one newspaper wrote, General Nogi's death marked "the completion of Japan's bushido of old. And while emotionally we express the greatest respect, rationally we regret we cannot approve. One can only hope that this act will not long blight the future of our national morality. We can appreciate the general's intention; we must not learn from his behaviour." In fact, the suicides represented a reassertion not just of the spirit of Bushido—the warrior spirit—but the revival of certain notions in the armed forces.

The Prince was just eleven years old. On hearing the news, he is said to have remarked with remarkable sangfroid—or perhaps numbed by the shock—that "Japan has suffered a regrettable loss." The boy was now without a mentor. His father was by now impossibly remote. His mother, beautiful, intelligent, and a Fujiwara princess scarred by her tumultuous marriage, had never played much part in his life.

The Prince spent two more years at the Peers' School before the deci-sion was made to create a special school around him. It was argued that he must be spared the bullying and other risks of being sent to an ordinary institution. The school was set up in the grounds of the Togu Palace, well away from the venality of the Akasaka Palace, with its air of Versailles decadence revolving around the new Emperor. Hirohito's new mentor was

Admiral Togo, the hero of the naval war with Russia. He was cast in a very different mold from the austere Nogi. A cheerful extrovert who enjoyed fraternizing with his men, he was put in charge of the boy at an age when children are more prone to ask questions; the Crown Prince was to be much less influenced by him—indeed by some accounts viewed the admiral with contempt.

Seven years of schooling followed, in the company of five other selected pupils chosen to give Hirohito companionship. His curriculum was a standard high school one: he dropped music, arts and crafts, and composition, at which he did badly, in favor of horseback riding and military science, both of which were to be useful in his later life. He was taught French badly and learned ethics under a famous scholar of the period, Shigetake Sugiura. Although not as absurd a figure as is sometimes made out, Sugiura was an ardent advocate of the Meiji doctrine of the inherent superiority of the Japanese over other races, particularly the "decadent" Chinese.

The Crown Prince was also introduced to his lasting passion, science: Professor Hattori, his biology teacher, inspired him by taking him out in a boat for specimen-collecting trips off Hayama, the imperial family's resort. At the age of 17 he was to achieve one of his life's ambitions by walking down the beach at Numazu and spotting a large red prawn. It was a new discovery, to be named the Sympathithae Imperialis. He was confirmed in his interest in marine biology, and under his tutor made a further contribution to the science by discovering several rare shellfish from a specially built boat.

Hirohito was hardly an extrovert. Yet he was not as cold and peculiar as some biographers make out. His interest in science was commendable and unusual at a time when it seemed the underpinning of the twentieth century; certainly no previous emperor had displayed such an interest. He was hardworking and disciplined, if not brilliant in his studies. He was a good student of military history. He was not keen on extramural activities, but this was hardly to be a disadvantage for an emperor who was to preside over the most intensely hardworking urban civilization in world history. The household was desperately keen that he should not take after his dissolute father whose character was bringing the imperial influence in politics into as sharp a decline as the Emperor Meiji's had elevated it.

Yoshihito's short reign was disastrous for the court's influence. He had suffered from meningitis as a child, which appeared to have triggered a progressive mental deterioration. As a young man he had overindulged his sexual appetites, and was a hard drinker. He was fond of dressing up in Western-style military uniforms, consciously imitating the wax mustache of

Kaiser Wilhelm II, and gave extravagant parties at his massive folly, the Akasaka Detached Palace. It was hard to begrudge him the pleasures of his short life. By 1916 he had grown increasingly eccentric. During one military parade he struck out at soldiers with his riding crop, told a soldier to dismantle his pack, then repacked it himself, and embraced an officer. On another occasion he rolled up his prepared speech opening the Diet and peered through it at Members of Parliament.

He had not always been a drunken, selfish debaucher: as a young man he had shown some independence of spirit, slipping out of the imperial summer house at Numazu Detached Palace to visit a local family, the Uematsus, where he would be given tea and cakes. He was clearly bored by the business of government, although perfectly capable of taking decisions. When his advisers came to see him he would often offer them a handful of cigarettes, saying, "That's for all your effort. Now, here, have a smoke." He enjoyed reading poetry and singing military songs, or attending small impromptu concerts of martial music staged by his guards. The Empress had developed from being a beautiful young woman into a formidable personality in her own right, and her husband would sneak into the pantry for a cup of sake, telling the servants not to say anything to his wife.

Hirohito's mother was an imposinglyly beautiful and intelligent woman, brought up in great simplicity on a farm. Elizabeth Gray Vining, one of the few Westerners who met her in later life, offers this portrait.

> She was a tiny lady, with a bright eye, a rather hawk-like profile, an expression of great sweetness, and an immense dignity. She was wearing a black silk dress with a V-neck filled in with a high-collared black lace guimpe, and little black kid slippers with jet beadwork on them showed under her long, full skirt. The only light note in her costume was a diamond and platinum pin at the point of the V in her dress. Inevitably she made one think of Queen Victoria, although there is nothing in the records to suggest that Queen Victoria was slender or that she had a sense of humor, which the Empress Dowager unquestionably had. The conversation never lagged. The Empress Dowager was in command of it throughout. Charming, vivacious, low-voiced, she asked questions, and introduced topics, her fingers turning and moving in her lap.

Hirohito from the first displayed a much lesser interest in sex than either his father or grandfather. At the age of 15, he first made love to a concubine sent by his father, an entirely standard sexual initiation. A year later he was already being prepared for marriage. In traditional Japanese style, he had no say in selecting his betrothed, who was selected by the senior members of the imperial household ministry. She was Princess Nagako, the 14-year-old daughter of Prince Kuniyoshi Kuni, a family which had frequently intermarried with the imperial line. She was small, full of charm, intelligent and cheerful—neither a beauty nor a wallflower.

She was also of the Satsuma clan—which quickly aroused the fury of the still powerful founder of Japan's military machine and head of the rival Choshu clan, General Aritomo Yamagata. It was soon put about that color blindness ran in Nagako's family on her mother's side. The argument advanced by Yamagata, then a peppery octogenarian, and others was that any son of the marriage would be expected to serve in the armed forces; learned articles were written asserting that color blindness was hereditary, and that a son born with it would fail the new military test to screen officers against the defect.

The bride's indignant father, Prince Kuni, was interviewed and advised by Yamagata and Prince Fushimi, the imperial household minister, to withdraw his daughter from the match. He flatly refused, writing at once to the Emperor with the threat of major scandal and his own suicide. "It was the imperial house itself that asked for my daughter's hand," he pointed out. "If the engagement is to be broken, it should be done by the imperial house. And I'd like to add that if that comes to pass, I shall be forced to answer to the insult to me and my family by first stabbing Nagako to death, and then committing suicide myself." He produced evidence to show that neither his wife nor daughter was color-blind.

The prime minister, who as a Choshu was on Yamagata's side, responded angrily that this was rude behavior and not something the imperial family should be subjected to. Yamagata wrote coruscatingly back, "Of course Prince Kuni is right in insisting that the engagement should be adhered to once entered into. But it should not be forgotten that the engagement was arranged, so to speak, behind our back. If we had been advised of the negotiations, we would have been able to offer our humble point of view beforehand. We are deeply distressed at the way things have turned out. . . ." Kuni promptly informed the Empress, having become convinced that Yamagata was doing no more than attempting to sabotage the marriage in order to further the claims of one of his own relations.

Yamagata at this stage made a fatal mistake. He suggested that Hirohito should go on a trip abroad, partly to get him out of the way of this court crisis, partly to broaden his horizons. Right-wing opinion was outraged that it was proposed that a future emperor should so depart from tradition as to leave Japan. Yamagata's "treachery" in suggesting such a thing became confused in the public mind with his intrigues at court, and demonstrations were held in favor of Prince Kuni and his daughter. When the Emperor Yoshihito was finally consulted on the matter by Baron Nakamura, minister of the royal household, he said elliptically, "I believe that even science is fallible." The Emperor had overruled his advisers, and Nakamura resigned.

Hirohito's trip abroad proved to be a milestone in his development. The great debate accompanying the decision to send him had a faintly comical quality. The prime minister was in favor of it, because he believed a modern monarch should have knowledge of the world outside. The dispatch of a Japanese fleet with the Crown Prince was also intended to underline Japan's newfound importance in the world. However, the ultranationalist right was aghast that he should have any contact with "barbarians." In addition, his father the Emperor was ailing, and it was feared that he might die while Hirohito was abroad; immediately after the Emperor's death, an accession ceremony is traditionally carried out during which the successor inherits the imperial regalia—the sword, the jewel and the mirror; yet it would take weeks for Hirohito to return from Europe to carry out this essential function. Some suggested that the Crown Prince should anyway show respect by not traveling while his father lay ill. Others suggested that there might be threats to the security of the Crown Prince abroad.

Yet on March 3, 1921, Hirohito left Japan regardless, aboard the battleship *Katari*. Neither his own nor his father's views are known: the decision was the outcome of the debate within the imperial court. His little squadron called at a host of ports, all of them, except Okinawa, British dependencies: Hong Kong, Singapore, Colombo, Aden, Suez, Port Said, Malta and Gibraltar. He was accorded 21-gun salutes at each: he basked in the new world status of Japan, but must have been left with an awesome impression of Britain's imperial power. He relished the freedom that the journey gave him after the rigors and formality of the Japanese court and of his schooldays.

On May 7 Hirohito arrived at Portsmouth, and was greeted by the 27-year-old Prince of Wales, tall, cheerful and informal. Prince Edward accompanied him onto the state train, which traveled to Victoria station, where King George V, the Duke of Connaught and the Duke of York (later George VI) were waiting. Hirohito spent three days at Buckingham Palace, where he was befriended by the Prince of Wales and was much taken by his relaxed approach and teasing of stuffy palace officials; even the king treated him as an equal. He was accorded a state dinner and an informal family lunch, at which the king frankly advised him about the duties of a sovereign.

Leonard Mosley tells an amusing, perhaps apocryphal, story of how Hirohito's host called in one evening. "The Japanese were amazed that the King of England should wander the corridors of his palace unescorted, half-dressed, tieless, and slap him on the back. 'I hope, my boy, that everyone is giving you everything you need,' said the King. 'I'll never forget how your grandfather treated me and me brother when we were in Yokohama. No geishas here, though, I'm afraid. Her Majesty would never allow it.'"

For a further four days he was the guest of the government at Chesterfield House, meeting the prime minister, David Lloyd George; royal writers were to write patronizingly of the tact with which the "heir to the most ancient and historic throne in the world" dealt with "the nephew of a cobbler from a distant Welsh village." Later he traveled to Scotland to go shooting at the Duke of Atholl's estate at Blair Castle, and joined in dancing the reels with local people. Hirohito considered this "genuine democracy without class distinction"—which gives a flavor of just how stratified contemporary Japan was.

On May 30 Hirohito returned to his ship for the short journey to Le Havre. He duly visited the sights of Paris, including the Champs-Élysées, the Eiffel Tower and the Bois de Boulogne. He went shopping, handling money for the first time, and buying a bust of Napoleon to add to those of his two other heroes: Lincoln and Darwin. He visited Versailles and saw a performance of *Macbeth*. He also visited Verdun and the Somme, the recent spilling ground of so much blood; he wandered about through the blackened trees and wooden crosses. "War is truly a cruel thing; anyone who admires war should come and see this place," he remarked. He went on to Belgium, Holland and Italy, where he had an audience with the Pope.

Hirohito returned to Yokohama on September 3, to a rapturous welcome. His father had not died in his absence, but his deterioration was plain to see. Hirohito and the Emperor Yoshihito had never been close; but there is little reason to suppose that the young man did not feel some affection toward his father—particularly after his intervention on the side of human feeling in the matter of his bride.

10 : Crown Prince

THE UNDISTINGUISHED REIGN OF EMPEROR YOSHIHITO IN FACT HAD BEEN a time of change and dislocation in Japanese society greater than those which occurred even during the Meiji period. In the space of a decade, the centralizing, absolutist nature of the Japanese state was transformed radically in four separate ways that promised an unraveling of the whole structure of authoritarianism. First, the period saw a rapid spurt in Japan's economic growth, dwarfing the early industrialization of the Meiji period. Second, the power of the Japanese army was momentarily checked and then reversed as a coalition of interests reacted powerfully against its growing overseas appetites. Third, economic and social change unleashed the first serious pressure for political reform in Japan from below. Fourth, the power of the Emperor himself declined sharply, although this was not reflected in the cult of emperor-worship, which certain interests were pushing intensively at the time.

All of these things were in their way encouraging developments and might, under normal circumstances, have led to the emergence of Japan as a young constitutional democracy. It was the country's bad luck, and to an even greater extent that of the rest of the world, that the experiment was so quickly to go sour and that the system set up by the Meiji oligarchs was so fatally skewed against normal constitutional evolution.

The First World War had been the forge which produced Japan's greatest rush to twentieth-century industrialization. At the beginning of the war there was a loss of confidence and a short-lived economic crisis. Then it became apparent that while overseas competition was declining, as the European powers turned their attention to vastly increasing war production, there was a huge demand for munitions and war supplies that Japan could meet. In just five years between 1914 and 1919, the number of factory workers in Japan increased from 1.1 million to 1.8 million, three quarters as many again as the total over the whole Meiji period. Electric power generation increased by 34 percent, electric motor capacity by no less than 200 percent, and the capacity of the copper industry by 44 percent.

Although Japan had to import nearly all of its coal and iron, its steel industry was largely created during the First World War. Japan had only eight steel plants with a capacity of more than 500,000 tonnes in 1914; by the end of the war it had 14, as well as 166 smaller plants, while three large plants had been built in Korea and Manchuria. The output of pig iron had increased from 240,000 tons to 580,000 tons, and of rolled steel, forgings and steel castings from 255,000 tons to 550,000.

Japan's economic growth was accompanied by a huge export penetration of Asian markets while the European powers were otherwise engaged. To achieve this, the Japanese had skillfully entered the war on the side of Britain and France: the purpose was to secure lucrative defense contracts and to enlarge the country's toehold on China. Within three months of the beginning of the war, the Japanese had seized German possessions in the Shantung Province, embarking upon the seizure of Tsingtao.

The nationalist and assertive new prime minister, Shigenobu Okuma, and his foreign minister, Takaaki Kato, were determined not to miss the opportunity provided by the First World War to attempt to turn the whole of China into a protectorate. After the fall of Shantung, the Japanese believed they had a stranglehold on China, and issued an ultimatum consisting of 21 Demands, against the wishes of their principal ally at the time, Britain, which wanted to preserve Chinese independence and its own privileges there. Among the demands was, predictably, the extension of Japan's rights in southern Manchuria; but the ultimatum went on to require that China should expel all foreign military and political advisers; that the Japanese police should be given authority over certain areas of the country; and that China should purchase more than half of its war material from Japan. The demands amounted to nothing less than an attempt to reimpose the old treaty port system on China by Japan; and although the latter eventually settled largely for an extension of its privileges in Manchuria, it indirectly threatened to withdraw from the war effort against Germany unless its "aspirations" were recognized. Britain did so, even though its colonial interests there were at stake.

Meanwhile the Japanese also moved in a new direction, occupying a host of German-occupied islands in the Pacific—whose sole purpose could only be to extend the strategic reach of the Japanese navy. These included the Marianas, Palau, the Carolines and the Marshalls. Studies were now initiated into the commercial possibilities of the South Seas, including South East Asia. The same period saw the birth of the concept of the "Greater East Asia Co-Prosperity Sphere." Japan argued that once China saw the advantages of stable government and prosperity to be derived from greater association with Japan, it would join in resisting any postwar attempt by the British to regain their influence.

One prominent businessman close to the government argued that Japan must now try "to develop the limitless natural resources of China and the industry of Japan by co-ordinating the two, so as to make possible a plan for self-sufficiency under which Japan and China might become a single entity." The remarkable mushrooming of Japan's imperial ambitions throughout this period once again underlined the continuity between the ideals of the Meiji Emperor and that of his successor, the Taisho Emperor. Now that Korea had been swallowed and Manchuria's eventual annexation virtually taken for granted, Japan's ambitions were to look to China and South East Asia.

Yet the immediate impact of the "21 Demands" was to revolt public opinion, particularly in the United States, as well as Britain, which for the first time began to formulate an image of Japan as a regional bully in outspoken press commentary particularly; the Americans were also alarmed by Japan's move into the Western Pacific. Even Yamagata realized that Japan had overstepped the mark, and had the foreign minister replaced.

While Japan's imperial aims thus grew during the First World War, the prestige of the army itself actually began to decline. It was a decade now since significant victories had been achieved. The army had been routed in its attempt to dictate its own budget in 1913; and there were other much more pressing demands such as social spending on the public purse. With Yamagata's death, the armed forces were becoming deeply frustrated; they had not taken part in the 1914–18 war, they feared their power was under challenge and they believed Japan to be on the brink of a militarist, imperialist destiny which civilian politicians were too feeble to take advantage of.

Another factor was the growth of industrial militancy. This was fueled by the accelerating pace of industrialization and the conditions of unbelievable penury in which workers were kept. In order to bring quick profits, workers were treated as slaves in all but name in many factories: female employees were literally penned into company compounds and not allowed to leave more than a couple of times a month. "Dormitory workers," as they were called, were not permitted to strike and could be punished physically for absenteeism. They could be asked to work day or night, and even had their leisure hours strictly controlled. The food was meager, the sanitation nonexistent, the quarters crowded, the bedding shared.

In the mines, conditions were, quite literally, satanic. Men earned some $20 a month, and the women $10. Some 30 miners died on average for every million tons of coal mined (in England the comparable figure was 10).

Given those conditions, it was unsurprising that when the economic boom showed signs of faltering, the "rice riots" of 1918, beginning as a series of raids on the houses of rice dealers, brought down the government of Count Masatake Terauchi and his replacement with the first commoner to run Japan, Takashi Hara. At least 100 people were killed and thousands arrested before the army regained control of the demonstrators. Hara had been the veteran liberal Prince Saionji's successor as leader of the Seiyukai party—although, surprisingly, enjoying a good relationship with Yamagata. The "Great Commoner" was quite unlike his contemporary, David Lloyd George, in Britain. Although in rivalry with the army faction, he was profoundly illiberal in his attitude to the unions and mass movements, and engaged a gang of *soshi*, professional bullies, that to some extent mirrored the fascist toughs in Italy.

However, he was a genuinely popular figure; his assassination in 1921 may have ended the career of the one civilian leader in a position to wrest power on behalf of the people from the three groups that dominated Japanese life—the bureaucracy, the army and the economic plutocrats. Above the three, as has been noted, the crown was undergoing a period of exceptional weakness: the Emperor Yoshihito lacked all personal authority, while the hold of the powerful oligarchic ministers of the Meiji period was visibly weakening: only Saionji was left alive, and the new generation of bureaucratic leaders lacked the authority of their predecessors.

The great flaw in the huge apparatus of power erected by the Meiji regime was beginning to become apparent. Throughout history, there have traditionally been three forces that legitimize the exercise of authority in the eyes of the people: the first and most common is heredity; the second, brute force; the third, consent, usually because the people have had the chance to express themselves through elections. Japan had been ruled for half a century by a mixture of hereditary right and brute force. The oligarchs had shielded their rule behind the Emperor's mantle of authority. With the Emperor weakened and their own power in sharp decline, some enlightened members of the oligarchy like Saionji recognized the desperate need for greater legitimacy based on the consent of the people. For otherwise—and particularly if civil disorder broke out throughout Japan, as it was beginning to—the third group, the armed forces, would step in.

There was no special reason why the armed forces should display restraint in Japan; traditionally the samurai class had been powerful; sovereignty in Japan resided not in parliament, nor the people, nor even the bureaucracy, but in the person of the Emperor, the commander-in-chief of the armed forces, to whom they owed direct allegiance. The oligarchs who had constructed modern Japan had jealously vested sovereignty in the Emperor in order to deny it to the people, to preserve their elitist power in a unique combination of the Führer-principle and that of absolute monarchy. They failed to realize that anyone else who gained the ear of the Emperor could perform exactly the same feat and govern through him. Because sovereignty was vested in a largely powerless individual, it could be hijacked more easily than in any country in the world. It can be said with pardonable exaggeration that the army had only to cultivate a constituency of one.

As Yoshihito's illness worsened, he became known as "the tragic emperor." Takashi Hara, the prime minister, who was charged with the problem of his deterioration along with the two remaining *genro* (elder statesmen), Prince Yamagata and Prince Saionji, became concerned that there was a danger to the throne. For one thing, the cult of emperor worship had reached new heights; the public knew nothing of Yoshihito's medical condition, but his lapses might become common knowledge. For another, the existence of a weak emperor meant that unscrupulous courtiers might try and influence his wife. "Recently it has got to the point where one must do everything through the Empress, and I am very concerned about the abuses that this might lead to in the future."

With painstaking thoroughness, Hara went through the processes of persuading first the Emperor himself, then his wife, then the Imperial Family Council, then the Privy Council, that the Emperor must give up his powers to his son, who could then become regent. On October 4, shortly after Hirohito's return to Japan, the shocked Japanese public learned for the first time of the remarkable mortality of the "divine" emperor.

This skillfully handled crisis coincided with the death of General Yamagata, one of the two remaining *genro*. An increasingly crusty old man, he had played a huge role in shaping not just Japan's emerging military class but also in forging the authoritarian nature of its constitution. The effect of his death upon the army was to be far-reaching: it at once removed the most powerful military figure at court, making the armed forces anxious about their possible loss of influence there; and it undermined the disciplinary hierarchy of the institution. Yamagata, for all his faults, was the only military authority who could keep the generals in check; no one now existed to perform this essential function.

The uncharted and turbulent waters Japan was entering upon were further demonstrated—in a bitter foretaste of things to come—on November 4 when the prime minister was assassinated by an 18-year-old right-wing fanatic. The remaining *genro*, Prince Saionji, as well as Hirohito himself, decided to go along with Hara's plans to make the young man 'regent' of Japan at a ceremony on November 25. Although Yoshihito, the Taisho Emperor, was to live for another five years, from that moment on Hirohito was in effect the apex of the emperor-system, and the absolute ruler of Japan in the public eye—even if he was far from being so in reality.

In defiance of those who viewed Hirohito as a dour young man with a prematurely aged outlook, he had acquired a cheerful new self-confidence as a result of his European trip. He attended the races in Tokyo, went to the rather tame nightclubs of the aristocracy, ate bacon and eggs for breakfast, and wore plus-fours at golf. In December he invited a group of young friends as well as a host of geishas to a homecoming party, opening a stock of Scotch whiskey given him by the Duke of Atholl. The bright young things danced, listened to music and respected Hirohito's welcoming remark, "For the next two hours please forget that I am Crown Prince. Let us not stand on ceremony." The palace chamberlains were shocked by the disrespect shown to Hirohito. The elderly Saionji, who had overseen the European trip, summoned him to give him a stern telling off for his behavior.

The timid Hirohito was crushed by the rebuke and never gave a similar party again. He was, after all, at the pinnacle of the most absolute monarchy the world had ever known, one which combined religious worship and obeisance with modern methods of propaganda and control. It seemed that the light of popular participation and liberalism might shine upon this towering structure of mystical authoritarianism for a brief instant at the very outset of the rule of this mildly open-minded young man; but the moment was to pass.

The youth that in effect ascended the throne in 1921 was in direct contrast to the grandeur of the office itself. He was introverted, retiring, and not a forceful personality. He was of only mild intelligence. His boyhood had been almost unbelievably stunted, giving him very little knowledge of conditions in his country; his foreign tour, contrived as it was, provided him with the only broad experience he had ever enjoyed in his life. He was, however, somewhat determined in character, a trait which had overcome some of his physical defects and permitted him to spend long hours in study. After his brief partying, he became dutiful in the extreme. His two main interests remained science and military history, while his upbringing made him deeply nationalist and racist in nature, imbued with views of the inherent superiority of the Japanese race. His outlook was leavened by the modern ideas of some advisers, notably Hara, before his death, and Saionji, who for a time became his closest mentor.

Hirohito approached his rule with formality, but a refreshing lack of pompousness and stuffiness, and an open mind toward the introduction of gradually more democratic principles into a ramrod-straight society. While little is known of his views at the time about Japan's imperial destiny, his visit to the battlefield of the First World War had made a major impression. There was certainly nothing about this quietly spoken, pleasant, dutiful young man, to suggest that, in the description of one recent critical biographer, he would emerge as "a cunning waverer and opportunist who used his military machine to conquer half the earth without ever taking full responsibility for its misdeeds." The adversity and struggle that had shaped the lives of his two fellow hate-figures of the mid-twentieth century, Hitler and Mussolini, hardly applied in Hirohito's case. Hirohito was to display much greater political skill than first seemed likely, in defense of Japan's interests at a time of great suffering for his nation. But it is to the system itself and to Japan's evolution as a society and economy that one must look for explanations of the next two decades, not to the inadequate individual that was at the nominal pinnacle of final authority.

PART III
AMERICAN HERO

11 : THE BIG COUNTRY

THE AMERICA IN WHICH DOUGLAS MACARTHUR EMERGED TO MANHOOD in 1901 was like him—strong, impetuous, self-confident and prepared to take on a larger world role. The wrenching divisions of the Civil War had begun to fade into history. The Union had been completed, its boundaries settled, except for a few grumblings from Mexico in the south. It was unified. A huge industrial revolution had swept across it, welding it together, creating unprecedented prosperity. Now a vigorous young nation was looking to taking its first steps in the world.

Before the Civil War, America's population was around 31 million; by the war's end it was 40 million; by 1880, some 50 million, by 1890, 63 million, by 1900, 75m—larger than that of any European country except Russia. Part of this growth was fueled by a high birth rate, but most by immigration, largely from Britain, Ireland, Germany and Scandinavia; over the next quarter century a further 15 million came, mostly from eastern and southern Europe.

To feed the population, agriculture expanded exponentially, assisted by the railroads snaking across the country taking farm products to lucrative export markets. The number of farms grew from 2 million in 1860 to 6 million in 1910. By 1900 50 million Americans lived on farms. Nearly half the working population was engaged on the land in 1880. Farm technology made this possible—the invention of cheap barbed wire to fence in the vast American outback, the windmill well to pump up water to irrigate dry land. The spread of cattle herds (and cowboys) across the high plains from the 1860s to the 1890s crowded out the buffalo and the Native Americans who lived off them. The development of the marsh harvester—the "wire binder"—and the combine harvester, originally drawn by horses, then by tractors, as well as new types of plow, harrow and seeder, accelerated the agricultural revolution.

But the development of the countryside was dwarfed by the industrialization and urbanization of America. By 1910 the percentage of those deriving a living from the land had fallen sharply to just a third. Between 1859 and 1919 American output of manufactured goods increased no fewer than 33 times. In 1860 America was the world's fourth largest manufacturing country: by 1894 it was in first place, producing three times as much as Britain, its nearest competitor, and half as much as all of Europe put together. With its huge resources, American energy consumption jumped from 2.4 million horsepower (hp) in 1870 to around 43 million hp 60 years later.

This expansion was made possible by the development of a cross-American internal market behind tariff walls and the state-subsidized breakneck growth of the American railway system. Direct government aid to rail between 1860 and 1890 was some $350m. By 1840 America had 3,000 miles of track compared with 1,800 in all of Europe (largely in Britain). This more than tripled by 1850 and rose again to 30,000 miles in 1860 and 164,000 miles by 1890, slowing a bit to 254,000 by 1916, a third of the world total. Steel followed in its wake. In 1844 huge deposits of iron ore were found in the Great Lakes region. With the introduction of cost-efficient ways of manufacturing steel, by 1873 production had expanded to 115,000 tons, then to 1.25 million tons in 1880 and 10 million tons in 1900. The price of steel rails plummeted from $160 a ton in 1875 to $17 a ton in 1898, thanks to greater efficiency.

As the American economy boomed, so did the country's big cities. Chicago, merely a fort with a few houses when Arthur MacArthur was a boy, was by 1848 a major port and by 1887 had 800,000 people, as well as America's first skyscrapers, rising up to ten stories high. New York, containing just 90,000 people in 1810, had grown to 800,000 in 1856, and then jumped to 3.5 million by 1900. New York's first skyscraper was the Equitable Building, eight stories high, completed in 1870. By 1915 skyscrapers 40 stories high were being finished. The country's vibrant attraction for immigrants was soon sewing a complex patchwork out of a formerly largely Protestant and English city: first Germans arrived, then Irish, then Italians, Greeks, and Jews. The Statue of Liberty was constructed when Douglas MacArthur was just eight, and Emma Lazarus wrote her famous verse:

> Give me your tired, your poor,
> Your huddled masses yearning to breathe free,
> The wretched refuse of your teeming shore.

The political scene after the Civil War was distinguished by obscure presidents and giant capitalist dynasties such as the steelmaker Andrew Carnegie, the financier J. Pierpoint Morgan and the oil tycoon John D.

Rockefeller. But when Douglas graduated, the age of the automobile had not yet arrived: Henry Ford was to make the first Model T in 1908.

When Arthur MacArthur arrived in Manila in 1898, an appointment of President William McKinley, along with his family, he felt he had at last received the recognition he deserved and for which he had worked in 30 years of provincial obscurity. His task was to liberate the Philippines from Spain. Indeed, from the first it was clear that his talents as a military commander had not deserted him. His advance force of nearly 5,000 men landed at Cavite, south of Manila, performing skillfully against the demoralized Spanish colonial forces: within nine days the Spanish commander in Manila had capitulated—at the princely cost of 13 Americans killed. MacArthur was appointed military governor of Manila; his eldest son, Arthur III, serving in a ship off Luzon, was witness to his father's triumph.

Peace with Spain swiftly followed. But the Americans showed no immediate inclination to hand over power to the rebel Filipinos themselves, who had fought a long and tenacious war against the Spanish colonial master. Under Emilio Aguinaldo, they launched a guerrilla war against the new American occupiers. McKinley had elaborated a new philosophy of American imperialism which, revealingly, Douglas MacArthur was later to claim would "guide my conduct in the occupation of a defeated enemy":

> The future of the Philippine Islands is now in the hands of the American people, and the Paris Treaty commits the free and franchised Filipinos to the guiding hand and the liberalizing influences, the generous sympathies, the uplifting agitation, not of their American masters, but of their American emancipation.
>
> No imperial designs lurk in the American mind. They are alien to American sentiment, thought and purpose. Our priceless principles undergo no change under a tropical sun. They go with a fiat: "Why read ye not the changeless truth, the free can conquer but to save?"

Arthur MacArthur came into his own: with a strategy of two-pronged attack he broke out of Manila and in a long series of engagements drove the 40,000-strong Filipino army back, bottling up the enemy forces within a year, and forcing Aguinaldo into hiding. He was appointed military governor of the Philippines after the withdrawal of General Ewell Otis. He was faced by a still considerable guerrilla insurrection.

MacArthur fought back with skill, eventually tracking down and capturing Aguinaldo, but also taking care to treat the Filipinos with magnanimity in order to secure their support. He set up a free public school system, replaced the severe Spanish legal system with an American-style one including the right of habeas corpus, built roads, set up a canal system and expanded the loyal Macabeke Scouts into the basis of a national army. The policy was that of benevolent imperialism (in an echo of today's rhetoric on Iraq). As MacArthur expounded it: "The idea of personal liberty allows a citizen to do within just limits whatever tends to his own happiness. That idea we are planting in the Orient. Wherever the American flag goes that idea goes. The fruition of that idea in the Philippines is merely a matter of evolution; and to my mind, a brief one. The Filipinos want precisely what we can give them . . . The planting of liberty—not money—is what we seek."

Back in Washington McKinley was becoming anxious about the situation in the Philippines, and decided to send a civilian emissary to check on whether the country's American military proconsul was governing wisely. The emissary was a perspiring barrel of a man: the nearly 350-pound Ohio judge William Howard Taft, a moderate and likeable lawyer who described Filipinos patronizingly as his "little brown brothers"—which prompted American soldiers to compose a celebrated racist song, "He may be a brother of William Howard Taft, but he ain't no brother of mine."

Arthur MacArthur showed the prickly side of his character: he was incensed by this challenge to his authority and implied rebuke, and not only failed to greet the portly judge when he arrived in the Philippines but gave him a tiny room as an office thoroughly ill-suited to his colossal girth, and conducted his relationship with the latter through correspondence, refusing to hold meetings with him at the proconsular Malacanan Palace. Taft was in turn understandably furious: "the more I have to do with M. the smaller man of affairs I think he is. His experience and his ability as a statesman of politician are nothing. He has all the angularity of military etiquette and discipline, and he takes himself with the greatest seriousness . . . General MacArthur in his correspondence assumes the position of lecturing us every time he gets an opportunity on the military necessities, and the obligation we feel under courteously to answer his communications involves a great waste of time and energy."

Taft described MacArthur as a "military martinet" whose attempts to censor journalists' stories were "revolting" and "utterly un-American."

Remote, haughty, a popular military hero in the United States, the general saw no need to pander to the bloated civilian pen pusher: he exhibited a family streak of political naivete: for had he sought to make friends with Taft, he might easily have secured that good-natured mediocrity's support.

As MacArthur's rule over the Philippines grew ever more imperious, Taft seized his chance to act. MacArthur now claimed that the archipelago was "the finest group of islands in the world. Its strategic position is unexcelled by that of any other position on the globe. The China Sea, which separates it by something like 750 miles from the continent, is nothing more or less than a safety moat. It lies on the flank of what might be called a position of several thousand miles of coast line; it is in the center of that position. It is therefore relatively better placed than Japan, which is on a flank, and therefore remote from the other extremity; likewise, India, on another flank. The Philippines are in the center of that position. It affords a means of protecting American interests which, with the very least output of physical power, has the effect of a commanding position in itself to retard hostile action."

Taft rightly believed that America's stewardship of the islands should be strictly limited in time and scope and in July 1901 he persuaded McKinley to recall MacArthur. The general appeared to be vindicated in senate hearings on the affair soon after; but he had made a dangerous enemy. Although given senior posts—the Department of the Great Lakes, the East and the Pacific—he never saw active service again.

With McKinley's assassination, Theodore Roosevelt became president and appointed his friend Taft secretary of war. Arthur meanwhile was dispatched on a grand tour of the Far East, taking Pinky and both his sons to Japan, China, Indochina, Burma, Malaya, Thailand, Ceylon and India; but he was passed over as chief of staff, although he was America's most decorated war commander and its senior general.

Some measure of young Douglas's disappointment at the circumstances of his father's return from the Philippines can be gauged from the fact that he makes no mention of it at all in his reminiscences, ascribing the dismissal to "the logical time for transfer from a military to a civilian government." But the seed of his later mistrust for the political class, epitomized by the well-fed Taft, had been born.

Douglas had the pleasure, though, of having his graduation witnessed by both his parents and spent a glorious summer in San Francisco at his father's headquarters on the Pacific Coast Command, where he witnessed his father's historic decision to expand Los Angeles harbor. He also had his first encounter with an enemy, tracking down a local escaped prisoner and pulling a gun on him. "You damn West Pointers," the man is said to have snarled at the youth.

The second lieutenant was further delighted to be posted to the Philippines, the scene of his father's triumphs. It was the first time Douglas had left his native shores, and he had plenty of time to consider the exciting challenges ahead on the 38-day trip across the Pacific: he was to oversee fortification and harbor improvements in Manila. On a foraging excursion into the jungle, he had his first baptism of fire:

> The place was dangerous, being infested with brigands and guerrillas. In spite of my early frontier training, I became careless and allowed myself to be waylaid on a narrow jungle trail by two of these desperadoes, one on each side. Like all frontiersmen, I was expert with a pistol. I dropped them both dead in their tracks, but not before one had blazed away at me with his antiquated rifle. The slug tore through the top of my campaign hat and almost cut the sapling tree immediately behind me. My foreman, a Regular Army sergeant and veteran of long years of service, came rushing up. He looked long and hard at the two dead men sprawled on the trail, at my crownless hat still smoking from the blast, at the broken tree behind me. And then, rolling his quid of tobacco into the hollow of his cheek, he slowly drew himself up to his full six feet of height, his heels clicking together, saluted, and drawled in his rich Irish brogue, "Begging thu Loo'tenant's paddon, but all the rest of the Loo'tenant's life is pure velvut."

He was there for a year, contracting malaria, but became a full lieutenant before returning to San Francisco and the Pacific command.

From there, in October 1905, his father took him as an aide-de-camp on his strategic tour of the Far East. President Roosevelt had been growing uneasy about Japan, and Arthur MacArthur's intelligence-gathering mission was therefore an important one. As Roosevelt had put it prophetically: "If Japan is careful, and is guided by the best minds in her Empire, she can become one of the leaders of the family of great nations; but if she is narrow and insular, if she tries to gain from her victory in the Russo-Japanese War more than she ought to have, she will array against her all the great powers, and however determined she may be she cannot successfully face an allied world."

Thus at the age of just 25 Douglas MacArthur unknowingly first came face-to-face with what was to be his destiny. The trip was a major opportunity for a young man who had only just started his military career to meet the greatest potentates in the region. His impressions on arrival in the great bay of Edo, with its tens of thousands of wooden houses crowding the waterfront and the great cone of sacred Mount Fuji in the background are not recorded. But the trip as a whole appealed to the high sense of romanticism in the young man:

> We traversed the path to Afghanistan, with the "King of the Khyber," Sir Bindon Blood; we rode the Grant Trunk Road of Kipling's Kim; we reached out from Darjeeling in trace of Sir Francis Younghusband's penetration of Tibet in search of the Grand Llama. We saw the strength and the weakness of the colonial system, how it brought law and order, but failed to develop the masses along the essential lines of education and political economy. We rubbed elbows with millions of the underprivileged who knew nothing of the difference between the systems of the free world and the slave world, but were interested only in getting a little more food in their stomachs, a little better coat on their backs, a little stronger roof over their heads.

In Thailand the king (son of the monarch of *The King and I* fame) offered to decorate him for fixing a fuse when the lights went out at a banquet. In Japan he "met all the great Japanese commanders: Oyama, Kuroki, Nogi, and the brilliant Admiral Heihachiro Togo—those grim, taciturn, aloof men of iron character and unshakeable purpose. It was here that I first encountered the boldness and courage of the Nipponese soldier. His almost fanatical belief in and reverence for his Emperor impressed me indelibly."

The young man was formally introduced to the impressive living deity, the Emperor of Japan, Mutsuhito, grandfather of Hirohito. He was struck by the great commanders of the Russo-Japanese war, two extraordinary men, General Maresuke Nogi and Admiral Heihachiro Togo, later to be Hirohito's guardians. MacArthur did not meet the little prince himself.

Arthur MacArthur thought he was doing his son a favor by taking him on a fantastic voyage of discovery. It was not clear that he was. The already almost insufferable lieutenant, top of his class at West Point, son of one of the foremost commanders in the American army, had now been exposed to one of the most exotic luxuries available to anyone outside royalty—a privileged existence aboard American warships, visiting absolutist courts, those of oriental god-rulers. Returning to the United States, his swollen head grew bigger still: as a youth gilded for greatness, he was appointed aide-de-camp to the President himself.

Theodore Roosevelt had started life as a sickly, nervous and awkward young man. After the death of his first wife when he was just 25, he had traveled to the badlands of Dakota, where he set up a cattle-herding business. There he beat up local toughs, shot grizzlies, captured three outlaws and boasted of wearing: "a sombrero, silk neckerchief, fringed buckskin shirt, sealskin *chaparajos* or riding trousers, alligator hide boots, and with my pearl-hilted revolvers and beautifully finished Winchester rifle, I shall be able to face anything."

He set out his philosophy:

> Like all Americans, I like big things: big prairies, big forests and mountains, big wheat fields, railroads—and herds of cattle too—big factories and steamboats and everything else. But we must keep steadily in mind that no people were ever yet benefited by riches if their prosperity corrupted their virtue. It is more important that we should show ourselves honest, brave, truthful, and intelligent than that we should own all the railways and grain elevators in the world. We have fallen heirs to the most glorious heritage a people ever received and each of us must do his part if we wish to show that this nation is worthy of its good fortune.

He was the big man standing up for the small man, and as such was one of the first practitioners of the new mass politics in the world. He launched a campaign of "trust-busting" to regulate big business, compelled the mine owners to negotiate with their unions, fought for the interests of small firms, and followed in Lincoln's tradition by encouraging black rights. He regulated the railways and sought to impose conditions on the food-processing and drug industries. He encouraged conservation.

Although these actions might have been expected to raise the hackles of the American right, he was also America's first great imperialist, possessed of a Palmerstonian vision of America as a force for good in the world. What was right for his country was right for the globe. His first large-scale intervention abroad was the creation of Panama out of a slice of Colombia to avoid paying the $25 million for canal rights demanded by the latter ("we stole it fair and square" boasted one wit); other Latin American interventions followed.

The young MacArthur was dazzled by the attention shown to him by this most overpowering of presidents:

> To an unprecedented degree, regardless of party, he had the support of the public. His vigor, courage, abounding vitality, his lack of Presidential

pomposity, his familiarity with all manner of men, even his loudness of action and utterance, stimulated all to raise themselves above the ordinary level of their ability and their desires.

He was greatly interested in my views on the Far East and talked with me long and often. I once asked him to what single factor did he attribute his extraordinary popularity with the masses. He replied, "To put into words what is in their hearts and minds but not their mouths. You must listen to the grass grow." When I became angered at an utterly unfounded criticism of him, dreamed up in the editorial room of a local paper, he said, "I like to have them talk well of me, but I would rather have them talk badly than not talk at all."

Another person who attracted my closest attention was the Speaker of the House of Representatives, Joe Cannon. He was the last to rule that august body with the autocracy of a czar. I would sit in the gallery and watch him with fascinated eyes as he wheedled, cajoled, bullied, and dominated the legislative leaders. But he was kindness itself, when I pleaded for more consideration for our native Indian tribes. One night I was on special duty at the White House during a dinner the President gave for the Speaker. The procedure was to gather the guests in the Red Room, then bring them in to meet the President in the Green Room. I brought the President to his accustomed place, then prepared to bring in the guests. The Speaker was surrounded by an eager group to whom he was declaiming in the most violent way. I knew the President was waiting and three times tried to break in without success. Finally, in desperation, I shoved aside a couple of ambassadors and a Senator or two, and, touching the Speaker's elbow, said, "Mr. Speaker, the President will receive you now." He just glared, looked me up and down, then, blowing the smoke from the big black cigar that was always in his mouth, barked in my face, "The hell he will!", and, to the delight of everyone but myself, continued his harangue. That night I lost any standing I might have had as a social arbiter.

12 : GROWING PAINS

THE YOUNG LIEUTENANT BEHAVED LIKE THE CROWN PRINCE AT SOME court. Arrogant, his head in the clouds, he neglected his studies at the elite School of Military Engineers in Washington to which he had been assigned. His superior officer observed:

I am sorry to report that during this time Lieutenant MacArthur seemed to take but little interest in his course at the school and that the character of the work done by him was generally not equal to that of most of the other student officers and barely exceeded the minimum which would have been permitted . . . Indeed, throughout the time Lieutenant MacArthur was under my observation, he displayed, on the whole, but little professional zeal and his work was far inferior to that which his West Point record shows him to be capable of.

Befriended by one of the four greatest presidents of the twentieth century, rubbing shoulders with the most powerful men in America, interlocutor with emperors and kings, the finest graduate from West Point since General Lee, the gilded youth was brought sharply down to earth by his superiors. He was appointed to a junior post in Milwaukee where, back in the real world of a provincial army posting, he seemed to go rapidly downhill. He neglected his duties to spend time with his parents. His father was by now deeply embittered by his premature retirement, and the household cannot have been a happy one, for MacArthur was soon seeking a transfer. His commandant wrote bitingly that his duties "were not performed in a satisfactory manner."

With his military world crumbling about him, his mother sought to get him a civilian job; but by then he had secured his wish—appointment as commander of the most junior company in Fort Leavenworth, Kansas—the very same company his father had commanded in 1885 in the place where Douglas's first schooling had begun 23 years before. It seemed a total comedown—an obscure outback command, almost in disgrace.

He was 28 years old, no longer the most promising young man in the American army, regarded by many of his new brother-officers as a snobbish dandy. Lieutenant Robert Eichelberger remembered first seeing him "standing a bit aloof from the rest of us and looking off in the distance with what I have always considered in other people to be a Napoleonic stance." Lieutenant George Marshall could not stand him—the birth of an undying enmity which was stronger initially on Marshall's side and then later on MacArthur's, and was fatefully to affect the latter's career.

The secretary of war, William Howard Taft, had passed over his old enemy, Arthur MacArthur, for the job of chief of staff; and in 1909 this incredibly brave, talented, but prickly and unbending soldier retired. He had caused a stir by announcing publicly, correctly but imprudently for his own career, that war with Germany was inevitable and that German-born recruits should not be accepted in the American armed forces. Even more prophetically he declared, "It will be impossible for Americans to keep the sea unless we meet quickly the desperate attack which Japan is now organising against us." President Roosevelt himself, no less, slapped him down.

He was so bitter that he told his wife that he wanted no military honors at his funeral, and willed not to be buried in Arlington National Cemetery. It is hard to judge whether this intelligent and talented commander in the field had been merely been dumped for political reasons, or whether he had gone slightly off the rails. A distinguished military career had ended in disappointment and vinegar. This rubbed off on his sensitive son, devoted to both his parents and himself facing his first professional setback.

Yet it was separation from them and a return to the beloved west of his childhood that provided the cure. For long a stuffed shirt, he became again a western cowboy, one of the guys, an officer in the saddle, a leader of men and a good comrade to his brother officers. He was transformed. He became a fine polo player, shone at poker, and was an astute manager of the Fort Leavenworth baseball team, cheating by buying two Texan professionals for 20 dollars to beat the Kansas City County Club, and on another occasion entertaining the latter to a large meal before the game while his men abstained. He was a superb junior officer, performing the jobs of quartermaster and engineer officer among others and writing a field manual. As throughout his life he drank little but would lead his company on loud renditions of, in particular, "Old Soldiers Never Die." Above all he excelled in getting the most out of his men.

It was a long posting for the now not-so-young lieutenant—more than four years, recalling his father's own years in the wilderness. It was broken only by a short tour of duty in the Panama Canal Zone, that exotic American base in the tropics, and then a visit to his old childhood home of San Antonio, Texas.

At about that time, however, he received news that his mother was seriously ill. Then disaster struck. MacArthur tells the story of the fiftieth annual reunion of his father's old regiment—the 24th Wisconsin, which he had led at the age of 17 up Missionary Hill. That day, September 5, 1912, was oppressively hot, and Arthur MacArthur had been ill:

> There were but ninety of them left as they sat around the table in Grand Army Hall retelling the old war stories and singing again the old war songs. Then the toastmaster called on my father. Still straight and commanding, he recalled the old days—they were again changing front at

Murfreesboro, crossing Peach Tree Creek at Atlanta, closing the gap at Franklin. "Your indomitable regiment," he continued, and then he faltered; his face grew ashen white; then he was down for good. Dr William J. Cronyn, the regimental surgeon, rushed once more to his side.

"Comrades, the General is dying," he said simply.

In the middle of the room the Reverend Paul B. Jenkins began to repeat the Lord's Prayer. And then those ninety old men who had followed him up Missionary Ridge and into the blazing fire of a dozen battlefields knelt by the side of their old commander and joined in. When the prayer ended, he was dead. The adjutant, Captain Edwin Parsons, took from the wall the battle-torn flag that he had so gallantly carried and wrapped it around the General. Captain Parsons stood in silence for a moment, gazing at his dead commander, then fell forward over the body and, within two weeks, passed on.

My whole world changed that night. Never have I been able to heal the wound in my heart.

He was not exaggerating: his father's career had been the single greatest influence in his life, stronger even than his mother's affection, and the general had died well before his time, aged 69. Although Douglas had shown his worth at Fort Leavenworth, he had singularly failed to live up to his father's expectations and had been absent from him in his final years. His mother's condition, unsurprisingly, became even worse, and she went to live with him at the Fort, where she clearly drove him to distraction.

He was rescued by the electoral defeat of the hostile Taft and by an unexpected appointment back to the heart of the nation's affairs, doubtless inspired by the guilt of senior military men at how his father had been treated and his untimely demise—virtually killed by the War Department. But it also reflected the young man's own self-redemption: he was appointed a member of the general staff under General Leonard Wood. When he left Fort Leavenworth, Sergeant Major Corbett provided a tribute "which perhaps I prize more than any other. Boys, he said as I left, there goes a soldier." The general staff was regarded as the brains of the army, and Wood was Secretary of War under a new American president, the Democrat Woodrow Wilson, who had been elected when Teddy Roosevelt, despairing of the mediocrity of his successor, the MacArthurs' old enemy William Howard Taft, ran again for president, so splitting the Republican vote. Now that Taft had fallen, MacArthur was getting another chance.

Washington provided a much more congenial environment in which Douglas could nurse his mother. But within a few months he was ordered on a mission by General Wood to report on a sudden crisis: the Americans had taken the city of Veracruz in Mexico in April 1914 to counter the seizure of power by General Victoriano Huerta, who had embarked on an anti-American pogrom south of the border. It seemed that war with Mexico beckoned. MacArthur's secret instructions were to reconnoiter and obtain "all possible information which would be of value in possible operations"— including a major American attack on Mexico. It was a James Bond–style mission, undoubtedly devised to test the young soldier.

In Veracruz he found the American army was virtually devoid of transport, including animals. He decided that the answer was to steal locomotives for the ample rolling stock lying idle in the city. Wearing military uniform, so as not to be shot as a spy, he got three Mexican railway men to lead him to the Jamapa River and, skirting the town of Alvarado while lashed to one of the men to prevent him running away and betraying him, finally found three locomotives in good condition.

On the return journey to report the find things went wrong: they were intercepted by bandits, who opened fire: MacArthur shot two of them. A few miles further on they ran into a band of 15 armed men: according to MacArthur three bullets went through his uniform and one of his Mexicans was injured in the shoulder, but he killed four and the rest fled. They grabbed a railway handcar to get away and were attacked by three men on horseback, one sending a bullet through MacArthur's shirt. He fired back and shot a horse from under one of his assailants which fell on the line ahead of the railcar; they had to remove it to proceed. At daylight, after a hazardous river crossing, MacArthur returned exhausted.

He was recommended for a Medal of Honor by General Wood for this action, but on the grounds that he had not acted under orders but on his own initiative, was not awarded it. Already a captain, he was promoted to major. It was the first indication of the superhuman courage of the talented young officer.

Back on the general staff, he found himself under orders from an earnest, highly intelligent young patron, the Assistant Secretary of the Navy, Franklin D. Roosevelt, preparing plans for mobilization in case America was sucked into the war that had broken out in Europe. MacArthur was commended by his superiors as "a high-minded, conscientious and unusually efficient officer, well-placed for posts requiring diplomacy and high-grade intelligence."

He got on well with the new Secretary of War, Newton D. Baker, who said he had a "swift and uninhibited mind." Baker appointed MacArthur his "press censor"'—his public relations officer. By all accounts he performed brilliantly at the job, his laconic intelligence and courtesy winning over the hardbitten journalists accustomed to being treated brusquely by haughty army officers. This experience was pivotal to one of MacArthur's greatest advantages in later life—his skill at public relations, of which he was certainly the first major practitioner in the American army, and historically exceeded only by Horatio Nelson and T. E. Lawrence. Long before most of his contemporaries, he understood the importance of image, of manipulating the news, of ensuring he was cast in the best possible light, of suppressing his mistakes in public. Always prone to posing and stylization, he saw in the press the means to secure a popular constituency way beyond his immediate military circle. He was even later to be denounced as merely a skilled PR man. The record of his other extraordinary achievements does not support this. But more than any military leader at the time he realized public relations was necessary to enhance and parade his achievements before the public: it also accorded with his natural vanity.

He secured a remarkable tribute from the journalists:

We of the Fourth Estate wish to address . . . to Major Douglas MacArthur, our appreciation of the way he has dealt with us for all these months in his trying position of military censor.

We feel no doubt of what the future holds for Major MacArthur. Rank and honors will come to him if merit can bring them to any man; but we wish to say our thanks to him for the unfailing kindness, patience and wise counsel we have received from him in the difficult days that are past.

Our needs have compelled us to tax that patience at all hours of the day and night. We have never failed to receive courteous treatment from him. Although the censorship imposed was but a voluntary obligation upon the press, it has been kept faithfully, and we feel that it has been largely because of the fair, wise and liberal way in which Major MacArthur exercised his functions that this was possible. He has put his own personality into the task.

On April 6, 1917, America declared war on Germany after two years of its merchant ships being sunk by U-boats; the sinking of the *Lusitania* was the final straw. MacArthur played a part in introducing the draft, and was then asked for his views on whether America's National Guard should take part in the war. He recommended in favor in an hour-long meeting with Secretary of War Baker and President Wilson, and that it be drawn from 26 states so "that it will stretch over the whole country like a rainbow." General William A. Mann was appointed to command the division and MacArthur, promoted to colonel, his chief of staff. He decided to serve in the infantry, rather than the elite engineers, so as to be in the thick of the fighting. Before he left Washington, the news came that General Frederick Funston, head of the American force at Veracruz and designated commander of the American expeditionary force in France, had died. MacArthur had to relate the news to the Secretary of War.

13 : THE RAINBOW DIVISION

ON OCTOBER 19, 1917, HE SET SAIL ACROSS THE U-BOAT–INFESTED Atlantic with the 27,000 men of the Rainbow Division on his first active service.

Life on board a troopship was a new and somewhat unnerving experience for the uninitiated. There were endless drills and efforts made to properly exercise the men. Space was cramped and each man was allowed forty-five minutes time a day on deck. Lifebelts were worn all the time. The ship was dark at night, with no smoking allowed in the open. In a running sea it is a real sensation to grope around decks in the darkness . . .

After being at sea for ten days we were within four days of our destination—St Nazaire. From then on all officers remained constantly at their posts. The air was like winter and the sea ice cold. We moved into an acute submarine and mine zone. All ships were zigzagging at a loss of a knot an hour. Captain Hasbrouk never left the bridge. Three days ticked off—long days that seemed like weeks. We had twenty-four hours more to safety when the wireless informed us that we had been spotted by enemy submarines who were moving in for the kill.

As night fell I went up on the bridge, but could see nothing in the black of an unknowing night. All we could hear was the deep voice of the skipper: "Rudder right, rudder left." It was bleak and nerve-racking, but I felt a glow in my heart knowing that the *Chattanooga*, commanded by my brother, Captain Arthur MacArthur, was out there in the escort watching over us. At long last, thank God, I saw the lights of Belle Isle. We steamed up the Loire and docked at St. Nazaire—our first glimpse of France.

By skillfully changing course 45 degrees the *Covington* had evaded the submarines, but on the way out they sank her.'

They ran aground 40 miles off St. Nazaire, but landed shortly afterward in cold rain. At the age of 37, after a glittering launch to his career and an equally inglorious setback, destiny had given MacArthur a second chance. A senior officer, with a solid reputation at headquarters, now possessed of considerable operational responsibility—Mann was ailing and quickly resigned and his successor admired MacArthur—he was determined not to stumble again. He had one huge advantage over his fellow staff officers: he had inherited his father's extraordinary courage.

But it was to be several months of frustration, training his raw men behind the lines in the dreary cold of a French winter with inadequate clothing and blankets near the American headquarters of Chaumont, before he saw action. He immediately established a reputation for meticulousness and flamboyance. His aide later wrote:

> He worked very early in the morning on his field plans. Alone, he made notes on a card, and by the time we met for a staff discussion he had the plans all worked out. He asked for our opinions but, more often than not, we all concurred with his. His plans invariably covered the optimum situation as well as the minimum. He was meticulous in organization and consummate in planning.

He quickly fell foul of the most intelligent staff officer working for Pershing, his old rival at Fort Leavenworth, George Marshall.

Mindful of his training in public relations, he established his own extraordinary style, which he put into practice when he was at last permitted to accompany his troops on their first engagement alongside the French—a night attack on German lines in February 1918. It was small-scale stuff, entirely typical of the Western Front, crawling forward from the frozen squalor of the trenches across no-man's land, the detonation of a hand grenade the signal for the attack, a quick and savage occupation of enemy trenches ended by a hand grenade thrown at the last German outpost. In the morning his men retired with 600 enemy prisoners, including a German colonel, and MacArthur was greeted by French soldiers offering absinthe and cognac; he was awarded a French Croix de Guerre and an American Silver Star.

Apart from his utter fearlessness—his leading troops into action was unusual for such a senior officer and much resented by his desk-bound fellow staff officers—his extraordinary attire was the most unusual thing about the raid: he wore a turtleneck sweater, riding breeches and cavalry boots. On his head was what was to become his famous "scrambled eggs" cap—a battered officer's parade-ground headgear—instead of a helmet. In his mouth was clamped an elegant cigarette holder. In his hands, instead of a gun, was a riding crop. The outfit was topped off by a four-foot scarf—a present from his mother. When he returned, with mud camouflage on his face and a hole in the seat of his riding breeches torn by barbed wire, he looked even more extraordinary. He was to be dubbed at once by the press the "Beau Brummel of the American expeditionary force."

The choice of clothing was, of course, a statement. MacArthur, by wearing no helmet or gas mask and not even carrying a gun, wanted to show that he was prepared to run even greater risks than his men, that danger should hold no terrors for them. He also wanted to display that he was a romantic cavalryman in an age of modern warfare and, more practically, wanted to be recognized by his men from a distance as their commander.

To most of the staff officers, who never accompanied their troops to the front, he was just a "show-off," and one setting a bad example by disregarding regulations in not wearing his helmet and gas mask, Moreover senior commanders should not thus put themselves at risk. Undoubtedly there was a huge element of one-upmanship in MacArthur's attire. He enjoyed exposing his brother officers as the bureaucrats bound to headquarters that he considered them to be; his was an eighteenth-century style of generalship. But the press loved it, as they were intended to: he was "the fighting Duke" and "D'Artagnan."

After his first experience of the front, he was confident enough to lead the Rainbow Division into an engagement on the night of March 9. As the Germans opened up with 40 batteries, he climbed up a scaling ladder.

> The blast was like a fiery furnace. For a dozen terrible seconds I felt they were not following me. But then, without turning around, I knew how wrong I was to have doubted for even an instant. In a moment they were around me, ahead of me, a roaring avalanche of glittering steel and cursing men. We carried the enemy position.

MacArthur was awarded the Distinguished Service Medal. Ten days later he had his comeuppance: he was gassed so badly that his sight was threatened.

Later that same month, as he recovered, the Germans embarked on their last full-scale offensive of the war, to capture Paris. The Rainbow was rushed to help the French in their defense of the city. For 82 days, MacArthur wrote, "the division was in almost constant combat." Back at headquarters Pershing's staff officers consistently poor-mouthed the flamboyant former commander, and the commander-in-chief finally paid him a visit, publicly berating his soldiers as "a filthy rabble." However, in Washington, his supporter Newton Baker, the Secretary of War, who read of MacArthur's exploits in the press and was also under pressure from the redoubtable Pinky, recognized the charismatic colonel by promoting him to brigadier-general.

The German offensive now reached its crescendo. To meet this the Rainbow was moved west to join the French Fourth Army defending the road to Chalons. MacArthur was immediately impressed by the French commander, General Henri Gouraud. He had formulated a new tactic to meet the German advance: he would vacate his forward trenches, leaving only a handful of "suicide squads" to put up token resistance and warn of the German advance. Then the French guns would fire further back with deadly accuracy on the Germans as they moved forward to occupy the French forward trenches. The Germans attacked on July 15: as they took the trenches, 1,000 guns opened up on them, pinning them down. They were repulsed, and the Germans' last great attack of the war was over.

MacArthur was awarded another Silver Star. But he was in uncharacteristically maudlin mood:

A few nights later a group of us toasted our victory in Chalons. We drank to the petite barmaids and sang of "Mademoiselle of Armentieres." but I found something missing. It may have been the vision of those writhing bodies hanging from the barbed wire or the stench of dead flesh still in my nostrils. Perhaps I was just getting old; somehow, I had forgotten how to play.

The Germans now retreated, with the Allies in pursuit. But it was relentlessly hard going. The Germans placed troops on slopes and in woods, opening up with machine guns and mortars from behind stone walls.

MacArthur pushed forward into the death trap:

The dead were so thick in spots we tumbled over them. There must have been at least 2,000 of those sprawled bodies. I identified the insignia of six of the best German divisions. The stench was suffocating. Not a tree was standing. The moans and cries of wounded men sounded everywhere. Sniper bullets sung like the buzzing of a hive of angry bees. An occasional shellburst always drew an angry oath from my guide. I counted almost a hundred disabled guns of various size and several times that number of abandoned machine guns.

Suddenly a flare lit up the area for a fraction of a minute and we hit the dirt, hard. Just ahead of us stood three Germans—a lieutenant pointing with outstretched arm, a sergeant crouched over a machine gun, a corporal feeding a bandolier of cartridges to the weapon. I held my breath waiting for the burst, but there was nothing. The seconds clicked by, but still nothing. We waited until we could wait no longer. My guide shifted his poised grenade to the other hand and reached for his flashlight. They had not moved. They were never to move. They were dead, all dead—the lieutenant with shrapnel through his heart, the sergeant with his belly blown into his back, the corporal with his spine where his head should have been. We left them there, just as they were, gallant men dead in the service of their country.

He won his fourth Silver Star. The Rainbow pushed forward regardless, taking 10,000 prisoners. MacArthur, who by now had won his fifth Silver Star, saw that the town of Metz was undefended. By taking this he believed he could cut through the Hindenburg Line and push into Germany itself. He was ordered not to. For the first but not the last time he was furious at the decisions taken by headquarters commanders so far from the front.

Taking refuge in a nearby chateau, he discovered ample food that had been left behind on the German retreat. A shell cut through the courtyard next to where he was about to dine. "All of Germany cannot make a shell that will kill MacArthur," he remarked. "Sit down, gentlemen, with me," he instructed the officers lying flat on the floor.

The American advance was now pinned down by fire from a ridge of hills known as the Coté de Chatillon. His commanding officer arrived. "Get me Chatillon, or a list of 5,000 casualties," he told MacArthur. "All right general, we'll take it" was the reply. He moved forward in a pincer under relentless fire. Of the 1,450 men and 25 officers that led the assault, only 300 men and 10 officers survived when the hills were taken. MacArthur himself was badly gassed again in the attack. Baker dubbed him "the greatest front-line general of the war," and recommended him for the Medal of Honor; instead he was awarded a second Distinguished Service Cross.

The army was ordered forward to Sedan. Thanks to a confusing order from headquarters issued by Colonel Marshall—"boundaries will not be considered binding"—one American corps blundered across the front of another, nearly resulting in a firefight between the two. After a delicious supper in an inn: "The proprietor had nothing but potatoes but what a feast he laid before me. Served them in five different courses—potato soup, potato fricassee, potatoes creamed, potato salad and finished with potato pie. It may be because I have not eaten for thirty-six hours, but that meal seems about the best I ever had." Hearing that troops were approaching his position, MacArthur got out of bed, dressed in his usual inimitable fashion, and was nearly taken prisoner by men of the approaching corps under Lieutenant Black who, however, recognized the most famous soldier at the American front.

Gouraud called him "the most remarkable officer I have ever known." General Menoher, his commanding officer, said:

> MacArthur is the bloodiest fighting man in this army. I'm afraid we're going to lose him sometime, for there's no risk of battle that any soldier is called upon to take that he is not liable to look up and see MacArthur at his side. At every advance MacArthur, with just his cap and his riding crop, will go forward with the first line. He is the source of the greatest possible inspiration to the men of this division who are devoted to him.

On Menoher's promotion, MacArthur was designated commander of 26,000 men at the age of 38 with the rank of major-general. But with the declaration of the armistice on November 11, all promotions were suspended.

The Rainbow was ordered into Germany as part of the occupation force. In the Rhineland he occupied the castle of Sinzig 25 miles south of Bonn, where suffering from post-battle exhaustion and the aftereffects of gas, he fell desperately ill with a throat infection, and then again with diphtheria. But he and his men had at last reached paradise.

There he had held court in a ragged brown sweater and civilian pants. A portrait painter called and painted him by candlelight.

> Young MacArthur looks like the typical hero of historical romance; he could easily have stepped out of the pages of the "Prisoner of Zenda," or "Rupert of Hentzau." He looked as though he were under thirty years of age . . . he is lean, light-skinned, with long, well-kept fingers, and is always

carefully groomed . . . He is a thoroughgoing brainy young man, distinctly of the city type, a good talker and a good listener, perfectly "daffy" about the 42nd Division, and, of course, positive that the 42nd Division won the Great War. He is quick in his movements, physical and mental, and is subject to changing moods; he knits his brows or laughs heartily with equal facility, and often during the same sentence.

The Prince of Wales visited, predicting that the Germans would rise up again. MacArthur was of the same opinion. When the Treaty of Versailles was signed the terms, he said, "look drastic and seem to me more a treaty of perpetual war than of perpetual peace." What impression the foppish, delicately featured young prince made on the battle-hardened MacArthur is not recorded. Less than three years after, the British royal was to host the young Hirohito on his official visit to Britain.

In March MacArthur was awarded the DSM in front of the assembled Rainbow Division and the following month he sailed for New York in great comfort.

We had a great trip over on the *Leviathan*. I gracefully occupied a $5,000.00 suite consisting of four rooms and three baths. It filled me with excitement to change my bed and bath each evening.

We reached New York on the 25th but where-oh-where was that welcome they told us of? Where was that howling mob to proclaim us monarchs of all we surveyed? Where were those bright eyes, slim ankles that had been kidding us in our dreams? Nothing—nothing like that. One little urchin asked us who we were and when we said—we are the famous 42nd—he asked if we had been to France.

Amid a silence that hurt—with no one, not even the children, to see us— we marched off the dock, to be scattered to the four winds—a sad, gloomy end of the Rainbow. There was no welcome for fighting men; no one wanted us to parade; no one even seemed to have heard of the war. And profiteers! Ye gods, the profiteers! He who has no Rolls Royce is certainly ye piker. And expensive living! Paris is certainly a cheap little place after all. I judge, too, that clothes are very, very high, for at the play the girls were absolutely unable to wear any. They looked well.

A ball was held in MacArthur's honor at the Waldorf Astoria.

I was in full uniform and in those days full uniform meant spurs and the works. I was dancing and the maitre d'hotel came over to me. He said it was against the rules to wear spurs on the dance floor. I said "Do you know who I am?" He said, "Yes, General." And I took my lady and we walked off the dance floor, and I have never set foot in that place again.

14 : THE AMOROUS SUPERINTENDENT

UNLIKE MANY BROTHER OFFICERS, WHO IMMEDIATELY FADED INTO OBSCUrity, MacArthur's battlefield successes had been too well reported for him to suffer a similar fate. The new army chief of staff, General Peyton C. Mack, offered him the prestigious job of superintendent of West Point with a mandate to revitalize the institution. An astonished and delighted MacArthur accepted and took up his new duties in June 1919. He and his mother moved into the superintendent's mansion 20 years to the day after he had first arrived at the prestigious academy. An authentic war hero, he looked a decade younger than his 39 years.

MacArthur's unusual personality soon imposed itself on the stuffy academy: he was informal by nature, impatient of ceremony and petty regulations, and penetratingly intelligent. His adjutant, Major William Ganoe, painted a vivid picture:

> He clung to his principle that rules are mostly made to be broken and are too often for the lazy to hide behind . . . He had a way of touching your elbow or shoulder, upping his chin with a slight jerk and crowding into his eye such a warmth of blessing, he made you feel you'd contributed a boon to the whole human race . . . Whereas you had no fear to let down your hair before him, you wouldn't think of slapping him on the back.
>
> The characteristic which made the greatest impression was his unwavering aplomb, his astonishing self-mastery. I had seen men who were so placid or stolid they were emotionless. But MacArthur was anything but that. His every tone, look or movement was the extreme of intense vivacity . . . As he talked, so he walked jauntily, without swagger. His gait and expression were carefree without being careless. He possessed a gifted leadership, a leadership that kept you at a respectful distance, yet at the same time took you in as an esteemed member of his team, and very quickly had you working harder than you had ever worked before in your life, just because of the loyalty, admiration and respect in which you held him.

Obedience is something a leader can command, but loyalty is something, an indefinable something, that he is obliged to win. MacArthur knew instinctively how to win it. [He was] all contradiction. He commanded without commanding. He was both a patrician and plebeian.

MacArthur was blunt on the need for reform, and farsighted in what he proposed: "Discipline no longer required extreme methods. Men generally needed only to be told what to do, rather than be forced by the fear of consequence of failure . . . Improvisation will be the watchword. Such changed conditions will require a modification in type of the officer, a type possessing all of the cardinal military virtues as of yore, but possessing an intimate understanding of his fellows, a comprehensive grasp of world and national affairs, and a generalization of conception which amounts to a change in his psychology of command."

McArthur proposed a radical set of changes: more subjects in the curriculum; more contact with the outside world; abolition of the elaborate social routine of summer camp in favor of training under regular army officers; the introduction of compulsory games for all cadets. "On the field of friendly strife are sown the seeds that upon other fields and other days will bear the fruits of victory," he had inscribed on the gate.

MacArthur only partly succeeded: he slammed up against the "privy council"—as he called it: the twelve-man academic board of greying old conservative military pedagogues (on which he had only two allies) who regarded him as their servant, rather than he their leader. Then MacArthur really began treading on toes. He proposed practical steps to ban "hazing"—the bullying of young cadets from which he himself had suffered; he introduced a new code of conduct and shut down the "beast barracks" where young cadets arrived for their initiation rituals. MacArthur's relentless attacks on the cherished practices of West Point were typical. He was the man of action of the First World War, and the least he could do at West Point was to shake things up. Mostly he was obstructed. He had however confirmed his reputation as a stirrer, a troubleshooter, an innovator, an officer of military spit and polish, a uniformed radical.

General Pershing, his venerable commander, and most of his clique of senior officers swore by the old ways and could not stand the man. They were determined to get him out before he further undermined their cherished institution. Pershing rated MacArthur as no more than "above average" in military efficiency in his official report, and rated him thirtyl-eighth in talent out of 46 brigadier-generals. "He has an exalted opinion of himself," he commented witheringly.

The old man's displeasure had not been provoked only by MacArthur's modernization of West Point: the young man was viewed as a cad on matters of the heart as well—which could hardly be justified on the facts (indeed, they pointed inescapably to the conclusion that Pershing himself was the cad). In 1917 the commander of the American expeditionary force in Europe had been entertained by a fabulously wealthy Gatsbyesque American couple in Paris, Walter Brooks, a Baltimore billionaire, and his wife Louise.

Brooks, despite his wealth, was a pompous and insignificant little man; his wife was the daughter of another plutocrat, Oliver E. Cromwell, and her stepfather, Edward Stotesbury, was a partner of J. P. Morgan with a fortune estimated at $150 million, one of the largest in the world.

Louise was everything her husband was not; although on the short side, she was pretty in a girlish, provocative way, with chubby cheeks, a playful smile and sparkling, alluring eyes. She radiated sex appeal. More than that: she adored sex, with all the abandon of one whose colossal wealth insulated her from any inhibitions or worries about what others might think of her.

The starchy old martinet Pershing, a widower who considered himself a ladies' man, was instantly smitten, and they became lovers. After a year of carrying on under Brooks's nose, "Black Jack" Pershing's roving eye caught that of a 20-year-old Romanian girl a third of his age. When Louise brazenly proposed marriage, the old goat left her. She turned her attentions to a young British admiral, Sir David Beatty, and caused the breakup of his marriage, then to an American senator.

On the Brooks's return to New York, she started to see Pershing again, this time acting as his hostess as he sought the Republican presidential nomination. Her separation from Brooks by now made this respectable. But her new romantic liaison was with 38-year-old Colonel John Quekemeyer, a staff protégé of Pershing, whom the old general looked upon as a son. Pershing favored the liaison.

Quite by accident she attended a social gathering at West Point in September 1921 and met its striking, aloof superintendent, a war hero to boot. There was an instant sexual chemistry between the two. It is far from surprising that the wealthy, flighty Louise fell for the handsome young general. What the highly intelligent, self-disciplined MacArthur saw in this bubbly young socialite remains more of a mystery: for he at once appeared to have viewed her not as a temporary bedmate but as a potential wife. MacArthur had long been persuaded by his mother's advice that he was wedded to his career, which would suffer if he married. There is no record of whether he had had occasional liaisons up to this comparatively late age in his personal life, although for a man of MacArthur's own passionate nature (as was soon to emerge) it would hardly be surprising if he had. But certainly there had been nothing serious.

Now he set himself at someone as unlike himself as it was possible to be—a vivacious, spoiled rich kid who took absolutely nothing and no one seriously. MacArthur, who had never been wealthy and must have felt the disparity in the glittering social circles he often brushed against, may have been attracted to the security that her wealth would confer—certainly his mother Pinky, who was initially delighted by the match, supported it for that reason, although Louise was later to call her "interfering."

He justified his overwhelming sexual passion for Louise in romantic terms: "Was ever such a romance in all this world before?" he wrote to her. "Some great destiny is involved in our union." On February 14, St. Valentine's Day, 1922, they were married. A newspaper headline proclaimed cheekily "Mars Marries Millions." Her brother reported next day her famous compliment, "He may be a general in the army, but he's a buck private in the boudoir." She had not made the mistake of sleeping with her intended before marriage, as had happened with Pershing. She had won her knight in shining armor at last. The inexperienced MacArthur was in a wholly new world, mistaking sexual ardour with the inexhaustible Louise for true love.

Pershing was beside himself with rage at MacArthur's stealing Louise from the heartbroken Quekemeyer. He took his revenge by cutting short MacArthur's term as West Point superintendent by a year and sending him on a posting to the Philippines. The scandal leaked into the newspapers. Pershing commented:

> It's all damn poppycock, without the slightest foundation and based on the idlest gossip. If I were married to all the ladies that gossips have engaged me to, I'd be a regular Brigham Young.

In June MacArthur was effectively dismissed from West Point, and in September the newlyweds sailed to Manila, MacArthur to take up the comparatively lowly post of Commander of the Military Division of Manila, his first task to map the torrid Bataan Peninsula at the mouth of Manila Bay.

Petty politicking at home had provided a new setback to the career of the meteoric young general, as it had to his father, and the Philippines were once again the backdrop. MacArthur's career now seemed headed toward respectable mediocrity well short of the top amid the dull provincialism of stodgy, sub-colonial American expatriate society in a tropical outpost at peace. It was to his credit that he chose not to dwell on the setback in his fortunes, but threw himself into his mundane tasks with his usual energy and vigor, professing himself honored to perform on his father's former stage.

Moreover, he personally believed in the possibility of the Philippines becoming a battleground in a future war with Japan. The army high command had ostensibly sent him to Bataan with the intention of discussing whether it would make a suitable defensive holdout in the event of an invasion of Japan overwhelming the thinly defended Philippines until a relief force could be organized.

Yet the prospect looked remote in that autumn of 1922. For Japan to the north was a cheerful, prosperous quasi-democracy under the prime ministership of the Great Commoner Hara and the constitutional rule of the young Prince Regent. Hirohito, who, with a beautiful young bride, had just come of age, ushered in a new and hopeful era after the uncertain rule of his erratic father.

15 : Eroticism, Grotesquery and Nonsense

THE REIGN OF THE YOUNG REGENT BEGAN ON A NOTE OF YOUTH, HOPE AND optimism that the dark undercurrents of politics did not justify. On April 12, 1922, Hirohito's young friend, the Prince of Wales, came to Japan on a state visit, to be greeted by the same shy young man he had encountered in Buckingham Palace—but this time endowed with the formidable authority of the regency. Edward was taken to Hakone, Kyoto, Nara and Nagashima, displaying an easy lack of convention that shocked many Japanese, particularly when on one occasion he posed as a coolie.

At the time there seemed every prospect that the reign would be one of increasing prosperity and calm. Japan's industrial base was larger than ever before. Its arts and society were undergoing an unprecedented enlightenment. Universal manhood suffrage was only three years away, and for the first time parliamentary institutions were making themselves felt in the life of the nation. Internationally Japan seemed intent on pursuing its aims through peaceful means. Prince Edward, visiting Japan, undoubtedly found Japanese deference and politeness profoundly comical; he cannot have found them threatening and dangerous.

The facade of Japanese constitutionalism was extraordinarily weak, like the flimsy, ubiquitous wooden houses in which ordinary Japanese lived. When times were good and the economic climate was favorable, it survived; when the winds of depression raged, it was to blow over with absurd ease, like those other ill-grounded regimes of Weimar Germany and the Third Republic in France. When the constitutional facade was gone, only industry and militarism were left, snarling at each other in a naked power struggle, with the bureaucrats serving as feeble umpires on the sidelines.

The real blame lay with those who, to entrench their own privileges, created a system that was not founded on popular or even middle-class support; indeed, the *zaibatsu* themselves, who were originally the extension of aristocratic authoritarianism into industrial and economic life, undermined any possibility of creating the solid middle class that is the bulwark of any democratic society. As in virtually no other industrial nation, not only was political power concentrated in the hands of a very few; so was economic power. In Japan there were just the industrial oligarchs and the toiling masses, as in some awful Marxist caricature, with precious little in between. In contrast to the traditional Marxist picture, the oligarchs were so relentless in suppressing every expression of popular and left-wing opposition that they could only be challenged by right-wing, nationalist populism—which made a powerful impression among ordinary people, certainly securing more support than the hated *zaibatsu* bosses could command.

Like some terrible foretaste or omen of the times to come, Hirohito's early regency was marked by a massive earthquake, on September 1, 1923. In Yokohama and Tokyo, devastation was immediately followed by raging fires. Yokohama was destroyed altogether, while half of Tokyo was razed to the ground. Some 100,000 died. The giant catfish under Japan that was supposed by legend to raise its back in anger when the humans above angered it had wreaked a terrible vengeance.

Worse was to come: the police used the earthquake as a pretext to crack down on a supposed conspiracy between Korean nationalists and Japanese communists to set up a revolutionary government in the aftermath of the earthquake. Many were arrested, many murdered, while angry mobs went in search of Koreans—the only significant immigrant community in Japan. Although the government was almost certainly in no way responsible for the massacres, it bowed to the pervasive racial and anticommunist sentiment of one sector of Japanese opinion.

The impact of the earthquake was to be partially assuaged in the public mind by an event of national celebration: Hirohito's wedding, repeatedly postponed, first through the opposition of Yamagata, then by the earthquake. On January 26, 1924, at the imperial palace in Tokyo, six years after the original engagement, the 22-year-old Hirohito and his 19-year-old bride were married; not until May did public festivities take place, in deference to the suffering caused by the earthquake. In August the imperial couple went on a month's honeymoon, and afterward they moved into the huge, over-the-top Akasaka Detached Palace, where Hirohito's father had spent so much of his short life.

The homely Nagako and the shy Hirohito were close from the first, spending much time together: she playing the piano for him and singing, the two of them listening to records together. The garden of the four seasons, to the south of the palace, where trees and plants bloomed throughout the year, became a favorite promenade. Hirohito set up a little laboratory inside the grounds of the palace, complete with a shed for raising animals and a field for growing plants. It seemed that he was at the height of his personal happiness. On December 6, 1925, a baby girl was born to the royal couple.

Only 10 days after Princess Teru Shigeko was born, the now incapacitated Emperor Yoshihito collapsed with a stroke. Another followed; he could no longer walk or talk properly. A year later, on December 25, 1926, he died of pneumonia at the age of just 47, during a fierce thunderstorm. The same night, Hirohito was given the sword and jewel of office—two of the three insignia of the throne, supposedly bequeathed by the Goddess Amaterasu—while another ceremony was held in the imperial sanctuary before the sacred mirror, which could not be moved.

The actual coronation of the new Emperor did not take place for another two years, in November, 1928. It was a staggering occasion, befitting the figurehead that the Meiji rulers had turned into a god-like, all-powerful entity and the leader of an increasingly self-assertive, nationalist country. It lasted no fewer than eight days. The coronation banquet itself lasted a whole day and was attended by 4,000 guests. The Japanese people showed a remarkable acquiescence toward the occasion, in spite of acute economic difficulties.

They seemed particularly to warm to the simplicity of the imperial couple. Many had heard of one of Hirohito's first reforms within his own household: he had abandoned the aristocratic ranking of ladies-in-waiting, a hotbed of courtly intrigue, making them all equal and permitting commoners to serve for the first time. He insisted, too, that ordinary Japanese, not classical courtly Japanese, be spoken in the palace. Above all, he showed that he and his wife would be a faithful couple, not a nominal one:

the Emperor would not indulge in concubines, as his father and grandfather had before him. He seemed in spirit with the times, reflecting a kind of divine simplicity magnified many times by the state propaganda machine. He was 27 at the time of his coronation; before that, although he was privy to the great decisions of state, it would be absurd to suggest that he had much influence over them.

Yet the same year an incident occurred that cast his role into a new perspective. It was a foreboding display of the power of imperial devotion occurring at the great Coronation Day parade on December 1, 1928, when more than 70,000 students and young people congregated in front of the huge walls of the imperial palace, beyond the moat. In the freezing December evening, as rain fell, the royal tent was suddenly dismantled. It was announced that the Emperor would appear without protection "in sympathy with the young people here." Promptly the students began removing their overcoats in reciprocation.

When Hirohito arrived at 2 A.M. he was wearing a military cape. Seeing the youngsters without their coats, he promptly stripped off his own, and the well-fed minions in attendance were obliged to follow suit. For nearly an hour and a half, the Emperor stood unprotected, saluting thousands of youths marching without their coats.

The events of the late 1920s and 1930s unfolded like Shakespearian tragedy. Japanese imperialism was firmly anchored in the ideals of the Meiji oligarchs. But there had been major divisions of policy on how fast and how far to proceed.

There was a consensus among the ruling groups in Japan—the bureaucracy, the armed forces and the business leaders—that further expansion was desirable, but no clear idea as to the best way of achieving it: the navy and many businessmen, for example, favored expansion southward; the army favored further expansion deep into China. For the moment caution prevailed. Under Japan's brief phase of parliamentary government, the middle-class electorate showed little inclination to be sucked into war— and briefly at that time public opinion counted for something. Business was cautious. The international climate was wrong. Japan's First World War allies had grown suspicious—and the British and the Americans still retained naval preponderance in Asia.

Politically, moderates under the influence of the business elites headed the government. After Hara's assassination in November 1921, four short-lived governments followed each other in swift succession before two major parties crushed the nominees of what was left of the Meiji bureaucracy in the general election of 1924. These were Takaaki Kato's Kenseikai party, and the assassinated Hara's Seiyukai party. In fact, each party was heavily dominated by the *zaibatsu*—Mitsubishi and Mitsui respectively. In the delicate power balance within Japan, it would be fair to say that real power had for the first time passed to big business in alliance with what little influence public opinion possessed.

The bureaucrats were on the defensive, although still entrenched in the ministries and, in particular, the imperial household. Their leader, the remaining *genrô*, Prince Saionji, was however on the side of reform. Beneath him higher and middle echelons in the bureaucracy seethed at their loss of control. They also resented the challenge to Japanese society represented by the forces of modernization and "licentiousness," and Japan's overseas moderation. The third power, the armed forces, was for the moment neutralized, but also harbored some of the most radically reactionary forces in Japanese society.

Kato and his successor as head of the Kenseikai, Rejiro Wakatsuki, were resolved to pursue Japan's quest for greater overseas influence by peaceful means. Kijuro Shidehara, the foreign minister, had moved to dispel the extreme suspicion of Japan generated by the notorious Twenty-One demands on China. Japan's new policy of noninterventionism was helped by the disastrous experience of Japan's expedition to Russia during the Civil War there in 1918. In alliance with the Americans, a 70,000-man force had blundered about, trying to secure national interests rather than defeat the Soviet forces. The Japanese had been given instructions to "facilitate the activities of Japanese officials and civilians" engaged in the "conduct of business and the development of natural resources." They were to "enhance Japan's position in its future competition with the Western powers in China."

Exasperated and pushed back by the Russians, the Americans withdrew in 1920. Alone and facing huge casualties for questionable objectives, the Japanese retreated from the Amur River in 1922 and in 1925 evacuated Northern Sakhalin, leaving behind them the enmity of the new Soviet state. This military debacle contributed to the low public standing of the Japanese army at the time. A moderate Minister of War, General Kazushige Ugaki, was appointed in 1924 to cut the army's strength by no fewer than four divisions.

Meanwhile, in China, Japan's previous aggression had made it enemies on all sides. In addition, its trade objectives there were coming into conflict with those of the United States. The British had refused to renew the Anglo-

Japanese alliance on the ground that Japan showed "little chance of industrial survival unless she can obtain control over the resources of China"—
and that would endanger Britain's own commercial objectives there.
Japan's international emissaries spoke bitterly of "the attempt to oppress
the non-Anglo-Saxon races, especially the colored races, by the two English-
speaking countries, Britain and the United States."

In the 1920s, Japan was alarmed by a sudden deterioration in its overseas security. President Woodrow Wilson had infuriated the Japanese at the
1919 Treaty of Versailles by deleting a clause asserting Japanese racial equality to America and the European powers. The disastrous 1922 Washington
Conference, which established a 5.5.3 naval balance between the United
States, Britain and Japan, was taken by the latter as an attempt to tie its
hands in permanent naval inferiority by the Anglo-Saxon powers, which had
hitherto been divided in their approach, with the British enjoying much
friendlier relations with Japan than the Americans. Worse, the agreement forbade the construction of American and British naval bases north of
Singapore and west of Hawaii—which made it possible for the first time for
Japan to contemplate attacking its Asian neighbors as well as the American-
dominated Philippines. The London Naval Conference in 1930 was effectively
to emasculate British naval strength in the Far East. Thus Japan lost its most
valuable restraining ally, Britain, and was left feeling isolated, insecure and
newly aggressive, as well as hostile to both Britain and America.

Yet Japan did not dare take on such enemies. Shidehara, the foreign
minister, argued eloquently in favor of the extension of Japanese influence
by non-military means. "Japan, being closest to China, has an advantage
by way of transport costs and she also has the greatest competitive power
because of her wages. It must therefore be a primary priority for Japan to
maintain the great market of China." Iwane Matsu, of the Japanese general staff, insisted that Japanese policy was "to substitute economic conquest for military invasion, financial influences for military control and
achieve our goals under the slogans of co-prosperity and co-existence." This
was hardly the language of peaceful diplomacy, but it did mark a greater
degree of Japanese caution than in the past.

The Tokyo spring of parliamentary democracy and restraint abroad contained the seeds of its own destruction. The growth in right-wing political
extremism had a long pedigree, dating back to the existence of the unemployed samurai class who had been behind the restoration of the Emperor in

1868, and then been stripped of its perks. The breeding ground was the city of Fukuoka, the closest point at which Japan approaches Asia, the starting point for the invasion of Korea by the Empress Jingu, as well as the attacks mounted by Hideyoshi in 1592, and the main operational base during the Russo-Japanese war. Fukuoka samurai had left their castle city to stage an attack on the home city of the Meiji statesman Iwakura as recently as 1874.

In 1881 a mass of samurai secret societies coalesced to form the Genyosha, dedicated to reverence of the Emperor, to furthering the interests of the nation, and to the rights of the people. The Genyosha did not believe, after Saigo's defeat in 1877, that an armed uprising was an option: the purpose of the society was to bring together like-minded extreme nationalists, particularly in the bureaucracy and the army, to promote its aims. There were a huge number of these, and the Genyosha was, literally, masonic in its network, furthering the business interests of its members, seeking intermediaries to act for sympathetic military and civilian leaders and, not least, resorting to systematic terror in pursuit of its aims.

Mitsuru Toyama was the Genyosha's best-known leader. Born of an impoverished samurai family, he spent his youth in tea houses and brothels; quite early on, he established for himself a curious autonomy and immunity from the law that allowed him to patronize not just homegrown terrorists but right-wing revolutionaries overseas. His two unwavering ideals were implacable opposition to Western interests and hatred of communism. In 1892 he reached an agreement with the government by which he was assured that it would pursue a strong foreign policy and increase military spending in exchange for Genyosha support. Toyama's strong-arm methods, with the assistance of *soshi* (toughs) from neighboring areas, terrorized the Fukuoka province; the election was the bloodiest in Japanese history, dozens being killed and several hundred wounded.

The police and home office closely cooperated with him, which was convenient, as the former would not launch attacks on public meetings themselves, but instead would turn up later to restore peace, arresting the victims of the attacks. At cabinet level, an unofficial alliance existed between the ministers of the interior, war and navy, who were happy to use the services of the Genyosha. The organization also provided the army with an unofficial foreign intelligence service. Contacts with anti-Manchu secret societies, nationalist groups in colonial territories and dissident Muslims in Central Asia were established and developed. In 1882 Toyama, with the help of the Kumamoto Sôaisha (Mutual Love Society), sent over 100 young men to China to gather information.

Parallel to the growth of the Genyosha (literally, Dark Ocean Society) and the Kokoryûkai (Black Dragon Society) was that of a clique of extremist philosophers, of whom the best known was Ikki Kita, later dubbed the father of Japanese fascism. Kita was an intellectual, not a man of action like Toyama. His book, *A Plan for the Resurgence of Japan* published in 1923 and promptly banned because of its egalitarian views, might be described as "socialist-imperialist." He jumped on the two most populist creeds of the time, the yearning for equality and the desire for national self-assertiveness, and welded them even more closely than Hitler and Mussolini had. He sought the establishment of a "revolutionary empire of Japan" through a military coup d'état, which would be founded on the indissoluble bonds between the Emperor and the armed forces, and whose mission would be to further Japanese expansion abroad.

Domestically his program was radical: politics would be suspended and the corrupting barriers between the Emperor and his people done away with. The rich would be expropriated of their land and financial dominance. The economy would be state-controlled and placed on a war footing. Land reform would be introduced in order to give protection to tenant farmers. Profit-sharing and an eight-hour day would be introduced into industry; and civil liberties would be permitted.

Kita's international views displayed the same kind of crazy, simple-minded plausibility. Britain, "a multimillionaire standing over the whole world," and Russia, "the great landlord of the northern hemisphere," needed to be expelled by the Asian nations headed by Japan. "Our several hundred million brothers in China and India have no path to independence other than that offered by our guidance and protection." Japan should "lift the virtuous banner of an Asian league and take the leadership in a world federation." Japan was not acting entirely out of altruism, of course: one reason for this struggle was that, for Japan, "great areas adequate to support a population of at least two hundred and forty or fifty millions will be absolutely necessary a hundred years from now." Even some recusant communists followed a similar line of thinking: Japan, on one account, had the task of leading "a progressive war for the peoples of Asia" against British and American capitalism.

Kita's ideas can be clearly traced in two later expressions. In the army, the Imperial Way Faction, led by General Sadao Araki, who became war minister in 1931, paid unashamed homage to them. But they became fashionable even in much more aristocratic circles. Prince Konoye of the venerable Fujiwara family and later to be a bitterly controversial prime minister, argued as far back as the 1920s that Britain and the United States were pursuing policies to keep down the "have-nots," condemning Japan "to remain forever subordinate to the advanced nations." It would be necessary, he concluded, "to destroy the status quo for the sake of self-preservation, just like Germany."

The Imperial Way faction had enormous influence among junior officers. Many were wedded to what became known as the doctrine of the Showa Restoration: the argument that, just as after the Meiji restoration the feudal princes, the *daimyo*, had had to surrender their lands to the Emperor, so the "feudal" industrial princes, the *zaibatsu*, must surrender their wealth to the Emperor. The popularity of such views extended from traditional samurai-background army officers through to the new class that had come up with the introduction of conscription. They were to comprise a pure form of nationalist communism, based on racism and imperialism.

The appeal of these ideas owes a great deal to the fact that the authoritarian system of Japan moved in with such relentless intensity against any formal mass movement of the left. The radical right—preaching social equality, nationalism, the unity of the Japanese people under the Emperor's mantle, hatred of capitalism, whether homegrown or abroad, the wish to lead the peoples of Asia in a crusade against the West—had come up with a creed of genuine mass appeal, particularly to the huge swathes of Japanese society that had suffered the ravages of industrialization and depression, many of whose children had been conscripted into the army. In Japan, the radical alternative to rule by big business and the bureaucracy became the egalitarian right, because the egalitarian left had been suppressed. This, in turn, was to put the fear of God into Japan's ruling class and helps to explain why they abandoned all good sense and calm in the whirlwind of events that began in the 1930s.

The ties between big business and the political parties were, of course, to be fatal for the latter and nearly so for the former. As long as Japan's economy was booming, such ties were acceptable. Elections were financed by large gifts from the *zaibatsu*, and politicians used open bribery to get themselves elected. The two leading parties traded accusations of corruption. The *zaibatsu* themselves were far from popular among the workers they employed and among the small business interests they habitually squeezed and crushed. In the countryside—where the bulk of soldiers were recruited—the powerful urban economic interests were identified not just with economic exploitation, but with the introduction of a new Japanese order that had destroyed centuries of tradition.

16 : DEVOURING MANCHURIA

FOR JAPAN THE FINANCIAL CRASH CAME EARLIER AND ENDED SOONER THAN elsewhere. In 1927, a minor bank failed; 36 more followed, bringing down scores of small firms with them. The *zaibatsu* gobbled up many of the hapless victims. The crisis stemmed to a great extent from the *zaibatsu* domination of the banking system, which had favored an expansionary monetary system even when this could not be sustained by real economic growth. The Nakatsuki government fell, and General Giichi Tanaka, of the opposition Seiyukai party, came to office. This first economic upheaval had the effect of beginning to discredit party politics, while increasing public hostility and contempt for the *zaibatsu*, particularly among the military class and the oppressed but conservative peasantry.

The crisis coincided with the challenge to Japan abroad. Many army officers were appalled by the government's hands-off approach to China: but in the same year it became apparent that Chiang Kai-Shek's Nationalist forces had gained control of the Yangtze Valley and were moving north to consolidate their hold over the country. The Japanese for the first time feared that a strong China was in the cards, which would undoubtedly threaten their interests in Manchuria. In the circumstances, many officers felt it would be a criminal dereliction of duty to continue Shidehara's policy of conciliation. The whole simplistic swirl of foreign policy weakness, corruption, democratic politics, big business exploitation and economic crisis began to fuse into a single obsession in the Japanese military mind: something must be done. The initial battle for control of Japan between the establishment and the far right was joined over the assassination of the Manchurian warlord, Chang Tso-lin.

Chang, the "Old Marshal," had been a loyal protégé of Japan's, a formidable and unscrupulous military leader in southern Manchuria from around 1920, controlling the southern city of Mukden. Chang had been supplied with Japanese arms, and was ready to cooperate with the Japanese; he was also firmly anti-Russian. However, he was deeply ambitious, and wanted to take over all of China. Japan's government at the time resolved to make him the puppet ruler of Manchuria, while discouraging his aims to the south. Accordingly, Japanese advisers were attached to Chang's staff, as much to keep an eye on him as to prop him up. Japanese troops were soon fighting alongside Chang when rebellions threatened. The alliance all but made Manchuria a Japanese protectorate by December 1925. With some 100,000 Japanese lives already lost protecting Japanese interests there, with so many subjects and commercial interests at stake, the Japanese forces, the Kwantung Army, became an occupying presence.

Within these constraints, Chang showed a measure of independence, setting up a Chinese-style education system to rival the Japanese one, permitting Chinese firms to compete with Japanese ones, renewing his interest in the rest of China. In 1926 he was self-confident enough to move down from Manchuria and occupy the capital, Peking. This alarmed the Japanese, who had no wish to get sucked into China's civil war at this stage and who did not want to make enemies of the man who might emerge as China's strongman, General Chiang Kai-Shek—even though they viewed him with deep suspicion.

General Tanaka, Japan's new prime minister, tried to deal directly with Chiang, securing a promise that his forces would stop short of Manchuria. When the generalissimo nevertheless attacked early in 1928, Japanese troops engaged his army. Chiang's forces advanced relentlessly to Peking, and Tanaka was forced to issue an ultimatum declaring that Japan would resist any encroachment on Manchuria with all the forces at its disposal. Simultaneously Chang was told that he must withdraw his forces from Peking into Manchuria, or risk having the border closed against him by the Japanese: this he did. The Japanese informed Chang that he would not be allowed to move south again. Their clear and moderate objective was to hold onto Manchuria and prevent its absorption into China's civil war.

There then occurred one of the most puzzling occurrences in the history of Japanese imperialism. As the defeated warlord returned from Peking to Mukden, a bomb was placed under his train on the orders of Colonel Daisaku Komoto, a senior officer of the Kwantung Army. Chang was seriously injured by the blast, and died shortly afterward. At first Chiang Kai-Shek was blamed: later the explosion was widely interpreted as providing a pretext for the Japanese invasion and annexation of Manchuria now that the only Chinese leader with real authority there was dead. The incident was significant as the first example of the Japanese army apparently acting off its own bat, without reference to the high command in Tokyo, much less the government or Emperor.

He had by now been the nominal head of his country for nearly six years, still strongly supported by the liberal Prince Saionji, whose mind belied his age, although his political power had sharply diminished. The prince profoundly loathed militarism, and had outlived his rival Yamagata. Saionji had openly criticized Hirohito's "lack of courage." Prince Kuni, Hirohito's father-in-law and a liberal aristocrat had said, in his dying words to his daughter, the Empress, 'The reigning Emperor is rather weak-willed at times. Therefore he will need your support. Be strong! Be strong!"

Hirohito was young, impulsive and of a reasonably liberal caste of mind. The young Emperor had already insisted that "a real military expansion" into Manchuria "would antagonize the Chinese," and had opposed it.

The prime minister of the time, General Giichi Tanaka, was summoned by the Emperor after the assassination and promised to take action against its perpetrators. Hirohito told him that "no matter what sort of man Chang Tso-lin may have been, he was the designated authority in Manchuria. It was very wrong of the army to have any hand in his assassination." Tanaka prepared a full report on the incident, which turned out to be a whitewash. Hirohito was furious. He asked the prime minister, "Does this not contradict what you told me before?" Tanaka replied that he could "offer a number of explanations for that." Then the Emperor said sharply, "I have no wish to hear your explanations," and left the room. The prime minister promptly resigned, having no choice in front of such an imperial snub.

Years later Hirohito was to regret his show of anger. "I was too young at the time." The Meiji constitution had firmly instructed the Emperor to follow the prime minister's advice on political issues. One minister at the time complained that "to treat the nation's prime minister so slightly, even once, is a serious matter. It would have been proper to remonstrate with His Majesty over this." Hirohito had behaved like a hotheaded young man, in defiance of the constitution that shackled him to impotence yet used his awesome imperial office as its backbone. He was chastened by the experience.

On this occasion, the militarists' tactic badly misfired and proved highly counterproductive to Japanese interests. Neither the Kwantung Army nor the Japanese high command made any move. Chang's son, Chang Hsueh-Liang—the "Young Marshal"—took over his father's army and promptly started to pursue a policy of opposition to Japanese interests, reaching an agreement with Chiang Kai-Shek in December, spurred by the widespread suspicion that the Japanese had, in fact, murdered his father. In China, there were boycotts of Japanese goods. A railway system favorable to the Japanese was ripped up by the Young Marshal. The Japanese were forced on the defensive, and in June 1929, grudgingly recognized Chiang Kai-Shek as the legitimate ruler of China.

There remains the intriguing possibility that Komoto had, after all, been acting with some kind of secret directive from the government: Chang had become a serious embarrassment to the Japanese and an obstacle to normal relations with China; his removal made possible agreement with Chiang. If Komoto—who narrowly escaped courtmartial—was acting under government direction, the primary objective was a moderate one. If, as is more likely, he was not, his gross insubordination had failed. The army hotheads, it seemed, had been rapped over the knuckles.

The setback to their cause was temporary: the beginnings of Japan's grim aberration, of the rush to extremism and madness, were only months away. The Emperor, as weak as any constitutional monarch, was being steered at that time by moderate party politicians, who were accused on all sides of corruption, believed to be in the pay of the detested business corporations, with only the flimsiest fig leaf of popular legitimacy. The country's huge conscript army was more powerful than it had ever been, and longed for the opportunity to intervene and give direction to Japan's affairs, now so feebly run by the politicians. In particular, as the military men saw it, such few colonial possessions as Japan had were in danger of being taken over by the renascent Chinese, aided by Russian Bolshevism and British and American imperialism. The army believed itself capable of winning any war it entered upon: what were the politicians waiting for?

In Manchuria, where so many Japanese lives had been lost and so many interests were at stake, the politicians were permitting the creation of an anti-Japanese state which in 1930 firmly declared its allegiance to Chiang Kai-Shek—presumably the man to push the Japanese out. The army, as has been seen, regarded itself as the direct descendant of the main Choshu faction behind the Meiji Restoration. It had direct access to the Emperor, bypassing the cabinet, and regarded itself as above the decisions of the government. The Emperor was a young man under the influence of "defeatist" advisers; loyalty to him did not entail allegiance to the corrupt influences around the throne, as numerous "loyal" samurai rebellions in the past testified. Japan's samurai purity was being corrupted by urban and internationalist influences.

While there undoubtedly were some moderate senior army officers, and some constitutionalists among them, these views were held not just by junior hotheads but by many senior members of the general staff. What happened over the next couple of years has often been described as the action of a few extremists. All the evidence suggests, however, that the general staff was directly implicated.

Two events shattered what restraints might have existed among army and civilian nationalists. The first was petty and absurd, the second deserving of sympathy. In 1930, at the London Naval Disarmament Conference, the Japanese delegation, which included the navy minister, agreed to a limit on the number of Japanese warships in the Pacific which was at once strongly contested by the naval general staff. Prime Minister Tanaka had resigned after the Emperor's criticism of his failure to prevent the assassination of Chang Tso-lin. His successor was the leader of the opposition, a feisty old man, Yuko Hamaguchi, known in political circles as "the lion." His war minister was the moderate General Ugaki, one of the last constitutionalists to hold the post. The government was tainted by being closely connected to Mitsubishi. The foreign minister, Jinnosuke Inouye, was the son-in-law of the head of that family, but had a reputation as a brilliant and honest economist in his own right.

Hamaguchi, who was acting as navy minister in Tokyo, immediately endorsed the recommendation of the London agreement, which also must have given satisfaction to Inouye, who wanted to cut military spending. The nationalists were appalled, claiming he had acted unconstitutionally in ignoring the views of the naval general staff (although the navy minister had himself reached the agreement). Senior army officers were appalled that their rival service appeared to be losing its autonomous power of political decision-making to the despised civilians.

Much more seriously, almost simultaneously, the world depression arrived. Japan had already had a foretaste of this in the 1927 wobble, and as a result was in a better position to face it than most countries in the industrial world. The view that the militarists seized power because of the strains induced by the depression is facile and demonstrably untrue. Yet the slump struck Japan in three very specific ways: first, it dealt a body blow to Japanese exports, which plunged between 1929 and 1931. In America the silk market collapsed, threatening many small farmers and plunging northern Japan into desperate poverty—which was further compounded by the failure of the 1932 rice crop that led to a major famine. Farmers staved off hunger by selling their daughters to the brokers that traveled the countryside on behalf of the big city brothels. The self-appointed representatives of the rural communities were the extreme nationalists who had hijacked the aspirations of Japan's traditionally miserable and repressed peasantry from the genuine peasant leaders so vigorously persecuted by local authorities and central government alike.

The depression also knocked the political argument from under the monopoly capitalists that dominated the political parties. In fact, urban

Japan was much less hard hit than rural Japan and was to recover quickly. But to the most radical sector of public opinion—the hard-hit peasantry and their right-wing champions—the corruption and domination of the oligopolistic monopolies were never more apparent. Their rotten, greedy, exploiting ways no longer even had success to point to as their pretext for eroding Japan's way of life.

Third, the peaceful approach to trade liberalization and negotiation was now exposed as a hollow sham: as countries rushed to put up trade barriers in the wake of the great depression, Japan had nothing to gain by continuing to endorse "open door" and "treaty port" systems—which it had always suspected were the shabby devices of Western colonial exploitation in the first place. Its policy henceforth would be one of creating its own self-sufficient trading block and expelling foreign colonialists from Asia. One prominent Diet member argued in 1931 that "economic warfare" was leading to the creation of "large economic blocks." Japan must create its own, using force to assure "its rights to a bare existence."

The army decided to act. The brush-dry tinder of Japanese extremism had been ignited by the fierce economic depression among the class from which its junior officers were drawn—the peasantry, bitterly opposed to the hated forces to urban cosmopolitanism. The Emperor must be rescued from his corrupt advisers. The nationalists acted on three fronts—through domestic terrorism, through preparation for a coup which intimidated successive civilian government into virtual submission, and through the pursuit of an independent, aggressive policy in Manchuria.

It is hard to exaggerate the climate of fear in which Japan was plunged by the whirlwind of far-right terror that was unleashed in 1930. In November of that year, Hamaguchi was shot by a far-right terrorist in the gothic splendor of Tokyo Station—nine years after Hara's assassination. Shidehara, who had returned as foreign minister, became acting prime minister until the following April, when Hamaguchi bravely returned to office in spite of his injuries, only to have to give way to foreign minister Wakatsuki. "The lion" died shortly afterward.

Only months after the assassination attempt, a group of senior army officers were discovered to be plotting a coup designed to put the war minister, General Ugaki, at the head of a military government. In March 1931 the moderate Ugaki learned of the plot—which became known as the "March Incident"—and denounced it. The conspirators included Major-

General Kuniaki Koiso, later to become prime minister, and the vice-chief of the general staff. On this occasion, as on others, many senior officers were involved, and all went virtually unpunished.

The "October Incident" followed months later: the plot this time was to blow up the entire cabinet and set up a military junta. Senior officers were again involved, and it was exposed only when some got cold feet. The ringleaders were held for a day or two, then posted outside the capital.

Unsurprisingly undeterred, the assassins and the plots soon started again. Early in 1932, Inouye, the former finance minister, linked to Mitsubishi, and Baron Dan, chief director of its rival, Mitsui, were assassinated by members of a fanatical right-wing sect calling itself "the League of Blood." On May 15 the 75-year-old Prime Minister, Tsuyoshi Inukai, who had succeeded Wakatsuke, was shot down in his official residence by nine young cadets. The killers were given prison sentences that tapered off within a few years. Early in 1934 a plot was discovered to bomb the cabinet of Inukai's successor, Admiral Saito, and to set up a cabinet headed by an unnamed prince of the imperial house. In August the following year, the deputy minister of war, Major-General Nagata, was slain by a sword wielded by a lieutenant-colonel. All of this was but a buildup to the most celebrated coup attempt of them all, that of February 1936.

But this catalog of terror and military fanaticism illustrates the conditions under which Japan's responsible decision-makers labored from 1930 onward. Right-wing murderers, aided and abetted by sympathizers in the police, the ministry of home affairs, the army, the bureaucracy and the judiciary, exercised vengeance against those of a different persuasion. The courage of those who fought back was to be commended. It is too much to say that extreme right-wingers actually took over the government in the early 1930s. But rarely have fanatical assassins so influenced a climate of opinion that to give authority to the armed forces seemed the only way both of appeasing and containing them. The squads of the right were the gallery to which the military figures that were progressively more in charge as the 1930s progressed were forced to play. Certainly, many senior military men worked hand in glove with the extremist groups that nurtured the killers and coup-plotters.

More to the point, decisive action against them was virtually impossible. Who would order such action? Tottering civilian cabinets or military-dominated administrations that owed their existence to the climate of fear? Who would carry it out? The home affairs agency, the police, the judiciary, or the army, riddled and infiltrated by the secret societies? The left, as will be seen, was ruthlessly suppressed, while the threat came from the right, and in particular the complexity of internal army politics at the time.

17 : THE MILITARY-INDUSTRIAL ALLIANCE

T HE STRUGGLE WITHIN THE ARMY DATED ALL THE WAY BACK TO THE AFTER-math of the First World War. Japan had participated very little in that war, except to serve in the profitable role of chief armorer for the Western powers—which had caused mixed feelings among its allies, the British and the French. Admiral Jellicoe, the British naval commander, commented acidly that, "apart from the selling of guns and ammunition to the Russians and ourselves, Japan is not taking a full share in the war."

In addition, the Japanese army had been hopelessly out of gear with the new concept of "total war" that had been experienced in Europe. Having taken no part in the war, and having failed to modernize its strategy and equipment, the Japanese army, built up by Aritomo Yamagata—which had considered invading Manchuria while its allies were otherwise occupied in the European war—had declined from a first-rate force to that of a second rank power by the end of the war.

Worse followed immediately, as far as the militarists were concerned: under pressure of the economic crisis, defense spending had slumped from nearly half of the budget to around a third between 1921 and 1923. In any event, the disastrous Japanese intervention in post-revolutionary Russia's civil war in support of the White Russian army in Siberia had muddied the image of the military class. Public opinion had been revolted by the expeditionary forces' association with Major General Von Ungern-Sternberg, the "cruel baron" commanding one of the White armies, who pledged to carve out a Greater Mongolia, restore the empire of Genghis Khan, and plant an avenue of gallows from Mongolia to China. Stopped short of these objectives, his forces hanged Jews, dismembered people, and roasted deserters alive. When Prince Saionji came to power in Tokyo, favoring the end of militarist competition between nations and espousing the principles of Versailles, the army was feeling deeply sorry for itself and resentful.

In these inauspicious conditions, the army began planning for the future. Yamagata, although still alive, was no longer in charge of day-to-day policy. His successor and protégé, General Katsura, was unpopular and lacked his authority. One of the most important of the new generals was General Ugaki, the moderate, down-to-earth minister of war who in October 1926 set up an "Equipment Bureau" designed to look at "the conversion of the industrial reserves of the nation to a war footing." The objective was to follow Lloyd George's example in setting up a ministry of munitions, and to prepare Japan for the time when the whole resources of the nation would have to be harnessed to the demands of modern war. The army, which as we have seen considered itself the vanguard of Imperial Japan, had been infuriated by the way industrial interests had decided to give low priority to munitions production because this was unprofitable.

During this period, the tension and competition between the armed forces and the industrial conglomerates was at its highest (the bureaucracy still loftily considered itself above both). The Japanese army wanted to modernize, and to be capable of harnessing the economic resources of the nation in the likely event that the country would have to go to war within a matter of years. The man in charge of the new bureau was Tetsugan Nagata, a brilliant staff officer, who in 1928 published the book that dominated Japanese military thinking over the following decade, *Total National Mobilization*, which argued the case for the creation of a "garrison state" calling upon every last resource of the nation in the event of war.

"The Resources Bureau," a kind of coordinating and planning adjunct (the equivalent of the British Committee for Imperial Defence), bringing together the prime minister, military ministers and the principal economic ministers, was set up at the same time. A national plan in the event of war was devised. In 1929 a series of exercises began to provide Japanese soldiers with the necessary experience of war: factories produced war material at full capacity; bombers buzzed the Osaka region, while antiaircraft fire blazed across the skies.

The Nagata plan, however, required partnership with the most powerful force in Japan: the *zaibatsu* industrial moguls. General Ugaki had spoken in 1929 of the need to tighten "the links between military forces and the industrial world." In exchange for *zaibatsu* help, the army was prepared to hand over its control of huge areas of war production. A historical compromise took place, in which the army's vision of using military force to secure raw materials and markets in order to compensate for the loss of these abroad and the erection of tariff barriers during the depression became attractive both to the *zaibatsu* and parts of the bureaucracy. The Important Industries Control Law was drafted to provide government support and rationalization for certain industries considered important to the war effort.

Partnership between the two was thus cemented: the military establishment was for the first time working hand in glove with the *zaibatsu*, and both together were now more powerful than either the bureaucrats or the government of the day: indeed, what gave the armed forces new impetus was the conversion of the industrialists to their cause through the collapse in world free trade. The industrialists recognized that military conquest was needed to secure supplies and markets; the armed forces recognized the industrialists were needed to provide the economic underpinning of the total war plans.

The dominant group in the army at the time, which favored this approach, was later to be derisively labeled the "Control Group" by its opponents. Nagata was its focus; around him he built up an informal apparatus called the Issekikai, a kind of loose secret society within the military. It included a young officer called Hideki Tôjô, later to become Japan's most notorious wartime prime minister; Tomoyuki Yamashita, the "Tiger of Malaya"; Daisaku Komoto, the celebrated assassin of Chang Tso-Lin; and two officers, Kanji Ishiwara and Seishiro Itagaki, architects of the "Manchurian Incident." So influential and senior had these officers now become that, although young rebels to begin with, they could now be said to represent the mainstream military thought of the establishment.

Their views were to predominate in the buildup to the Pacific War and thereafter: while the concept of young hotheads leading their elders astray may have been true at the time of the Manchurian Incident, it emphatically was not to be so in the later 1930s. The high command, with a few notable exceptions, was fully informed and aware of most of the major military actions that took place after 1936. The Issekikai was so close to the high command that even in the early 1930s it is hard to believe that both Chang's assassination and the Manchurian Incident did not have the approval of senior figures in the war ministry—although, as we have seen, not of the civilian cabinet or the Emperor himself.

What the Control Group, the army high command, and their new allies among the *zaibatsu* could not have predicted was the rumbling discontent among the lower ranks of officers which threatened in the 1930s to ignite into a military coup, resulting in an attempt to impose an authentic kind of Japanese fascism and social revolution. A brand of egalitarian anti-*zaibatsu* socialism combined with fanatical nationalism and devotion to the Emperor had already been preached by Ikki Kita in his book *A Plan for the*

Regeneration of Japan; its advocacy of a Showa restoration to overthrow the "business *daimyo*" and parcel out their fiefdoms to the Emperor, just as the nobles had done in the nineteenth century, had led to its initial suppression. Although violently anti-Communist, business and government leaders feared that its doctrines could find deeper roots in Japan than "alien" communism, which was anyway being ruthlessly suppressed by the police.

Kita's theories found fertile ground among the junior ranks of the officer corps in the later 1920s and early 1930s. The Japanese army had undergone profound social transformation since Yamagata's reforms. From being an elite commanded by Choshu-descended samurai, it was now a largely conscript army, only 15 percent of whose officers were samurai-descended (although this included many of the most senior, causing a much resented class distinction with junior officers). The Choshu were only a small minority among these. The ranks of the army were drawn from the very poorest backgrounds in the remote mountain regions—the class worst hit in the slump of the 1920s. The younger officers, reflecting the extreme resentment among their men, deeply disliked the more glamorous officers and their failure to proceed with such enterprises as the occupation of Manchuria. The junior officers held parliamentary government in deep contempt, viewing it as a nest of corruption, manipulated by the *zaibatsu*.

Above all, they hated the *zaibatsu*, whom the army commanders in the mid-1930s—once the young Turks of their day, now the military establishment—had now forged a pact with. The *zaibatsu* represented the huge impersonal economic forces which had brought radical change to the previously static and peaceful Japanese countryside, draining its young men into alien and immoral urban life, then emptying the villages of their young women, who were sold off by starving peasant farmers as prostitutes in the cities. It was in reaction to this pact between the military and the *zaibatsu* establishment that the young officers' movement, now dubbed the Kodo-Ha—"Imperial Way" school—virtually seized power within the army in 1932, starting the countdown to the coup attempt of 1936.

The key organizer of the faction was Mitsugi Nishida, a disciple of Kita's, and a charismatic officer. The hero of the Imperial Way group, which considered itself the direct descendant of Saigo's romantic samurai tradition—even though very few of its supporters were warrior-descended—was General Sadao Araki, the head of the Kôdôgikai, a 40,000-strong civilian-military organization. He had preached the case for the invasion of Manchuria after the assassination of Chang Tso-Lin. He was a brilliant man, highly civilized with a tough exterior: he had strong, broad features and a handlebar mustache. He served as a young man in Russia and loathed communism, which he viewed as the principal threat to Japan. "There is a shining sun ahead for Japan in this age of Showa," he proclaimed. The aborted coup in October 1931 had as its aim the installation of Araki; in an astonishing move to placate the armed forces' dissidents, he was appointed war minister in December of that year.

The new minister enacted radically different plans to those of Nagata and the Control Group. He believed that war with Russia was imminent, and devoted himself to the immediate and short-term rearmament of Japan to "strike north" against the Russians; he drove a coach and horses through Nagata's painstaking, long-term preparations, breaking off the alliance with the *zaibatsu*. Nagata was transferred out of Tokyo to become a regional commander. Araki revived the traditional art of sword-making, to provide individual swords soldiers could be proud of, rather than the mass-produced kind introduced by Yamagata. Japan's agents were sent abroad to make large-scale purchases of arms and equipment.

The *zaibatsu* were thrown into confusion and fear by this unexpected turn of events. On the one hand, they welcomed the new government's repression of Communist agitators; on the other, talk of social revolution, equality and the Showa restoration alarmed them, as did the decision to freeze the *zaibatsu* out of developing Manchuria. There seemed the prospect of an outright national socialist government which would introduce a policy of widespread nationalization: it is hard to exaggerate the loathing felt by junior officers for the *zaibatsu*, who were believed to be linked with international Jewry, communism and foreigners generally. The radical officers could unleash violently antielitist forces in Japan.

Hirohito and the bureaucracy also distrusted the younger officers. However, in spite of their extremism, they did not share the Control faction's addiction to war with China, being satisfied with the occupation of Manchuria and favoring the occupation of resource-rich Siberia. In Manchuria there was a genuinely idealistic attempt to keep the *zaibatsu* out: the Kwantung Army, in which Imperial Way officers were predominant, preached the principle of "state capitalism." This failed, largely because the army lacked the resources to develop Manchuria on its own: so a new industrial conglomerate, Nissan, was set up to develop the region. Nissan differed from the old *zaibatsu* in having been founded on genuine principles of joint-stock ownership, with shareholdings distributed among thousands, rather than a single family. But a prominent minority of the old *zaibatsu* bought Nissan shares through intermediaries. In northern China, the Imperial

Way group was unable to keep out the *zaibatsu*, which ran the region's mines through the North China Development Company.

The young officers thus posed a major and real threat to the most powerful interests in Japan: the now hugely swollen *zaibatsu*, which had gorged themselves on the smaller companies during the recession; the bureaucracy and imperial court; and the senior army establishment (not to mention the navy). It is a remarkable irony of history that if the Imperial Way faction had prevailed, Japan might have gone to war with Russia, not China, during the 1930s, and in the climate prevailing then, it is hard to see either America or Britain showing any readiness to go to Stalin's help. The Pacific War might have been averted; indeed, Hitler might have decided to open up a second front in the east, rather than attack France.

The gigantic interests this upset combined to fight back. Araki, caught between the pressures from below and the hostility of Japan's most powerful groups, fell ill and was forced to accept a nominally superior job as Supreme War Councillor, relinquishing the war ministry to General Senjuro Hayashi, from the Control Group, who promptly sent for Nagata. Collaboration with the *zaibatsu* resumed, the total war program was put back on the rails, and the focus of Japan's policy shifted back from the 'strike north' option with Russia to the 'strike south' option of war with China. The junior officers were seething, all the more so when one of their number was replaced as inspector-general of education. A lieutenant-colonel burst into Nagata's office on August 15, 1935, and shot the éminence grise of the Japanese army.

From that moment on, both sides prepared for a showdown: the army establishment, with the backing of the *zaibatsu*, waited for the young officers to overreach themselves and provide an excuse for their suppression as an organized group within the army; at the same time, the military establishment was aware that by rushing to the aid of the civilian authorities when a coup was staged, it would effectively be confirmed in control of the nation, along with its *zaibatsu* allies, who were persuaded of the economic benefits of the army's policy of expansionism. Unaware that they were about to fall into a trap, the Imperial Way officers launched their conspiracy—and were suppressed, while being used as fall guys for the army elders' seizure of power.

Internationally, the day when Japan embarked upon the fateful course that led to Hiroshima and Nagasaki, and the day that the outside world came to learn of the extraordinary tensions besetting what to outward appearances was a rather earnest industrial power, was September 18, 1931, the start of the "Manchurian Incident." This was far from being the spontaneous affair later alleged. The view taken by the principal planners of the Kwantung Army, Seishiro Itagaki and Kanji Ishiwara, had for some time been that Japan's presence in Manchuria was deteriorating dangerously. The young Marshal, Chang Hsueh-Liang, was now formally committed to Chiang Kai-Shek and was spreading anti-Japanese propaganda. Chinese commercial interests were competing against Japan in Manchuria, and winning. Manchuria's treasure trove of food, raw materials and space was in danger of being lost by default—or at least by the pussyfooting of Shidehara at the foreign ministry.

Throughout the summer, campaign plans were drawn up, in consultation with the general staff in Tokyo. It is highly disingenuous to believe that Japan's senior military figures were ignorant of these preparations. By the beginning of September there was some evidence that Japanese foreign office officials in Manchuria, as well as senior government circles, were buzzing with rumors about the military preparations. Both the Prime Minister, Wakatsuki, and the Foreign Minister, Shidehara, protested energetically to the new War Minister, General Minami, and also to the Emperor. At the instigation of the *genro*, Prince Saionji, Hirohito sent for Minami and flatly instructed him that the army had to be restrained.

Minami thereupon behaved with all the deviousness that might be expected from one fully in on the army's plot to seize Manchuria. He dispatched a letter to the commander of the Kwantung Army instructing him to abandon any plans for "direct action" against the Chinese. Major-General Yoshitsugu Tategawa was instructed to carry the message. A less suitable candidate could hardly be imagined: he had been implicated in the March Incident and was closely involved with the army nationalists. Instead of flying with the letter, he traveled by boat to Korea and then by train to Mukden. There he was met by a colleague who had also been involved in the March Incident, and taken to a geisha house where he got drunk, his letter still upon him.

That same night the "Manchurian Incident" began. The Kwantung army commander, Shigeru Honjo, claimed that the Chinese had planted a bomb on the South Manchurian railway north of Mukden. In fact, it was detonated by the Japanese. Even in the unlikely event that the Chinese had been responsible, the reaction of the Japanese was grotesquely disproportionate: it consisted of a full-scale attack on Chinese troops in Mukden. Within hours the city itself had been occupied after heavy fighting. Honjo, in a clearly premeditated move, was already rushing reinforcements to Mukden and asking the Japanese army in Korea to send men. Changchun to the north was taken hours later. After that, at last, General Tategawa delivered his letter.

On September 20 the war minister, the chief of staff and the director of military education went to the Emperor to rubber-stamp the occupation of Manchuria and the crushing of Chinese resistance there. They insisted that there could be no going back. By the end of the year, virtually the whole territory was under Japanese control: Chang Hsueh-Liang, the young Marshal, had fled south of the Great Wall of China, and the feared Russian invasion had not materialized. The Wakatsuki government was left spluttering in embarrassment and fending off a great storm of international opprobrium. Prince Saionji's second-in-command complained afterward that "from beginning to end the government has been utterly fooled by the army."

Kawahara, in his biography of Hirohito, paints a pathetic picture of the Emperor at the time:

Hirohito's military attaché was about to enter the emperor's chambers one day during this period when he heard a sad soliloquy from beyond the door. "Again, again . . . they're at it again. Once again the army has gone and done something stupid, and this is the result! Wouldn't it be simpler just to give Manchuria back to Chang Hsueh-Liang?" The aide was left with a vivid image of his troubled sovereign, alone in his room, pacing back and forth, muttering to himself. Indeed, it was the Emperor's habit to wander up and down the room, talking to himself, when he was troubled or upset about something.

The course of events leads to no other conclusion than that the whole occupation had been plotted by the officers on the spot, with the approval and connivance of the army high command, headed by the Minister of War, General Minami: the incident of the courier, the advance planning, the preparations for reinforcement, the immaculate nature of the campaign itself, its prompt endorsement by the military chiefs in Tokyo—all of these suggest connivance from top to bottom. Equally it is impossible to doubt the sincere opposition of the prime minister, foreign minister and the Emperor to the venture.

The consequences of the occupation of Manchuria were quickly felt. In February 1933, the Lytton Commission investigating the causes of the Manchurian Incident discreetly but firmly censured Japan, and the General

Assembly of the League of Nations condemned Japan by 42 votes to one (Japan's). The Japanese delegation promptly walked out. Manchuria was renamed Manchukuo and the last Emperor of China, Pu Yi, installed as head of state. Pu Yi was treated as a joke by the Kwantung Army commanders who really ran Manchuria, and was humiliated on his sole visit to Tokyo in 1935, being kept apart from his family and treated as a clear subordinate of Hirohito. His "palace" was an old salt exchange.

In the international community, Japan was treated with extreme suspicion, which seemed further justified by the country's slide toward war with China. By the time of its withdrawal from the League, Japanese army units had advanced on Jehol and Hopei provinces, with the pretext of securing Manchuria's defenses. Deeply concerned by the trend, in 1932 Hirohito asked Tsuyoshi Inukai, his 75-year-old prime minister to initiate contacts with China behind the army's back. The Emperor warned Inukai that "the army's interference in domestic and foreign policies, and its willfulness, is a state of affairs which, for the good of the nation, we must view with apprehension." A small mission was dispatched to China, but the army learned of the arrangement through a sympathizer, the chief cabinet secretary.

Meanwhile Makato Inukai was preparing, with the Emperor's agreement, an imperial rescript to restrain the armed forces in Manchuria and China. It was feared that such a rescript would lead to outright disloyalty and perhaps mutiny by many of the younger officers engaged in the campaigns there; many court officials were reluctant to approve the idea, while even the moderate Prince Saionji feared the effects of the Emperor descending into the political fray. Nevertheless it seems certain that a command was being prepared when, with perfect timing, Inukai was shot dead by nine naval and army cadets on May 15, 1932. Hirohito never again considered the idea of issuing a rescript.

Admiral Makato Saito, Inukai's successor, was the first of a succession of prime ministers who believed that the military tiger should be ridden rather than restrained. "Everything will be all right," Saito remarked shortly after taking office, "so long as we old men are here to put on the brake." However the extent to which Japan's imperial aims were expanding in accordance with the army's wishes was revealed in December 1934, when a memorandum was drafted for the cabinet by the Army, Navy and Foreign ministries which stated that China was to be brought into a grouping, along with Manchuria, with Japan as the "nucleus." Noninterference in Chinese affairs must cease, according to this document. Japan must "exploit internal strife" in order to overcome China's "anti-Japanese attitude." Chiang Kai-Shek must be induced to appoint persons friendly to Japan to certain offices within the government.

A year later, China's border provinces with Manchuria were placed under the control of a separate regional government under Japanese domination, the Hopei-Chahar Political Council. The Japanese empire had grown a little bigger for "defensive" reasons. The Japanese justified their expansion by claiming that there was no recognizable political authority in China at all. Yet it was beyond doubt that Manchuria could have been defended from any conceivable military attack from China. Japan quite simply did not need a new buffer strip along the boundaries of its buffer Manchuria, taken to buffer Korea, itself a buffer against aggression. In fact, this theory of accumulating buffers was spurious. Japan's absorption of a slice of China was naked aggression, pure and simple, and sanctioned by the highest authorities in government, albeit reluctantly so by the Emperor. Hirohito at that stage seemed to be almost alone in trying to make a stand against the militarist tribe: the bureaucracy and the officials of the imperial household seemed resigned both to a continuing expansion of the Japanese empire abroad and the growing extremism in Japan's domestic political scene.

18 : BLOOD ON THE SNOW

D URING THE EARLY HOURS OF THE MORNING ON FEBRUARY 26, 1936, A HEAVY fall of snow deepened the huge drifts already buttressing the thick walls of the Imperial Palace. The scene was one of desolation and tranquillity, with barely a person to be seen or a vehicle on the road. Many of the principal officials of the court were long since in bed. Two senior figures, the Grand Chamberlain, Kantaro Suzuki, and the Lord Privy Seal, Admiral Saito, recently demoted as prime minister, had been attending a dinner party at the American embassy, after which they stayed on for a film, *Naughty Marietta*, a light comedy.

At the dinner they discussed the results of the parliamentary elections, just five days earlier. These had been remarkable. In the last opportunity before the Pacific War for popular consultation, Japan's limited electorate had shown its preferment, even in a climate of hysterical nationalism, not for the extreme right but for the more moderate of the two main parties, the Minseito, which won 205 seats to the Seiyukai's 174; the small parties of the legalized left also did well. If it had been left to ordinary Japanese, there probably would have been no Pacific War; but their influence was slight.

At about two in the morning, in the guards' barracks closest to the

Imperial Palace, members of the First Army Division and the Third Regiment of the Imperial Guard were summoned to their parade grounds. Four officers were in charge of these detachments: Captain Teruzo Ando, Captain Shiro Nonaka, Lieutenant Yasuhide Kurihara and Captain Ichitaro Yamaguchi. Ando was duty officer for the Third Infantry Regiment that day, and Yamaguchi duty officer for the First Infantry Regiment. The regimental commanders had gone home in the evening.

A large part of the First Army Division was known to be seething with right-wing discontent, and the whole division was accordingly to be transferred to Manchuria in April, to lessen any danger from that quarter. Most of the soldiers were from miserably poor backgrounds, peasants' sons who had only just joined the army and had expected a grim winter. They had been given the rudiments of training, and been taught that they must obey the orders of their officers just as if they were obeying the Emperor himself. The soldiers were told they were going to the Yasukuni Shrine, or embarking on night maneuvers. Blindly these illiterate, brutalized young men did as they were told. Some 1,300 were assembled at various points around the Imperial Palace.

At four in the morning, under cover of darkness, the soldiers divided into nine squads and embarked upon a carefully planned rampage of murder. One group went to the residence of the War Minister, General Yoshiyuko Kawashima. They were challenged by the duty guard officer; he told them the general had a cold. The young officers stormed into his bedroom and read him a copy of their manifesto, called the Great Purpose: "With due reverence, we consider that the basis of the divinity of our country lies in the fact that the nation is destined to expand under Imperial Rule until it embraces all the world. . . . It is now time to expand and develop in all directions. . . ."

Many observers subsequently believed that Kawashima had been appraised of the plot in advance and supported it. For almost every act of insubordination by junior officers there seemed the possibility of acquiescence and even instigation by senior officers; it was always convenient for them to test the waters of insurrection and then wash their hands of responsibility in the event of failure. In any event, Kawashima did not resist, and did not overtly oppose the plot. He was to become a kind of hostage and mediator for the rebels, receiving visits from a host of senior officers over the next three days.

A second group of mutineers occupied the police station directly across the road from the Imperial Palace, forcing the policemen on duty there to surrender. A third group went to Admiral Suzuki's residence. He awoke at the commotion and tried to seize his sword. "Are you His Excellency?" a soldier asked. Suzuki asked why they had come.

A sergeant said, "No time. We're going to shoot."

"Go ahead and shoot," said Suzuki irritably. Three officers shot him, then one knelt by the body to deliver the coup de grace.

His wife screamed: "Don't do it, I'll do it," and they desisted. Afterward they knelt in front of the body and saluted it.

Captain Ando told the hysterical Mrs. Suzuki, "I am particularly sorry about this but our views differ from His Excellency's, so it had to come to this." Suzuki, remarkably and fatefully, was to survive to become the man charged with the distressing patriotic responsibility of Japan's surrender in 1945.

A 300-strong contingent surrounded the prime minister's residence, killing four policemen at the gate. The premier, Admiral Keisuke Okada, who was in his dressing gown, took refuge in a disused storeroom while his brother-in-law, Colonel Matsuo, attempted to ring for help, then escaped the house. He was caught by the soldiers, mistaken for the prime minister, and put up against a wall and shot. Okada emerged from his hiding place and was hidden by two maids in a cupboard under a pile of laundry. Another detachment of rebels arrived at the foreign minister's house, surprised him asleep in bed, and shot him three times, slashing at him with a sword as well.

About 200 soldiers surrounded the house of the Lord Privy Seal, Saito. He was shot down in his nightgown while his distraught wife attempted to protect him with her body. They fired again and again, riddling his body with bullets and wounding his wife with sword cuts. General Watanabe, the inspector-general of military training, was shot down at his home and his throat was cut. Outside Tokyo, a former Lord Privy Seal narrowly escaped assassination when his granddaughter warned him and led him up a hill in the dark, losing his pursuers below. Saionji, who was also on the death list, had been tipped off beforehand and had taken shelter in the house of his local police chief.

Half an hour later, the Emperor was awoken to hear of the carnage. "So they've finally made their move," he remarked. His chief military aide, General Shigeru Honjo, witnessed a rare display of imperial rage. When the War Minister, General Kawashima, arrived at the palace, having been escorted through by the rebels surrounding the gates, he told Hirohito, "The conduct of these officers is indeed disgraceful; yet it arises from their sincere devotion to Your Majesty and to the nation. It is hoped that Your Majesty will understand their feelings." He insisted on reading the rebel manifesto to the Emperor.

Hirohito was furious: "They have murdered our closest advisers. What possible justification can be found for the brutality these officers have shown, no matter what their motives? We order the immediate suppression of these rebels." Honjo suggested the Emperor might reconsider the word rebels. "Soldiers who act without our orders are not our soldiers. They are rebels," retorted the Emperor. As the prime minister was believed to have been killed, the Emperor appointed the minister of home affairs to run the government and accept the resignation of the cabinet. When General Kawashima resigned, he wrote to the Emperor implying that he knew nothing of the plot. Hirohito exploded. "Does the war minister think that this letter absolves him? It's this kind of thinking that makes the army so bad."

Meanwhile Okada's son-in-law, after donning the obligatory topper and morning dress, managed to reach the Imperial palace to inform the Emperor that the prime minister was still alive and in hiding behind rebel lines. Hirohito was delighted. He had ordered Kawashima flatly to "end this incident as soon as possible."

Yet, although it seemed just possible that the senior military leadership knew nothing of the intended coup, their immediate reaction was to support it. Kawashima issued a statement saying: "The motives behind the uprising have been made clear to the Emperor. We recognize that your acts are a manifestation of your loyalty to the state." General Sadao Araki, the army's most controversial right-wing general, labeled the insurgents "restoration troops." By the evening the rebels were elated, with such formidable backing from the high command. It seemed that the senior generals behind the Emperor were unwilling to take them on, and would eventually accept the situation; it was important that they should remain in position until a military government took over.

Hirohito, who all day had been grumbling at General Honjo, was appalled at the attitude of the army high command, which issued a statement blithely saying that Tokyo had been placed "under the jurisdiction of the First Division." Honjo, who may have been implicated in the coup, failed to tell the Emperor the news that nothing was being done to control the rebels, adding to his frustration and fear that his opposition to the coup was not being relayed to the outside world.

The following morning martial law had been declared by Lieutenant-General Kashii, who himself was in sympathy with the insurgents. He insisted that "all occupying troops must return to their original corps. These are His Majesty's orders." The impatient Hirohito summoned a meeting of the senior princes of his household; his suspicion was that one at least was in league with the plotters, who would not scruple at deposing or even killing him and installing a successor. The finger pointed to his younger brother, Prince Chichibu, the commander of the Eighth Division at Hirosaki, nearly 1,000 miles north of Tokyo.

Chichibu had befriended Captain Ando in a previous command, and both admired Ikki Kita's right-wing diatribe, *A Plan for the Regeneration of Japan*. The news that Chichibu was coming on his own initiative to Tokyo had caused considerable disquiet among the Emperor's retainers. Professor Hiraizumi, a right-wing but loyal theorist from the University of Tokyo, was dispatched to meet the prince at Minakami station; the professor accompanied the prince to Ueno station, where two truckloads of the imperial guard were waiting to ensure that he had no opportunity to talk to the rebel leaders. No contact was made on the journey to the imperial palace, and when he saw his brother at last over a meal, he assured him he had no connection with the plot—something which was later confirmed by one of the plotters. It was said afterward that the Prince had changed his mind on hearing of the murders; another explanation is that he realized Hirohito had sufficient force on his side to prevail. Later in the day the Emperor met other members of the imperial family, asking them all to pledge their allegiance.

Meanwhile the desperate Honjo continued to try and plead the rebels' cause, almost certainly reflecting the views of the entire army high command. The insurgents "should not necessarily be condemned . . . because they were thinking of the good of the nation."

Hirohito replied angrily. "How can we not condemn even the spirit of these criminally brutal officers who killed my aged subjects who were my hands and feet? To kill these aged and venerable men whom I trusted the most is akin to gently strangling me with floss-silk." Their only excuse, in the Emperor's view, was they had had not acted "for selfish reasons." In response to the Emperor's orders, some 25,000 men had at last taken up positions surrounding the rebels, with machine guns and tanks at the ready. The First Fleet had been assembled in Tokyo Bay with its guns aiming at the rebel positions.

By the morning of the third day, the rebels were dispirited and desperately cold. They realized that, in view of the forces arrayed against them and the Emperor's implacability, their days were numbered. One ringleader asked, through an intermediary, whether an imperial messenger might be sent to witness their ritual suicide. The response was fast and furious. As Honjo reported:

"His Majesty is extremely angry. He said that if they wanted to commit suicide, they should go ahead and do it, but sending an imperial representative is out of the question. Furthermore, he said that if the division commander had done nothing about the incident, he does not know where his duty lies. I have never heard His Majesty issue so stern a censure. He gave strict orders that the rebellion be suppressed immediately at any cost."

A leaflet was dropped by aircraft over rebel positions. It urged bluntly, "Return to your units. It is not yet too late. All who resist are rebels. We will shoot them. Your families weep to see you becoming traitors." Japan's best known radio announcer, Shigeru Nakamura, reinforced the message: "You may have believed that the orders from your superiors were right and in obeying them absolutely, your motives were sincere. However, His Majesty the Emperor has recommended all of you to return to your home units . . . You must not defy His Majesty for, in doing so, you will be branded traitors for all time. Since even as I speak it is not too late, lay down your arms and return to barracks. If you do, your offenses will be pardoned."

Tanks rumbled ominously through the streets. In dribs and drabs, rebel units began to desert, and no attempt was made to stop them. Captain Nonaka, the most senior, shot himself. Ando tried to kill himself, while other officers surrendered, believing they would be treated leniently, as was the precedent. In fact the main plotters were quietly executed, under the express orders of the Emperor.

Hirohito's steady nerve had largely contributed to the demise of the plot. In the days after the coup, its extensive ramifications became apparent: Prince Chichibu clearly was implicated. The Emperor's secretary, Marquis Kido, privately worked against the plot beforehand, but did not inform the Emperor of what he knew. Kawashima was implicated, and Honjo may have been. A major shakeup of the senior ranks of the army now took place. Several thousand unsuitable officers were purged.

Yet in spite of the strong hand he seemed to hold, Hirohito now flinched. Later, he said that "since we fear a repetition of this kind of incident if we do not accede [to the army's demands] we want to take their view into consideration." The Emperor, it seemed, had won a battle only to lose the war.

How had this extraordinary reversal come about just after his most dramatic display of decisive action? Later he was to admit, "In some sense I was violating the constitution in my rebuke of Prime Minister Tanaka at the time of the Chang Tso-lin incident, and in the stand I took in the February 26th Incident." On both occasions he seems indeed to have shrunk from the consequences of his boldness with remarkable speed. In fact, the February 26 revolt was a much more complex affair than at first appeared.

As in some elaborate conspiracy theory, the truth of the outcome of the February 26 "incident" was that although the visible coup had been crushed, a military coup had taken place unnoticed on a much wider scale. Far from proving that the government had reverted to the hands of the civil authorities, the slow response of the armed forces to the Emperor's desperate appeals for action exposed how dependent he was on their support: the military chiefs who had at last come to rescue him after three tense days from being a virtual hostage of the extremist officers now held him, and what remained of constitutional government in Japan, in the palm of their hands.

There had been complicity by senior army men in the coup, who certainly knew it was coming and did nothing to stop it when the attempt was made. They could pose as the men who rushed to the Emperor's defense— not before he was given convincing evidence of just how defenseless he was without their protection. In addition, permitting the abortive coup to take place had the considerable advantage of allowing the junior officers who had been an irritation to the generals for more than a decade enough rope to hang themselves with.

The impact of the real coup—the coup behind the coup—was felt immediately. From then on, the political parties ceased to enjoy any effective power; the bureaucracy was sidelined; the Emperor's protests were barely heard; and his every decision was affected by the fear that extremist militarists would stage another coup—and this time no one would come and save him. The choice of prime minister, while not actually dictated by the army, became irrelevant: power was in the hands of the war minister, whose threat to resign was invariably enough to bring the moderates to heel. The prime minister was not an outright army nominee until the 1940s; but he might as well have been, because the real prime minister, both in defense and domestic matters, was the war minister.

With the crushing of the February coup, the Control faction was firmly in charge. A massive purge ran through the army to rid it of the Imperial Way faction. The war minister was given the power to appoint, transfer, promote and relegate every officer in the army. Army ministers were henceforth to be chosen from the rank of active generals—making it impossible for governments to find retired generals who disagreed with current military thinking to do the job. The army had not been so centralized since Yamagata had conceived it. The first army minister after the coup was Hisaichi Terauchi, a formidably tough-minded man who immediately set out the three missions of the army as enforcing discipline, safeguarding national defense and reforming the administration. The main purpose of the last task was to make money available for military expansion.

The new prime minister, Koki Hirota, was a former foreign minister and nominee of Prince Saionji, whose power was all but at an end. When he formed his cabinet, he found Terauchi exercising a veto over each of his appointments. "The military is like an untamed horse left to run wild," Hirota told a friend. "If you try to stop it, you'll get kicked to death. The only hope is to jump on it from the side and try to get it under control . . . Somebody has to do it. That's why I've jumped on." He didn't stay on it for long and while he did, merely stayed in the saddle while it careered recklessly away. Realizing this, he resigned after only a few months.

Saionji, flexing his old, tired counsel of moderation for the last time, tried to install one of Japan's constitutionalist generals, Ugaki, as prime minister. The Kempeitai, the country's sinister riot police, stopped Ugaki's car on the way to the Emperor in an attempt to intimidate him. Ugaki pressed on, but the army refused to nominate a minister of war to serve with him. One of Terauchi's cronies instead took control: this was General Senjuro Hayashi, a tough-minded soldier with no political skills, whom both the main parties joined in opposing. Faced by outright political opposition in parliament, he resigned after just four months. This was a modified defeat for the army: if the civilians could not have their preferred candidate, they could at least block an out-and-out military reactionary.

A compromise was needed: this turned out to be Prince Fumimaro Konoye, surely one of the most inappropriate choices ever made for a nation at a time of extreme national crisis. Konoye's basic qualification for the job, from the army's point of view, was that he was a rabid nationalist and a political lightweight with no support in parliament. Related to the Emperor, and descended from Japan's oldest family, the Fujiwaras, he had considerable influence at court. Yet his ideas were shallow and silly, and he lacked any popular power base: he was merely, at first, a useful front man for military rule. Later, he acquired the courage and wisdom of experience. He had a weak and attractive personality; idle and easygoing, he treated the Emperor as a chum, which endeared him to the friendless Hirohito. He was tall, good-looking, and a womanizer, as well as a hypochondriac.

Sir Robert Craigie, British Ambassador in Japan in 1937, described Konoye vividly:

> His expression denotes neither energy not determination, but rather a sense of philosophic doubt. Calm and unruffled in all circumstances, he is by disposition phlegmatic. His eyes are his best feature, denoting intelligence and political acumen, combined with a touch of laziness. The profile is disappointing and does not bear out the promise of the striking full face. These facial contrasts fit in with his enigmatic character. There were moments when his actions showed a touch of genius. Time and again one was impressed by acts of statesmanship, only to be irritated just as often by his apparent lack of firmness in leadership, and his failure at times of crises to use his strong personal position to curb the extremists. His Japanese friends were completely baffled by many of his actions, wondering whether he really stood for what he was supposed to represent—a moderating influence—or whether, unknown to his more responsible friends and followers, he was a totalitarian at heart and rather enjoyed giving the army its long rope.

For the political parties, his attraction was that, although a rather eccentric nationalist, he was not in the army's pocket. He was reasonably intelligent, and like many without a political power base, believed he had more political authority than he had—although he was not so obtuse as to fail to understand when he was being manipulated, which provoked frequent crises of conscience, usually overcome.

With the seizure of power by the Control Group, committed to the annexation of China and supported by the major *zaibatsu*, events moved rapidly. A statement of principles was drawn up, known as the Foundations of National Policy. This asserted that Japan must "eliminate the tyrannical policies of the powers in East Asia" and substitute "cordial relations . . . founded on the principles of coexistence and co-prosperity." Economic expansion was to be achieved by creating a strong coalition between Japan, Manchuria and China.

While the views of the Imperial Way faction urging war against the Soviet Union were now discredited, the army recognized the need to leave forces in Korea and in Manchuria that were big enough to deter Russian attack. The army must also be strong enough to retain "ascendancy in the Pacific," said the principles. "Self-sufficiency" was required in important resources and materials needed for the nation's defense and its industry. As far as the Japanese army in China was concerned, this represented a green light to move ahead and conquer the country; the Chinese reached much the same conclusion as well.

19 : INTO CHINA

THE RESULT WAS THE HISTORIC CLASH AT THE MARCO POLO BRIDGE, JUST north of Peking, on July 7, 1937, which is seen as the beginning of Japan's war with China. It is more difficult on this occasion to blame the Japanese unreservedly for starting the fighting. Both sides had decided the time had come for a showdown. Chiang Kai-Shek, overconfident but rightly suspicious of Japanese intentions, was spoiling for a fight. Equally, the Japanese felt that the time had come to teach China a lesson: unless the cocky generalissimo was dealt with, head-on, he might become a more formidable foe. They believed that China would collapse under a Japanese onslaught like a paper tiger—the Japanese chief of staff, General Sugiyama, assured the Emperor the campaign there would take a month to finish.

The *zaibatsu* favored war with China in order to secure their industrial schemes in the north of the country and, ruthlessly, to destroy the Chinese capacity to resist militarily and compete economically further south. Some generals favored war in order to secure the minor nuisance to the south before undertaking the far more hazardous task of confronting the colossus to the north—Russia. For Japan, the Chinese adventure was to be the biggest miscalculation in its history.

The Marco Polo incident itself was trivial. Just before midnight, as a small group of Japanese soldiers under the command of Captain Setsuro Shimizu were resting on the banks of the Yuntung River, a volley of shots rang out. One Japanese private went missing in the dark. The shots may have been fired by Chinese nationalists, but more probably were the work of Communist agitators intent on making mischief for Chiang Kai-Shek. The missing private turned up shortly afterward; but the Japanese took advantage of the incident to demand a Chinese withdrawal from the strategic Marco Polo bridge and the railway bridge beside it. The Chinese refused. The Japanese tried to search a small town at their end of the bridges, only to be fired upon by Chinese troops. Gunfire and casualties began to spread.

On learning of the incident Chiang Kai-Shek declared privately, "The time has come now to make the decision to fight." He announced that his country had reached its "final critical hour." The Japanese were no less ready to make a stand. The high command considered it would be wise to move against China now, while Russia was in the throes of one of Stalin's great purges. Tojo, the chief of staff of the Kwantung Army, had argued a month earlier: "Judging the present situation in China from the point of view of military preparation against the Soviet Union, I am convinced that if military power permits it, we should deliver first of all a blow upon the Nanking regime to get rid of the menace at our back. If our military power will not permit us to take such a step, I think it proper that we keep a strict watch on the Chinese government that they do not lay a single hand on our present undertakings in China until our national defense system is completed." Chiang Kai-Shek's recently concluded agreement with the Communists to fight the Japanese had strengthened him and made the latter nervous.

An invincible force had encountered an immovable object. The fighting quickly spread. The extent of Japanese war preparations was revealed by the speed with which troops were rushed from Korea and Manchuria. General Sugiyama, the minister of war in Prince Konoye's government, poured troops in from the mainland. Konoye, with the support of the navy and foreign ministers, tried to object. Hirohito asked plaintively, "Isn't this the Manchurian Incident all over again?"

Sugiyama threatened to resign, bringing down the cabinet if he was overruled. He got his way; the armed forces could hardly have staged a more blatant seizure of power if they had grabbed control by force. The Emperor, prime minister and cabinet were all shown to be less powerful than the army. Japan was under a military dictatorship. Only the *zaibatsu* could have frustrated the armed forces by denying them the essential supplies they needed; but at this stage big business stood foursquare behind the army, seeking to secure its interests in northern China as well as to destroy strategic competition from the Chinese.

Whatever the rights and wrongs of the Incident itself, Japan's actions now amounted to outright aggression. Talks between the two countries broke down after a few weeks and full-scale fighting broke out after Chinese militia at Tungchow rebelled against their Japanese officers and massacred 200 civilians. In August fighting broke out between Japanese and Chinese forces in Shanghai, and Japanese reinforcements were rushed into the city in an engagement that lasted three months before the Chinese Nationalist military forces were expelled.

The fighting was full-scale, and there could be no pretense that it was not coordinated from Tokyo: the officers in the field were not the primary instigators of the war against China. The Japanese invasion of China was to last for eight years and to claim the lives of some 3.2 million Chinese soldiers and perhaps as many as 10 million civilians; the Japanese lost around 1 million in the fighting. It was to be the greatest conflict across one country the world has ever seen, before or since.

The war was initially fought on two fronts: the north, and soon around Shanghai. By November 1937, the Japanese army was already down the Yangtse driving toward the Chinese Nationalist capital of Nanking, a bustling city in a loop on the southern bank of the river, with a permanent population of around 250,000 people, but now also teeming with some three times as many refugees. Nanking was perhaps China's main cultural center, with a university and several institutions of higher learning. Chiang Kai-Shek decided it was too exposed, however, for serious resistance, and his soldiers, along with about half of the city's current inhabitants, withdrew to regroup in the interior. On December 12 the last Chinese detachments fled, and the following day the Japanese moved in. One of the worst atrocities of the war followed, in which tens of thousands were murdered and as many women were raped in an orgy of carnage and lust that lasted several days.

A 62-year-old Chinese railway official described what happened: "They shot at everyone on sight. Anybody who run away, or on the streets, or hanging around somewhere, or peeking through the door, they shoot them— instant death." Three days after the Japanese entered the city, according to Hsu Chuan-ying, there were bodies everywhere. "I saw the dead bodies lying everywhere, and some of the bodies were very badly mutilated. Some of the bodies are lying there as they were shot or killed, some kneeling, some bending, some on their sides and some just with their legs and arms wide open." On one street, he started counting the corpses and after reaching 500 decided there "was no use counting them."

The Japanese soldiers went into the supposedly protected refugee zone of Nanking and arrested anyone with rough hands, which might have been caused by carrying rifles. Prisoners were arrested and roped together in groups of ten and fifteen and marched away—no fewer than 1,500 on a single day. The refugees, themselves in terror thanks to these incursions, could hear machine guns chattering through the night, although there was no fighting in the city.

Rape was the accompaniment to murder. "The Japanese soldiers—they are so fond of raping, so fond of women that one cannot believe," said Hsu.

"There was a mass round-up of women between thirteen and forty, most of whom were gang-raped." Hsu visited a house in which three women, two of them young girls, had been raped. One, he said, had been violated on a table, "and while I was there blood on the table was not all dry yet . . ." According to international estimates, some 30,000 women in Nanking were raped, and many killed and mutilated afterwards.

Hsu belonged to the Chinese equivalent to the Red Cross, and when the Japanese got around to burying the bodies—fearing that their decomposition would create an epidemic—he was appalled by how many were tied together with rope or wire. "It is our sacred practice to have a dead body all unloosed if it is tied. We wanted to unloose everything and bury them one by one. But with these wires now it is almost impossible to do that. In many cases these bodies were already decayed so we would not be able to bury them one by one. All we can do is simply to bury them in groups." Hsu reckoned some 43,000 people were buried over the following few weeks, but the real figure was probably much higher, as the Japanese forbade the Chinese relief officials to keep records.

Miner Bates, an American professor at the University of Nanking, gave a picture of the murderous duplicity of the forces that had taken over the city. Posters were put up asking Chinese to volunteer as workers for the Japanese army's labor camps. "If you have previously been a Chinese soldier or if you have worked as a carrier or laborer in the Chinese army," said the authorities, "that will all be forgotten and forgiven if you join the labor corps." According to Bates, two hundred or so men enlisted on the university campus "and were marched away and executed that evening."

Looting was systematic. "On one occasion I observed a supply column, two-thirds of a mile long, loaded with high-grade redwood and blackwood furniture." A large number of buildings were burnt: stores, churches, embassies, houses were set alight, their flames illuminating the dark nights while the machine guns chattered. "We could not see any reason or pattern in it," said Bates. International opinion, informed by the significant expatriate community in the city about these events, was profoundly shocked, nowhere more so than in the United States, whose citizens read the horrific eyewitness reports of Americans there.

From the first day not only the world press (although not the censored Japanese press), but the Japanese foreign office was flooded by descriptions of the rape and vigorous protests. No fewer than 70 representations were forwarded to the Japanese embassy in Nanking by the International Rescue Committee. A note on December 27—10 days after Matsui admits he entered

Nanking—said bluntly, "Shameful disorder continues and we see no serious efforts to stop it. The soldiers every day injure hundreds of persons most seriously. Does not the Japanese army care for its reputation?" The embassy officials were visited by scores of foreigners and were largely excused from blame. Miner Bates testified, "These men were honestly trying to do what they could in a very bad situation, but they themselves were terrified by the military and could do nothing except forward these communications through Shanghai to Tokyo."

The messages certainly arrived in Tokyo and were the object of intense diplomatic concern there. According to Bates, the American embassy in Nanking had shown him messages from the American ambassador in Tokyo, Joseph Grew, "in which he referred to these reports in great detail and mentioned conversations in which they had been discussed between Grew and officials of the Gaimusho, including Mr. Hirota." Apart from the Japanese embassy, which was next door to the university campus, on which many of the worst atrocities occurred, the American, British and German embassies were sending a stream of messages which were forwarded to Tokyo. Counselor Hidaka of the Japanese embassy protested in person to General Asaka and sent a report to the foreign ministry, which was forwarded to the ministry of war and the general staff.

Prince Konoye and other Japanese leaders believed that Chiang Kai-Shek would sue for peace after the fall of his capital and offered the Chinese stringent terms, which one part of the Nationalist leadership was disposed to accept. If so, the "Chinese Incident" would have been won reasonably satisfactorily by the Japanese in five months—although not the one month promised to the Emperor.

Yosuku Matsuoka, Japan's notorious foreign minister under Konoye, summed up the Japanese attitude to China:

"China and Japan are two brothers who have inherited a great mansion called East Asia. Adversity sent them both down to the depth of poverty. The scapegrace elder brother (China) became a dope fiend and a rogue, but the younger (Japan), lean but tough and ambitious, ever dreamed of bringing back past glories to the old home. He sold newspapers at street corners and worked hard to support the home. The elder cheated the younger out of his meager savings and sold him to their common enemy. The younger in a towering rage beat up the elder—trying to beat into him some sense of shame and awaken some pride in the noble traditions of the great house. After many scraps, the younger finally made up his mind to stage a showdown fight. And that is the fight now raging along the North China and Shanghai fronts."

Instead Chiang spurned the proposals, and in January 1938, the Japanese announced there would be no further negotiations. The Chinese secured a minor success in Shantung in April, but their main army was nearly encircled by a brilliant Japanese flanking maneuver at Hsuchow on the Peking-Nanking railway. The Japanese offensive continued to push ahead with fair success that year.

But an unpleasant shock was to await them. Confident of defeating China, the Japanese began to turn their attention to their more serious foe, Russia. That summer, the Japanese came close to a major engagement with Russian forces at Changkufeng Hill, on the border between Korea, Russia and Manchuria. At this stage the war was being fought by the army under a new war minister, General Itagaki, virtually without reference to the civilian cabinet. But the Emperor retained some influence. Appalled by the prospect of war on two fronts with China and Russia—which some generals favored, believing they could beat both—he summoned the war minister and the army chief of staff. Although Hirohito's powers were severely circumscribed, with the onset of war he had formally taken up his powers as commander-in-chief. As Kawahara recounts:

> In response to the prospects of a long-term conflict, a military headquarters was set up in the imperial palace, and inevitably the Emperor was kept very busy. Night and day he was beset by worries over the outcome of the military action, and began to look haggard. Hirohito was a man of delicate sensibilities. Worry soon took its toll, and as he so often did in such circumstances, he began talking to himself. Sometimes, when reports from the field were good, he would feel even more exhausted—perhaps due to the sudden release of tension.
>
> His aides were concerned and suggested he go to the imperial residences at Hayama or Nasu for a rest, but as one of them said later, "His Majesty was very scrupulous in his duties and although we urged him to take a rest, he was reluctant to do so." Perhaps his reluctance stemmed from an embarrassing incident that had occurred at the time of the outbreak of hostilities between Japan and China. Hirohito had gone to Hayama for some recreation and to pursue his interest in marine biology. Although he received reports of the Marco Polo Bridge incident, he did not return to Tokyo immediately. Instead he remained in Hayama for three days, much to the disgust of certain factions within the military.
>
> There was some grumbling, though nothing more serious than, "Imagine! For the Emperor to be fooling around with worthless little ani-

mals at such a crucial time!" and, "If he has so much free time, I wish he'd spend it learning more about military matters. . . ."

It seemed then, that Hirohito's "reluctance" was a reluctance to get involved with the military. But thereafter he virtually gave up the research and experiments that he conducted with so much obvious pleasure. "It is my only hobby," he'd once said in his defense.

Still, from time to time he would summon his old biology mentor, Professor Hattori, to the palace, and would at least have a chance to listen to his lectures.

Thus Hirohito, in his typically diffident, hesitant, unconvincing way, may have been trying to disassociate himself from responsibility for starting the war with China.

The military chiefs, while contemptuously brushing aside the objections of Konoye's civilian cabinet, could not be quite so dismissive of the Emperor's express anger. This made itself felt on the occasion of the Russo-Japanese clash. "Really, the army's behavior is outrageous," he told General Itagaki. "Be it at Lukouchiao at the time of the Manchurian Incident, or just recently at the Marco Polo Bridge, they ignore the orders sent out by central command and all too often go their own way, employing despicable, inexcusable methods. They are our forces, yet we find their conduct disgraceful, not to say impertinent. Henceforth not one soldier will be moved without our explicit orders."

Itagaki was shaken. "I can never enter His Majesty's presence again. I must resign." The chief of staff, Prince Kan'in, also sought to quit. Prince Konoye persuaded them to withdraw their resignations. Had they not done so, the government would have fallen and an outright military coup might have followed, which the Emperor was determined to avoid at all costs.

This incident encapsulated the dilemma and tragedy of Hirohito's personal responsibility for events. There can be little doubt of his opposition to the steady escalation of Japan's military involvement in Asia, which was voiced at virtually every step forward. Usually Hirohito objected for sound pragmatic reasons. But this did not make him a calculating opportunist. Such justifications were the only ones likely to cut much ice with the armed forces; a general statement of principle against expansionist policies would have been brushed aside as a sign of weakness. However, when it came to outright confrontation, the Emperor was now to back down on every occasion until 1945 because he believed he could better influence events at the center of power than by being cast out (he believed that his assassination or enforced abdication in favor of the more pliant Prince Chichibu was always a possibility). He may have been right.

Yet, in giving way, he lent his immense personal authority to militarist-inspired decisions as effectively as if he had been deposed and a new Emperor found. He could not escape his share of responsibility—which might, indeed, be considered the highest of any of his subjects—for decisions which he privately opposed but publicly approved. We shall never know what might have happened if the Emperor had placed his massive prestige on the line in opposing one of the key decisions of the imperial army, denying them the imprimatur of acting in his name, because he never tried.

The army in fact obeyed the Emperor's will and pulled back from confrontation with the Russians. The wisdom of his counsel was to be underlined within a year in May 1939, on one of the most desolate reaches on earth. The Nomonhan region, on the border between Manchuria and Outer Mongolia, was a large, undulating grassy plain. Mongolian forces supported by the Russians began to stage incursions across the Halha River, which the Japanese had designated the boundary of Manchuria. The Russians may have been testing Japanese resolve on ground of their own choosing. The Kwantung Army took the bait and rushed forces to the border, launching a major expedition to cut Mongolian-Russian supply lines. Soon a full-scale engagement was under way between Soviet and Japanese forces involving aircraft, tanks and heavy artillery.

The contest was unequal from the start: the Russians had overwhelming force and much better transport facilities. They pushed the Japanese back to the Halha River. In spite of one coup by the air force in destroying 120 Russian planes at Tomsk—thereby risking escalating the conflict into a full-scale war between the two nations—the Japanese suffered an overwhelming and humiliating defeat, their routed army losing some 20,000 dead and the same number of injured at the hands of Soviet forces commanded by the most brilliant of Russian military leaders, Marshal Zhukov.

It was Japan's great good fortune that the Russians were in no mood for full-scale war. The Japanese had attacked and, with one great swipe of the Russian bear's paw, had been repulsed and bloodied. The incident persuaded the Japanese high command of the need to pursue softer options further south. It should have alerted the militarists to the fact that when confronted with a force as well prepared as itself, the vaunted invincibility of the Japanese war machine soon evaporated.

In China, the war continued through 1938 with a string of Japanese victories, none of them decisive. They captured Hangkow in the autumn and landed at Bias Bay in the south to seize Canton with remarkable speed. At this stage, Chiang was again expected to sue for peace, and the Japanese hinted they were ready for an agreement. Throughout the conflict, Japan showed no desire to occupy the whole of China—a probably impossible objective—merely to turn it into a vassal state. To their astonishment, Chiang later rejected their terms from his new capital of Chunking, although some of his lieutenants made their peace. The war settled into a longer, slower phase of Japanese advances and Chinese retreats, with fewer dramatic victories and Japanese forces continually harassed by Mao Tse-Tung's Communist guerrillas. The Japanese always had the upper hand; but final victory remained utterly elusive.

Three features of the war deserve attention. The first was that, from an economic viewpoint, the war did not deliver the goods. For decades the Control Group of the Japanese army had pressed for the creation of a Japanese-dominated "Co-Prosperity Sphere" with China as the obvious economic framework for the development of the Far East. In the year since the world depression had closed off international markets, the *zaibatsu* had come to believe that China could provide the resources needed for continued economic growth. However, the immense dislocations of the war and the hostility of the Chinese prevented the emergence of a new market for exports on the mainland. Even the development of natural resources in the areas the Japanese controlled proved disappointing, with industries and mines lying idle for much of the time.

This led the *zaibatsu* to look with new favor on the arguments being propounded by the navy and some in the army that South East Asia was a more promising prospect for economic penetration, both in terms of the treasure chest of oil and raw materials there, and of better markets. It was argued that Japanese supremacy through domination of the sealanes was more attainable than victory in the vast land war in China. Thus Japan's gaze shifted first from Russia to China, then from the latter to an old theater of interest, South East Asia.

Second, even as late as 1940 there was no reason to suppose that Japan was on course for war with the United States and the other Western powers. Certainly the Japanese army and navy had been greatly strengthened to deal with such a contingency; but the objectives remained confused, and conflict was far from inevitable. The invasion of China had been an opportunistic one based on a gross miscalculation of the country's military weakness, entered into almost by accident. The war had provoked no more than occasional outbursts of indignation from Western foreign ministers and the press; yet no major country was going to fight for China, in spite of the vast scale and horror of the carnage there. If Japan had concentrated on China alone, it would probably have prevailed in the long run, and created a huge Asian empire.

A third key aspect of the Sino-Japanese war was its systematic brutality. The Rape of Nanking, described earlier, gave only a foretaste of this, being the rule rather than the exception. The angel of death now rode across China. The town of Pingting, said an eyewitness, was turned into a base "sending soldiers north and south, east and west. . . . Those coming from the front would rest a day or so and rape and loot. . . . Anyone whose clothes had any resemblance to those of a soldier was killed on the spot without questions." At Wuhu during the first week of occupation, according to an eyewitness, "the ruthless treatment and slaughter of civilians and the wanton looting and destruction of the homes of the city far exceeded anything ever seen in my 20 years experience of China. . . . The soldiers seemed especially to seek Chinese women for violation."

At Kaifeng "women dare not go on the streets as they are attacked even in broad daylight in their homes, or dragged off the street to their homes by Japanese soldiers. I never guessed I would ever come into contact with such awful wickedness that is occurring day by day. Multiply anything you have heard about them by 20 and it is only half the truth. Small boys are kidnapped and along with young women are shipped by train to the east. . . ."

At Kihrien 2,000 civilians were killed. "I never thought I should witness such suffering and live." In Hangchow: "Our beautiful Hangchow soon became a filthy, battered, obscene place . . . a city of dread . . . robbery, wounding, murder, rape and burning . . . Japanese military police did their best to help us foreigners but for the city at large there was no help."

Terror in the towns and villages of the Yangtse basin combined with the destruction of homes, food stocks and the means of making a living to create a sea of refugees. Some three quarters of the one million people in Nanking fled before the Imperial Army. Perhaps as many as 20 million Chinese were forced to seek survival elsewhere, and no one knows how many died.

No single explanation accounts for the astonishing scale of the atrocities. At least nine major influences were involved:

(1) Racism. This undoubtedly played a major role in the attitudes of ordinary Japanese. The country's racial supremacy over other peoples was deeply inculcated. To cite just one example: at the 2,600th anniversary

of the start of the reign of Jimmu, Hirohito's distant mythical ancestor, Baron Hiranuma, a former prime minister and master of ceremonies, declared that Japan was a uniquely superior country "because foreign kings, emperors, presidents, are all created by man but Japan has a sacred throne inherited from the Imperial ancestors. Japan's imperial rule is therefore an extension of heaven. Man-made dynasties collapse, but the heaven-created throne is beyond the power of mere mortals."

In fact, Japanese attitudes toward the Chinese were somewhat ambivalent. Toward other Asian races pure contempt was displayed: the peoples of South East Asia were beyond consideration, barely human at all. Westerners were viewed with hatred inspired by their colonial record; they were inferior, but had subjugated much of Asia and so were regarded with some awe, also for their sheer physical size; this was supposedly offset by the superior intelligence of the Japanese and their unique minds. Japanese soldiers had on occasion to be reminded not to be intimidated by the size of Westerners. The Chinese had long been viewed as Japan's cultural siblings and rivals: they had Confucianism and Buddhism in common. Perhaps because of this the Japanese army was particularly intent on establishing its superiority through mass murder.

(2) The amorality of Japanese religion and ethics. Because Shintoism laid no stress on the individual conscience, but rather on conforming to a collective view within a hierarchy headed by an Emperor and rigorously structured beneath him, there was no room for the individual to question the will of the collective. Right was what a soldier was ordered to do; to disobey was to do wrong. There was no overriding moral absolute to set this against.

(3) The brutal way of life of the ordinary Japanese peasant, who made up the bulk of the rank-and-file of the Imperial Army. Certainly the utter impoverishment of Japan's peasant families, coupled with the tradition of absolute subservience to the authorities in the villages, helps to explain the routine sadism and lack of humanity of ordinary soldiers. The harshness of discipline in the imperial army, the savagery with which officers treated NCOs and ordinary men, and with which the former, many of whom became officers later in the war, treated the ranks must be added to this. All the same it is hard to believe that random brutality was in the nature of ordinary Japanese any more than any other race—although people accustomed to ill-treatment and a brutish life hardly understood that there was anything wrong in applying the same standards to people accustomed to a more civilized life.

(4) The *Essence of the Imperial Rescript to Soldiers and Sailors* was an injunction of absolute loyalty. "The soldier and the sailor should consider loyalty their essential duty . . . A soldier or sailor in whom this spirit is not strong, however skilled in art or proficient in science, is a mere puppet; and a body of soldiers or sailors wanting in loyalty, however disciplined it may be, is in the emergency no better than a rabble . . . with single head fulfill your essential duty of loyalty, and bear in mind that duty is weightier than a mountain, while death is lighter than a feather."

(5) The indiscipline of the Japanese army. The army expanded with astonishing speed before 1937, growing from 24 divisions to 34 the following year, 41 in 1939 and 50 in 1940. Previously soldiers had had at least two years' training; now they received only a month or two basic training before being put in the field. The Japanese military police were few in number, and their prime purpose was intelligence work, not the policing of ordinary troops. In fact, the Japanese army, in contrast with its image of iron discipline, was often shabbily ill-disciplined, with officers and NCOs resorting to violence as the only way of controlling their men.

(6) The Japanese army's penchant for rape, particularly in China, was also a product of the wretchedly low status accorded Japanese women, which was multiplied exponentially in relation to the women of other races. The situation became so bad that the Japanese authorities began to round up whole villages of women, setting up brothels in Korea and some parts of China, thus limiting off-duty activity. The Korean "comfort girls," whom it was established in 1992 served in government—organized bordellos—were expected to service anything up to 30 Japanese a day. For the ordinary soldier, rape was one of the few pleasures in a comfortless and deprived life in which he could expect to reap very few of the spoils of war.

(7) Military training, which in Japan, as might be expected, went to extremes in exaggerating the standard military drill of dehumanising the individual, humiliating him and forcing him to conform to a group with the wider purpose of winning a war. This leads to inevitable excesses in any war, from those perpetrated at My Lai in Vietnam to the more systematic atrocities carried out by the Russians in Afghanistan. Yet nowhere—except perhaps in the still inexplicable holocaust in Cambodia in the 1970s—were they on such a vast scale as those inflicted by the Japanese on the Chinese and during the Pacific War.

(8) The nature of the fighting. The war in China was of a particularly vicious and bloody nature. The Chinese Nationalists fought savagely and gave little quarter; and when Mao's guerrillas entered the fray, they conducted a no-holds-barred campaign of a kind that left the Japanese defensive, frightened and vicious. The traditional response to such tactics—whether in China, or later in Malaysia and the Philippines—was at the time to terrorize the villages that were necessary to supporting the guerrilla fighters, usually by massacre and the burning down of hamlets, or the extraction of information from captured insurgents through torture.

In addition, the sheer degradation of the ordinary Japanese soldier under extreme privation and, later military pressure, played a major part. One Japanese prisoner on one of the Pacific Islands explained:

Japanese troops had been under such conditions that they were not normal human beings at the time when the cannibalism took place. [The conditions included] continuous standing in swamp water up to the armpits, suffering from malaria with 40 degrees of fever and such lack of food, particularly vitamin B, as to cause night blindness . . . They were also reduced to such a state of delirium that their only reaction was to discharge their rifles in the general direction of any sound that they might hear. In committing dreadful acts of cruelty and violence against others, many of the soldiers of the Imperial Army were taking revenge in advance for their own imminent deaths.

The desperation of the ordinary soldier should not be underestimated: According to a military surgeon stranded in the Philippines, Tadashi Moriya, there were two ways to avoid starvation. One was bats:

We tore off the wings, roasted them until they were done brown, flayed and munched from their heads holding them with their legs. The brain was relishable. The tiny eyes cracked lightly in the mouth. The teeth were small but sharp, so we crunched and swallowed them down. We ate everything, bones and intestines, except the legs. The abdomen felt rough to the tongue, as they seemed to eat small insects like mosquitoes. We never minded that, and devoured them ravenously . . . Hunger is the best sauce, indeed, for I ate 15 bats a day.

An officer reported he saw a group of soldiers cooking meat. When he approached, they tried to conceal the contents of the mess tin, but he had a peep of them. A good deal of fat swam on the surface of the stew they were cooking, and he saw at once that it couldn't be the karabaw meat. Then I had the news that an officer of another unit was eaten up by his orderly as soon as he breathed his last. I believe the officer was so attached to his orderly that he bequeathed his body to his servant, and the devoted orderly faithfully executed the last will and testament of his lord and master and buried him in his belly instead of the earth.

(9) Japan's Bushido creed was harsh in the extreme: death was viewed as beautiful, beheading a noble way to die, surrender as deeply shaming and those who engaged in it beneath contempt.

The perpetration of atrocities was systematic, a deliberate tactic ordered from above. At the outset of the war with China, when many of the worst atrocities, including the Rape of Nanking, took place, the Japanese army was not noted for its indiscipline. Indeed, the vigorous purge of junior officers carried out after the attempted putsch of February 1936 meant that it was more centralized than ever before: atrocities on the scale that occurred could not have taken place without the knowledge and tacit approval, if not outright orders, of the authorities at the top, although there were certainly officers that disapproved of and condemned these actions.

The Bushido tradition advocated respectful, even chivalrous treatment toward the enemy. Nogi's behavior toward his defeated Russian foes in the Russo-Japanese war was the most recent example. There was room for mercy in the creed of Bushido—but it was not the tactic adopted by Japanese army commanders to win the war with China. Bushido was perverted in the military training of the 1930s: its self-sacrificial doctrines were retained, while its code of honor was discarded in the interests of a much more modern doctrine—that of "total war," which envisaged treating whole nations, not just soldiers, as combatants, and favored using every method available—including torture, murder, deceit, and booby-trapping —to win. The "total war" theorists, at the very summit of the Japanese army, believed there were no limits to combat—a thoroughly twentieth century doctrine with no connection at all to traditional Bushido.

Several participants in the Rape of Nanking alleged that they were acting under orders; and one of the underlying concepts in the "China Incident" was the Japanese idea of a "war of punishment" inflicting brutality on an organized, massive scale. Anything that could hasten victory was permissible, and deliberate savagery was believed to be a tactic that would spread sufficient terror to do just that.

Yet this was seriously to misunderstand the Chinese character. Brutality convinced the Chinese that surrender to the Japanese would be a more terrible fate than continued fighting; resistance stiffened. Certainly, even after the Control Group purged the Imperial Way rebels and centralized decision-making, the Japanese army was more prone to being led from below than most.

Some form of responsibility can be ascribed. Take the Rape of Nanking. It is not clear to this day who in fact gave the orders for the mass murder, rape and looting that engulfed the city after it was abandoned by Chinese Nationalist forces. The implication given by the Japanese generals in the postwar investigations is that the carnage was either on a much smaller scale than is commonly supposed, or that it was the action of troops on the ground. Was it the ordinary soldiers? Was it the NCOs and middle-ranking officers? Was it the divisional commanders in the field, General Nakajima, Major-General Heisuke Yanagawa, and Prince Asaka (Hirohito's uncle by marriage)? Was it General Matsui, the commander-in-chief in China? Was it the army high command in Tokyo? What did the government and the Emperor know?

From the available evidence it is possible to make a relatively precise judgment about which of these basic seven links in the chains of command were involved. Given the prevailing conditions of discipline at the time—and Nanking occurred before the degeneration of the Japanese army and intense military pressure of the following few years—it seems certain that ordinary soldiers were not acting under their own initiative. The scale of the pillaging, the length of time it went on and the absence of disciplinary action against the ranks all point in the same direction. Similarly, nowhere else had NCOs and middle-ranking Japanese officers up till then felt free to permit their men to go on a rampage. A Japanese private, Shiro Asuma, and other Japanese ex-servicemen insisted after the war that they were acting on orders from above.

The three main divisional commanders were certainly aware of what was happening, and are believed to have issued the specific orders for it. General Matsui, who was condemned to death by the Tokyo War Crimes Tribunal for his part in the Rape, was, in the view of one of Hirohito's biographers, Edward Behr, "the one Japanese general who was appalled by the Nanking atrocities and did his best to prevent them." In fact, Matsui's role was more ambiguous. Not being a divisional commander on the spot, he lacked the necessary authority to rein in his generals. Indeed, Nakajima, Tanagawa and Asaka were all intimately connected with the Control Group and Issekikai, the army within an army that now effectively ran Japan, whose most prominent member was General Tojo. It is possible that

Matsui was in effect powerless, and too frightened to challenge the author- ity of the Emperor's uncle. Matsui denied that the Rape ever took place.

The carnage was no spur-of-the-moment matter, but continued for at least a fortnight. During that time, there is no record of orders having been issued from Tokyo to stop it, although 80 officers were transferred a couple of months later from Nanking. Almost certainly, the Emperor in his new war headquarters must have learned of the Rape of Nanking. His foreign minister, Hirota, and prime minister, Konoye, were informed but powerless to stop it.

Hirohito's biographer, Kawahara, passes over the Rape without com- ment—but does not deny that the Emperor knew. Kawahara asserts that "[w]hen Hirohito heard the reports he was violently angry. He went to see the war minister Sugiyama to protest and to ask him to take immediate steps to tighten up the discipline in the army. At the same time Counselor Hidaka and others in Nanking visited local army leaders in order to urge them to do something. General Matsui, commander-in-chief, admitted that those under him seemed to have behaved outrageously. When Hidaka asked him whether perhaps the ordinary troops had not heard their supe- riors' orders, he muttered darkly that it seemed the superiors themselves were sometimes to blame."

From the evidence presented here, and contrary to the views of some historians, it seems likely that the Rape of Nanking was ordered by the Control Group in Tokyo, now committed to winning the China conflict in as short a time as possible through the "war of punishment" tactic. Those orders were directly executed by the divisional commanders in the field. Matsui, powerless, it must be assumed, turned a blind eye and later joined in the general conspiracy of silence to deny that the Rape had ever occurred (he thus bears major responsibility). It seems probable that the Emperor and prime minister protested so violently that an official inquiry fol- lowed—much too late—and those chiefly responsible were transferred, while their superiors remained in office.

There was no change of policy from the war of punishment, however. Atrocity followed atrocity across China, although no single incident was as widely observed internationally and independently reported as the Rape of Nanking. The extent to which deliberate brutality was, in fact, the policy of the ruling military group is revealed in this remarkable exchange with Matsui's nominal subordinate, General Akira Muto, who was very much his minder on behalf of the Control Group. Muto was to serve later as head of the Military Affairs Bureau, as Japanese army commander during the brutal occupation of Sumatra, and as chief of staff during the Rape of

Manila. Muto outlined to his interrogators that it was deliberate Japanese policy not to take any prisoners.

". . . Of course, you took prisoners from the Chinese armies?"

"No. The question of whether Chinese captives would be declared prisoners of war or not was quite a problem, and it was finally decided in 1938 that because the Chinese conflict was officially known as an 'incident' that Chinese captives would not be regarded as prisoners of war."

"As a matter of fact, the 'Chinese incident' was a war, was it not?"

"Actually, yes, but the Japanese government looked upon it as being an incident."

"So that you carried on a policy of not treating the Chinese captives as prisoners of war?"

"Yes."

In fact large numbers of prisoners were taken, and most were executed or became forced laborers. This was logical to the Japanese military mind. Prisoners were beneath contempt, deserving only death for failing to fight to the end, Chinese ones doubly so. Besides, the army, which had very few supplies and was expected as a matter of policy to live off the land, lacked the wherewithal to feed them. Nevertheless the very decision to call the war an "incident" was at least in part a hollow attempt to justify the most flagrant violation of human rights and the Geneva Convention. Responsibility for this must extend all the way up to the government in Tokyo and to the Emperor himself.

Two further atrocities of the Sino-Japanese war—the biggest theatre of the Second World War and possibly the largest conflict of all time—bear comment. The first was Japan's notorious Unit 731, set up by imperial decree as an "Epidemic Prevention and Water Purification Supply Unit" under General Shiro Ishii. The real purpose of the unit was to develop methods of scientific, chemical and bacteriological warfare, testing these on human beings. Between 3,000 and 10,000 died in its experiments. Brackman sums up the activities of Unit 732:

> The Japanese experiments in bacteriological warfare, it was alleged, included infecting prisoners with diseases, freezing portions of their bodies, and exposing prisoners to fragmentation bombs. Chinese women were infected with syphilis to develop vaccine. Prisoners were infected with plague, typhus, typhoid, haemorrhagic fever, cholera, anthrax, tularemia, smallpox and dysentery. Prisoners were given doses of horse blood and had their livers destroyed by prolonged exposure to X-rays. Allied prison-

ers were dissected alive. POWs were tied to stakes and canisters of bubonic plague and other horrible viruses exploded nearby while Japanese army technicians in protective clothing, holding stopwatches, measured how long it took the prisoners to die. The experiments were carried out in Manchuria and on the outskirts of Nanking, and included the bombing of Chinese cities with plague.

These horrific experiments, compared to similar ones in Germany, affected a proportionally small number of victims and were insignificant to the Japanese war effort. One remarkable Japanese air raid which dropped infected rats killed nearly 2,000 of their own people. But these experiments marked a peculiarly grisly turn of the screw. It seems certain that Hirohito personally supported the Unit, although there is no clear evidence that he knew of the human experimentation there.

Another repugnant aspect of the war was the Japanese army's resolve to finance a large quantity of its costs through the drug trade. This decision was taken at the very top. The China Affairs Board, set up by Prince Konoye, oversaw a $300 million trade in opium deliberately revived in China by the Japanese army both as a means of raising money and demoralizing the Chinese population. Although narcotics were almost extinct in central China itself in 1917, the Japanese in Manchuria took over the Young Marshal's lucrative drugs business, set up huge poppy plantations, and ran and licensed the dens that sold heroin (there were 600 in Peking alone).

Although most of the horrors associated with Japan's war on China were instigated and carried to extremes by Japanese armies in the field, most were approved by the Control Group in Tokyo. Both in Tokyo and the field, the "war of punishment" was deliberate policy. Funding it through the opium trade was deliberate policy. The Korean "comfort girls" and the press-ganged brothels were official policy. The attempt to subdue all of China was deliberate policy. All of these decisions were taken at the highest level of the army, with the civilian government, where necessary, ignored. The Emperor, when he knew, gave his grudging consent because he could not veto them, and may have even believed in the necessity of some of them. He certainly approved of the decision to go to war with China—with the usual reservations. He made clear his view that the conflict must be brought quickly to an end—which proved not to be possible.

20 : THE EAGLE STIRS

GIVEN TIME AND EFFORT, JAPAN WOULD PROBABLY HAVE SECURED ALL OF China. But the bogging down of the army in China and the poor economic returns made the *zaibatsu* impatient. They turned to their closer ally, the traditionally weaker power in the Japanese military establishment, the supposedly "moderate," navy. At that stage, the die was cast. As late as 1939 the Pacific War was entirely avoidable: America was not willing to fight for China, however savage and large-scale the fighting there. With the *zaibatsu*'s decision to align itself with a minority of the army and the bulk of the navy in their grand vision of a "southern strike" into South East Asia, war became inevitable. Ironically, the China-obsessed mainstream army leaders joined the civilians and the Emperor in worrying deeply about the consequences of such an extension of the war. Prime responsibility for the invasion of South East Asia—which caused the Pacific War—thus lay with the navy and the *zaibatsu*.

Much more serious than the issue of responsibility as applied to the largely powerless Emperor, dragged along in the wake of his government's decisions, was the role of the other major player in 1930s Japan—the *zaibatsu*, which alone had the power to block Japan's march to war. As we have seen, the evidence suggests not just acquiescence by the *zaibatsu*, who now had a virtual stranglehold over the Japanese economy, but their active encouragement. The business interests, starved of overseas markets, were determined to find them and also secure supplies of strategic raw materials with the help of their military friends.

The *zaibatsu* had revived their alliance with the Control Group, both crushing the hated "Imperial Way" hotheads in their army. The mainstream of the army, hand in glove with the *zaibatsu*, took the decision to go to war and use the hellish methods with which it was prosecuted. And the *zaibatsu* were left to run the huge archipelago of forced labor in the mines and the factories of occupied China (and not least the narcotics trade: Mitsubishi controlled supply and distribution of drugs in Manchuria, while Mitsui controlled it in South China; the two squabbled for turf in the rest of occupied China).

By 1939, as general war broke out in Europe, the outcome of the war in China had proved a disappointment both for the army and the *zaibatsu*.

The treasure trove of China had been much smaller than the *zaibatsu* had been led to expect: raw materials were barely available outside Manchuria. The Chinese market, except for opium, provided poor pickings: a proper manufacturing base was lacking and in that impoverished, war-torn and terrorized land, consumption was low. The war had deprived Manchuria, with its abundant raw materials, of its labor force: most of Mukden's factories were idle. Some 500,000 Japanese had died in two years of fighting.

The catalyst for Japan's ill-starred venture into South East Asia was the trend of events in Europe. Japan's attitude toward Europe was entirely opportunistic. Its military alliance with Britain had fallen apart after the First World War, and with its walkout from the League of Nations, relations between the Western powers and Japan were on a wary and suspicious footing. This encouraged the Japanese to make common cause with Germany and Italy, the Axis powers who also were in bitter rivalry with Britain, France and the United States and shared Japan's deep distrust of the Soviet Union. The Japanese persuaded themselves that they shared a common cause with Germany and Italy as "have-not-nations" in opposition to the British and American "empires." All three wanted their own empires. In 1936 the three signed the Anti-Comintern Pact, directed against Russia.

The Japanese military attaché in Berlin, Lieutenant-General Hiroshi Oshima, pursued a vigorous policy of friendship with Hitler, whom he deeply admired, even at one stage suggesting that Japan would join Germany in fighting Britain and America. "Perhaps we could call on the war minister to reprimand him," commented an exasperated Hirohito, who was unenthusiastic about an alliance with Germany. On another occasion the Emperor buttonholed the war minister. "Is it not a usurpation of imperial authority for the military attaché to promise, on his own, our military co-operation with Germany? I am further disturbed by the fact that the army seems to support him on this issue, and I am displeased that you have failed to bring the matter up at cabinet meetings." Nevertheless, Germany and Japan seemed to be drawing ever closer together.

In August 1939 Hitler dropped a bombshell by concluding a non-aggression pact with Japan's foremost enemy—the Soviet Union, which now could reinforce its armies in the East to face Japan. The shocked Japanese Prime Minister, Baron Hiranuma, resigned, remarking "the situation in Europe has taken a strange and complex new turn." Hirohito, who had long distrusted the Germans, argued forcefully, "In foreign affairs our goal should be maintaining a harmonious relationship with England and the United States. Furthermore, the foreign minister should act in a manner more clearly consistent with constitutional provisions." The foreign minister at the time was a departure from the moderate tradition of that institution: Yosuke Matsuoka was a verbose nationalist, who had also engineered the appointment of one of his military allies, General Hata, as the new war minister. Relations between Germany and Japan were now severely strained for a time.

But in the early summer of 1940, as Hitler's armies overran continental Europe, Japan was anxious to join forces with the winning side. There were two immediate consequences: first, the triumph of the Nazis in Europe suggested to the Japanese that the facade of parliamentary democracy—and by now it was no more than that—was outmoded. Fascism was seen as the new wave. Prince Konoye, once again prime minister, formally dissolved the political parties and set up a mass movement "designed to assist the Imperial throne." In fact the parties had long counted for little, and Japan had been a virtual military dictatorship since 1936; but now even the pretence was gone.

Second, in September 1940, the tripartite Axis Pact was signed. The essence of the pact for Japan was that it committed Germany to coming to its aid in the event of an attack by the United States. Defeat in France had virtually removed Japan's other rival in East Asia, Britain, as a serious challenger in the Pacific; at the same time Britain had bowed to Japan's demands to close one of the main supply routes to Chiang Kai-Shek's beleaguered army in China—the Burma Road.

Hirohito was unhappy with the Axis Pact, remarking, "[E]ven if we wait to see what happens between Germany and Russia, there will still be time for an alliance" and insisting, "Surely the United States will embargo imports of oil and scrap iron to Japan by way of retaliation. What will happen then?" Another time he said angrily, "No matter how you look at it, this will be ruinous for the army. They won't wake up to the situation until Manchuria and Korea have been lost." With Britain crippled and America neutralized, Japan began to consider the feasibility of further colonial advances—even though it had yet to absorb China.

In June 1941, Germany, which had been urging Japan to strike against British and French interests in Asia, invaded Russia. The Japanese were delighted: with Britain, France and the Netherlands now on their knees, their Asian interests were ripe for the picking; the Soviet Union's attentions were entirely taken up in Europe. America would not risk war with Germany by seeking to block Japan's aims in Indochina and the Pacific. It was now or never toward creating a truly enormous empire in southern

Asia. The region had oil, tin, bauxite, nickel, and rice—all the things most desperately needed by Japan's expeditionary force in China and, more importantly, by the *zaibatsu*, who took the view that, with Japan's export earnings at an all-time low and no money available to buy raw materials, they had to be seized instead.

The army and the navy, meanwhile, had joined with the *zaibatsu* in a nearly unstoppable alliance. The navy's War Guidance Office had long been advocating the "strike south." "Finally, the time has come," it declared. "This maritime nation, Japan, should today commence its advance to the Bay of Bengal. Moss-covered tundras, vast barren deserts—of what use are they? Today people should begin to follow the grand strategy of the navy." A cautionary note was sounded by Admiral Yamamoto, who prophetically told Konoye in mid-1941: "If I am told to fight, regardless of the consequences, I shall run wild considerably for the first six months or a year, but I have utterly no confidence for the second and third years. Now that the situation has come to this pass, I hope you will work for avoidance of an American-Japanese war."

A month after the launch of Hitler's Operation Barbarossa offensive into Russia, the Japanese made their move into Indochina, little foreseeing that it would make war with the United States inevitable. There is no doubt, though, that Hirohito was genuinely troubled by the venture. He told the Lord Privy Seal, Marquis Kido, who had emerged as his chief adviser, "I am not at all pleased when we act on our own and take advantage of the other side's weakness like a thief at a fire. However, in order to deal with the unsettled conditions we find in the world today, it would not do to be beaten because we failed to attack when we had the chance. . . . I only hope you will show prudence in the execution of your plans."

Like the British in Burma, the Vichy government in France had been bullied into closing the supply route across Indochina to Chiang's forces. Nevertheless, in July 1941, Japanese forces occupied French bases in southern Indochina, being welcomed into them by the Vichy government, which had little alternative. It seemed that the occupation could be only a prelude to the invasion of Malaya, the Philippines and the Dutch East Indies. The British responded by promptly reopening the Burma to China road in a gesture of defiance against Japan's unprovoked expansionism. The Japanese were later to claim that this made the occupation of Malaya and the East Indies inevitable. But in this case the chicken seems clearly to have preceded the egg: they had no pretext for occupying French Indochina in the first place, because both the British and French supply routes to Chiang had already been closed.

The United States, Britain and Holland responded by imposing an embargo on the supply of oil, iron and steel from any of their territories or dependencies to Japan. Japanese assets in the United States were also frozen.

It took some time for the Japanese to realize that America was serious: their reaction then was to conclude that war with the United States was inevitable—and that the Americans had brought it on themselves. Admiral Nagano, the naval chief of staff, summed up the Japanese view at an historic cabinet meeting on September 3: with the country now starved of oil, the Allies could only become stronger and Japan weaker. "Although I am confident that at the present time we have a chance to win the war, I feel that this opportunity will disappear with the passage of time." Tojo was less certain, believing that victory was by no means certain, but that Japan had no other choice. The Emperor prodded Konoye into a frantic last-minute effort to talk peace with the Americans.

It was to become apparent over the next few months, however, that the Japanese were right about one thing, at least: peace was now impossible because the Americans were resolved to go to war except in the unlikely event of Japanese capitulation to humiliating demands. In occupying French Indochina, the Japanese had miscalculated disastrously (although they would plead that there had been no clear-cut signal from Washington to lay off). That single act, taken with the approval of all Japan's main power centers—the Emperor and his household (grudgingly), Prince Konoye, the cabinet, the army, the navy, the *zaibatsu*, the bureaucracy—represented the crossing of the Rubicon.

Why did the United States, which had watched in passive disapproval while Japan's massive war effort against China proceeded, react with alacrity and firmness to the Japanese occupation of French Indochina, which, almost alone of the advances of the past decade, took place with the acquiescence of the country concerned and largely without bloodshed? Two explanations have about equal weight. With the move into Indochina, Japan now clearly threatened South East Asia; it was firmly against America's strategic interest that Japan should have a clear dominance over the Western Pacific, and be able to call upon huge supplies of strategic raw materials in any further colonial adventure.

Yet there was a second reason. Roosevelt was by now anxious to enter the European war, having been convinced by Churchill of the dangers of German hegemony over continental Europe. This in part explains why the Americans were prepared to tolerate the war with China, but not the invasion of Indochina. Roosevelt must have known the imposition of sanctions against Japan rendered war virtually inevitable; and the Japanese attack on Pearl Harbor, coupled with Hitler's ritual declaration of war on America (which was not necessary under the Axis Pact, since Japan had not been first attacked), made it possible for the United States promptly to enter the European war.

That this was uppermost in Roosevelt's mind is supported by the way the great bulk of American forces were promptly assigned to the European theater, not to the Far East—much to General MacArthur's disgust. Roosevelt was to treat the war with Japan almost as a sideshow. Confident that he would prevail there in the end, the American President's initial attentions went far beyond Asia.

The four months after the embargo was imposed were marked by frantic Japanese preparation for war coupled with Hirohito's equally frantic search for peace. The Emperor's motives were twofold: a manifest reluctance to resort to war, and his considerable doubts that Japan would win. Admiral Nagano, the naval chief, had told him in July that a total victory was out of the question. "Indeed, we're not even sure of winning." On September 6 the draft plans for war were approved before the Emperor. But he insisted that every last diplomatic effort be made. He told Konoye, in Kawahara's account:

"Judging from these plans, the first priority is preparation for a war. Diplomatic negotiations are relegated to second place. I get the feeling that war is the master, diplomacy the slave. What do you think?" He explicitly ordered, "War preparations and diplomacy should not be given equal footing. Diplomatic efforts must take precedence." He then summoned Chairman of the Joint Chiefs of Staff Sugiyama and questioned him at length regarding the southern campaign and its prospects. Sugiyama told him, "So long as it is only South-east Asia, we can settle the matter in about three months."

The Emperor's reply was sharp. "You were war minister when the China Incident broke out and you told me it would be settled within a month. Now it is four years later and it is still going on, is it not?" Sugiyama's excuse was that China's interior was so vast, but Hirohito pressed him further: "You say China's interior is vast. Tell me, is not the Pacific Ocean even bigger? What makes you so sure it will only take three months?" Sugiyama could only hang his head in silence. But the Emperor was by no means finished. He wanted to know more about the army's plans. "Are you absolutely certain you can win?" he demanded.

"I cannot say absolutely, but I can say that in all probability we will win. However it is impossible to be sure," Sugiyama equivocated.

"I see!" said the Emperor in an uncharacteristically strong voice.

The following day the cabinet approved two fateful resolutions. First, "in order to preserve the Empire's self-sufficiency and self-defense, Japan is determined not to back away from war with the United States, Britain and the Netherlands; consequently, war preparations are to be completed by the end of October." Second, "parallel with the above, and in an effort to satisfy the Emperor's demands, Japan will exhaust all diplomatic means with respect to the United States and England."

The head of the privy council, standing in for the Emperor, addressed a number of questions to the navy minister on behalf of Hirohito. The Emperor had been advised not to put these questions himself. After they had finished, he angrily drew out a poem by the Meiji Emperor:

I believed this was a world
In which all men were brothers
Across the Four Seas.
Why then do the waves and winds
Arise now in such turmoil?

The military chiefs assured him they would make an effort for peace. Prince Konoye had been pressing for a summit with Roosevelt, which the Americans played along with for a while, to buy time, although they suspected that the Japanese intention was to "spring a Munich."

However the Americans were being simultaneously appraised of Japanese preparations for war by MAGIC, the codename for a remarkable breakthrough in cracking Japanese communications codes which was to serve superbly throughout the Pacific War. In September, Roosevelt drew up terms for a settlement which the Japanese could not accept. The Americans underlined that they required not just a withdrawal from Indochina, but from China itself, now viewed as an unacceptable act of expansion, which seemed a deliberate attempt to goad the Japanese. Konoye's fallback position was to offer a retreat from Indochina in exchange for lifting the embargo, in other words a return to the status quo ante July. The prime minister had a secret meeting with the American ambassador in Tokyo, Joseph Grew, to press for the summit; Cordell Hull, the American Secretary of State, was unimpressed.

On October 12 Konoye met Tojo, the war minister and by now the acknowledged chief of the Control Group in the army, and urged him to withdraw "some" troops from China. Tojo flatly refused, and it is certain that the Americans would have rejected such a half-measure. By then it seems that Hirohito himself had accepted that war was inevitable, telling Kido realistically that "in the present conditions I think U.S.–Japanese negotiations have little hope of success."

On October 14, Tojo sent an ultimatum to Konoye, urging his resignation for his failure to report that there were serious divisions within the navy as to the advisability of war (Konoye suggested that the navy as a whole was against war, something Tojo disputed). Konoye, faced by the prospect of the government falling, recommended that a moderate, Prince Hikashikuni, succeed him. This relative of the Emperor later claimed that he told Konoye to go ahead and form another government, sacking Tojo. This would have called the army's bluff. It might also have led to the outright military coup that the Emperor feared above all else. Instead, Hirohito appointed Tojo prime minister, with the memorable remark to the snake-like Kido, who had proposed the war minister, "It is just as they say, you can't control a tiger unless you enter its lair."

Hideki Tojo was the son of a famous general under Emperor Meiji. Even for a Japanese, he was short. He made a virtue of dressing as unprepossessingly as the ordinary Japanese soldier: unpolished shoes, baggy pants, unironed uniform. He was in striking contrast to his predecessor as war minister, General Araki, an inspired and loquacious public speaker. Tojo would speak briefly and exactly to the point. He was both an able administrator and an effective field commander. He first rose to prominence as head of the military police in the Kwantung army in Manchuria, becoming commander of Japan's mechanized forces in China and then being promoted to vice-minister of war in the first Konoye Cabinet. His abilities impressed Konoye, and he was appointed air force chief, immensely strengthening that arm. Konoye appointed him war minister in his second and third cabinets, under pressure from army extremists.

Tojo was highly effective, reimposing discipline on the faction-ridden army, dissolving the separate infantry, cavalry and artillery divisions, as well as the engineering and air commissariats so that the army was more unified and able officers could be transferred from one branch of the army to another at speed. Tojo's experience in China had taught him the value of air power, mechanization and blitzkrieg tactics, and he introduced a "modern weapons" department into the army. He was possessed of a brilliant military mind, and was a masterly strategist. He was tough, determined, utterly loyal to Japan and the Emperor and somewhat lacking in imagination.

Konoye later sadly told his aide that he had been let down by Hirohito.

> When I used to tell the Emperor that it would be a bad thing to start the war, he would agree with me, but then he would listen to others and afterward tell me I shouldn't worry so much. He was slightly in favor of war and later on he became more war-inclined. Eventually he started believing that I was no expert on strategy or military matters generally. As prime minister, I had no authority over the army and there was only one person I could appeal to: the Emperor. But the Emperor became so much under the influence of the military that I couldn't do anything about it.

Konoye's verdict is damning, but also self-serving. It is true that by this stage, Hirohito was reconciled to war: he had displayed his own sometimes prescient doubts about the recklessness of the military and he now accepted, in view of America's refusal to back down, that his country could not yield and save face. In this he reflected the views of almost everyone but Konoye—the man who, however, had presided over both Japan's decisions to invade China and to occupy Indochina.

Japan was far advanced with preparations for all-out war as long before Pearl Harbor as July 1940, when the manufacture of luxury goods was prohibited. The sale of stocks of luxuries was stopped in October. Non-essential industries were prepared for the quick shift to war production. Eighteen months before Pearl Harbor, driving for pleasure was banned. In mid-1941 private cars were stopped from using the streets. Rubber-soled *tabui* had disappeared from the shops two years before the war in order to accumulate reserves of rubber; oil and iron ore were also being stockpiled.

For several years, useful materials like metal plumbing fixtures were being stripped from private homes. Nails, bottle caps, spectacle frames and hat pins were seized. Two weeks before Pearl Harbor members of the powerless Japanese parliament, the Diet, were forced to take buses to their sessions. Other signs of war preparations were the absence of coffee; the extinguishing of neon lights in the Ginza; the introduction of "Service Day for the Development of Asia"—a kind of family fast day every month; a ban on the polishing of rice, which made it smaller. In 1940 rice, salt, sugar matches and other daily necessities were rationed—even though the war with China did not justify this. Women were forbidden to wear smart clothes or style their hair.

By November 2, Hirohito was meeting with his chiefs of staff over the direct operational planning for war, and showed knowledge of the date and location of the navy's strike against Pearl Harbor. When Japanese negotiators met the Americans on November 7, their demands had stiffened perceptibly. On November 26 the Americans reiterated their demand to the Japanese for withdrawal both from China and Indo-China. Roosevelt warned his top admirals to prepare for war. Stimson, the American Secretary of War, recalls that Roosevelt told them, "We were likely to be attacked as early as next Monday (December 1st), for the Japanese are notorious for making an attack without warning." Roosevelt believed this would come in the Southern Pacific, because Japanese ships were assembling at Shanghai.

At a fateful meeting of senior statesmen on November 29, Konoye was bafflingly, perhaps duplicitously, ambiguous.

I deeply regret that I have not been able to do anything towards the adjustment of Japanese-American relations despite my efforts from last April onwards. I beg to express my appreciation to the present cabinet for zealously striving to attain this end. To my great regret, I am forced to con-clude, on the basis of this morning's explanation by the government, that further continuation of diplomatic negotiations would be hopeless . . . Still, is it necessary to go to war at once, even if diplomatic negotiations have been broken off? Would it not be possible, I wonder, while carrying on matters as they are, to find a way out of the deadlock later by persevering to the utmost despite the difficulties?

All the other senior men present spoke against war. Admiral Yonai said tortuously: "If I may use a vernacular expression, let me say that in our efforts to avoid going broke in the future we are in danger of bankrupting ourselves at once." Former Prime Ministers Hirota, Hiyashi, Abe and Wakatsuki said much the same.

Hirohito's doubts were raised at this eleventh hour by Prince Takamatsu, his younger brother, who reported to him on November 30 that the navy "will be very pleased if a war can be avoided." The Emperor promptly summoned the navy minister and chief of staff as well as Tojo, and was assured that they had no doubts. Kido reported, "When the Emperor questioned them, they answered with conviction, so he told me to have the prime minister proceed as planned."

Some time between early September and the end of November, the Emperor's mind had decisively altered in favor of war; he may have been persuaded by what he saw as the obduracy of the Americans. With the exception of a few elderly bureaucrats and a minority within the navy, all of Japan's power structures were now reconciled to the desirability and inevitability of war. The decision was a national one, not that of a militarist clique. Ordinary Japanese, of course, were not consulted, merely exhorted. Public opinion in the United States, while revolted by Japanese atrocities in China and approving Roosevelt's firm line, had very little idea that war was impending, or even likely. It took Pearl Harbor to change that.

At a meeting on December 2, Nagano and Sugiyama told Hirohito that the night of December 8 provided the best opportunity because, among other things, it would be Sunday, when the Americans were at ease and their ships in port. December 8 was a Monday in Tokyo and the rest of Asia, and a Sunday in Hawaii, across the International Date Line. Some Japanese historians now say that Nagano informed Hirohito the attack would be on a Monday, when Americans would be weary after Sunday revels—which seems improbable.

On December 2, 1941, Admiral Yamamoto, commander of the Japanese fleet, and one of those who harbored the most serious doubts about the desirability of war, sent out his coded order, "Ascend Mt. Nitaka! 1298," meaning that the attack on Pearl Harbor should proceed for December 8th. The Japanese fleet had already left the Kuriles and was in the Northern Pacific. At 6 P.M. Washington time, President Roosevelt followed the advice of a last-minute intermediary and sent a personal message to Hirohito asking for a withdrawal from Indochina without spelling out the need for a withdrawal from China. The note was held back by Japan's military censors, reaching the American ambassador in Tokyo, Joseph Grew, 12 hours later. At midnight December 8, Tokyo time, he tried to relay the message to the Emperor, but, absurdly, was told by the foreign minister that Hirohito could not be disturbed.

The Japanese declaration of hostilities against the United States was transmitted to the Japanese embassy in Washington, to be handed over at 1 P.M. the following day. Supposedly because of delays in the transmission, it was in fact handed over to Cordell Hull by the Japanese ambassador, Admiral Nomura, at 2:20 P.M. Half an hour before, Hull, along with Roosevelt and the Navy Secretary, had been appraised of the Japanese attack on Pearl Harbor.

At the age of 41, Hirohito had reached the turning point of his whole life with the decision to launch the Pacific War. The god-Emperor had unleashed a whirlwind of titanic proportions, which would cause the deaths of tens of millions and alter the lives of hundreds of millions.

A much more vigorous, self-confident man now, prone to arrogance, headstrong with the adulation of his huge military machine and the unqualified obedience of millions of his subjects, ignoring his wiser advisers, he was at the height of his personal authority. The awkward, shy, almost disabled little boy, the retiring student of marine biology, the agonized talker to himself were for a time no more. He was the ruler of a united people.

How harshly should history judge him for the decision to go to war? Herbert Bix, whose *Hirohito and the Making of Modern Japan* is perhaps the best crafted indictment of Hirohito, sets out the case clearly. He quotes the outgoing Prime Minister, Prince Konoye, on the subject of the Emperor's responsibility:

> Confronted with military strangulation by oil embargoes and the choice of admitting defeat in China, thereby abandoning a large part of his continental empire and probably destabilising the monarchy he had inherited, Hirohito opted for his third alternative: war against the United States and Britain. Like most of his top commanders he believed that Germany would triumph over Britain as it already had over all of Europe. If certain strategic schedules were quickly achieved, Japan would be able to counter superior American productive capacity and force at least a standoff with the United States. Having made his choice, Hirohito dedicated himself totally to presiding over and guiding the war to victory at all costs. It was a most demanding and absolutely vital role.

Yet there are complex issues to be disentangled. At each stage in Japan's slide toward domination by the military and the creation of a Far Eastern Empire, Hirohito had resisted, justifying his own eventual grudging compliance in terms first of his need to continue to act as a moderating influence and second of remaining the supreme embodiment and unifying symbol for his nation and people.

The endgame before Pearl Harbor was no different. In September he had objected to the turn of events: the Japanese occupation of Indochina had set in motion American economic strangulation. Faced by the decision whether to retreat and abandon Indochina and China, or go to war against the United States and Britain, he made the second choice. It is undeniable that given what had gone before, his choice was not only logical, but must have seemed the only one possible for him to make.

With Konoye's peace initiative failing to yield results, the war party was in the ascendant. For him to try and block it was probably impossible and might even have cost him his crown. Any attempt to do so would have required historical statesmanship and courage: and whatever else Hirohito was, he was certainly not cast in a heroic mold.

That is not quite the same as arguing, as some do, that he sought war, wanted war, or believed in war with the United States and Britain. Indeed he had desperately sought to avoid this—not least for fear that Japan might lose. Given his reluctant but fateful assent to a policy of Japanese imperial expansion at the expense of its Asian neighbors, he had now been put into a position where his country must either humiliatingly retreat or go to war with the Western powers that had unreasonably—in his view—decided to block this. But the conclusion he had reached was that the American stand made war inevitable.

So the great game began between these two mighty antagonists on either side of the enormous Pacific lake, neither coveting the territory of the other, but fighting for domination of the region. Two more different antagonists can hardly be imagined. On the one side was a vibrant young democracy of great industrial strength with a tiny standing army recently swollen by the recruitment of hundreds of thousands of conscripts which—except in the Philippines—had never fought beyond the boundaries of its own hemisphere.

On the other was a country in the second flush of industrialization, effectively under military dictatorship with a centuries-old warrior tradition molded into highly disciplined armed forces fanatically loyal to a living national symbol, the Emperor. Japan had crushingly defeated one great power, Russia, and its battle-hardened forces had conquered Formosa, Korea, Manchuria and much of China. Ironically, it was actually America, with a small standing army, that had been closer to the samurai tradition of an elite professional army than the new Japan, which had exchanged the traditional concept of a warrior elite for brutalized conscript armed forces. The feudal and the new worlds were locked into a mighty tussle for control of the world's greatest ocean and landmass, and of the majority of the world's population that dwelled on Asia.

PART IV

THE OLD MAN OF CORREGIDOR

21 : GENERALISSIMO OF WASHINGTON

WHILE THIS YOUNG MONARCH WAS PUTTING HIS NAME TO THE MOST fateful gamble in his nation's history a superannuated, aging American general 21 years his senior was eking out his years before retirement as a paid mercenary for a third-rate foreign power, ludicrously attired in Gilbert and Sullivan self-designed comic opera uniforms, a few hundred miles to the south.

How had the lean, energetic war hero we left in the autumn of 1922 come to this sorry pass? Douglas MacArthur's career at that time was, admittedly, in the doldrums. The victim of his own naïve romantic streak, disapproved of for his reformism by the old men of the American army and for his choice of marriage partner by its frisky patriarch, General Pershing, he had been left to languish mapping the dense jungle of the Bataan Peninsula—a mosquito-infested hellhole in which he could little have imagined he would play so fateful a role.

Nor, in the provincial social round of Manila American expatriate life, could he have imagined that his dream of wedded bliss would so quickly turn to ashes. For vibrant, teasing, partying, sophisticated, sexy Louise, accustomed to the smartest set in New York and Paris, found the life of an army officer on an overseas posting very different from what she had imagined. Although the great Bay of Manila is a spectacular natural setting, the sprawling jumble of impoverished one-story dwellings that was the city offered little of interest apart from a few luxurious villas, hotels and government buildings.

She quickly became bored. The Philippines, she wrote home, were "extremely dull." She was not diverted by her two small children. MacArthur doted on them, playing with them whenever he had the time in the large garden of his picturesque house built into the city walls. The General taught young Walter to ride (he fell off once), and showed sympathy for little Louise, who caught malaria.

His wife tried to create the social excitements she craved. She became a part-time policewoman and arrested a man for whipping his horse. She poked gentle fun at MacArthur, whom she openly called "Sir Galahad." MacArthur himself intensely disliked socializing. While Louise immersed herself in the pseudo-colonial partying of the islands, he confined himself to occasional dinner parties with the governor-general, Leonard Wood, MacArthur's former patron, at which Louise would complain bitterly of Pershing's decision to exile her husband.

Early in 1923 MacArthur was summoned back to America by a telephone call saying that his mother was critically ill—and Louise made no secret of her delight at returning. There MacArthur sought out the Secretary of War, John Weeks, and begged to be ordered home: but Weeks would not defy the powerful Pershing. Louise asked her colossally wealthy stepfather, Edward T. Stotesbury, to raise the matter directly with President Calvin Coolidge. It was all to no avail. MacArthur had to return after ascertaining that his mother was on the road to recovery.

Back in the Philippines he and Wood set about trying to draft a defensive strategy for the islands, toying with the idea of a Swiss-style militia. He was put in command of the Philippine Division, an amalgam of the Philippine Scouts and the 31st American military regiment. MacArthur showed no trace of racism in his command, dealing easily with Filipino officers, as well as renewing his acquaintance with his old friend Manuel Quezon: such tolerance was unusual for an American commander of the time.

His success in the job led Wood to press Washington for promotion. Weeks replied that "his turn will come in the early future." Meanwhile Pinky, who had staged a remarkable recovery, went directly to the source of the trouble, Pershing. In a letter that must have had MacArthur squirming with embarrassment when he learned of it, she cheekily patronized the most famous general in the American army:

> It was a real joy to see you on Saturday looking still so young and wonderfully handsome! I think you will never grow old . . . I am presuming on long and loyal friendship for you—to open my heart in this appeal for my Boy—and ask if you can't find it convenient to give him his promotion during your regime as Chief of Staff. You are so powerful in all Army matters that you could give him his promotion by a stroke of your pen! You have never failed me yet—and somehow I feel you will not in this request . . . Won't you be real good and sweet—the "Dear Old Jack" of long ago—and give me some assurance that you will give my Boy his well earned promotion before you leave the Army, God bless you—and crown your valuable life—by taking you to the White House. Faithfully your friend—Mary P. MacArthur.

The crotchety old soldier at last promoted MacArthur to two-star major-general—the youngest in the American army, and a position too senior to be compatible with service in the backwater of the Philippines.

In January 1925 the couple sailed back, to Louise's intense relief. Relations between them had settled down to a mutually wary level. Louise, fabulously rich all her life, was not one to do her husband's bidding. MacArthur was deeply impatient at her lack of punctuality. On his return there was a further disappointment: he was posted to command the Fourth Corps in Atlanta, Georgia, another provincial backwater. There, in the deep south, there remained simmering resentment of Arthur MacArthur's Civil War record. Arriving in church, Douglas was humiliated to see three quarters of the congregation walk out in protest. He immediately demanded a transfer, and was sent to command the Third Corps in Baltimore, Maryland, a more agreeable backwater. Family tragedy overshadowed this modest improvement in MacArthur's fortunes: his brother Arthur, who had embarked on a successful naval career, died of appendicitis.

One of MacArthur's first and most disagreeable duties was to serve at the court-martial of an old friend, the flamboyant American air force pioneer, Billy Mitchell. He was the grandson of a friend of MacArthur's grandfather, son of an officer who had served with his father, and a friend of Douglas since boyhood. Mitchell, much like MacArthur in character, believed regulations were there to be challenged, but took this conviction much too far. He publicly attacked senior officers for negligence over a string of air disasters, and predicted that "any offensive to be pushed against Japan will have to be made under the cover of our own air power . . . In the future, campaigns across the sea will be carried on from land base to land base under the protection of aircraft." He was to be vindicated by events.

MacArthur sat grimly through the court-martial, which lasted seven weeks, during which Mitchell publicly aired his ideas, without saying a single word, merely exchanging looks with Louise, who dutifully attended. It is not known how MacArthur voted, but Mitchell was narrowly convicted. MacArthur was later to be viewed with deep suspicion by many air force officers under his command, to whom Mitchell was a hero, although the latter bore no grudge. It seems that counsels of professional caution had prevailed over MacArthur's usual romantic impulses, although few believed that the airman actually deserved acquittal for his gross insubordination. MacArthur later claimed that he had played a moderating role in court behind the scenes.

He meanwhile reluctantly participated in the gregarious social life of Baltimore county, where Louse owned an estate appropriately called Rainbow Hill. But this posting was routine and dull for the most part, with the army under pressure to reduce its budget. In spite of his youth in his job, he chafed for a more challenging role. This came unexpectedly in September

1927 when he was offered the job of President of the American Olympic Committee after the unexpected death of the incumbent to preside over the American effort in the games in Holland the following year. With his passion for athletics, he instantly accepted.

At that stage it became apparent that all was not well in his five-year-old marriage. When Quekemeyer, whom Louise perhaps regretted not marrying, died, she wrote a grief-filled letter to Pershing. She had become fed up with the provincialism of army life and had tried to persuade her husband to enter civilian life in a well paid job in her stepfather's firm, J. P. Morgan. MacArthur refused, and in a barbed speech referred to the "barbarism of ostentatious splendor"—an apt description of Louise's background. She had tried to buy MacArthur out of the profession he revered above all else: faced by having to pick between his two loves, he preferred the latter. It is not enough to dismiss the marriage as an empty one, as most have done: it had survived a comparatively long time between two incompatibles, presumably because each had enough affection for the other to try to make it work. But Louise by now had had enough of the matrons of Baltimore and decamped for the glitter of New York.

Soon afterward MacArthur left for Holland unaccompanied. There the later celebrated journalist and author William L. Shirer reported that he had been "rather impressed by the general":

> He seemed above the stripe of what I had imagined our professional soldiers to be. He was forceful, articulate, thoughtful, even a bit philosophical, and well read. Only his arrogance bothered me.

MacArthur threw himself into the task as though he had a war to win. "We are here to represent the greatest country on earth. We did not come here to lose gracefully. We came here to win—and win decisively." He was as good as his word. The American team won more awards than the two runners-up combined, and set seven world records as well as 17 Olympic records. On his return he wrote a toe-curlingly purple account of the Games to President Coolidge which ended with sentiments that were pure MacArthur—romantically reaching for the moon:

> To set the cause above renown,
> To love the game beyond the prize,
> To honor, as you strike him down,
> The foe that comes with fearless eyes.
> To count the life of battle good,

And dear the land that gave you birth,
And dearer yet the Brotherhood
That binds the brave of all the Earth.

What the notoriously taciturn Coolidge thought of this torrent can be readily guessed (one story about Coolidge had one of two ladies at a lunch telling him, "We had a bet, Mr. President, that we could get you to say more than three words during the meal." "You lose," the reply had been). The contrast between MacArthur's verbal hyperbole and the terse sparseness of Emperor Hirohito's poetry is striking.

MacArthur was now to display another characteristic unusual in a military man—a direct interest in politics. The distinction between the military and politics in America has traditionally been more blurred than in most democracies. Since George Washington there has been a long tradition of military men, usually after a long and distinguished career, taking an interest in politics. General Pershing, who had abortively sought the presidency himself, was one such. MacArthur, however, decided to go on record not as a partisan, but to denounce the dangers threatening America and the world. As MacArthur later wrote:

> Back in Baltimore, I publicly expressed my fears that pacifist and other alien ideologies were causing America to repeat the errors of the past.
>
> With the Red menace in Russia, Poland in disorder, Romania threatened with secession, France fighting in Morocco, Nicaragua in revolution, Mexico in confusion, and civil war in China, it did not seem unlikely that our streets would again be filled with marching men and our country again have need of our military services. . . . My firm belief in the necessity for adequate military preparation gained for me, in those uneasy days of the '20s and early '30s, the lasting hostility of two powerful groups in the United States, the Communists and the pacifists.

For the commander of the Third Corps, such apocalyptic sentiments were unusual, to say the least. It was also interesting that MacArthur, although from his experience in the Philippines worried about the possibility of war with Japan, was more concerned about a threat from the left at home. The seeds were sown of the great controversies that were later to engulf that turbulent career: at the age of 50 MacArthur was at last emerging from his military cloister and tasting the heady allure of politics. Like Hirohito, he identified the enemy as the pacifists and Communists on the left. Equally striking was the fact that he voiced these sentiments before the sudden crash on Wall Street was to plunge America into years of the Depression.

Meanwhile, Louise had refused to accompany him to Holland and was seen with a string of men in New York. On his return he saw little of her: it seems likely that the imminent breakup of the marriage was a source of deep disappointment to MacArthur, who craved female companionship: he had also grown attached to the two children. When he was ordered back to the Philippines soon after to take command of all the forces there, Louise refused to go with him.

Six months later she filed for divorce on the mutually agreed but ridiculous grounds that he had failed to support her—one of the wealthiest women in America! But she announced bravely to the press, "I have the greatest admiration and respect for General MacArthur."

In his new job, MacArthur found himself getting on uneasily with the governor-general of the Philippines, the aristocratic and erudite Henry L. Stimson; but he also renewed his friendship with Manuel Quezon. His main preoccupation remained how to defend the islands against a still hypothetical Japanese threat: his army consisted of 17,000 badly trained and equipped American and Filipino troops and just 18 aircraft. MacArthur called this "pitifully inadequate." Stimson was recalled to become Secretary of State in February 1929 by the newly elected President Herbert Hoover, who had noticed the ascending star of the bright young anti-Communist, General MacArthur.

In the autumn of 1929 the Wall Street Crash suddenly heralded the end of the Roaring Twenties. Hoover faced a very different outlook: bleak depression and lengthening unemployment queues. MacArthur did not have long to wait for the call: in the summer of 1930 he was offered the job of chief of engineers—the highest tribute from Hoover, himself an engineer. MacArthur's task was to embark on public works projects to mop up some of the unemployment resulting from the Crash.

To everyone's astonishment, MacArthur refused. He was holding out for the highest stakes of all: chief of staff. To the new Secretary of War, Patrick J. Hurley, he wrote a letter dripping with flattery. In August 1930 Hoover and Hurley awarded him the post: MacArthur, aware of the difficulties of holding the job in the teeth of a depression, showed unexpected modesty.

> I knew the dreadful ordeal that faced the new Chief of Staff, and shrank from it. I wished from the bottom of my heart to stay with troops in a field command. But my mother, who made her home in Washington, sensed what was in my mind and cabled me to accept. She said my father would be ashamed if I showed timidity. That settled it.

He returned to press accolades as the "d'Artagnan of the army," taking up his residence at Quarters Number One at Fort Myers, across the Potomac River. Pinky, his 77-year-old mother, moved in with him; he was no longer alone.

Unknown to his mother, there was another presence. In Manila at a boxing match, he had glimpsed an apparition of perfect, unsullied beauty: a 16-year-old, the daughter of a Scottish businessman by a Filipino: her name was Isabel Rosario Cooper, and she was—inevitably—a chorus girl. MacArthur was instantly smitten: as with Louise his strong romantic urge merged with his sex drive. She called him "Daddy" and he called her "darling one" and "my baby girl." He wrote desperately how he craved her "deep lips" and "soft body' He said he would die without her. On leaving Manila to take up his new command, he bought her a ticket to follow him discreetly, imagining that she would probably melt into the fleshpots of Shanghai along the way.

When instead she arrived he set her up in a smart apartment with a huge supply of provocative underwear and a poodle for companionship. There he would visit her as often as he could. She was beautiful: one independent observer described her (there are no photographs):

> I thought I had never seen anything as exquisite. She was wearing a lovely, obviously expensive chiffon tea gown, and she looked as if she were carved from the most delicate opaline. She had her hair in braids down her back.

Technically, MacArthur was doing no wrong: he was divorced and she was just of legal age. But the inevitable happened: growing bored of life in an apartment pleasing him when he happened to call, she started going out and having liaisons of her own. She set off on holiday to Havana, with its bright lights and racy lifestyle. Then she fell in love with a law student. MacArthur lost interest and in January 1934 gave her a ticket to return to Manila. He indicated in no uncertain terms that the affair was over. But she wanted more money; and by that time MacArthur had become one of the most hated and controversial figures in Washington.

MacArthur cut a dash from the moment he became chief of staff. He surrounded himself with bright young officers of which two—Dwight Eisenhower and George Patton—were to ascend to much greater prominence. He was easygoing, loquacious and enjoyed intellectual challenge. He was no stickler for military convention, wearing a Japanese kimono at his desk occasionally, and sometimes sporting a jeweled cigarette holder. He was denounced as a poseur by officers irritated at these affectations: but they were part of the showman in

MacArthur, the public relations practitioner that realized modern society craved something out of the ordinary, the trademark and props of an actor—which would have been intolerable in a less talented man.

He had taken office at a time of appalling economic crisis: as war clouds loomed abroad, the cry was for America's tiny military to be much further reduced. The armed forces consisted of just 132,000 men, fewer than those of either Greece or Portugal and little more than $300 million was spent on defense. Its equipment included only 12 postwar tanks, .50 calibre machine guns, and World War One mortars. America's armed forces ranked sixteenth in the world. President Hoover sought to cut them further in order to balance his budget and spend more on job creation. MacArthur refused to attend the 51-nation disarmament conference in Geneva, declaring that "the way to end war is to outlaw war, not disarm." He paid visits to France, Turkey, Romania, Hungary, Poland and Austria, where the small size of the American army was sneered at.

MacArthur was a whirlwind of activity. He elaborated his own strategy, which was farsighted for the time:

> It was plain to see that modern war would be a war of massive striking power, a war of lightning movement, a war of many machines, yet a war with its cutting edge in the hands of but a few skilled operatives. We had learned at bitter price the lesson of the last war, that one new innovation, the perfected machine gun, had foiled plans and planners, and had driven great armies into a stalemate of mud and trench. It was easy for the professional mind to foresee the armored task force of bombing planes, tanks, and supporting motorized columns reviving mobile war.

MacArthur enacted a national industrial mobilization plan and a plan for the general mobilization of manpower in the event of war. He based the defense of America on his "Four-Army plan." He set up the independent air arm which eventually became the United States Air Force. He established a school for an independent armed land force which was to be the embryo of America's armored divisions. For the romantic who had sauntered through the killing grounds of the First World War in cavalry boots and riding crop, all of this was visionary and modernizing after years of stagnation under less imaginative stuffed-shirt generals. He laid the foundations for the huge military machine that was to win the Second World War.

This was not obvious at the time because he lacked the money to pay for any but its earliest implementation. He was a dynamic and inspired leader, and Eisenhower, for one, was captivated (at this stage):

In my opinion, he has the capacity to undertake successfully any position in government. He has a reserved dignity—but he is most animated in conversation on subjects interesting him . . . He is impulsive—able, even brilliant—quick—tenacious of his views and extremely self-confident.

But it was as a political general that he was to make the most—and most hotly contested—impact. As Eisenhower also observed:

Most of the senior officers I had known always drew a clean-cut line between the military and the political. Off duty, among them-selves and close civilian friends, they might explosively denounce everything they thought was wrong with Washington and the world, and propose their own cure for its evils. On duty, nothing could induce them to cross the line they, and old army tradition, had established. But if General MacArthur ever recognized the existence of that line, he usually chose to ignore it.

America was in the throes of perhaps the greatest crisis since the Civil War. The Great Depression had not just plunged millions of Americans into misery: it had called into question the very American dream. The unqualified belief in business and wealth creation, the ostentatious good living of the 1920s, were all under fierce challenge from millions of Americans who had lost their livelihoods and their savings. The puritanical pro-business sentiments of presidents like Coolidge and Hoover had been made to look hollow. Abroad, the logic of communism, amplified by American scaremongers, seemed almost to have been justified by the Great Depression: the final crisis of capitalism predicted by Karl Marx seemed under way. Global revolution might follow as unrest spread across the globe in the wake of economic disaster. In America the liberal politician, Franklin Roosevelt, was assembling a team of "socialists" to seek power in the 1932 presidential election.

In these circumstances, with politics taking a dangerously radical turn and with a seriously circumscribed president, MacArthur saw himself as a crucial buttress for the forces of order—even the man whose destiny might be to save America. The very survival of the republic seemed at stake. MacArthur's small army was one of the few forces that stood between the nation and communism or anarchy. His opponents, however, saw him as a potential dictator, "one of the two most dangerous men in America," as Roosevelt dubbed him (the other being the demagogic Louisiana governor Huey Long)—even a military putschist. The inflammatory simplicism of his views did nothing to dispel the impression that he also believed he was a man of destiny whose time might yet come.

In June 1932, MacArthur addressed students at the University of Pittsburgh in terms that seemed to find an echo in the later era of his near-namesake, Senator Joe McCarthy.

Pacifism and its bedfellow, Communism, are all about us. In the theaters, newspapers and magazines, pulpits and lecture halls, schools and colleges, it hangs like a mist before the face of America, organizing the forces of unrest and undermining the morals of the working man. Day by day this canker eats deeper into the body politic.

For the sentimentalism and emotionalism which have infested our country, we should substitute hard common sense. Pacific habits do not insure peace or immunity from national insult and aggression. Any nation that would keep its self-respect must be prepared to defend itself.

Every reasonable man knows that war is cruel and destructive, and yet very little of the fever of war will melt the veneer of our civilization. History has proved that nations once great, that neglected their national defense are dust and ashes. Where are Rome and Carthage? Where Byzantium? Where Egypt, once so great a state? Where Korea, whose death cries were unheard by the world?

This was highly inflammatory stuff in the middle of a dangerous economic crisis, all the more so coming from America's top soldier, and must have been carefully considered before delivery (it is unlikely he had cleared it with Hoover). As MacArthur wrote later:

The reaction against these concepts was prompt and tremendous. I was roundly denounced not only by pacifists and Communists, but even on the floor of Congress itself. A small group in that august body fancied themselves far better strategists than any general. I was harassed ceaselessly in the effort to force me into acceptance of their appeasement views. I was slandered and smeared almost daily in the press. The propaganda spared neither my professional attributes nor my personal character. It was bitter as gall and I knew that something of the gall would always be with me.

MacArthur was jeered by the 300 students present, one of those occasions when the young were probably right.

It was soon apparent that MacArthur was playing for high stakes: the real game was about to begin. Even before his incendiary speech, some

10,000 "bonus marchers" had arrived in Washington the previous month. The object of their protest was peaceful and constitutional. They were veterans from the First World War, and they had a legitimate demand: made jobless in the Depression, they wanted to redeem immediately a bonus of around $1,000 payable on their deaths or in 1945, whichever came first, which had been approved by Congress in 1934. Legislation had been introduced into Congress to permit them to obtain this.

The marchers, styling themselves the Bonus Expeditionary Force, set up makeshift unsanitary camps on the wasteland around Washington, in particular on an ill-drained piece of land beside the Potomac called Anacastia Flats. They also squatted in a number of derelict buildings along Pennsylvania Avenue which had been condemned to make way for new public buildings. The marchers soon swelled to 25,000 in number and showed no intention of departing: it was the largest and biggest demonstration Washington had ever seen up to then. Their leader was an eloquent former sergeant who had served in France, Walter Waters, from Oregon. The demonstrators staged daily marches to the Capitol, the White House and other government buildings.

As the weather grew hotter, conditions worsened for the men and their families living by open drains. Although supplied with a minimum of food and medicine, their plight deteriorated. At last the bill passed the House of Representatives, but was rejected in the Senate, which was righteously angered by this attempt to coerce through mob rule. Congress then adjourned for the summer. The President appealed for the Bonus Marchers to go home, and offered them the money to do so. The liberal governor of New York State, Franklin Roosevelt, did the same. Many of the marchers took up the offer and drifted away.

But a hard core of around 8,000 remained. Hoover and even the Washington police chief, Pelham D. Glassford, had initially felt some sympathy for the marchers. Yet as tempers frayed and acts of violence became common, along with petty criminality by the marchers against Washington residents, this goodwill began to evaporate. MacArthur had much less time for men "abandoning the plea for justice and adopting in its place threat and coercion." He had taken the precaution of instructing his deputy chief of staff, General Van Horn Mosely, an officer of virtually fascist sympathies and a deep anti-Semitic streak, to move six tanks down from Fort Meade, Maryland, to his headquarters at Fort Myers, and to order reinforcements to Washington. MacArthur's view of the seriousness of the situation grew more and more apocalyptic. He wrote later:

In these days of wholehearted national unity, it is hard to believe that thirty years ago the President of the United States lived in danger, and that Congress shook with fear at the sight and sound of the marchers. It is hard to believe, too, that government employees and other citizens of Washington who bore witness to the tawdry street battles cheered the stoning of the Washington police force.

The movement was actually far deeper and more dangerous than an effort to secure funds from a nearly depleted federal treasury. The American Communist Party planned a riot of such proportions that it was hoped the United States Army, in its efforts to maintain peace, would have to fire on the marchers. In this way, the Communists hoped to incite revolutionary action. Red organizers infiltrated the veteran groups and presently took command from their unwitting leaders.

MacArthur was convinced that Communists had taken control of the marchers:

But the hard core of the Communist bloc not only stayed, but grew. The Federal Bureau of Investigation reported that an examination of the fingerprints of 4,723 Bonus Marchers showed that 1,069 of them were men who had criminal records ranging from drunkenness to murder and rape. Not more than one in ten of those who stayed was a veteran. By this time Waters had been deposed and the Communists had gained control.

In fact the Veterans Administration claimed that nine tenths of the marchers had been ex-servicemen and that two thirds had served overseas. The chief of staff was later to cite the evidence of senior Communists as evidence in his favor. Earl Broeder, the American party leader, had declared that "the bonus revolutionary force in Washington is the most significant beginning of the mass struggle against the deepening consequences of the crisis." John T. Pace, another of the party's leaders, said in 1949:

I led the left wing or communist section of the bonus march. I was ordered by my Red superiors to provoke riots. I was told to use every trick to bring about bloodshed in the hopes that President Hoover would be forced to call out the army. The communists didn't care how many veterans were killed. I was told Moscow had ordered riots and bloodshed in the hopes that this might set off the revolution. My communist bosses were jumping with joy on July 28 when the Washington police killed one veteran.

MacArthur added wryly, some would say paranoically:

During the Bonus March Communist threats continued to be made against responsible officials. I was to be publicly hanged on the steps of the Capitol. It was the beginning of a definite and ceaseless campaign that set me apart as a man to be destroyed, no matter how long the communists and their friends and admirers had to wait, and no matter what means they might have to use. But it was to be nineteen years before the bells of Moscow pealed out their glee at my eclipse.

Glassford, the police chief, had asked soldiers to support the police and twice MacArthur had refused. In fact, with the departure of most of the marchers, the threat had markedly decreased. But the authorities were determined to take the initiative and ordered the evacuation of the buildings they had occupied on Pennsylvania Avenue. Most left peacefully, again belying MacArthur's claim that they were extremists.

Waters, their leader—whom MacArthur wrongly said had been replaced by Communists—went to see Hurley, the Secretary of War, on the afternoon of July 26 and found MacArthur with him. Both were in intransigent moods, MacArthur furiously pacing the room. Hurley told Waters bluntly, "we are interested only in getting you out of the district and we have plenty of troops to force you out." Waters asked that his supporters be allowed to retire with dignity if confronted by the army, not be driven out "like rats." MacArthur impatiently gave him that assurance.

It was clear that the armed forces commander had decided that the moment of truth had come and that the authorities had made the first move toward a showdown: up to now the marchers had been guilty of no more than random acts of violence and turning their camp into a scene of squalor. If the authorities had done nothing, most of the marchers would gradually have drifted away, although a minority might have chosen confrontation.

On the morning of July 28 a handful of the marchers reoccupied a building that they had previously evacuated. The police went in at lunchtime to get them out and a scuffle ensued. Glassford, who was in charge of the operation, was hit with a brick, while another policeman suffered a fractured skull. Four other policemen were slightly injured. This was still small-scale stuff. But the police had become jittery, and when marchers moved on the Capitol as usual, fighting broke out and the police opened fire, shooting two marchers, one of whom died.

At this stage the police, fearing they were losing control, asked MacArthur to use his troops. But the order had to come from the White House, and Hoover refused unless the police request was made in writing. This the police chief did, saying that unless the army intervened it would be "impossible for the police department to maintain law and order except by the free use of firearms. The presence of federal troops in small number will obviate the seriousness of the situation, and it will result in far less violence and bloodshed." That was MacArthur's cue. His high-handed order to the marchers to leave two days earlier had provoked the situation. He later claimed that "a mob 5,000-strong began to move up Pennsylvania Avenue toward the Treasury Building and the White House. The police were outnumbered five to one." In fact, although the mood of the crowd was turning ugly, there was no unified march, only a series of scuffles by milling, dispirited, embittered, heat-dazed protesters.

MacArthur went one stage further. Together with Hurley, he went to see Hoover to urge the imposition of martial law. MacArthur now clearly saw himself as the man of the moment. "MacArthur has decided to go into active command in the field. There is incipient revolution in the air," he declared to one of his aides. He understandably believed there was a Communist revolution gathering and that the weak and unpopular man in the White House—MacArthur was disparaging about Hoover in private—was no match for the situation. Martial law would give MacArthur effective control of the capital and, with the President incapacitated and Congress away, the government. If a showdown had to be fought with the Communist extremists, he would win it.

Then what? With the possibility of Roosevelt winning the presidential election, backed by liberals, pacifists and Communists, MacArthur might have seen it as his duty to prolong martial law, taking advantage of Hoover's weakness; elections might even be postponed. Other similar confrontations had already occurred elsewhere. In Italy Mussolini had taken power in 1922 to avert a Communist takeover: extraordinary measures were required in the face of extraordinary dangers.

But to MacArthur's cold anger, Hoover refused to declare martial law and insisted that the army should act "in support of the police" to restore order in the capital and push the protesters back to Anacostia Flats. MacArthur was seething, yet he had no choice constitutionally but to obey the President. He ordered the 16th Infantry Brigade to cross the Memorial Bridge from Fort Myers. A young commander, George Patton, headed the tanks. Extraordinarily, MacArthur decided to take personal charge of the operation: for a chief of staff to supervize a domestic policing operation was unprecedented: Eisenhower, his politically savvy aide, was deeply dismayed. MacArthur ordered his valet to find a full dress uniform for the occasion. Soon the written order arrived:

> The President has just now informed me that the civil government of the District of Columbia has reported to him that it is unable to maintain law and order in the District.
>
> You will have United States troops proceed immediately to the scene of disorder. Cooperate fully with the District of Columbia police force which is now in charge. Surround the affected area and clear it without delay.
>
> Turn over all prisoners to the civil authorities.
>
> In your orders insist that any women or children who may be in the affected area be accorded every consideration and kindness. Use all humanity consistent with the due execution of the order.

General Percy L. Miles, in charge of the 16th Infantry Brigade, gave his own instructions:

> The cavalry will make a demonstration down Pennsylvania Avenue. The infantry will deploy in line of skirmishers in the rear of the cavalry. You will surround the area and evict the men in possession there. Use care and consideration toward all women and children who may be in the area.

He too resented MacArthur's insistence on taking charge of the operation. The two army officers caught up with the bandaged Glassford, who was directing the police, and far from "cooperating with the District of Columbia police force which is now in charge" as ordered to by Hoover, took charge themselves.

MacArthur put it with characteristic bluntness: he was going "to drive the veterans out of the city. We are going to break the back of the BEF"— as though he were talking about an enemy army, not a ragged group of unarmed American demonstrators. He cited orders from Hoover in his support; no such orders had been issued.

The cavalry advanced on the marchers with the flats of their sabers exposed, the infantry behind them with their bayonets drawn. Tear gas was poured down on the demonstrators, to be met by desultory volleys of stones and the waving of sticks as they retreated. MacArthur was taken aback: the "Communist revolution" did not occur; these desperate men, nine tenths of whom he alleged were not veterans but members of the "Communist block," a fifth of whom he said had criminal records, did not fight back, or make a stand to be mown down. Sadly, dispiritedly, they retreated before the overwhelming show of force. Only a few were hurt, no one was killed—which said as much for their peaceful intentions as for the army's excellent discipline. The Communist revolution had turned out to be a dud.

Arriving at the bridge leading to the camp at Anacastia Flats, MacArthur received an emissary of Waters who asked for time to evacuate the women and children from the camp so that they should not see the swords and bayonets. MacArthur agreed and ordered his men to stop for dinner for two hours as night fell. Hoover, who was opposed to the troops crossing the bridge and occupying the camp and had given no orders that this be done, asked Hurley to instruct MacArthur not to cross.

Hurley sent instructions by two emissaries, one of them the hardline General Moseley, who claimed he had delivered the message to MacArthur, who he said had been visibly angered. But Eisenhower and Miles, much more reliable witnesses, denied that he had been given the order—although Eisenhower also reported that MacArthur had declared himself "too busy" to receive orders. Another witness claimed that Moseley suppressed the order. Moseley is also believed to have told the officer delivering the duplicate order to "get lost" and he disappeared for three hours before reaching MacArthur. There must be some question of whether Moseley was acting on his own initiative, or on MacArthur's prior instructions.

MacArthur's forces crossed the bridge: the few remaining marchers set fire to the camp as a last protest. The chief of staff returned to the War Department as reservists and police occupied the camp, meeting little resistance; wild allegations of deaths and that a seven-year-old boy had been wounded trying to rescue his pet rabbit were exposed as fabrications. After reporting to Hoover and Hurley, MacArthur held a triumphal press conference:

> If President Hoover had not acted when he did he would have been faced with a serious situation. Another week might have meant that the government was in peril. He had reached the end of an extraordinary patience and had gone to the very limit to avoid friction before using force. Had the President not acted when he did he would have been derelict in his duty.

He denied that he had said the United States faced "incipient revolution." But Hoover was incandescent that his orders had been ignored and that

MacArthur had briefly taken charge. The president upbraided MacArthur the following day and the latter offered to resign as chief of staff—an offer he knew would be refused, as it would have made Hoover's political position even less tenable.

MacArthur had been frustrated by two things: the marchers were not an organized Communist conspiracy and dispersed peacefully at the end; and the backlash from the civilian opposition was fast and furious. Roosevelt and other liberal politicians understood exactly what had happened: MacArthur was thunderously denounced. As he remarked bitterly later:

> The most extravagant distortions of what had occurred were widely circulated. I was violently attacked, and even blatantly misrepresented before Congress. Speeches pictured me in full dress uniform astride a fiery white charger, bedecked with medals, waving a bloody saber, and leading a mad cavalry charge against unarmed and innocent citizens. Of course there was absolutely no foundation for such statements. There was no cavalry charge. There was no fiery white charger. There was no saber. There was no full dress uniform. There were no medals. I wore the same uniform as the troops. When I challenged such distortions, they were merely shrugged off with the expression, "it was only politics." Franklin Roosevelt once said to me, "Douglas, I think you are our best general, but I believe you would be our worst politician." With his rare sense of humor, I wonder which side of that remark he thought was the compliment.

MacArthur's argument that the government would have been in peril a week later had he failed to act was not only specious, it was an admission that the government was in no real danger on July 28 itself. He had exaggerated the threat. The only arguable benefit to emerge from the whole fiasco was to show how viciously the government would lash out if confronted by any challenge to the social order in the Depression—even a legitimate one by its own veterans. It served as a warning light to the suffering millions in America.

The major consequence of the whole affair was the precise opposite to the one MacArthur had intended. Public opinion was appalled. Hoover had proved himself incapable of responding to the giant challenges raised by the Depression and had apparently shown that he would resort to crude repression if necessary. The American people flocked to the polls to turn the Republicans out of the White House and to put that extraordinary figure, Franklin D. Roosevelt, into power.

22 : THE TWO GIANTS

MACARTHUR WATCHED WITH GRIM APPREHENSION AS ROOSEVELT SWEPT to power with nearly 23 million votes to Hoover's fewer than 16 million, and the Democrats seized control of both houses of Congress. To MacArthur it almost seemed that the very forces of communism and revolution had won at the ballot box.

Roosevelt, a patrician who had worked with MacArthur in the past and was so wily that he had secured the support and respect of New York's legendary Tammany Hall powerbrokers, made an unlikely revolutionary. But he was surrounded by radical and extremely young advisers and he had won office with all the skills of the world's finest demagogue—hugely charismatic, projecting optimism and a broad smile, declaring that "the only thing we have to fear is fear itself." He proclaimed a New Deal for America and used as his campaign song, "Happy Days are Here Again." His mandate and his control of Congress gave him virtually dictatorial power, and he promptly demanded more—emergency powers "as great as the power that would be given to me if we were in fact invaded by a foreign foe."

He promptly threw himself into extending Hoover's interventionist policies to such huge programs as the Tennessee Valley Authority. But his most significant step was to close the banks, then reopen them under the Emergency Banking Restructuring Act, which liquidated 1,000 insolvent banks and gave the promise of government support to the rest, in exchange for a shareholding in the banks—in effect, the banking system was nationalized. This restored confidence. Roosevelt also laid down the foundations of a welfare state—which because of the absence of funding remained small throughout his presidency. He continually denounced the business community, even using the office of the presidency to harass his opponents.

His second election was a walkover—28 million votes to 17 million—although economic recovery remained painfully slow. By 1940 he had won another landslide—27 million to 22 million—against an appealing Republican challenger, Wendell Willkie. Lifelong Republicans could only watch, powerless to act, as this elected dictator (the Democratic majority in Congress was 334 to 89 and in the Senate 75 to 17 in 1936) acquired unheard-of power and extended the role of government in America to entirely new dimensions. Although many regarded Roosevelt as little more than a Fascist or a Communist, his great achievement was to defuse the potential for extremism in America. Unscrupulous and even brutal at times, he was essentially a moderate and a constitutionalist. Yet he made the struggling American people feel that they had their own man in the White House—which was remarkable for a man born with a silver spoon in his mouth. His superb public relations skills carried the mass of the American people with him, even as recovery was painfully slow in coming: otherwise the pressure for revolution, disorder on the streets or even a military solution might have become overwhelming.

In his relations with MacArthur Roosevelt displayed the political skills for which he was famous—indeed, one of the foremost practitioners in world history. He could have chosen to confront this unbending Republican, the standard-bearer of the right who had crushed the Bonus Marchers, by dismissing him (he still had a year of his term as chief of staff to run). Instead Roosevelt conscripted MacArthur, appealing to his sense of patriotism and duty while, like a boa constrictor, squeezing the credibility he had with his supporters completely out of him, leaving him a lifeless shell. He first mesmerized, then swallowed, the general. MacArthur's attitude to Roosevelt reflects his confusion in dealing with this political grand master:

> He became the leading liberal of the age. Whether his vision of economic and political freedom is within the realm of fruition, only future history can tell. That his means for accomplishment won him the almost idolatrous devotion of an immeasurable following is known to all. That they aroused bitterness and resentment in others is equally true. In my own case, whatever differences arose between us, it never sullied in the slightest degree the warmth of my personal friendship for him.

Roosevelt, indeed, seems to have been the only mortal MacArthur considered his equal, or even his superior. The President's first move was to appeal to MacArthur for help: he asked the army to administer the Civilian Conservation Corps, a job creation program for the young unemployed which aimed to enroll 300,000 people within six months.

MacArthur was seduced, in spite of the doubts of many brother officers: "My time with the Civilian Conservation Corps has been a real inspiration for me. It was a type of human reconstruction that has appeal to me more than I sometimes admit." However, many people inside the new administration were gunning for him; Harold Ickes, the waspish Interior Secretary, intensely disliked him, as did many administration figures who referred to him as "the man on the white horse." (He had in fact ridden on a white horse at Roosevelt's inauguration, in place of the indisposed General Pershing—not against the Bonus Marchers, as his enemies frequently alleged.)

News now leaked of a Wall Street financier's plot to start a new bonus march of half a million veterans, with the object, ironically, of putting MacArthur into the White House in a kind of a military coup—which MacArthur, who had never been approached, laughed off.

Ickes and the army's enemies wanted Roosevelt to slash the military budget, arguing that it should reduce its high command from 105 senior officers to just 15. The Bureau of the Budget proposed a military budget for 1934 of just $190 million—a third less than that proposed by the outgoing Hoover administration. MacArthur was appalled: he went to see Roosevelt:

> I felt it my duty to take up the cudgels. The country's safety was at stake, and I said so bluntly. The President turned the full vials of his sarcasm upon me. He was a scorcher when aroused. The tension began to boil over. For the third and last time in my life that paralyzing nausea began to creep over me. In my emotional exhaustion I spoke recklessly and said something to the general effect that when we lost the next war, and an American boy, lying in the mud with an enemy bayonet through his belly and an enemy foot on his dying throat, spat out his last curse, I wanted the name not to be MacArthur, but Roosevelt. The President grew livid. "You must not talk that way to the President!" he roared. He was, of course, right, and I knew it almost before the words had left my mouth. I said that I was sorry and apologized. But I felt my Army career was at an end. I told him he had my resignation as Chief of Staff. As I reached the door his voice came with that cool detachment which so reflected his extraordinary self-control, "Don't be foolish, Douglas; you and the budget must get together on this."
>
> Dern [the Army Secretary] had shortly reached my side and I could hear his gleeful tones, "You've saved the Army." But I just vomited on the steps of the White House.

The result was a budget of $278 million—still far too small in MacArthur's estimation. He nevertheless had been won over by Roosevelt's charm, and went frequently to see him in private. When congressional hearings were called to examine the following year's budget MacArthur broke all constitutional precedent by asking Congress to approve more than the Budget Bureau had proposed—$305 million compared to $289 million. He pointed out that the army had only 12 modern tanks in service and just six times as many men as the New York Police Department. In an illuminating exchange of ruffled vanity, a congressman, picking over the defense budget, read out the appropriation for lavatory paper and asked: "General, do you expect a serious epidemic of dysentery in the U.S. Army?"

MacArthur replied, "I have humiliated myself. I have almost licked the boots of some gentlemen to get funds for the motorization and mechanization of the army. Now, gentlemen, you have insulted me. I am as high in my profession as you are in yours. When you are ready to apologize, I shall be back."

But it was all to no avail. In 1935 Congress awarded the army $284 million—exactly the amount the Budget Bureau had sought—although MacArthur's tactic may have been designed to prevent even this being pruned.

With that rebuff behind him, MacArthur was assailed by a new indignity in the summer of 1934: he had had enough of the constant sniping of the venomous columnist Drew Pearson, who had described him as "dictatorial, insubordinate, disloyal, mutinous and disrespectful of his superiors in the War Department." MacArthur sued. But Pearson found out about his affair with Isabel which the general had just broken off. Isabel sold 23 intimate letters from MacArthur to Pearson and offered to go into the witness stand against him (the embittered Louise had been too shy to do so). She was prepared to say that he habitually referred to Roosevelt as "that cripple in the White House" and that he had remarked of Hoover that he was "a weakling, but I finally put some backbone into him."

MacArthur had done nothing illegal, but feared the ridicule the publicity would create. Worse, his aged mother would hear of the affair. He paid Isabel $15,000 to keep quiet and dropped the libel action. She married her boyfriend, and moved to Hollywood. Ickes and Pearson believed that MacArthur had had her murdered. In fact she failed to become a film star and, impoverished, committed suicide in 1960 aged just 47.

Roosevelt, having utterly neutralized MacArthur, could have seized the chance of being rid of him when his traditional four-year term was up. But for reasons that are still unclear—perhaps further to diminish his reputation on the right, perhaps out of a grudging respect, perhaps so that he could appoint his own choice to succeed MacArthur—he gave him a further year in office.

The chief of staff resumed sparring with Congress: with Germany and Japan both rearming, the dangerous state of America's armed forces had at last become apparent. MacArthur sought a budget of $361 million and an increase in troop levels of 40,000, but the Budget Bureau reduced the demand to $331 million. To his own surprise he got $363 million—more than his original request—and all 40,000 men. "The turn has at last been reached," he exclaimed exultantly. He went out with a valedictory address to his beloved Rainbow Division veterans:

> They died unquestioningly, uncomplaining, with faith in their hearts and on their lips the hope that we would go on to victory . . . They have gone beyond the mists that blind us here, and become part of that beautiful thing we call the spirit of the unknown soldier. In chambered temples of silence the dust of their dauntless valor sleeps, waiting, waiting in the Chancery of Heaven the final reckoning of Judgment Day. "Only those are fit to live who are not afraid to die."

Roosevelt offered him a wonderful present to speed him on his retirement (he was still only 54, a comparatively young general and capable of making mischief in the army): the post of governor-general of the Philippines where a Filipino, his old friend Manuel Quezon, had just been elected president of what was in effect an independent government. The post would get MacArthur, with his troublesome penchant for meddling in politics, out of the way and into a gilded cage.

But MacArthur had also been offered two jobs as, in effect, a paid mercenary: running the Chinese army, by the country's dictator, Chiang Kai-Shek; and running the Philippines armed forces, which were still American-led, by Quezon. The first he regarded as an impossible task: pulling together the armies of several warlords and working under the notoriously capricious Chiang. The second offered the prospect of an active retirement in his beloved Philippines. Telling Roosevelt he could not resign as a soldier (which accepting the governor-generalship entailed, one of the devious President's many calculations) he accepted the second offer. Roosevelt was furious. MacArthur, the best-known general in the army, would remain on active service and a rallying point for political opponents. He said farewell with grace, however, meaning not a word of it: "Douglas, if war should suddenly come, don't wait for orders to come home. Grab the first transportation you can find. I want you to command my armies."

In an act of brutal pettiness, the moment MacArthur left Washington by rail to sail from San Francisco, the President relieved his chief of staff two months before he had promised and installed his own nominee, General Malin Craig. MacArthur had been deprived of his departing and arriving honors as chief of staff and a four-star general. According to Eisenhower, MacArthur heard this news with "an explosive denunciation of politics, bad manners, bad judgment, broken promises, arrogance, unconstitutionality, insensitivity, and the way the world had gone to hell."

As he traveled to Manila, MacArthur had plenty of time to reflect on the twists of fate. He had enjoyed one of the most brilliant careers in American military history, becoming chief of staff at the age of 50. Now he was prematurely and effectively retired at just 55, a man of vigor and intelligence still at the height of his powers acting as a mercenary for a foreign government (he had ensured he would be paid a performance bonus of $250,000 on top of his actual salary of $15,000 and $15,000 a year expenses—a giant leap for a man on $7,500 a year up to then and a huge amount of money for the time, at last bringing the prospect of wealth to the impecunious MacArthur).

Moreover, while still enjoying the respect of those that worked for him, and probably believing he had saved the American army from virtual extinction during the Depression years, his professional reputation was in ruins. He had been vilified by his many enemies to the American people as "the man on the white horse" with a bloodied saber, who had repressed his own impoverished combat veterans. He had presided over the worst years for the American military in history, with spending sharply cut until the turning point of 1936. He had seemingly lacked the courage to stand up to Roosevelt and his cronies and resign. The verdict of many, as he well knew, was that one of the youngest chiefs of staff of the American army had also been one of the worst.

Up to the final stage in MacArthur's career, he seems a largely two-dimensional figure: a man of huge intellect and leadership qualities certainly, but one of limited vision—a highly capable and exceedingly brave soldier, but no more. The flamboyance, the grandstanding, the showing off in battle, the self-promotion, the leading of his men from the front in the First World War were all highly attractive in a dashing soldier, but were hardly suggestive of real depth to the man. His reforms at West Point were those favored by most enlightened younger soldiers of the time. His flair for public relations made him a figure thoroughly in touch with the age, but again suggested a certain superficiality about his persona.

His controversial career as chief of staff exhibited him in a much more critical, even harshly unattractive, light: he became positively obnoxious to many. His railing against communism at the time of the Great Depression shows him to have been a political neophyte possessed of a crude and unsympathetic approach not just toward ex-servicemen with legitimate grievances, but American liberals and those suffering the terrible effects of the recession alike.

His actions during the Bonus March bordered on the unconstitutional, and it was more by luck than by design that they did not lead to a bloodbath of unarmed and innocent people in central Washington: he had displayed a crass defect of most soldiers confronted by the complexities of a tricky political confrontation—to treat ordinary fellow citizens as though they were an enemy. His attempt to fight for defense appropriations through the unfavorable climate of Depression America was admirable, and he should be credited for discerning the international storm clouds just over the horizon. With his departure to become a generalissimo in the Philippines, a touch of the ridiculous now also attached to this seemingly simplistic, right-wing martinet in the twilight of his career.

Now professional annihilation loomed, albeit of a particularly comfortable kind, as organizer of a fledgling army in an American protectorate. Having exceeded his father in achievement, he was one of the youngest has-beens in American history. Only the possibility that his predictions of imminent war might turn out to be true excited him: for he had planted himself in the front line of any potential war with Japan—where indeed, earlier that year, in a fateful shift of power, the military had hardened its grip around the throne of Emperor Hirohito. Nine months after MacArthur's arrival in Manila, Japan invaded China.

Personal problems of the most painful kind were also on his mind as he made that long journey across the Pacific. His 84-year-old mother, who had been indisposed before, but had rallied so many times, was seriously ill, and had broken her arm. She was confined to her cabin and nursed by MacArthur's devoted sister-in-law, the widow of Arthur, Mary. MacArthur faced the prospect of personal loneliness along with professional oblivion. But on the same voyage, he was introduced to an unmarried 35-year-old woman, Jean Faircloth from Tennessee.

Her attractions were not immediately obvious: she was tiny—five foot two—and slender, with a bony, toothy, wide-mouthed smile that bordered on the goofy. Her distinctive high cheekbones gave her a slightly cadaverous look. But she had a lively and cheerful personality, and from the start got on extremely well with the general. She possessed a quick intelligence and preparedness to accommodate his every whim that had been noticeably missing from his previous two female partners. Unlike independent and wayward Louise, she was prepared to devote herself to MacArthur; unlike Isabel, she was mature and intelligent—not a sex object at all. She was attractive, motherly without dominating him and a kind of army adjutant all at the same time.

She herself was captivated by the military life, and MacArthur as an ex–chief of staff inspired awe in her at first. She had substantial independent means, having inherited some $200,000 from her father, a prosperous Tennessee businessman. She had the same conservative political instincts as MacArthur, having worked for the Daughters of the Confederacy and the Daughters of the American Revolution.

MacArthur, perhaps sensing and fearing the loneliness that otherwise lay in prospect, would meet her frequently for breakfast on the voyage before returning to his ailing mother's cabin, where he would spend the rest of the day. A month after his arrival in manila Pinky died of cerebral thrombosis. He was devastated and deeply depressed for as long as a year.

Now he needed adult companionship: and an adult was waiting in a Manila hotel. Jean Faircloth had an extraordinary ability both to provide the equality of an intelligent and self-confident woman and yet to look up to MacArthur and give him the devotion of a daughter or a mother. When they were married in New York in April 1937, MacArthur declared, "[T]his is for keeps." He turned out to be right. Ten months later a child was born, Arthur.

The couple made their home in a splendid penthouse on the top floor of the Manila Hotel, a magnificent wood-paneled building overlooking the Bay. There at last MacArthur found conjugal happiness, and the down-to-earth Jean was delighted to settle into the conventionality of Manila expatriate society, unlike the glamorous Louise. She also seemed able to put up with MacArthur's psychological quirks. He reveled in the unaccustomed role of father, spoiling the little boy shamelessly.

He led a routine life in his luxury pad, barely indulging in alcohol, his one vice being smoking cigarettes through elaborate holders, as well as a variety of pipes including the corncob that was to become so celebrated, and a cigar in the evening. Lieutenant Sidney Huff offered a vivid picture:

> The General lighted a cigarette—this was before his pipe-smoking days—and immediately put it down on his desk and started walking back and forth across the room . . . He stuck his hands in his hip pockets as he paced, his jaw jutted out a little and he began talking in that deep, resonant voice—thinking out loud. From time to time he paused beside the wide mahogany desk to push the cigarette neatly into line with the edge of the ash tray, and to glance over at me. "Do you follow me, Sid?" he asked, swinging into his pacing stride again. Or sometimes he would stop at the

desk to line up a dozen pencils that were already in a neat pattern—or to turn them around and push the points carefully into line. But always he went back to pacing and to thinking out loud.

While inspiring devotion in a small coterie, MacArthur was aloof and unsociable toward outsiders: Filipinos respected him, but members of the American community were often offended by his lack of gregariousness or democratic affability toward them. He was imperious and vain, changing three times a day to present an immaculate appearance in the sultry Philippine climate. Yet he had shown an ability in public relations that was far in advance of most soldiers of his time.

The solution to the extraordinary paradox of MacArthur's personality was probably quite simple: he was nice to anyone that was of use to him— be they his closest lieutenants or journalists. Toward the rest he was indifferent, as befitted the natural leader he believed himself to be, and one of high intelligence, which was undoubted.

The controversial former chief of staff had not yet outrun his bad luck. Lured by the islands he loved so well and the prospect of becoming a rich man for the first time, MacArthur had set himself an impossible task. The Philippines were simply not defensible. On arriving MacArthur lied glibly to Quezon about the virtues of the moth-eaten Orange Plan, which provided for a retreat to the Bataan Peninsula in the event of an overwhelming invasion in the hope that reinforcements would arrive from the United States within six months:

> I was in complete disagreement with the Orange Plan when I became Chief of Staff but I realized at once I would be wasting my time in trying to educate others to my point of view. I, therefore, short-circuited it by seeing the President personally and telling him that if mobilization became necessary during my tenure of office that my first step would be to send two divisions from the Atlantic coast to reinforce the Philippines . . . that I intended to defend every inch of those possessions and defend them successfully. This being the case, the Orange Plan was a completely useless document . . . the man who is in command at the time will be the man who will determine the main features of the campaign. If he is a big man he will pay no more attention to the stereotyped plans that may be filed in the dusty pigeon holes of the War Department than their merit warrants.

MacArthur was being absurd: the entire American army consisted of just three divisions. There would be no reinforcement. His second plan was, however, realistic and with Eisenhower he set about implementing it. The two best minds in the American army perhaps ever came up with the idea of setting up a regular force—920 officers and 100,000 recruits—and a huge militia, 40,000 of them to be trained every year. The idea was to create an enormous reserve which, if the islands were invaded, would be able to become a gigantic guerrilla army, harassing any enemy occupier out of the country.

The problem was money: it would cost $80 million—a colossal sum for the impoverished Philippines, and the United States was unwilling to pay. A year later the price tag had risen to $105 million. Another difficulty was that the organization was not in place to start training the militia until 1937. Finally, Filipinos spoke eight different languages and 87 different dialects. MacArthur's and Eisenhower's ideas were not in error: they were simply impossible to put into practice.

Where they were wrong was in suggesting that the archipelago could be defended at sea by just 50 motor torpedo boats and a handful of decrepit aircraft. The reason was not just that they could obtain nothing better, but that they grossly underestimated the Japanese. Both MacArthur and Eisenhower, remembering the lessons of Gallipoli in the First World War, considered amphibious operations to be impossible to stage successfully: they believed that guerrilla warfare could not be defeated—it would take 100,000 soldiers to defeat 20,000 insurgents, according to the textbooks; and they regarded the Japanese armed forces as a joke: worse, they did not believe that Japan would wage war. "I do not agree with those who predict an imminent war," declared MacArthur in the summer of 1937. "The complete state of preparedness of practically all nations is the surest preventative of war." This was MacArthur at his blustering worst.

What he was right about was his perception of the Philippines as being of key strategic importance. His views were widely dismissed in Washington as MacArthur having gone native. With his father having served there and he on his fourth tour of duty, he could be attacked as merely defending his patch. Yet he argued:

> What I am doing is far more than merely accomplishing the security of the Philippine islands . . . We are actually building up [the] fatally weak left wing of our Pacific defense. We have never secured our Navy base here and the Navy has never really been able to concentrate here. All this will be changed now . . . Our real Pacific line should extend from Alaska to the Philippines. This would call for a naval base in Alaska. When this is accomplished, our line—Alaska, Philippines—will lie athwart every trade

route in the Pacific and give us complete control of the Pacific problem . . .
The old defeatist line of Alaska, Hawaii and Panama, was in my opinion
fatally defective . . . it pitched the potential battle areas on our own coast
and, second, destroyed the maneuvering potentialities of the fleet . . .

The American general staff begged to disagree: they did not regard the
Philippines as particularly important, being much further from the
American coast than the nearest point with Japan. In any event they considered the archipelago indefensible, consisting of more than 7,000 islands
with a coastline longer than that of the United States. Luzon alone had 250
miles of possible landing beaches.

But they also missed the point: the Philippines were a potential Trojan
horse in the midst of any possible Japanese attempt to dominate the Pacific—
the Japanese were compelled to occupy them to secure victory in Asia, as they
straddled the lines of communication to the south; and they were also a huge
possible stationary aircraft carrier for any American assault on Japan: if the
Philippines fell into enemy hands, the Japanese mainland would become virtually indefensible. About this MacArthur was absolutely right; but this particular argument was to rage for nearly a decade.

Meanwhile MacArthur was left twisting in the wind, starved of funds
from Washington to create his guerrilla army. He took refuge in impressing
his boss, Manuel Quezon, godfather to Arthur. He accepted the extraordinary rank of field marshal from Quezon (in fact he suggested the idea)
which no American soldier had ever held before, sporting a self-designed
uniform of black trousers, a white tunic regaled with gold braid and medals
and a cap laden with gold braid surmounted by an American eagle. All of
this made him an object of derision among Americans, some of whom
thought he had gone mad, but it seemed to impress Quezon.

The Philippine leader accompanied MacArthur on a visit to the United
States in January 1937. They stopped at Tokyo on the way. There Quezon
was received by Emperor Hirohito, with MacArthur in attendance. Very
little is known about this meeting, which was largely one of protocol. It
was the first time the two men had set eyes on each other.

The 37-year-old was at the height of his authority as god-Emperor,
although real power was of course exercised by the military clique that had
been in absolute control for nearly a year. Hirohito at the time was a tight-
lipped, dutiful, disciplined and inscrutable icon, with a trace of arrogance in
his impeccable courtesy. He must have viewed Quezon, a man who for all his
intelligence and political cunning was a bon vivant who enjoyed making love

and gambling through the night in Manila, with contempt. MacArthur—tall, formal, austere and official—may have made a better impression: but he was in his late fifties, past his prime, an unlikely threat to the invincible Japanese. To MacArthur the emperor was little more than an object of curiosity. He viewed the god-Emperor as a purely constitutional monarch, and Japan as a military paper tiger. And yet he knew that Japan was the only country that posed a threat to the Philippines. Later he was to write of the visit:

> Cooped up within the narrow land mass of their four main islands, the Japanese were barely able to feed their burgeoning population. Equipped with a splendid labor force, they lacked the raw materials necessary for increased productivity. They lacked sugar, so they took Formosa. They lacked iron, so they took Manchuria. They lacked hard coal and timber, so they invaded China. They lacked security, so they took Korea. Without the products these nations possessed, their industry could be strangled, millions of their laborers thrown out of work, and an economic disaster precipitated that might easily lead to revolution.
>
> They still lacked the nickel and minerals of Malaya, the oil and rubber of the Dutch East Indies, and the rice and cotton of Burma and Siam. It was easy to see that they intended, by force of arms if necessary . . . to establish an economic sphere completely under their own control. There was nothing in the Philippines they coveted except its strategic position, and Quezon was hopeful to the very end that his country might escape the blow. He was cordially received in Tokyo, but the old friendship toward me had been replaced by a thinly veiled hostility.

The somewhat comical pair then proceeded to Los Angeles, Quezon landing at once to enjoy life in New York, ignoring the irate President. When MacArthur sought an invitation for himself and his boss to see Roosevelt, he was told they would have just five minutes of the President's time. The meeting lasted five hours, with Quezon demanding full independence for the Philippines in 1938. The exasperated President refused and decided that MacArthur's antics in the Philippines were not just comical but dangerous and provocative to the Japanese. He ordered him to give up his command and return to America.

MacArthur, who received the order upon his arrival in Manila, was shocked:

> Your letter has amazed me. The action suggested would constitute my summary relief . . . Considering rank and position it can only be interpreted

as constituting disciplinary action . . . my good name and professional reputation are threatened by the proposed action . . . almost forty years of loyal and devoted service should insure for me the same just treatment and reasonable consideration that our army has traditionally and rigidly observed toward even its rawest recruit.

He handed in his resignation from his beloved U.S. army as of December 31: he would continue to serve Quezon in a purely private capacity. He had been outwitted by Roosevelt again: the President had finally eased MacArthur out of the army and neutralized his influence there, and he could disown any of MacArthur's subsequent actions in the Philippines as those of a private citizen.

Yet there were wider implications: by the time he received Roosevelt's orders, the strategic situation in the Far East had worsened dramatically: Japan had invaded China, and MacArthur now believed it was Japan's intention to attack the archipelago. The invasion had two other huge implications: Quezon watched in horror as China's supposedly strong army collapsed under the impact of the Japanese attack. He looked through MacArthur's bluster and saw the grim reality: poorly paid and ill-trained Filipino reservists would be no match for Japan. America was unwilling to pay for the Philippines' defense and had effectively written off the islands. After all, if Quezon wanted independence he could look to his own defenses. He realistically decided that the Philippines should not, after all, make a stand and looked upon MacArthur, who now no longer represented the United States but was merely his own employee, as sadly diminished.

Quezon traveled again to Tokyo, on his own this time, to ask whether the Japanese might consider "neutrality" for the islands; and he opposed MacArthur's militia strategy, arguing that it would merely antagonize the Japanese. On one occasion he refused to see MacArthur. When the general was informed, he said to the President's secretary: "Some day your boss is going to want to see me much more than I want to see him."

Eisenhower could smell the decay surrounding his beleaguered chief: always something of an opportunist, he had no intention of staying around as mate aboard a sinking ship. His career would be adversely affected if he remained with a quixotic aging general no longer serving in the United States army in a country that was likely to lose any confrontation with Japan. At the end of 1939 he left. He had long decided, in a thinly veiled barb at MacArthur:

There are no "great men" as we understood that expression when we were shavers. The man whose brain is so all-embracing in its grasp of events, so infallible in its logic, and so swift in formulation of perfect decisions, is only a figment of the imagination.

MacArthur privately resented this act of betrayal for the rest of his life: he was later to describe Eisenhower as "the best clerk I ever had." But prima donna that he was, he was no fool: the two remained professional friends, corresponding frequently. Sadly, in Eisenhower's place, MacArthur now began to acquire the medieval court his autocratic style of leadership had always been prone to. As MacArthur was no longer viewed in Washington as being even in the American army, many of the American officers available to him on secondment to the Philippine army were pretty mediocre, and lasted with him throughout the tumultuous years that followed.

Replacing Eisenhower as his right-hand men were Lieutenant-Colonel Richard Sutherland, a hard, tough, brusque Yankee grandee who did not suffer fools gladly; Sidney Huff, a former naval lieutenant promoted to lieutenant-colonel; and Colonel Charles Willoughby, a large German-born American whose original name had been Karl Weidenbach, who spoke in a thick German accent and openly admired dictatorship. These men were useful executives, highly efficient in carrying out the boss's orders; but they were no intellectual match for MacArthur, who henceforth retired further into his inner conviction that he was always right and, moreover, a child of destiny. As he told a bemused Theodore White, then a junior journalist at *Time* magazine, "It was destiny that brought us here, White, destiny! By God it is destiny that brings me here now."

23 : CORREGIDOR AND BATAAN

WITH THE OUTBREAK OF WAR IN EUROPE IN SEPTEMBER 1939, NEITHER MacArthur nor Washington could have been under any illusions about the approaching danger. Yet as MacArthur showered requests for military assistance upon Washington he was met with a blank refusal. Part of the trouble was that MacArthur was no longer an American general. Another part was that the Americans not only considered the Philippines indefensible but felt that if they should enter the war, they should concentrate their main effort on Europe. Nothing happened.

Another year and a half passed. By May 1941, the demoralized MacArthur wrote to the new chief of staff that he would return home if no help was offered. His interlocutor was none other than his old adversary from the days of Fort Leavenworth and the Chaumont clique around General Pershing in the First World War, George C. Marshall. With confrontation with Japan fast approaching, the army could clearly not dispense with MacArthur's abilities. A month later Marshall responded: he had decided

> That your outstanding qualifications and vast experience in the Philippines make you the logical selection for the Army in the Far East should the situation approach a crisis. The Secretary has delayed recommending your appointment as he does not feel the time has arrived for such action. However, he has authorized me to tell you that, at the proper time, he will recommend to the President that you be so appointed. It is my impression that the President will approve his recommendation.

The following month the appointment was confirmed: MacArthur was back as a lieutenant-general in the highest echelons of the American army.

The same month the Japanese had occupied part of Indochina after bludgeoning the Vichy government in France to allow them in: they now threatened all of Indochina. Roosevelt's reply—after first placing MacArthur in charge of a unified Philippine defense—was to freeze Japanese assets in America and to declare an embargo on oil, iron and rubber exports to Japan. The British and the Dutch joined the embargo. The Japanese were surprised by the vigor of the American response, and were left with no alternative but ignominious retreat or an invasion of Malaysia and the Dutch East Indies to obtain these resources.

The Philippines were in the way. On hearing the fateful news, MacArthur said to his chief of staff, "I feel like an old dog in a new uniform." Sutherland told him, "You know, general, it adds up to an insurmountable task." But Quezon was overjoyed by MacArthur's new appointment, concluding that the Philippines at last had the active support of the United States. MacArthur took the view that the Japanese invasion would come in April 1942 after the monsoon: he had nine months to prepare. But American supplies were still slow in coming—just 6,000 new troops arriving in December out of a promised 50,000, along with a handful of dud mortar shells, and a few tanks. The promised aircraft never arrived.

Yet MacArthur, at last recognized after years of neglect from Washington, was now in a trance of optimism, believing preparations would be in place by the spring. His plan was, as usual, daring in the extreme: scorning the old

Orange Plan, which called for a retreat into Bataan, he proposed to attack the enemy as it landed on the beaches. This involved placing the army's supply depots on the central plain of Luzon, outside Manila. There had been a huge number of "immigrants" arriving from Japan, who were really Japanese soldiers spying out the land; as war approached many left. Meanwhile huge convoys of Japanese ships passed the islands, staging exercises.

MacArthur decided, as a precaution, to move the 35 B-17s based at Clark Air Field, 70 miles north of Manila, down to Del Monte air base on the island of Mindanao where they would be out of range of Japan's aircraft. But Lewis Brereton, his air force commander, knew this to be unpopular among his pilots, as there were no rest facilities there, and ignored the order until a furious Sutherland berated him on December 4. Brereton sent only 16 of the aircraft down south.

At 4 A.M. on the night of December 8 (December 9 in Hawaii) MacArthur was awoken by the news of the Japanese attack on Pearl Harbor. He was told that "considerable damage" had been inflicted and that an invasion of the Philippines "in the near future" was a strong possibility. MacArthur read his Bible for a while in shock. Like other American commanders, he had believed Hawaii to be virtually impregnable: the Japanese could not risk an assault there, and could not cross the Pacific without being detected.

As numbed officers congregated in MacArthur's office, Brereton said it was his intention to attack Formosa by air. MacArthur had not arrived but Sutherland told the air force commander to wait. Brereton, a timid man, made no real attempt to persuade MacArthur. "Our task is defensive, but stand by for orders," MacArthur told him. Meanwhile reports came in of an attack on a seaplane and two patrol boats in Davao by Japanese aircraft. Fighters also strafed a radio station on the north of Luzon. But MacArthur did not hear of these attacks until 10 A.M., three hours after they occurred. Brereton had sensibly scrambled his B-17s into the air in case of a dawn attack, but they were now running short of fuel and had to land. The mystery was why the Japanese had not yet attacked. By 10 A.M. the uncharacteristically indecisive MacArthur had at last issued the order authorizing the air force to attack Formosa.

While the B-17s were refueling, Brereton also ordered all his P-40 fighters to land for refueling at Iba airfield—whereas he should have taken the precaution of keeping at least half in the air while the others refueled, or made them land south, out of Japanese range. Why had MacArthur delayed so long in giving the order to attack? He later claimed:

When this report reached me, I was still under the impression that the Japanese had suffered a setback at Pearl Harbor, and their failure to close in on me supported that belief. I therefore contemplated an air reconnaissance to the north, using bombers with fighter protection, to ascertain a true estimate of the situation and to exploit any possible weaknesses that might develop on the enemy's front.

There are suggestions too that he thought the Japanese might consider the Philippines neutral under Quezon's Commonwealth government and would therefore not be attacked. His own orders were clear: not to initiate offensive action against the Japanese from the Philippines—but then those orders had been drafted before Pearl Harbor, which no one expected. He could hardly argue that Japan and the United States were not now at war. Quezon may also have asked him, in several frantic telephone calls that morning, to hold his fire. But he was an American general now, not Quezon's poodle. MacArthur later claimed that the idea of attacking Formosa was never even raised with him:

> Sometime in the morning of December 8, before the Clark Field attack, General Brereton suggested to General Sutherland a foray against Formosa. I know nothing of any interview with Sutherland, and Brereton never at any time recommended or suggested an attack on Formosa to me. My first knowledge of it was in a newspaper dispatch months later. Such a suggestion to the Chief of Staff must have been of a most nebulous and superficial character, as there was no record of it at headquarters. The proposal, if intended seriously, should certainly have been made to me in person. He has never spoken of the matter to me either before or after the Clark Field attack.
>
> As a matter of fact, an attack on Formosa, with its heavy air concentrations, by our small bomber force without fighter cover, which because of the great distance involved and the limited range of the fighters was impossible, would have been suicidal. In contrast, the enemy's bombers from Formosa had fighter protection from their air carriers, an entirely different condition from our own.

It was not a decision to be lightly made: Japanese aircraft would have heavily outnumbered American ones if they did attack Formosa. MacArthur certainly hesitated too long. The failure of the Japanese to strike at dawn turned out to be a result of the heavy fog over the air bases at Formosa, but MacArthur did not know that.

1. Emperor Mutsuhito—stern creator of modern Japan, who ruled on earth as well as reigned as a god.

2. His grandson, the slight and diffident Crown Prince Hirohito, 1921.

3. Douglas MacArthur in the First World War, most decorated American general and death-defying Beau Brummel of the trenches, in his trademark cap and scarf.

4. MacArthur showing the strains of combat as he is decorated by Pershing, soon to become a bitter critic.

5. A rare intimate picture of Hirohito and Nagato.

6. "Mars marries millions"—MacArthur and his fabulously wealthy first wife, Louise Cromwell Brooks, 1925.

7. The man on the white charger—Hirohito on his mount at military maneuvers, 1931.

8. The man who charged the Bonus Marchers—MacArthur directing his soldiers in Washington, July 1931.

9. The first fateful step—the 1931 Japanese occupation of Manchuria.

10. Blood on the snow—Tokyo coup attempt of 1936.

11. After the bombing—Kweilin, China, 1940.

12. Brilliant planner of Pearl Harbor, Yamamoto, the whole world in his hands—but not, he knew, for long.

13. Drifting into war—vacillating prime minister Konoe, rabid foreign minister Matsuoka, pragmatic navy minister Yoshida, fanatic war minister Tojo, 1940.

14. Pearl Harbor, 1941—day of Japanese infamy
and infamous American unpreparedness.

Facing page:
15. *Top,* MacArthur's bunker—the
Malinta Tunnel on Corregidor.

16. *Bottom,* judgment of Solomon—
Roosevelt (center) approved both the
rival plans of MacArthur (left) and
Nimitz (right).

17. He had returned—MacArthur just after landing on Leyte in the Philippines, 1944.

18. The fire bombing of Tokyo. 100,000 perished in a capital reduced to ashes.

19. Nagasaki, the second atomic bomb—both were unnecessary, in MacArthur's view.

20. Into the jaws of the lion—MacArthur lands at Atsugi accompanied by Sutherland (second from left).

21. Surrender at sea—Shigemitsu signs as MacArthur watches aboard the USS *Missouri*.

22. Studied insolence—Shogun MacArthur slouches as Emperor Hirohito pays homage.

23. A god descends to his people—Hirohito touring Japan, 1946.

24. His finest hour—MacArthur watches the shelling at Inchon with faithful Whitney (left) and General Mark Almond, 1950.

25. Masking mutual contempt—Truman and MacArthur at Wake Island.

26. Old soldiers never die—MacArthur's plea to America, 1951.

27. New York's gratitude—MacArthur's tickertape parade, but after that his campaign for vindication faltered.

28. Don't get sucked into Vietnam, young man—MacArthur in his autumn years advises Kennedy, 1961.

29. Rising above the clouds—a tranquil Hirohito aged 77, 1978.

Misjudgement turned into tragedy. When the fog cleared and the Japanese took off, they did so in time to find the B-17s and the P-40s laid out in line. Some 110 Japanese aircraft reached Iba airfield and destroyed the 16 P-40s there as they lay in the open. Another 82 Japanese aircraft were heading toward Clark base shortly after twelve o'clock, when the air crews were settling down to lunch. A radio commentator had just broadcast unconfirmed reports that the Japanese were bombing Clark, which raised a hearty laugh among the airmen. Out of the clear blue sky the Japanese appeared, looking, according to the crew of the one B-17 still in the sky, like a thunderstorm. A whole squadron of B-52s was destroyed on the ground, although two others were fortunately in the air off Manila Bay. It was a shattering blow and would render air bases on the north of the island out of commission and virtually without fighter protection.

Brereton soon after had to order most of his remaining aircraft to Australia and Java. The few remaining fighter aircraft fought on, against vastly superior Japanese air power. Deprived of air cover the Philippines were sitting ducks for Japanese air attack: three days later the huge American naval base at Cavite was blown up. On December 16 it was the turn of the Manila docks.

Meanwhile news had arrived that two of the biggest Allied ships in the western Pacific, the British battleship *Prince of Wales* and the cruiser *Repulse*, had been sunk by air attack. Conventional ships simply could not operate without air defense. Tom Hart, the American navy commander in the Philippines, decided to withdraw his remaining naval forces from the islands. MacArthur was mortified. The old defensive plan for the Philippines was in tatters because after the catastrophe at Pearl Harbor the navy had decided it could not maintain a supply route to the Philippines: the army would thus eventually run out of supplies.

MacArthur furiously argued that the navy should send its aircraft carriers, which had avoided destruction at Pearl Harbor, to aid the Philippines. In cables he urged direct air attacks on Japan itself:

> The mass of enemy air and naval strength committed in the theater from Singapore to the Philippines and eastward, established his weakness in Japan proper and definite information available here shows that entry of Russia is enemy's greatest fear. Most favorable opportunity now exists, and immediate attack on Japan from north would not only inflict heavy punishment but would at once relieve pressure from objectives of Jap drive to southward. Heavy air attack on Jap objectives would not only pull in much of present widely dispersed air strength but could destroy much of

their exposed oil supply. A golden opportunity now exists for a master stroke while the enemy is engaged in over-extended initial air effort.

These were ingenious tactics, but the navy did not respond. In shock after Pearl Harbor, unwilling to risk the precious aircraft carriers, Washington had decided to dispense with the Philippines. After the disastrous way in which he had allowed part of his air force to be destroyed, MacArthur too had been written off as a superannuated has-been, no longer a serious general.

As MacArthur waited for the inevitable land invasion, he surveyed the wreckage of everything he had striven for. His inadequate air defenses were destroyed or gone. The islands were blockaded by sea and the navy had all but left. He had worked for more than six years to build up a Philippine defense force, but his militia was still only half-trained and now demoralized.

He was not free of blame for the disasters at Iba and Clark airfields, but Brereton's incompetence and sheer bad luck had also been culprits. The chief cause lay with America's military planners, who had supplied far too little far too late, in spite of MacArthur's entreaties. Nevertheless he was presiding over a colossal military failure, one to cap what seemed his record of disaster as army chief of staff: the mounting Philippines debacle looked ominously like another Pearl Harbor or Singapore in the making. He was 61 years old and witnessing his worst ever professional setback.

MacArthur had immediately and correctly appraised the danger to his forces: if the Japanese landed in strength in Luzon, his army of 70,000, while numerically strong, could do nothing but delay the inevitable. The Japanese had tanks and aircraft. MacArthur, now deprived of the aircraft and ships that could have blocked the landing, had no more than raw recruits. For two weeks after Pearl Harbor the Philippines enjoyed an unreal respite, while a handful of diversionary landings were staged which MacArthur correctly interpreted as an attempt to get him to divide up his forces. To his disappointment the 12 submarines left on the islands proved incapable of inflicting much damage on Japanese warships in Manila Bay, due to dud detonators on the torpedoes.

On December 22 a force of 80 Japanese landing craft carrying some 20,000 troops beached at Lingayen Gulf well to the north of Manila. Two days later 7,000 Japanese troops were landed at Lamon Bay. The Japanese were closing in two giant pincers to take Manila. MacArthur, now that the unreal interlude was over, was at his decisive best: he had long realized that to send his inexperienced men to fight in the open on the Plain of Luzon would be madness: his army would disintegrate under Japanese air and tank attack. The Japanese, for their part, expected him to dig in and defend Manila. But this was equally hopeless, in MacArthur's view.

Both armies on north and south Luzon were instead ordered to retreat to the Bataan Peninsula, where they could hold out until the promised reinforcements could be brought up: it was the old, discredited Orange Plan dusted out and put into effect. He ordered Quezon to leave at once, at 2 P.M. on Christmas Eve, for the stronghold of Corregidor, an island two miles off the tip of the Bataan Peninsula.

He and his family, who had already celebrated a muted early Christmas for little MacArthur's sake, left only a little later for the five-hour trip 30 miles across the Bay. As they crossed the calm waters they could see the smoke of hundreds of fires burning munitions and supplies that might have been of use to the Japanese, while a large oil depot at Cavite was still alight, producing a thick plume of smoke. It was a deeply surreal Christmas Eve. Reaching Corregidor, MacArthur installed himself in Topside, the officers' house on the top of Malinta Hill.

From there he directed by telephone one of the most superbly executed retreats ever staged in history. The chief difficulty was that his armies were divided in two: if the northern one retreated too fast the advancing Japanese could intercept and cut the southern forces off from reaching Bataan. MacArthur instructed General Jonathan Wainwright, the commander of the northern army, to build a line of defense, wait for the Japanese to mass for an attack, then retreat and build another line ten miles back. In this way they could stagger and delay the Japanese advance without losing significant casualties. Some 180 bridges were blown en route. General Masaharu Homma, the Japanese commander, advanced just as MacArthur had expected, but was held up by the defensive lines, allowing the smaller southern army to slip into Bataan ahead of the northern. Even that curmudgeonly old critic of MacArthur's, Jack Pershing, called it "a masterpiece—one of the greatest moves in all military history."

The two armies—the 28,000-strong northern army and the 15,000-strong southern one, once 160 miles apart—rendezvoused at Calumpit bridge, spent two days crossing the river, then blew it up and withdrew to the next river crossing at Layao, where they destroyed the bridge on January 6, 1942. By then 80,000 troops had arrived safely in Bataan—5,000 American soldiers and 65,000 Filipinos. There were, in addition, some 26,000 civilian refugees. Manila was declared an open city.

The Japanese were astonished—they had expected to have to fight for Manila until the last moment. The Japanese general staff in Tokyo noted that "the Japanese commanders could not adjust to the new situation." It had been "a great strategic move" on MacArthur's part. Those on this superb retreat were not to know that many of them might have ultimately been better off dead fighting in the open.

On one count, though, MacArthur could be badly faulted: only the fortnight before the Japanese landings, instead of filling the peninsula with supplies, he had left most outside Manila in pursuit of his strategy—when he still had the air power—of attacking the Japanese as they landed. It had proved impossible to move most of these in time. Now the peninsula was greatly overpopulated and food had to be half-rationed.

Three days later the Japanese staged their first air attack on Topside, which lasted nearly four hours. MacArthur coolly watched it in his soft military cap, until forced down on his stomach beside a hedge by his orderly who held his own helmet over the general's head: a piece of shrapnel tore off the back of the orderly's hand and another dented the helmet.

With his home destroyed, MacArthur was forced to take shelter in the deep tunnel he had himself built under Malina, which was overcrowded, unhygienic and uncomfortable during air raids. But he insisted in spending most of the time in a house outside the tunnel. The best adapted to the new circumstances was the three-year-old Arthur, who became fondly known as "sergeant" by the troops. He walked happily up and down the tunnel singing "The Battle Hymn of the Republic," or crying out, "Air raid, air raid."

Meanwhile the real fighting was taking place on the defensive front line of Bataan as the Japanese chipped away at the bulk of the Philippine and American troops. It was a grim contest, but the defenders held out. The Allied forces were split across the peninsula into a First Corps, commanded by Wainwright, and a Second Corps, commanded by General George Parker. There was a gap in between on the flanks of Bataan's main mountain, which Wainwright considered impenetrable. But 500 Japanese soldiers got through and Sutherland, MacArthur's acerbic chief of staff, mistakenly ordered Wainwright to pull back, leaving most of his artillery behind. The Japanese landed troops behind the backs of both armies. Wainwright launched brilliant attacks eliminating both beachheads.

MacArthur, during the days of the siege, showed exceptional courage. As his aide Huff wrote:

> Everybody on the staff tried to persuade the general to keep away
> from the entrance or at least to wear a helmet during raids. He paid no

attention to us. We put up big telephone poles, strung with cables, along the approach to the tunnel to prevent suicide bombers from crashing the entrance, and we erected flash walls at an angle to prevent them from "skipping" a bomb inside where it would set off our ammunition and blow up the whole place. MacArthur, however, kept right on walking outside to look—sometimes angrily and sometimes scornfully—at the enemy craft wheeling overhead.

But he also irked his men with boastful declarations. He even kept on with an erroneously triumphal refrain:

From various sources hitherto regarded as reliable General MacArthur has received persistent reports that Lieut Gen Masaharu Homma, Commander-in-Chief of the Japanese forces in the Philippines, committed Harakiri . . . The funeral rites of the late Japanese commander, the reports state, were held on Feb 26 in Manila . . . An interesting and ironic detail of the story is that the suicide and funeral rites occurred in the suite at the Manila hotel occupied by General MacArthur prior to the evacuation of Manila. Help is on the way from the United States. Thousands of troops and hundreds of planes are being dispatched. The exact time of arrival of reinforcements is unknown, as they will have to fight their way through Japanese lines. It is imperative that our troops hold until these reinforcements arrive.

MacArthur expressed his concern that Homma had "messed up" his apartment at the hotel. Most controversial of all was his refusal to visit Bataan more than once, on January 10, when he told anyone who asked, "Help is definitely on the way. We must hold out until it comes. And again later."

MacArthur never went back to Bataan—surely not for lack of courage, which was most untypical for a commander who usually relished visiting the front line—but because he couldn't bear to tell his anxious men he had been wrong.

Help was not on the way. The lie was not MacArthur's—he had firmly believed that it was. The lie was that of his old sparring partner Franklin Roosevelt. The latter's legendary capacity for mendacity excelled itself this time. His chief of staff, General George Marshall, assured MacArthur in January that Roosevelt and Churchill were

looking toward the quick development of strength in the Far East so as to break the enemy's hold on the Philippines . . . Our great hope is that the development of an overwhelming air power on the Malay Barrier will cut the Japanese communications south of Borneo and permit an assault in the Southern Philippines. A stream of four-engine bombers, previously delayed by foul weather, is en route . . . Another stream of similar bombers started today from Hawaii staging at new island fields. Two groups of powerful medium bombers of long range and heavy bomb-load capacity leave next week. Pursuit planes are coming on every ship we can use. Our definitely allocated air reinforcements together with British should give us an early superiority in the Southwestern Pacific. Our strength is to be concentrated and it should exert a decisive effect on Japanese shipping and force a withdrawal northward . . . Every day of time you gain is vital to the concentration of the overwhelming power necessary for our purpose. Furthermore, the current conferences in Washington . . . are extremely encouraging in respect to accelerating speed of ultimate success.

In fact, a number of ships tried to run the Japanese blockade to get supplies through to Bataan. Just three made it—but they only got as far as the southern Philippines. Not a single American ship or warplane got through to Bataan, and only a few submarines made the passage—even though American ships were running Hitler's Atlantic Blockade all the time.

It is usually assumed that Washington was right in writing off Bataan as a lost cause: yet the navy, which was so cautious, never really put the matter to the test. Had supplies reached Bataan, MacArthur's forces might have been able to hold out indefinitely: they were never defeated in battle. The decision to abandon 80,000 men was certainly a grave one, and it is far from certain that the war department was right even on military grounds. Maintaining such a huge pocket of resistance behind Japanese lines would certainly have given the Japanese pause for thought. After the realization dawned that instead they had been abandoned, Quezon expostulated furiously about Roosevelt: "Come, listen to this scoundrel! *Que demonio!* How typical of America to writhe in anguish at the fate of a distant cousin, Europe, while a daughter, the Philippines, is being raped in the back room!"

MacArthur tried to dissuade him from giving himself up to the Japanese. The general cabled Roosevelt for support. The President responded to Quebon with the most breathtaking lie of all.

I can assure you that every vessel available is bearing . . . the strength that will eventually crush the enemy and liberate your native land. The people of the United States will never forget what the people of the Philippines are doing these days and will do in the days to come. I give to the people of the Philippines my solemn pledge that their freedom will be retained and their independence established and redeemed. The entire resources in men and materials of the United States stand behind that pledge.

Only a week later he was forced to admit that nothing could be done at this stage. The understandably irate Quezon threatened to ask Japan for a neutrality agreement, which in practice would have given the Philippines similar status to France's supine Vichy government—the right of the Japanese to walk over the Philippines as a conquest in all but name. MacArthur shook Washington by appearing to endorse this call:

> Since I have no air or sea protection, you must be prepared at any time to figure on the complete destruction of this command. You must determine whether the mission of delay would be better furthered by the temporizing plan of Quezon, or by my continued battle effort. So far as the military angle is concerned, the problem presents itself as to whether the plan of President Quezon might offer the best possible solution of what is about to be a disastrous debacle.

Roosevelt replied soothingly:

> Although I cannot at this time state the day that help will arrive in the Philippines . . . vessels . . . have been filled with cargo of necessary supplies and have been dispatched to Manila. Our arms, together with those of our allies, have dealt heavy blows to enemy transports and naval vessels . . . A continuous stream of fighter and pursuit planes is traversing the Pacific . . . Extensive arrivals of troops are being guarded by adequate protective elements of our navy.

The following day Quezon acquiesced and agreed to leave for Australia. Roosevelt conveyed to MacArthur a terrible order to fight to the death.

> American forces will continue to keep our flag flying in the Philippines so long as there remains any possibility of resistance. I have made these decisions in complete understanding of your military estimate that accompanied President Quezon's message to me. The duty and the necessity of resisting Japanese aggression to the last transcends in importance any other obligation now facing us in the Philippines.
>
> I therefore give you this most difficult mission in full understanding of the desperate nature to which you may shortly be reduced.

MacArthur rose to the challenge: "I have not the slightest intention in the world of surrendering or capitulating the Filipino forces of my command. I intend to fight to destruction on Bataan and then do the same on Corregidor." Privately he summed it up with bitter accuracy: "never in history was so large and gallant an army written off so callously." The general prepared to die with his troops. He even considered shooting Jean and Arthur if they refused to leave the island without him. Both Roosevelt and Eisenhower believed the outcome to be inevitable, although Marshall disagreed. The possibility of surrendering Bataan never occurred to MacArthur—not least because he knew how the Japanese treated their prisoners. Better for him to go down gloriously after all the humiliations they had inflicted on the Americans, British and Dutch in Asia.

MacArthur wrote:

My heart ached as I saw my men slowly wasting away. Their clothes hung on them like tattered rags. Their bare feet stuck out in silent protest. Their long bedraggled hair framed gaunt bloodless faces. Their hoarse, wild laughter greeted the constant stream of obscene and ribald jokes issuing from their parched, dry throats. They cursed the enemy and in the same breath cursed and reviled the United States; they spat when they jeered at the Navy. But their eyes would light up and they would cheer when they saw my battered, and much reviled in America, "scrambled egg" cap. They would gather round and pat me on the back and "Mabuhay Macarsar" me. They would grin—that ghastly skeleton-like grin of the dying—as they would roar in unison, "We are the battling bastards of Bataan—no papa, no mama, no Uncle Sam."

They asked no quarter and they gave none. They died hard—those savage men—not gently like a stricken dove folding its wings in peaceful passing, but like a wounded wolf at bay, with lips curled back in sneering menace, and always a nerveless hand reaching for that long sharp machete knife which long ago they had substituted for the bayonet. And around their necks, as we buried them, would be a thread of dirty string with its dangling crucifix. They were filthy, and they were lousy, and they stank. And I loved them.

Events took an extraordinary turn. The government of Australia, which was virtually defenseless before Japan, had fallen out with Churchill when demanding the recall of the Australian division fighting at El Alamein in north Africa. Churchill flatly refused: the Australian prime minister, John Curtis, desperately wired the Americans for help. Churchill came up with an idea. As he wrote in his memoirs:

When I was at the White House at the end of December, 1941, I learned from the President and Mr. Stimson of the approaching fate of General MacArthur and the American garrison at Corregidor. I thought it right to show them the way in which we had dealt with the position of a Commander-in-Chief whose force was reduced to a small fraction of his original command. We had ordered Gort to leave Dunkirk and deprive the Germans of a needless triumph.

The president and Mr. Stimson read the telegram with profound attention, and I was struck by the impression it seemed to make upon them. A little later in the day, Mr. Stimson came back and asked for a copy of it, which I promptly gave him.

Thus Churchill saved MacArthur.

Before Quezon left, he agreed to pay MacArthur for his services in the Philippines, as well as a bonus for his seven commanders: the total figure was a colossal $500,000. MacArthur accepted the money, although he believed he would be dead before he could enjoy it: it was intended for Mary and Arthur.

24 : "I SHALL RETURN"

O N FEBRUARY 23 ROOSEVELT ISSUED THE ORDER FOR MACARTHUR to travel to Mindanao and then on to Melbourne. MacArthur had a momentary breakdown, threatening to resign his commission and enlist as a private on Bataan, but the following day he said that for the sake of his men he had no alternative but to obey a direct presidential order which was now repeated even more insistently. MacArthur deluded himself that Roosevelt would be true to his pledge to allow MacArthur to return and save his men.

On the evening of March 11, he entrusted the fateful command to General Wainwright.

Jonathan, I want you to understand my position very plainly. I'm leaving for Australia pursuant to repeated orders of the President. Things have reached such a point that I must comply with these orders or get out of the Army. I want you to make it known throughout all elements of your command that I'm leaving over my repeated protests . . . If I get through to Australia you know I'll come back as soon as I can with as much as I can. In the meantime you've got to hold. Good-bye, Jonathan. When I get back, if you're still on Bataan, I'll make you a lieutenant general.

MacArthur described the scene on the dock:

> Darkness had now fallen, and the waters were beginning to ripple from the faint night breeze. The enemy firing had ceased and a muttering silence had fallen. It was as though the dead were passing by the stench of destruction. The smell of filth thickened the night air. I raised my cap in farewell salute, and I could feel my face go white, feel a sudden, convulsive twitch in the muscles of my face. I heard someone ask, "What's his chance, Sarge, of getting through?" and the gruff reply, "Dunno. He's lucky. Maybe one in five."

The convoy consisted of four P.T. low-slung 75-foot speed-boats that were some of the few remaining craft on Bataan. Suffering from claustrophobia MacArthur had refused to travel by submarine, which would have been quicker and safer. His thoughts as he left his men were in turmoil: he had wanted to stay on and fight to the death, and he doubted the brave but alcohol-dependent Wainwright could do the job. But he believed that only by leaving could he obtain the help necessary for the garrison to survive: it was a dilemma straight out of the Old West.

The little party made an extraordinarily dangerous trip through Japanese lines to Cuyon Island, where they rendezvoused, then on to Del Monte on Mindanao, where after a long wait a rackety airplane was all that Australia could muster to take MacArthur and his family to land near Darwin (a Japanese air raid was in progress on the town's airstrip as he arrived). He flew by air over Jean's protests to Alice Springs, in the central outback, and then took a rudimentary train to Melbourne.

At Darwin his enthusiastic reception had brought him to nervous and emotional collapse for at least the fourth time in recent months (the first was following news of Pearl Harbor; the second after his arrival in Corregidor; and the third the occasion of Roosevelt's order to leave Corregidor). He broke down again in Melbourne: He discovered that Roosevelt had lied once more: there was no army in Australia waiting to return him to Bataan: there were just 32,000 troops altogether, including the Australian army. There was no navy, fewer than 100 working aircraft, and no tanks. "God have mercy on us," MacArthur said when he realized the true predicament.

On arrival in Australian territory he had said:

> The President of the United States ordered me to break through the Japanese lines and proceed from Corregidor to Australia for the purpose, as I understand it, of organizing the American offensive against Japan, a primary objective of which is the relief of the Philippines. I came through and I shall return.

Those three last words were a public relations stroke of genius: they instantly became the cornerstone of the MacArthur legend, one of the most famous utterances by a general in history.

For the second surprise on his arrival in Australia—almost as unexpected as the first—was the realization that he, the man who had been tricked into abandoning tens of thousands of his own troops and who had pulled off a spectacular retreat from the advancing Japanese had become a hero: not just any hero, but probably the greatest hero of the war so far, a towering figure of resistance.

Unlike the British General Perceval who had surrendered Singapore, he had held on grimly, month after month, against irresistible force—the only spoke in the wheel of the relentless Japanese advance. It had been a new Alamo, the stuff of legend, a second Dunkirk, defeat dressed up as victory. The 62-year-old general so long dogged by failure had become the symbol of resistance to Japanese aggression in the Far East. In Australia he was living proof of America's commitment to defend the continent, which was why Roosevelt had sent him there.

It was a bittersweet experience. For while MacArthur's Filipino troops had revered him as "Macarsar," many of the American troops had grumbled bitterly at their absent commander on Corregidor (even though he was sharing their privations there). A famous piece of doggerel (to the refrain of "The Battle Hymn of the Republic") was aimed at MacArthur, and stung him deeply at the time:

> Dugout Doug MacArthur lies ashakin' on the Rock
> Safe from all the bombers and from any sudden shock
> Dugout Doug is eating of the best food on Bataan
> And his troops go starving on . . .
> Dugout Doug, come out from hiding
> Dugout Doug, come out from hiding
> Send to Franklin the glad tidings
> That his troops go starving on!
> We're the battling bastards of Bataan:
> No mama, no papa, no Uncle Sam,
> No aunts, no uncles, no nephews, no nieces,
> No rifles, no planes, or artillery pieces,
> And nobody gives a damn.

MacArthur made a hugely important friend in Australia, Lord Gowrie, the able and percipient British governor-general, himself a war hero and winner of Britain's highest decoration, the Victoria Cross. Along with the tough and honest Australian prime minister John Curtin, Gowrie was one of the key figures in the defense of Australia from Japanese attack, which seemed increasingly imminent as frequent air raids were staged. Gowrie wrote that "with the enemy at the gates," he was "enormously impressed" by the general. He considered him "a very brave man, full of energy and thoroughly inspired with the offensive spirit and a great leader of men . . . his showmanship particularly contains an appeal to the masses," which Gowrie judged to be enormously important. Gowrie's particular role was as a direct channel of communication to Winston Churchill, who became an almost starstruck admirer of MacArthur and impressed his view on the more sceptical Roosevelt.

MacArthur was awarded the Medal of Honor at last. In his new position as commander of the Far East, he urged Wainwright to break out of Bataan and join the guerrillas operating in Luzon. But Wainwright's exhausted men could do no such thing. He had enough food to last only until April 15. They surrendered on April 9. For a further 27 days Corregidor held out under intense artillery fire and air attack. On May 5 the Japanese landed in force and, although at first driven back, put five light tanks ashore and threatened to fire right into the tunnel which contained 1,000 injured men. On May 6 Corregidor's 11,000 defenders surrendered. The first phase of the Pacific War was over: the brave stand of those on Bataan and Corregidor had broken the otherwise unbroken string of Japanese victories. The Japanese now took their revenge, taking the Bataan prisoners on their terrible "death march," which caused some 15,000 to perish.

At least 131,000 murders by the Japanese in the Philippines during the occupation between 1942 and 1945 were accounted for by the later Tokyo war crimes tribunal. The real figure was almost certainly many times higher. The Philippine counsel at the trial, Pedro Lopez, claimed in his opening statement that for the "hundreds [who] suffered slow and painful death in dark, foul and lice-infested cells . . . the quick, scientific mass extermination in the lethal gas chambers at Camp Dachau would have been a welcome alternative."

Lopez listed an appalling catalogue: Lucas Doctolero was crucified, nails being driven through his hands, feet and skull, on September 18, 1943. A blind woman was dragged from her home on November 17, stripped naked and hanged. In Manila, 800 men, women and children at St. Paul's College were machine-gunned. At Calamba, 2,500 people were bayoneted or shot dead. At Ponson in the south, 100 people were bayoneted inside a church while 200 outside were hunted down like game and killed. At Matina Pangi, 169 villagers were lined up and bayoneted or shot. A Japanese directive commanded, "When killing Filipinos assemble them together in one place as far as possible, thereby saving ammunition and labor." Getting rid of the bodies was "troublesome." Two recommended solutions were to "throw them in a river or put them in a house and blow it up."

For seven days in April and May 1942, 76,000 American and Filipino troops from Bataan and Corregidor were marched 120 kilometers to POW camps. Some 15,000 died. American Staff Sergeant Samuel Moody said that the only food they received on the march were the stalks of sugarcane they grabbed from the side of the road or the morsels thrown at them by Filipinos. They drank from the water holes of animals and from ditches. "We were beaten. The men were bayoneted, stabbed; they were kicked with hobnail boots . . . If any man lagged to the rear of the road, fell off to the side, he was immediately bayoneted and beaten." Bodies littered the road. "I saw many dead men, many of whom were my friends. I also saw two dead women, one of whom was pregnant. Many times I could look ahead and see my friends stabbed and beaten. Quite often I could hear the groans of men behind me that had received beatings from someone in the rear."

In the first few months of war, everything had gone Japan's way. The day after Pearl Harbor, the British battleships *Prince of Wales* and *Repulse*, accompanied by several destroyers, set out for Singapore to intercept Japanese forces being landed on the Kra Peninsula, the thin slice of land between Thailand and Malaya. Japanese fighter-bombers found the ships and in two hours sank them both. "In all the war, I never received a more direct shock," Churchill admitted afterward. Guam, meanwhile, had fallen to Japanese forces. Wake's defenders fought back heroically but in a fortnight the island fell after supplies had failed to get through. The garrison at Hong Kong put up an epic struggle, and lasted out until Christmas Day. The Gilbert Islands soon fell.

Just four days after Pearl Harbor, the Japanese launched their two biggest offensives so far: against Malaya and the Philippines. The Japanese deployed speed, courage and tactical brilliance throughout the Malaya campaign, landing at a series of points along the undefended coast. The defenders, mostly ill-trained Indian troops under British command, were demoralized to find that Japanese forces had thrust between them and their supply base at Singapore, threatening to cut them off, and most fled south in confusion to avoid such a fate. In fact they could probably have resisted by retreating deeper into the peninsula and outflanking the smaller Japanese forces. But by January 15 the Japanese Twenty-Fifth Army had advanced 400 miles in five weeks and was within a hundred miles of the apparently impregnable British stronghold of Singapore.

On January 31 the last troops in Malaya retreated across the causeway between Singapore and the mainland. The British force on the island was a massive one: around 45 battalions, outnumbering the Japanese army's 31, under the control of General Arthur Percival. Singapore's garrison had however been supplied with the wrong ammunition, which rendered the batteries facing the Malay coast virtually inoperative. The more impressive sea batteries were redundant because the threat came from the coast of Johore, just one mile to the north.

On February 8 the Japanese attacked in overwhelming strength against Percival's forces, which were necessarily strung out across 30 miles of vulnerable shoreline. The overstretched defenders on the north west coast of the island were overwhelmed and fell back. A week later the Japanese had advanced to secure control of the reservoirs on which the city, whose population was now swollen by refugees to 1 million people, depended. The following day Percival surrendered, and was photographed carrying the Union Jack in defeat, in what was to be labeled the greatest disaster in British military history.

It was certainly a defeat: 130,000 troops had yielded to a force half their number. Yet it is hard to see what else Percival could have done: to have fought on would have been to invite a lingering and horrific end for his forces, with no hope of relief. Just conceivably, a swift counteroffensive by his forces when the Japanese landed, or before the water shortage began to bite, might have been possible against the inferior Japanese forces: but they had the advantage of higher morale and superior momentum. The real lesson of the defeat was the danger of dependence on "fortress" bases, particularly ones as exposed as Singapore: an "impregnable" garrison was much more vulnerable, once its supply lines were cut off, than a series of bases. This was a lesson the Japanese themselves were to learn later in the war.

Percival's defense of the island can hardly be classed as imaginative or heroic. But the superior determination, mobility, firepower and sheer energy of the Japanese forces had put the defenders off balance in much the same way as Hitler's blitzkrieg tactics had in Europe. Dunkirk had been a defeat, although the evacuation of the British Expeditionary Force rendered it heroic. For Singapore's defenders, there was no such consolation, only shame and the horror of becoming prisoners of the Japanese (many Indians taken there went over to the Japanese forces).

Japan's invasion of the East Indies had begun on December 16. Japanese tactics consisted of amphibious landings along the whole 2,000-mile length of the East Indian archipelago: Borneo and the Celebes were attacked in January, Timor and Sumatra in February, Java in March. The fighting was wholly unequal from the start. The Dutch defenders were ill-equipped, outnumbered and had very little support from the local people. Small detachments of Australian troops provided the only semblance of a struggle. But the great bulk of Australia's forces were fighting with the British in the Middle East and in Malaya. In fact, there was now only the thinnest of lines of defense between the invading Japanese forces and Australia.

On February 27, the Japanese fleet appeared off Java with the clear intention of landing forces there. What remained of the allied naval force in the region had assembled under Admiral Doorman to attack the Japanese fleet. The two fleets met in the Battle of the Java Sea, which began late in the afternoon: two heavy and three light cruisers and nine destroyers on the Allied side confronted two heavy and two light cruisers and 14 destroyers on the Japanese side. After exchanging massive bombardments, the Japanese employed long-range torpedoes, forcing the Allied fleet to break away from the engagement.

In darkness, Doorman sent half of his fleet to refuel, but retained the other half in an attempt to attack the Japanese and prevent them from landing. He bore down on part of the fleet, only to be surprised by the rest of it, which ambushed his ships with their torpedoes. It seemed the Japanese were unstoppable navally, as well as on land. What neither side knew was that the Battle of the Java Sea was to be the only decisive Japanese naval victory throughout the Pacific War.

Within a fortnight, Java surrendered. Sumatra capitulated soon afterward. In Burma the formidable British military presence threatened to collapse almost as easily; but General Alexander was determined to fight back. He had no option, however, in the face of Japanese superiority but to stage a spectacular 600-mile retreat—the longest in British history—across Burma, pursued by the Japanese, who were stopped from chasing him into India only by the monsoon season.

It is not hard to see the explanation for the spectacular Japanese successes in just four months. The Japanese had the advantage of surprise; of well-disciplined, well-armed fighting men willing to endure extreme physical rigor; and of a brilliantly conceived and executed strategy of amphibious landing. With the exception of the garrison in Singapore, their opponents were ill-prepared, ill-equipped, unsupported, and strung out in a variety of small bases which could be picked off at will. The Allies had little air support; after the destruction of the American Pacific Fleet, Japan could move virtually at will through these paradisiacal South Sea islands soon to be turned into living hells. Doorman's defeat represented the end of the last substantial naval force in the region capable of withstanding the Japanese. With Penang, Hong Kong, Singapore, Bataan, Rangoon, and Malaya under their control, with India and Australia under threat, with all the oil, rubber, tin and bauxite that they needed, with Britain and America humiliated, the Japanese triumph had been as spectacular as any in the history of warfare.

They had stumbled over only one obstacle in the hurricane fury of their advance: the Philippines. Even there, the culpable unpreparedness of their enemy and the fury of their attack at first seemed to repeat the pattern of Pearl Harbor and Singapore. Their onslaught was to be only marginally affected by the fighting in the Philippines. Yet out of it was to grow a legend which did as much as anything to affect the course of the Pacific War and of Japan's postwar history.

In May 1942, it seemed to the Japanese that all their goals had been rewarded with success. The British and the Americans had been routed. The Russians had not entered the war against them. Japan's allies in Europe were victorious. The Japanese were on the winning side. A quarter of the world had been conquered in less than six months.

As the last beleaguered survivors of the Philippines surrendered, the first indication came that the Japanese might not, after all, be militarily superhuman or invincible. One of America's foremost aircraft carriers, the USS *Hornet*, had succeeded in bringing a number of B-52 bombers to raid Tokyo, the spectacular Doolittle raid, which shocked the Japanese high command; most of the pilots ran out of fuel and crash-landed in China.

On May 7, two other carriers, the *Yorktown* and the *Lexington*, were sent to intercept the Japanese invading force near Port Moresby. In the Battle of the Coral Sea, the Japanese carriers *Shoho* and *Shokaku* were badly damaged, while the *Lexington* had to be abandoned. The attempt to capture Port Moresby was blocked. Yamamoto now determined to provoke a naval battle in order to destroy America's carriers. His fleet set sail for the island of Midway, near Hawaii, with the intention of provoking an American response.

By this time the Americans had assembled a fleet which, although smaller than the Japanese one, was respectable. It consisted of three carriers, bearing some 180 aircraft, with cruiser and destroyer escorts. The Japanese had five carriers, with superior battleship escorts, and some 272 aircraft. However, the Americans also had heavily armored bombers, Flying Fortresses, stationed on Midway itself. The battle began with a Japanese air raid on Midway, which resulted in the destruction of two thirds of the fighters stationed there. The Americans responded by playing for time as they brought up their carrier fleet, using the few remaining aircraft at Midway to launch attacks on the Japanese fleet. Thinking they had caught the Japanese napping, American torpedo bombers homed in on the Japanese, only to be shot down by zero fighters; the Japanese fleet remained largely intact.

During the second wave of American bombing, largely by accident, 37 Dauntless dive-bombers from the USS *Enterprise*, which had temporarily got lost, turned toward the scene of the fighting to see the zero fighters engaged in action with the torpedo-bombers. Their chief, Lieutenant-Commander Wade McClusky, personally led his aircraft in a surprise attack on the vulnerable Japanese carriers. In the space of five minutes, three of the carriers were destroyed; the fourth fled, only to be found that same afternoon, and sunk.

The Battle of Midway marked the turning point in the naval war; with America's far superior war production machine, the odds were already lengthening against Japan in the long term. The Americans were to produce 20 carriers against the six produced by the Japanese over the following two years. Midway had been a close thing, a battle won almost by accident. But it signalled to the Americans that victory was possible in the Pacific. It rendered the diversion of precious war resources to the Pacific theater sensible. And at that stage the Americans made a number of crucial decisions that were to determine the course of the Pacific War.

The first was to aim for Japan itself as the central strategic objective. There was no intention of merely rolling back the Japanese conquests; the aim was nothing less than to strike at the home islands themselves and extract an unconditional surrender, as Roosevelt made clear at his summit with Churchill in Casablanca early in 1943. The strategy was to neglect the limbs, and strike at the heart.

This led to the second key choice: how to get there: along the rocky and desolate atolls of the northern Pacific, or by regaining the major islands of the East Indies now held by the Japanese? Finally, there was the fiercely controversial strategy adopted by Roosevelt to concentrate the bulk of American forces in Europe—even though the Japanese attack on Pearl Harbor had been primarily responsible for the American entry into the war and most directly threatened American interests.

The first choice—to aim for Japan itself—won enthusiastic support. The second created a major inter-service row that at times threatened seriously to damage the American war effort in the Pacific. At the heart of it was the decision to give MacArthur, who had expected control of the entire Pacific area of operations, only half the cake: the chief of naval staff, Admiral King, insisted on setting up a separate Pacific Ocean Area Command under Admiral Chester Nimitz. MacArthur later wrote angrily,

Of all the faulty decisions of the war, perhaps the most inexplicable one was the failure to unify the command in the Pacific . . . It cannot be defended in logic, in theory, or even in common sense. Other motives must be ascribed. It resulted in divided effort, the waste, diffusion and duplication of force, and the consequent extension of the war and added casualties and cost. The generally excellent co-operation between the two commands in the Pacific, supported by the goodwill, good nature and professional qualifications of the numerous personnel involved, was no substitute for the essential unity of direction of centralized authority. The handicaps and hazards unnecessarily resulting were numerous, and many a man lies in his grave today who could have been saved.

MacArthur volunteered to serve as the subordinate commander, despite his seniority, if the commands were unified. The crucial Battle of Leyte Gulf was nearly to be lost as a result of faulty coordination between the two commands. The division of commands meant that while Nimitz and the navy pressed for an "island-hopping" strategy across the northern atolls to Japan, MacArthur remained committed to the southern route, which also led to the Philippines, to which he had a close emotional attachment and had vowed to return. MacArthur was later bitterly to accuse the navy of failing to send him support and supply ships when he needed them, and of wasteful frontal assaults on minor island targets where the Japanese were well dug in. Against that, the protagonists of island-hopping, the navy, could argue that their route to Japan was much more direct and involved assaulting much smaller garrisons than that proposed by MacArthur.

In the end a messy compromise was reached between the northern and southern routes. MacArthur had the best of the argument, convincing the Joint Chiefs of Staff that victory over Japan was not possible without ending Japanese control of the major islands flanking the Pacific: "island-hopping" would merely lead to an overextension of American forces which would be vulnerable to attack from the Japanese-occupied south. Moreover, the kind of large American armies needed for the occupation of Japan could not be moved into place without control of the major territories necessary to support them; an army could not live off barren rock.

There was a great deal of special pleading on both sides. But it is hard not to conclude that while a thrust along the line suggested by MacArthur was essential, the northward route was not in fact indispensable—although there was something to be said for the two-pronged attack eventually adopted (it threw the Japanese off balance and confused them: they could never be sure where to concentrate their forces). Almost certainly, MacArthur was right in urging a unified command: ironically, the American row exactly mirrored Japan's notorious inter-service hatreds and preference for different avenues of military advance.

The navy was given charge of the first major American advance in the war, the attack on Guadalcanal, the strongly fortified Japanese outpost off eastern New Guinea, while MacArthur was given charge of the invasion of New Guinea itself and the attack on Japan's command center in the south at Rabaul. Even as MacArthur began to plan his campaign, American tactics were thrown into confusion by a major Japanese landing at Buna with the objective of crossing the nearly impenetrable mountain jungle of southern New Guinea in order to seize Port Moresby, the capital. Simultaneously, the Japanese responded furiously to the almost unopposed American landing on Guadalcanal: the Japanese regarded this as a major test of their strength, and threw everything they could into it.

The capture of Port Moresby threatened to bring Japan even closer to Australia and to provide air bases capable of striking into the Northern Territory. MacArthur was determined to avoid this at all costs. It had seemed impossible that the Japanese could cross the rugged and ferociously hostile Owen Stanley range. A force was sent under General Blamey to cross the jungle-clad mountains in reverse and try to cut off the supply line of the invaders. Almost simultaneously, the Japanese were ordered to return to Buna, as troops were rushed to the Guadalcanal battle. The Japanese fought a desperate race back to Buna, to avoid being outflanked by Blaney's forces, and broke through to form an enclave along the coast. With incredible difficulty, the Americans at last overwhelmed this and won their first land battle against the Japanese, at a cost of some 3,000 dead and more than 5,000 wounded.

Meanwhile, Guadalcanal had become an epic. After establishing their beachhead, the marines had to be supplied down a treacherous channel through which ships came under fire on three sides. On August 8, the Japanese surprised an American flotilla, sinking four cruisers and destroying another. The Americans hit back on August 24, sinking a carrier, a cruiser and a destroyer. However, Japanese reinforcements poured in as the fighting spread on the island, and became ever more intense and bloody. In October the Americans surprised one of the Japanese carrier convoys known as the "Tokyo Express"; two days later the Japanese came off best in the Battle of Santa Cruz. In November during the Battle of Guadalcanal the Japanese were bloodied; a fortnight later, the Japanese failed in a major attempt to intercept the American supply convoys to Guadalcanal. Only in February, after frenzied fighting, was the epic and pyhrric struggle over: the Japanese force was evacuated.

The tide had turned, painfully and bloodily, in the Allies' favor. There was to be much criticism of the Allies' decision to fight so bitterly for Guadalcanal at such at appalling cost, not least from MacArthur. Yet at that stage in the war, a grim battle of attrition against the Japanese was almost inevitable, to drive home the message that they were not invincible, after all. After Guadalcanal, the Imperial Army was never to take the offensive again in the Pacific. It fought bitterly to hold on to what it had acquired.

MacArthur outlined the new tactics now adopted:

> The calculated advance of bomber lines through the seizure of forward bases meant that a relatively small force of bombers operating at short and medium ranges could attack under cover of an equally limited fighter force. Each phase of advance had as its objective an airfield which could serve as a stepping stone to the next advance. In addition, as this air line moved forward, naval forces under newly established air cover began to regain the sea lanes, which had been the undisputed arteries of the enemy's far-flung positions. Ground, air and sea operations were thoroughly co-ordinated. It was a new type of campaign—three-dimensional warfare—the triphibious concept.
>
> It was the practical application of this system of warfare—to avoid the frontal attack with its terrible loss of life; to bypass Japanese strongpoints and neutralize them by cutting their lines of supply; to thus isolate their armies and starve them in the battlefield; to, as Willie Keeler used to say, "hit 'em where they ain't"—that from this time forward guided my movements and operations.
>
> ... The lack of naval aircraft carriers affected and hampered the Southwest Pacific operations most seriously. ... The very essence of our so-called "island-hopping" method of advance depended upon securing air control over the area covered in each forward step. In the present state of development of the art of war, no movement can safely be made of forces on sea or land without adequate air protection. The limit of such protection in our case was the possible radius of operation of our fighter planes. This radius has to be measured from the actual location of our ground air bases. This required the seizing or construction of such new bases at each forward movement.

Colonel Matsuicho Juio, senior intelligence officer of the Eighth Army Staff, later claimed:

> This was the type of strategy we hated most. The Americans, with minimum losses, attacked and seized a relatively weak area, constructed mine-

fields and then proceeded to cut the supply lines to troops in that area. Without engaging in a large-scale operation, our strongpoints were gradually starved out. The Japanese army preferred direct assault, after the German fashion, but the Americans flowed into our weaker points and submerged us, just as water seeks the weakest entry to sink a ship. We respected this type of strategy for its brilliance because it gained the most while losing the least.

The next target was Rabaul, with its large naval base, airfields and supply depots. MacArthur was determined to engage the enemy as infrequently as possible as he moved up the coast of New Guinea, leapfrogging to the next airstrip and leaving Japanese forces outflanked with their supplies cut off. In fact the campaign proved much slower and more arduous than expected, requiring a series of landings and difficult amphibious operations. But one by one his targets were picked off. Woodlark, Kiriwina, and Nassau Bay were seized virtually without casualties. MacArthur's forces then marched on Salamanua, a major base which the Japanese evacuated. Thanks to a brilliant encircling move, MacArthur then forced the Japanese to withdraw also from Lae. The Japanese put up stiff resistance at Finschhafen, which fell on October 2. The bulk of New Guinea was now in Allied hands.

Meanwhile a parallel assault was being mounted by naval forces along the Solomon Island chain to the north. The Russell Islands fell in February, New Georgia in June and Vella Cavela in August. Japanese counterattacks were unsuccessful. By October the northern forces were ready to attack Bougainville, the final stepping-stone to Rabaul. The American navy was poised to form one part of the pincer, MacArthur's forces the other, in Operation Cartwheel, which was intended to surround the Japanese stronghold.

The American air force was now securing victories through a new policy of low level bombing. In the Battle of the Bismarck Sea, Flying Fortresses sank four destroyers and a convoy of transport ships. In another aerial engagement in April, Admiral Yamamoto was shot down. MacArthur's advance was then slowed by a probably unnecessary landing on southern New Britain; his Australian forces became bogged down in arduous fighting in the Huon Peninsula.

At the end of 1943 Stalin, Roosevelt and Churchill approved a new strategy in Teheran, which allocated greater resources to the Pacific War, and persuaded Admiral Nimitz to go on the offensive in the Northern Pacific, in open competition with MacArthur's forces further south. The general was meanwhile given specific goals: the seizure of Kavieng, New

Ireland and Manus, further to encircle Rabaul. Meanwhile Nimitz wasted no time in making a landing on the Marshall Islands in January 1944 and seizing its western point, Eniwetok, in a bloody battle in February.

MacArthur decided to bypass Kavieng, leaving it to wither on the vine, and seize Manus with relatively light casualties. By this stage tens of thousands of Japanese had been killed, while some 100,000 had been left behind by the Allied advance. American planners then decided that an outright assault on Rabaul, which was encircled, was unnecessary. It could be neutralized by air bombardment and left behind. MacArthur was instructed to seize the Admiral Islands and advance a full 600 miles to Hollandia, along the coast of northern New Guinea. His air force caught the Japanese air force at Hollandia napping at the end of March, destroying 300 aircraft; then, with a huge invasion fleet, the Allied forces landed there, taking the Japanese entirely by surprise and forcing most to flee to the hills.

The Japanese, horrified at the two-pronged attack, now resolved an attempt to contain it in one major gamble: lure American naval forces into a trap, where they could make use of their control of airspace and the protection of shore-based guns. The project was called Operation A-go. However, the American naval forces made no move towards the Japanese fleet, preparing to concentrate on island-hopping in the north. On June 19–21, the Japanese fleet, which had decided to pursue the Americans, met its match. The Battle of the Philippine Sea, which became known colloquially as the Marianas Turkey Shoot, saw the sinking of three Japanese carriers, while two others were severely damaged. Some 330 Japanese planes were lost.

Immediately afterwards, Saipan was landed upon and after a fierce battle was seized; in July Guam and Timor also fell after heavy fighting, in which 60,000 Japanese and at least 5,000 Americans were killed. The Japanese fleet was now no further threat for several months. MacArthur's forces moved forward much more quickly and self-confidently to Biak, Noemfoor Island and Sansapor. The Americans now effectively controlled the whole of New Guinea, and were only 500 miles from reaching the Philippines.

PART V
FIGHTBACK

25 : To the Philippines

THE JOINT CHIEFS OF STAFF REVIEWED THE SITUATION. IN THEIR OPINION there was little reason, with the seizure of the Marianas, which brought American aircraft within strategic bombing distance of Japan, to get bogged down in a long campaign to liberate the Philippines. Better for MacArthur's land forces to be brought under Nimitz's control, for Formosa to be seized and for an invasion of Japan proper to be prepared. On January 26 Roosevelt traveled to Pearl Harbor to meet MacArthur, the only senior commander who recommended landing in the Philippines.

MacArthur, who by now was a legendary figure in America, as much for his Bataan campaign as for his penchant for wading ashore under enemy fire on the occasion of major landings, made a theatrical entrance alongside the cruiser *Baltimore*, carrying the President. He arrived in a large open-backed limousine with a police escort. He wore a brown leather services jacket, dark glasses and his "scrambled egg" floppy campaign hat. He was applauded by the sailors as he came on deck to meet Roosevelt for the first time in seven years. MacArthur was shocked by the change in the President's appearance. "He was just a shell of the man I had known."

Admiral Nimitz was already there. He was much less enthusiastic about the naval strategy for seizing Formosa than MacArthur was about seizing the Philippines. MacArthur stated the moral obligation to free the Philippines; but he had more important and rational arguments to hand as well:

> I was in total disagreement with the proposed plan, not only on strategic but psychological grounds. Militarily I felt that if I could secure the Philippines it would enable us to clamp an air and naval blockade on the flow of all supplies from the south to Japan, and thus, by paralyzing her industries, force her to early capitulation. I argued against the naval concept of frontal assault against the strongly held island positions of Iwo Jima or Okinawa. In my argument, I stressed that our losses would be far too heavy to justify the benefits to be gained by seizing these outposts. They were not essential to the enemy's defeat, and by cutting them off from supplies, they could be easily reduced and their effectiveness completely neutralized with negligible loss to ourselves. They were not in themselves

possessed of sufficient resources to act as main bases in our advance . . . To bypass isolated islands was one thing, but to leave in your rear such a large enemy concentration as the Philippines involved serious and unnecessary risks.

MacArthur's arguments won the day: in September instructions were issued for American forces to aim for the Philippines. It was to remain MacArthur's conviction to the last that Iwo Jima, Okinawa and a direct invasion of Japan were unnecessary, much less the atomic bombs dropped in order to obviate the need for such an invasion. With its fleet on the defensive and the Philippines in American hands, he declared that Japan could be strangled economically, becoming the biggest of all examples of his wither-on-the-vine philosophy, and forced to sue for peace.

As American forces prepared for the landings there, the Japanese rounded up their remaining naval forces for a final attempt to stop the invasion: a large Japanese fleet opposed the American fleet at Leyte Gulf in October. The battle, the largest in world naval history, raged for several days and was a close call for the American fleet, part of which had been mistakenly sent off on a wild-goose chase in search of the Japanese carriers, largely as a result of poor coordination between Nimitz's forces and MacArthur's. In the end, however, the Japanese fleet lost four carriers, including their flagship, three battleships, six heavy cruisers, three light cruisers and ten destroyers. The Japanese fleet was all but destroyed.

The way was open for the landings on the island of Leyte, two thirds of the way down the Philippine archipelago. MacArthur memorably described the scene. There were:

> ships to the front, to the rear, to the left, and to the right, as far as the eye could see. Their sturdy hulls plowed the water, now presenting a broadside view, now their sterns, as they methodically carried out the zigzag tactics of evasion.
>
> We came to Leyte just before midnight of a dark and moonless night. The stygian waters below and the black sky above seemed to conspire in wrapping us in an invisible cloak, as we lay to and waited for dawn before entering Leyte Gulf. Phase One of the plan had been accomplished with little resistance. Now and then a ghostly ship would slide quietly by us, looming out of the night and disappearing into the gloom almost before its outlines could be depicted. I knew that on every ship nervous men lined

the rails or paced the decks, peering into the darkness and wondering what stood out there beyond the night waiting for the dawn to come.

MacArthur waded ashore, as was his wont, the following morning. The landing proved remarkably successful, but the Japanese followed up with four counteroffensives, throwing so many aircraft into the fighting that American control of the air seemed in danger. For a while it looked as if the offensive was stalled, until American aircraft succeeded in sinking a major Japanese convoy carrying reinforcements to Leyte in November. Even so, the Americans remained bogged down in a massive quagmire of mud for several weeks until MacArthur came up with a bold plan to stage a further landing in December at Ormoc behind Japanese lines. The landing was successful and panicked the Japanese. The impasse was broken.

The same month, the small outpost of Mindoro was attacked and seized with high casualties. An invasion force of 200,000 men was assembled to move on Luzon, the main Philippine island. The Japanese were now fighting a war of attrition, to delay invasion of the home islands. The American fleet supporting MacArthur, under Admiral William Halsey, suffered several setbacks: a typhoon wrecked several ships; an attack on Formosa's airfields was frustrated by the weather; and in January a series of Kamikaze attacks sunk a battleship, two cruisers and a destroyer. But the bulk of the forces landed without opposition.

The Japanese garrison of some 27,500 men retreated to mountain fastnesses in the center of the island. Even against light resistance, though, the Americans made slow progress, as General Krueger, their commander, feared a breakout from the mountains to cut him off in the rear. MacArthur ordered Krueger to move faster on Manila where the Americans feared that thousands of prisoners of war were about to be butchered. Two further landings were staged to complete the encirclement of the capital. In a spectacular raid, a contingent of MacArthur's army rushed into central Manila, scattering the Japanese forces, to free some 5,000 prisoners.

However, the fight to rid the capital of its 20,000 troops, the recapture of Corregidor and Bataan, and the attempt to get the Japanese out of the central mountains were to take several bloody months. The casualty rate was high: some 80,000 Japanese lost their lives on Luzon alone, compared to 7,300 American and Allied troops. With the southern Philippines liberated, Borneo fell also.

After the conclusion of the epic battle for the Pacific, Japan's struggle in the western part of its empire was almost a sideshow. In April 1944, the

Japanese launched Operation Ichi-go to try and regain the initiative in China. This proved so successful that it seemed that Chiang Kai-Shek's forces might at last be overwhelmed, although they just managed to hold their own until the end of the war.

Another offensive, U-go, had as its objective a thrust from Burma into India, as a preemptive strike against what seemed to Japan to be an inevitable British offensive after the successful penetration of Orde Wingate's Chindits. On March 6 General Mutaguchi led a major Japanese force across the Chindwin river into India, making for Imphal and Kohima, two cities that commanded the approaches to the Indian plain. General William Slim, the British commander, had expected such a thrust and his defenses were well entrenched in the two cities. Try as they might, the Japanese could not take them in spite of the closest and fiercest fighting of the war. On June 22, after the monsoon had arrived, Mutaguchi finally conceded defeat and led his bedraggled forces back across the swampy roads into Burma before they became impassable. Only 20,000 out of 85,000 Japanese survived from the original invasion force.

The battleship *Yamato*, with an escort of a cruiser and eight destroyers, set out on a suicidal mission to delay the American landings. On April 7 she was located by American aircraft and pounded mercilessly, before capsizing with 2,300 sailors on board. The cruiser and five of the destroyers were sunk. Thus ended the last naval engagement of the Pacific war. More effective were the attacks by some 900 Kamikaze aircraft, which wrecked three destroyers and two ammunition ships. Over the following five months, the Americans lost 14 destroyers and some 5,000 dead.

In February 1945 the Americans had attacked Iwo Jima—just eight square miles of land. Its supposed importance was to be in providing an emergency landing point for crippled American bombers, 900 miles from Tokyo; the fate of captured airmen in Japanese hands was not calculated to boost the morale of the raiders. The 23,000 Japanese there fought to the last man, inflicting over 20,000 casualties on the Americans and holding up their progress for a month.

At Okinawa the resistance was if anything more intense. The island's significance was that it would be the ideal forward base for invading Japan. Of the Ryukyu Island group, only Okinawa had enough airfields and natural anchorages for the massive concentration of ground forces needed to take the mainland. Okinawa had three-lane airstrips at Naha, Yontan and Kadena, and two smaller ones at Yonabaru and Machinato. There were two fine anchorages on the east side of the island. The Japanese were determined not to give up such a prize lightly. Although they were eventually defeated in the face of overwhelming American superiority, it was at such a cost that the defenders considered it a victory.

At that point the purpose of Japan's army commanders was to compel the Americans to abandon their goal of unconditional surrender and negotiate a peace. The kind of carnage that would result from an invasion of the Japanese mainland would, in the view of the commanders, force the Americans to the negotiating table. Japan's leaders were often portrayed as insane fanatics determined to fight to the finish. Yet their objective was not entirely unrealistic. There may have been a point at which the casualties inflicted on the Americans may have forced them to start compromising.

Okinawa rammed the message home. Altogether, the Americans suffered around 20,000 deaths and 53,000 wounded, as well as 26,000 non-battle casualties. No fewer than 763 aircraft were lost and 368 ships knocked out, of which 38 were sunk. The Japanese losses were immense, of course: more than 100,000 dead, and 7,800 planes and 16 ships destroyed. Many of their aircraft were lost in Kamikaze attacks on American ships. (Kamikaze does not mean suicide, but "divine wind," a reference to the sudden typhoons that destroyed the last attempted invasions of Japan from the sea, those of the Mongols). There were more than 1,900 such attacks from Japanese aircraft. The large majority failed: some pilots got cold feet, many were shot down, many attacked the first ships they saw—usually minor vessels. The Ohka piloted bomb proved a flop because the aircraft carrying them were sitting targets; the Shinyo suicide speedboats also proved relatively easy to intercept.

Japanese infantry tactics proved to be brilliantly coordinated. Okinawa's rocky, rugged terrain turned out to be ideal for defense, and the Japanese made the most of the opportunity: they brought to bear the greatest concentration of artillery encountered by the Americans throughout the Pacific War. A huge network of caves and underground passages provided shelter against the Allied naval and aerial barrage, and gave the advantages of flexibility and surprise. A pattern of the fighting was for the advancing Americans to come under artillery attack, while the Japanese sheltered underground from bombardment. Then, as the American infantry advanced over exposed ridges, the Japanese would come out of their caves and tunnels and open fire from heavily fortified positions.

The fight for Okinawa would almost certainly have taken a considerably higher toll but for two blunders by the Japanese. Under pressure from

Tokyo for a success, the Japanese commander, General Ushijima, launched a disastrous counteroffensive against superior forces which considerably weakened his 32nd Army. A second offensive, this time at the instigation of his chief of staff, Lieutenant-General Cho, who believed that the spiritual superiority of the Japanese army would cause American resistance to crumble, fatally debilitated the Japanese forces. By mid-June large numbers of Japanese were for the first time surrendering, although Ushijima and Cho took their own lives in the classic manner.

MacArthur was dryly to observe that the total killed on both islands was greater than that in the whole of his campaign from Papua New Guinea to the Philippines. As we have seen, MacArthur had argued against frontal attacks on the islands, saying they were inessential to his strangulation plan. The other American commanders had resolved to use Okinawa's anchorages as the staging point for their invasion of Japan.

In March 1945 preparations began in Japan for the defense of the mainland—Operation Ketsu-go. It assumed that the Americans would invade Japan's southern island of Kyushu with fifteen divisions in October (in fact America's planned Operation Olympic called for ten divisions to arrive in November). Under Ketsu-go it was intended to muster no fewer than fifty-eight infantry divisions, made up of 2.6 million from the regular army, backed up by 3.65 million reservists and a volunteer militia of 28 million. Obviously, not just the militia and reservists but also much of the regular army was poorly trained and ill-equipped. But after Okinawa's 110,000 had shown what they could do, the prospect of an invasion of Japan, and the likely resistance and casualties, was awesome.

At 9:30 A.M. on June 16, the joint chiefs of staff arrived at the White House to give President Truman the results of a two-day appraisal of the task of invading Japan. General George Marshall outlined the plan for the first attack, Operation Olympic, to go in on November 1, 1945, with 816,000 troops; this would be followed by an invasion of Honshu around Tokyo with 1,172,000 men on March 1, 1946. Stimson told Truman that "a landing operation would be a very big, costly and arduous struggle on our part . . . The terrain, much of which I have visited several times, has left the impression on my memory of being one which would be susceptible to a last-ditch defense." The somber warning given by the chiefs of staff was that a million American lives were likely to be lost in the operation.

A month later, Truman was given an even more dire message by MacArthur, the head of American Forces in the Far East. He warned that the Japanese could resort to guerrilla warfare in the event of an invasion and that a campaign might last ten years. No estimate of the extent of American casualties could be given; nor was any made of the likely number of Japanese dead and wounded, either by MacArthur or by the Joint Chiefs of Staff. But air raids on Japanese cities had already taken some 700,000 lives before August 1945. Military casualties could be reckoned at upward of a million, with civilian casualties a multiple of that.

The epitaph on the Pacific War must be that Japan's defeat was inevitable, inherent in its very successes in the early stages of the war. The Japanese had played for the highest stakes: by destroying the American fleet at Pearl Harbor, they had ensured that the war would be fought to the finish. They grossly underestimated the American will to resist, believing that their superior motivation would overcome the spirit of the supposedly pampered and indolent Americans. They also underestimated the power of American industry to produce ships and guns at a vastly faster rate than themselves. As a group of offshore islands, Japan was especially vulnerable to naval attack to cut off its supply routes, and once the tide had turned in the sea war, Japan's defeat was only a matter of time.

The early Japanese successes were secured by surprise, fanaticism, lightning tactics, and above all through the softness of their targets. They had caught the Americans unprepared, sleeping at anchor. They had exposed the weakness of the British forces in Asia while the bulk of the country's war effort was concentrated in Europe. The Dutch were a walkover. Only the Australians put up serious resistance. The local populations of the areas they occupied did not support their old colonial masters, and were at worst hostile to them and at best indifferent, except in the Philippines. (In fact the Japanese occupation decisively weakened the hold of the colonial powers in the postwar period). Having for the most part secured easy victories across an empire one and a half times larger than that of Nazi Germany at its most extensive, they were highly vulnerable to serious attack. Only ferocity and determination prevented greater Japan from collapsing much more quickly than it did.

That said, both MacArthur and Nimitz staged tactically brilliant campaigns, reversing the Japanese occupation much faster than Washington dared hope. Japan's six-month wonder would have ended far more quickly than it did had the Americans given strategic priority to the Pacific campaign. Instead Roosevelt had from the first accorded priority to the European threat—even though Japan's attack had caused the United States to enter the war. Accordingly, only 29 divisions of some half a million men were to serve at any one time in the Pacific theater, only a third of them full combat divisions. Japan had around the same number engaged in the Pacific War and a further 2 million or so committed to China. By contrast, in Europe, the United States had some 4 million men. There were around the same number of British forces, and some 12 million Russians ranged against some 10 million Germans.

The position in Europe was so desperate and critical that Roosevelt's decision was understandable. In retrospect, though, had American forces been more evenly divided between the two theaters, the American success in the Pacific might have been much speedier. It was all the more remarkable that MacArthur and Nimitz achieved so much with so little—virtually an even fight with the occupying Japanese. Although overwhelming American firepower played a major part in the final stages of the war with Japan, that was far from being the case at the beginning. The Americans won a hard and fair fight. The two key questions as far as American strategy was concerned were whether anything was achieved through having competing lines of approach and whether a policy of economic strangulation would have worked.

26 : Dance of Death

WITHIN JAPAN AS THE WAR PROGRESSED, THE MAIN POWERS IN THE LAND, the bureaucracy, the imperial household and the Emperor himself, were, as we have seen, steadily declining in influence. Hirohito's reservations about the desirability of war have already been noted. After the decision to go to war, he seemed to regard it as his duty to dedicate himself to prosecuting the war effort as vigorously as possible. Many observers of Japan have noted as a national characteristic the ability to press for one course of action, be frustrated, and then prosecute the reverse course with equal fervor. The Emperor was in this mold, which in truth is also a characteristic of a weak mind, not overendowed with intelligence.

The exasperation with Hirohito that both Konoye and Kido felt during the war, when the Emperor who had had such misgivings about going to war seemed at times to be in thrall to Tojo's fervor, can thus be explained, and not in terms of an evil or Machiavellian personality, which nothing in Hirohito's actions before or after the war suggests he was.

Kawahara, his biographer, writes:

> Hirohito had signed the declaration of war on December 8, in spite of his reservations, under pressure from the military. After hostilities began, he

felt duty-bound to support the war effort. He put aside his former misgivings and, along with the nation, concentrated on the task of defeating the Allies. After the outbreak of the China war, Hirohito had given up golf; thereafter he also gave up horseback riding. Apart from a visit to the Grand Shrine at Ise and one to the Nasu Detached Palace, Hirohito did not leave Tokyo until the war ended. He lost seven or eight kilos, as he subsisted on wartime rations. Toward the end of the war, when the news was all bad, he suffered a nervous breakdown. He would forget that he had watered his plants and water them again. He took to pacing up and down his room, and railing impotently against the military, to the despair of his aides.

It is certainly true that Hirohito did his best for the war effort and indulged in celebrations at Japanese victories; little else could be expected of the head of a nation at war, with soldiers dying in his service, even if he believed that conflict had been the consequence of misguided policies. Short of abdicating, Hirohito could hardly have indulged himself in open criticism or expressions of sadness at Japanese victories. Kido, his chief adviser, found him "poised and serene and I detected not the slightest anxiety in his behavior," following Pearl Harbor. The Emperor was "very cheerful after the fall of Singapore, attributing the successes of the operation to advance planning."

Yet in February 1942, only three months into the war, Hirohito was talking of peace, although more as one dictated to the Allies than as the consequence of negotiation. Still, in Japan's jingoistic climate, it was a surprising thing to do. He told Kido: "Let us not lose any opportunity to end the war. It would not be good for humanity if the war were prolonged and the tragedy spread. If it does go on, the army will get worse. We have to consider the situation carefully and plan accordingly."

Hirohito's prime reservations about the war were concerned with its winnability, not its morality. There is no record of whether the Emperor was aware of the atrocities committed in China, Malaysia and the Philippines, although he showed no emotion to Kido when informed of the Bataan Death March afterward.

With the Battle of Midway the tide began to turn for the first time in the direction Hirohito had always feared; but he remained cool. "It's really regrettable. It's a shame. But I've given orders to the chiefs of staff not to lose our sense of combat, not to become passive as far as operations are concerned." Early in 1943 Buna was lost. Hirohito remarked that the operation "must be rated a failure but if this can be the basis of future success it may turn out to be a salutary lesson." By April 1943, Hirohito was striking a more querulous, gloomy note:

You make all sorts of excuses like thick fog and so on, but this should have been taken into consideration beforehand. I wonder if the Army and the Navy talk to each other at all? . . . We can't win with this kind of lack of co-operation. If we go on fighting like this we will only make China rejoice, confuse neutrals, dismay our allies and weaken the Co-Prosperity Sphere. Isn't there any way, somehow, somewhere, of closing in on a United States force and destroying it?

Two months later he told Tojo harshly, "You keep saying the Imperial Army is invincible but whenever the enemy lands, you lose the fight. You have never been able to repulse an enemy landing. If we don't stop them somewhere, where, I ask you, will it all end?" After the Japanese withdrawal from Guadalcanal, the Emperor scolded, "The military underrated the Allies; their sacrifice was in vain." Hirohito undoubtedly reflected the views of both the bureaucracy and the imperial household. But for long no criticism of the war effort was to be heard from the *zaibatsu* ministers in the government, whose alliance with the armed forces remained intact as defeat followed defeat.

Under Prime Minister Hideki Tojo the illusion was created that Japan was turning into a military dictatorship. In fact, with the exception of Tojo's appointment, the government remained much the same as it had always been—a mixture of interest groups—the armed forces, the economic super-bosses, and the bureaucrats.

Tojo was firmly in the driving seat, but the *zaibatsu*, in particular, were always in a position to block government decisions. Tojo depended on the goodwill of the *zaibatsu* to meet the huge demands of modern warfare. Three months before Pearl Harbor, after a year of intense debate, the *zaibatsu* had scored a spectacular victory in opposing an attempt by some military leaders to subject them to the control of wartime bureaucracy. The Major Industry Association Ordinance was drawn up appropriating power over specific industries to the Industrial Control Associations—in effect giving the cartels absolute control over war material, labor and capital in their industries, with instructions to rationalize smaller firms. This was like appointing a wolf to round up a flock of sheep.

The *zaibatsu* now had the power to gobble up or render dependent their small competitors. This they certainly did, vigorously. The big four *zaibatsu* doubled their percentage of production from 12 percent to 24 percent in the first four war years of 1941–45, absorbing hundreds of smaller firms. The war years also produced a much larger reliance on heavy industries to produce war material; by the end of the war, heavy industry accounted for four fifths of Japan's industrial output, compared with around half at the outset. Heavy industry was entirely dominated by the *zaibatsu*.

Under the new provision, big business control over the economy was actually strengthened. Increasingly it began to seem that the *zaibatsu* dictated policy to the military, rather than the other way round. There is no evidence to suggest that they were a restraining influence on the armed forces of the period—the high noon of Japan's aggression abroad—until late in the war.

With Japan's early war successes, the *zaibatsu* moved in behind the soldiers to control the mineral treasures of the East Indies and channel raw materials to Japan. As we have seen, the "Total War" group in the Japanese army, which was now in control and whose senior representative was Tojo, believed in close collaboration with the *zaibatsu*. The group recognized that it would only achieve its expansionist aims in alliance with the cartels. In turn, the *zaibatsu* recognized that their interests could be furthered only by co-operation with the army, in importing the raw materials and finding markets through conquest that had been denied through world recession. The partnership was one of mutual dependence.

As the war developed, however, Tojo and the other military chiefs began to look for a system of central control of production that would result in less autonomy, profiteering and stockpiling by the *zaibatsu*. However, the cartels fought back bitterly to retain their growing share of the spoils. Early in 1943 Tojo sought a measure giving him "special powers" over the economy; but he was forced to accept a series of reforms giving the *zaibatsu* greater powers than ever. First, his cabinet was enlarged to include more representatives from business. Second, an advisory council of seven leading cartel representatives was set up by him. Third, the *zaibatsu* were given control of the administration of a new ministry of munitions, nominally headed by Tojo but in fact run by the deputy minister, Nobusuke Kishi, later to become a postwar prime minister. Forth, a Mitsui executive, Ginjiro Fujihara, was appointed to the cabinet in November 1943, as a kind of *zaibatsu* minder for Tojo.

The search was on for a way to extricate Japan from the war; by early 1944 this involved Kido as well as the virtually disgraced figure of Konoye, for some time an advocate of early peace. The Emperor, having been a relatively late convert to the war, now seemed reluctant to believe it was definitely lost: he persuaded Tojo, who was growing ever more isolated, to take on the roles of foreign minister and war minister in order to streamline the Japanese war effort. Presiding over this immense bureaucratic empire, Tojo had no alibis when Nimitz's forces astounded Japan by taking Saipan in mid-1944. The Americans were now within bombing distance of Japan itself. In the Emperor's eyes the army had made a severe mistake in committing Japan to defend Rabaul in the south and neglecting the defense of Saipan, close to home and much more important strategically. Tojo had no choice but to resign after the fall of Saipan as his cabinet enemies, now joined by the *zaibatsu* representatives, combined to force him out.

Kido and Konoye were discussing ways at this stage of initiating peace talks, and even of forcing Hirohito's abdication in favor of his youngest brother, Prince Takamatsu, who unlike the more bellicose Chichibu, had always inclined toward the peace faction; but they merely represented a tiny minority in the government. A moderate, General Koiso, was appointed to succeed Tojo. With the beginning of the Allied campaign to liberate the Philippines and to start massive aerial bombardment of Tokyo, all hope of turning the tide evaporated. The question for the armed forces, their *zaibatsu* allies and the bureaucracy was how to secure the best possible peace terms.

In January 1945, it seemed that Hirohito too was beginning to favor talks—very late in the day. "Now a decisive battle will have to be fought on Leyte as Luzon has been lost. . . . We will have to conceal this from the people. . . . It's reported that the U.S. army intends to land at Luzon. The war situation in the Philippines is extremely grave."

In March the saturation raid on Tokyo was staged which killed some 100,000 people (more than were to die initially at either Hiroshima or Nagasaki). Eight days later, Hirohito tored the city and remarked sadly to Kido: "After the Great Kanto Earthquake, everything was so totally, cleanly burned and destroyed that one did not feel a sense of shock. But this is far more tragic. It pains me deeply. Tokyo has become 'scorched earth'."

In May a large part of the imperial palace was burned down, although the shrine of the sacred mirror was spared. The Meiji Shrine was destroyed the same night. The government now had to confront reality. Tojo and the army continued to urge resistance, arguing that America could be lured into a truly bloody invasion of Formosa which would force them to negotiate terms. Tojo also tried to secure the appointment of General Hata, the war minister, as prime minister, to succeed the caretaker Koiso. Hirohito, knowing that a new prime minister would have to assume responsibility for the surrender, compelled a distinguished elder statesman, Admiral Kantaro Suzuki, survivor of the death squads of the February 1936 coup, to take the job. All but the army were now reconciled to the inevitability of defeat.

In these dark days, one section of the elite was still carefully protecting its interests. The *zaibatsu* had turned decisively against the war. For them the danger had begun with Tojo's attempts to wrest control of war production from them at the height of the Pacific War, which they bitterly and successfully resisted. They were now appalled by the destruction wrought by the B-29s upon their property, and feared that workers would begin to revolt. They pressed for the "nationalization" of industry and for setting up an "industrial army" among the workforce subject to military discipline, and thus banned from strikes or absenteeism.

Under the terms of the nationalization proposal, the state agreed temporarily to underwrite the major industries and to restore them to the *zaibatsu* after the war; formal ownership would remain in *zaibatsu* hands, as would operating control of the companies concerned. The state would be responsible only for their losses and the costs of reconstruction. Army officers were given the task of organising a huge civilian militia into which the whole nation was effectively conscripted, to prevent any insurrections against the elites responsible for having reduced Japan to rubble. T. A. Bisson summed up the relationship between the army and the *zaibatsu* as the war came to an end:

> During the corse of the Pacific War American official propaganda placed such emphasis on the "military dictatorship" which allegedly ruled Japan as to distort beyond recognition the role which the *zaibatsu* monopolies were playing both in the politics and economy of the country. On the political side, it is sufficient to note that Japan's last two wartime cabinets under premiers Koiso and Suzuki were thoroughly dominated by a coalition of the imperial palace guard and representatives of the *zaibatsu* monopolies aided by a number of bureaucrats. The military and naval men in these cabinets played second fiddle to the nominees of the conservative *zaibatsu*-monarchist combination within the Japanese oligarchy, while the bureaucrats accommodated themselves to the stronger force.
>
> A similar misapprehension exists with respect to the Japanese economy. Since the military were all-powerful, the propaganda line runs, they dictated to the *zaibatsu* the terms on which the national economy worked—in effect they "nationalized" industry. Nothing could be further from the truth. Full domination of Japan's wartime economy by representatives of the *zaibatsu* was expressed on two levels: first, in their control of the direc-

tion and scope of the government's wartime economic policy and, second, in the vast increases effected in the plant and capital expansion of the monopoly concerns.

One further absurdity was to ensue: Japan had lost most of its empire and been cut off from its forces in the parts left behind. The country was now being subjected to the most awesome and savage punishment. The saturation bombing of Tokyo, carried out from American and British carriers as well as the Marianas, Iwo Jima and Okinawa, had destroyed nearly half the built-up area of some 60 cities. The large urban sprawl from Tokyo to Yokohama lay in ruins; Osaka, Nagoya and Iwaki were devastated. There was not the slightest chance that Japan could break out of its encirclement. Its major industries had virtually come to a halt, its fleet was confined to port, and it was dangerously short of supplies and spare parts. While the ruins of their country lay around them, however, Japan's army chiefs would still not acknowledge defeat to their own people.

Suzuki, the new prime minister, was no friend of the militarists; but he too felt unable to accept the inevitable, and clutched at one last straw. That straw was Russian mediation on Japan's behalf. It was a ludicrous hope: the Russians were Japan's worst traditional enemy. Suzuki offered to hand over southern Sakhalin, the northern Kuriles and northern Manchuria to Russia, as well as a handful of cruisers and raw materials from the south (which the Japanese could not deliver: the supply lines there had been cut). In return they hoped Stalin might be induced not just to mediate with the West, but also to provide Japan with desperately needed oil for the last battle which, the Japanese believed would compel the Americans to accept a negotiated peace.

Suzuki's proposal was a non-starter. The Russians had long looked upon Japan with intense suspicion; they had already agreed to declare war on Japan after Hitler's defeat. They stood to gain much in such a war. When Suzuki took office, the Russians told him they would not renew their neutrality pact with Japan. The Prime Minister pleaded with them to reconsider, and would not take the repeated brush-offs, nor the sound advice of the Japanese ambassador in Moscow, for an answer. In July, with the fall of Okinawa, the government tried to send Prince Konoye, one of their elder statesmen, to Moscow to seek Russian mediation with America. The Russians brusquely brushed the proposal aside, although Stalin reported it to the Americans at Potsdam.

27 : LITTLE BOY AND FAT MAN

ON APRIL 12, 1945, VICE PRESIDENT HARRY S TRUMAN HAD BEEN
fulfilling his routine duty of presiding over the Senate; when the sitting ended he dropped into the office of the speaker of the house, Sam
Rayburn, for a bourbon and water, only to be rung by President Roosevelt's
secretary and invited to "come over." Once there, he was ushered to the
study of Eleanor Roosevelt, the president's wife, who told him immediately that her husband was dead.

Two hours later, at seven o'clock, Truman was sworn in. As cabinet
members filed out, Stimson held back. "Mr. President, I must talk to you
on a most urgent matter," he said. "I want to inform you about an immense
project that is under way—a project leading to the development of a new
explosive of almost unbelievable destructive power." With those cryptic
words, the old man left, leaving behind an exhausted and bewildered
President in his first hours in office.

Over the next few weeks he was to learn a great deal more. On April 25
Stimson and General Groves arrived for an interview they had requested on a
"highly secret matter." Straightaway, Stimson told Truman that he wanted to
discuss a bomb equal in power to all the artillery used in both world wars.
He went on, "Within four months we shall in all probability have completed the most terrible weapon ever known in human history, one bomb
which could destroy a whole city. Although we have shared its development with the United Kingdom, physically the U.S. is at present in the position of controlling the resources with which to construct and use it, and no
other nation could reach this position for some years. Nevertheless, it is practically certain that we could not remain in this position indefinitely."

In Stimson's view it was morally essential that the United States win the
race for the bomb. "We may see a time when such a weapon may be constructed in secret and used suddenly and effectively . . . with its aid even a
very powerful, unsuspecting nation might be conquered within a few days
by a very much smaller one . . . The world in its present state of moral
advancement compared with its technical development would be eventually
at the mercy of such a weapon. In other words, modern civilization might
be completely destroyed." He ended by saying that, despite all the draw-

backs, he still favored its being used against Japan. Truman agreed at once on the necessity of continuing the work, but left the final decision on using the bomb against a live target until he was forced to make it.

On July 6, Truman left for Potsdam. With his wife Bess and his daughter Margaret, he had been attending a concert on the White House lawn given by an army band. As soon as it was over he went indoors, bade the women goodbye, and left for Union Station. Seven hours later a special presidential train drew into Newport News, Virginia, where his heavy cruiser, the *Augusta*, was anchored. On that journey across the Atlantic, under threat of attack by a rogue submarine, he had many hours to ponder the further progress Stimson had reported to him four days before on the development of the bomb, and the suggestion that the Japanese be given one last chance before it was dropped.

The town of Potsdam outside Berlin is small, bourgeois and pleasant, endowed with a superb baroque villa, the Sans-Souci palace, and a comfortable, staid conference center. In July the weather had been warm and agreeable. As limousines shuttled between Harry Truman's three-floor stucco residence, Winston Churchill's comfortable house and Josef Stalin's fine villa, it was hard to believe that a war which had taken millions of lives had raged all around them and ended just two months before.

On the morning of July 17, Truman had enjoyed an ample breakfast when a convoy of cars arrived outside his residence. There emerged possibly the most famous living face in the world, a short, plump, genial, boyishly energetic 69-year-old, Winston Churchill, to pay his respects for the first time to the new American president. Truman had been advised to treat Churchill warily: the British leader, according to the president's advisers, had enormous charm, but was a die-hard reactionary whose main war aim was to restore the status of the British Empire; indeed, Truman had heard from his staff more criticism of Churchill than of Stalin, whom the Americans regarded vaguely as "a hard nut to crack" but not a particularly sinister figure. The President's advisers had been far more concerned with breaking the stranglehold of British imperialism than with any threat posed by the Soviet Union.

To both their surprises, the plainspoken Missourian found himself getting along famously with the bluff aristocratic imperialist, who was equally blunt and, rather than using his wartime experience to patronize the inexperienced American, tended to seek and agree with his views. Churchill, desperately frustrated by the way Roosevelt had ignored his concerns about Stalin at Yalta, was keen to recruit the new President to his side. American thinking on the dangers posed by the Russians had evolved just a little since Yalta. Truman was gratified by the way Churchill listened to him. Stalin, who had suffered a minor heart attack, was a day late in arriving at the conference.

After the British prime minister departed, Truman toured the ruins of Berlin, a city reduced virtually to rubble. Later he recalled, rather flatly, that he had seen "a demonstration of what can happen when a man over-reaches himself." When the President returned to his villa, Stimson, the secretary for war, was waiting to hand him a telegram from the Pentagon. It read, employing a tasteless code, "Operated on this morning. Diagnosis not yet complete but results seem satisfactory and already exceed expectations. Local press release necessary as interest extends great distance. Dr. Groves pleased. He returns tomorrow. I will keep you posted."

Truman replied, "I send my warmest congratulations to the doctor and his consultant."

Four days later he received a full eyewitness report from the Manhattan Project's director, General Groves. The world's first testing of an atomic bomb had taken place before dawn on the morning of July 16 at Alamogordo, New Mexico, one of the remotest desert locations. It was cold, and occasional shafts of lightning lit up the desolate eeriness of the pace. There were over four hundred people present, most of them around 20 miles away. At 5:25 A.M. the observers lay facedown in trenches. Groves was near the scientific director of the project, J. Robert Oppenheimer.

Ten seconds from the intended blast, a green flare shot up; five seconds later, another followed. At 5:30 precisely the words, "I am become death, the destroyer of worlds," from the sacred Hindu text, flickered into Oppenheimer's mind as he viewed the first atomic detonation in history.

The *New York Times* observer was to describe the scene later: "A light not of this world, the light of many suns in one" struck the surrounding hills.

It was a sunrise such as the world had never seen, a great green super-sun climbing in a fraction of a second to a height more than 8000 feet, rising ever higher until it touched the clouds, lighting up earth and sky and all around with dazzling luminosity. Up it went, a great ball of fire about a mile in diameter, changing colors as it kept shooting upward, from deep purple to orange, expanding, growing bigger, rising as it was expanding, an elemental force freed from its bonds after being chained for billions of years. For a fleeting instant the color was unearthly green, such as one only sees in the corona of the sun during a total eclipse. It was as though the earth had opened and the skies had split. One felt as though he had been privileged to witness the Birth of the World—to be present at the moment of Creation when the Lord said, "Let there be Light."

Subsequently, many were to argue that what had been witnessed was the first glimpse of the end of the world.

The explosion had produced a temperature of 100 million degrees Fahrenheit, over three times that at the center of the sun, and ten thousand times the sun's surface temperature. The light had been brighter than a thousands suns. All life within a mile of the focus of the explosion had been killed; the soil had turned into a white-hot saucer 500 yards in diameter. The scaffolding by the bomb had been vaporized. The billowing nuclear cloud had plumed 40,000 feet into the air; thirty seconds after the explosion, a hurricane-force wind tore through the camp where most of the observers were, followed by a deafening roar. When peace returned, the scientists ran out of their bunkers, dancing and whooping with joy.

When Stimson had finished reading Groves's report to Truman, the President grinned. He had, he said later, "an entirely new feeling of confidence." The following day he was told that the bomb would be ready for use by early August. Truman was delighted and calmed after days of increasing restlessness listening to "endless debates on matters that could not be settled between Churchill and Stalin." Stimson also showed the report to the British prime minister, and told him that Stalin would be informed of the existence of the bomb without being apprised of details.

Later that day Churchill and Truman met. The British leader told the president that in his view the bomb was "a miracle of deliverance." He listed four reasons: it might make the invasion of the Japanese mainland unnecessary; it might end the war "in one or two violent shocks"; it could—and in this Churchill showed extraordinary perceptiveness—save Japanese honor; and it would avert the need to ask Stalin for help in subduing Japan. Churchill's views complemented Truman's own. The inevitable could be stopped now only by a rare outbreak of good sense on the part of Japan's government.

It was Winston Churchill, with the characteristic brilliance that underlay an appearance raddled by decades of success, frustration, democratic politics, bonhomie and decision-making, who had made the most apposite, if crafted, remark about the bomb. When Stimson had shown him the report of the test, the British prime minister, mildly apprehensive on the eve of an election which he believed he would win (and didn't), read the report somberly. "Stimson, what was gunpowder? Trivial. What was electricity? Meaningless. The atom bomb is the Second Coming in wrath."

Churchill in fact knew a great deal about the project, to which British scientists had made a major contribution. But his remarks, even if prepared, had the ring of truth. Churchill's second judgment came later, summarizing what had been agreed at Potsdam about the bomb. The British prime minister asserted that, "while the final decision lay in the main" with America's new president, Harry S Truman, Churchill fully supported it. "The historic fact remains, and it must be judged in the after time, that the decision whether or not to use the atomic bomb to compel the surrender of Japan was never an issue. There was unanimous, automatic, unquestioning agreement around the table."

On July 26, 1945, Japan was given its last chance. In the names of President Truman and the British and Chinese governments—Stalin had been deliberately excluded—the Potsdam Declaration was issued. The main points were, first, a threat:

> The result of the futile, senseless German resistance to the might of the aroused free peoples of the world stands forth in awful clarity as an example to the people of Japan. The might that now converges on Japan is immeasurably greater than that which, when applied to the resisting Nazis, necessarily laid waste to the lands, industry and the methods of life of the whole German people. The full application of our military power, backed by our resolve, will mean the inevitable and complete destruction of the Japanese armed forces and just as inevitably the utter devastation of the Japanese homeland.

Second, there was an offer:

> The time has come for Japan to decide whether she will continue to be controlled by those self-willed militaristic advisers whose unintelligent calculations have brought the Empire of Japan to the threshold of annihilation, or whether she will follow the path of reason.

The conditions followed:

> The following are our terms. We will not deviate from them. There are no alternatives. We shall brook no delay.
> There must be eliminated for all time the authority and influence of those who have deceived and misled the people of Japan into embarking on world conquest, for we insist that a new order of peace, security and

justice will be impossible until irresponsible militarism is driven from the world;

Until such a new order is established and until there is convincing proof that Japan's war-making power is destroyed, points in Japanese territory to be designated by the Allies shall be occupied to secure the achievement of the basic objectives we are here setting forth;

We do not intend that the Japanese shall be enslaved as a race or destroyed as a nation, but stern justice shall be meted out to all war criminals, including those who have visited cruelties upon our prisoners. The Japanese government shall remove all obstacles to the revival and strengthening of democratic tendencies among the Japanese people. Freedom of speech, of religion and of thought, as well as respect for the fundamental human rights shall be established.

The occupying forces of the Allies shall be withdrawn from Japan as soon as these objectives have been accomplished and there has been established in accordance with the freely expressed will of the Japanese people a peacefully inclined and responsible government.

In furtherance of these aims, the Declaration called for the immediate surrender of all Japanese armed forces—"The alternative for Japan is prompt and utter destruction." The declaration reflected some of the infighting between Stimson, the veteran who felt his views were being bypassed, and the new secretary of state, James F. Byrnes, a Democratic party power broker with little experience of foreign affairs.

As such the document was badly flawed, perhaps fatally so. There was no mention in it of the sine qua non for a Japanese surrender: maintenance of the imperial system. Stimson had favored this, but Byrnes, in deference to American public opinion—two-thirds of which favored Hirohito's arrest or execution, according to a Gallup poll—was opposed. Stimson, his personal aide, Ambassador Averell Harriman, and Britain's new Labour foreign secretary, Ernest Bevin, all believed, in the latter's words, that "the Emperor was the institution through which one might have to deal to effectively control Japan."

Truman was more simple-minded: at a party aboard his ship on the return journey, he was exhilarated by the testing of the bomb. America, he said, had "developed a revolutionary new weapon of such force and nature that we do not need the Russians or any other nation." The bomb was acquiring an unstoppable momentum. For hard-line Japanese, however, the absence of any reference to the Emperor suggested that his office might indeed be abolished—although the more perceptive realized that the omission and reference to the "freely expressed will of the Japanese people" was an indication that he would be allowed to continue.

The second flaw was the cavalier attitude adopted toward the Russians. Certainly, it seemed like the answer to a prayer for the Americans to be able to contemplate the defeat of Japan without having to ask the Russians for help in opening up a second front to attack Japan from the north. Yet the United States had already begun quietly to encourage the Russians to prepare for the possibility of intervention, in case the option of the bomb was not available in time. The Russians were hardly unjustified in being resentful and suspicious at the way the Americans had behaved, however richly Stalin deserved it for his high-handedness at Yalta.

Finally, the Declaration made no reference to the bomb itself. An obsession with security was partly responsible; the fear of looking ridiculous if the bomb should fail to work was another cause. The Americans were also concerned that they would not be believed if they inserted such a warning. Yet Japanese intelligence was already vaguely aware of the American work on the bomb. While the Japanese would probably have publicly dismissed its existence, privately they might have paused for thought. Certainly, "prompt and utter destruction" was too vague a euphemism even to hint at the bomb's existence, and was taken to refer to the saturation bombing of Tokyo and other cities.

President Truman had thus made mistakes which compounded the tragedy that followed. The bulk of the blame, though, must be ascribed to the Japanese: they missed their chance. As soon as the terms of the Declaration reached Tokyo, they had been delivered by the foreign minister, Shigenori Togo, to the Emperor. Hirohito read the Declaration slowly, asking questions. Togo agreed with the Emperor that on certain key points the terms marked a substantial climbdown from the "unconditional surrender" requested in the Cairo Declaration issued by Roosevelt. Hirohito asked whether the terms "were the most reasonable to be expected in the circumstances."

Togo agreed that they were: "in principle they are acceptable." If that had been the end of it, peace would surely have been achieved and Hiroshima and Nagasaki spared. But at that stage the Emperor was not in charge. The cabinet had met earlier and the prime minister, Kantaro Suzuki, a member of the imperial household elite, had decided to prevaricate, probably in the forlorn hope that the Russians would mediate with the Americans. A day later, at a press conference, Suzuki said the government would *mokusatsu* the declaration—meaning that they would "treat it with silent contempt," "ignore it," "kill it with silence." Suzuki was responding to an officially promoted journalist's question and reading from a prepared text. He had unwittingly pronounced the death sentence on Hiroshima and Nagasaki.

Stimson, in Potsdam, gave the Allies' response: "In the face of this rejection, we could only proceed to demonstrate that the ultimatum had meant exactly what it said. For such a purpose the atomic bomb was an eminently suitable weapon."

On the early morning of August 6, 1945, Second Lieutenant Morris Jeppson of the U.S. Air Force was making his way along a narrow catwalk in the center of a B-29 bomber cruising at around 9,000 feet at a speed of 205 miles an hour. He was in the bomb bay of the aircraft, which was empty save for a single large metal casing. It was pleasantly cool—18 degrees Celsius, 66 Fahrenheit. As the aircraft moved evenly along, Jeppson reached the bomb casing and carefully unscrewed three green safety plugs, exchanging them for three red ones. There was no hitch: they fitted perfectly. The world's first atomic bomb to be used in conflict had been armed.

He moved back along the catwalk and reported to Captain William Parsons, the naval officer who was one of the most influential planners behind the Manhattan Project. Parsons was profoundly relieved. The replacement of the safety plug had completed an extraordinary night's work. Less than four hours before he had been down in the bomb bay with Jeppson, who had been holding a flashlight. Parsons had inserted a charge of high-quality gunpowder wired with an electrical detonator into a breech behind the "bullet"—a uranium cylinder shaped like a tin of soup some six inches long.

The detonator was programmed to set off the powder, which would propel the bullet down a 52-inch barrel 900 feet a second into the center of a uranium ring, and a device made of plutonium-239 would begin emitting neutrons, starting off the chain reaction. After two minutes of preparation Parsons had been ready to perform the most delicate task. He had to assemble the four sections of explosive together, then connect up the detonator. He had tightened up the breech plate, front and rear. The green plugs had remained in place to ensure that the bomb could not be detonated by an accidental electrical charge. Now it was live.

Parsons in turn informed the mission commander and pilot of the *Enola Gay*, Colonel Paul W. Tibbets, who turned to gaze in silence at the clear early morning sky over the unending blue expanse of the Pacific. The sun had risen only two hours before in a staggering display of incandescent pink. It was Tibbets who bore the ultimate responsibility for the success or failure of the most important mission ever undertaken by an American aircraft, before or since.

Two hours before, Tibbets had been round the aircraft on a tour of inspection, handing over the controls to his copilot, Captain Robert Lewis. The mission commander encountered Technical Sergeant George (Bob) Caron, a friend from the old days of the B-29 training program. After nearly a year of intensive training on this project, Tibbets directly addressed the subject of the mission for the first time. He asked Caron whether he had guessed what they were doing. "Colonel, I don't want to get put up against a wall and shot," replied the other wryly.

"Bob, we're on our way now. You can talk."

Caron asked whether they carried "a new super-explosive . . . a chemist's nightmare." Tibbets shook his head.

Caron asked if it was "a physical nightmare."

"Yes," Tibbets told him.

"Are we splitting atoms?" Caron asked, recalling a popular scientific magazine he had once read. Tibbets said nothing.

Now that the bomb was fully armed, he switched on the intercom and addressed the crew, answering Caron's question. "We are carrying the world's first atomic bomb." He paused. "When the bomb is dropped, Lieutenant Beser [the radio officer] will record our reactions to what we see. This recording is being made for history. Watch your language and don't clutter up the intercom. Bob," he told Caron, "you were right. We are splitting atoms. Now get back in your turret. We're going to start climbing." A few minutes later, at twenty minutes to seven, the aircraft carrying the bomb, the *Enola Gay*—named after Tibbet's mother—started to climb to its bombing height of 30,000 feet.

Moments before, First Lieutenant Jacob Beser had frozen as he saw the Japanese early warning signal sweep by the aircraft on the radar, once, twice, and then lock into a constant pulse, indicating that they had a fix. Beser decided not to cause unnecessary stress by informing the crew, or even the captain. There was nothing to be done.

Even at this late stage, Tibbets had no final idea of their objective. It could be one of three cities: Hiroshima, Kokura, or Nagasaki. As recently as May 12 the list had been much longer, with Nagasaki excluded and Yokohama and Kyoto included. On August 2 General Curtis LeMay, chief of staff of the strategic air forces, had dismissed the preferred target of Kyoto. "It wasn't much of a military target, only a lot of shrines and things of that sort there; and anyway riling people gets you nowhere—it's just not profitable."

Thus was Japan's Florence spared: destroying the sacred imperial city would have created a vendetta for generations to come. LeMay had told Tibbets that, in view of the large number of troops and weapons concentrated at Hiroshima, it was "the primary." Tibbets, relieved, told him he had always preferred it. The following day the list had been finalized. Primary: Hiroshima; secondary, Kokura; tertiary, Nagasaki. All that remained in determining which target the bomb would actually fall upon was whether conditions were right.

Captain Claude Eatherly, a good-looking, voluble Texan, was in charge of the Straight Flush, the reconnaissance flight detailed to check on weather conditions at Hiroshima. The aircraft reached the beginning of the projected bombing run—the "initial point"—at a height of 30,000 feet, traveling at 235 miles per hour. There was nothing but thick cloud. Moments later, a huge hole some 10 miles wide appeared directly over the city of Hiroshima. The reconnaissance aircraft over Kokura and Nagasaki reported that conditions were faultless there too. The Straight Flush sent a coded message to Tibbets: the weather had determined that the primary target, Hiroshima, had been chosen.

Eatherly, who was under orders to return to base at Tinian Atoll, asked his crew whether they wanted to wait for the *Enola Gay*'s arrival "and then follow him back to see what happens when the bomb goes off." Crew members hotly debated the subject. Eatherly suddenly realized that if they didn't get back to Tinian by two o'clock they would miss the afternoon poker game. The flight engineer told the commander they might not have enough fuel to make it, which would force them to land on Iwo Jima. That decided it. Anyway, where was the interest in seeing one bomb drop? "What would we see?" pointed out Eatherly. For the sake of a poker game, the crew of the reconnaissance plane decided to skip the dropping of the world's first atom bomb on a live target. Hardly less casually did the fates responsible for weather conditions over Japan condemn one city to hell on earth, sparing another. At a height of 26,000 feet, the *Enola Gay* set course for Hiroshima.

As the *Enola Gay* reached the initial point, already overflown by the Straight Flush, Tibbets, now piloting the aircraft again, knew they had only three minutes to get to the target. The easy part would be evading any Japanese antiaircraft fire, finding the target and dropping the bomb. The difficult part would be surviving it. No one could predict how serious the shock waves from Little Boy would be at 30,000 feet. In the plane, Tibbets alone knew of a conversation he had had nearly a year earlier with Oppenheimer, the father of the bomb. The scientist had told him baldly, "Colonel, your biggest problem may be after the bomb has left your aircraft. The shock waves from the detonation could crush your plane. I am afraid that I can give you no guarantee that you will survive." His aircraft's most intensive practice had been in executing the turn necessary for a quick get-away, which would be as sharp as safe flying permitted.

With a minute to go, Tibbets ordered "on glasses." Nine members of the twelve-man crew put on the thick Polaroid glasses they had been issued to protect their eyes from the nuclear flash. Tibbets, Major Thomas Ferebee, the chief bombardier, and Jacob Beser, the radio officer, kept theirs off in order to do their jobs. They seemed home, they were coming over Hiroshima. "Stand by for the tone break and the turn," said Tibbets. Ferebee's bomb aligner focused on the Aioi Bridge, the aiming point. "I've got it," said the bombardier, turning on the automatic synchronizer for dropping Little Boy, which let out a low-pitched hum, the "tone break."

The die was cast. Little Boy could not be stopped now. At seven seconds past 8:15 A.M. the bomb doors opened and it fell off the retaining hook. The aircraft leapt up 10 feet after shedding its 9,000-pound load. Ferebee shouted, "Bomb away," and saw it fall. Tibbets rammed the *Enola Gay* into the right-hand turn he had practiced. The crew members were pinioned to their seats by the violence of the movement. Forty seconds later, at 8:16 A.M. Little Boy det-onated 890 feet above the ground, just 800 feet from the target bridge, over a clinic. At the exact instant of the first explosion, a fireball 84 feet wide formed around a core millions of degrees in intensity. From the *Enola Gay*, Tibbets said he could savor the brilliance of the explosion. "It tasted like lead."

Bob Caron, in his tail gun, blinked at the flash, then opened his eyes and, in his words, took "a peep into hell." He observed a huge mass of compressed air that could actually be seen rushing outwards and upwards at the speed of sound towards the aircraft. It looked like "the ring of some distant planet had loosed itself and was coming up towards us." The mass of air caught the plane with a roaring explosion, which Tibbets at first assumed was a direct hit from a Japanese antiaircraft battery. The plane jumped violently. Caron yelled, as he saw another circular mass of air accelerating toward the air-craft. "There's another one coming!" Again the plane was violently shaken.

Tibbets, wrestling with the controls, was calm now. He understood what had happened. "That was the reflected aftershock, bounced back from the ground," he told the crew. "There won't be any more." The plane had settled, and Tibbets realized that they had survived the forces which the scientists had been unable to guarantee would not destroy the plane.

Caron described the awesome sight from his rear turret as the plane moved away. He saw

> a column of smoke rising, rising fast. It has a fiery red core. A bubbling mass, purple-grey in color, within that red core. It's turbulent. Fires are springing up everywhere, like flames shooting out of a huge red of coals. I am starting to count the fires. One, two, three, four, five, six . . . fourteen, fifteen . . . It's impossible. There are too many to count. Here it comes, the mushroom shape that Captain Parsons spoke about. It's coming this way. It's like a mass of bubbling molasses. The mushroom is spreading out. It's maybe a mile or two wide and half a mile high. It's growing up and up. It's maybe level with us and climbing. It's very black, but there is a purplish tint to the cloud. The base of the mushroom looks like a heavy undercast that is shot through with flames. The city must be below that. The flames and smoke are billowing out, whirling into the foothills. The hills are disappearing under the smoke. All I can see now of the city is the main dock and what looks like an airfield. That is still visible. There are planes down there.

28 : WHEN THE SINGING STOPPED

ON THE FINE MORNING OF AUGUST 6, 1945, THIRTEEN-YEAR-OLD YOSHITAKA Kawamoto dressed himself in his neat black school uniform, with its flat cap and Prussian-modeled tunic buttoned up to the collar. He was known as a happy, sensible boy, a little shy perhaps, of middling height for his age. He was the apple of his mother's eye, in a family where the father had died young. She saw to it that the impeccable standards of dress and appearance prescribed by the harsh discipline of the school were fully observed. His hair was crew-cut almost to fuzzy baldness, his face scrubbed and washed, his shoes jet-black.

As Yoshitaka affectionately kissed her goodbye and trotted out of the low, wooden house, Mrs. Kawamoto's pride must have been tempered with the apprehension of any mother of her generation. She was sad that he was leaving the house, although it allowed her to get on with her chores—as she had not been able to when he was very young. She was concerned, too, that nothing should happen to him on the long journey to and from school, but

Yoshitaka was quite grown up by now, and not a child to do foolish things. His mother also entertained a looming fear for the future: at fifteen years of age, boys were expected to go and work in the munitions factories based on the outskirts of town; a couple of years later they would become eligible for military service.

But it was rumored that the war was ending. Surely it could not continue for four more years? The idea seemed impossibly remote to her on this peaceful August day in the growing heat of the morning. Once during the previous night, she had heard the distant sound of air-raid sirens from Hiroshima, but the family lived too far from the center to take refuge in a shelter. Two hours later the all-clear had sounded.

Anyway, Hiroshima had never been bombed.

The Kawamoto family lived in a traditional Japanese wooden house on one of the flanks of the mountain range that tumbled down to the placid waters of the Inland Sea like a hand with its five fingers stretched out; Hiroshima was crammed into a couple of gaps of flat terrain between the fingers. As everywhere in the rocky islands of Japan, land was at a premium. Houses and farms were crowded onto whatever spaces the mountains and ocean would allow.

The Kawamotos knew they lived in the loveliest spot of all: they overlooked Miyajima island, a short ferry ride away. There, one of Japan's most spectacular and sacred Buddhist shrines crouched over the water. It was a monastery complex, built out on piles which left only a foot or two of clearance from the surface at high tide. The building was a harmonious, human-proportioned wooden edifice painted in dull red with pleasant, broad rooms for meditation and prayer and narrow, covered catwalks connecting up the different piers; the ubiquitous curving thatch of Japanese Buddhist roofs lent the construction a symmetric harmony.

A stage where Japan's ritualistic Noh theater was occasionally performed protruded over the water from the left-hand side of the temple. To the right there was a fine, turreted red shrine, resembling a giant carnival hat, dating back only a few years. Young deer roaming in a gully behind the temple were shooed away as dirty pests by local people. The surrounding village was small and poor. The island rose up behind; other shrines, none as important or spectacular as the floating monastery, protruded from the sloping forests above.

The Kawamoto family frequently took the ferry to visit the shrines, to enjoy the peace and because these were sacred places. A few hundred yards from the temple a Shinto arch was skewed lopsidedly into the water, like a monster musical note that had somehow become embedded in the sea.

Yoshitaka was taken once at nighttime, to witness the lighting of the lanterns at the temple. Ten thousand of them would sparkle out over the still waters of the Inland Sea, giving the monastery the ghostly quality of a mysterious vessel afloat on the darkness of the surface of the water, a myriad of pinpricks of light illuminating mellow red timbers. When the Kawamotos visited the shrine, they had never felt such inner calm: Yoshitaka had been old enough for some years now to understand such things, to appreciate peace and beauty.

Yoshitaka Kawamoto trotted dutifully along the four kilometers of dusty streets to the station. Other diminutive uniformed cadres were also falling into line as instructed, forming an improvized march. Japan was a deeply militarized society, and the discipline of small boys, as Yoshitaka was later to reflect, "was spartan, with the object of turning us into tough soldiers." Even so, there was some banter and playful barging about as friends met each other on the way to the station; the friendships formed in youth—the only age when advancement and deference do not determine relationships—are to many Japanese the most lasting, and provide the greatest pleasure in their declining years.

But that morning Yoshitaka was in a serious frame of mind. He was well regarded by the teachers in his class—in as far as their stern injunctions to be aloof from their pupils allowed them to express favor. He had been passing his exams with good marks. The teaching was tough, thorough and unimaginative, a matter of learning by rote, and the punishments were severe. There had been no school treats or holidays during these war years, and Yoshitaka could hardly remember a time when Japan was not at war. If he performed well, he would be able to serve his country, like many of the soldiers who came to the streets of Hiroshima from the nearby base, one of the key supply posts for Japan's overseas army in China.

He would be proud to serve his country. He had been taught from the beginning that Japan's enemies, the Americans and the British in particular, were devils: hardly human at all, barbaric beyond belief. His homeland was under threat from their aggression. He was pleased to be a boy doing well in Hiroshima's best school, with the chance even of becoming an officer in the imperial army. He was in the seventh grade, his first year in middle school. The school had 280 pupils, making it one of the largest in the city. The little train that took the children the 13 kilometers to Hiroshima was rudimentary in the extreme, with narrow wooden benches from which Yoshitaka gazed across to the small wooden ships that plied the Inland Sea against a backdrop of islands and mountains scattered haphazardly across the horizon.

He breathed an inward sigh of relief that he was one of the even numbers in the roll call of his class. The odd-numbered pupils were on duty that day, constructing firebreaks between the rows of wooden houses. Each day the rota alternated between the even and odd numbers. It was hard, backbreaking work, particularly in midsummer. It had been going on for several months, because there were rumors that the foreign devils were to mount air attacks.

But none had come. Some pupils, echoing their parents, complained that the destruction of houses to make room for the breaks was unnecessary—not within earshot of the older boys and the teachers, of course. But Yoshitaka thought that any precaution which could save lives was surely necessary. The homes of Hiroshima, like those almost everywhere else in Japan, were small wooden structures: a widespread fire would lead to disaster. The teachers said building the firebreaks would mean that a bomb explosion would be a small, contained affair which might burn down a few houses but would not become a general conflagration. The firebreaks were just shallow trenches. Yoshitaka had wondered whether burning material might be swept by the wind from one house to another across the trenches. But there was no wind that day in Hiroshima, and the weather would bring none.

As he climbed down the iron steps of his railway carriage onto the platform of Hiroshima Station, Yoshitaka Kawamoto was delighted to see Wada, one of his friends. They laughed and chatted, grabbing at each other's satchels as they fell into line together for the short walk to the school. They passed the entrance of the girls' school, speeding up as they went—any boy caught pausing there would get into terrible trouble. The system was strictly segregated, and any contact with the opposite sex except under regulated school or parental supervision was severely punished.

Minutes later, they reached the school, just in time for morning assembly at 8 o'clock. Wada was in a different class, and they exchanged "see yous" as they joined the ranks of students dictated by grade and seniority standing before the headmaster. As always, they were exhorted to work hard and strive harder for their Emperor, the homeland and the war effort. The headmaster told them that the all-clear had been sounded after the air-raid warning of nearly an hour before. Yoshitaka, like many others, had been on the train and not heard it. None of the boys took much notice: air-raid warnings were common occurrences, but nothing ever happened. He had heard older people talking about the fearsome damage inflicted by air raids on Tokyo, but the capital was a long way away.

As the headmaster spoke on the assembly ground outside the school, a single drone could be heard. The eyes of the boys followed the small speck that they knew to be an enemy aircraft. The sky was blue above, although there was cloud in the distance. The tiny insect moving across their field of view was far more compelling, more hypnotic than the headmaster's exhortations. No air-raid alarm sounded, which was curious, but what possible harm could a single aircraft do? It was obviously a reconnaissance plane, and much too high for antiaircraft fire, of which there was none.

The pupils were divided into two groups, the odd-numbered classmates marching off to join the firebreak construction teams, the even-numbered ones entering the school building. There were forty-nine pupils in Yoshitaka's class, in a long, low room with a single window. A blackboard and teacher's desk stood at one end. The thirteen-year-old took his place standing by his desk, until ordered to sit by the "elder student"—the senior prefect in charge of the class. He was an odious youth, extremely tough and stern, who would hit virtually every member of the class in sadistic fury at least once a day, waiting for each to make the mistake or display the minor insubordination they inevitably would.

He ordered them to perform the silent Shinto tribute that was the prelude to lessons every day. Yoshitaka closed his eyes, along with all his classmates, apparently in prayer, but wondering what had happened to that reconnaissance plane that had passed overhead.

The boy thought he heard a noise, the insistent rising and falling hum of an aircraft. He tensed; he heard the prefect telling them to remain with their eyes closed until he returned, and heard the scraping of a chair as the tyrannical senior rose to leave the room—almost certainly to go to the lavatory. Yoshitaka's desk was right in the center of the classroom, with a row of desks on either side. The window was toward the front.

He opened his eyes, which he had been forbidden to do. If the senior came back quickly—as well he might, he could be setting them up— Yoshitaka would surely be struck severely. A friend near the window called out to him in a quiet voice, so that the rest of the class would not hear, that he could see a B-29. Yoshitaka was excited, craning his head to see the rectangle of sky visible from the window. Other boys were looking too. He rose from his seat to get a better view.

When Yoshitaka Kawamoto rose from his desk to look at the B-29, most of his friends had their eyes closed in silent tribute, expecting the ruthless class senior to return any minute. An instant later, looking out of the window, Yoshitaka saw "a pale, intense light, which was bluish in color." This eerie experience lasted a full two or three seconds. Yoshitaka remembers hearing nothing. The pressure from the bomb hurled him to the ground. His seated companions were not so lucky: their legs were doubled up and crushed beneath them where they sat.

When Yoshitaka woke up, he couldn't see anything at all. He was in pain, with something very heavy pressing upon him, holding him down. He became aware of the pitiful sound of ten or so injured children singing. He joined in. The boys had been rigorously forbidden to shout things like "Help me" or "Save me" in an emergency, so they sang the school song instead. They wanted to alert those outside the collapsed building to the fact that they were still alive. Yoshitaka thought there had been a gas explosion.

One by one, the voices stopped. It became more and more quiet, until only Yoshitaka's voice was left. "When I realized that I was the only one left singing the school song," he later told the author, "you cannot imagine my terror."

Gradually smoke seemed to be entering the confined space in which he was pinned down in the rubble of the school, and Yoshitaka felt he was stiffening. He understood that the building had been flattened; he knew he was in danger. With a desperate burst of strength, he managed to lift himself out of the debris, pushing aside the rubble. He was in the open air. As he rose, he saw incalculable devastation around him. Above, a huge cumulonimbus cloud hung over the city.

Like all the other children of his class, Yoshitaka had been taught an emergency drill. Don't run away, he had been instructed, check for serious injuries first. He found that a piece of wood was stuck in his left arm, which was bleeding. He tried to stem the flow with a rough tourniquet torn from his shirt. His front teeth were bleeding—four of them broken. He was covered in scratches.

The boy stared at the neighboring wooden buildings, many of them crushed like his school. There were fires all around, rapidly moving toward the nearby wreckage, spreading like liquid, burning the chestnut trees. Yoshitaka wanted to run, but he had been taught not to go alone, to take someone else. So he looked around him. He began to search the rubble of his school in an effort to find somebody alive.

With a start, he found his friend Wada. The boy's skull was split open and one eye had come out of its socket. He couldn't speak, although he was clearly trying to, biting his lip. Like all the other children he had a black identification tag, which he was trying to push with his chin, presumably wanting Yoshitaka to give it to his mother. The boy took it. Wada waved feebly, and Yoshitaka thought his movements were an attempt to tell him to leave immediately. The fires were now approaching. Yoshitaka didn't know where to run, but he headed for the furthest point from the fire. He looked back and saw Wada's one eye still fixed on him. They had been the same age. The elderly Yoshitaka still dreams about it.

The fleeing boy was experiencing the stuff of nightmares, a piece of hell come alive. Fires were spreading all around. Amid the smoke and the devastation people wandered, some with skin flayed from the raw and bleeding flesh of their arms and bodies hanging down grotesquely from their fingers and limbs. In the confusion Yoshitaka was surrounded by stumbling figures, shouting out that they should move toward the wind, not away; he didn't know why. As the boy began to run, agonized figures on the ground clutched at his legs and feet, grabbing them feebly. Yoshitaka had to kick them aside in order to continue. Suddenly he saw someone he recognized through the smoke: his school's deputy headmaster, pushing a cartload of injured. He followed the spectral figure with its wheelbarrow of suffering for a moment, until they were swallowed up in the smoke.

Yoshitaka's throat was burning with thirst in the intense heat. He had to drink, desperately. He saw that he had reached the Hiroshima River: he plunged into the water which was filled with a "truly huge number of drifting bodies." But he was past disgust: he pushed them aside to make room to stand and drink. It didn't matter, in the intense relief of the cooling water. He climbed out of the river and collapsed on the bank. He was by a bridge some three kilometers from his school.

When the boy recovered consciousness, he saw groups of survivors and relief workers stumbling through the smoke, helping the wounded. They passed him by, oblivious. He viewed the terrible injuries of the survivors, many with their skin blistered. Another cart filled with wounded people was pushed by. He tried at first to get up and help, but he was too weak. Consciousness slipped away again.

He awoke at 7 o'clock that evening in a makeshift hospital ward where the injured lay in rows on the ground. He learned later that army trucks had come through the city shortly after he lost consciousness, and a soldier called Haijan, engaged in the grisly task of sorting the living from the dead, had felt his pulse beating and had put him in a truck filled with barely moving bodies, instead of the one detailed to dispose of the dead.

Yoshitaka Kawamoto's first reaction was that he was incredibly lucky to be alive. Haijan, who had saved the boy's life, passed his bed and patted him on the cheek. He was in acute pain, and desperately thirsty: his throat and mouth were scorching hot. Eventually a medical orderly came down the ward. People all around were crying out for water. As the orderly moved from bed to bed, he nodded or shook his head, permitting his patients to have water or not. Yoshitaka learned later that those the doctors thought were about to die were allowed to have water; those likely to survive were denied it. He never found out why, although the water made people vomit and probably weakened them. A soldier took pity on the boy as he pleaded for water and went to a nearby ice box, finding a piece of ice for him to suck on.

At eight o'clock Yoshitaka was examined again, and the decision was made to transfer him, along with other badly injured victims, to an uninhabited island in Hiroshima Bay. Dazed and uncomprehending, he was brought ashore to a dismal tent-city of the injured and the dying. There he lay for several days, growing weaker on the pitiful rations of food and water the injured were given. Around him, thousands died. He could only presume his end was not far off.

Weeks later, his mother reached him. Living so far from the hypocenter of the blast, she had survived it unscathed and immediately gone searching for her son. It had taken many days of touring hospitals; eventually she heard of the camps on the islands in the bay and hired a fishing boat to visit them one by one. When she found him she took him away to a house in the hills beyond Hiroshima. He was a piteous figure: ten days after the blast he had lost all of his hair; his face and body were black for three months, while he bled regularly from his nose and mouth. He vomited constantly.

For a year, Yoshitaka lay at death's door. There were no medicines and food was short. His mother sought to cure him with herbs and root extracts. Later he would claim that his mother's love "was the medicine." He had been incredibly fortunate—to have been just 800 meters from the hypocenter of the world's first atomic explosion and lived. He was the only one of 40 members of his class still alive forty-five years later, and one of only 4 survivors out of the 280 pupils of his school.

On the ground about 80,000 people—a quarter of the population— were killed instantly or mortally wounded, a third of them soldiers. The clinic directly beneath the blast (at the bomb's "hypocenter") was razed to the ground, its occupants vaporized. Most of those within a one-kilometer radius died at once or within a couple of days, their skin ripped off and their internal organs severely damaged. Within two kilometers most people were badly burned. Three or more kilometers away, the injuries were largely limited to skin burns.

The heat was such that granite surfaces within 1,000 yards of the hypocenter melted; bubbles formed on the surface of tiles less than 600 metres away. The bodies of several thousand soldiers were burned into the parade ground of Hiroshima Castle; in some cases, shadow imprints of people were all that remained on the ground or on buildings. Hats were burned into peoples heads, kimonos printed onto bodies. At the hypocenter itself the blast pressure was 35 tonnes per square yard. The shock wave traveled outward at 445 yards per second—and was still powerful enough at 30,000 feet to toss a plane about like a leaf. As the column of the explosion rose, it sucked burning air into its base in a nuclear wind which roared across the largely wood-constructed city. Virtually every wooden building within a radius of two miles was burned.

Anyone within 935 yards of the bomb received a dose of some 700 rads—about 1,500 times the normal safe level of radiation—and 100 yards beyond that a dose of 400 rads, at which about half of those exposed usually die. Three fifths of the deaths at Hiroshima were caused by burns, one-fifth by blast injuries, and one-fifth by radiation. Rescue workers coming into the city experienced residual radiation. An area 19 miles wide was also exposed to a cloudburst which lasted for two hours. The rain was contaminated and black.

Huge numbers suffered from some form of acute radiation sickness over the following five months, usually with nausea, vomiting and diarrhea, insomnia and delirium, hair loss, internal and external bleeding, inflammation, blood diseases, and general failure of the organs. Keloids—grotesque skin growths—formed one to four months after the explosion. After 1947 leukemia became common, reaching a peak in the 1950s. After 1960, as the incidence of leukemia declined, other cancers among survivors increased.

A year after the explosion it was reckoned that 119,000 had died, with 31,000 seriously injured and 48,000 slightly wounded; 4,000 people were missing. Some 55,000 buildings were totally burned and 7,000 destroyed by the blast itself. More than four fifths of central Hiroshima was devastated by the explosion, reduced to a scarred atomic desert.

The second bomb was equally devastating. At 1:56 A.M. on August 9, another B-29 called *Bock's Car* took off from Tinian Atoll carrying a plutonium bomb slightly more powerful than the one dropped on Hiroshima.

The aircraft's usual pilot, Fred Bock, was flying an observer plane behind. In his place was Major Chuck Sweeney, a cheerful Boston Irishman, and the bombardier was Captain Kermit Beahan. The bomb, nicknamed Fat Man because of its shape, was targeted for Kokura.

Fate rolled its dice, however, and spared the city. With the bomb doors open at a height of 31,000 feet, Beahan looked for the target point—the city's arsenal. But industrial haze and smoke from a fire obscured it. "No drop," he shouted. Once again they flew over the target area; once again the view was obscured. Antiaircraft fire opened up. The plane went over a third time, as Japanese fighters began to climb into the sky. Beahan could still not see the arsenal through the haze. "No drop," he called again.

Sweeney decided to make for the second objective—Nagasaki, Japan's historic center of Christianity. Sweeney had only enough fuel to make a single run over the city before he returned to land on Okinawa. Puffy white clouds had moved in over Nagasaki, but a break showed the outline of the city stadium. Beahan trained his bombsight on it. Fat Man fell for forty seconds before detonating at twenty past eleven in the morning.

The hypocenter of the blast was the Urakami branch of Nagasaki prison, where 134 prisoners and wardens were vaporized. Some 30,000 people were killed instantly, and 120,000 were to die altogether. Unlike Hiroshima, only 16 percent of the victims were involved with the war effort, and only 3 percent were soldiers. Nagasaki was, in effect, Mitsubishi's company town: out of 1,700 in its steelworks, 1,000 died.

The most vivid eyewitness description of the afterblast came from Tatsuichiro Akizuki, a local doctor:

> The sky was as dark as pitch, covered with dense clouds of smoke; under that blackness, over the earth, hung a yellow-brown fog. Gradually the veiled ground became visible and the view beyond rooted me to the spot with horror.
>
> All the buildings I could see were on fire: large ones and small ones and those with straw thatched roofs. Further along the valley Urakami Church, the largest Catholic church in the East, was ablaze. The technical school, a large two-story wooden building, was on fire, as were many houses and the distant ordnance factory. Electricity poles were wrapped in flames like so many pieces of kindling. Trees on the nearby hills were smoking, as were the leaves of sweet potatoes in the fields. To say that everything burned is not enough. It seemed as if the earth itself emitted fire and smoke, flames that writhed up and erupted from under ground. The sky was dark, the ground

was scarlet and in between hung clouds of yellowish smoke. Three kinds of color—black, yellow and scarlet—loomed ominously over the people, who ran about like so many ants seeking to escape. What had happened? Urakami Hospital had not been bombed—I understood that much, but that ocean of fire, that sky of smoke! It seemed like the end of the world.

The plight of the victims was pitiable:

Ten or twenty minutes after the smoke had cleared outside, people began coming up the hill from the town below, crying about and groaning, "Help me, help!" Those cries and groans seemed not to be made by human voices; they sounded unearthly, weird. About ten minutes after the explosion a big man, half-naked, holding his head between his hands, came into the yard toward me making sounds that seemed to be dragged from the pit of his stomach. "Got hurt sir," he groaned; he shivered as if he were cold. "I'm hurt."

I stared at the strange-looking man. Then I saw it was Mr. Kenjiro Tsujimoro, a market gardener and a friendly neighbor to me and the hospital. I wondered what had happened to the robust Kenjiro . . . His head and his face were whitish; his hair singed. It was because his eyelashes had been scorched away that he seemed so bleary-eyed. He was half-naked because his shirt had been burned from his back in a single flash . . .

After Mr. Tsujimoro came staggering up to me, another person who looked just like him wandered into the yard. Who he was and where he had come from I had no idea. "Help me," he said, groaning, half-naked, holding his head between his hands. He sat down, exhausted. "Water . . . water . . ." he whispered . . .

As time passed more and more people in a similar plight came up to the hospital—two minutes, twenty minutes, an hour after the explosion. All were of the same appearance, sounded the same. "I, hurt, hurt! I'm burning! Water!" They all moaned the same lament. I shuddered. Half-naked or stark naked, they walked with strange slow steps, groaning from deep inside themselves as if they had traveled from the depths of hell. They looked whitish, their faces were like masks. I felt as if I were dreaming, watching pallid ghosts processing slowly in one direction—as in a dream I had once had in my childhood.

These ghosts came on foot uphill toward the hospital from the direction of the burning city and from the more easterly ordnance factory. Worker or student, girl or man, they walked slowly and had the same mask-like face. Each one groaned and cried for help. Their cries grew in strength as the people increased in number, sounding like something from the Buddhist scriptures, re-echoing everywhere, as if the earth itself were in pain.

To quantify human suffering and death seems obscene. To weigh one person's life is a task for God, not man. To weigh the fates of hundreds of thousands goes beyond blasphemy, it might seem. Yet for the practical purpose of reaching a decision in war, men, however inadequate, have to make such judgments all the time.

So it was with the decision to drop the bomb. At one level, anyone introducing a weapon capable of destroying the world, and of contemplating the destruction of 120,000 people at a stroke, is flouting every bound of conventional humanity. Yet if there is every reason to believe that the lives of countless more will be saved by such actions, there may be felt to be little alternative.

Such inhuman calculations are the very essence of decision-making in war, although probably no single decision has yielded so drastic a result in so short a space of time as that to drop the bomb. The politicians and generals waging war find it difficult to ascribe different moral values to different weapons. Although the bombs inflicted a particularly ghastly kind of death on many people, it is hard to suggest that the injuries were worse than those inflicted by, say, conventional ordnance or incendiaries in the "normal" course of war.

There was much concern among the scientists who helped to perfect the new technology about its use against a country that was a long way from acquiring similar technology. Yet victory through the ages has gone to nations with more advanced weaponry. The view was taken in Washington that the development of nuclear technology was inevitable: better that responsible, democratic hands should wield it first. The technology could not be suppressed, but those that might be tempted to use it irresponsibly could be deterred.

When Truman had to make the decision whether or not to drop the bomb, he was doing so in the harshest circumstances possible: a world at war. However agonizing the decision, it would be hard to find a more clear-cut rationale than the situation in which the American President believed he found himself. His first duty in war was to proceed to victory at as limited a cost as possible to his own countrymen and soldiers. That is not the only duty, of course: even in armed conflict certain rules have to be respected (for example, regarding the treatment of civilians and prisoners of war), and a democratic leader has a duty to wage war as humanely as possible.

The nature of the Second World War was such that the decision had already been taken that the mass-killing of civilian populations was decided upon virtually as soon as bombing began to play a major part in warfare. One statistic may help to place even the atomic bombs in perspective: the saturation bombing of Tokyo had killed 100,000 people, injured at least 412,000, destroyed 2 million dwellings and rendered between 9 and 13 million people homeless. These figures are well above the totals for Hiroshima and Nagasaki.

The circumstances that Truman had to consider seemed clear-cut. There was no reason to expect anything other than last-ditch, bitter resistance to any invasion of Japan. The Americans expected to suffer upward of a million deaths as a result of the invasion; Japanese casualties were likely to be very much higher. The battle of Okinawa had already displayed the savagery of the resistance likely to be encountered in an invasion. Further saturation bombing raids in advance were likely to take many more lives than even the previous ones had. And the Japanese had been offered, and had rejected, a last chance to settle—although in hindsight there had been serious errors in the nature of the offer made.

Last but not least, the enemy had waged an aggressive war in which millions had died in open conflict, had savaged millions of others to death through brutal occupation policies, and had shown none of the natural constraints to prisoners and subject peoples that could be expected of humane combatants. The weakest link in this powerful chain of reasoning was whether a serious attempt at a negotiated peace with Japan would have produced results not far different from the eventual terms of surrender and occupation. General MacArthur later asserted that Japan would have submitted to a naval blockade.

Truman had been given what he considered to be an instrument likely to end the war. He believed that use of that weapon would cause suffering only a fraction as great as that which would accompany a messy landing on Japan; even after the bombs were dropped, the Japanese army wanted to fight on, but was overruled by the Emperor. Truman felt he would have to answer to the American people had the bomb not been used, and a million of his countrymen and several million Japanese had died in an invasion. In the circumstances, it seemed that no other decision was possible. What Truman could not have guessed, but Churchill had grasped, was that in dropping the bomb he had also performed an incalculable service to the very elements of the Japanese power structure most responsible for the whirlwind of carnage unleashed by the Pacific War.

29 : SURRENDER

WHEN HIROHITO HEARD REPORTS OF THE DESTRUCTION OF HIROSHIMA, he was, for the first time since February 1936, goaded into decisive action, overruling the views of his advisers, the army, or the cabinet.

No matter what happens to my safety we must put an end to this war as quickly as possible, so that this tragedy will not be repeated . . . Since it has reached the point where such new weaponry is being deployed, we cannot continue this war any further. It is impossible. We no longer have the luxury of waiting for an opportune time to begin negotiations. We must concentrate our efforts on ending the war quickly.

On August 8, the Russians declared war on Japan, and their armies swept brutally into Manchuria, quickly gaining total control: the Kwantung Army melted before them. The "Manchurian Incident" had at last turned full circle: nemesis was complete. The following day Fat Man was dropped on Nagasaki. Incredibly, even though Japan was surrounded on all sides, with Russia, America and Britain against it, and was now losing Manchuria in addition to the rest of its empire, even though many major cities had been reduced to rubble, even though two atomic bombs had been dropped, the country was still not to yield without a struggle. Many senior army officers did indeed seem to believe that annihilation was preferable to surrender. The next few hours were to be the Emperor's finest, after a bad war, and the army's most demented.

The chief protagonist of peace was Shigenori Togo, the foreign minister, who was utterly outspoken and unfearful in his quest. He was arrogant, intellectually self-confident, and at 62 a comparative youngster in Japanese politics. Suzuki, the prime minister, a moderate from the imperial household elite, was at the age of 77, verbose, befuddled, vague and often indecisive. They were the only two civilian members of Japan's top policy-making body at this stage, the Supreme War Council. Incredibly, the day before Nagasaki, this group had failed to meet because one of its members had "more pressing" business than to discuss war and peace.

On Thursday, August 9, at eight o'clock, Togo had arrived at Suzuki's house. The day was already hot. Suzuki agreed that the council must meet, and Togo went to call on his sole military ally, the navy minister and former premier, Admiral Yonai. The council met at 11 o'clock, just half an hour before the Nagasaki bomb exploded. Suzuki opened the proceedings by recommending that the government accept the Potsdam terms. Yonai, a moderate who years earlier had been forced out of office as prime minister because he opposed the alliance with Germany and Italy, also urged acceptance. Togo's position was well known. The only condition the moderates sought from the allies was some reassurance on the position of the Emperor.

The other three flatly opposed surrender unless a number of other conditions were met as well: a nominal occupation force; Japan's right to try its own war criminals; and the demobilization of Japanese troops by their own officers. The purpose was clear: to try and preserve the illusion to the Japanese army and people that the country had not in fact surrendered. Face was still everything—even worth fighting to the death for. The leader of the hardline faction was, unsurprisingly, the war minister, General Anami, a stolid serving officer of no great imagination, lacking in Tojo's messianic fervor, but respected by his men. The army chief of staff, General Umezu, and the navy chief, Admiral Toyoda, were also opposed to surrender.

Togo angrily rebuffed Anami, saying the Allies would refuse to negotiate such terms. Umezu retorted that the Japanese had not yet lost the war and could still inflict great damage on the enemy. Togo answered that Japan would certainly not be able to withstand a second assault. At one o'clock, the council adjourned, deadlocked. At two-thirty a meeting of the full cabinet began. Togo again argued the case for peace. Anami replied with stubborn self-delusion:

> Our men will not lay down their arms. And since they know they are not permitted to surrender, since they know that a fighting man who surrenders is liable to extremely heavy punishment there is really no alternative for us but to continue the war. . . We must fight the war through to the end, no matter how great the odds against us.

He was supported by the conservative Home Affairs Minister, Genki Abe, who said he could not guarantee civil peace if the order was issued to surrender. However, the *zaibatsu* ministers were unanimously in favor of peace. The ministers of agriculture, commerce, transport and munitions argued that the country was now finally exhausted. At ten o'clock, the cabinet adjourned, having failed to resolve its differences and reach the necessary unanimity.

There was nothing for it. Togo and Suzuki realized that the Emperor would have to intervene—even though there was no provision in the constitution for him to do so. At ten minutes to midnight, the Emperor arrived to take his place at a further meeting of the Supreme War Council, which was also attended by Cabinet Secretary Hisatsune Sakomizu and the president of the privy council, Baron Kiichiro Hiranuma. They met in an 18-foot by 30-foot bunker, which was hot and stuffy, in uniforms and morning suits. Togo once again set out the case for surrender, Anami for fighting on. Hiranuma, a silly old man, aligned himself with the hardliners, though he had no formal vote. Anami settled back in his seat with satisfaction; the war party was beginning to prevail.

Suzuki rose suddenly: "Your Imperial Majesty's decision is required as to which proposal should be adopted," he said. Anami was caught off guard. The Emperor, speaking as prearranged, declared that continuing the war could only result in the annihilation of the Japanese people and an extension of the suffering of all humanity. It was obvious that Japan could no longer fight, and its ability to defend its own shores was doubtful. "That it is unbearable for me to see my loyal troops disarmed goes without saying . . . But the time has come to bear the unbearable . . . I give my sanction to the proposal to accept the Allied Proclamation on the basis outlined by the foreign minister." Then he left the room. Suzuki proposed that His Majesty's decision be adopted as the decision of the council. There was no dissent from Anami.

At around two in the morning the cabinet met and resolved to accept the Potsdam Declaration "with the understanding that the said declaration does not comprise any demand which prejudices the prerogatives of His Majesty as a sovereign ruler." That morning, Anami summoned his senior officers. "We have no alternative but to abide by the Emperor's decision. Whether we fight on or whether we surrender now depends on the enemy's reply to our note. No matter which we do, you must remember that you are soldiers, you must obey orders, you must not deviate from strict military discipline. In the crisis that faces us, the uncontrolled actions of one man could bring about the ruin of the entire country." An officer asked if the war minister was actually contemplating surrender. Anami slammed his swagger stick down on the table. "Anyone who isn't willing to obey orders will have to do so over my dead body," he told his men—and in Japan this was no mere figure of speech. Japan waited for the reply throughout the following day and the morning of August 11.

That morning, a group of hard-line officers met to consider the next step. Lieutenant-Colonel Masuhiko Takeshita, General Anami's brother-in-law, presided. Among the officers present was a pale, thin-faced fanatic, Major Kenji Hatanaka. It was resolved that the imperial palace be seized and the Emperor placed under the "protection" of the hard-liners. Suzuki and Togo were marked down for assassination, as was the Emperor's chief adviser, Marquis Kido. It was February 1936, all over again.

Just past midnight on August 12, the Allies' reply was heard: the Japanese acceptance was agreed to, on the condition that the Japanese government and the authority of the Emperor would be "subject to" the Supreme Commander of the Allied Powers. Anami and Hiranuma saw Suzuki immediately afterward and persuaded him that this demand was unacceptable and that Japan must fight on. Togo, the foreign minister, was appalled when he heard that the prime minister had changed his mind and had Kido summon the elderly Suzuki to tell him that surrender was the express wish of the Emperor. Suzuki bowed to imperial authority, and reversed himself once again.

Meanwhile, Anami, who had been put under intense pressure from his fanatical juniors, was wondering whether to ask Japan's senior officers to appeal as a body to the Emperor to reject the Allied terms. To his astonishment, General Umezu, the army chief of staff, then told him that he had changed his own hard-line opinion and now favored surrender. But by next day, August 13, Umezu had reverted to his previous position, and the supreme war council was divided again, three-to-three, on whether to accept the Allies' final terms. The cabinet also split along predictable lines. The ordinary people of Japan were, of course, not consulted, nor is there any way of knowing their opinions, whether a yearning for peace, a sense of profound shame and the desire to fight on—or a mixture.

Throughout the day, rebellious groups of officers began to organize. A number of them went over to see General Anami, requesting that martial law be declared and the allied terms rejected. The war minister was noncommittal. At 10:30 the following morning, the Supreme War Council was again convoked. Once again, the split was three-three. The Emperor now spoke, while those present sobbed quietly. It was an absolute pronouncement from what Japanese labeled the Voice of the Crane (an imperial command which, like a crane, could still be heard in the sky after the bird has passed):

> Although some of you are apprehensive about the preservation of the national structure, I believe that the Allied reply is evidence of the good intentions of the enemy. The conviction and resolution of the Japanese people are, therefore, the most important consideration. That is why I favor acceptance of the reply . . .

If we continue the war, Japan will be altogether destroyed. Although some of you are of the opinion that we cannot completely trust the Allies, I believe that an immediate and peaceful end to the war is preferable to seeing Japan annihilated. As things stand now the nation still has a chance to recover.

I am reminded of the anguish Emperor Meiji felt at the time of the Triple Intervention. Like him, I must bear the unbearable now and hope for the rehabilitation of the country in the future . . .

As the people of Japan are unaware of the present situation, I know they will be deeply shocked when they hear of our decision. If it is thought appropriate that I explain the matter to them personally, I am willing to go before the microphone. The troops, particularly, will be dismayed at our decision. The war minister and the navy minister may not find it easy to persuade them to accept the decision. I am willing to go wherever necessary to explain our action.

I desire the Cabinet to prepare as soon as possible an Imperial Rescript announcing the termination of the war.

Following the meeting, Anami informed his brother-in-law, Takeshita, that he would abide by the imperial decision. In addition, he would not resign from the government—thus drawing the final responsibility for the army's acceptance of the Emperor's decision upon himself. If he had resigned, the government would have fallen and the country been plunged into chaos. Whether Anami secretly accepted that Japan had no realistic alternative, but had been going through the motions on the army's behalf, or whether he felt he must obey a direct command of the Emperor can only be surmised. The war minister summoned another meeting of his senior officers. The atmosphere in the room was electric. He told them that:

One of a soldier's chief virtues is obedience. The future of Japan is no longer in doubt, but nor will it be an easy future. You officers must realize that death cannot absolve you of your duty. Your duty is to stay alive and do your best to help your country along the path to recovery—even if it means chewing grass and eating earth and sleeping in the fields!

The fanatical Major Hatanaka, meanwhile, was calling on the head of the Eastern District Army, the redoubtable General Tanaka, who had command of the main military force in Tokyo. Tanaka, a decisive man with fine handlebar mustaches, was surprised by the young officer, who burst into the room in a high state of tension. Tanaka's adjutant seized the handle of his sword, fearing that Hatanaka might be prepared to kill the general. Tanaka rounded on the major furiously as soon as he entered. "Why did you come here? I know what's on your mind! I don't want to hear it! Leave at once! Get out!" Hatanaka, after a moment of wild-eyed reflection, left and went to find another hard-line young officer, Lieutenant-Colonel Masataka Ida.

The two had a conversation of Shakespearean intensity. Ida told Hatanaka he intended to commit *sepukku*. Hatanaka cried, "Yes! That would indeed be a beautiful and correct thing to do."

"It is the only correct thing to do," replied Ida. Hatanaka then informed Ida he was planning a coup. "Don't you think that's a more beautiful thing to do than cutting your belly open?"

"Success would be more beautiful. But the war minister says there is no chance of success. The Emperor was determined to end the war. A fire on which water has been poured will not burn again. That is the way of life."

The cabinet spent most of the remainder of the day arguing fruitlessly about the exact wording of the surrender rescript. The argument was over the phrase, "The war situation grows more unfavorable to us every day," favored by the navy minister, Admiral Yonai, and "the war situation has not developed to Japan's advantage," favored by General Anami. Both were massive understatements; in the end, Anami's wording prevailed.

That night, at around 11 o'clock, Hirohito himself twice recorded the rescript announcing surrender. No Emperor had ever broadcast before. No ordinary Japanese had ever previously heard the voice of their living god. In doing so, he was to render it impossible for ordinary soldiers to claim that they had not received his direct order to surrender. It could not be argued that "treacherous" advisers had issued the order in his name. The message itself was astonishing. It was the first time in Japan's thousands of years of recorded history that the nation had been defeated and was to undergo occupation: surrender up to that point had been considered an act of shame beyond measure. But if the Emperor ordered it, even the unthinkable could be borne—indeed became the duty of ordinary Japanese.

The announcement was carefully crafted in order to preserve the country's self-respect. More than that: the myth of Japan's undefeat was for the first time propagated. In 1945, the argument that Japan's armies had not been defeated, merely forced to yield by the atomic bomb—the "new and most cruel bomb"—was born in the Emperor's surrender broadcast:

> We declared war on America and Britain out of our sincere desire to ensure Japan's self-preservation and the stabilization of East Asia, it being far from our thoughts either to infringe upon the sovereignty of other nations or to embark on territorial aggrandizement.
>
> But now the war has lasted for nearly four years. Despite the best that has been done by everyone—the gallant fighting of the military and naval forces, the diligence and assiduity of our servants of the state, and the devoted service of our one hundred million people—the war situation has developed not necessarily to Japan's advantage, while the general trends of the world have all turned against her interest.
>
> Moreover, the enemy has begun to deploy a new and most cruel bomb, the power of which to do damage is, indeed, incalculable, taking the toll of many innocent lives. Should we continue to fight, not only would it result in an ultimate collapse and obliteration of the Japanese nation, but it would also lead to the total extinction of human civilization.
>
> Such being the case, how are we to save the millions of our subjects, or to atone ourselves before the hallowed spirits of our imperial ancestors? This is the reason why we have ordered the acceptance of the provisions of the Powers of the joint declaration.
>
> We cannot but express the deepest regret to our allied nations of East Asia, who have consistently cooperated with the Empire towards the emancipation of East Asia . . .

The government, rather than the Emperor, was of course responsible for the broadcast's contents. But a number of points stand out immediately. First, there is no mention of surrender. In fact, Japan is presented as taking the initiative "in effecting a settlement of the present situation by resorting to an extraordinary measure." To simple Japanese, dependent on official lies and propaganda for information, it would be hard to resist the conclusion that Japan itself had initiated the quest for peace out of its own sense of humanity. Further, the Emperor merely accepted the provisions of the joint declaration by the Allies. This might have been a commercial transaction for all the remorse shown. To ordinary Japanese who wished to delude themselves—a great many to their credit did not—this was no surrender.

Second, Japan emphatically did not admit—as it does not officially to this day—to having done any wrong. On the contrary, it declared war on Britain and America "out of our sincere desire to ensure Japan's self-preservation and the stabilization of East Asia, it being far from our thoughts either to infringe upon the sovereignty of other nations or to engage in territorial aggrandizement." Even for someone who accepts the Japanese version of events—that its legitimate colonial expansion had inadvertently over-provoked the Western powers—this statement is a startling piece of effrontery in describing what had happened over the previous 15 years. It would be hard to view the creation of what was probably the largest, if one of the shortest-lived, empires in human history as not infringing upon the sover-eignty of others or engaging in territorial aggrandizement. For Japan to express its regret to its "allies" in East Asia, for surrendering to them and the West, after years of systematic murder, rape and looting of their region, which inflicted millions of deaths, was barefaced to a degree. Japan was apologizing for removing the jackboot from the necks of its colonies.

Third, Japan did not acknowledge military defeat, only that the war had "not necessarily developed" to Japan's "advantage," while world trends had turned against her interests. The string of devastating reversals along two fronts in the Pacific and a third in India and Burma might never have hap-pened: what had happened was that a 'new and most cruel bomb' had been deployed which might lead to the obliteration of the Japanese nation. Undefeated in the field, morally in the right, Japan had to yield before the inhuman perfidy of the enemy. The country had its alibi for defeat.

Finally, Japanese were exhorted to enhance the "innate glory of the Imperial state"—the very regime which had led them into the present humil-iation and devastation. Thus ordinary Japanese, cocooned from reality by wartime propaganda, were now to believe that the Pacific War was largely the consequence of Western hostility to the peaceful, idealistic Japanese state which had been intent on liberating the peoples of Asia; and that Japan had sued for peace in the interests of avoiding overwhelming human suffering after the horrific nuclear attacks at Hiroshima and Nagasaki, which wholly eclipsed any alleged excesses by the Japanese forces in the past. In this ver-sion Japan, of course, had not been decisively defeated. The bombs had purged Japan of both the shame of defeat and its guilt for starting the war and committing innumerable atrocities on a scale never seen before.

Throughout the broadcast there was no hint of guilt, regret, remorse or acknowledgment of error. Japan was not to blame for the war, but its course had gone a little wrong recently and the bomb threatened the nation with extinction. So peace had been agreed upon. That was all. The bombs wiped the slate clean: they were as cathartic and purgative of shame and guilt for the nation as the committing of suicide would be for a Japanese individual. Those blinding flashes of bluish white light, and the immense suffering they caused, were as cleansing and "beautiful" a method of absolving a nation of guilt as the rites of *seppuku* for a warrior that had been defeated or dishonored.

The tapes were hidden carefully away, and the Emperor left the broadcasting studio with tears in his eyes. But he apparently had little to cry about: Japan had not acknowledged its surrender. It is legitimate to ask whether the whole huge pretence was not merely the necessary face-saving for a people brainwashed into a doctrine where loss of pride was all, whether the vast majority of ordinary Japanese knew defeat for what it was and yet preferred to go about it with dignity, rather like the action of a businessman who has suffered financial ruin still dressing in impeccable suits and leaving his home dutifully for the office each morning.

There must certainly have been an element of this for ordinary Japanese. Yet the sheer extent of the lie leads to the conclusion that a large part of the Japanese establishment convinced itself, in spite of all the evidence to the contrary, that its propaganda was indeed true: Japan could have fought on had the bombs not been dropped. Certainly many senior army officers believed this even after Hiroshima and Nagasaki. Japan was undefeated, and could still hold its head high.

Even the broadcast went too far, in the opinion of one section of the army. The conspirators, led by Major Hatanaka, had a simple plan: to use the imperial guards, the personal bodyguards of the Emperor, to seize control of the imperial palace and isolate the Emperor; to block the surrender broadcast; and to win over the Eastern Army, commanding Tokyo and its surroundings. The first snag, however, was that the commander of the imperial guards, General Takeshi Mori, would not join the conspiracy. Hatanaka soon sorted that out: at one o'clock in the morning he went into Mori's office and shot him; another insurgent decapitated his brother-in-law, who was present. The conspirators attached the dead commander's seal to their orders for securing the palace, which were promptly carried out.

Lieutenant-Colonel Ida, the top-ranked conspirator, was sent to secure the support of the Eastern Army, which he failed to obtain. The duty officers preferred to wait until General Tanaka, the commander, who had gone to bed, turned up in the morning. Meanwhile a number of senior officials were rounded up and imprisoned in a shed. Lieutenant-Colonel Takeshita was sent to secure the support of his brother-in-law, the war minister, General Anami, who just at that moment was preparing to kill himself in atonement for assuming the responsibility of surrender on behalf of the Japanese army.

Again, there was a mixture of Shakespearean tragedy and almost comic pathos about the scene as Takeshita was invited by his brother-in-law to join in a protracted drinking session while he prepared himself for death. Madness raged outside as Anami grew drunker and drunker while Takeshita found himself unable to screw up the courage, in the presence of imminent death, to urge the minister to join in the coup. The official Japanese account of events takes up the story as Anami welcomes Takeshita:

It was hard for Takeshita to believe, looking at the calm, healthy, ruddy face of his brother-in-law, that here was a man who had spent days in the exhausting and dispiriting business of trying to secure the best possible terms for his vanquished army and who, now, having done so, was considering when to kill himself.

"Sit down, sit down," said Anami, and told the maid to bring some taller glasses, as though Anami felt too impatient, that night, to deal with the thimble-sized sake cups that a man may not even fill for himself; etiquette demanded that he lift the cup while a companion filled it for him.

He folded the papers that lay on the table and put them away in a small cupboard behind him. After he had poured some sake for his guest and himself, he said, "As you probably know, I decided some time ago to commit *seppuku*. I intend to do it tonight."

"Yes," said Takeshita. "I knew this afternoon that you had decided. Under the circumstances, I will not attempt to dissuade you."

"I am glad to hear it," said Anami. "When I heard that you had come so unexpectedly, I was afraid that you might try to stop me. I am glad I was mistaken. I bid you welcome—you have come at an opportune moment."

Anami refilled the glasses and talked genially on. He seemed content that he had done his best for the army entrusted into his care and for the country he had sworn to defend. He seemed satisfied that his work was done, relaxed, almost jovial.

Takeshita, on the other hand, as Anami talked on, grew sadder and more apprehensive. He was thinking of Hatanaka and of the revolt that had been planned for two o'clock; he felt guilty that he was doing nothing to stop what could only end in defeat—and more death. But now that Anami, in grandeur and tranquillity, had made up his mind to die, could Takeshita bring him back to earth again with details of a sordid little insurrection in the army that Anami had fought, and was now preparing to die, for?

Anami laughed, "You know, I had my vitamin injection tonight the same as I always do. When the maid asked me, I could hardly say I didn't want it because I was going to die. Could I now?"

Some two hours of steady drinking and talking later, Lieutenant-Colonel Ida went to the war minister's residence to find out what had delayed Takeshita

"Now come on," said Anami, "pull yourself together, and let's drink our sake. I don't know how long it will be before we have our next sake party together—in some other place." He laughed heartily at his joke.

The others joined him. The drinking resumed. Anami's round face grew rosier.

"If you drink too much," said Takeshita, in a worried tone, "your hand might slip, you might not succeed in killing yourself."

"Don't worry," Anami replied genially. "I haven't drunk too much yet. Besides, drink helps because it improves the circulation—the blood will flow more quickly. And don't forget I'm a fencer! Fifth grade. No, I'm not likely to fail. Relax!" Anami's hearty laugh rang out.

His guests smiled, as etiquette demanded.

Meanwhile, rebel units had set fire to the prime minister's official residence—although Suzuki had been spirited away in the nick of time. Marquis Kido's house had been attacked. At four in the morning General Tanaka, the loyal commander of the Eastern Army, arrived at his office, arrested those of his officers who were in on the plot, and then drove up to the imperial palace. By now the party sent to kill Suzuki was on its way to his private house. By a matter of minutes, because the rebels took a wrong turning, Suzuki escaped the trap to the house of a friend. The infuriated soldiers burned the house down instead.

At last, some time after five o'clock, General Anami committed *seppuku*:

The War Minister rose and put on a white shirt. "This was given to me" he said, "by the Emperor when I was his aide-de-camp. He had worn it himself. I can think of nothing I prize more highly—and so I intend to die wearing it."

Anami then pinned his decorations to a dress uniform and put the uniform on, after which he removed it, folded it properly, and laid it in front of the Tokonoma, "When I am dead," he said, "will you drape the uniform over me?"

Takeshita nodded, unable to speak; Ida felt his eyes fill with tears.

Anami took a photograph of his second son, Koreakira, who had died at the age of twenty-one during the China Incident, and placed it on top of his folded uniform in front of the Tokonoma.

When Takeshita returned, after seeing Okido, he paused in the corridor, behind the kneeling, but upright, figure of the war minister. Then Takeshita also dropped to his knees. Anami had drawn the dagger across his belly and was now, the dagger in his left hand, looking for the carotid artery on the right side of his neck.

Anami began to sway. The dagger swept across his neck, and a torrent of blood pulsed out. Yet Anami's body was still erect.

"Shall I help you?" asked Takeshita, in quiet, almost inaudible tones.

"No." There was nothing unusual about the War Minister's voice; he might have been answering the most ordinary of questions. "Leave me."

Takeshita went out into the garden. Ida lay sobbing on the bare ground. . . .

More than an hour after he had committed his act of *seppuku*, General Anami still knelt in the same place, his body still erect. The blood still flowed from his wounds.

"Aren't you in agony?" Takeshita whispered.

But there was no reply. The war minister seemed to have lost consciousness. Takeshita took the dagger that lay beside him and thrust it deep into the right side of Anami's neck. The body fell.

General Tanaka, meanwhile, had brushed past the armed sentries at the palace and told the rebellious officers there they were now under his control. He then marched into the *gobunko*, the imperial library, where the Emperor had been sleeping lightly through the night, oblivious to the events around him. The building had been shuttered and barred by the flapping, elderly imperial chamberlains. Tanaka was allowed in when he informed them that the coup was over.

Major Hatanaka, whose men had failed to find the tapes of the imperial broadcast, had by now broken into the offices of the broadcasting station, in an attempt to seize ten minutes of air time. After Tanaka had freed the Emperor and apologized for the "disrespect" his late arrival might have caused him, bowing five times, he also found Kido, who had been hidden in a small room under the imperial household ministry. Hatanaka, having failed to intimidate the broadcasting staff into giving him air time, returned to the outside of the imperial palace with a fellow conspirator, Lieutenant-

Colonel Shiizaki. The one on a motorcycle, the other on a white horse, they tried to distribute leaflets calling for a general insurrection.

Shortly before noon, when the Emperor's broadcast was due to go on the air, Hatanaka shot himself on the patch of green near the Sakshita Gate of the palace. Shiizaki stuck a sword into his stomach, and then shot himself in the head. Major Koga, Tojo's son-in-law, who had been guarding the body of General Mori through most of the night, cut his stomach open in the shape of a cross.

Colonel Ida, who had so often pledged to commit suicide, was placed under guard, and failed to do so. Takeshita, Anami's brother-in-law, lived on to become a senior general in Japan's postwar Self-Defense Force. The heroic Tanaka shot himself through the head on August 24, possibly because he felt himself responsible for the air raid damage to the imperial palace and the Meiji Shrine. Sporadic resistance continued around the country after the Emperor's broadcast, particularly at Atsugi air base, at which General MacArthur was shortly to land. But on the whole the docility with which the imperial army submitted to the Emperor's command to surrender was remarkable.

Japan's death throes had been agonized and protracted. The tragi-comedy of the coup attempt had demonstrated two things: how only a handful of strategically placed officers could influence not just the direction of the army, but the destiny of the Japanese nation; it was remarkable how men like Hatanaka and Ida, with the support of only a tiny number of officers, had nearly wrested power from the central government.

The second lesson was that in spite of the fanaticism of a few at the head of the army and further down, in fact the overwhelming majority were only too ready to invert a lifetime's training and lay down arms. The long-standing fear of the Emperor and his moderate advisers that any real opposition to the army vanguard would result in civil war was shown to have been unfounded. This must raise the question whether an imperial rescript against the militarists in the late 1930s might have worked; the Emperor and his advisers were perhaps the victims of their own trapped and timid perceptions in the imperial palace hothouse. The Emperor's command had, in the end, been obeyed.

How can the Emperor have felt, during that long night before Japan's surrender, while unknown to him the shades and spirits of Japan's dying army grappled for its soul, only to be chased away by the morning light, and his minister of war ritually drank sake and prepared to commit suicide? The immediate outlook could not have been bleaker for that remote, detached, shy little man, with his rarefied tastes, suppressed emotions, and sudden bursts of anger. He had recovered now from his nervous breakdown of mid-war, leading a life of spartan simplicity, rising at seven, to wash and read the newspapers, pray, and eat a breakfast of black bread and oatmeal, before working until noon and eating a lunch of cooked vegetables and dumpling soup. Afterward he would return to work and indulge in a short walk. He had no real friends and neither smoked nor drank; his family had been moved out of Tokyo, and he turned in early each evening.

He slept lightly, and the image must surely have recurred to him that night of the destruction of Tokyo, which he had himself witnessed from one of the few constructions left standing amid the burne out shells of the wooden buildings of the capital. More than 100,000 had been killed in Tokyo alone, while 2 million families had been rendered homeless. The majority of people were sleeping in flimsily constructed shelters of corrugated iron and charred wood. Closer to home still, on May 24 the imperial palace had been hit. The main part of it dated from 1884, taking four years to build, out of cypress wood. It had beautifully painted doors, screens and ceilings, with chandeliers imported from Europe. The main building was entirely gutted, its copper roofs collapsed in on its treasures. Thirty-three firemen had died trying to put out the blaze.

Six months earlier, the Emperor had moved his quarters into the *gobunko*, with its underground shelter 100 meters to the northeast. Hirohito had been heartbroken as the fire raged; his main concern had been to protect the palace shrine, some 200 meters to the west of the main palace. The shrine, however, was spared, as was the vault containing the sacred mirror. In the same raid, however, the Meiji Shrine had been burned and the Ise shrine had also been damaged. He wrote soon afterward:

> I probably should have brought the imperial mirror from Ise and the imperial sword from Atsuta here so that I could take care of them myself. But in deciding when to move them, I must act cautiously and take into account the effect it would have on the people's morale. Still, if worse comes to the worse, I feel I have no choice but to guard the sacred objects myself and share them with whatever fate has in store.

He was an Emperor whose empire was in ruins, surrounded by a devastated city, in a nation ravaged by war and two atomic bombs. He bore the ultimate responsibility. Most of the ideals he personified had been destroyed. Japan, the land of the select, was about to be occupied by barbarians. The Japanese empire was eliminated. The "unbeatable" Japanese army was decimated. His country was enduring unprecedented hardship and suffering even for a land that was no stranger to natural calamities.

He had come to office with high aspirations to restore the imperial throne to its former influence after the rule of his idiot father, when it had been a plaything for competing court factions and grubby civilian politicians. Hirohito had tried to do his duty, to restore the authority of himself and his imperial household at the apex of the huge bureau-authoritarian structure of the Japanese state. But events had conspired tragically against him.

On three occasions in his rule, he had exercised direct imperial authority: when he had dismissed the prime minister on the occasion of the murder of Chang Tso-lin; on the occasion of the February 1936 revolt; and again now, at the time of surrender, to prevent Japan's darkest hour turning blacker still. Saionji and the others had advised him that to interfere more would endanger his throne, his life even. He should have acted to issue a rescript to prevent Japan's drift toward war in the mid-1930s, as Prime Minister Inukai had advised. That was the time when the downhill slide could have been stopped.

The slide had been the culmination of a mass of errors which seemed inevitable at the time. There was the crown's refusal to permit the growth of truly representative institutions, for fear that they might have been manipulated by the left during the dangerous period of the late 1920s. There was the decision to curb the insolent young officers of the Kwantung Army in Manchuria, which merely gave power to their superiors in Tokyo, who were just as determined to embark on a course of imperial expansion—in the disastrous direction of China. There was the fatal alliance of the army and the *zaibatsu*, born largely of the consequences of world recession, which was too strong for the Emperor or his household to resist.

There was the disastrous decision to invade China itself, the war that the then chief of staff, General Sugiyama, had promised the Emperor would take a month to win, and was still unwon after eight years and millions of casualties. There was the navy's new strategy, and the cockiness of the admirals that they could destroy the American fleet and force Roosevelt to a negotiated settlement. There was the awesome miscalculation of the Konoye government that the invasion of South East Asia would be quietly accepted by the international community. So many miscalculations by the armed forces, by his advisers.

His own instincts had usually been right, but they had not prevailed. He had been right to try and stop the armed forces seizing the initiative in foreign policy. He had been right in his doubts about the China war. He had been right to worry about the consequences of invading Indochina.

He had been right to try and avert the Pacific War through diplomatic means, for fear that Japan would not in the end prevail. Only at the height of the madness of war, as the tide turned against Japan, had he somehow become convinced by Tojo that if Japan redoubled its efforts, it might win, buttressing the war party to the extent that even the faithful Kido had despaired and considered the desirability of forcing him to abdicate. Yet Kido failed to understand that it had been Hirohito's sacred duty by his ancestors and Japan's soldiers to pursue the war to a successful finish once it had been declared. He had had no alternative. Now all was in ruins.

Yet Hirohito was no longer the pathetic victim of a nervous breakdown, racked by guilt, of preceding months. With the decision to surrender, he was more at peace than for years. His country had at last turned the page: there was something to look forward to. Peace was about to come. He believed that Japan could recover, as it did from earthquakes and all kinds of natural disaster. He could not have faced the judgment of his ancestors had he been called upon to account for his reign today: even his demented father, Taisho, had presided over an era of peace and prosperity by contrast to the hurricane rule of his son.

But the Emperor still had a chance to restore his country to greatness. With the dropping of the bombs, the enemy had assumed the entire burden of blame for Japan's defeat on its own shoulders. True, the war had not been going well—all Japanese recognized that. Yet the country had not been defeated, even though it could not hope to prevail against "the new and most cruel" bomb. There would be misery, suffering and humiliation throughout the land, particularly for the army. Who knew how the barbarian conquerors of Japan would behave in occupation? But Japan had salvaged its honor. It could be no part of Bushido to undergo complete national self-immolation against impossible odds. With the imperial system preserved and honor intact, Japan could be rebuilt.

As General Anami prepared for death that night, he left two suicide notes of no great moment. As an afterthought, he wrote on the back of the second, "I believe in Japan's sacred indestructibility." In a note to his brother-in-law, he wrote, "It's true. The dead are dead, the living face hardships that are beyond our power to foresee, but if they work together, and if each does what he can, I believe that Japan will be saved." Like Hirohito, he knew that Japan had been given the fresh start it needed to recover and rebuild by the atomic bombs.

The Emperor was a light sleeper, but he slept more soundly than on any night in recent months, satisfied too to have exercised his imperial power so decisively both in the cause of saving Japan's honor, and of saving lives.

PART VI
AMERICAN SHOGUN

30 : Conqueror

A S THE WAR ENDED AND THE DIMINISHED FIGURE OF HIROHITO REELED from the magnitude of the tasks just undertaken, another man was grimly reflecting on the tasks ahead. The war had been an extraordinary one in the career of Douglas MacArthur. At its beginning he had been a retired and derided minor figure on the American stage. Now at the age of 65 he was one of the best known men in the world, a figure of towering heroism and stature, who had at last lived up to his own expectations of himself. After the holdout at Bataan, he had staged a dramatic military comeback fighting his way across thousands of miles of island territory with dazzling success and light casualties, arguing with his superiors every step of the way.

Now he made them recoil with fury as he criticized the decision to drop the atom bombs on Hiroshima and Nagasaki: it was MacArthur's view that Japan had been already on the point of surrender, which he believed could come as early as September 1, 1945. George Kenney recorded that "everyone I talked to in the War Department and even among the air command disagreed with MacArthur's view that the war would soon be over. The consensus was that Japan would hold out possibly for two more years."

With Tokyo reduced to rubble, most Japanese munitions factories obliterated, and the country starved of all raw materials it is hard to see how this view could be sustained. Harry Hopkins, Roosevelt's trusted special envoy, reported from Manila that "Japan is dead and the Japanese know it." Japanese industrialists told the government that war materials could be provided "for a few days more" only.

In late July MacArthur had been told of the successful testing of the atom bomb. He was appalled. He felt it was "completely unnecessary from a military point of view." Nevertheless he did as he was ordered and went ahead with preparations for a huge American invasion of mainland Japan, involving 1.4 million GIs based in the Philippines and a further 1 million to come. It was said that the Japanese had prepared 5,000 Kamikaze aircraft and that securing Kyushu would cause more than 250,000 American casualties. "Operation Olympic" was intended to land 750,000 men on the island of Kyushu in November 1945, and Operation Coronet would follow. But

MacArthur told his chief of staff, Sutherland, in the summer of 1945, "Dick, don't spend too much time planning for Olympic and Coronet. If you can get a way to drag your feet do so, because we are never going to invade Japan." This was before MacArthur learned of the existence of the bomb.

With the Russians likely to enter the war and Japan devastated, MacArthur was sure that it was imminently over. He had meanwhile been appointed Supreme Commander of the Allied Powers (SCAP) and therefore the probable head of the intended military occupation of Japan. He was almost certainly right in believing the planning for the invasion and the dropping of the bombs on Hiroshima and Nagasaki to have been unnecessary, although Washington was acting in all sincerity in believing that this would shorten the war and save hundreds of thousands of Allied servicemens' lives.

With the Japanese decision to surrender, he prepared himself for the biggest task in his life, one never performed by an American before or since: proconsul of a defeated nation, military dictator of 75 million people. This was an entirely political appointment and it was far from clear that a man whose entire career had been in the military—and as a conservative wherever he had strayed into politics—was the right man. But the dying Roosevelt had favored MacArthur over the more narrow-minded and unimaginative naval candidate, Chester Nimitz. At the time Washington still believed a full-scale invasion was necessary, and that a military man would have to take charge. When Harry Truman took office, he was too inexperienced to make any change in the command structure. So it fell to Douglas MacArthur to become the first foreign ruler in the 2,000-year-old history of Japan.

The man who was expected to lead millions of troops up the Japanese mainland and exact victor's retribution upon the most merciless fighters in the Second World War now performed one of the most extraordinary coups de theatre in his entire colorful career. He decided to arrive virtually alone in the teeth of the just-surrendered and still-smouldering Japanese military machine. The new American shogun was to land nearly a century after the fall of the last Tokugawa one, and in style.

On August 30, 1945, less than a month after Little Boy was dropped, a C-54 aircraft, the *Bataan*, took off from Okinawa, bearing the commander of American forces in the Far East, General Douglas MacArthur, and his chief aides across a clear, calm blue sky.

If he was nervous, MacArthur tried not to show it. He paced up and down the aircraft, talking about his priorities in the exercise of the awesome powers that in a few hours were to pass to him. He dictated staccato, apparently random thoughts:

First destroy the military power . . . Then build the structure of representative government . . . Enfranchise the women . . . Free the political prisoners . . . Liberate the farmers . . . Establish a free labor movement . . . Encourage a free economy . . . Abolish police oppression . . . Develop a free and responsible press . . . decentralize the political power . . . Could he, for the first time in modern history, accomplish that miraculous phenomenon: a successful occupation of a defeated nation?

It amounted to a blueprint for the reshaping of a whole Asian society. In fact, this extensive list of priorities had been transmitted to MacArthur the day before from Washington under the title, "Initial Post-Surrender Priority for Japan," reflecting years of planning at a high level and bearing President Truman's personal stamp of approval.

MacArthur then took a nap. His faithful ally, General Courtney Whitney, described by his detractors as a "stuffed pig with a mustache," and generally viewed as pompous and rude, woke him up to admire what MacArthur commented under his breath was "beautiful Mount Fuji." The plane began the descent to land at Atsugi Air Base outside Tokyo.

MacArthur's action appeared to be one of absolute foolhardiness. General Eichelberger, in charge of the advance party at Atsugi, and one of MacArthur's most hardheaded colleagues, repeatedly tried to persuade the commander in chief to abandon the venture. The dangers of landing with only minimal protection in the heart of the Kanto Plain southwest of Tokyo, where 300,000 well-armed Japanese troops were based, and where acts of insubordination and refusal to acknowledge defeat had been commonplace, were only too apparent. Atsugi had been a training base for kamikaze pilots, many of whom had refused to surrender. A mutiny there after the Emperor's broadcast had sputtered on for days.

Yet MacArthur ordered his own party to take off their guns before the aircraft landed. He believed the arrival of the Americans unarmed would make it less likely that they would be attacked; moreover, it would rub in the fact "to the oriental mind" that the Japanese had been defeated. MacArthur would come as a conqueror, not as a fighter. General Whitney takes up the story:

We circled the field at little more than treetop height, and as I looked out at the field and the flat stretches of Kanto Plain, I could see numerous antiaircraft emplacements. It was difficult not to let my mind dwell on Japan's recent performances. The war had been started without a formal declaration; nearly everywhere Japanese soldiers had refused to give up until killed; the usual laws of war had not been complied with; deadly traps had frequently been set. Here was the greatest opportunity for a final and climactic act. The antiaircraft guns could not possibly miss at this range. Had death, this insatiable monster of the battle, passed MacArthur by on a thousand fields only to murder him at the end? I held my breath. I think the whole world was holding its breath. But as usual he had been right. He knew the orient. He knew the basic Japanese character too well to have thus gambled blindly with death. He knew and trusted that national spirit of traditional chivalry called "bushido."

The plane nestled down on the field and MacArthur got out. He paused for a second or two to look about him. The sky was a bright blue, splotched with patches of fleecy clouds. The sun beating down on the airfield made the concrete runways and apron shimmer with the heat. There were several other United States planes on the field, and the few armed Allied troops in the area seemed a frighteningly small force. A handful of officers waited to greet him. The senior was General Eichelberger, who strode forward to meet MacArthur. They shook hands and MacArthur said in a quiet voice: "Bob, from Melbourne to Tokyo is a long way, but this seems to be the end of the road."

The showman with dark glasses and corncob pipe who had probably been as responsible as any for Japan's defeat descended the aircraft steps and set foot on enemy soil. Awaiting him on the airfield was, according to Whitney, a collection "of the most decrepit looking vehicles I have ever seen—the best means of transport the Japanese could round up for the trip into Yokohama." MacArthur was given the place of honor in an ancient American Lincoln; the other American officers climbed aboard the cars behind, some 20 armed American soldiers joining the convoy immediately after the commander in chief.

A fire engine "that resembled the Toonerville Trolley" started with such a loud backfire that the Americans ducked. Then, like "a sequence in a dream fantasy," in Eichelberger's words, the worn-out procession of clattering, sputtering vehicles started moving down the 20-mile drive to Yokohama along a gauntlet of Japanese soldiers—two divisions of some 30,000 men— with their backs to the procession.

The Japanese officials accompanying the American party explained that this was a gesture of respect: they were guarding MacArthur in the manner they guarded the Emperor. The real purpose, for MacArthur as for the Emperor, was to protect him from renegade forces or any gesture of disrespect. Whitney was far from certain that the entire bizarre sequence, from the landing to the procession, was not some symbolic expression of hatred—"I could not help wondering whether the Japanese intended it as a gesture of defiance, whether they felt a strong guard like this was really necessary, or whether there was some other deep-seated, mysterious, ulterior motive." The cars kept breaking down along the route, rendering the Americans sitting ducks. Eichelberger did not draw an easy breath until the journey ended.

They found Yokohama like a ghost town, deserted and boarded up. At the city's splendid New Grand Hotel, the staff instantly prostrated themselves before MacArthur. At dinner, Whitney warned his boss that his steak might be poisoned. He laughed and replied, "No one can live forever."

Churchill was later to venture the opinion that "the outstanding accomplishment" of any commander during the war was General MacArthur's "landing with such a small force of troops in the face of several million Japanese soldiers who had not yet been disarmed." He later wrote, "[O]f all the amazing deeds of bravery of the war, I regarded MacArthur's personal landing at Atsugi as the greatest of the lot." This typically flamboyant—and in the view of some, unnecessary—act of courage by the general in fact paid ample returns: it started the occupation off on exactly the right note, underlining that the Americans came bearing a message of peace and for conciliation, not vengeance of the kind the Japanese expected (and had every reason to expect), after their own behavior to conquered peoples and to captured Americans.

The Japanese historian, Kazuo Kawai, wrote:

> It was an exhibition of cool personal courage; it was even more a gesture of trust in the good faith of the Japanese. It was a masterpiece of psychology which completely disarmed Japanese apprehensions. From that moment, whatever danger there might have been of a fanatic attack on the Americans vanished in a wave of Japanese admiration and gratitude.

After this, the actual Japanese surrender ceremony was something of an anticlimax, in spite of MacArthur's attempts to orchestrate a grand finale. In one poignant piece of symbolism, he invited General Jonathan Wainwright, who had surrendered to the Japanese at Corregidor after MacArthur had left the island, and General Arthur Percival, the former British commander at Singapore, to meet him and then witness the surrender.

The reunion with Wainright was emotional. As the local CBS correspondent told it,

When Wainwright's car arrived outside the New Grand Hotel, General MacArthur dashed out of his office and across the lobby to greet the emaciated, hungry-looking scarecrow who was approaching. Without waiting for the formality of a salute, General MacArthur grabbed Wainwright's hand and put his arm around his shoulder in a half embrace . . . General MacArthur was marked with more emotion than I ever saw the general display . . .

MacArthur was shocked by his old comrade's appearance.

He was haggard and aged. His uniform hung in folds on his fleshless form. He walked with difficulty and with the help of a cane. His eyes were sunken and there were pits in his cheeks. His hair was snow white and his skin looked like old shoe leather. He made a brave effort to smile as I took him in my arms, but when he tried to talk his voice wouldn't come. For three years he had imagined himself in disgrace for having surrendered Corregidor. He believed he would never again be given an active command. This shocked me. "Why Jim," I said, "your old corps is yours when you want it."

Two days later, on September 2, a cloudy Sunday morning, MacArthur's naval rival, Admiral Nimitz, climbed aboard the massive 45,000-ton battleship, the USS *Missouri*, anchored some 18 miles off Tokyo Bay. Under a huge Stars and Stripes, the Japanese delegation came aboard onto the crowded deck; thousands of seamen watched them while cameramen found angles from every conceivable part of the superstructure.

The Japanese delegation was less impressive than MacArthur might have expected. The Emperor, of course, would not attend. The Prime Minister, Prince Higashikuni, was the Emperor's uncle and had used his royal blood as a pretext for staying away. His deputy, and the real strongman in the government, Prince Konoye, also made his excuses. The short straw was drawn by the foreign minister, Mamoru Shigemitsu, a tough old idealist who had lost his leg in a bomb attack 15 years before, and who appropriately enough was a vigorous anti-militarist. For the army, General Yoshijiro Umezu, the chief of the army general staff, the figure who had vacillated and then urged Japan to fight on, was ordered to attend. When he had first heard this he had gone pale with anger and threatened to commit *seppuku*, until the Emperor himself prevailed upon him to attend.

The Japanese looked grim and diminished in their morning dress and top hats and uniforms, standing stiffly to attention as an American army chaplain said a prayer and "The Star-Spangled Banner" was played on a tinny, scratched record. They were joined by MacArthur, Nimitz, Halsey, Wainwright and Percival. One of the Japanese delegates recorded the experience:

They were all thronged, packed to suffocation, representatives, journalists, spectators, an assembly of brass, braid and brand. As we appeared
on the scene we were, I felt, being subjected to the torture of the pillory.
There were a million eyes beating us in the million shafts of a rattling
storm of arrows barbed with fire. I felt their keenness sink into my body
with a sharp physical pain. Never have I realized that the glance of glaring
eyes could hurt so much.

We waited for a few minutes, standing in the public gaze like penitent
boys awaiting the dreaded schoolmaster. I tried to preserve with the utmost
sangfroid the dignity of defeat, but it was difficult and every minute
seemed to contain ages. I looked up and saw painted on the wall several
miniature Rising Suns, our flag, evidently in numbers corresponding to the
planes and submarines shot down or sunk by the crew of the battleship.
As I tried to count these markings, tears rose in my throat and quickly
gathered to the eyes, flooding them.

MacArthur approached the microphones. He had thought about his
speech carefully: the terrible overuse of purple passagery that was his worst
rhetorical enemy threatened to overwhelm the solemnity of the occasion:

[A]s I prepared to receive the surrender of the mighty warlords of the
Far East, I wished that my pen were wielded by one on such intimate terms
with words—those immortal heralds of thought which at the touch of
genius become radiant—that at my call they would convey my feelings in
terms that would satisfy the ultimate sources of reason, history and interpretation. For I have a consciousness that in the events culminating at this
immortal moment lie those truths which at last are transplanted into epics
and lyrics, and those exalted terms which we find on the lips of the great
seers and prophets.

Was the day beclouded by mists and trailing clouds? Were there lone
trees cresting Tokyo's shores against the moving sky? Were there voices of
waters falling far up within some wild ravine racing into the bay? Were there
nearby fields where bees were buzzing? I cannot remember, but this I do—
the all-embracing pride I felt in my country's monumental victory. Its future
seemed to gleam as though seen through the optimistic gates of youth . . .

Fortunately good sense prevailed and MacArthur was uncharacteristically brief and to the point. He received a little support from above in
orchestrating the climax to the ceremony. The sun suddenly broke through

the clouds as he had finished speaking, and a steady drone could be heard, turning into a deafening roar as 400 B-29 Super-Fortresses and 1,500 fighters zoomed overhead. MacArthur's broadcast to the American people that day was even oddly moving and thoughtful:

Today the guns are silent. A great tragedy has ended. A great victory has been won. . . .

A new era is upon us. Even the lesson of victory itself brings with it profound concern, both for our future security and the survival of civilization. The destructiveness of the war potential, through progressive advances in scientific discovery, has in fact now reached a point which revises the traditional concepts of war.

Men since the beginning of time have sought peace . . . Military alliances, balances of power, leagues of nations, all in turn have failed, leaving the only path to be by way of the crucible of war. We have had our last chance. If we do not now devise some greater and more equitable system, Armageddon will be at our door. The problem basically is theological and involves a spiritual recrudescence and improvement of human character that will synchronize with our matchless advances in science, art, literature and all material and cultural developments of the past two thousand years. It must be of the spirit if we are to save the flesh.

What can the Japanese officials who first met General Douglas MacArthur at Atsugi, and then at the surrender ceremony, have thought of him as they gaped up at this tall, balding man, on the threshold of old age, with his curious trademarks of floppy military hat, corncob pipe and dark glasses, and a studied battlefield informality, usually standing at ease, rarely wearing a tie or a jacket, extremely articulate, even hypnotic in the monologues that were the despair of his staff, who could hardly ever get his meetings to end on time? The first impression was one of fear, that the victorious commander would exact revenge; the second, born of MacArthur's conciliatory attitude, one of cautious approval, mixed with awe.

The Japanese diplomat present, Toshikazu Kase, observed:

What stirring eloquence and what a noble vision! Here is a victor announcing the verdict to the prostrate enemy. He can exact his pound of flesh if he so chooses. He can impose a humiliating penalty if he so desires. And yet he pleads for freedom, tolerance, and justice. For me, who expected the worst humiliation, this was a complete surprise. I was thrilled beyond words, spellbound, thunderstruck. "For the living heroes and dead martyrs of the war this speech was a wreath of undying flowers."

The third great setpiece after MacArthur's dramatic arrival at Atsugi and the surrender ceremony was the shogun's meeting with the Emperor. On his relationship with Hirohito would hinge the outcome of the occupation in Japan. In constructing this MacArthur, more than his political masters in Washington, played the dominant role. Washington, at that time still in the hands of the second-generation New Dealers, had four dominant objectives for the occupation: to preserve Japan from disintegration and, worse, the possibility that communism would come to power out of the rubble; to draw the teeth of militarist Japan, so that it could not threaten Asia and the United States again; to break up the great monopolist *zaibatsu* rightly seen as the underpinning of Japanese militarism; and to liberalize a feudal society and implant democracy.

These were the instructions that they gave MacArthur and they were not at all unpalatable to him, even though he was a conservative Republican by conviction. As a Teddy Roosevelt–style trustbuster and paternalist, he too favored breaking up the semi-socialist giant capitalist monopolies to allow smaller private enterprise to flourish; and he regarded himself as a liberal and a Democrat politically. There is a revealing incident described by an officer at a dinner in Manila before the war, when Sutherland, his chief of staff, let loose his primitive right-wing view that the United States should have been a dictatorship in wartime.

General MacArthur listened for a while and then told Sutherland he was wrong; that democracy works and will always work, because the people are allowed to think, to talk, and keep their minds free, open, and supple. He said that while the dictator state may plan a war, get everything worked out down to the last detail, launch the attack, and do pretty well at the beginning, eventually something goes wrong with the plan. Something interrupts the schedule. Now, the regimented minds of the dictator command are not flexible enough to handle quickly the changed situation. They have tried to make war a science when it is actually an art.

He went on to say that a democracy, on the other hand, produces hundreds and thousands of flexible-minded, freethinking leaders who will take advantage of the dictator's troubles and mistakes and think of a dozen ways to outthink and defeat him. As long as a democracy can withstand the initial onslaught, it will find ways of striking back and eventually it will win. It costs money and at times does look inefficient but, in the final analysis, democracy as we have it in the United States is the best form of government that man has ever evolved. He paused and said, "The trouble with you, Dick, I am afraid, is that you are a natural-born autocrat."

However, there were many in Washington who thought that the Emperor should be deposed and put on trial for his responsibility in the war: they reflected a huge swathe of domestic opinion—probably the overwhelming majority, as well as the views of most American allies.

But MacArthur vehemently disagreed: he believed the Emperor was essential to maintaining stability in Japan. The occupation, he felt, could not govern against the Emperor, only through him. The origin of this view can be found in the counsels of Brigadier Bonner Fellers, MacArthur's military secretary, a deeply-read student of Japan whose cousin Gwen was married to a Japanese diplomat, Hidenari Terasaki. Fellers held extremely enlightened views for an American of the time, condemning the saturation bombing of Tokyo as "one of the most ruthless and barbaric killings of noncombatants in all history." Just a week before Japan surrendered, he wrote:

> The war in Europe was both political and social while the war in the Pacific was racial . . . the white man as overlord of the Orient is finished . . . The American position in the Orient cannot be founded upon the theory of white supremacy. The Oriental must be placed on the basis of absolute equality with our people . . . There must be no taboo because of race.

In a brilliant pre-surrender paper he argued that

> [a]n absolute and unconditional defeat of Japan is the essential ingredient for a lasting peace in the Orient. Only through complete military disaster and the resultant chaos can the Japanese people be disillusioned from their fanatical indoctrination that they are the superior people, destined to be the overlords of Asia. Only stinging defeat and colossal losses will prove to the people that the military machine is not invincible and that their fanatical leadership has taken them the way of disaster . . .
>
> There must be no weakness in the peace terms. However, to dethrone, or hang, the Emperor would cause a tremendous and violent reaction from all Japanese. Hanging of the Emperor to them would be comparable to the

crucifixion of Christ to us. All would fight to die like ants. The position of the gangster militarists would be strengthened immeasurably. The war would be unduly prolonged; our losses heavier than otherwise would be necessary . . .

An independent Japanese army responsible only to the Emperor is a permanent menace to peace. But the mystic hold the Emperor has on his people and the spiritual strength of the Shinto faith properly directed need not be dangerous. The Emperor can be made a force for good and peace provided Japan is totally defeated and the military clique destroyed.

The Government must have a system of checks and balances. The Emperor must be surrounded by liberal civilian leaders. The military must be limited to an internal police force, responsible to civil authority . . .

This became a blueprint for what followed—with one important exception: the Japanese had not suffered "absolute and unconditional defeat." They had been defeated by atom bombs against which, of course, there had been no defense, as the Emperor had made clear.

To Kennan on one occasion, MacArthur claimed that the occupation's most spectacular achievement "lay in the fact that it was bringing to the Japanese two great appreciations which they have never before perceived and which were designed to revolutionize their thinking, namely, democracy and Christianity." To him, Japan "formed the western outpost of our defenses, protected by Christianity and military power." He believed that "an astonishing number of the Japanese people—already estimated at over 2 million" had moved to embrace "the Christian faith as a means to fill the spiritual vacuum left in Japanese life by the collapse of their past faith." The "spearhead of Christianity" would transform "hundreds of millions of backward peoples."

For MacArthur the reason for protecting the Emperor was absolutely straightforward: he believed that he had no choice, and he may have been right:

There had been a considerable outcry from some of the Allies, notably the Russians and the British, to include him in this category [as a war criminal] . . . When Washington seemed to be veering toward the British point of view, I had advised that I would need at least one million reinforcements should such action be taken. I believed that if the Emperor were indicted, and perhaps hanged, as a war criminal, military government would have to be instituted throughout all Japan, and guerrilla warfare would probably break out. The Emperor's name had then been stricken from the list.

In his advice to the joint chiefs of staff, relayed through a top secret message on July 25, he had gone further:

> Destroy him and the nation will disintegrate . . . Civilized practices will largely cease and a condition of underground chaos and disorder amounting to guerrilla warfare in the mountainous and outlying regions will result. I believe all hope of introducing modern democratic methods would disappear and that when military control finally ceased, some form of intense regimentation, probably along communistic lines, would arise from the mutilated masses . . . It is quite possible that a minimum of a million troops would be required which would have to be maintained for an indefinite number of years. In addition, a complete civil service might have to be recruited and imported, possibly running into a size of several hundred thousand. I have gained the definite impression from as complete a research as was possible to me that [the Emperor's] connection with affairs of state up to the time of the end of the war was largely ministerial and automatically responsive to the advice of his counselors.

Although MacArthur's views were so strong and so definitive that he must bear prime responsibility for the decision, he was preaching to the converted. In spite of the clamor of public opinion for Hirohito's head—in June 1945, 33 percent of Americans wanted Hirohito executed (although only half of those polled knew his name; there were those who thought it was Tojo, Hara-Kiri, Tito, Chiang Kai-Shek and Yoko Hama)—Truman endured intense pressure from State Department insiders not to punish Japan, but to preserve the imperial institution in the face of the danger from socialism and communism—indeed to enlist it in the fight against communism.

The Defense Department took the same view, only more so. With both great departments of government pointing the same way, while the Americans were anxious to extricate themselves from further commitments in men and money and the commander on the spot was emphatically recommending the preservation of the imperial institution, the President could have taken no other decision, however disagreeable to ordinary Americans who had witnessed the Japanese atrocities of the past few years. Who can say that they were all wrong? If Hirohito had been forced out, Japan might indeed have been plunged into widespread bloodshed and social disintegration.

A question mark hangs over the issue of the Emperor's abdication, as opposed to his forcible removal, trial or execution, or the abolition of the emperor-system. It must be doubted that any serious upheaval would have taken place if the Emperor had been prevailed upon to abdicate in favor of his young son. There is evidence that Hirohito considered this. On August 29 Hirohito told his closest adviser, Marquis Kido, that he was willing to "resign from the throne" in order to save his "subordinates from prosecution." Kido, the fussing, alarmist courtier as always, feared that this would undermine the emperor-system and feed "the tide of republicanism and democracy." Both the Emperor's brothers, Prince Chichibu and Takamatsu, made veiled suggestions that they would consider putting themselves forward as regent should Hirohito abdicate in favor of his young son, Akihito.

If he had, the main benefits of the decision to retain the Emperor and his throne would have remained exactly the same, as Homer Dubs, a Japan expert consulted by the American government, wrote at the time. "It makes no difference whether he was inclined toward peace or war. It is the office, not the individual, that is important in Japanese eyes; the essential matter is to remove from the minds of the Japanese people their belief in the sanctity of the Emperor. That cannot be done unless the Allies prove to them that they are able to uproot even their divine rulers . . . The present U.S. practice of refraining from criticizing or blaming or touching the Emperor in any way plays into the hands of the nationalistic Japanese. They can declare to their people that even the Americans respect and are awed by the inviolable mikado."

The consequences of the decision to preserve both the imperial institution and its incumbent—taken like so many other decisions at the time as the lesser of two evils—went much deeper than MacArthur and his superiors either intended or foresaw. The retention of the Emperor was to signal to the Japanese that, however strongly the Americans pledged to change the country on the surface, they would tolerate the survival of the system. The throne was the very incarnation and embodiment of the power struggle, the pinnacle of usually formal authority in a body politic that was entirely hierarchical from top to bottom. Retaining the Emperor meant retaining the concepts of authority, respect and subservience.

MacArthur strode mightily, as we shall see, to turn Hirohito into a constitutional monarch. But something else happened. The Japanese had a long history of elevating the Emperor "above the clouds," at one remove from politics, yet nevertheless regarding him as the linchpin of the whole edifice of deference and authoritarianism. There would be no difficulty at all in removing the Emperor from politics—a relatively recent innovation of the Meiji period. Indeed, as we have seen, Hirohito's real powers were heavily circumscribed: throughout the previous two decades, his role as a symbol was far more important to the militarists than his usually meddlesome exercise of actual power. Stripping him of his powers while retaining him as a symbol made little difference to the real structure of Japanese power. Beneath him the system would continue.

A constitutional monarchy is one in which sovereignty is firmly rooted in the people, and the monarch rules only as long as he is respected by the people; indeed the survival of a modern constitutional monarchy depends on its ability to retain popularity and outwit its republican opponents. In Japan, after a brief left-wing flourish of opposition to the Emperor in the initial postwar period, a protective consensus immediately formed around him. The monarch was a little more powerless than before; but his power had always rested on the symbolism of his throne as the apex of the social, political and economic structure, not upon the man.

There seems to have been a conscious blurring in the minds of MacArthur and his American masters of the difference between putting the Emperor on trial and of getting him to abdicate. The first would have had dramatic consequences, the second more limited repercussions. What served Hirohito in good stead was his documented record of reluctance to go along with the militarists. More persuasively, the Americans felt that he was too useful a tool for them to dispense with. Any direct conflict with the Emperor would run the risk of precipitating civil war, with fanatical Japanese attacks on the Americans. But with the Emperor acquiescing in the American occupation, nationalist feeling was effectively neutralized. The fiction could be maintained that the country was not under occupation. The Emperor still ruled: he was merely being advised by the Americans, as his predecessors had for so many centuries by the shoguns who really ruled the country.

The American decision to preserve both Hirohito and his office was bitterly opposed by some of America's allies. Although the British understood and even privately agreed, Ernest Bevin, the foreign secretary, refused to pull America's chestnuts out of the fire. "I do not want us to recommend to the Americans that the Emperor should be preserved. They would no doubt like to get such advice, then say they had reluctantly concurred with us." China favored putting the Emperor on trial. Australia's foreign minister had placed Hirohito on the list of criminals he wanted to see stand trial. New Zealand felt the same way.

Predictably, the Russians were most adamant in their demands for Hirohito to be deposed and prosecuted—a view MacArthur interpreted as an attempt to weaken Japan and create a state of social tension from which the country's Communists would benefit. The Soviet pressure paradoxically had the effect of strengthening American support for MacArthur's pro-Emperor stand. Joseph Grew, the American Secretary of State, came down flatly and determinedly on MacArthur's side. Truman confirmed the order.

The Japanese perspective was significantly different. To Hirohito and his advisers the Emperor had been allowed to remain on his throne not just to preserve order and continuity in Japan, but because the fiction that Japan had not actually been defeated could thus be maintained. If the Americans had not removed the Emperor from office and put him on trial, or even merely forced him to abdicate, this was an acknowledgment that the Emperor had not been guilty in his declaration of war and pursuit of Japan's national interests. Even the victors, it seemed, showed that they respected his innocence in this respect. He had been let down by the military clique he had opposed before the war because they had failed to deliver the victory they had promised, not because they had been intrinsically wrong in pursuing Japan's imperial expansionism which had ultimately led to the war with America.

Shortly after the surrender broadcast the Prime Minister, Kantaro Suzuki, had "sincerely apologized" to the Emperor on behalf of the government for failing to achieve victory. In September Hirohito had written to the 12-year-old Crown Prince Akihito that the armed forces had concentrated too much on "the spirit" and had neglected science during the war (a favorite theme of Hirohito)—hardly an admission of moral guilt. The Americans and the British, he said, had been taken too lightly. He had accepted defeat, he wrote "to preserve the needs of our people." Akihito dutifully observed in his diary, no doubt reflecting his father's views, that Japan lost the war because of its scientific backwardness, and because the Japanese lacked the team spirit shown by the Americans.

In this interpretation, Hirohito's preservation on the throne was an acknowledgement by the victors that Japan had not been wrong in its objectives, and Hirohito had been right to place the blame for losing the war on the advisers who had so ill-served him (as well as the weapon against which there was no defense). Hirohito's own defense, being hurriedly prepared in case he was indicted as a war criminal, was designed to show how he had opposed the war only because he felt it could not be won—not because he believed it to be wrong. The great fear of the Japanese in the early weeks of occupation was that MacArthur would not retain the imperial institution or that—almost as bad—the Emperor would be put on trial and exposed as having approved the key decisions of the war and therefore revealed before his people as fallible, because the war had been lost—or both. The apprehensions Hirohito showed before the meeting stemmed at least as much from these two considerations as from fears as to his own personal safety.

Thus the stage was set for that extraordinary first meeting between the Mikado and the American shogun. The symbolism of Japan's Emperor meeting his country's first foreign conqueror was, of course, immense. The upstart democratic power, less than 170 years old, was usurping the oldest autocratic system in the world. A mere mortal would be overpowering a divinity. But in human terms the encounter was no less poignant. Superficially, the differences between the two men could hardly have been greater: the pampered, almost physically handicapped weakling who had enjoyed supreme power for nearly two decades was meeting a man whose entire life had been one of action, and one who had fought his way across a quarter of the world in opposition to the Emperor's own forces. Hirohito had never seen military action; MacArthur had been in the thick of it, dodging bullets from France to Corregidor to the South Pacific, risking his life innumerable times.

Yet Hirohito was not in entirely unfamiliar territory as he walked from his car into the American embassy on September 27: for three centuries his forefathers had been spiritual adornments to the real power exercised by military dictators, the Tokugawa shoguns, who themselves had become figureheads for their own chief ministers. During the decade before the war— and particularly in the five years after the suppression of the February 1936 coup which in practice marked the final ascent to power of militarism in prewar Japan, Hirohito, while endowed with great formal authority, had very little choice but to endorse—while occasionally querying—the decisions put before him by his militarist chief ministers. Was his prostration before another military figure, this time an American one, to be so different?

MacArthur's own career had also been roller coaster—from triumph in 1918 to virtual exile in 1924, to triumph again in 1930, to ignominy in 1932 to virtual disgrace in 1941, followed by meteoric redemption the following year. Both men had suffered from extraordinary reversals of fortune. There was a surprising similarity of temperament too: both had been reared in conditions of almost stultifying orthodoxy—Hirohito by the martinets of the imperial court, MacArthur in the severe surroundings of military outposts and barracks. Yet beneath the immaculate exteriors of both lay inner natures that sought private escapes—MacArthur toward women, his love of poetry as a young man and feel for words (something the poetry-loving Hirohito also prided himself upon), the Emperor toward science. It was to come as a surprise to many that the tiny, modest, cosseted god-ruler should be able to get on well with the towering, vain, flamboyant, overbearing man of action. It should not; it was a meeting of different kinds of gods, nothing less.

31 : PROCONSUL

MACARTHUR WAS NOW PLACED IN ONE OF THE MOST REMARKABLE POSItions of any man in world history. He had been given sole charge of a country of 80 million people with a unique tradition of obeisance, deference and hierarchy. He was the first foreign ruler and occupier in 2,000 years of Japanese history. His absolute power on September 2, 1945, can be paralleled with that exercised by Pizarro in Peru, Cortes in Mexico and Clive in India after the defeat of their absolute systems of government. He was perhaps the only example of a true viceroy, appointed to rule over another land, and a huge one at that, in America's history of avowed opposition to colonialism. He was Japan's new shogun, dwarfing the Emperor in power. He had charged himself with no less a task than the transformation of a warlike despotism into a modern, democratic state. Three questions arise: how had it come about that a single individual from a democratic country was given such dictatorial powers to shape the new Japan? Why, specifically, was MacArthur chosen? And was he the right man for the job?

The answer to the first question was straightforward enough: drastic and effective central authority was clearly essential for Japan, in the condition of destruction and potential mass starvation to which it had been reduced. Some kind of military occupation authority was inevitable. In Germany a four-power division between the Allied victors had been established. In Japan the Americans had been in the driving seat, and were determined not to share power with their allies in the Pacific War—the British, the Australians and others—nor, more pressingly, to give the Russians a toehold. From the first, Japan was viewed as a potential bulwark against the Russians.

As early as August 16—a fortnight before the surrender—the Russians insisted that they be given an occupation zone on Japan's northern island of Hokkaido. They complained that the Americans had been urging them to attack Japan just days before the two atomic bombs were dropped; the Americans retorted that the Russians had been a long time about it, and that they had secured their two immediate strategic aims—the conquest of Manchuria and the occupation of the Kurile islands north of Japan. The Americans insisted that the Russians could not be involved in Japan itself except in a nominal capacity and asked that their aircraft be allowed to overfly the Kuriles. In Moscow the American ambassador, Averell Harriman, was convinced that the Soviet demands were mere feints, an attempt to embarrass the Americans so that, in return for a Russian hands-off policy on Japan, the United States would agree to leave Hungary, Bulgaria, Romania and the Balkans alone. With more justice, the British government also demanded a role in the running of Japan.

The argument among the three main Allied victors steadily escalated. When Harriman on October 24 secured a meeting with Stalin, who was supposedly under internal challenge and had dropped from view for several days, the Soviet leader bluntly diverted the conversation away from Europe to Japan. He wanted a consultative committee including the Russians to be set up along the lines of those administering Hungary and Romania. He said he was angered by the way MacArthur had treated his representative in Tokyo, General Kuzma Derevyanko, like "a piece of furniture." He insisted that a joint Allied commission should have the power of veto over the Supreme Commander of the Allied Powers in Tokyo.

Yet Stalin's attitude convinced Harriman that he was not serious about demanding a voice in Japanese affairs—understandably, in view of the almost negligible contribution the Russians had made to the war effort against Japan—but that America would have to give something. The Americans accepted a purely nominal measure of influence in Bulgaria and Romania in exchange for allowing much the same to Russia over Japan: a Far Eastern Commission in Washington was set up, along with a smaller Allied Council for Japan in Tokyo. Neither had much real power. The Allied Council comprised of America, Russia, China and the British Commonwealth. It had the right to consult with MacArthur "the exigencies of the situation permitting." But he was not obliged to accept any of its recommendations, and he had "controlling" power.

MacArthur was from the first deeply opposed to any Russian influence in Japan; when Derevyanko, the liaison officer, tried to assert the Soviet right to occupy Hokkaido, MacArthur refused. The envoy became "abusive," suggesting that Stalin could have the supreme commander dismissed at any time and that Russian forces would move in regardless. The American commander told him that if a single Soviet soldier entered Japan without permission, Derevyanko, as head of the Russian mission, would be jailed.

"By God, I believe you would," the Russian replied. There was no Soviet move.

MacArthur was even angrier when he heard of the two consultative bodies agreed to by Washington, particularly when the State Department suggested that he had agreed to them. The general insisted that "I had not an iota of responsibility for the decisions" and that his views had not been sought. He was contemptuous of both bodies, and ignored them. He later wrote:

> The very nature of its composition and procedures eventually made the Far Eastern Commission ineffective. All four of the major powers had a veto. It took time for the commission members to convene, and it took an even longer time for them to make a decision once they had convened. As it turned out, they usually confined themselves to approving actions which the occupation had already taken on its own initiative. From the start, the Russian members tried to turn the commission into a propaganda instrument through derogatory speeches and statements designed to obstruct orderly government in Japan. . . .
>
> The Far Eastern Commission became little more than a debating society, and when a peace treaty was finally signed with Japan, it died a quiet death. Not one constructive idea to help with the reorientation and reconstruction of Japan ever came from the Far Eastern commission or its satellite, the Allied Council. This latter body was, by its terms of reference, solely advisory and consultative. But it was neither the one nor the other, its sole contribution being that of nuisance and defamation.

American contempt for the interference of its allies, it seems, far preceded the Iraq war more than half a century later. The truth was that the Russians were much more interested in Europe and were keen only to score points off the Americans in Japan so as to assert their control over Eastern Europe; the Americans, with their overwhelming preponderance of military force in Japan, were determined to run it themselves, according to their own precepts, half idealistic, half self-interested. They were anxious to avoid a repetition of the supposed fiasco of the four-power occupation of Germany; MacArthur, in particular, strongly asserted his right to exclusive American control.

Much the same applies as to why MacArthur himself was chosen as America's viceroy. He was the right man in the right place. He was the principal, although by no means the only, senior commander in the Pacific War (both Admirals Nimitz and Halsey played major roles). The most pressing problems in occupied Japan were of a military, logistical and organizational nature, which seemed to rule out a civilian authority and to require a kind of military dictator. MacArthur was decisive, high-profile and likely to impress the Japanese, who were not used to more democratic figures. He had frequently quarreled with Roosevelt, who nevertheless respected him.

Truman, instead, hated him, but recognized that he could not stop his appointment, which was also supported by virtually all the generals in the European theater and Washington, who were determined not to have MacArthur, with his huge public cachet, in the foreground. Truman's views on MacArthur, according to Harold Ickes, his interior secretary, included "some pretty vigorous Montana epithets." Two weeks before appointing his Supreme Commander, the American President had written witheringly of "Mr. Prima Donna, Brass Hat, Five-Star MacArthur. He's worse than the Cabots and the Lodges—they at least talked with one another before they told God what to do. Mac tells God right off. It's a very great pity we have stuffed shirts like that in key positions. I don't see why in hell Roosevelt didn't order Wainwright home and let MacArthur be a martyr. Guess he was afraid of the Sabotage Press-McCormick-Patterson axis. We'd have had a real general and a fighting man if we had Wainwright and not a play actor and a bunco man such as we have now."

In September, Truman recognized that he had no choice but to appoint MacArthur, and Ickes agreed. "Politically he couldn't do anything else. The blame is due to Roosevelt. I remarked that Roosevelt had made a mistake in taking MacArthur away from the Philippines; that he should have left MacArthur to clean up his own mess and taken Wainwright out. Truman agreed, saying that Wainwright was a better soldier. He knows, as do others, that the Philippine campaign under MacArthur was a fiasco."

Was he the right man for the job? Truman's judgment seems unnecessarily harsh. MacArthur was a man of towering virtues and dizzying defects. He was an authoritarian figure, unusual for an American, which served him in immense good stead in a country like Japan. He had tremendous physical courage. He was undoubtedly one of the great military strategists and commanders of the Second World War. He possessed superb organizational qualities which were suited to a country in the immediate aftermath of defeat. He had a theatrical sense of showmanship that invited sneers, but was suited to modern leadership as well as to enhancing his public reputation when the media had become all-important for the first time. He knew and cared about Japan and Asia. He had a huge reserve of charismatic idealism and genuinely believed he could reform Japanese society from top to bottom.

Finally, he was much more of a realist than is commonly assumed; while indulging in well-publicized arguments with his masters in Washington, in fact he adapted his views and tacked as necessary when he felt it was expedient: his cussedness over Korea brought about his dismissal in 1951; yet he had survived for six years as dictator of Japan—itself a remarkable achievement.

His defects were as transparent as his abilities: he was vain, peremptory and in some respects, curiously naive. He was to set up a caste of colonial overseers in Japan that was to dismay many of his visiting fellow countrymen. He was remote and preferred to rule through a coterie of sometimes sycophantic yes-men (the so-called "Bataan Gang").

If the relationship between the Mikado and shogun had now been established, reinventing Japan's government was a still greater task. When MacArthur arrived it seemed that the Americans had intended to rule directly through their own colonial government. This would have been as disastrous as removing the Emperor. For one thing, MacArthur apart, many of those who served under him were woefully inadequate to the task: some like Sutherland and Willoughby, were highly efficient executives, capable of carrying out orders in brutal, efficient fashion, but absolutely blind to the political sensitivities of administering a hostile and dejected people. Others, like Courtney Whitney, were court flatterers, men MacArthur required for fawning adoration, not to run a country of 80 million people.

MacArthur, on his arrival, had issued three peremptory proclamations on September 3, setting up his administration and making English the official language of government, instituting military courts and declaring military-issued currency to be legal tender. The foreign minister, Mamoru Shigematsu, promptly went to see him to implore him this was not the way to do things: the Japanese government, he insisted, would act as his administration and carry out whatever he decreed. He listened, and scrapped the proclamations.

Washington went along with this, although it set out in detail the policies MacArthur was to follow, as an order to him: this was JCS 1380/15, an 8,000-word document. Within the parameters of this directive, MacArthur was free to act as dictator of 80 million people in Japan and some 32 million in the Philippines and the Marianas. Some biographers have suggested that he did no more than carry out Washington's instructions. This displays a fundamental ignorance both of MacArthur's character and the logistics of running a country like Japan with only a skeleton staff. He had the power to act in Hirohito's name, to dissolve parliament, to suspend political parties and remove public servants. He wanted to turn Japan into "the world's greatest laboratory for an experiment in the liberation of people from authoritarianism military rule and for the liberalization of government from within." The guidelines of his policies, true, had been laid out by the War, Navy and State Departments, and he was technically answerable to President Truman, Secretary of State James F. Byrnes and Secretary of War Robert Patterson.

But Ambassador William J. Sebald, the State Department's man on the spot, had no illusions about the extent of his power. "Never before in the history of the United States had such enormous and absolute power been placed in the hands of a single individual." Sebag had to ask MacArthur's permission even to visit the Emperor. Truman himself stated in his instructions, "You will exercise our authority as you deem proper to carry out your mission. Our relations with Japan do not rest on a contractual basis, but on unconditional surrender . . . your authority is supreme." MacArthur put it more bluntly still: "Sometimes my whole staff was lined up against me. But I knew what I was doing. After all, I had more experience than they. And most of the time I was right."

When the Japanese cabinet at one stage threatened to resign, he declared:

> If the cabinet resigns en masse tomorrow it can only be interpreted by the Japanese people to mean that it is unable to implement my directive. Thereafter Baron Shidehara may be acceptable to the Emperor for reappointment as prime minister, but he will not be acceptable to me.

With the state of communications at the time, it was quite simply impossible for Washington to run Japan on a day-to-day basis from thousands of miles away. On one occasion MacArthur described himself as a "sovereign" on a level with Truman or the kings of England.

That was just how he behaved. Taking a leaf out of Hirohito's prewar experience, he withdrew into remote autocratic seclusion. This was entirely deliberate: it was partly because MacArthur actually understood the sensitivities he would ruffle as a foreign potentate appearing in public with his retinue, seeming to lord it over the Japanese people. It was partly a matter of temperament: MacArthur was no politician, he did not glory in pressing the flesh and meeting baggety-assed provincial politicians. He was always at the forefront of his men in battle, but that was in position of command. He shunned the compromises and false bonhomie of democratic politics. Social life bored him rigid.

He ran his own staff like a medieval monarch. Whitney, his fawning acolyte, was made head of the Government Section of SCAP—which in practice meant that MacArthur ran it. Colonel Laurence Bunker, an extreme right-winger, acted as official chief of staff, controlling access to the shogun, while Lieutenant-Colonel Charles Kades, a New Deal liberal, provided a balance. Colonel William Marquat ran the huge Economic and Scientific Section. The army chief of staff was General Robert Eichelberger, one of MacArthur's former military subordinates whom, however, he treated cavalierly in Japan. General Sutherland, MacArthur's former chief of staff, although invited to the surrender ceremony, had long since fallen out of favor for disobeying MacArthur's instructions to get rid of a mistress the boss disapproved of.

Behind this incestuous circle of key advisers he ruled through issuing instructions to the Japanese government. As he had predicted, his regal low profile, austerity and remoteness made a powerful impression on the Japanese people, accustomed to servility and the lordly ways of their masters. He displayed a thoroughly un-American formality and lack of approachability, and was regaled as an oriental despot in return.

MacArthur was showered with around 500,000 letters during his rule, many of them venerating him as a "living savior" as well as hundreds of gifts, including a kimono and a sash from one man containing 70 million stitches, to symbolize each of the Japanese people he ruled over, which had been painstakingly embroidered for three years. One Japanese newspaper declared the nation was "making a god of General MacArthur." At times it seemed indeed to be going to his already oversized head.

Most of the American occupiers were a good deal less popular than the shogun. "Little America" inhabited the small part of Tokyo left unscathed by the air raids. The occupiers shopped at well-stocked PXs while many Japanese starved. One colonel's wife noted:

> There was always a crowd of Japanese outside the PX . . . watching the customers come in and out, flattening their noses against the show windows, gazing in silent awe at the display of merchandise: the souvenirs, candy bars, cameras, milkshakes, shoes, wool sweaters, silk kimonos and guaranteed curios of the Orient.

John C. Dower, whose magisterial study of the defeated Japanese nation, *Embracing Defeat*, is unlikely to be surpassed, wrote of the new colonial class:

> Daily reminders of American superiority were unavoidable. The most redundant phrase in the defeated land, posted in public places and reiterated

in a myriad public and private settings, was *Shinchugun no meirei ni yoru*—
By order of the Occupation Forces. Petty as well as grand activities were governed by directives from GHQ and encumbered by all the tedious paperwork and micromanagement this entailed. Numerous stores, theaters, hotels, buildings, trains, land areas, and recreational facilities like golf courses were designated "off limits" to Japanese. Ordinary SCAP officers and civilian officials who would have lived plain middle-class lives at home resided in upper-class houses requisitioned from their owners, hardly the most persuasive demonstration of respect for the rights and property of others. There, they might employ three, four, five, or even six servants, all paid for by the Japanese government (cook, "boy," maid, gardener, nursemaid, and laundress was considered an ideal roster). Bowers, an irrepressible aficionado of Kabuki, managed to obtain two personal cooks, one for Western-style and the other for Japanese-style cuisine. "I and nearly all the occupation people I knew," he later mused, "were extremely conceited and extremely arrogant and used our power every inch of the way . . ."

Young Americans in their twenties or thirties, short on practical experience and unversed in the native language, were empowered to tell more elderly Japanese how to conduct their business and rearrange their minds. Individuals who did not speak a second language judged the intelligence of those they dealt with by their competence in English and joked about their pidgin-English mistakes. Americans accused of crimes against Japanese were tried by their own government, not in local courts, and their crimes went unreported in the press. Indeed, any criticism of the alien overlords whatsoever was forbidden. The mass media were not permitted to take issue with SCAP policy or speak negatively of any of the victorious Allied powers, nor were they allowed to mention that they were operating under such restraints.

Although as a rule the victors conducted themselves with far greater discipline than the Japanese military had exercised in occupied areas of Asia, assault and rape inevitably occurred. None of this was reported in the press, and more than a few incidents went unreported to the police as well. Victims had little faith in the possibility of fair redress. After the occupation, mass-circulation magazines ran articles about rapes by American servicemen, and Japanese men resentfully recalled incidents of being randomly, almost whimsically, assaulted in public. The sexual opportunities enjoyed by men affiliated with the occupation forces, including foreign journalists—with their gifts of tinned goods, chocolates, nylon stockings, cigarettes, and liquor—humiliated and infuriated Japanese males. GIs regarded themselves as experts on "babysan's world" and, in a racial idiom they found amusing, joked that this gave them a unique "slant" on Japan. Some spoke with contempt of the "gook girls." Mixed-blood children became one of the sad, unspoken stories of the occupation—seldom acknowledged by their foreign fathers and invariably ostracized by the Japanese.

In numerous such ways, the contradictions of the democratic revolution from above were clear for all to see: while the victors preached democracy, they ruled by fiat; while they espoused equality, they themselves constituted an inviolate privileged caste. Their reformist agenda rested on the assumption that, virtually without exception, Western culture and its values were superior to those of "the Orient." At the same time, almost every interaction between victor and vanquished was infused with intimations of white supremacism. For all its uniqueness of time, place, and circumstance—all its peculiarly "American" iconoclasm—the occupation was in this sense but a new manifestation of the old racial paternalism that historically accompanied the global expansion of the Western powers. Like their colonialist predecessors, the victors were imbued with a sense of manifest destiny. They spoke of being engaged in the mission of civilizing their subjects. They bore the burden (in their own eyes) of their race, creed, and culture. They swaggered, and were enviously free of self-doubt.

MacArthur himself refused to police his men's sexual needs. "Soldiers will be soldiers," he remarked. On seeing a young GI and a Japanese girl in flagrante in a doorway he observed:

> They keep trying to get me to stop all this. I won't do it. My father told me never to give an order unless I was certain it would be carried out. I wouldn't issue a no-fraternization order for all the tea in China.

There was a tragicomic side to these all-too-human problems. As early as August 19 the outgoing prime minister, Fumimaro Konoye, fully expected the American occupiers to have the same needs as Japanese soldiers in Korea with their "comfort women." He instructed the deputy police chief for Tokyo to "please defend the young women of Japan" by setting up facilities to provide prostitutes for the GIs to prevent the harassing of chaste women. These were advertized

> As part of urgent national facilities to deal with the postwar, we are seeking the active cooperation of new Japanese women to participate in the great task of comforting the occupation force.

A Recreation and Amusement Section was set up, with the girls required to take an oath:

> Although our family has endured for 3,000 years, unchanging as the mountains and valleys, the rivers and grasses, since the great rending of August 15, 1945, which marked the end of an era, we have been wracked with infinite, piercing grief and endless sorrow, and are about to sink to the bottom of perilous, boundless desperation . . .
>
> The time has come, an order has been given, and by virtue of our realm of business we have been assigned the difficult task of comforting the occupation army as part of the urgent national facilities for postwar management. This order is heavy and immense. And success will be extremely difficult . . .
>
> And so we unite and go forward to where our beliefs lead us, and through the sacrifice of several thousands of "Okichis of our era" build a breakwater to hold back the raging waves and defend and nurture the purity of our race, becoming as well an invisible underground pillar at the root of the postwar social order . . .
>
> We absolutely are not flattering the occupation force. We are not compromising our integrity or selling our soul. We are paying an inescapable courtesy, and serving to fulfill one part of our obligations and to contribute to the security of our society. We dare say it loudly: we are but offering ourselves for the defense of the national polity. We reaffirm this. This is our proclamation.

Each of the girls heroically serviced between 15 and 60 soldiers a day, at around 15 yen or a dollar a time—about the price of a packet of cigarettes. Different quarters were allocated for officers, white soldiers and black soldiers. There were some 33 R and A section centers in Tokyo and a further 20 elsewhere around the country. As VD rates soared, this public-sector prostitution was abolished although its private counterpart continued, occupying anything up to 70,000 girls eager to support themselves and their families in the desperate conditions of postwar Japan.

MacArthur's immediate priority on arrival was alleviating the appalling conditions he found. He rose magnificently to the occasion. Nearly 3 million servicemen and civilians had died in the war—around 4 percent of the population—while 4.5 million had been disabled. Four fifths of all ships and one third of machine tools had been destroyed. A third of Japan's total wealth and up to half its income had been lost. Some 666 cities had been substantially destroyed by bombs, rendering around a third of the population homeless: two thirds of Tokyo and Osaka lay in ruins, as did nine tenths of Nagoya. Some 9 million people were homeless. Hunger stalked the land: a professor of German at the elite Tokyo High School died of malnutrition. Most people survived on a third of the 2,200 calories a day regarded as the minimum necessary. Disaster followed: in the three years after 1945 some 650,000 people contracted serious hygiene-related diseases and around 100,000 died. Some 146,000 died of tuberculosis in 1947.

The attractive side of the viceroyalty was immediately on display with MacArthur's arrival in Japan. He knew and loved Asia, even Japan. Considering that he was the main American commander in one of the most difficult and savage campaigns in military history, he displayed a truly amazing sense of leadership and refusal to court popularity in the gentleness of his initial occupation policy toward a defeated nation and in his efforts to win the Japanese over with kindness. The nearest parallel of a military figure pursuing policies he believed to be right that flew in the face of the convictions of his natural supporters was that of General de Gaulle in France during the Algerian crisis. They shared many other characteristics: vast egotism, aloofness, masterful public relations and a sense of destiny which was eventually to prove their undoing.

It is worth recalling the climate of American opinion in which MacArthur was working. A year before, a Gallup poll showed that 13 percent of all Americans favored exterminating all Japanese. Another survey three months before the surrender showed that a third of Americans were in favor of executing Emperor Hirohito without trial, while a majority favored convicting him as a war criminal. Senator Theodore Bilbo of Mississippi urged MacArthur to sterilize all Japanese. An adviser to the State-War-Navy Co-ordinating Committee, one of Washington's senior policymaking bodies, urged the "almost total elimination of the Japanese as a race;" Japan should be bombed so savagely that there would be "little left of its civilization." Congressman John Rankin of Mississippi denounced the Japanese as "savage apes." Senator Richard Russell suggested that the American Indian was a "chivalrous cavalier" in contrast with the "bestial Japs."

From the moment he arrived in Japan, the commander of so many Americans who had been killed, tortured or ill-treated by the Japanese army showed a lofty disdain for these frothings: his policy was to show magnanimity in victory, as Churchill had urged, to win the trust of the Japanese people. For MacArthur,

> Japan had become the world's greatest laboratory for an experiment in the liberation of a people from totalitarian military rule and for the liberalization of government from within . . . Yet history clearly showed that no modern military occupation of a conquered nation had been a success.

He went on with moving good sense which should perhaps now resound with the American occupiers in Iraq:

> Military occupation was not new to me. I had garrisoned the West Bank of the Rhine as commander of the Rainbow Division at the end of World War One. At first hand I had seen what I thought were basic and fundamental weaknesses in prior forms of military occupations: the substitution of civil by military authority; the loss of self-respect and self-confidence by the people; the constantly growing ascendancy of centralized dictatorial power instead of a localized and representative system; the lowering of the spiritual and moral tone of a population controlled by foreign bayonets; the inevitable deterioration of the occupying forces themselves as the disease of power infiltrated their ranks and bred a sort of race superiority.
>
> If any occupation lasts too long, or is not carefully watched from the start, one party becomes slaves and the other masters. History teaches, too, that almost every military occupation breeds new wars of the future. I had studied the lives of Alexander and Caesar and Napoleon, and, great as these captains were, all had suffered when they became the leaders of the occupation forces. I tried to remember the lessons my own father had taught me, lessons learned out of his experience as military governor of the Philippines, but I was assailed by the greatest misgivings. With such hazards as I anticipated, could I succeed? My doubts were to be my best safeguard, my fears my greatest strength.

Only a military man could have shown such wholesale contempt for the views of the country he served: MacArthur stood foursquare against most public and congressional opinion in the United States; he was trading, to a great extent, on his immense wartime reputation: it confused many conservatives in America that the very man most responsible for victory in the Pacific War, and a man admired as an opponent of New Dealers within the administration, should hold such conciliatory views toward the Japanese.

Yet it was a fine reflection both on the man and American values, as well as the American army, that his exercise of dictatorial arrogance should have been extended in the cause of harmony, magnanimity and democratic values. MacArthur also found himself under intense pressure from the Russians for a more vindictive policy; he scorned this. The Americans' other major war allies, the British, applauded his magnanimity, although they were to take the view that the Americans would have done well to dispense with the whole cumbersome process of the Tokyo Trials in favor of the summary execution of the major war criminals—not including the Emperor.

MacArthur's second staggering—and undisputed—success was administrative: within a matter of days he had established a working administration over a nation that was shocked, destroyed and helpless: and within a matter of weeks he was fighting a major emergency—the threat of mass starvation—successfully, while coping with one of the biggest movements of population the world has ever seen: the return of the 8 million or more Japanese stranded in their now collapsed empire.

Both were models of soldierly improvization. MacArthur came upon a country bereft of raw materials and food, thanks both to the success of the Allies' military blockade during the closing months of the war and Japan's loss of empire. Rice, which had usually been imported, was in desperately short supply; the internal transport system was nonexistent. The harvests of 1945 had been poor. Japan's stockpiles of wartime supplies had been looted by government officials and the major industries. Hyper-inflation had taken root, fueled by the government's attempt to discharge its obligations at the end of the war through printing money. Army kitchens were promptly set up by MacArthur to feed hundreds of thousands of starving people. He then seized some 3.5 million tons of food stockpiled by the American army in the Pacific as an emergency measure to see Japan through the winter of 1945–46.

The Appropriations Committee of the House of Representatives was indignant at his seizure of army supplies to feed America's former enemy. MacArthur responded with lofty disdain, but admirable logic:

> Under the responsibilities of victory the Japanese people are now our prisoners, no less than did the starving men of Bataan become their prisoners when the peninsula fell. As a consequence of the ill treatment, including starvation of Allied prisoners in Japanese hands, we have tried

and executed the Japanese officers upon proof of responsibility. Can we justify such punitive action if we ourselves in reversed circumstances but with hostilities at an end, fail to provide the food to sustain life among the Japanese people over whom we now stand guard within the narrow confines of their home islands? To cut off Japan's relief supplies in this situation would cause starvation to countless Japanese—and starvation breeds mass unrest, disorder and violence. Give me bread or give me bullets.

The repatriation of overseas Japanese forces was pursued with no less efficiency: it took a year to finish the job, but a small armada of nearly 400 ships, manned by the Japanese under American supervision, brought them in, against a background of deep local hostility from the once occupied peoples. To his reputation as a man of courage and an able strategist, MacArthur had now added that of supremely competent administrator. Having taken the necessary measures to cope with the immediate postwar emergency and set the country on the road to recovery, MacArthur embarked with dictatorial vigor on the hugely ambitious program of transforming a whole nation.

Two key factors limited the American room for maneuver in the first place, and dulled MacArthur's reforming drive. The first was the fact that the bombs, so terrible in their immediate devastation, nevertheless provided an alibi. They had permitted the Japanese to lay down arms with honor. How could any nation not armed with the bomb hope to prevail over or hold out against a foe possessing, and willing to use, so terrible a weapon of destruction? For Japan to fight on after Hiroshima and Nagasaki would have been to invite total annihilation—something no reasonable man could expect (although a few fanatics did). Further resistance was futile. The view could be upheld that Japan had not been formally defeated, that its fighting men remained unvanquished.

In the closing months of the war, Japanese propaganda suggested to ordinary people that the country's forces were not being pushed back across the Pacific, but that they were staging a series of tactical retreats to concentrate on defending their homeland from American invasion. Utter confidence was always publicly expressed: the Japanese would repulse an invasion and eventually defeat the enemy. But against the bombs there could be no victory: Japan had no alternative but to surrender and live to fight another day, expressing no regret for the decision to go to war. The ruling classes of Japan—the bureaucracy, the *zaibatsu* and the army—could claim that they were not in error in initiating the war, and that therefore they had every right to retain their dominant position in Japanese society—although the power of the military, which had misjudged and lost the conflict, was temporarily eclipsed.

The suffering caused by the bombs assumed truly mythological proportions in Japanese histories of the Second World War: it became the dominant theme of all textbooks and was assiduously propagated in films, books, schools, television programs and commemoration ceremonies. The devastation at Hiroshima and Nagasaki, moreover, completely overshadowed and seemed to wipe the slate clean of all the atrocities which Japan committed in the war. Many responsible Japanese were genuinely horrified at the scale of the savagery and admitted moral responsibility for it, and many ordinary people were only too aware of what the Japanese army had been capable of. But these views were eclipsed by the enormity of the Allies' moral callousness in dropping the two bombs; extremism against the Allies had been shown to be justified, because an enemy capable of using the bomb was capable of anything. The bombs, in the view of many senior Japanese, including some impeccable antimilitarists, decisively tilted the moral scales in Japan's favor.

It is to MacArthur's credit that, realizing this, he sought to reverse the process by treating the Japanese with such dignity and gentleness that many ordinary people were won over to the view that the enemy was not vengeful after all. Even so, for a great number, probably a majority, MacArthur's humanity could not reverse the perception of a truly barbaric enemy prepared to use the most terrible of all weapons—one never so far used again in conflict—to defeat the enemy. To this day the decision to drop the bombs remains hotly contested on moral grounds in the West; how much more bitter must be the lingering resentment at its use among the majority of Japanese?

All of these perceptions are reinforced by an examination of the views of the Japanese themselves as the avalanche of controversy about the bombs gathered pace, both before and after the occupation.

The second key background factor stemmed directly from the first. The country was under American occupation: but unlike Germany and Italy, it had not been defeated on its own soil. The position of Japan after 1945 resembled that of Germany after the First World War. Then, civilian politicians had negotiated a surrender following the crushing defeat of the German forces in France before Allied forces could break into, and occupy the country. Its armed forces remained largely intact. In military and nationalist circles there grew up the legend of the *dolchstoss*, the Stab in the Back. The view was taken by the nationalist right that Germany had been betrayed by its civilian leaders and that, had the war continued, its undefeated armies could have regrouped and yet inflicted a crushing blow on their opponents. The anger of the German right had been further fanned by the humiliating terms inflicted at the Treaty of Versailles. The flame of nationalist hate was kept alight, while Germany rearmed in secret, as its humiliation, and subsequent economic miseries, were blamed by the increasingly popular Nazis on the treachery that led to Germany's suing for peace in 1918.

In both Germany and Italy after 1945, however, no such interpretation was possible. Allied forces had grimly fought their way up the long Italian peninsula to gain control, and the Italian army had quickly surrendered; German forces were pushed back into the Fatherland, and utterly, convincingly and devastatingly defeated. Hardly any German or Italian could have been ignorant of the scale or completeness of that defeat. Moreover, in both cases, the ruling parties had been intimately associated with aggressive war, totalitarian methods and failure, and were chased ignominiously from office. Mussolini was executed by a lynch mob, and Hitler was killed in the ruins of Berlin in 1945. Fascism and Nazism were both utterly spurned and discredited.

Neither of those things was true of Japan in September 1945. Japan's huge mainland armies remained intact, asked to surrender by the Emperor for a reason everyone understood—the invincibility of the bomb; the victorious American occupiers had not crushed those armies. There had been no punishing war of attrition up the Japanese mainland to convince ordinary Japanese of the superiority of the American fighting machine, of the inevitability of defeat. Japan had been conquered by a handful of American scientists. For the Japanese, if the boot had been on the other foot and they had discovered the bomb first, they would have won.

Moreover, the ruling ideology and political movement was not discredited in any way. Japanese absolutism was very different, as we have seen, from Nazism and Fascism. Far from being passing, ephemeral populist movements which could be jettisoned at the end of the war, Japan's very history, tradition and culture had themselves evolved into the expansionist, military-minded machine that precipitated the Pacific War. Militarism represented the goals of Meiji Japan taken to an extreme but logical conclusion, whereas Nazism and Fascism were always perversions of the national ideals of Germany and Italy, alien growths on the body politics.

It was convenient for the Japanese ruling class to attempt to isolate the militarists and blame the war solely on their fanaticism, even for a period to ostracize and disown them (although even this only took place to a limited degree). Tojo and his cronies were equated with Hitler and Mussolini. Yet the militarists were part of a consensus that affected both the bureaucracy and the business class; Japan could not have gone to war without their support and acquiescence. Certainly the armed forces were the driving force, the engine, of Japan's movement toward war; but, to extend the metaphor, the business classes comprised the hull of the ship around the engine, and the bureaucrats the crew manning the ship; without the three, war would have been impossible.

The occupation itself ended the Japanese illusion that the country could not be defeated. Instead of running the country directly, however, and setting up new political parties and organizations to take over the running of the system, as happened in Germany, the Americans decided, fatefully, to run the country through the same governing machine that had been in place when the surrender was announced. It was rather as if Admiral Doenitz's transitional regime in Germany, or Marshal Badoglio's in Italy, had been asked to continue. MacArthur did not take over the functions of Japan's major government departments; instead he permitted those same offices to remain in being, and set up a parallel or shadow administration to issue orders to them.

MacArthur himself was SCAP—Supreme Commander of the Allied Powers: the same name was applied to his bureaucracy. It was divided into 14 staff sections, roughly in parallel with the major Japanese ministries. The most powerful of these were the Government Section, the Civil Information and Education Section, the Economic and Scientific Section, and the International Prosecution Section. Very few of MacArthur's officials could speak Japanese: before they arrived to take up their posts, the Japanese had set up a Central Liaison Office, which consisted of foreign office personnel whose role was to act as intermediaries between MacArthur's parallel administration and the Japanese government. MacArthur's officials would issue directives, known as SCAPINs, which were sent to the Central Liaison Office, translated, and handed onto the appropriate ministry for action. MacArthur made it clear that his directives were the ultimate source of authority in Japan, and were intended to be obeyed. But the Central Liaison Office and the ministries frequently "misunderstood" his instructions, provided erroneous translations, or even ignored them.

For political reasons, MacArthur preferred to cultivate the myth that his occupation forces were merely "advising" the government and "suggesting" changes—partly in order to persuade the Japanese not to scrap his reforms the moment the Americans withdrew. However, this allowed those lower down Japan's administrative hierarchy to take the American pretense at face value, and ignore the "advice" or reject the "suggestion." MacArthur had set up 46 observer teams of young officers, one in each of Japan's prefectures, to check and ensure that SCAP directives were being carried out. In practice it was extremely difficult for the teams to keep abreast of the initiatives or intricacies of Japanese local administration, in another language. The young Americans had no direct powers to ensure compliance at a local level, merely to observe and report to their superiors, who would take action only in the light of what was politically convenient.

Though the Japanese accepted and respected the authority of MacArthur as Japan's new shogun, in practice they were a people with long centuries of schooling to avoid the implementation of central directives in the provinces and villages (pre-war totalitarian control only went back over the previous half century). Moreover, Japan's long tradition of overmighty advisers nominally subservient to a supreme authority was to make MacArthur's edicts easier to avoid. In practice, his humane, democratic approach was an island in a sea of indifference or outright hostility. The bureaucracy, the industrialists and the local officials the occupation authorities had to work through were in fact the very bricks and mortar of the hierarchical and hugely conservative Japanese system of government that MacArthur was trying to change.

A further constraint on MacArthur's efforts was that not only was he answerable to Washington—itself divided over how to treat Japan—but his own organization was deeply fissured over the same issue. SCAP was not, in truth, the best kind of colonial administration, and was almost entirely staffed by people who had no such experience (in contrast, for example, to the British and French colonial service). Most were recruited in the United States: at the top there were a number of career staff officers, a large number of demobilized army officers, many adventurers, and the inevitable carpetbaggers trying to profit financially from the occupation. Many of the administrators were genuinely idealistic—leading to MacArthur's complaint that Washington had sent him "a boatload of New Dealers." The most prominent among these were Charles Kades, a New York lawyer, Alfred Hussey, a Harvard graduate, and Thomas Bisson, an able economist.

MacArthur had a penchant for appointing military figures as heads of department: a brigadier-general ran the Education Section, a general the Economic and Scientific Section, and Major-General Courtney Whitney, MacArthur's most trusted crony, ran the key Government Section (in addition to being SCAP, MacArthur was Commander-in-Chief, Far East, presiding over the Far Eastern Command [FECOM]). At the summit of the hierarchy was the so-called Bataan Gang—MacArthur's most trusted and protective advisers dating back to his struggles to defend the Philippines. The Bataan Gang jealously guarded access to MacArthur, and competed bitterly among themselves. One hostile observer, George Kennan, commented acidly that the atmosphere of intrigue at the top was reminiscent of "the latter days of the Court of Emperor Catherine II, or of the Kremlin under Stalin." The principal intriguers were Whitney, who in spite of his pompous exterior was the principal reformer within SCAP, and General Charles Willoughby, the head of G-2, the military intelligence section, a vigorous and crusading anti-Communist who viewed Japan as essential to containing the Kremlin's ambitions.

SCAP functioned in a swirl of social life: loud-mouthed colonial types experienced for the first time the pleasures of servants and supremacy over another race. Kennan, who loathed MacArthur, provided a graphic picture of the ambience. SCAP, he felt, was a parasite, displaying "monumental impassiveness to the suffering and difficulties of [the Japanese]." The Americans in Tokyo were "startlingly Philistine," monopolizing "everything that smacks of comfort, elegance, or luxury," and exhibiting "idleness and boredom." The "monotony of contemporary American social life, its unbending drinking rituals, the obvious paucity of its purposes and its unimaginative devotion to outward convention in the absence of inner content or even enjoyment" were "pathetic." The "shrill cackling wives" of MacArthur's officials behaved as though the purpose of the war had been so that they might have "six Japanese butlers with the divisional insignia on their jackets."

Kennan agreed that "many of the Japs deserve a worse fate than to have the tastes and habits of American suburbia imposed upon them," but in his view the American occupation was not "intelligible." Kennan's critique could as well have applied to any society under colonial tutelage, and the Americans in Japan were no worse, and in some respects much better, than their equivalents in the traditional European empires. Certainly the behavior of the GIs, except for the occasional rowdiness or sexual forwardness, caused little complaint among ordinary Japanese. Yet some of Kennan's criticisms hit their target.

32 : VISIONARY

I T WAS IN THE ROLE OF POLITICAL AND SOCIAL REFORMER THAT MACARTHUR was to fail massively, although not in every respect. Politics, of course, is the art of the possible, and in seeking to transform the entire basis of Japan's social and economic order, which he termed "feudal." MacArthur had probably set himself a superhuman task. It was his wont, too, to proclaim reforms only half achieved, or not achieved at all, as great victories when he realized he could do no more. Moreover the climate of opinion among his political masters in Washington was to change dramatically within three years, halting the few real reforms MacArthur instituted in their tracks.

Because of his colorful personality, outspokenness and penchant for snubbing American political leaders, particularly the President, the impression was given—to MacArthur's own satisfaction—that he was much more of a lone wolf, his own man, than was in fact the case. In practice, although he sometimes mischievously played politics with Washington and frequently contravened and ignored minor directives from the American capital, throughout the occupation there is no single major occasion on which he defied a direct order from Washington. He was on a long lead and took advantage of the lack of interest shown by the Truman administration in Japan during the first two years of the occupation; but he took care never to break the connection.

Nevertheless he took personal satisfaction in such theatrical gestures as defying a direct order from Truman to attend a ticker-tape reception in his honor in the United States. He was too busy, he cabled, the situation in Japan was too critical. Not only did this offend the President, for whom MacArthur from the first could scarcely conceal his contempt, it was designed to display his superiority over the other generals who had indulged in such shows of vainglory. MacArthur's critics contend that throughout the occupation he was primarily concerned with using Japan as a stepping-stone for running for president back home.

MacArthur lived in the American Ambassador's residence, known as the Big House, along with Jean and Arthur. He would rise at 7 A.M., breakfast with the two of them, and exercise. He would read the papers and then his mail, writing replies to letters on the reverse side or initialing them for his subordinates' attention. Whitney would ring from the Dai-Ichi Building, SCAP's headquarters, to brief him on important happenings.

Not until 10:30 or 11:00 would MacArthur leave for the office in a 1941 Cadillac, with an escort of two soldiers in a jeep. Traffic was stopped and lights changed to green as the Cadillac performed the five-minute journey every morning. Crowds of Japanese and Americans would gather around the main entrance to the Dai-Ichi Building to watch MacArthur enter and leave at the appropriate times. In his phoneless office, MacArthur would confer with Whitney, and dictate letters and dispatches in his usual flowing manner. The writer John Gunther said of his style, "It is astonishing that anyone who talks as well as MacArthur could write so badly . . . It is not merely that his style is pompous. It is worse than that." MacArthur would then start meeting people, lighting up his pipe, pacing the floor and talking interminably, to the despair of his subordinates.

At 2 P.M. he would return for a late lunch, the only occasion during the day when he would entertain. His wife Jean would greet him with a cheery "Hello, General" as she waited with visitors. Without pausing for a drink they would go and eat in haphazard fashion at table with no placement prepared—something which shocked stuffy diplomats and officials. Gunther attended one such lunch:

> What struck me most was his lightness, humor and give-and-take. The mystique of the great commander so surrounds MacArthur that one is apt to forget how human he is. I expected him to be oracular, volcanic and unceasing. He was all of that, but something less too: he laughed a good deal, enjoyed jokes, told some pretty good ones, permitted interruptions, and listened well . . . MacArthur ate almost nothing but drank several cups of coffee with heaping spoonfuls of sugar. Part of the time he looked directly at us or his wife; part of the time he talked with his face gazing steadily, fixedly, out of the window to his right. What was he looking for, looking at?

Like Churchill, after lunch MacArthur would take a one-hour sleep, then relax by reading the paper or chatting to his wife. At about five o'clock he would return to his office, where he would subject his grumbling staffers to a further three or four hours' work (they would already have put in a full day). When someone complained to him that he was "killing" his staff, he replied, with near-Japanese callousness, "What better fate for a man than to die in the performance of his duty?" He would return home at 8:30 or 9 o'clock, where he would eat a light snack and then go and watch a film, which any member of SCAP could attend. He enjoyed newsreels, westerns or light comedies. Then he would resume his walking and talking, usually along the first floor of the embassy, using his long-suffering wife as audience until one in the morning, by which time she was almost asleep.

It is extremely difficult to ascertain what MacArthur himself really thought at any one time, because, subtle military politician that he was, he changed his views depending on the audience he was addressing. But there seemed to be at least three obvious strands running through his policy. He was a passionate and committed constitutional democrat, which motivated him radically to reform the authoritarian nature of Japanese society.

He was, within that framework, a conventional American right-winger. In the American army he might be viewed as something of a liberal, but not in anyone else's political lexicon. He mistrusted New Dealers, hated Communists, but recognized he sometimes had to work with those of a very different persuasion, like Franklin Roosevelt; he had not ascended the very pinnacle of the army hierarchy by being incapable of compromise when necessary.

Finally, he was a fervent Christian. This underpinned both his mission and his anti-communism: he sought genuinely to transform Japan spiritually, placing him in opposition to more cynical conservatives on his staff.

MacArthur was undaunted in his initial zest for reform. How far, in fact, had the reform process got in those three short years, and how lasting were its achievements? The answer was that MacArthur and the reformists had tried their damnedest, and achieved a surprising amount, but not enough. MacArthur had never had any illusions about the size of the task he had set himself in trying to change the underlying ethos of Japanese society. His critics were entirely wrong to suggest that his heart was not in the venture. He wrote later:

> Supposedly, the Japanese were a twentieth-century civilization. In reality they were more nearly a feudal society, of the type discarded by Western nations some four centuries ago. There were aspects of Japanese life that went even further back than that. Although theocracy was a system of government that had been thoroughly discredited by 3,000 years of progress in the Western world, it still existed in Japan. The Emperor was considered a divine being, and the average Japanese subject dared not even lift up his eyes to view his ruler. This God-Emperor was absolute. His word was final. He was bolstered in power by a small group of families who controlled the military, the apparatus of government and the economy. There was no such thing as civil rights. There were not even human rights. The property and the produce of

the average Japanese individual could be taken away from him in whole or in part as its suited the ruling cliques. Between 1937 and 1940 more than 60,000 people were thrown into prison for "dangerous thinking," by the secret police. Indeed, an American viewing Japan would be more inclined to class it as more nearly akin to ancient Sparta than to any modern nation . . .

When I moved my headquarters into the Dai Ichi Building, I made a public statement that "SCAP is not concerned with how to keep Japan down, but how to get her on her feet again." I underlined again and again that we had several missions. It was true that we intended to destroy Japan as a militarist power. It was true that we intended to impose penalties for past wrongs. These things had been set out in the surrender terms. But we also felt that we could best accomplish our purpose by building a new kind of Japan, one that would give the Japanese people freedom and justice, and some kind of security. I was determined that our principles during the occupation would be the same principles for which our soldiers had fought on the battlefield.

MacArthur's genuine reformist idealism should never be underestimated. The outcome can be assessed by looking at the achievements in each of the areas and targets SCAP had set itself, as listed on the aircraft that carried MacArthur to Japan as supreme commander for the first time, and as dictated the day before by the Truman administration.

First destroy the military power. Punish war criminals. Build the structure of representative government. Modernize the constitution. Hold free elections. Enfranchise the women. Release the political prisoners. Liberate the farmers. Establish a free labor movement. Encourage a free economy. Abolish police oppression. Develop a free and responsible press. Liberalize education. Decentralize the political power. Separate church from state.

These tasks were to occupy me for the next five years and more. All were eventually accomplished, some easily, some with difficulty. But as the reforms progressed and freedom increasingly came to the Japanese masses, a unique bond of mutual faith developed between the Japanese people and the Supreme Commander. As they increasingly sensed my insistence upon just treatment for them, even at times against the great nations I represented, they came to regard me as not as a conqueror but as a protector.

The first category of MacArthur's reforms was retributive. The Supreme Commander also made little secret of his distaste for war reparations, which many economists, Keynes among them, had, in Germany's case, identified as a major cause of the Second World War.

In 1945, Truman had appointed Edwin Pauley, a former Gulf Oil magnate and Democratic Party fund-raiser not, just to exact reparations but to reform the industrial structures of Germany and Japan. Pauley drew up ambitious plans to transfer basic industries from Japan to South East Asia, arguing that "as Japan began to recover there would be more local strength" to prevent aggression for economic motives. This crackpot idea was to redress the uneven balance between Japan's industrial strength and that of the Asian mainland. The intention was to transfer iron and steel mills from Japan to Manchuria, which had the necessary raw materials of coal and iron ore: this would give China the kind of industrial production which Japan would be forced to respect.

Pauley and his chief adviser Owen Lattimore, a respected Asian expert, concluded early on in the occupation that MacArthur, who resented their intrusion on his turf, was little disposed to help. In December 1945, Pauley advanced a program to seize "Japanese excess capacity" which might later contribute to "economic imperialism." He called for the seizure of 27 of the most important machine-tool manufacturers, producing roughly half of Japan's total, as well as restructuring the aerospace, ball-bearing and shipping industries and slashing steel production from 11 million tons to 2.5 million. Truman promptly approved the reforms, saying that "these should be implemented as soon as the necessary details are worked out."

The program was quite clearly punitive, and almost certainly unworkable, imposing restraints upon industrial development that no country could accept in the long term. MacArthur was deeply opposed from the first. Under duress, he agreed to transport some 1 million machine tools to mainland Asia, but carried the Pauley reparations package no further. The recipients of Pauley's initial generosity began to quarrel bitterly among themselves.

By 1947 the Truman administration was beginning to have second thoughts, and another mission led by Clifford Strike, a prominent engineering manufacturer, suggested that it was "neither sensible nor desirable" to adhere to the Pauley program. Japan had to be left with "enough industry so that the Japanese economy will be self-sustaining." Strike argued that Japan possessed limited, if any, excess industrial capacity. Pauley indignantly retorted that Strike's recommendations would amount to a "complete repudiation of U.S. reparations policy."

In October 1948, American officials stressed that those countries that still sought reparations should begin to move Japanese industrial plants to the former colonies under a tight timetable. Most were physically unable to do this, and the reparations program was terminated. It had achieved almost nothing, was opposed from the beginning with eminent good sense by MacArthur and, if carried through, would have been thoroughly bad policy.

The next category of reform objectives was to be the most important of all: a concerted assault upon the four elites of Japanese power: the military cliques, which MacArthur wanted to destroy; the monopolist *zaibatsu*, the enemies of a "free economy"; the country's "oppressive police state"; and the bureaucrats, through decentralising the political power. All four groups, moreover, were to be the targets of a massive purge of those primarily involved in the militaristic rush to disaster in the 1930s and 1940s.

MacArthur subsequently argued that he considered the purge a mistake from the first. He "doubted its wisdom." However, SCAPIN 550, issued by him and his staff in January, 1946, contained a strong commitment to weed out the guilty men among the ranks of politicians, bureaucrats, military officers, corporate executives, local government officials, teachers, theater producers, filmmakers, educators, university professors and police chiefs. No fewer than 2.5 million people were to be affected. Those purged were accused of "participation in, or support of, military aggression and overseas imperialism; dissemination of ultra-nationalist propaganda; claims of ethnic superiority and attempts to act on them— assuming leadership of other Asiatic races, for example, or excluding foreigners from trade and commerce; advocacy of totalitarianism; the use of violence and terror to achieve political ends and crush opposition to the regime; an insistence on the special status and prerogatives of the soldier." The subjects' public views during the era of Japanese expansion in the late 1930s—and dating sometimes as far back as 1931 and the Manchurian Incident, as well as during the Pacific War— were under inspection.

A further objective of the purge was the destruction of Japan's constellation of far-right societies, and the banning of their members from government employment. These included not just the Black Dragon Society (the Amaru River Society), but the Bayonet Practice Promotion Society, the White Blood Corpuscle League, the Anti-Foreigner Similar Spirits Society, the Society for the Ultimate Solution of the Manchurian Question, and the Imperial National Blood War Body.

The centerpiece of the purge consisted in asking everyone in Japan in the affected offices to fill out a questionnaire, detailing military service, membership of political organizations and past careers. A central screening committee examined these: however the penalties for covering up past misdeeds were not severe. In 1947–48, the questionnaire was no longer required, and only outside evidence could disqualify a person from office. SCAP, moreover, sought to ensure that those removed did not return to their jobs, purged them from other types of work, and debarred their relatives from holding similar offices and thus acting in their stead. The Japanese argued that this represented visiting the sins of the fathers upon the sons.

The effects of the initial purge were fairly severe. The Home Ministry lost 34 senior officials, the Imperial Household 118, 170 peers were removed from the upper house, while only 10 percent of Diet members were deemed eligible for reelection in April 1946. The purge was implemented with special harshness in the army, the former enemy of the civilian ministries, which were in charge of carrying out SCAP's edicts. Yet the impact was largely confined to old people whose careers were coming to an end; within a year or two evasion was widespread. As Meirion and Susie Harries point out,

> Evasion took many forms. There was the anticipatory move—the early retirement enabling the potential purgee to retain pension rights, or the hasty transfer from a purgeable position to a non-purgeable one. (The U.S. army found itself unwittingly employing considerable numbers of the Home Ministry's former "thought police" who had the foresight to quit their employment immediately after the surrender.) There was the simple failure to screen—thirty-six new members, some of them highly dubious, entered the House of Peers in March 1946 without any examination of their eligibility. And there was the failure to screen diligently: in December 1946 the Ministry of Education called upon the Tottori Prefecture Screening Committee for teachers to resign. Out of 4,700 candidates screened, the Screening Committee had seen fit to reject only six, and the ministry, as it put it, doubted "the wholeheartedness with which the committee was pursuing its task."

In October 1948, NSC/3/2, which effectively marked the death-knell of the MacArthur reforms, put the purge into rewind. Several cases of "relatively harmless" purgees were permitted to return to public office, including most of the businessmen affected. An Approved Persons Board began reinstating purgees—150 in the first 14 months of office, some 10 percent of those applying, then 30 percent and 90 percent in subsequent years.

By 1951 some 177,000 people had been de-purged—more than two thirds of the original total affected. Many of the rest were now past retirement; only 9,000 people remained on the banned list. The Potsdam Declaration had specified that "there must be eliminated for all time the authority and influence of those who have deceived and misled the people of Japan." Only a tiny proportion were in fact eliminated. By 1952, there were 139 former purgees in the house of representatives while two years later one of their number, Ichiro Hatoyama, became prime minister. Denazification in Germany was a much more thorough and lasting process.

The attempt to single out individuals for blame for Japan's wartime excesses involved a measure of rough justice, and was arguably less important than the reforms needed to transform the armed forces, the police, big business and the bureaucracy.

The most thorough and successful reform was, of course, practiced upon the first. It took three forms: writing into the constitution a specific provision by which Japan "renounced war"; disbanding the imperial army; and turning Japan's defense forces into a largely passive organization imbued with democratic values. The insertion of the "no war" clause into Japan's constitution was one of MacArthur's prime achievements, yet he denied the responsibility was his at all, but that of the prime minister, Shidehara. MacArthur recounts that the latter came to him to thank me for making what was then a new drug in Japan, penicillin, available in aiding his recovery from serious illness.

He then proposed that when the new constitution became final it should include the so-called no-war clause. He also wanted it to prohibit any military establishment for Japan—any military establishment whatsoever. Two things would thus be accomplished. The old military party would be deprived of any instrument through which they could some day seize power, and the rest of the world would know that Japan never intended to wage war again. He added that Japan was a poor country and could not really afford to pour money into armaments anyway. Whatever resources the nation had left should go into bolstering the economy.

I had thought my long years of experience had rendered me practically immune to surprise or unusual excitement, but this took my breath away. I could not have agreed more. For years I have believed that war should be abolished as an outmoded means of resolving disputes between nations. Probably no living man had seen as much of war and its destruction as I had. A participant or observer in six wars, a veteran of twenty campaigns, the survivor of hundreds of battlefields, I have fought with or against the soldiers of practically every country in the world, and my abhorrence reached its height with the perfection of the atom bomb.

When I spoke in this vein, it was Shidehara's turn to be surprised. His amazement was so great that he seemed overwhelmed as he left the office. Tears ran down his face and he turned back to me and said, "the world will laugh and mock us as impracticable visionaries, but a hundred years from now we will be called prophets."

This account has not been seriously contradicted, although Shidehara was believed to have been anticipating MacArthur's own wishes. To the American it was essential that the provision appeared to originate from the Japanese; otherwise it might be repealed after the occupation ended. Shidehara and some of his peace party may genuinely have thought the article desirable, and it was supported by a large swathe of public opinion in Japan, which was understandably sickened by war and resented the army as an oppressor force.

MacArthur himself at the time leaned primarily to the view that Japan was in no danger of attack from Russia, while Russia understood that America would retaliate overwhelmingly. He considered that a police force and a symbolic American presence would be enough to secure Japan's defenses in the event of a Russian attack. He believed Japan should be supported through American bases at Okinawa and the Pacific, which could best deter the Russians if necessary. Provided Japan was not altogether demilitarized, he did not believe the Russians would attack.

The no-war provision was a remarkable one in any constitution, doubly so in Japan's. It read:

> Aspiring sincerely to international peace based on justice and order, the Japanese people forever renounce war as a sovereign right of the nation and the threat or use of force as a means of settling international disputes. In order to accomplish the aim of the preceding paragraph, land, sea and air forces, as well as other war potential will never be maintained.

The disarming of Japan was achieved through prodigious organization by MacArthur's forces. The demobilization and repatriation program, involving some 8 million Japanese, has already been touched upon. In addition all arsenals, ammunition dumps and advance depots had to be located; much of this was booby-trapped against an American invasion and highly volatile. Ammunition frequently exploded, parachute flares ignited and on one occasion a cave full of propellant charges blew up, killing dozens of Japanese workmen. Another massive explosion took place at Tatayama airfield, when an ammunition dump blew up.

Tanks, guns, antiaircraft equipment and aircraft were cut open with blowtorches. Ships were distributed among the victorious nations and some were scuttled or used in American atomic tests. The Americans captured 120,000 bayonets, 81,000 rifles and 2,200 automatic weapons. All of Japan's air defenses and combat aircraft were destroyed. Japanese airfields were to be turned over to agricultural purposes, and no Japanese permitted to pilot even civil aircraft. The vast and formidable arsenal of civil defense equipment was confiscated, including baseball bats, crossbows, guns, plumbing pipes, explosive arrows and primitive bazookas. However, in the fortnight between Japan's surrender and the beginning of the occupation, vast quantities of munitions were spirited to secret depots in the hills, with the intention of providing an arsenal for a future "secret army" akin to that in Germany after the First World War. In the event, none was needed.

SCAP also sought to enforce a policy intended to prevent Japan rearming: no reserves, no arms imports and no arms production were permitted. Atomic energy equipment was confiscated: nuclear scientists were arrested and all nuclear-related material seized. Japan's four cyclotrons were destroyed on Washington's orders—to MacArthur's fury. A ban was imposed on all industrial activity geared to war and a ceiling set on production of steel, oil, rail equipment, ball-bearings and machine tools. These levels were set at a tenth of the levels of the Japanese armaments program of the 1930s. Finally, the Americans formally disbanded the Japanese army, navy and air force.

All three of these far-reaching attacks on the militarists were to prove partly illusory, although it would be mistaken to assert that they had no effect. The constitutional ban on war, it turned out, was far from being a prohibition on defense spending. Vice President Richard Nixon was to call it, with dismaying candor, an "honest mistake" as early as 1953. MacArthur made it plain at the time:

> Should the course of world events require that all mankind stand to arms in defense of human liberty and Japan comes within the orbit of immediately threatened attack, then the Japanese, too, should mount the maximum defensive power which their resources will permit. Article 9 is

based upon the highest moral ideals, but by no sophistry of reasoning can it be interpreted as a complete negation of the inalienable right of self-defense against unprovoked attack.

MacArthur was soon to recommend that a defense force of ten divisions be set up, with corresponding sea and air elements. However, the importance of Article Nine as a block on Japan's path to remilitarization should not be underestimated: the bitterest political and street-fighting of the postwar period were to revolve around this very issue, and that of the relationship with America, which was to divide Japanese society as no other, tearing away the facade of Japan's so-called "consensus society" for a time.

The destruction of war material was, of course, irreversible. But some was saved, and the long-term ban on stockpiling, importing and producing ordnance and weapons, even in some limited respects for nuclear purposes, was ignored by the end of the occupation—not least by the Americans who needed weaponry for the Korean War. It could not be enforced on post-occupation Japan. The limits on heavy-industry production were similarly ignored.

Behind the scenes, moreover, at least one part of the occupation forces ensured that the dissolution of the Japanese war machine was only partially successful. The man who achieved this was General Charles Willoughby, head of military intelligence (G2) and the occupation's most powerful military commander after MacArthur. Willoughby was born of a Prussian military family, as Charles Von Tscheppe-Weidenback. He was tall, good-looking, authoritarian and possessed of a powerful temper. After Japan's defeat, for Willoughby, the prime task was to fight communism; he considered the anti-militarist provisions of the occupation wasteful. His sympathies were often on the borderlines of fascism. He argued that Mussolini had been right to invade Ethiopia, thus "wiping out a memory of defeat before re-establishing the traditional military supremacy of the white race." After retiring in the 1950s he served as an adviser to Spain's General Franco—the "second greatest general in the world."

Willoughby set up a "loyalty desk" inside SCAP to scrutinize the civilian machinery of the occupation bureaucracy and to weed out "leftists and fellow-travellers." Willoughby's unit succeeded in forcing out several reformers: the great Japanese scholar, Thomas Bisson, was hounded out of SCAP and lost his job at Berkeley after the occupation. Willoughby also supported Joseph McCarthy's witch hunts by providing "evidence" of the "guilt" of some of his political opponents inside SCAP. Within Japan in 1947 he admitted he had acted under a top-secret Pentagon order to preserve the nucleus of the Japanese general staff and to maintain the records of the army and navy. This ran directly counter to SCAP's official instructions.

By January 1946 there were still some 190 Japanese generals and admirals pursuing "occupation objectives"; many were engaged in the process of "historical research" on a major project set up Willoughby in cooperation with General Seizo Arisuc, head of Japanese military intelligence at the end of the war. The results never emerged. Arisue and another senior officer, Tokushiro Hattori, former private secretary to Tojo, were engaged in setting up what was in effect their own general staff of some 50–60 senior officers throughout Japan.

Further down the ranks, "Local Assistance Bureaus" were set up consisting of entire companies supposedly engaged in helping demobilized soldiers, but in fact acting as clandestine army units. "Farms" were also set up along military lines by veterans, consisting of entire military detachments staffed by officers. Tanks were used as tractors, education was militaristic, and army drill was still maintained, as was discipline.

Willoughby himself took control of records set up by the former army authorities which fully documented the soldiery of the old imperial army. When the time came to re-create a Japanese army, the men and material were in place. The whole process irresistibly recalled the setting up of Germany's secret Wehrmacht after the First World War (and may now be being repeated in Iraq). Prophetically, the *London Times* had predicted on August 27, 1945, that

> The way is . . . opened for the propagation of the myth, which proved so formidable a factor in the rise of the Third Reich, that the army had not been conquered, that the war was lost by poor civilian morale caused by the Allies' employment of an unfair weapon . . . It will be strange indeed if the Japanese General Staff does not endeavor to "go to ground" as the German General Staff did in 1918.

The assault by MacArthur on the anti-democratic parts of Japan's internal security apparatus—the various police forces—did not entirely fail, either, although it was heavily modified with the passage of time. Even MacArthur admitted the "extraordinarily difficult" nature of the problem. The "Thought Police," responsible for internal repression and the detention of some 60,000 dissidents, had been well entrenched in the home affairs ministry. The civilian police, who were less feared, had been ruthless in the suppression of public meetings and worked in league with the right-wing secret societies. The Kempeitai were a kind of local gestapo who acted with maximum brutality against dissidents.

One of MacArthur's first acts had been to free the country's political prisoners, held in conditions of horrific suffering. His second objective was to break the centralized stranglehold of the home affairs ministry and strengthen the power of local government. He demanded the decentralization of the police forces, as well as, of course, outright abolition of the Kempeitai and Thought Police.

Every town with a population of more than 5,000 was given the right to have its own police force which was no longer answerable to the central government. This created a mass of problems: some towns could not afford a proper force and pay fell accordingly among the police, leading to corruption; it was hard to coordinate between rival forces. Indeed, after the occupation had ended, the Japanese government moved quickly to re-create a national police force, of a rather more responsible kind than before— although not entirely devoid of the characteristics of the prewar period. Local autonomy as decreed by MacArthur in other spheres of administration was more successful, building upon the traditional Japanese unit of the village; but the home affairs ministry regained a considerable measure of control after the occupation ended.

The scale of MacArthur's assaults upon the political interests that ruled Japan was thus extremely limited. The bureaucracy was purged, although later most of the purgees were allowed to return. The police were reigned in and the home affairs ministry was decentralized to a limited extent, although this was later largely reversed. But for the most part, the occupation operated through the prewar bureaucracy, which had cleverly pinned the blame for the war on the militarists and posed as the natural ally of the Americans. There was no substantial administrative reform.

MacArthur's attempts to tie down the bureaucracy were confined to constitutional reform designed to make it accountable to parliament. This was only partially successful, although the changes secured were significant. By and large the power of the bureaucracy was hardly diminished by the occupation; in some respects it was considerably strengthened because it regained its position as primus inter pares among Japan's elites: the armed forces were now discredited, and the zaibatsu, suffering from wartime devastation, were keeping their heads down.

33 : THE ASSAULT ON PRIVILEGE

THE AMERICAN ASSAULT UPON THE THIRD LEG OF POWER IN JAPAN—THE *zaibatsu*, the monopoly capitalists who had steadily increased their stranglehold over the Japanese economy before and during the war—was much more determined, and led to the greatest controversy surrounding the occupation. As we have seen, the *zaibatsu* shared equal responsibility with the armed forces for Japan's slide towards war. It was the profound conviction of most of the reformists within SCAP that unless the great combines were broken up, real democracy in Japan was impossible, and no middle class would be created, much less a free-market economy. Indeed, Whitney's supporters probably placed more emphasis upon this than any other reform.

Thomas Bisson, the economist, later pilloried and hounded by Willoughby, argued convincingly that the *zaibatsu*, far from opposing Japanese aggression, helped to channel its direction to serve their interests— into China and South East Asia in particular. During the period of wartime mobilization, he argued, they used the "control associations" to establish a stranglehold over raw materials and further increase their control over industry. Bisson argued that, contrary to the *zaibatsus'* attempt to pin all wartime responsibility on the armed forces, they worked hand in hand with the military to mold Japan's economy for war during the pre-Pearl Harbor years. "If the *zaibatsu* are permitted to survive the conditions of defeat, they will continue to dominate Japan's postwar government. With the experience gained in this war, they will be able to prepare even more thoroughly for their next attempt to conquer East Asia by force of arms."

Between 1931 and 1941, the *zaibatsus'* share of key industries related to war preparation rose from 15 percent to an astonishing 72 percent. By 1945, the major ten *zaibatsu* controlled three quarters of industry, finance and commerce in Japan, possibly more, through the skillful manipulation of financial holdings, than even at the height of the Meiji period. Another American economist working for SCAP, Eleanor Hadley, pointed out that Mitsubishi's family holdings in relative terms were "the equivalent of a single American conglomerate comprising U.S. Steel, General Motors, Standard Oil of New Jersey, Alcoa, Douglas Aircraft, Dupont, Sun Shipbuilding, Allis-Chalmers, Westinghouse, AT&T, RCA, IBM, U.S. Rubber, Sea Island Sugar, Dole

Pineapple, U.S. Lines, Grace Lines, National City Bank, Metropolitan Life Insurance, Woolworth Stores and the Statler Hotels."

MacArthur himself was in no doubt about the malevolent effects of the *zaibatsu*. "The world," he argued, "has probably never seen a counterpart to so abnormal an economic system. It permitted the exploitation of the many for the sole benefit of the few. The integration of these few with government was complete and their influence upon government inordinate, and set the course which ultimately led to war and destruction." MacArthur took the bull by the horns in October 1945, asking the four major giants of Japanese business and industry—Mitsui, Mitsubishi, Sumitomo and Yasuda—to submit plans for their own dissolution. The idea, as ever, was to give the impression that the Japanese had virtually administered their own reform, as well as to evoke the principle at the time of the Meiji Restoration, when the *daimyo* offered their lands to the Emperor.

Needless to say, the proposal drawn up by the companies—the Yasuda Plan—was almost wholly cosmetic. They proposed that the holding companies of the four corporations be dissolved, and that family members resign from the boards of major subsidiaries. Family shares in the holding companies would be sold to a "liquidation commission," and the proceeds invested in 10-year bonds as compensation for the losses suffered by the families. Although superficially attractive, the flaws were obvious from the start: there was nothing to prevent people acting for the families at one remove buying up the shareholdings. The subsidiaries were to remain intact. No attempt would be made to break up the smothering monopolies that the subsidiaries exercised over Japanese industry and commerce.

Shigeru Yoshida, Japan's postwar prime minister, lent his backing to the plan. He asserted that the *zaibatsu*, far from profiting from the war, had been kept out of Japan's conquered lands by the jealous army, and also that the *zaibatsus'* investment in wartime production gave rise to meager profits. This was true only of Manchuria initially. MacArthur, his hands full, initially welcomed the Yasuda Plan and issued SCAPIN 244, which liquidated the holding companies as proposed. But the supreme commander had his doubts, and either on his own initiative or in response to the concerns of the "China crowd" in Washington, which was appalled by the limited nature of these reforms, asked for an advisory group of antitrust experts to be dispatched from Washington.

This group, under the chairmanship of Professor Corwin Edwards, took only a few months to reject the Yasuda Plan. Edwards was convinced of the need to reform the *zaibatsu*—"the guys principally responsible for the war . . . and a principal factor in the Japanese war potential." For decades the *zaibatsu* had enforced "semi-feudal relations between employer and employee, held down wages, and blocked the development of labor unions"; they had retarded "the rise of a Japanese middle class," which was necessary as "a counterweight to military despotism." The low wages permitted ordinary Japanese had stifled domestic consumption and led to the drive for exports. The power and influence of the giant industrial combines made them primarily responsible for Japan's atrocious behavior overseas.

Edwards was no fellow traveler, or even radical. He vigorously opposed nationalizing the *zaibatsu* or promoting worker control. Instead, he advocated selling stock to small firms and controlling the old monopolies with rigor through antitrust legislation limiting the size, scope and ownership of the new businesses. MacArthur, although initially hostile to the Edwards reforms, which he viewed as a criticism of his own measures, soon espoused the cause with vigor.

The three principal recommendations of the Edwards mission, if fully implemented, would almost certainly have revolutionized the Japanese business world. First, the holding companies were to be dissolved, along with their subsidiaries; the leading *zaibatsu* bosses were to be prohibited from reacquiring them. Second, a Holding Companies Liquidation Commission was set up to dissolve any over-large enterprise: it proposed to break up 325 of Japan's biggest companies in the first instance.

Third, a Fair Trade Commission was set up to implement a new anti-monopoly law outlawing "unreasonable restraints of trade" and unfair methods of competition, in an effort to assault the huge, intricate network of *zaibatsu* control—the inter-corporate security ownership, family ties and interlocking directorates. All shareholdings in the companies defined as being an "excessive concentration" of economic power were to be sold by the Liquidation Commission on the open market, at very low prices, in order to encourage the spread of small and medium enterprises and individuals. A crushing levy of up to 100 percent on war profits was imposed, while steep increases in inheritance tax were instituted and the economic assets of fourteen leading *zaibatsu* families were to be frozen while preparing for sequestration (although this in fact happened only to some 56 people).

It was an imaginative and ambitious program, on paper. Undoubtedly MacArthur's heart was in it. But a victory against the towering combines of Japanese business power was far, far harder to achieve than one against the war machine. MacArthur's frontal assault was first softened and absorbed by the concealed resistance of the Japanese bureaucrats who were supposed to implement the reforms, but were in fact very close to the *zaibatsu* themselves; it was then lost in the jungle thickets of Japanese business practices, which were virtually incomprehensible to the outsider; and it was finally repealed when Japanese business found allies among American business and right-wingers who waged a vicious propaganda battle that ended up depicting MacArthur—of all people—as being the dupe of Socialist and Communist forces.

The first two stages are described eloquently by Meirion and Susie Harries:

On paper SCAP looked like making a clean sweep. All the major *zaibatsu* families and their appointees and all key officials of other designated companies (plus their relatives to the third degree) were to be prohibited from working in any company within their own combines or for that matter in any other capacity in the business world. But in practice less than two thousand business figures were ever designated as purgees, and not all of those were actually removed from their jobs.

Moral issues aside—and there were many who saw the destruction of hugely successful business concerns as criminally wasteful, smacking of anarchy, or worse, communism—did the proposals of the Edwards Mission ever have a chance of working? It seems that in fact the men in SCAP's Economic and Scientific Section had taken upon themselves a virtually impossible burden. To dismantle permanently even one of the *zaibatsu* business empires would have required more time, more staff and above all far more experience of Japanese business's law and methods than they possessed. They might identify and dissolve the principal holding companies at the top of the pyramid readily enough, but when they moved against the myriad subsidiaries, the complexity of the task defeated them.

The first line of *zaibatsu* defense was the claim, which could never be disproved, that all the documentation necessary for the efficient reorganization of the companies had been destroyed in the bombing. If ESS surmounted this hurdle, they were soon hopelessly tangled in a web of contracts, loans and accounts, joint and nominee shareholdings, common directorships, family ties and Oyabun-Kobun patterns which held the business world together; as fast as they severed connections, the strands rejoined silently behind them.

"In dominating men or being dominated by them," wrote Shungaku Matsudaira in 1850, "the issue turns simply on the question of who has the initiative." Anticipating dissolution, large companies fragmented stockholdings secretly among dummies from whom they could later reclaim them. The delay in implementing the economic purge gave its targets time not only to nominate and groom successors but to fortify the corporations' defenses and put snares into the path of the attackers. The initiative was something the *zaibatsu* never lost, from the Yasuda Plan onward.

The Japanese bureaucracy undoubtedly understood the workings of the business world, having interacted closely with it throughout Japan's modernization. But by virtue of this very intimacy and the benefits it had brought, they could hardly be expected to cooperate in guiding SCAP's men through the maze. Yoshida himself was a doughty defender of traditional business methods. "It is a great mistake to judge the *zaibatsu* as having done only bad things. Japan's economic structure today was built by such old *zaibatsu* as Mitsui and Mitsubishi. It can be said that the prosperity of the Japanese people has depended in great part upon the efforts of these *zaibatsu*. Thus, it is doubtful that the dissolution of these old *zaibatsu* will really benefit the people."

Nor, indeed, was there support for SCAP from the sector these reforms were intended to benefit. MacArthur's ambition was to develop a lassez-faire economy in the American tradition, in which small and medium-sized enterprises would compete freely in an open market. But the notion of individualistic internal competition, foreign in any case to the Japanese group orientation, was virtually incomprehensible to a nation preparing to force its way back into international markets against stiff external resistance. Besides, such independent entrepreneurial talent, and there was little enough, as had existed before the war, had been obliterated by bombing, blockade or by the postwar economic collapse. When the Holding Companies Liquidation Commission put the dissolved corporations' assets on the market, there were no other businesses, nor a large enough middle class, with the money to buy them even at reduced prices. It is believed that almost all the "redistributed" stocks were repossessed either by the original *zaibatsu* under false names, or by black marketeers "laundering" their profits.

These delaying tactics in fact enabled the *zaibatsu* to survive through to the third stage which coincided with the major crisis of the American occupation and forced MacArthur entirely to change policy.

There were two further major assaults upon economic privilege undertaken by MacArthur. The first was to be one of the few really lasting achievements of the occupation, and was also to have a profound effect upon the country's political system. As we have seen, the plight of the peasants in Japan was a wretched one: most worked in the service of small farmers as poor as themselves. One prominent member of SCAP, Edwin Martin, described the position succinctly:

So long as the 47 percent of the Japanese people living on farms are barely able to survive, they will continue to be a source of cheap labor and cannon fodder. They will be an uneducated and dissatisfied group, seeking a way to better their lot without too much regard for the morality of the means, or understanding of the probable consequences of their acts.

Once again the Japanese administrators formulated wholly inadequate proposals. MacArthur demanded more far-reaching action. Absentee landlords were expropriated, their land being purchased by the government and sold to tenants at prewar prices—in effect, the land was given. Owners were allocated 7.5 acres for their own house, and were allowed to rent out 2.5 acres. These patches might seem ridiculously small, but in mountainous Japan only 2,000 farmers had more than 100 acres, and few had more than ten; a 7.5 acre farm was a respectable size (this gives an idea of the sheer scale of rural poverty); over the years of the reform almost a third of all land was expropriated in this way, benefiting a similar proportion of Japanese peasants.

The new rural class was, for the first time, not living at levels of absolute poverty and was deeply conservative, transferring its allegiance to right-wing parties and becoming one of their chief props. Japan thus neatly sidestepped what was to be the source of major political instability in the rest of Asia—the existence of a peasant underclass—and also buttressed the country's ruling parties. Later, the existence of these hundreds of thousands of smallholders, whose rice prices were supported by governments which owed their existence to the peasants, would bring its own problems. But at the time, MacArthur's land reform was successful in improving the lives of millions of wretchedly poor Japanese, undermining the militarist class which had been rooted in the peasantry—and bolstering conservatism.

The third area of economic reforms touched an area of intense controversy: the power of organized labor. Politically repressed and fragmented into small-scale unions that were usually merely a tool of management, the unions were practically nonexistent at the end of the war. Idealists in SCAP considered this an affront to the natural rights of labor. The Civil Liberties Directive of October 4, 1945, ordered the Japanese government to abolish all laws restricting freedom of the press, thought, speech, religion or assembly. This permitted unions to begin organizing. With MacArthur's decision to free political prisoners, many former Communists and union leaders emerged from jail.

In December 1945, a trade union law was passed guaranteeing Japanese workers the right to organize trade unions, to collective bargaining, and to strike. No fewer than 14 labor relations bills were passed, setting up all the customary machinery of Western industrial relations, including labor exchanges, vocational training and arbitration machinery. In April 1941, the Labor Standards Law was enacted, setting out minimum standards for safety, hygiene, wages, overtime, working hours, holidays, sick leave and accident compensation. Forced labor was abolished, and the employment of women and children was regulated.

Between 1945 and June 1949 the number of union members rose from just 707 to 6,655,483. Two giant union federations sprang into being: Sodomo, the Socialist General Federation of Trades Unions, and Sanbetsu, the Communist National Congress of Industrial Unions. The new laws were enforced, and quickly led to the equivalent of an earthquake in Japan's deeply conservative social structure. This enabled MacArthur's right-wing critics in Washington to pillory him and force him to change course in such a way as effectively to smother the power of organized labor in Japan almost as completely as in prewar years.

The third major category of reforms alongside the punitive ones and the attacks on Japan's vested interest were constructive. Chief among them were MacArthur's attempts to modernize the constitution, to institute rule by representative, decentralized government, to create a genuinely free press, to liberalize education and to separate religion from the state.

MacArthur's constitutional reform was the most dramatic direct imposition of American power during the occupation. As in other matters MacArthur wanted the new constitution to be drawn up by the Japanese, to endow it with wider authority. Virtually as soon as the occupation began, in October 1945, a group under Prince Konoye, the deputy prime minister, began to examine constitutional reform. Within weeks, however, it became clear that Konoye himself might be indicted as a war criminal, and his group was quietly wound up.

A new body was set up instead under the minister of state, Juji Matsumoto, a prominent opponent of the militarists in the prewar period. He believed, along with many other members of the old oligarchy, that Japan's problems had arisen because of the militarists' departure from the spirit of the Meiji constitution. To him, constitutional reform meant reasserting the supremacy of the old Meiji institutions. On February 1, 1946, the Matsumoto committee's recommendations were released to the press, falling far short of American intentions for democratic reform.

Two days later, MacArthur, who was backed by a firm directive from Washington on the matter, ordered a group under General Whitney to draw up their own proposals for a draft constitution. The two worst features of the Matsumoto committee's proposals were, in MacArthur's view, the continuing, power vested in the Emperor and the refusal to submit legislation to proper parliamentary control. MacArthur insisted on three main points: the Emperor could stay on as head of state, but must be responsible to the people; feudal institutions—such as the peerage—must be abolished; and war was to be proscribed. The members of government section worked on the few books and constitutional treatises they could get their hands on; one drew on extracts from a book by Lincoln; another drew on the writings of the Abbé Sieyes; another found an authority on constitutional law in the library of Tokyo University. Within ten days they had assembled the outline of a constitution for a nation of 75 million people.

The methods used to ensure Japan's acceptance of the draft were those of Al Capone. At 10 A.M. on February 13, 1946, General Whitney led a delegation of his constitutional committee to the home of the foreign minister, Shigeru Yoshida, who was waiting with Matsumoto, his secretary, Jiro Shirasu, and a foreign ministry official. According to the American account of the meeting:

> General Whitney sat with his back to the sun, affording best light on the countenances of the Japanese present who sat opposite him. He cut short any analysis of the Matsumoto draft by stating flatly that it was "wholly unacceptable to the Supreme Commander as a document of freedom and democracy" and gave the Japanese 15 copies of SCAP's own draft. "At 10:10 o'clock General Whitney and the undersigned left the porch and went out into the sunshine of the garden as an American plane passed over the house. After about fifteen minutes Mr. Shirasu joined us, whereupon General Whitney quietly observed to him, "[W]e are out here enjoying the warmth of atomic energy"—which Whitney later described as a "psychological shaft."

This was pressure of the crudest kind. At ten minutes to eleven Whitney returned to the house and told the Japanese that unless they adopted the SCAP draft, two things would follow: the Emperor's fate would be reviewed, including the possibility that he might be tried as a war criminal; and SCAP would submit its proposals to a referendum, which might undermine the power of the conservative clique then in control. "Mr. Shirasu straightened up as if he had sat on something. Dr. Matsumoto sucked in his breath. Mr. Yoshida's face was a black cloud," summarized Whitney. "The Japanese acted as though they were about to be taken out and shot."

The constitution, crude though well-intentioned, contained the essential underpinnings of democracy. The Diet was set up as Japan's sole legislative body, and was given the final say in approving the budget, as well as powers of scrutiny over the cabinet, a majority of which now had to be drawn from the Diet. An independent judiciary was established, with the power to review all legislation passed by the Diet. Local government was to be decentralized and elected. A bill of rights was drawn up, enshrining freedom of speech, thought, religion, assembly and the press. Discrimination on grounds of race, nationality, creed, or political opinion was outlawed. Universal manhood suffrage was introduced. Women were given the right to vote and the right to choose their husbands, as well as to divorce.

Above all, the Emperor was stripped of his temporal power and on January 1, 1946, issued a rescript renouncing divinity. "The ties between us and our people have always stood upon mutual trust and affection. They do not depend upon mere legends and myths. They are not predicated on the false conception that the Emperor is divine."

The rescript was believed to have been suggested by a tutor in English to Crown Prince Akihito, Reginald Blyth, who acted as a kind of intermediary, and even spy, for SCAP in the Emperor's household. Harold Henderson, Head of the Education, Religion and Fine Arts Department of SCAP, actually dictated it to Blyth. The Japanese to this day insist the rescript was largely the work of Prime Minister Shidehara. On Kawahara's account:

> For years the target of attacks by militarists and right-wingers for his pro-Western sympathies, Shidehara saw the concept of a divine emperor as not only antiquated but also as the cause of great suffering. The prime minister began drafting the announcement in English. He chose English because the imperial rescript he was preparing was more for the consumption of the GHQ and foreign countries than for the Japanese themselves. On top of that, he actually felt more comfortable writing in English than Japanese.

On December 28 he showed the finished draft to Hirohito, who nodded his approval, saying it was "just fine," though he wanted to add as a preface a reference to the Emperor Meiji's Charter Oath of Five Articles, which had set the guidelines for the Japanese state in 1868. The completed rescript was published and broadcast on January 1, 1946, and has come to be known as "The Emperor's Proclamation of his Humanity." The rescript was far more limited than it appears on first reading. The Emperor remained at the center of Shinto worship, as he had before; as far as the Shinto priests were concerned, there was no change in their treatment of him. Moreover, Hirohito's unbroken connections with his distant ancestors had not been changed; he had merely divested himself of the concept that he was a living god—which had been played up by the militarists, but was not at the center of the Meiji notion of the imperial ascendancy.

The constitution made him subordinate to the will of the people: authority flowed from them to him, not the other way round. Government was "a sacred trust of the people, the authority for which is derived from the people, the powers of which are exercised by representatives of the people and the benefits of which are enjoyed by the people."

However, the new constitution was MacArthur's, imposed upon the Japanese people. What gave it strength was the support it secured among ordinary Japanese, who relished their new role in checking and controlling their masters of many centuries. This upheaval, in practice, was to be remarkably circumscribed, but the democratization of Japan was to be one of MacArthur's finest achievements.

MacArthur's three other constructive reforms were to free the press; to liberalize education; and to separate church and state, a process already begun by the imperial rescript renouncing his divinity. Freedom of the press was enshrined in the constitution and it was to work in practice in a very circumspect way. The reforms of education and religion—the two great propaganda bulwarks of the militarist state in the 1930s—were ambitious, and like so much else about the SCAP program, only partially successful. The reform of education was one of the central planks of MacArthur's reforms. Even before SCAP had stated its demands, some 116,000 teachers were sacked, and large numbers of new teachers brought in, many of them victims of past militarist purges.

In April 1946, a teachers' manual was issued preaching revolutionary doctrines for education: it suggested teachers use their own initiative in the classroom, experiment with new methods and encourage pupil participation. In addition, the ministry of education set up a program of "teacher reorientation," which included a five-week course of lectures on the militarists' role in the prewar period. Under the terms of the reform as dictated by SCAP, education now existed to promote the individual; the ministry of education's monopoly over teachers, textbooks and the curriculum was to be eased, and local education boards were given responsibility for these matters; pupils were given a freer choice of subjects. The Meiji education structure was reformed: there were now to be six years of elementary education and three of middle school, which were compulsory, plus the option of three years at senior high school—the American system at the time. History and geography courses were shorn of their nationalist overtones, and *shushin*—moral teaching—abolished altogether and replaced by civics and social studies courses.

In the sphere of physical education, radical reform took place:

> Military methods were eradicated from the way that students gathered, marched, saluted and attended school. Teachers were told that they should "be careful not to fall into vain formalization, regulation, discipline or uniform instruction . . . stress must be laid on the sportslike or play-like treatment of subjects for study."

Competitive sports replaced coordinated exercises, while schools were now able to pay attention to weather conditions, stamina and the ages of children when compelling them to take part. Five- to eleven-year-olds were no longer to be taught judo, kenyo, kyudo, walk with measured tread, play at soldiers, warships, and fish torpedoes; their elders were reprieved from learning halberd practice, navy march, stronghold of iron, shout of triumph, bayonet exercise, and hand-grenade throwing.

The ministry of education's monopoly of textbooks was abolished in 1948; instead a "textbook authorization committee" allowed independent authors to write them, and schools made their own selection. In practice, the ministry retained a veto power over the contents of textbooks. Moreover, it proved far easier to reform Japan's education system on paper than in reality. Many old teachers quietly returned to the schools. Although the militarist message was no longer preached, most teaching was to remain rigid and unimaginative, and discipline was to stay strict; the textbooks were to remain far from satisfactory, particularly in relation to accounts of the Pacific War.

In respect of religion, there was intense pressure from the Christian evangelist groups, to which MacArthur paid particular attention, for the radical transformation of state Shinto. As one commentator explained it, Shinto is the only religion in the world which constrains its followers to practice every vice recommended by Satan. No other religion, no matter how barbarous may be its adherents, glorifies lying, cheating, stealing, rape, plunder and pillage on the wholesale scale of shintoism. No other barbarous religion outlines a religious and racial destiny which contemplates the extermination of the entire remainder of the human race.

MacArthur saw his task as being to strip Shinto of its militarist trappings, and to ensure the separation of church and state. In the Shinto directive of December 1945, he cut off government funding for Shinto and its shrines; made illegal the semicompulsory shrine levies upon ordinary Japanese, forbade public servants from attending ceremonies in an official capacity; and curbed Shintoist indoctrination in the schools.

Pupils were no longer required to bow toward the imperial palace, while the shrines at which the imperial rescript on education and the Emperor's portrait were kept were removed. Schoolchildren were no longer forced to go on compulsory trips to Shinto shrines, which were also prevented from employing former soldiers as priests. Government officials were forbidden to participate at military funerals. The national holidays celebrating Shintoism were abolished.

However, SCAP was scrupulous in not seeking to eradicate Shintoism as such. MacArthur himself, with his fervent Christian beliefs, embarrassed his own officials by invoking Christian ideals throughout the occupation—which also seemed to conflict with the attempt to separate church and state. He encouraged missions from American Bible societies to distribute the Good Book. MacArthur told the young Billy Graham that the Emperor was considering becoming a convert to Christianity, and taking his people with him; there were later rumors that Hirohito was thinking of becoming a Catholic. In fact, Christianity made few converts during the occupation: the Catholics increased their numbers from around 20,000 in 1941 to 157,000 in 1951.

MacArthur messianically exaggerated the number of converts to Christianity. On one occasion he claimed there were some 2 million Japanese embracing "the Christian faith as a means to fill the spiritual vacuum left in Japan's life by the collapse of their past faith." This Christian spearhead "would transform" hundreds of millions of backward people in Asia. In 1947 he hailed the fact that three major Asian nations had Christians as their leaders—in Japan, the socialist Tetsu Katayama, in China Chiang Kai-Shek, and in the Philippines Manuel Roxas. Yet all three soon lost their jobs.

MacArthur's zeal probably did little harm; the Japanese may even have been impressed by his religious faith. The great failing of his reforms in this sphere, as in others, was believing that awe for the Emperor and ingrained beliefs could be eliminated at the stroke of a pen. The Shinto-militarist association was driven underground, and many ordinary Japanese were probably glad to be rid of it. But many thousands of Japanese still subscribed to it openly, waiting for the opportunity to reassert it.

Press reform too was a strictly limited affair. At first, at the end of the war, there was a sigh of relief when Japanese military censorship was lifted and newspapers reveled in a newfound freedom to publish. But although MacArthur established press freedom, he imposed his own more relaxed controls. "News must adhere strictly to the truth . . . there should be no destructive criticisms of the Allied Forces of Occupation," went one SCAP directive: American black-marketeering, theft, rape and drunkenness were subjects that could not be discussed, although some Japanese euphemisms for American soldiers got through: "blue eyed nationals" and "men with nine-inch footprints" were described as committing such crimes. American censorship extended to emotional descriptions of Hiroshima and Nagasaki; overall, it proved a poor example for the Japanese press, which was to exercise a curious kind of self-censorship in reporting, as though it feared the consequences of excessive frankness.

34 : THE TOKYO TRIALS

PERHAPS THE MOST DISAGREEABLE ASPECT OF MACARTHUR'S SHOGUNATE —as he himself made clear—was the imposition of justice on Japan's war criminals. Hirohito had been correct about one thing: his being spared undermined the whole basis for the legal travesty that was the Tokyo War Crimes Trial, perhaps the most disgraceful and least important achievement of the American occupation.

It needs underlining from the outset that there was nothing ignoble or flawed about the original American intention to hold such a trial, as a Far Eastern equivalent of the Nuremberg tribunal. The British favored the illegal, but speedy and efficient execution of the principal war criminals. The Americans had wider goals: to help construct the kind of future international order in which a framework existed to judge and condemn "international criminals" and aggressors. There were more understandable motives behind the trials as well: it would serve to satisfy public opinion that the monsters of Nanking, Bataan, and Burma were receiving due punishment: it was entirely natural for ordinary people in the Allied nations, and particularly in America, to demand retribution—particularly in view of the perceived "softness" of the occupation policy itself.

Yet underlying the Tokyo trials was a cynical American calculation that a war crimes tribunal would mask, and to some extent compensate for, the American decision to preserve the postwar power structure in Japan. The actual decision to hold such a trial does not appear to have been taken until late in the day; the legal basis for it was missing. Henry Stimson, one of the driving forces behind the Tokyo trials, and other liberals pointed to the 1919 Convention of the League of Nations and to the 1928 Kellog-Briand Pact by which war had been discarded as an instrument of national policy in order to buttress the contention that "aggressive war" was illegal. The trouble is that waging aggressive war had never before been a crime; for who but the victor could judge who was to blame in any war? In addition, how could individuals be judged responsible for the actions of a state?

This last point became crucial in relation to the Emperor. The difference between the actions of a nation, or a whole institution such as an army, and those of an individual was that not just that the former were usually the result of collective decision-making, but that it was virtually impossible to decide who actually was responsible for taking, and who for opposing, them. The Emperor's own position amply illustrated this: the balance of the evidence points to the fact, as we noted in the last chapter, that he resisted much of the slide into war and only went along reluctantly. Nevertheless, all Japanese actions in the war took place in his name: if the Emperor was to be absolved, even more complex calculations would have to be made to determine the guilt of his subordinates.

It was easy to pinpoint General Tojo, the militarist prime minister, as having been responsible for waging "aggressive war" through his own public statements. (Even so, Tojo's defense was that he had been waging defensive war.) Many other potential war criminals like General Matsui, in charge of the Japanese forces during the Rape of Nanking, may not have been directly responsible for initiating the massacres, or may have been incapable of stopping them. They, however, were to be blamed for being the "men in charge" when the atrocities were carried out—a perfectly fair allocation of responsibility, even if there was little evidence to link them directly to the killings. But if this principle of responsibility at the top applied to them, why not also to the Emperor? If he was absolved, why not they?

A poignant cause was that of Prince Konoye, who played so central a role in the events leading up to the war and thereafter. As we have seen, although his position was ambivalent and he was thoroughly mistrusted by MacArthur and other SCAP officials, the bulk of the evidence suggests that he spent the crucial months before the war trying to avert it; indeed he was so confident that the Americans would identify him as the leader of the peace party during the conflict that he believed they would entrust him with a major role in the reconstruction of postwar Japan.

But it soon became apparent that MacArthur was distancing himself from the prince, and on December 6 he was asked to report to Sugamo Prison as a suspected war criminal ten days later. The day before he was due to arrive, he swallowed a cyanide capsule. Robert Fearey, a former SCAP official, described the thinking behind Konoye's indictment thus:

> Atcheson (MacArthur's civilian deputy) called me into his office and told me, "I've had a call from General MacArthur and he has noticed that all these major war criminals have been arrested and tried, or are about to be tried, in Germany, and here we have arrested no major war criminals in Japan, they're still walking the streets. This isn't right. So would you please draw me a list of 10 to 12—or whatever the number was—of people who should be arrested and then arrest them." Together with Herb Norman, a Canadian working for the intelligence branch of SCAP, we drew up a list of 10 people we thought should be arrested as major war criminals, and gave it to Atcheson, who gave it to MacArthur and the next day they were arrested, headlines all over the place.
>
> Maybe a week later, MacArthur said, "There must be more than ten." So I produced another list, and on it was Prince Konoye, not because we felt he was a war criminal who should be tried and convicted, but because he had been Prime Minister at critical phases over many years when Japan had gone into North China, and his involvement was important from the military point of view. The understanding between us was that we would get word to Prince Konoye that we did not regard him as a war criminal like the others, that we only wanted him as a material witness and felt that we had to do this because of the positions he had held . . . I am afraid that word of this did not get to Prince Konoye in time. Someone forgot to tell him.

Based thus on a very shaky legal premise, largely in fact because of the decision to exclude the Emperor from prosecution, the justice dispensed at the International Military Tribunals Far East (IMTFE) was arbitrary and based on evidence that would never have stood scrutiny in a proper court of law. To Arnold Brackman, a young UPI correspondent who later wrote the best account of the trial, the issue was straightforward: countless crimes were committed, someone had to pay for them. The men in the dock were steeped in guilt. That alone was justification enough for the trial. The trial was justified in terms of natural right and punishment. It was entirely correct that the victors should extract justice from the vanquished, and self-evident to most nations except the Japanese that they had been the aggressors in the war, and had conducted it with wholly excessive savagery.

But in terms of legality, something more was required. A clear legal framework had to be constructed for the trial. It was not. There is an indisputable case for arguing that waging aggressive war and mass murder under cover of war are crimes, indeed the severest form of crime. Yet neither was outlawed internationally at the time. Even the Geneva Convention on the treatment of prisoners of war did not have the force of international law. Moreover, the evidence had to be sifted and the defense given a chance to rebut it properly (due process); instead, the procedures of the trial were crude in the extreme; for example, at the end of two years' work on the trial, the prosecution had found a wealth of new, incriminating evidence and asked for the opportunity to rebut the defense's case. The defense argued, with some justice, that this would constitute a retrial; but the request was granted and the defense was given just 10 days to rebut the new evidence in its turn.

Meirion and Susie Harries also point to the huge translation difficulties suffered by the defense:

> Out of a total staff which by January 1946, had swollen to seventy, only five could read Japanese, and Keenan (the chief prosecutor), had no option but to request the Japanese government to supply 50 or so English-speaking Japanese nationals—"Hobson's choice," as he put it. Eventually some two hundred Japanese nationals were employed on the staff of the IPS, which may have contributed to the constant breaches of security that plagued the trial; the British list of proposed defendants, for example, was leaked to the press almost as soon as it was notified to Keenan.
>
> The swamp of translation difficulties was to swallow up prosecution and defense alike. Turning Japanese into English, and vice versa, with the precision of nuance required by lawyers is virtually impossible. Japanese as a language bears no relation to English or any other European language, and the process of translating it is more like describing a picture in words—

creating an equivalent, not a replica. Not only is it difficult, it is also particularly time-consuming. In a tone of near desperation the head of IPS translation, after trying to explain to uncompromising attorneys why accurate translation of one page of double-spaced foolscap took one linguist two days, concluded by warning, "unless reasonable time is allowed for translations (days or weeks not hours) the language division will be forced either to delay the court proceedings or to turn out a succession of rush jobs that will embarrass the prosecution by not holding up in court."

In the face of such difficulties, the associate prosecutor from England, Arthur Comyns Carr, KC, found his first few weeks in Tokyo a time of intense frustration. "This is a frightful job you have let men in for," he wrote to Attorney-General Sir Hartley Shawcross, whose representative he was. "I have already been here as long as you said the whole trip would take, and there is no sign of the proceedings even beginning. On my arrival I found the Americans with a huge staff engaged in an enormous research with a stack of documents which have never even been listed or translated."

There were no level playing fields as far as the prosecution and defense were concerned.

Shortly after the prosecution phase closed, the tribunal convened a tripartite conference with the prosecution and defense to discuss ways of speeding up the trial. Webb suggested, for example, that the time available for the defense of each individual accused should be fixed at two days. But Bruce Blakeney, speaking for the defense as a whole, made their discontent plain: "It was of course our friends of the prosecution, not we, who drew this indictment . . . 55 counts, covering 17 years of time and half a world of space." It was they who put in evidence running the gamut from the celebrated and portentous fire-cracker incident at home to the theft of Mrs. Wang's pig in Far China, all of which the defense were going to have to rebut.

The Tribunal, however, was unsympathetic, and responded with various new devices for saving time. Most significantly, it tightened up the rules on the nature of the evidence it would accept. A "best evidence" rule was introduced—which meant that dubious or unproven evidence of the type which had been readily accepted in the prosecution phase was turned down when submitted by the defense. And the Tribunal claimed the right to reject evidence which it regarded as irrelevant to the case. This latter point was to be hotly contested, and perhaps demonstrates most graphically why in the interests of justice, a nation should not be judge in its own cause.

The "trial of the century" was staged in Ichigaya, the hilltop headquarters for the Japanese army during the war, now transformed into an ultramodern courtroom. It was of awesome dimensions. The trial lasted for two and a half years. Judges from 11 Allied nations presided. Some 200,000 spectators attended altogether. More than 400 witnesses were called and 779 documents were introduced in evidence. There were usually about 1,000 people in the court at any one time. The Australian presiding judge, Sir William Webb, was generally agreed to have been as fair as possible under the circumstances.

The American chief prosecutor, Joseph Keenan, a distinguished anti-Mafia lawyer who had once prosecuted Al Capone, was in the autumn of his career, a heavy drinker, frequently unintelligible, and knowing nothing of Japan. His British deputy, Sir William Comyns Carr, was more legally punctilious, but drew up a complex and thorough indictment that was responsible for much of the slow progress of the trial. As a legal process, it was a shambles, and quickly turned into an embarrassment and a bore for the occupation authorities.

In political terms though, there was evidence that Western public opinion was satisfied that its demands for retribution had been met through holding the trial—although the occupied nations of the Far East (in particular China and the Philippines) thought that the judgment did not go far enough. As far as Japan itself was concerned, the trial was almost certainly counterproductive, helping to smudge the nonvindictive image of the American occupation that MacArthur was so keen to establish, while providing a platform for the Japanese militarists to provide a far-fetched, but just credible defense of their actions.

The man whose testimony most successfully caught the imagination of the Japanese public was the country's most guilty war criminal, the principal head of the militarist faction, Hideki Tojo, prime minister during the crucial years of the war. His evidence is worth quoting from extensively, because in so many respects it was to form the subsequent views not just of Japanese nationalists, but of mainstream political leaders defending Japan's role in the Pacific War.

Tojo had been given the right to prepare a formal affidavit which took three days to read in court: it was a masterly defense of the militarists' cause. He then endured three days of cross-examination at the hands not of John Filhelly, an experienced criminal lawyer who had prepared extensively for the interrogation, but of Keenan himself, who had undertaken no such work and had overridden his junior at the last moment. Filhelly was furious and stalked out of the courtroom, never to return. Keenan may have been acting purely out of jealousy, after months of visible frustration in court; or he may simply have felt that it was the chief prosecutor's job to interrogate the chief defendant. Either way, he played straight into the tough, wily former prime minister's hands.

Tojo blew his nose ostentatiously before entering the witness box—a major insult in Japan, where nasal excretions are viewed as no different from others. His lawyer, Ichiro Kiyose, read out a statement asserting that Japan had "neither planned nor prepared beforehand for the war against the United States, Britain and the Netherlands." Japan had held "neither territorial ambition nor the idea of economic monopoly" in China. The Allied nations had provoked Japan's attack on the Anglo-American forces; before the attack, Japan "had scrupulously prepared to deliver the lawful notification of war to the United States of America prior to the commencement of hostilities."

The Greater East Asia Co-Prosperity Sphere had been set up to "secure political freedom for all peoples of Greater East Asia." It was "groundless . . . sheer imagination" to suppose that Japan had been ruled by militaristic cliques. Tojo himself "neither gave orders for, tolerated, nor connived at any inhuman acts." Tojo's 60,000-word defense asserted that it was "absolutely without foundation" that he had any preconceived notion or plan for aggression, "and so far as I know no member of the cabinet had any such belief." Japan had been provoked into a war not of its choosing by the obduracy of others. The Americans had frustrated Konoye's peace initiative in 1941; the Russians had broken the Neutrality Pact. "Never once was an unfriendly act directed against the Soviet Union [by the Japanese] despite the pressure exerted by the Germans."

On the contrary, it was the Allies who had engaged in the "military encirclement" of Japan. "It was clearly discernible that the U.S. was exerting itself feverishly in military expansion." Japan was pushed into the war by economic strangulation—an aggressive act long before Pearl Harbor—indeed, in Tojo's view, an unofficial declaration of war. If Japan had yielded, its interests would have been crushed. "Japan relied upon America and Britain for the major portion of her imports of essential materials. Once these were cut off, the very existence of the nation was endangered." To Tojo, the purpose of sanctions was to force Japan to pull her troops out of China:

If we swallow the American demands, totally giving up the stationing of our troops in China and withdraw them wholesale, what will ensue after that? Not only would Japan bring to naught those sacrifices and those efforts paid for in the course of the China Incident of more than four years' standing, but also Chinese contempt for Japan will ever expand if we retire from China unconditionally because of United States duress. Relations between Japan and China will grow worse, coupled with the thoroughgoing resistance against Japan maintained by the Communists . . . Repercussions or loss of prestige will be keenly felt in Manchuria and Korea . . .

Viewed in this dim light, a compromise with the U.S. became too insurmountable to apprehend. . . . Japan had made concessions to the U.S. to almost unbearable limits so that the negotiations might be successfully concluded, and yet the U.S. showed no signs of responding to them and that government did not move an inch . . . [America had been] waging an economic war against Japan while at the same time keeping her out of actual war [so as to] reap the fruits of victory over Japan without resorting to an act of war.

By the autumn of 1941, in Tojo's view, Japan's position could only be helped through extreme measures, because of the extremities in which she found herself.

If Japan could not solve the fatal situation by means of diplomacy, then there would be no way remaining for her but to take up arms and break through the economic and military barrier flung around her . . . There was a danger of an exhaustion of liquid fuel and, on the other hand, during the second half of the following year the strength of the American navy would be vastly augmented . . . The High Command considered that the month of November was the most conducive time for a successful operation; December possible, but difficult; and in January quite impossible of performance.

Tojo suggested that Japan had no alternative but to fight; and thus must seize the initiative. But he claimed that the army was always realistic about the possibility of defeat.

It was apparent that we could not be too hopeful of winning against the two greatest powers in the world. Japan had no alternative but to advance to the Pacific and Indian Oceans, holding up strategic points, occupying regions for military resources and repulsing enemy attacks to the best of our ability and spirit to the last ditch.

On the issue of Hirohito's role in the decision to start the war, Tojo recounted how he broke the decision to go to war to the Emperor on November 2, 1941.

While presenting the submission I could see from the expression of His Majesty that he was suffering from a painful sense of distress arising from his peace-loving faith. When His Majesty had listened to what we had to submit, he was grave and thoughtful for some time, and then he declared, "Is there no way left but to determine, against our wishes, to wage war against America and Britain in case our effort in American-Japanese talks should fail to break the deadlock?" Then he continued: "If the state of affairs is just as you have stated now, there will be no alternative but to proceed in the preparations, but I still do hope that you will further adopt every possible means to tide over the difficulties in the American-Japanese negotiations." I still remember quite vividly, even today, that we were awe-stricken by these words.

Tojo accepted full responsibility not for starting the war, but for losing it. "I feel that it devolved upon myself as Premier. The responsibility in that sense I am not only willing but sincerely desire to accept fully."

The cross-examination by Keenan was, predictably, a shambles. He began with the bludgeon. "Accused Tojo, I shall not address you as general because, as you know, there is no longer any Japanese army."

A series of absurd exchanges followed, playing into Tojo's hands. Tojo was asked if he was ashamed of Japan's alliance with Nazi Germany. "No, I do not entertain any such cowardly views," the general retorted. Keenan asked whether it was obvious that the Vichy government in France "was under the control of the Hitler government." Tojo returned the ball with devastating precision. "I was well aware of the fact that the Vichy government was governing under the German occupation, but I consider the Vichy government as the legitimate government of France. It is just as the present Japanese government, operating under the American government, is the legitimate government of Japan." Then they got into an argument about the merits of an Emperor against those of an elected president.

An exasperated Webb asked, "What is the relevance of this, Mr. Chief Counsel?"

Keenan replied, "But, Mr. President, if it is offensive in any way to take a few moments in this courtroom in this historic trial to let the people here know the authority of the United States government, I shall not press the point. I shall go immediately to something else on a further indication from the court."

"Go immediately to something else," Webb retorted.

"I believe the court means that it would like to have me do so, it is not a command."

"It is the acceptance of an invitation by you," replied Webb dryly. "We do not want to hear any more questions of that type."

More such farce was to follow. Keenan asked, "Would you agree with me, Mr. Tojo, that aggressive wars are crimes?"

"We are certainly getting no help from this type of cross-examination," said Webb in exasperation. Keenan replied that he was "not so stupid" as to believe that Tojo's reply would settle the issue, but was Webb attempting to prevent the prosecution getting Tojo to admit that he was guilty of the crime of aggression? Webb set him straight in no uncertain terms:

> "He was not invited to make an admission of guilt. Now the position is this: his honest and reasonable, though mistaken, belief in a state of facts is a defense. His opinion or belief as to the law is not a defense and irrelevant except on the question perhaps of mitigation, if he is found guilty. The only man found guilty of aggressive war, and aggressive war alone, at Nuremberg [Rudolf Hess] was not sentenced to death; so Nuremberg may have thought that belief as to the law, mistaken belief, may be a circumstance of mitigation, but they did not say so. I am only stating the fact. If I am asked whether I think aggressive war is a crime, and I say that I think it is not a crime, am I guilty of anything?" Keenan's question was overruled.

Even the prosecutor could not bowl Tojo such easy balls all the time and the ex-premier's answers became particularly unsatisfying on at least three occasions. Questioned about Pearl Harbor, he answered that he "really didn't know" that the Japanese fleet had set sail for Hawaii in November. He met Hirohito several times during the first week of December but did not, he claimed, discuss the impending attack on Pearl Harbor. "I spoke with him on greater matters than that, on war itself as a whole, which included that matter." On this explanation, Hirohito was not appraised of the detail that Pearl Harbor would be attacked, but was kept informed of the general decision to go to war. Indeed, Tojo confessed that the Emperor had "assented, though reluctantly, to the war . . . none of us would have dared act against the Emperor's will."

This was a bombshell. It suggested that a simple no from Hirohito could have averted the war. It flew in the face of the defense of almost all the accused that the Emperor could not have stopped a decision to go to war even if he was aware of its full inevitability. Astonishingly, Keenan, faithfully reflecting MacArthur's instructions not to have Hirohito dragged into the proceedings, then used an intermediary to consult Marquis Kido to prod Tojo to correct his remark and absolve the Emperor from blame— something that the former prime minister, fanatically loyal and deeply regretting his slip, was delighted to do.

This was accepted in the following exchange on January 6, when Keenan suddenly brought up the subject:

"While we are discussing the subject matter of emperors, it might be an appropriate moment to ask you a few questions on the relative positions of yourself and the Emperor of Japan on the matter of waging war in December of 1941. You have told us on repeated occasions made known to you that he was a man of peace and did not want war, is that correct?"

"I was then speaking to you of my feeling towards the Emperor as a subject, and that is quite a different matter from the problem of responsibility, that is, the responsibility of the Emperor."

"Well, you did make war against the United States, Great Britain and the Netherlands did you not?"

"War was decided on in my cabinet."

"Was that the will of the Emperor Hirohito, that war should be instituted?"

"It may not have been according to his will, but it is a fact that because of my advice and because of the advice given by the high command, the Emperor consented—though reluctantly—to the war."

The interpreter said, "The first part should be corrected: 'It might have been against the Emperor's will'."

Tojo continued, "The Emperor's love and desire for peace remained the same right up to the very moment when hostilities commenced, and even during the war his feelings remained the same. The Emperor's feelings in this regard can be clearly ascertained from the imperial rescript given on the eighth of December, 1941, declaring war . . . That is to say, the imperial rescript contains words to this effect: this war is indeed unavoidable and is against my own desires."

Incredibly, the prosecution and the American authorities had colluded with Japan's foremost war criminal to keep evidence incriminating to the Emperor out of court, further undermining the already shaky basis for the trial.

Tojo's composure broke only once, on the issue of the treatment of prisoners of war: "I don't recall what kind of orders were issued at the time, so I am unable to give an exact reply," he fumed. He had been war minister at the time; his attitude was totally unconvincing. Did not the imperial general staff discuss the issue of POWs? he was pressed. "I do not remember well." Brackman sums up the subsequent exchange:

Was for example, the Bataan death march ever discussed? "I do not remember." Well, as prime minister and war minister Tojo toured the Philippines—were there rumors? "There were rumors." Who was responsible for the march? "General Homma would naturally be responsible." Did Tojo or anyone in the government discuss the march with Homma? "I do not know if this matter was ever discussed." (Homma had been tried by the Americans as a war criminal shortly after the Japanese surrender; he was convicted and executed in the Philippines.)

Were copies of Allied protest notes about the mistreatment of prisoners sent to the Emperor, or was the Emperor informed in any way about Allied complaints of Japanese inhumanity towards prisoners and others? "No, he was not," said Tojo firmly. Why not? Wasn't the Emperor the commander-in-chief of the imperial Japanese armed forces? "The Emperor was busy and had a great deal of work so I did this [handling Allied protests] on my own," he replied. "Consequently the Emperor is not responsible in connection with this matter."

Was Tojo responsible as premier and war minister for the treatment of prisoners of war? "Yes," he said without hesitation. "I was responsible for their treatment." When was the Prisoners of War Bureau set up in the War Ministry? "Immediately after the outbreak of war," Tojo confirmed. Which war? "The Greater East Asia [Pacific] War," he said. Why was it set up? "This is according to international law." Then why was there no such bureau during the China war? "It was not necessary during the China Incident," he answered. What bureau was set up to handle Chinese prisoners? "There was no organization set up to deal with Chinese prisoners."

How did Tojo explain the atrocious behavior of the Japanese army and navy? "I am astounded at the truth regarding atrocities that is now being revealed in the newspapers," he said. "If the Japanese had followed the Emperor's instructions, these atrocities would never have happened."

Tojo slept on these words, and the following day, March 24, 1946, told his Sugamo interrogator that he would like to amplify his remarks. He returned to the subject of atrocities. "We did not suspect that such things had happened." Addressing himself to history, he added, "The Emperor especially, because of his benevolence, would have had a contrary feeling. Such acts are not permissible in Japan. The character of the Japanese people is such that they believe that neither heaven nor earth would permit such things." His concern, he said, is that "the world [will] believe that these inhuman acts are the result of the Japanese character."

Keenan was later praised by the Japanese for his role in exempting the Emperor from prosecution. Webb opposed the imposition of death sentences on the grounds that all the accused were no more than "accomplices in crime" to the leader in crime, the Emperor. Here the blunt Australian put his finger on the weakness of the whole proceedings: either the top man was to be held responsible, regardless of whether he knew of the details of the crimes, along with his chief ministers; or they should have been absolved of all but specific instances in which they could have been said to have approved, instigated or committed crimes (of which there were very few).

The tribunal acted with a greater degree of balance than was apparent from its proceedings. In November 1948, no fewer than 45 of the 55 charges against the accused were thrown out. But the 10 remaining counts were deemed violations of international law then in existence. On the primary charges, the tribunal came to the conclusion "that the conspiracy to wage aggressive wars has been made out [and] that these acts are . . . criminal in the highest degree." On the issue of atrocities and crimes against humanity, the tribunal was unequivocal (and surely right):

> During a period of several months the tribunal heard evidence, orally or by affidavit, from witnesses who testified in detail to atrocities committed in all theaters of war on a scale so vast, yet following so common a pattern in all theaters, that only one conclusion is possible—the atrocities were either secretly ordered or willfully permitted by the Japanese government or individual members thereof and by the leaders of the armed forces . . . Massacres were freely committed as a means of terrorizing the civilian population and subjecting them to the domination of the Japanese.

The tribunal emphasized, however, that the Japanese military alone was not responsible for conventional war crimes and crimes against humanity. "The Japanese government conducted ill-treatment of prisoners of war and civilian internees (including Asian conscripted laborers) by failing and neglecting to punish those guilty of ill-treating them or by prescribing trifling and inadequate penalties for the offense," the judgment held. "The government also attempted to conceal the mistreatment and murder of prisoners and internees." In conclusion, the judgment summarized the view of the majority of the IMTFE as follows:

> Those far-reaching plans for waging wars of aggression, and the prolonged and intricate preparation for and waging of these wars of aggression were not the work of one man. They were the work of many leaders acting in pursuance of a common plan for the achievement of a common object. That common object, that they should secure Japan's domination by preparing and waging wars of aggression, was a criminal object. Indeed, no more grave crime can be conceived than a conspiracy to wage a war of aggression or the waging of a war of aggression, for the conspiracy threatens the security of the peoples of the world, and the waging disrupts it . . . the tribunal finds that the existence of the criminal conspiracy to wage wars of aggression . . . has been proved.

What good came of the trial? It had accumulated a mass of evidence about Japan's responsibility for the war, and had exposed the unconvincing denials of those who sought to duck their responsibility for the vast dimensions of the war's savagery. It had satisfied, and even damped down, through boredom, the clamor for revenge after the war in most Allied countries, if not Japan's American conqueror. But it had wholly failed to impress ordinary Japanese. To them the court was a fix, the kind of justice inevitably meted out by victor upon vanquished—although many Japanese were impressed by the limited extent of the retribution actually imposed. Some senior figures rejoiced in the trial, believing it had pinpointed responsibility where it belonged—with the militarists.

Many ordinary Japanese, however, admired the demeanor and dignity of the accused, respected Tojo for his directness—the British Ambassador, Sir Alvary Gascoigne, reported that Tojo had stood up to his accusers "like a true Japanese"—and at least half accepted the justification offered by the defendants for going to war. It is also true to say that a sizeable minority were shamed by the revelations of Japanese brutality in the occupied territories. MacArthur himself was angered that Tojo had not been better cross-examined and afterward ruefully admitted that the effect of Tojo's testimony on the Japanese public was "pretty profound."

Seven of the defendants were sentenced to death including, obviously, Tojo. The others were General Kenji Doihara, a professional sponsor of terrorism and clandestine work abroad, who had been commander of the Kwantung army in Manchuria and of Singapore and then many of the POW camps; Baron Koki Hirota, a follower of Toyama, the founder of the Black Dragon Society, and foreign minister during the Rape of Nanking and prime minister while the invasion of South East Asia was planned; General Seishiro Itagaki, a former minister of war in charge of many of the worst POW camps; General Heitaro Kimura, a former army commander primarily responsible while the Burma railway was being constructed; General Iwane Matsui, formally in charge during the Rape of Nanking—although almost certainly not directly responsible—and General Akira Muto, who played a key role in both the Rape of Nanking and the Rape of Manila, as well as running POW camps in Sumatra. All the rest were convicted, and all who lived that long were pardoned after six or seven years except for the ruthless General Kenryo Sato, who spent a further year in prison. One defendant, Mamoru Shigemitsu, was soon to become Japan"s foreign minister.

The seven were executed on December 22, 1948, six years to the month after Pearl Harbor. The Japanese were bitter at the refusal of the Americans to permit them an honorable death through beheading rather than the squalor and indignity of hanging. General Sato complained: "Aside from the question of whether it was right or wrong to sentence six generals and one premier to death, why were they not sentenced to be shot to death? Even if the tribunal sentenced them to be hanged, MacArthur was empowered to review the sentences . . . MacArthur did not have even a scintilla of the so-called compassion of the warrior."

Brackman described the grim event:

> December 22nd was a cold day and the dead leaves of the paulownia tree blew across the empty courtyard separating the prison block from the death house. From afar, the other prisoners could see the Sugamo Seven shuffle slowly over the frozen earth of the exercise yard for the last time, each handcuffed to a guard. "Without intending to do so," Yoshio Kodama noted in his diary, "I found my eyes turned away from them . . ." The condemned men spent their final day and evening writing farewell letters and in prayer as Hanayama prepared them for their journey. Muto alone admitted that he had "surges of fear" and confided to Hanayama that "the others have them, too."

At 11:30 four of the prisoners—Doihara, Matsui, Tojo and Muto, in that order—each handcuffed to two guards, entered the makeshift chapel, lit candles, burned incense and, almost inaudibly, chanted Buddhist scripture. They shook hands with one another, softly uttered the word sayonara, and accompanied by Hanayama, wended their way across the courtyard to their appointment. Matsui, at seventy the oldest of the quartet, now reconciled to his fate, raised a cry of resignation and defiance: "Banzai! Banzai! Banzai!" The others joined him.

Hanayama left them at the door of the death chamber, which was ablaze with light. Along one wall were two men in dark suits and two generals in uniform—the Australian, American, Chinese and Russian members of the Far Eastern Commission, whom MacArthur had summoned as witnesses. No Japanese was present other than the condemned men. Unlike the authorities at Nuremberg, MacArthur had barred all photographers and even banned official photographs as documentary evidence that the executions had been carried out . . . MacArthur had spared them the ultimate indignity of having their pictures in death splashed across the world's front pages . . .

The only known eyewitness account of the executions is Sebald's memoirs. "They seemed to shuffle as they walked, and each face was a vacant stare as it passed me," he wrote. A single word from the officer of the guard crackled: "Proceed!" The traps were sprung. The executions moved so swiftly from life to death—it took one and a half minutes—that as Hanayama recrossed the courtyard to return to his chapel cell and to administer the last rites to the second group, consisting of Itagaki, Hirota and Kimura, he heard a "loud crash" and involuntarily looked behind him. To Sebald the traps "sounded like a rifle volley."

The fate of those old men aroused only pity and some admiration among ordinary Japanese. It would have been better if they had been summarily shot in 1945, as the British had urged. MacArthur himself had accepted the distasteful necessity for the trial and believed that the preservation of Hirohito's position depended upon it. He spurned Webb, the Australian presiding judge, in his certainty of Hirohito's guilt. Nevertheless the supreme commander was revolted by the proceedings and dismayed by their impact upon Japanese public opinion. Almost certainly, the trial was counterproductive, in securing sympathy and support for the accused while not convincing many Japanese that they had done criminal wrong. Yet those executed and imprisoned had been, with one or two exceptions, guilty men.

PART VII
FALL OF THE SHOGUN

35 : Counter-Attack

TOWARD THE END OF 1947 A NEW WIND BEGAN TO BLOW FROM WASHINGton. When MacArthur first took over Japan, there could be little doubt of the sincerity of his ambition to transform Japanese society. He embarked on a whirlwind of far-reaching reforms with vigor and energy. Within a couple of years, they were beginning to falter as a result of the subtle resistance mounted by the Japanese government, which had most of the direct responsibility for implementing the reforms. A year or two later the chief opponents of the reforms were to be found within the American administration itself.

Because of MacArthur's bravura public relations performance, it did not become fully apparent that by 1950 only a minority of the initial reforms had been enacted, even if these were deep and far-reaching. It is fair to say that America won the war, and Japan won the occupation. Before embarking on a review of the spheres in which the reforms failed, it is necessary to see how over the space of a few years, the attitude of MacArthur's bosses in Washington toward the reforms changed radically, and in a way that was to influence American foreign policy for decades to come.

At the end of the Pacific War, policy toward Japan had been the subject of a major debate in the State Department which in those days, as ever, was deeply divided by territorial responsibilities. The main argument was between the "China crowd," which favored the reemergence of a modern China, many of whom sympathized with the reformist aspirations of Mao Tse-Tung's Communist party, and the "Japan crowd," many of whom had intimate knowledge of the country and favored purging the militarists while reviving the country in its Meiji form as a bulwark against the threat of communism sweeping Asia. The China crowd was in the ascendant in the immediate postwar period, as Dean Acheson's moderate views acquired influence in the State Department, when George Marshall became Secretary of State. China hands like Philip Jessup argued that it would be foolish to support the collapsing war efforts of Chiang Kai-Shek and the Kuomintang against Mao, for fear of driving the Chinese Communists into the hands of the Russians.

In February 1949, however, 50 senators urged the Americans to send combat advisers to help Chiang Kai-Shek. The defense department and joint chiefs of staff joined the debate, urging support for the Nationalists to prevent the Soviet Union expanding its influence through the Chinese Communist party. MacArthur also took part, suggesting that if Taiwan were lost so too would be the whole American defense position in the Far East. "America would have to move its defensive line back to the western coast of the continental United States"; yet, characteristically, the rhetoric also contained a muted message: MacArthur did not urge military assistance for the Nationalists.

Acheson was to defy this pressure, his subordinates urging a policy of quite extraordinary moderation against the gut anti-communism of the Japan crowd and their allies in the armed forces. The China crowd argued that a Communist victory there was inevitable, but that it would take years for Mao to consolidate his hold on the country. Ultimately, if American policy toward China were accommodating, the full force of Chinese nationalism "could be turned against the Russians. There is no point in doing anything for Chiang" whose forces were now "only slightly less important than Yugoslav royalists." This was hotly contested by the "Japan crowd."

The process of splitting the Chinese Communists away from Russia was to take some 15 years, but it was indeed to occur. The Sino-Soviet split began as early as 1960, while exactly a quarter of a century later President Nixon and his Secretary of State, Henry Kissinger, inaugurated a new policy of American alliance with China against Russia. The attitude of the China crowd toward imperial Japan was one of outright hostility: believing China to be moving toward revolutionary reform, they saw no reason why the oligarchs of Japan should be preserved under American occupation. While this group was dominant in Washington, MacArthur's reformists, under the driving hand of Courtney Whitney, were in the ascendant.

The pressure for a radical change in Washington had been mounting long before the civil war in China came to its denoument. Indeed, Acheson's moderation in its closing stages was to prove to be a final triumph before a wave of anti-communist hysteria engulfed the State Department, dominating it throughout the Cold War. The architect of the new policy toward Japan, as toward the Soviet Union itself, was a brilliant foreign service officer, George Kennan, who from the first was deeply critical not just of his seniors in the State Department, but of MacArthur in Japan. Kennan had served as charge d'affaires in Moscow in 1946, when he wrote a long and eloquent dispatch to the State Department about the danger posed by the Soviet Union—a danger being underrated by the United States but long understood by Churchill and other Western European politicians.

In 1947 he published a brilliant article in the American establishment journal *Foreign Affairs*, under the pseudonym "X," arguing for military, political and economic containment of the Soviet challenge; it argued that the threat could be controlled through peaceful means—in contrast to the belligerent rumblings of hysterical anti-communists at the time; and it urged that America rebuild the power base of its two defeated enemies, Germany and Japan, in an effort to counter the Soviet block. In Europe, Kennan's prescriptions were later adopted as the Marshall Plan.

Kennan was no crude anti-communist: in many respects he agreed with the hands-off approach toward China urged by Acheson's followers; he suggested that America should adopt a low profile there and "sweat it out." He did not believe the Nationalists could succeed, even though he doubted the Chinese Communists would be able to restrain the ideological fervor of their movement or to prevent a degree of dependence upon Moscow. But he did argue that Japan and Germany were essential to the containment of communism. Both should be strengthened "to a point where they could play their part in the Eurasian balance of power and yet to a point not so far advanced as to permit them again to threaten the interests of the maritime world of the West." Kennan's arguments were to form the cornerstone of America's subsequent Cold War foreign policy; they seemed to convince even Acheson, who in May 1947 argued that America had a duty to rescue the two "great workshops of the world—Germany and Japan."

But the Kennan thesis also legitimized a crude world view which was to come to the fore both in Washington—where it reached its ugliest expression in McCarthyism—and in Japan. An alliance of powerful economic forces, the Japan crowd, and of military interests, viewed the country as potentially America's best ally in Asia and as a "jumping-off point" for American military resistance to the Soviet Union. Ex-President Herbert Hoover, its archetypal exponent and an influential voice still, argued that in Asia Japan provided "the real ideological dam against the march of communism."

In May 1946, after a visit to Tokyo, Hoover issued a furious attack on SCAP policies, while carefully absolving his old friend, MacArthur, from blame. In January 1947, *Newsweek* magazine launched a campaign of bitter opposition to reform in Japan, accusing SCAP of playing into Russia's hands; it quoted a Japanese businessman as asking why, "when America could have all Japan working in its own interests, it is now engaged in weakening the country so as to leave it as an eventual prize for the Russians?" Although as a hero of the American right MacArthur was protected from these attacks, he angrily rebutted the *Newsweek* allegations, taking up the cudgels on behalf of his reformist subordinates. But the general was also coming under some modest initial fire himself.

In September 1947, the Policy Planning Staff in Washington issued a top secret 37-page document which called for a radical revision of policy toward Japan. It summarized its contents as follows:

> A major shift in U.S. policy toward Japan is being talked about under cover. Idea of eliminating Japan as a military power for all time is changing. Now, because of Russia's conduct, tendency is to develop Hirohito's islands as a buffer state. The peace treaty now being drafted would have to allow for this changed attitude.

One official from the office of the Assistant Secretary of State for Occupied Areas wrote in horrified rebuttal that the new approach resembled "the reinstatement of Schacht, the directors of Farben and the Ruhr on the grounds that compared with the SS or the Communists they were the strongest force in Germany for stability and moderation." The occupation had sought to promote democracy and modest economic reform, while also trying to contain Soviet expansionism. Yet to seek "the latter by abandoning the former" was "to argue that democracy must be abandoned in order to be defended." Alas, this simplistic switch toward the belief that any opponent of communism, however repugnant, was a natural ally of the United States was to plague American foreign policy for the next 30 years.

Kennan now took off his gloves toward MacArthur, whom he accused of encouraging "Communist penetration of Japan." He argued in October 1947 that, owing to wartime destruction and "the loss of its markets and raw material resources in Soviet-dominated portions of the mainland, with highly unstable conditions prevailing in China, in Indonesia and Indochina, and in India, and with no certainty as to the resumption of certain traditional exports to the dollar area, Japan faces, even in the best of circumstances, an economic problem of extremely serious dimensions."

MacArthur's reformers, aware of the danger that their program would be scrapped by Washington, began arguing frantically for an immediate peace treaty to permit America's withdrawal from Japan before the reforms were put into reverse. Kennan argued fervently, on the contrary, that if the country were turned "back to the Japanese" prematurely, there would be economic disaster, inflation, "near anarchy, which would be precisely what the Communists want." The following month the Secretary of State, George Marshall, added his imprimatur to Kennan's views. The survival of the non-Communist world, he declared, depended on rebuilding "the two nations we have just destroyed."

MacArthur's enemies had first begun to coalesce in Washington in 1947. The initial shot fired was by Harry Kern, *Newsweek*'s foreign editor, who had been pro-Japanese throughout the 1930s and blamed Chiang Kai-Shek, absurdly, for manoeuvering Roosevelt into forcing Pearl Harbor upon the Japanese. Kern was a small-minded right-winger who believed that MacArthur's reforms would hand Japan over to the Communists. In January 1947, *Newsweek* launched its campaign, criticizing the economic purge which drove some 30,000 "active, efficient, cultured and cosmopolitan" managers from office and would destroy the basis of "the entire Japanese economic structure." This would play into the hands of the Russians: "We Americans could have all Japan working in our interest" but instead were now "engaged in wrecking the country so as to leave it as an eventual prize for the Russians."

Kern's principal ally was a New York lawyer, James Kauffman, who at the start of 1947 was commissioned by the American business community in Tokyo to write a report which was bitterly opposed to MacArthur. Kauffman obtained a copy of FEC 230, which contained MacArthur's anti-*zaibatsu* reforms, and bitterly attacked these as "socialist and unAmerican." The country was in deep trouble "much to the delight of senior Russians who are attached to the Soviet Embassy in Tokyo." In similarly crude terms, Kauffman wrote: "The high command in Japan has failed to take advantage of the services of experienced businessmen which have been offered. It has accepted the advice of mediocre people and listened to the siren song of a lot of crackpots . . . not only financial institutions, but all business is to come under the knife of the economic quack." A copy of the report was leaked to *Newsweek*, which indulged in similar polemics.

The third of MacArthur's principal enemies was the Under-Secretary for War, General William Draper, whom Kern tried to promote as an alternative supreme commander to MacArthur. Draper sent a copy of the still classified anti-*zaibatsu* report to Senator William Knowland, who denounced it in the Senate. He also circulated a memorandum apparently originating within SCAP attacking MacArthur as vain and stupid and interested in Japan only as a stepping-stone to the presidency of the United States.

MacArthur's reply was vigorous and intelligent: for him the *zaibatsu* were the bitter opponents of free enterprise. The real conflict in Japan, he said, lay "between a system of free competitive enterprise . . . and social-ists of one kind or another." The monopolists were a form of "socialism in private hands." Thus he cunningly and accurately stuck the collectivist label on the big business interests being promoted by Kern.

Draper, as army under-secretary, persuaded his boss, Kenneth Royall, to deliver the celebrated speech in San Francisco on January 6, 1948, arguing that the reforms should be put into reverse and that the assault on business there should be brought to an end. He said that "the men who were the most active in building up and running Japan's war machine—militarily and indus-trially—were often the ablest and most successful business leaders of that country, and their services would in many instances contribute to the econom-ic recovery of Japan." This was equivalent to suggesting that the Nazis and the Wehrmacht were the men best suited to rebuilding Germany after the war.

America's interest, Royall argued, was to build a Japan "strong and stable enough to support itself and at the same time . . . serve as a deter-rent against any other totalitarian war threat which might hereafter arise in the Far East." The army had quite clearly decided that American policy towards Japan must be reversed in the interests of the struggle against com-munism. It must be assumed that President Truman had some advance knowledge of so keynote a speech.

MacArthur, however, firmly defended his position:

> Traditionally [a people] exploited into virtual slavery by an oligarchic system of economic feudalism under which a few . . . families directly or indirectly have controlled all of the commerce and industry and raw mate-rials of Japan, the Japanese are rapidly freeing themselves of these struc-tures to clear the road for the establishment of here or a more competitive enterprise—to release the long suppressed energies of the people towards the building of that higher productivity of a society which is free.

"Amazing strides," said MacArthur, had been made toward industrial rehabilitation and recovery. By 1948, however, a prominent member of the State Department, W. W. Butterworth, had joined the army's opposition to SCAP reform: he argued that Japan would have to recover "through the normal operation of merchant greed, not idealist reforms." In February, MacArthur reacted to the combined assault on him by the army, the State Department, a large part of the American media and the senate by attacking "the traditional economic pyramid" and suggesting that unless the *zaibatsu* were reformed, "there is not the slightest doubt that their clearing away will eventually occur through a bloodbath of revolutionary violence."

The law on deconcentration was pushed through the Diet: some 300 companies, controlling over half of Japan's commerce and industry, were scheduled for possible dissolution. MacArthur's enemies reacted furiously: George Kennan, who had joined their number, visited Japan and issued a 42-page commentary attacking SCAP as a parasite gorging on Japan which took up a third of the country's budget; Kennan argued against radical reform. Draper and Percy Johnson, Chairman of the Chemical Bank, led a delegation to Japan in March which argued passionately that Japan must be made economically "self-supporting as soon as possible" and that the reforms, the anti-*zaibatsu* law and the purge must be ended.

MacArthur was defiant and firm: he told Sir Alvary Gascoigne, the head of the British mission, that "America's tycoons" such as Royall and Draper, opposed the anti-*zaibatsu* law because they thought it would hinder their own business interests. MacArthur insisted that he would not obey orders from "a mere under-secretary." But the supreme commander's position was already being undermined from within, not through his own fault: Japan's economy was a shambles; and union militancy was growing to a level at which it could be portrayed as a serious Communist threat.

MacArthur had hardly been slow to respond to the problem of the unions. As far back as spring 1946, "production control"—the seizure of factories and mines by workers who formed cooperatives to manage them—was under way. In April and May of that year, large demonstrations had taken place, with workers demanding bigger fuel rations, wage increases and the resignation of the government. On May 19, a huge crowd outside the prime minister's residence and in front of the imperial palace alarmed the authorities. MacArthur issued one of the toughest proclamations of his period of office, a warning against mob disorder or violence by "undisciplined elements," that threatened order in postwar Japan. The Japanese government must act, he warned, or SCAP would. The government accordingly took measures against the far left. Later MacArthur denounced "strikes, walkouts or other work stoppages which are inimical to the objectives of the occupation." Union leaders were threatened with arrest.

MacArthur was exceeding his brief: the principal targets of the occupation were supposed to be Japanese militarists, not union members; and most of the strikes in Japan were peaceful. Moreover MacArthur's declaration had clearly violated the new right to strike. On January 1, 1947, he banned a one-day general strike as a "deadly socialist weapon." SCAP then collaborated with the government in passing laws to ban strikes by public sector workers, to abolish collective bargaining in the public sector, and to control labor militancy in the private sector. Labor activists were purged from industry. The action of the authorities suggested a move back toward the repression of the 1920s and 1930s. Yet MacArthur's conservatism in this field was not enough to satisfy his right-wing opponents in America.

His authority began decisively to falter only in the spring and summer of 1948, when he rashly allowed his name to go forward to the Republican nomination for president. He had a flimsy campaign organization and on the eve of the Wisconsin primary came under attack from a rising star, Senator Joe McCarthy, as an old man hopelessly out of touch with American politics. At the Republican convention, MacArthur won just seven votes on the first ballot. The general's many enemies were jubilant and for the first time MacArthur's fighting spirit seemed to ebb. MacArthur remained personally popular as a hero in America but was seen as a political lightweight by the professionals.

A Deconcentration Review Board was set up by Draper, with the backing of the army and the State Department. In May the board went through more than 300 companies targeted by the occupation. Virtually every one was exempted from the anti-trust legislation. Edward Welsch, helplessly in charge of the Anti-Trust and Cartels division of SCAP, concluded bitterly that

> [w]hat was initially considered . . . a major objective of the occupation (had) become . . . a major embarrassment . . . Without formally questioning the desirability or broad purposes of the policy, it was decided to take measures which would minimize the actions prepared for carrying out the policy. The facts of the last war faded . . . and conjectures on the next war took their place.

At the same time it seems clear that MacArthur was close to some kind of emotional breakdown as his plans were emasculated and his power savagely reined back. He fervently tried to prove his anti-Communist credentials by beginning what was described by a British embassy observer as an "almost hysterical . . . witch-hunt" in Japan. The press became shrilly anti-Communist and anti-labor.

General Willoughby was the driving force behind the campaign, through his counterintelligence corps. CIC argued that the strikers were being idealistically motivated: the truth was that Japan's precarious economic condition, as well as rising prices and food shortages, had led to a growing number of strikes and demonstrations. But MacArthur's response was decisive: public sector workers were finally stripped of their right to strike and bargain collectively with the threat of "anarchy, insurrection and destruction" being cited by the authorities. When the Japanese government implemented these measures, there were walkouts throughout the country. SCAP instructed the government to arrest the strikers, trade union activists and Communists. Even the British, usually America's allies in the Far East Commission, were appalled by this resort to frankly dictatorial powers.

When Sir Alvary Gascoigne, head of the British mission and regarded as a close friend by MacArthur, protested to the supreme commander, he "shouted at me without stopping for one-and-three-quarter hours." MacArthur accused the British of taking sides "with the Kremlin" and of "betraying" America. Britain was helping the Russians to "corrupt labor and cause disruption and chaos." Sir Alvary described the meeting as his "most painful duty in Japan." MacArthur's biographer, Clay Blair, believed MacArthur was undergoing a personal crisis under the impact of his loss of real power:

> What was happening to MacArthur? The available evidence seems to indicate not only extreme paranoia, but (a frequently related symptom) illusions of grandeur. He had stripped the Emperor of his divinity, but now MacArthur, replacing the Emperor as absolute rule of Japan, appeared to be assuming a god-like posture himself. He was aloof, withdrawn, monastic. Other than Whitney, few men saw him. He refused to hold press conferences. American or foreign reporters which criticized a SCAP policy were harassed or evicted from Japan.
>
> The press was absolutely forbidden to publish anything other than favorable stories on SCAP. When he or SCAP were criticized in United States newspapers, he (or Whitney) would draft and send verbose and baroque replies—even to the smallest and least significant journals—often unwisely adding fuel on a fire that would have died of its own accord. The staff treated

MacArthur with awed reverence. To visiting journalists (John Gunther, for one) MacArthur was "the greatest man alive" or "too enormous, too unpredictable," "the greatest general in history," "the greatest man since Christ." MacArthur himself would say that, "My major advisers have now boiled down to two men—George Washington and Abraham Lincoln."

At about the same time—mid-1948—SCAP shifted the focus for its purges from right to left: some 10,000 suspected Communists were removed from the public sector, the media and the educational system; around the same number were purged from positions in industry.

The coup de grace was administered in October 1948, when the National Security Council issued directive NSC 13/2, ordering MacArthur to press no more reforms upon the Japanese government, and to relax existing measures which pressed upon its economy. The reform of Japan was now a thing of the past: the country was to be treated as a major ally. One of MacArthur's aides complained bitterly, "Seldom can a defeated nation have had such an important role allocated to it so soon after its defeat." After just three years the attempt to transform the authoritarian, hierarchical basis of Japanese society into something resembling a modern democracy had been officially halted. As we have seen, the dropping of the bombs, the decision to reform Japan through its existing institutions, and the return of the Emperor-system had placed huge handicaps on the reform effort from the outset.

Many blamed MacArthur for the failure. Yet it should be underlined that he had thrown himself with energy and vigor into the reform process, in spite of the constraints, and had vigorously tried to fight the opponents of reform back home.

In June 1950, as tensions over Korea mounted, MacArthur purged the whole central committee of the Japan Communist Party, as well as the editorial staff of Akahata (Red Flag), the party newspaper, which was banned shortly afterwards. The U.S. chamber of commerce distributed pamphlets entitled "How to Spot a Communist" and "Communism, a World Threat." In alliance with Willoughby's anti-communist crusade was the Special Investigation Bureau, staffed largely by former members of the Thought Police, which expanded from 150 members in 1948 to 1,700 under Mitsusada Yoshikawa.

The Japanese government had already decided "informally" to maintain a "police force" of 25,000 men and to set up a gendarmerie as big. Hitoshi Ashida, a leading politician who was chairman of the constitutional amendments committee of the House of Representatives, argued at the time that "para-military" forces were needed to protect Japan from left-wing subversion and civil unrest. By 1948 the American Defense Secretary, James Forrestal, had ordered the Department of the Army to commence limited rearmament in Japan.

General William Draper, a leading member of Forrestal's team and a staunch anti-Communist who had also pressed for enlisting Germany in the anti-Communist struggle, claimed in March, 1948, that there was a "general trend in recent department thinking towards the early establishment of a small defensive force for Japan, to be ready at such times as the American occupation forces leave the country." MacArthur's former Pacific War aide, General Eichelberger, argued that "dollar for dollar, there is no cheaper fighting man in the world than the Japanese. He is already a veteran. His food is simple."

That summer, the authorities decided in principle to set up a force of 150,000 troops to engage Russia in what many American planners saw as an inevitable war on two fronts—Europe and Asia. However, just the act of setting up such an army could provoke the Russians; it was therefore necessary to label this a "national police force." An American military report at the time pointed out that "even though created originally for the maintenance of domestic law and order, an augmented Civilian Police would be vehicle for possible organization of Japanese armed forces at a later date and could initiate manpower registration records."

There is evidence to suggest that both MacArthur and the prime minister, Yoshida, bitterly fought the pressure for rearmament from Washington. MacArthur suggested that the Japanese

> would not be willing to establish an armed force of their own unless we forced them into it. This we should not do . . . Japanese rearmament is contrary to many of the fundamental principles which have guided SCAP ever since the Japanese surrender . . . abandonment of these principles now would dangerously weaken our prestige in Japan and place us in a ridiculous light before the Japanese people.

As late as 1950, MacArthur argued that for Japan to have an army would cause "convulsions" in Australia, New Zealand, Indonesia and the Philippines. Yoshida was an out-and-out opponent of the militarists, though highly conservative politically. Both believed that America could deter the Russians in the Pacific much more effectively from the Pacific islands.

However, with the outbreak of the Korean War, MacArthur's rearguard action against the Pentagon proved no longer tenable. In July 1950, he ordered

Yoshida to set up a "National Police Reserve" of 75,000 men to stand in for the first division of the American Eighth Army sent to Korea. Willoughby proposed that Colonel Hattori be put in charge of the new force, but MacArthur quashed him. The force was created without reference to the Japanese Parliament. It was dressed in American-style uniforms, based in American barracks, and trained by American instructors. Three thousand senior ex-officers were recalled, and most of the men were former veterans. The "police" were equipped with rifles, light machine guns, mortars and light tanks. Willoughby described it as "the army of the future."

In 1951 John Foster Dulles, in charge of negotiating the peace treaty with Japan, pressed for American bases in the country and the setting up of a Japanese army of 350,000 men, as well as an Asia-Pacific Defense Pact. In April 1951, Truman fired MacArthur, and in September the peace treaty granting Japan its independence was signed: it recognized Japan's "right of individual or collective self-defense." provided for the country to enter into collective security arrangements with its Asian neighbors, offered Japan American protection in the event of attack, and gave America the right to station forces in Japan indefinitely.

Yoshida insisted that as the American umbrella would not last forever, "we must undertake to build up a safe defensive power of our own gradually." In August 1952, the National Supply Agency was set up to plan for Japan's defenses under a "civilian" head with a decidedly dubious pedigree: Tokutaro Kimura, a former member of many right-wing secret societies, who had been purged by MacArthur and only two years before sought to set up a "Patriotic Anti-Communist Drawn Sword Militia." Two months later the National Police Reserve was expanded to 110,000 men and merged with Japan's burgeoning naval force into the National Security Force. The "police force" now disposed of medium tanks and heavy artillery.

In November 1953, the visiting American Vice President, Richard Nixon, made his "honest mistake" speech in which the wholly new direction of Japanese rearmament was exposed: "We believe now as we believed then in the principle of disarmament. We believe in peace . . . But on the other hand we recognize that disarmament under present world conditions by the free nations would inevitably lead to war and, therefore, it is because we want peace and we believe in peace that we ourselves have rearmed since 1946, and that we believe that Japan and other free nations must assume their share of the responsibility of rearming since 1946 . . . It must be admitted that the primary responsibility for Japan's defense must rest upon Japan and the Japanese people."

Nixon was pushing at an open door, albeit one that the Japanese government was hoping to give the impression it was unlocking reluctantly, partly to assuage domestic public opinion, which was distinctly uneasy at Japan's decision to rearm. In March 1954, the Mutual Defense Association Agreement was signed between America and Japan. The same year, the Diet passed the law officially establishing Japan's new armed forces. The Self-Defense Agency Law created the Japanese Self-Defense Agency, which was a ministry of defense under another name. The Self-Defense Forces Law set up permanent armed forces, which already existed in embryonic form. The army alone was to be 130,000 strong, although three conditions remained: that it would be a professional army, with no conscripts; that it would not be sent overseas; and that it would be under civilian direction.

The navy, like the army, had been assiduously preparing for its reentry on the national stage. Admiral Kichiburo Nomura was the man who held the flame aloft in the dark days following Japan's surrender: he had been the celebrated ambassador to the United States who delivered Japan's declaration of hostilities too late after Pearl Harbor, and the butt of American fury at the time. Barely a year after the Japanese surrender, Nomura drew up proposals for a Japanese "coastguard force" to cope with a severe outbreak of piracy along the coast from China, Russia and Korea.

MacArthur responded at once, and by March 1948 a 10,000-man Marine Safety Board was set up, later to become the Maritime Safety Agency. Two years later Japanese mine-sweepers helped the Americans to clear a path for a landing north of Wonsan in Korea—the only time Japanese armed forces had been used for any purpose abroad after the Pacific War. In October 1951, the Americans offered the Japanese 18 frigates and 50 landing craft as the nucleus for a new Japanese navy.

In 1952 the restrictions on the construction of war materials were relaxed and the industry was going full throttle by 1953. In January of the following year the Air Self-Defense Force came into being and pilots were permitted to train again. The turnaround in America's initial solemn commitment never to allow Japan to rearm was virtually a 180-degree one: the three services had been brought back into being, largely staffed by the officers and men of the old imperial armed forces.

In four significant ways, however, the position of the armed forces was now very different to that before the Pacific War: First, they had been demoted to be the junior of the three main partners in government (the bureaucracy, the economic giants and the armed forces). Second, they remained objects of intense suspicion among ordinary Japanese. For decades after the Pacific

War, it was a sign of relatively low social status to belong to the armed forces; to that extent pacifists had made much of the running among post-war Japanese. Third, the constitutional prohibition against waging aggressive war did commit the armed forces to be scrupulous about avoiding overseas entanglements. Fourth, defense spending in Japan, while far from small, remained a relatively low priority by comparison with that of other major industrial nations.

Thus, while MacArthur's attempts to neutralize Japan, turning it into the "Switzerland of Asia," as he called it, had foundered just three years after his departure from Tokyo, his efforts were not entirely in vain: Japan, while far from disarmed, was a hesitant military power for decades to come. MacArthur's wholesale opposition to Japanese rearmament was genuine, and reflected his background and judgment of the country and the dangers rearmament might pose; he was virtually alone on the American anti-Communist right in holding the view he did. He was overwhelmed by an unstoppable coalition formed by the anti-Communists now dominant in Washington, their followers under his own command, industrial interests and the Japanese establishment. On this issue, he went down fighting, and salvaged some of his original goals.

SCAP's lurch to the right was accompanied by a similar one in Japanese politics that was to define the political complexion of the country over the next 40 years. The emergence of a Communist threat—both the real one in Asia and the mythical one in Japan—as well as the dramatic change of direction in Washington, prompted Japanese conservatism to reassert itself. The Social Democratic party, which had enjoyed a brief spell in power during the occupation, split, and was never to return to power again. The middle-of-the-road Ashida cabinet fell and the Liberal Democrat party was formed from a coalition of the two main right-wing parties, coming to power under its tough-minded leader Shigeru Yoshida.

The mold of Japanese politics was thus set for decades to come. MacArthur was belatedly to claim the credit over the next few months for crushing communism, breaking the power of the unions and splitting the Socialists. In fact he had been largely forced to do so by Washington. Japan had harked back to prewar oligarchy Meiji rule with the virtual collapse of MacArthur's power; from 1948 on, he was largely a figurehead, just as the Emperor had been over the previous two years; the new shogun, always exerting his power discreetly during the occupation, was Yoshida. MacArthur may have convinced himself that the move to the right was really necessary in view of the challenges within Japan. He cannot have believed this: he had fought tenaciously and long for real change in Japan during the period when he was the most powerful man in Japan.

The intense bitterness he felt at the turn of events is reflected in his reminiscences, which make virtually no mention of the way in which his reforms were turned upside down and emasculated; like the idealist he fundamentally was, he boasts of his program of change as though it had actually been fully carried through. MacArthur, who had won so many battles, had been decisively defeated by a large and formidable combination of conservative and military enemies in Washington, by Willoughby's fifth column within the SCAP hierarchy, and finally by the most formidable power of all, even in national defeat—the Japanese ruling class, determined to frustrate any real change in the system of government established by the Meiji oligarchy. The Japanese elite effectively obstructed most, though not quite all, of the significant reforms.

On the most crucial issue—the dissolution of the *zaibatsu*—no visible progress at all had been made by the end of the occupation: the Japanese economic and industrial structure was virtually the same as during the middle of the Pacific War—when the *zaibatsu* were considerably more powerful than they had been during the 1920s. The Japanese economy was still dominated by a handful of massive, furiously competing, yet also cooperating megaeconomic giants. Virtually the whole shape of Japan's economic success, and expansion, was governed by this single fact during the postwar years.

As for the other traditional centers of power in Japan, the bureaucracy had survived virtually intact, and was to re-embark upon a new golden age of oligarchic dominance, while the militarists had been relegated to a much lower place on the ladder of power—but had by no means been eliminated, as had been the intention. A fourth estate had also entered into the power structure: the political class, which while much more significant than before the war, was in no sense truly sovereign. In any democracy, it is true that the elected politicians are usually only the first among equals at a table which also accommodates the bureaucracy and the business class, the trade unions, the armed forces (and the security services) and the press. In Japan the model was fatally skewed, even after MacArthur's frenzied attempts to reform it: the *zaibatsu*, by virtue of their huge concentration of economic power, and the bureaucracy were clearly the primi inter pares, with the political leaders a distant second; the armed forces were now fourth. Neither the unions nor the press counted for anything.

The final verdict on MacArthur must be favorable. He came from a deeply conservative background, the U.S. army. He had fought the Japanese with tenacity and brilliance. Yet in his stewardship he not only resisted the attempt by many of his fellow countrymen to give the Japanese a taste of their own vengeful values, but made the only attempt in the country's history to set up the kind of democratic, popular values that would block the awesome hold of its traditional power structures. For over two years, he fought with remarkable vigor on behalf of the idealists beneath him.

He was crushed by an unholy alliance of the Japanese private sector and bureaucracy, genuine anti-Communists in his own administration, and the military-industrial complex in the United States. His subsequent attempts to suggest that he agreed with these three groups did him no credit, and must have been regretted later. As in Bataan, he lost against overwhelming odds. But, as there, what survived from his struggle was by no means negligible: the relegation of the army to lower status and the tenacious flowering of democracy, in particular.

Another turning point was reached with the arrival early in 1949 of Joseph Dodge, a conservative economist whose "nine commandments" were drawn up to introduce free-market economics into "New Deal" Japan. The budget was balanced. In April 1949 a fixed exchange rate was introduced of 360 yen to the dollar, undervaluing the yen to stimulate exports. The ministry of commerce and the board of trade were merged to create the superministry of Japanese economic growth and control during the 1950s, the Ministry of International Trade and Industry, Miti. The anti-*zaibatsu* laws were relaxed and government powers were increased. Government spending was controlled.

The result was predictable: the economy lurched towards depression as welfare provision was tightened, bankruptcies spread and unemployment rose. The conservative American magazine *U.S. News and World Report* called the policy "economic suicide" and said that Japan was "on the verge of an economic depression." It was saved by the boom in demand for Japanese products as a result of the Korean War, which pumped $2.3 billion into the economy in three years, or as much as had been received in aid during the entire occupation.

36 : HUMANIZING THE EMPEROR

MACARTHUR HAD PROPHETICALLY REMARKED, ON BECOMING SCAP, that if the occupation lasted more than three years it would be undone. To a great extent he was proved right: the last two years had been disastrous for his reforms, which had largely gone into reverse thanks to an unholy alliance of right-wing Japanese and American business interests.

Yet the most remarkable transformation of all occurred in the shogun's relationship with the Emperor. Having arrived as conqueror and magnanimously and patronizingly extended a helping hand to his defeated foe, MacArthur was to see Hirohito's star rise as his own began to wane— although he would not acknowledge this, even to himself. The shuffling little Mikado in the black morning coat was to prove a far shrewder politician than the all-powerful shogun. MacArthur never foresaw this: from the first he sought to absolve Hirohito from war guilt so as to preserve a working government through which he could administer Japan. MacArthur proved all too successful. He backed the weakened postwar Hirohito because he believed he could control him.

The shogun had sought to protect Hirohito from indictment as a war criminal. But his support of the Emperor actually went much further. As has been seen, not just in the imperial household, but throughout Japan, the possibility of Hirohito's abdication in favor of his son was seriously floated for all 1946. Even at the end of the war, the Japanese cabinet had considered the issue, not because they believed Hirohito to be guilty of warmongering, but simply so that he would take responsibility for what had occurred and draw a line under it.

There was good precedent: Emperor Uda, who had reigned in the ninth century, had abdicated; Hirohito's own father had been pushed aside when he became incapable. Prince Higashikuni, the Emperor's uncle and the first prime minister after the defeat, urged the Emperor to abdicate. A number of responsible senior figures also urged that he step down, including the constitutional scholar Soichi Sosaki and a celebrated Buddhist sage, Hajime Tanabe. In June 1946 the poet Miyoshi Tatsuji accused the Emperor not of starting the war, nor of "responsibility for defeat in war" but of being "responsible for betraying the loyal soldiers who had laid down their lives in battle for him."

General Fellers, however, made it clear to these eminent Japanese that this was out of the question. As far as he was concerned, he informed senior Japanese officials:

> It would be most convenient if the Japanese side could prove to us that the Emperor is completely blameless. I think the forthcoming trials offer the best opportunity to do that. Tojo, in particular, should be made to bear all responsibility at his trial. In other words, I want you to have Tojo say as follows: "At the Imperial Conference prior to the start of the war, I had already decided to push for war even if His Majesty the Emperor was against going to war with the United States."

Brigadier Elliott Thorpe, MacArthur's intelligence adviser, explained the thinking behind this decision:

> [O]therwise we would have had nothing but chaos. The religion was gone, the government was gone, and he was the only symbol of control. Now, I know he had his hand in the cookie jar, and he wasn't any innocent little child. But he was of great use to us, and that was the basis on which I recommended to the Old Man [MacArthur] that we keep him.

The problem surfaced again in 1948 as the Tokyo trial came to an end: many Japanese now argued that abdication would not result in Hirohito being brought to trial, but that he should be made to suffer some retribution when some of his most faithful ministers were being executed. Fellers, who by now had retired, considered this a disastrous idea. Abdication

> would be a victory for all Communists and especially the Russians who hold it is naïve to claim that Japan can be democratized so long as the Emperor remains on the throne. [It] would be a blow to the MacArthur occupation as the General's success has made the very best use of the Emperor's prestige and personal leadership.
>
> . . . His abdication, especially if it coincided with the announcement of war crimes punishments, would, in the eyes of the world, identify the Sire as one of the military clique. This of course is absolutely untrue. It would reverse public opinion in this country [the United States] which is beginning to turn to the impression that the Emperor was not responsible for the war. Abdication would fix the Sire's place in history as one who sympathized with the war criminals and, as a gesture of his sympathy for them, gave up his throne . . .

Today Japan is absorbing the terrific impact of Western civilization. She needs, in fact Japan must have, the stabilizing influence which only the Sire can give. He is part and parcel of the new Japan which is surely emerging. He must help Japan's re-entry into the family of nations.

At the end of the occupation itself, Marquis Kido, Hirohito's former chief adviser, himself urged the Emperor to abdicate "in compliance with the truth." Otherwise "the imperial family alone would have failed to take responsibility." Kido's intervention was hugely significant: he had attended all the wartime imperial meetings and there was no doubt in his mind, at least, of the proactive role of the Emperor in the prosecution of the war. But Hirohito refused, and even declined to make a formal apology when he formally resumed sovereignty after MacArthur's departure.

By abdicating, Hirohito would have performed a selfless act and formally accepted all responsibility for the events leading up to the war. Of course he would not have performed the supreme sacrifice of those executed as war criminals. Yet his penance would have been of the same order, by imperial standards. Truly then Japan would have been purged of its war guilt. Even if abdication was not on the cards, there were many who believed he should formally have issued a rescript accepting responsibility for the war.

The debate emerged in public when in May 1948 the chief justice of the supreme court, Shigeru Mibuchi, said: "If at the end of the war the Emperor had of his own accord issued a rescript accepting responsibility, it would have moved the Japanese people very deeply." Hirohito defended his decision not to abdicate to a palace official: "I am like a canary whose cage has been opened and someone says, 'Fly away!' Where should I fly to? If I have a song to sing, why should I waste it on places where the wind may blow it away?"

A month later the president of Tokyo University, Shigeru Nanbara, was more outspoken still:

I believe the Emperor ought to abdicate. And I am not the only one; this is an opinion shared by educators throughout Japan, from elementary school teachers to university professors. The only thing is, he needs to consider the repercussions this would have among the Japanese people, and should time his announcement carefully. His abdication should be carried out without any pressure from politicians or citizens. It should be a spontaneous act that comes from within himself.

Even as loyal a supporter of Hirohito as Kawahara concludes:

> That Hirohito escaped trial at the Far Eastern War Crimes Tribunal
> was solely because it was politically expedient for America and the
> Occupation forces. But this by no means absolves him. As noted earlier,
> there is a feeling that if he had apologized and taken public responsibility
> just after the war, the matter would be behind Japan . . . I suspect that
> when all is said and done, historians will have this to say about Emperor
> Hirohito: he may have been of pure and noble character, but for some rea-
> son he never found it in himself to accept responsibility for the war.

The continuation of Hirohito in office graphically underlined Japan's
refusal to accept responsibility for the war, echoing the surrender broadcast
and foreshadowing every subsequent refusal to apologize. Hirohito's decision
not to go was no mere act of omission but a positive assertion that Japan felt
it had done no fundamental wrong. Given the readiness of the Japanese themselves to accept Hirohito's abdication after a decent interval, and the historical precedents, MacArthur's dire warnings about the dangers of insurrection
and communism can be dismissed as hyperbole. The right could argue that the
war had changed nothing: the continuity of Hirohito's rule had been maintained, and indeed had prevailed against the country's military occupiers.

If the Emperor had accepted responsibility not just in the privacy of
MacArthur's office—which he did—but publicly and renounced his throne,
the Japanese people would have been given an incontrovertible demonstration of the fact that the country had been wrong to initiate the Pacific War.
Instead, just as in the surrender broadcast, he did not admit public guilt
and neither, therefore, did Japan. Once again, Hirohito, for all his private
common sense, had failed his people. For the American occupiers, it was
remarkable that the man in nominal charge of the war effort should have
been allowed to stay, breaking precedent not just with the fall of the Kaiser
and the Austro-Hungarian Emperor after the First World War, as well as
that of Hitler and Mussolini in the Second, but of the treatment of defeated
enemies virtually throughout history.

Hirohito's survival in office had another, equally profound, more subtle impact. It suggested to many in the Japanese hierarchy that although the
form of government had changed, its substance, the hierarchical pyramid
of power, had not. It was all very well for a foreign-dictated constitution to
assert that Hirohito's authority derived from the will of the people. But
Japan's vast panoply of authoritarianism and deference had traditionally

depended very little on the written word—and one imposed by outsiders at that. If the majority continued to believe in the Emperor's status as the pinnacle of authority in Japan, then the situation was much as before.

The Emperor's power had always been symbolic, justifying the awesome cataract of subjugation of the system beneath him. He was now more powerless still, but if the symbol stayed, so did the system. Of course, government could now be removed by election; but Japan's democracy was quietly modified to ensure that the same conservative forces remained permanently in office. Hirohito had been largely a figurehead before the war, although possessed of some reserve powers he proved deeply reluctant to use. After the war he was formally deemed a figurehead, and stripped of those powers. But behind the scenes it is hard to believe that he did not act much as before: exercising his influence through his advisers, and occasionally venturing a private opinion which would certainly carry great authority. However, his government and advisers would now have been extremely careful not to divulge the existence of such views and opinions.

Why did MacArthur so doggedly support the Emperor against the calls for his abdication? He could not argue that the imperial institution would be threatened and with it the cohesion of Japan: a boy-Emperor and a prince regent would preserve the tradition, as had happened in the 1920s. The answer must be that MacArthur believed that by keeping Hirohito, who was now discredited and questioned by his own countrymen, he would have a freer hand to do as he chose during the occupation.

The Emperor was determined to frustrate this. Grateful as he was for being allowed to survive in office, he decided to start creating his own constituency of popular support by touring the country. The remote god-figure now sought to create a popular movement in his favor to match that of the Meiji Emperor, who had similarly crisscrossed the land in 1872. The purpose was twofold: to dispel lingering public hostility to him as a result of the war; and to begin to emerge as an independent public figure in his own right from under MacArthur's shadow. It was a superb piece of politics and public relations, at first bitterly opposed by court officials but enthusiastically supported by MacArthur, who did not realize the full implications. The Emperor was effectively running for office, as leader of the Japanese resistance to the occupation. It was an extraordinary inversion: while MacArthur was behaving like a remote oriental potentate, Hirohito was running like an American politician for office.

With the concept of lèse-majesté abandoned, the Emperor came under fierce personal attack from left-wing opponents, as well as caustic derision from foreign journalists: this was to work almost wholly in his favor. One Communist candidate for the Diet orated gratingly that "MacArthur is the naval. Why? Because it is situated above the penis [the Japanese word for this closely resembles the royal 'we']."

Mark Gayn, the correspondent of the *Chicago Sun*, described Hirohito as a "pathetic little man, compelled to do a distasteful job, trying desperately to control his disobedient voice and face and body." The Emperor, he said, was "about five feet two, in a badly cut, grey striped suit, with trousers a couple of inches too short. He has a pronounced facial tic, and his right shoulder twitches constantly. When he walks, he throws his right leg a little sideways, as if he has no control over it. He was obviously excited and ill at ease, and uncertain what to do with his arms and hands." This was to miss the point, however. For the great mass of ordinary Japanese, it was enough that the Emperor had descended from the clouds and sought their approval. In the desperate times after the war, his shabby appearance and humility exactly matched the mood of the day and reflected the suffering of the people.

His household was reduced from 8,000 to 1,000, after General Whitney told the Emperor's staff "we've no room for royal parasites here." One imperial official's wife described the plight of these rejected courtiers. "Everyone lived on the black market. One sold what precious possessions one still possessed, article by article, in exchange for food. We called it onion-skin living. An appropriate description. Each layer of your belongings you peeled off and sold made you weep." The Emperor's advisers propagated the image of an ascetic emperor—which was nothing less than the truth. He had cut down to five cigarettes and a single meal of rice a day. His daughters were pictured washing dishes

Hirohito and his advisers recognized that the Emperor must now be exposed to the people, in a series of walkabouts around the towns and factories of the country. For a man in his mid-40s who had never had any contact with common people, his decision was not without courage, and must have been painful at first. He still shrank from physical contact with his subjects, preferring to bow; and his conversation was appallingly stilted, making him the object of countless jibes: "Ah so," his standard reply, meaning "really," became his trademark. Huge crowds turned out to see him: at Kawasaki, Osaka and Nagoya, people thronged as though he were an American presidential candidate, treading on his toes, clawing at his clothes. Hirohito and his entourage frequently camped in government offices, classrooms and railway carriages. He was to all intents and purposes running for reelection.

Hirohito's discovery of the most banal aspects of everyday life was to make his itinerant conversation unintentionally funny. As he surveyed the ruins of Hiroshima, he observed, "[T]here seems to have been considerable damage here." However, his remark on the condition of the peasantry became a classic of royal insensitivity and pathos:

> Peasants in their own way lead happy lives. One cannot say that members of the aristocracy are always happy. I enjoyed freedom when I was on a tour of Europe. The only time when I feel happy is when I am able to experience a similar feeling of freedom . . . so peasants should think about the pleasantness of nature out there for them to enjoy and not merely dwell on the uncomfortable aspects of their lives.

The tours began in February 1946. He went to every part of mainland Japan. He attracted derision from American journalists, who entirely missed the point of his campaign, but adulation from ordinary people, who were witnessing the one-off passage of a god, his very simplicity and clumsiness a sign of his otherworldliness. The *Nippon Times* wrote adoringly:

> The Emperor's present attempt at humanizing himself fortunately has not been marred by any mishaps . . . it isn't everybody who can take a fan between his toes and fan himself. Not only can Emperor Hirohito perform this stunt but he is able to do so while swimming. He can also swim in the rain holding an open umbrella in one hand.

Those who laughed at the Emperor's lack of sophistication merely exposed their own. Kawahara, his Japanese biographer, describes the impact of the procession:

> The Emperor they were seeing now, warm of countenance and unaffected in attitude, contrasted sharply with the solemn monarch in military uniform they had seen before. People could hardly believe it. In Osaka, Nagoya, and other cities on his itinerary, crowds of thousands got out of hand and pressed forward to see Hirohito, trapping him in a sea of humanity. Anxious police could only look on in trepidation as he had his feet trampled on, and his buttons torn off. On one such day he said to his chamberlain when they got back to their lodgings for the evening, "The people were really wild again today, weren't they?" His face broke into a smile.

The term "lodgings" is somewhat grand to describe where Hirohito really had to stay. Since virtually no part of Japan had been untouched by the war's devastation, he and his entourage bedded down where they could, sometimes in the formal reception room of the local government office, or in a public hall, an elementary-school classroom, or even in a railroad car stopped for the night on a railroad siding. The chamberlain worried about how Hirohito might bathe, but the Emperor himself was unconcerned. "I can go ten days without bathing. It doesn't matter," he insisted.

Even in the palace he was in the habit of bathing only once every two or three days, and always a very quick bath at that. While he was in Shikoku his relatively infrequent bathing made for an amusing incident. A certain innkeeper in the town of Uwajima, honored that the Emperor was planning to stay at his inn, spent a great deal of money refurbishing the baths in his establishment. He waited with anticipation for the imperial visit, but was disappointed when Hirohito arrived and went straight to bed without bathing.

Two of the Emperor's doctors decided to use the bath in his place, thinking it a waste not to use the water that had been heated up for the occasion. But once they got in, they noticed that the water was draining rapidly, and before long they had to get out. It seems that the innkeeper, disappointed that the Emperor was not going to use the bath, pulled the plug when he found two mere court doctors in the water. There was another reason for the innkeeper's anger: after the Emperor finished the bath he was supposed to have taken, the innkeeper had promised local dignitaries that they could then bathe in the same water. And to the innkeeper's dismay, there they were, all lined up in their morning coats, awaiting their turn.

The Emperor's travels through Japan yielded any number of anecdotes. Once, for example, he marveled at the practicality of an inn. "These inns are really designed so that it is easy for people to stay in them." Hirohito was prepared to bear many inconveniences and hardships. Once he visited a coal mine 500 meters underground to thank the miners for their work. To greet people in remote farming and fishing villages, he would tramp along the paths between rice fields, and visit fishermen off-loading their catch.

Since time and again he disingenuously lifted his soft-brimmed hat in salutation, by the end of each day it would lose its shape, and each evening it fell to his young page or chamberlain to straighten it out again.

By the end of 1947, when Hirohito traveled to Osaka, his reception was ecstatic, thousands joining in waving flags, clearly regarding Hirohito as a symbol of national pride during the American occupation—although this sentiment could not be openly expressed. Hirohito's visit to Hiroshima on December 7, 1947—symbolically, six years to the day after Pearl Harbor, a reminder of how much worse the Americans had behaved toward Japan than the latter to America on the Day of Infamy—was the clearest expression of this cheeky, covertly anti-American nationalism: children were waiting

> and standing beside them were a few mothers, their faces scarred with keloids, who held children in more or less serious stages of disfigurement. While the cameras clicked and turned and the crowd pushed in more and more excitedly, the Emperor listened, hat in hand, to a short explanation of what had happened to this group. He murmured a few "Is that so's" and made as though to speak into a microphone that was being held out toward him. Then his lip trembled and with a short bow, he turned back to his car. At this point, the crowd went berserk. Shouting banzais at the top of their voices, the people rushed forward, their eyes shining and all their mask of unemotionalism wiped off their faces. [Imperial] Household officials and police were jostled and trampled on before he got back to his car. None of the crowd touched the Emperor, but many of them seemed happy just to touch the body of his car.
>
> Our party went ahead at the next stop, on to the improvised plaza where the mayor, the city officials and a crowd of 50,000—a quarter of the city's present population—were waiting to welcome him . . . Here again you could see people weeping with emotion . . . The Emperor mounted a rostrum . . . and once again was photographed from every angle. [Pulling a slip of paper from his pocket] he read a short simple speech. . . . At the city hall he climbed up to the roof where the mayor was waiting with a map showing the city as it was, as it is, and as it is planned that it will be . . . A pair of field glasses rested on a purple handkerchief for the Emperor's use, but he did not touch them. For the first time that day he was obviously overcome with nervousness and seemed anxious to get away.

With remarkable political agility, Hirohito had become the focus of opposition of American rule: the shogun was a harsh, unbending, remote ruler of Japan, the Mikado the personification of the ordinary Japanese people. MacArthur, who was in fact giving freedom to the Japanese people, was now regarded as the autocrat; Hirohito, who had never been a democrat in his life, became the popular embodiment of the Japanese people. It was a colossal historical irony: the hereditary Emperor had politically outwitted the meritocratic representative of American democracy. If MacArthur had won round one, Hirohito had decisively won round two.

But it would be a historical mistake to argue, as some do, that MacArthur's shogunate was a failure. On the contrary, it was one of the boldest political experiments ever undertaken by a single man and the fact that it was only three quarters, or even half, successful does not reflect badly on MacArthur and was itself of huge importance. In less than six years he had attempted a peaceful revolution in a country of 80 million people that was essentially locked into a medieval time warp politically and culturally, whatever its industrial and scientific progress during the twentieth century.

He was seeking to overturn 2,000 years of history in a moment. He had reinstated democracy and freedom of the press, both of which Japan had briefly glimpsed during the 1920s; he had attempted to end the Emperor's divine status and reduce him to the position of constitutional monarch. He had introduced a far-reaching land reform which had broken the back of the old feudal families behind the Meiji Restoration and had created a conservative class of peasant smallholders who were the best supporters of the new democracy.

He had staged a major assault on the bulwarks of Japanese economic life, the great monopolies, which dominated the industrial economy and had backed the militarists in their ascent to prewar power. He had attempted to break the back of militarism, dismantle the war machine and destroy their weapons. He had tried to purge the militarists and their sympathizers from positions of power.

All of this was done in the context of a victor's sensitivity probably unparalleled throughout history. While the victims of Japanese aggression cried out for vengeance, he had behaved with restraint, mercy and respect for Japanese traditions and institutions. After the appalling cruelties inflicted by the Japanese upon their subject peoples, the American occupation could have been brutal and vengeful, leaving bitter hatreds among ordinary Japanese. Instead, although there were grossnesses and excesses by Americans in Japan, MacArthur left a legacy of awed respect for himself as shogun. He had come as a conqueror, and acted bravely as a liberator. It was a staggering achievement by any standards: the fact that he was not successful in many areas of his bold reforms and that he was ultimately ambushed by conservative Japanese institutions and by business interests in America should not detract from the greatness of what he attempted. He was perhaps the most merciful and enlightened conqueror in history.

As early as March 1947 MacArthur had met journalists to tell them it was time that the occupation ended.

> The time is now approaching when we must talk peace with Japan. The military purpose [of the occupation] has been, I think, accomplished. The political phase is approaching such completion as is possible under the Occupation . . . The third phase is economic . . . But this is not a phase the Occupation can settle. We can only enforce economic strangulation.

The truth was that he was desperate to get out before his reforms unravelled. MacArthur's free hand in Japan had been brought to an end: faced by an alliance of the State Department, the Defense Department and Truman, MacArthur was now a lame duck. There was even an attempt to have him replaced as supreme commander by Kennan and Dean Acheson, the aristocratic, crusty Secretary of State who detested MacArthur, by General Maxwell Taylor, but this failed.

As his authority ebbed and the measures introduced by Dodge brought the Japanese economy to a standstill, MacArthur fumed with impatience for a peace treaty to end the occupation before his reforms were undone. He also watched developments in Washington with dismay. He blamed his own country for the collapse in the Chinese Nationalist resistance to Mao Tse-tung's Communists:

> In China, Generalissimo Chiang Kai-shek was gradually pushing the Communists back, being largely aided and supplied by the United States. For some unaccountable reason, the Communists were not looked upon with disfavor by the State Department, who labeled them "agrarian reformers." Instead of pushing on to the victory that was within the Generalissimo's grasp, an armistice was arranged, and General Marshall was sent to amalgamate the two opponents . . .
>
> After months of fruitless negotiation, he withdrew without tangible results, and the war for China resumed. But in this interval of seven months a decisive change had taken place. The Generalissimo had received no ammunitions or supplies from the United States, but the Soviets, working day and night, reinforced the Chinese Communist armies. The great mass of military supplies we had sent them at Vladivostok during the latter stages of the war, none of which had been used, was largely transferred to the Communist force, so that when hostilities were resumed, the balance of power had shifted. They pressed their advantage to the fullest, and finally

drove the Generalissimo's forces out of continental Asia onto Formosa. The decision to withhold previously pledged American support was one of the greatest mistakes ever made in our history. At one fell blow, everything that had been so laboriously built up since the days of John Hay was lost. It was the beginning of the crumbling of our power in continental Asia—the birth of the taunt, "Paper Tiger." Its consequences will be felt for centuries, and its ultimate disastrous effects on the fortunes of the free world are still to be unfolded.

He was not alone in his opinions: a young congressman, John F Kennedy, wrote:

During the postwar period began the great split in the minds of our diplomats over whether to support the Government of Chiang Kai-shek or force Chiang Kai-shek as the price of our assistance to bring Chinese Communists into the government to form a coalition.

Our policy in China has reaped the whirlwind. The continued insistence that it would not be forthcoming unless a coalition government was formed was a body blow to the National Government. So concerned were our diplomats and our advisors . . . with the imperfections of the diplomatic system in China after twenty years of war, and the tales of corruption in higher places, that they lost sight of our tremendous stake in a non-Communist China.

Representative Walter Judd, a right-wing American Asia specialist who had served as a missionary and doctor in China, led the charge of those who alleged that the Truman administration had "lost" China.

I argued that you can't save Europe in the end unless you save Asia too. You have got to contain both ends of the barrel if you want to contain either. The Truman policy in Europe was to help independent and friendly governments, even like the Greek Government . . .

But Truman did the exact opposite in Asia. He tried to appease Communism. He sent [General George C.] Marshall to China to tell the Chinese we wouldn't help them unless they took the Communists into their government . . .

. . . Because Russia assumed that we were going to support our ally, Chiang, after the war as he had faithfully and at great cost supported us and our wishes during the war, Russia signed an agreement with

Nationalist China on, as I recall, August 15, 1945 in Moscow. After all, we'd won, and Chiang was on top in China. It never occurred to them, I think, that we weren't going to stand by Chiang after the war, or that we would walk out on him as we had on Poland and East Germany, now their satellites. So Russia promised in the treaty to give postwar aid only to the Nationalist Government of China.

Obviously from Mao's own speeches the Russians tried to keep him from starting a civil war in China, but he was determined to seize control of China, so he fought and, with our desertion of Chiang, he won. When the Russians saw that we weren't going to support our own ally, China, well, they didn't support it either. They shifted their aid from Chiang to Mao. I can't really blame them for breaking their word to Chiang, after our action, because if we didn't have brains enough to support our own side, we couldn't expect them to support our side. They knew our power, they knew we had just exploded atomic weapons. Clearly they weren't going to challenge the United States. But although we had overwhelming power, we told them we wouldn't use it. And there is no such thing as power if you don't have the will to use it.

Whether or not MacArthur, Kennedy and Judd were right, China was lost. Washington also decided effectively to write off not just Formosa but South Korea as well, where following the Japanese surrender Russia had occupied the country north of the 39th Parallel, and the Americans had struggled to preserve the south. The Russians had installed a stooge, Kim il-Sung. A right-wing dictator, Syngman Ree, took over the south while the Americans steadily withdrew their forces to under divisional strength.

MacArthur realistically informed Washington that America had no chance of defending the south with such a small force, and recommended total withdrawal.

> In the event of any serious threat to the security of Korea, strategic and military considerations will force abandonment of any pretense of military support . . . We must increase the strength of the XXIV Corps decidedly or turn the U.S. interest in the Korean occupation over to the State Department for handling.

By June 1949 all American forces had left, except 500 military advisers. In January 1950 Acheson explicitly stated that South Korea was outside America's line of defense:

that runs along the Aleutians to Japan and then goes to the Ryukyus [chiefly Okinawa]. We hold important defense positions in the Ryukyu Islands, and these we will continue to hold . . . The defense perimeter runs from the Ryukyus to the Philippine Islands . . . So far as the military security of the United States is concerned, it must be clear that no person can guarantee these areas [outside the line] against military attack. Should such an attack occur . . . the initial reliance must be on the people attacked.

MacArthur had said the same thing a year earlier:

Our defensive positions against Asiatic aggression used to be based on the west coast of the American continent. The Pacific was looked upon as the avenue of possible enemy approach. Now . . . our line of defense runs through the chain of islands fringing the coast of Asia. It starts from the Philippines and continues through the Ryukyu Archipelago, which includes its main bastion, Okinawa. Then it bends back through Japan and the Aleutian Island chain to Alaska.

But that had been before the fall of Communist China. With the Nationalist evacuation to Formosa, MacArthur may have changed his mind, although he did not say so publicly. The Americans of course had little interest in the survival of Rhee. Korea's strategic importance was that it was only 90 miles off the coast of Japan. This was as true in 1949 as 1950, and MacArthur should have voiced his concerns then: he may have felt there was no hope of persuading Acheson, and that it was easier to defend Japan on the mainland than over the straits in Korea.

The fall of China deeply disturbed American public opinion: Acheson dispatched a tough old state department lawyer, John Foster Dulles, as his personal representative to scout out the situation for himself. Dulles startled MacArthur by claiming he believed the South Koreans could defend their state, and then by declaring that the United States would defend South Korea if she were attacked. As this was clearly impossible without American troops based on the peninsula, MacArthur thought little more of it. Only a month earlier he had declared, "I do not believe a shooting war is imminent."

37 : KOREA

A FEW DAYS AFTER DULLES'S VISIT, ON SUNDAY, JUNE 25, THE TELEPHONE rang in MacArthur's bedroom. He took up the story:

> It rang with the note of urgency that can sound only in the hush of a darkened room. It was the duty officer at headquarters. "General," he said, "we have just received a dispatch from Seoul, advising that the North Koreans have struck in great strength south across the 38th Parallel at four o'clock this morning." Thousands of Red Korean troops had poured over the border, overwhelming the South Korean advance posts, and were moving southward with a speed and power that was sweeping aside all opposition.
>
> I had an uncanny feeling of nightmare. It had been nine years before, on a Sunday morning, at the same hour, that a telephone call with the same note of urgency had awakened me in the penthouse atop the Manila Hotel. It was the same fell note of the war cry that was again ringing in my ears. It couldn't be, I told myself. Not again! I must still be asleep and dreaming. Not again! And then came the crisp, cool voice of my fine chief of staff, General Ned Almond, "Any orders, General?"

By June 27 the tanks of the 150,000 strong North Korean army were outside Seoul. MacArthur desperately reported to Washington "complete collapse is imminent" and proposed to evacuate American nationals. He was in for a real surprise: Truman had decided to fight: MacArthur, as commander in chief of the Far East, was ordered to send American air and naval units to Korea, while a 13-nation force was put together under authority from the United Nations, which Russia was boycotting because of its refusal to oust the Chinese nationalist delegation there.

MacArthur is said to have exclaimed, "I don't believe it." Later he wrote:

> Thus, step by hesitant step, the United States went to war against Communism in Asia. I could not help being amazed at the manner in which this great decision was being made. With no submission to Congress, whose duty it is to declare war, and without even consulting the field commander involved, the members of the executive branch of the government agreed to enter the Korean War. All the risks inherent in this

decision—including the possibility of Chinese and Russian involvement—applied then just as much as they applied later.

Not that he opposed the decision: he had simply never believed it was in Truman to declare war—and he feared the difficulties involved in fighting now that the Americans had evacuated Korea.

But he was not a man to refuse a call to arms: he had "peeled ten years from his shoulder," one aide reported. Faced with the slow death of his shogunate in Japan he had lately looked every one of his 71 years. The high hopes of this greatest of all American proconsuls in September 1946 had been gradually strangled by his combined enemies—men like Dodge, Dulles, Kennan, Willoughby and their Japanese allies and, though he would not admit it, the Emperor himself, working behind the scenes. He faced disappointment and retirement as his time in Japan drew to a close.

Now, by accident, as in the Philippines, he had been given a whole new glorious lease of life: he found himself in the front line of the first real engagement of the Cold War. The challenge was a startling one: the most popular general in America, the hero of the Pacific war, had been turned to again by his nation in its hour of need. He was rejuvenated. Truman, who had been under pressure in the United States for his appeasement of Communists, had had to turn to the very general he hated most. MacArthur happened to be on the spot; but most Americans believed he was the only man capable of rising to the challenge.

This he did, gloriously. Within two days, again displaying the breathtaking courage he was capable of, he had flown in the unarmed *Bataan* to Suwon airfield, 70 miles south of Seoul, where he was met by Rhee. There he commandeered a black Dodge and several jeeps to tour the front for eight hours. One of the journalists with him reported that they

> drove through the swirling, defeated South Korean army and masses of bewildered, pathetic civilian refugees for a firsthand look at the battlefront . . . Throughout the journey, the convoy constantly risked enemy air action, against which there was no adequate protection . . . The crump of mortars was loud and clear, and the North Koreans could have seriously endangered the party with gunfire from only moderately heavy artillery.

MacArthur wrote:

> Seoul was already in enemy hands. Only a mile away, I could see the towers of smoke rising from the ruins of this fourteenth-century city. I pushed forward toward a hill a little way ahead. It was a tragic scene.

Across the Han, Seoul burned and smoked in its agony of destruction. There was the constant crump of Red mortar fire as the enemy swooped down toward the bridges. Below me, and streaming by both sides of the hill, were the retreating, panting columns of disorganized troops, the drab color of their weaving lines interspersed here and there with the bright red crosses of ambulances filled with broken, groaning men.

The sky was resonant with shrieking missiles of death, and everywhere were the stench and utter desolation of a stricken battlefield. Clogging all the roads in a writhing, dust-shrouded mass of humanity were the refugees. But among them there was no hysteria, no whimpering. Here were the progeny of a proud and sturdy race that for centuries had accepted disaster imperturbably. As they painfully plodded south, carrying all their worldly belongings on their backs, and leading their terror-stricken but wide-eyed, uncrying children, I watched for an hour the pitiful evidence of the disaster I had inherited.

In that brief interval on the blood-soaked hill, I formulated my plans. They were desperate plans indeed, but I could see no other way except to accept a defeat which would include not only Korea, but all of continental Asia.

The first priority was to land troops from Japan. Truman authorized him to do so within 48 hours. MacArthur rushed three divisions of the American Eighth Army to South Korea, instructing their advance guard to delay the North Koreans for the time needed to bring in reinforcements. This worked and in late July the North Koreans were brought to a stop outside the defensive line 15 miles from the port of Pusan. MacArthur had secured himself a last-minute toehold as troops poured in from the 12 allies.

But MacArthur had no intention of staying on the defensive: when Averell Harriman, an old friend of MacArthur whom Truman diplomatically sent as his special envoy, arrived, the general asked for the First Marine Division to be sent out:

> I cannot believe that a great nation such as the United States cannot give me these few paltry reinforcements for which I ask. Tell the President that if he gives them to me, I will, on the rising tide of the fifteenth of September, land at Inchon and between the hammer of this landing and the anvil of the Eighth Army, I will crush and destroy the army of North Korea.

On August 23 he convinced senior commanders of his plan: He promised, "I realize this is a 5,000 to 1 gamble. But I am used to taking such odds . . . We shall land at Inchon . . . and I shall crush them!"

It was by any standards an almost lunatic risk. Inchon had no beaches, and the attacking force would have to land on the piers against an entrenched enemy: the tides were 32 feet, one of the highest in the world, and on only two days would be high enough to go in: withdrawal of the force once landed would be nearly impossible. On the first tide an offshore islet would have to be captured before the main landings could be made on the second. "We drew up a list of every natural and geographic handicap—and Inchon had 'em all," said one officer. MacArthur argued that surprise was everything:

> The very arguments you have made as to the impracticabilities involved [confirm my faith in the plan], for the enemy commander will reason that no one would be so brash as to make such an attempt. Surprise is the most vital element for success in war . . . the Marquis de Montcalm believed in 1759 that it was impossible for an armed force to scale the precipitous river banks south of the then walled city of Quebec, and therefore concentrated his formidable defenses along the more vulnerable banks north of the city. But General James Wolfe and a small force did indeed come up the St. Lawrence River and scale those heights. On the Plains of Abraham, Wolfe won a stunning victory that was made possible almost entirely by surprise. Thus he captured Quebec and in effect ended the French and Indian War. Like Montcalm, the North Koreans would regard an Inchon landing as impossible. Like Wolfe, I could take them by surprise.

MacArthur believed he would have the advantage precisely because the North Koreans would not expect such an attack: and Inchon was only 30 miles from Seoul. MacArthur was proposing the most difficult military action of them all—an amphibious military landing to cut off the enemy's supply lines and trap their army in south Korea.

On September 15 the landing was made, with MacArthur watching from one of the ships. Two days later he went ashore, where he was violently sick as the tension drained away when he appreciated the success of the landing. He exposed himself recklessly to enemy fire. Geoffrey Perret, one of his biographers, may have been right in writing:

> There was one day in MacArthur's life when he was a military genius: September 15, 1950. In the life of every great commander there is one battle that stands out above all the rest, the supreme test of generalship that places him among the other military immortals. For MacArthur that bat-

tle was Inchon. The landing produced all the results he had promised. By the end of September Seoul had been recaptured, the Eighth Army had broken out from the Pusan perimeter and the Inmun Gun was destroyed. The survivors were fleeing across the thirty-eighth parallel with UN forces in hot pursuit. The most fitting conclusion to MacArthur's life would have been to die a soldier's death in the waters off Inchon at the height of his glory, with his legend not simply intact but magnified beyond even his florid imaginings. There was only way it could go from here—down.

Just over 500 Americans had been killed and 2,500 wounded against enemy losses of 30,000-40,000. By September 26 Seoul had fallen. American forces broke out of the Pusan beachhead and trapped a further 50,000 North Korean troops between the two pincers, the remaining 50,000 fleeing northward. Soon the total captured rose to 130,000. It had been one of the swiftest, boldest and most decisive military triumphs in history—achieved by a 71-year-old general who had not seen active combat for six years. Of all the glories of the MacArthur legend, this was certainly the greatest.

MacArthur was now ordered to destroy the North Korean armed forces:

> Your military objective is the destruction of the North Korean armed forces. In attaining this objective, you are authorized to conduct military operations north of the 38th parallel in Korea. Under no circumstances, however, will your forces, ground, air or sea, cross the Manchurian or USSR borders of Korea and, as a matter of policy, no non-Korean ground forces will be used in the northern provinces bordering the Soviet Union, or in the areas along the Manchurian border. Furthermore, support of your operations, north or south of the 38th parallel, will not include air or naval action against Manchuria or against USSR territory.

This was clear enough. MacArthur divided his army in two because of the inaccessibility of the rocky mountain interior. They were to march north and rejoin across the narrowest part of the peninsula above the North Korean capital of Pyongyang.

Truman, faced with a difficult mid-term election in November, arranged to fly and meet MacArthur at the Pacific atoll of Wake Island, to bask in the reflected glow of victory. It had long been apparent that the two men loathed each other. Truman regarded MacArthur as a right-wing Republican stuffed shirt and MacArthur considered Truman an insignificant provincial politician unworthy of the mantle of Roosevelt, for whom he had a grudging respect.

On October 15 they met, not as President to subordinate—MacArthur ordered his aircraft to circle so that Truman would land first and have to welcome him as the arriving VIP, and he decided not to salute but to shake Truman's hand in an act of studied insolence—but rather as one head of state meeting another. Truman had no message of substance, nor did he seek to give orders to MacArthur: he merely asked questions, while the assembled Washington cameramen clicked away.

The only significant question he asked was whether MacArthur felt there was any danger of Chinese or Soviet intervention in Korea. MacArthur replied:

> Very little. Had they interfered in the first or second months it would have been decisive. We are no longer fearful of their intervention . . . Only fifty to sixty thousand could be gotten across the Yalu River. They have no air force. Now that we have bases for our air force in Korea, if the Chinese tried to get down to Pyongyang there would be the greatest slaughter.

Truman made no comment: he had no information to the contrary.

Neither man touched on their only disagreement to date: MacArthur a few weeks before had flown to Formosa, where he had met Chiang Kai-Shek for the first time. There he had turned down a Nationalist offer of three divisions to help in Korea, as Washington had instructed him that nothing was more likely to bring the Communist Chinese into the peninsula. But he had irritated Truman by making semi-public criticism of the American policy of policing the Straits of Formosa to prevent either Formosa or mainland China from launching an attack on the other. MacArthur later argued that this had allowed the Chinese to remove the bulk of their mainland army away from the coast to the Korean border.

MacArthur's role in Formosa was shrouded in mystery, but is the key to his dismissal (not his advocacy of a belt of nuclear waste to cut off Korea from China, a suggestion which Truman himself seriously considered at one stage). Representative Judd makes it clear that MacArthur was far from alone in his advocacy of a daring Taiwanese attack into China to take the pressure off Korea:

> Some of us House Members went down to see Mr. Truman in December of that year—four Democrats and four Republicans. As I recall, Nixon was one of the Republicans. I largely organized the group and

wanted it to be bipartisan. It was right after the Chinese Communists had come into the war in Korea. We wanted Truman to allow the Chinese on Formosa to make trouble in Red China's rear or flank. The Chinese were killing our boys in Korea. They knew perfectly well it was safe to intervene because Mr. Truman, through Attlee, had given assurance that we would not go beyond the Yalu River. We would not attack China, so China was freed to attack us . . . Well, the eight of us went down to see President Truman and we asked him, why not use these Chinese troops? I had always opposed using white boys on the mainland of China—or the mainland of Asia—against non-Caucasians . . .

Well, Mr. Truman, when we proposed that, I remember the sentence so well, said, "We will if we have to." That is, we will use Chiang Kai-shek if we have to. There was our policy toward a faithful ally—all in one sentence. The Chinese knew this. They knew that we didn't want to treat them as allies; we hated their guts; we really hoped their island of Formosa would disappear. But if necessary to save us, we'd use them, let them shed their blood to save ours. And some still wonder why Asians don't trust us.

. . . If the Chinese Communists had had some fear that he might, I'm sure they wouldn't have entered the Korean war. It was the fact that they knew they were secure at home which opened the door to Korea for them. They knew because we assured them, directly and indirectly, that they didn't have anything to fear, we wouldn't let Chiang move against them. Chiang could at least have tied them down at home, that's the point. If we were considering only our own boys in Korea, he could have made the Chinese Reds hesitate. Neither Russia or China has risked war for itself.

Judd added that when MacArthur went to Taiwan

[a]ll hell broke loose against him here in Washington, although he was merely discharging his responsibility to defend the area. I have reason to believe from very high Chinese authorities that his trip was what saved Quemoy and Matsu. We had previously urged the [Nationalist] Chinese to withdraw from the Tachen Islands which was their lookout, up close to Shanghai. From it they could monitor everything that went into and came out of Shanghai. But we had put pressure on them and again they followed our advice and evacuated their troops. We also urged them to pull out of Quemoy and Matsu and they were reluctantly preparing to follow our advice when MacArthur went over, took a look and said to the Chinese (he didn't know about this pressure from Washington), "You must hang on to

the islands. If you're going to defend Taiwan, Quemoy and the Matsu are your outposts. The first thing every military outfit does when it camps at night is to set out its sentinels. These islands are your sentinels. If they start anything against Taiwan, they've got to do it from the mainland ports; with those offshore islands, you're tipped off ahead of time." So the Chinese government bucked up after MacArthur's suggestion, held its own against us and wouldn't evacuate.

So once more Chiang Kai-shek got cussed and I'm sure MacArthur got cussed too—but thank God the Chinese listened to MacArthur instead of to the State Department boys who were still demanding that step by step we turn all of China over to the Communists.

It has been suggested, although there is no firm evidence, that MacArthur believed a Taiwanese attack on the mainland might even be successful in toppling the overstretched Chinese Communists already fighting on the Korean front; and that MacArthur had an astonishing grand design for establishing a giant protectorate of both liberated China and Japan under his vice-royalty. If so, this would have been one of the greatest empires in history, in terms of population and extent, and would have marked an astonishing climax to his career. But apart from the claims of a few ardent MacArthur supporters and bitter detractors, there is no documentation to support this. MacArthur was nothing if not imaginative and ambitious, and such a dream might not have been out of character; yet there is nothing to suggest this was the true reason for his dismissal.

But both MacArthur and Truman showed ignorance of the danger at Wake. MacArthur said afterward of the Wake conference:

> I had been warned about Mr. Truman's quick and violent temper and prejudices, but he radiated nothing but courtesy and good humor during our meeting. He has an engaging personality, a quick and witty tongue, and I liked him from the start. At the conference itself, he seemed to take great pride in his historical knowledge, but, it seemed to me that in spite of his having read much, it was of a superficial character, encompassing facts without the logic and reasoning dictating those facts. Of the Far East he knew little, presenting a strange combination of distorted history and vague hopes that somehow, some way, we could do something to help those struggling against Communism.

> The conference at Wake Island made me realize that a curious, and sinister, change was taking place in Washington. The defiant, rallying figure

that had been Franklin Roosevelt was gone. Instead, there was a tendency toward temporizing rather than fighting it through. The original courageous decision of Harry Truman to boldly meet and defeat communism in Asia was apparently being chipped away by the constant pounding whispers of timidity and cynicism. The President seemed to be swayed by the blandishments of some of the more selfish politicians of the United Nations. He seemed to be in the anomalous position of openly expressing fears of over-calculated risks that he had fearlessly taken only a few months before.

Ten days later MacArthur proposed advancing to a new line 40 miles north of Pyongyang, which was about to fall, and then to "secure all of North Korea." MacArthur was chafing at the restrictions imposed by Washington on his ability to use air power to prevent enemy aircraft from raiding across the Manchurian border and to bomb hydroelectric plants in North Korea along the Yalu River between Manchuria and Korea, as well as the supply center at Racin in north-east Korea.

However, the Chinese had already infiltrated some 100,000 men into the mountainous Korean territory between the two American armies, and chose this moment to punch at America's most extended units in the far north. MacArthur was by now deeply concerned: he estimated that there were some 56 Chinese divisions in Manchuria—nearly half a million men, as well as 400,000 reservists.

Washington sent an order half-tying his hands:

> In the event of the open our covert employment anywhere in Korea of major Chinese Communist units, without prior announcement, you should continue the action as long as, in your judgment, action by forces now under your control offers a reasonable chance of success. In any case, prior to taking any military action against objectives in Chinese territory, you will obtain authorization from Washington.

MacArthur ordered the bridges across the Yalu to be bombed—but Washington countermanded this and ordered him not to bomb within five miles of the border. When MacArthur furiously protested, he was ordered to bomb "the Korean end" of the Yalu bridges—a clearly nonsensical order, and one which exposed American pilots to fire from China without being able to reply. As the Yalu was soon to freeze over, the whole dispute was somewhat academic—although his tactic would have squeezed the Chinese army's lines of communication. MacArthur angrily threatened to resign his command.

Meanwhile some 200,000 fresh Chinese troops were infiltrated across the unbombed bridges by November 26. The day before MacArthur flew audaciously along the line of the Yalu to see for himself. He saw nothing:

> When we reached the mouth of the Yalu, I told Story to turn east and follow the river at an altitude of 5,000 feet. At this height we could observe in detail the entire area of international no-man's land all the way to the Siberian border. All that spread before our eyes was an endless expanse of utterly barren countryside, jagged hills, yawning crevices, and the black waters of the Yalu locked in the silent death grip of snow and ice. It was a merciless wasteland. If a large force or massive supply train had passed over the border, the imprints had already been well-covered by the intermittent snowstorms of the Yalu Valley. I decided to have Walker await withdrawing until actual combat might indicate its necessity.

The following day saw the worst setback for American forces since the Second World War. The Chinese, under a brilliant and ruthless commander, General Lin Piao, had concentrated in immense strength, taking advantage of the cover of the winter, and holed up secretly in hamlets and caves along the rugged mountains of the Korean backbone that MacArthur always believed to be uninhabitable and impassable. Some 300,000 hungry, poorly equipped young troops fell upon the American force, outnumbering it ten to one, from the front, sides and rear, threatening to cut off and surround it. MacArthur, caught by surprise and stunned out of his usual jaunty self-confidence, wired to Washington, "We face an entirely new war."

With foolhardy stubbornness—perhaps for the first time betraying the inflexibility of his years—he continued to order the Americans to move forward for four days before bowing to the inevitable and ordering their withdrawal—in the nick of time for the beleaguered American Tenth Corps, which had to fight its way heroically eastward through the massed Chinese forces toward the port of Hungam. In a celebrated incident, when the Americans were blocked by a deep gorge, aircraft lowered a whole bridge across it to help them on their way. The Seventh Fleet picked up the survivors and carried them down to Pusan. To the south another Allied army was forced back across the 38th Parallel.

A rattled President Truman himself said at a press conference that nuclear weapons might be used against China and that this was for MacArthur to decide—only to withdraw the threat under British pressure. In fact the retreat had been superbly handled with a high but not overwhelming casualty rate of 25 percent killed or wounded—around 13,000, compared with, for example, the 66,000 lost in the "victory" of Okinawa. Nevertheless, it was a devastating setback, resulting in the near loss of the entire peninsula to the Chinese army.

MacArthur was immediately blamed by much of the world press for failing to predict the attack and, much less fairly, for having "provoked" it—although it should have been obvious that so massive an offensive (eventually involving nearly 1 million men) had been months in preparation, long before his own limited northward thrust—which had anyway been authorized by the high command. The extraordinarily accurate Chinese knowledge of troop deployments in Korea had been furnished by two British spies in Washington, Kim Philby and Anthony Burgess, and a colleague in London, Donald Maclean. In January 1951, Seoul fell again, this time to the Chinese, and they continued down to a line about halfway across South Korea.

By this time a fresh American commander, General Matthew Ridgway, had arrived in Korea to replace General Walker, who had been killed: he was an energetic, courageous fighter. The following month he boldly launched a counterattack, saying that the Chinese were exhausted, and recaptured Seoul and all territory up to the 38th Parallel: MacArthur, who in the wake of the Chinese offensive had been uncharacteristically defeatist and flustered, was beginning to be regarded by Washington as dispensable in view of Ridgway"s successes. But, having been offered troops again by Chiang Kai-Shek, MacArthur urged a more aggressive course upon Truman.

> Should a policy determination be reached by our government or through it by the United Nations to recognize the state of war which has been forced upon us by the Chinese authorities and to take retaliatory measures within our capabilities, we could: (1) blockade the coast of China; (2) destroy through naval gunfire and air bombardment China's industrial capacity to wage war; (3) secure reinforcements from the Nationalist garrison on Formosa to strengthen our position in Korea if we decided to continue the fight for that peninsula; and (4) release existing restrictions upon the Formosan garrison for diversionary action, possibly leading to counterinvasion against vulnerable areas of the Chinese mainland.
>
> I believe that by the foregoing measures we could severely cripple and largely neutralize China's capability to wage aggressive war and thus save Asia from the engulfment otherwise facing it.

Washington, however, did not want to widen the war. Indeed Truman had come to the conclusion—after at one stage fearing that the Allies might have to abandon Korea altogether—that the objective of the war should be to secure South Korea up to the 38th Parallel.

MacArthur ran into a storm of opprobrium, which he answered with such vigor that Truman considered dismissing him there and then, but settled instead for a grudging order insisting that any such statements be cleared first with Washington. The President himself was locked in a furious partisan struggle with the Republicans, who had performed well in the mid-term elections, accusing him of being "soft on communism," and MacArthur's constant string of indiscretions was resented bitterly by Truman.

On February 11 MacArthur proposed a new, bold plan to:

> clear the enemy rear all across the top of North Korea by massive air attacks. If I were still not permitted to attack the massed enemy reinforcements across the Yalu, or to destroy its bridges, I would sever Korea from Manchuria by laying a field of radioactive wastes—the by-products of atomic manufacture—across all the major lines of enemy supply . . . I would make simultaneous amphibious and airborne landings at the upper end of both coasts of North Korea, and close a gigantic trap. The Chinese would soon starve or surrender. Without food and ammunition, they would become helpless. It would be something like Inchon, but on a much larger scale.

It was turned down. Learning that Truman was trying to arrange a secret ceasefire along the 38th Parallel, MacArthur issued a public statement lambasting the Chinese and also calling for a ceasefire, which effectively torpedoed the secret initiative, as the enemy could not afford to be seen responding to an American call. Truman was livid.

It seems clear that by now MacArthur had decided on provoking the President into dismissing him: he knew that the best possible outcome of the war—restoration of the status quo ante—would be inglorious and saw no future in commanding the American army there any longer; moreover, he saw the glimmer of a chance of standing for the presidency. On April 5 a story was printed in the London *Daily Telegraph* that MacArthur had told a British visitor that

> United Nations forces were circumscribed by a web of artificial conditions . . . in a war without a definite objective . . . It was not the soldier who had encroached upon the realm of the political [but the reverse] . . . The true object of a commander in war was to destroy the forces opposed

to him. But this was not the case in Korea. The situation would be ludicrous if men's lives were not involved.

At the same time the House minority leader, Congressman Joe Martin, wrote into the congressional record a letter that he had received from MacArthur on March 20. MacArthur commended Martin on his views about using the Chinese Nationalists which he suggested were in conformity with the tradition of "meeting force with maximum counterforce . . . it seems strangely difficult to some to realize that here in Asia is where the communist conspirators have elected to make their play for global conquest . . . if we lose the war to communism in Asia the fall of Europe is inevitable . . . as you point out, we must win. There is no substitute for victory."

MacArthur's insistence that this was "private" correspondence does not ring true: he must have expected so serious a missive to be used by a senior Republican for partisan purposes. Truman regarded this as an outright contradiction of his new policy of seeking an armistice—which indeed it was. Although later the administration was to float wild allegations, depicting MacArthur as a warmonger prepared to start the Third World War, who wanted to use nuclear weapons against China (even Truman considered this possibility), the issue of dispute was this comparatively narrow area of disagreement, and the actual act of insubordination not a matter of life and death at all but this limited but deliberate needling by MacArthur against the President.

On April 11 Truman summoned the press to the White House and announced MacArthur's dismissal—before word of it had reached him, for fear that he would take the opportunity of resigning first ("The sonofabitch isn't going to resign on me. I want him fired" declared Truman). As MacArthur put it later:

> The actual order I received was so drastic as to prevent the usual amenities incident to a transfer of command, and practically placed me under duress. No office boy, no charwoman, no servant of any sort would have been dismissed with such callous disregard for the ordinary decencies.

MacArthur told his wife, "Jeanie, we're going home at last."

In all the controversy surrounding his dismissal a number of points stand out: first, and most clearly, at issue was not simply a matter of a general straying into politics and disobeying the orders of his commander in chief, as Truman was later to assert. MacArthur had interfered in politics ever since he had been army commander in the Philippines, and arguably even before that. He was constantly making political pronouncements. His office as Japan's shogun was a political one. All of this was acceptable. The problem was simply that he disagreed with Truman's new policy on Korea, and was determined to make his views known— and yes, he almost certainly was courting dismissal. He may have concluded that with Washington now backing Ridgway as effective commander in Korea, he had nothing to lose—he would be dismissed sooner or later anyway.

But he genuinely believed that it would be disaster to fight the Korean War with the limited objective of restoring the position to what it had been before the North had attacked the South—thereby rendering the sacrifice of so many men in vain and encouraging other Communist aggressors to believe the West was too supine to defeat them. "There is no substitute for victory," he insisted. In spite of the reverses suffered since the Chinese had entered the war, MacArthur insisted that given the proper commitment of resources and the will, the war could still be won, Korea could still be freed. It was not the demented, crazed, warmongering policy it was made out to be.

Looking back at MacArthur's decision to try and free the Korean peninsula before the Chinese intervention, it was clearly absurd to say, as Truman's supporters later did, that he "provoked" the Chinese into war. He did not cross the Yalu nor bomb on the north side of it, and the massing of a million men along the mountains had taken months of planning. Almost certainly the Chinese had decided to intervene when the American drive up the peninsula began after the Inchon landing.

Once MacArthur's forces had been driven back below Seoul, and the American fightback began, it was not illegitimate nor wild-eyed to seek to widen the war against China by encouraging the Nationalists to attack the Chinese coast and launching his own air attacks on Chinese bases supplying the troops in North Korea. Bold, maybe, even rash—but not illegitimate: it had been the Chinese who had widened the war and committed unprovoked aggression against the Americans by attacking the armies in North Korea in force: these had not crossed the border into China. MacArthur may even have been right that the Chinese, who had just ended their war with the Nationalists and now suffered a setback in South Korea, were exhausted and would sue for peace. He insisted that he did not contemplate sending a single American soldier into Chinese territory.

Would these actions have triggered the Third World War? This seems unlikely: the Russians were highly unlikely to have come to China's rescue, as their caution elsewhere suggested. The Chinese and American armies were already at war in Korea, and this did not trigger wider hostilities for the good reason that the battered Chinese armed forces were in no shape to take on any more (China at the time of course had no nuclear weapons).

Judd provides poignant insights into his dismissal: "Dulles said, 'On the way out, my plane passed his in the air as he returned. We talked back and forth,' not by telephone then, but by morse code, 'and there was not one word of bitterness from the General. I asked him for advice and he gave me concrete suggestions as to what it would be most useful for me to do and say when I got to Tokyo. His whole concern was for the success of his mission out there.' Dulles said, 'I never had greater admiration for a man. Under such provocation, he still uttered not a word of personal bitterness; he considered only the cause of his country'. He added, 'As long as America can produce men of that stature and caliber it will be safe.'"

Judd remarked cuttingly: "Mr. Truman made a decision not to win the war in Korea when we were in the fourth quarter and finally in the lead. He decided not to go ahead, but pulled out our star quarterback, MacArthur. This was one of the greatest mistakes in history and he won't be able to escape responsibility for it, even as his original going into Korea was one of the great decisions of history for which it will give him full credit."

In practice Truman's policy of caution, formulated in the winter of 1951, did not result in an end to the war—far from it. More were to die before the war ground inconclusively to a stop in July 1952 than had been killed during the whole of MacArthur's command. A quick victory might well have saved these men's lives. Truman's policy was at least partly dictated by fears that the Soviet Union would take advantage of a major war in Korea to stage an attack in Europe—for example over the Berlin issue. Yet the war of attrition continued anyway, defying Truman's expectation that a quick armistice was in the cards in Korea, and Stalin did not attack. But Truman was not to know that. On this fundamental disagreement did the break come. Hindsight probably slightly favors MacArthur: but neither of the two men's positions were unreasonable, and Truman had the decisive authority, as MacArthur well knew.

38 : Old Soldiers Never Die

B Y THE END OF THE SECOND WORLD WAR, MacArthur, FROM BEING A slightly absurd and controversial right-wing former chief of staff, had become one of the most famous men in the world. The occupation of Japan caused him to exhibit a complex personality unsuspected by most of those who knew him in the prewar years. Here was a man whose courage and determination had become a byword for defiance of the Japanese military juggernaut against all the odds—although there were those who criticized his abandonment of command in Corregidor under direct orders from President Roosevelt. His brilliant leapfrogging strategy across the South Pacific had secured a string of victories at a minimum cost in casualties—unlike the appallingly bloody progress of more conventional commanders across the North Pacific.

He was a soldier who had opposed the dropping of the two atom bombs on Japan and preached peace, disarmament and social reform. He was a man whose lofty patrician remoteness—for which he was so much criticized by those he snubbed—seemed absolutely natural to the deferential nation he presided over. He was a leader who forgave his principal enemies in war and indeed turned them into the principal instruments of his rule. The bugbear of American liberals and left-wingers, hated by Roosevelt's New Dealers, had now apparently turned into an antimilitarist, anti–big business, land-reforming progressive. The transformation was truly extraordinary—and he only got away with his occupation reforms because of his previous credentials on the American right.

With the invasion of Korea, MacArthur did a backward somersault from being a far-seeing social reformer in Japan to demon of the American liberal left to darling of the American right again. He was the man who had supposedly provoked the Chinese invasion of Korea; who had urged hot pursuit into Chinese territory and nearly precipitated a world war with the most populous country on earth; who may have been plotting planning a double pincer from Korea and Formosa into Communist China; who had been prepared to use nuclear material (although not, as he was wrongly accused, nuclear weapons) against China—a position also shared by his chief detractors in the Truman administration. This was the warmonger who had brought the world to the brink of war with global communism at a time when America itself was in the grip of an anti-Communist witch hunt and paranoia.

As we have seen the reality was somewhat different, and MacArthur's actions in Korea were logical and defensible, if certainly lacking the caution that dictated the inconsistencies and policy flip-flops of the Truman administration. If indeed, as this study suggests, he did contemplate a two-pronged attack on China, he was certainly characteristically guilty of "thinking the unthinkable." But perhaps this is the role of the military man, as it is the role of his political masters to restrain him, as indeed they did.

Was he being completely unrealistic? On the face of it the project, while far-fetched, was by no means unfeasible, and in this author's view Stalin was unlikely to have gone to war to help Mao, against whom he had previously sided with Chiang Kai-Shek. Certainly, though, an attack on China would have been a huge gamble, and had it gone wrong the damage to American interests would have been colossal. But the transformation of MacArthur back from statesman-like ruler of Japan into a crazed right-winger was complete, fairly or not, and the image continued to stick to him throughout the rest of his life.

MacArthur also believed, though, that he was not finished: he had another great battle yet to fight. He had deliberately provoked Truman into dismissing him—that much seems clear—because he had no wish to be slowly pushed off center stage as Ridgway took command in Korea; he now aimed for the supreme prize. With a coherent vision—the need to resist communist aggressors in Korea and elsewhere—he would take his case to the country and perhaps secure the ultimate prize, the presidency. Now from a position of fame, he would carry his cause to the American people.

An upsurge of popular sympathy for MacArthur perhaps unprecedented in American history greeted news of the dismissal. On August 16 MacArthur flew back to San Francisco aboard the *Bataan*. He stopped at Hawaii on the way, where a crowd of 100,000 greeted him. In San Francisco nearly a million people awaited him. A crowd as big welcomed him to city hall the following morning, to hear him say:

> I was just asked if I intend to enter politics. My reply was no. I have no political aspirations whatsoever. I do not intend to run for political office, and I hope that my name will never be used in a political way. The only politics I have is contained in a single phrase known well to all of you—"God Bless America!"

Reaching Washington there were 12,000 waiting. The following day he delivered the most electric speech of his life, and one of the greatest ever delivered in American history, to a joint session of Congress.

History teaches with unmistakable emphasis that appeasement but begets new and bloodier war. It points to no single instance where the end has justified that means—where appeasement has led to more than a sham peace. Like blackmail, it lays the basis for new and successively greater demands, until, as in blackmail, violence becomes the only other alternative. Why, my soldiers asked of me, surrender military advantages to an enemy in the field? I could not answer.

Your fighting sons are splendid in every way . . . Those gallant men will remain often in my thoughts and in my prayers always. I am closing my fifty-two years of military service. When I joined the Army, even before the turn of the century, it was the fulfillment of all my boyish hopes and dreams. The world has turned over many times since I took the oath on the Plain at West Point, and the hopes and dreams have long since vanished. But I still remember the refrain of one of the most popular barrack ballads of that day, which proclaimed, most proudly, that "Old soldiers never die. They just fade away." And like the soldier of the ballad, I now close my military career and just fade away—an old soldier who tried to do his duty as God gave him the right to see that duty. Good-bye."

He was interrupted by 30 ovations. Afterward he emerged to a crowd of 500,000 in Pennsylvania Avenue, as air force jets flew overhead in tribute. He traveled to New York. There the largest ticker-tape parade the city had ever staged greeted him, and it took seven hours for his car to cross the fewer than 20 miles of motorcade through the millions of spectators. Were these supporters of his political stand against the President, or merely greeting the return of the most romantic American hero of the Second World War?

On May 3, 1951, he testified before a joint session of the Senate Foreign Relations and Armed Services Committees. It was a characteristically magisterial performance:

The inertia that exists! There is no policy—there is nothing, I tell you—no plan, or anything! Could America continue to fight in this accordion fashion—up and down—which means that your cumulative losses are going to be staggering. It isn't just dust that is settling in Korea, Senator . . . it is American blood. Now there are only three ways that I can think of, as

I said this morning. Either pursue it to victory; to surrender to the enemy and end it on his terms; or what I think is the worst of all choices—to go on indefinitely and indefinitely, neither to win or lose, in that stalemate; because what we are doing is sacrificing thousands of men while we are doing it.

Senator Brien McMahon probed his weak point:

The Joint Chiefs and the President of the United States, the Commander in Chief, has [sic] to look at this thing on a global basis and a global defense. You as a theater commander by your own statement have not made that kind of study, and yet you advise to push forward with a course of action that may involve us in that global conflict.

The administration's heavy guns, desperate to stop the MacArthur juggernaut, were wheeled in. General Omar Bradley, the chief of staff, was summoned to defend Truman's position. In so doing he attempted to demolish MacArthur's arguments, but he did so to such an extent that he appeared no more than a White House stooge, causing the powerful Senator Robert Taft to declare that he had lost all confidence in Bradley's military judgment.

At the congressional hearing, Bradley declared that MacArthur intended to "involve us in the wrong war, at the wrong place, at the wrong time, and with the wrong enemy." This somewhat glib characterization has largely become the accepted verdict of history. But it was more complex than that. MacArthur had been quite explicit in his speech before Congress about his policies—"to neutralize the sanctuary protection against the enemy north of the Yalu, an economic and naval blockade of China, air reconnaissance of China's coastal areas and of Manchuria" and—most controversially—permitting Chiang Kai-Shek's Nationalist forces in Formosa to stage raids on the mainland. In the past he had also urged widespread bombing and naval bombardment to destroy China's "industrial capacity to wage war."

The Truman administration had chosen to interpret this, half-justifiably, as a declaration of war against Communist China. Perhaps the most sensitive aspect of the MacArthur plan was the proposal for Chiang to raid into China, and the evidence here is still circumstantial: there is no record of what MacArthur really discussed with Chiang on his visit to Formosa. In any event this ran entirely contrary to American policy hitherto, which had involved the abandonment of Chiang Kai-Shek as a lost cause and, in the opinion of some American right-wingers, active support for Mao's Communists as progressive agrarian reformers.

Again, the evidence is circumstantial, but the evidence of a former China hand, Congressman Walter Judd, is interesting in suggesting that MacArthur was in fact urging his supporters to seek a total overthrow of Mao's Communists, only recently precariously installed. If so, the epic decision to dismiss MacArthur becomes much more understandable as the result of a titanic conflict within the American administration between those who sought to roll back the loss of China and those who sought to live with it. This is probably the key to the whole controversy over his dismissal.

MacArthur continued his triumphal progress across America for a year, his statements getting more incautious and extreme, accusing Truman of "heading toward a communist state with as dreadful certainty as though the leaders of the Kremlin were charting the course." He supported Senator Robert Taft for the presidency. Truman, bowing largely to his Korean war failures, withdrew from standing for reelection.

Taft now made it to be known that MacArthur was his favored vice-presidential running mate and as such would be made "deputy commander in chief." On July 7 MacArthur delivered the keynote address at the Republican convention—which by common consent was one of the worst speeches of his career, mixing stale hyperbole with flatness of tone. In a single speech he had ruined his chances. When Taft failed to secure the nomination, he urged his supporters to vote for MacArthur.

But in the cruelest irony of all, they went to Dwight Eisenhower, MacArthur's former subordinate, a moderate, shrewd, highly political general unlike the incautious MacArthur. It was, at 72, the end of the line for a career that had undergone seven roller coasters. He did his reputation no good by offering Eisenhower gratuitous advice after he had won the presidency, now advocating that China should be bombed and nuclear waste laid around North Korea unless Stalin accepted the reunification of both Germany and Korea.

By 1955 he was reverting to more thoughtful mode, pressing for nuclear weapons to be renounced on both sides. When the armistice was reached in Korea, he declared prophetically, "This is the death warrant for Indochina." In 1961 he visited the newly elected President Kennedy and advised him that no American soldiers should be committed to Vietnam—advice Kennedy should have heeded. The same year he traveled back to the Philippines, where he was greeted by 2 million people. In April 1964, following a visit by President Lyndon Johnson in the hospital, he died, aged 84, and was buried at his own memorial in Norfolk, Virginia.

His last speech to the West Point cadets he loved so much had been made in 1962 and was one of his finest:

Duty—Honor—Country. Those three hallowed words reverently dictate what you ought to be, what you can be, what you will be. They are your rallying points; to build courage when courage seems to fail; to regain faith when there seems to be little cause for faith; to create hope when hope becomes forlorn. Unhappily, I possess neither that eloquence of diction, that poetry of imagination, nor that brilliance of metaphor to tell you all that they mean. The unbelievers will say they are but words, but a slogan, but a flamboyant phrase. Every pedant, every demagogue, every cynic, every hypocrite, every troublemaker, and, I am sorry to say, some others of an entirely different character, will try to downgrade them even to the extent of mockery and ridicule.

But these are some of the things they do. They build your basic character; they mold you for your future roles as custodians of the nation's defense; they make you strong enough to know when you are weak, and brave enough to face yourself when you are afraid. They teach you to be proud and unbending in yourself when you are afraid. They teach you to be proud and unbending in honest failure, but humble and gentle in success, not to substitute words for actions, not to seek the path of comfort, but to face the stress and spur of difficulty and challenge; to learn to stand up in the storm but to have compassion on those who fail; to master yourself before you seek to master others; to have a heart that is clean, a goal that is high; to learn to laugh yet never forget how to weep; to reach into the future yet never neglect the past; to be serious yet never to take yourself too seriously; to be modest so that you will remember the simplicity of true greatness, the open mind of true wisdom, the meekness of true strength.

They give you a temper of the will, a quality of the imagination, a vigor of the emotions, a freshness of the deep springs of life, a temperamental predominance of courage over timidity, an appetite for adventure over love of ease. They create in your heart the sense of wonder, the unfailing hope of what next, and the joy and inspiration of life. They teach you in this way to be an officer and gentleman . . . This does not mean that you are warmongers. On the contrary, the soldier, above all other people, prays for peace, for he must suffer and bear the deepest wounds and scars of war. But always in our ears ring the ominous words of Plato, that wisest of all philosophers, "Only the dead have seen the end of war."

The shadows are lengthening for me. The twilight is here. My days of old have vanished tone and tint; they have gone glimmering through the dreams of things that were. Their memory is one of wondrous beauty, watered by tears, and coaxed and caressed by the smiles of yesterday. I listen vainly, but with thirsty ear, for the witching melody of faint bugles blowing reveille, of far drums of musketry, the strange mournful mutter of the battlefield. But in the evening of my memory, always I come back to West Point. Always there echoes and re-echoes in my ears—Duty—Honor—Country.

Today marks my final roll call with you. But I want you to know that when I cross the river my last conscious thoughts will be of the Corps—and the Corps—and the Corps.

I bid you farewell.

MacArthur's political career seems amply to have vindicated Roosevelt's judgment that he was a brilliant general and an appalling politician. His final act in Korea would have been understood in Japan, where one of the greatest heroes of recent history was the great warrior Saigo, who committed hara-kiri rather than compromise his principles of honor with the corruption of politics. MacArthur was much more a natural Japanese hero than an American one. The American shogun had died as just that—a great warrior, a moderate, wise and principled military ruler, a shogun.

Hirohito was 63 when MacArthur died, and went on to live until the age of 88, only four years longer than his shogun, until January 7, 1989. On the face of things, he had emerged the survivor from their extraordinary relationship: MacArthur's shogunate lasted less than six years in a reign that effectively spanned 66 years. Hirohito ruled for 38 years after MacArthur's departure. During that time it seemed that all traces of the American occupation were steadily effaced from Japan.

MacArthur's dismissal by Truman had come as a body blow to the Emperor. There is no doubting the genuine outpouring of shock and dismay in Japan when the news came through. This was due to four things: the genuine affection in which this extraordinary, imperious, un-American Japanese-style ruler was held, both by the Japanese power elite and by ordinary people, who believed he was their champion against the predatory ruling classes; the fear of the elites that he might be replaced by something worse—a more democratic reformer; the fear among ordinary people that a hard right-winger might now take over; and the manner of his dismissal.

Nothing could have underlined the difference between the American and Japanese way of government up to then more clearly than the brutal manner of MacArthur's replacement. This seemingly all-powerful, god-like figure was removed in a few terse phrases by the democratically elected President of the United States. A prime minister might fall the same way in Japan—but not the man to whom the Emperor himself deferred. On hearing the news at an official reception, the Prime Minister, Shigeru Yoshida, was visibly shocked and had to rest for half an hour to compose himself.

The Asahi newspapers, traditionally liberal, expressed Japanese sentiments the next day:

> We have lived with General MacArthur from the end of the war until today . . . When the Japanese people faced the unprecedented situation of defeat, and fell into the *kyodatsu* condition of exhaustion and despair, it was General MacArthur who taught us the merits of democracy and pacifism and guided us with kindness along this bright path. As if pleased with his own children growing up, he took pleasure in the Japanese people, yesterday's enemy, walking step by step toward democracy, and kept encouraging us.

Mainichi wrote:

> MacArthur's dismissal is the greatest shock since the end of the war. He dealt with the Japanese people not as a conqueror but a great reformer. He was a noble political missionary. What he gave us was not material aid and democratic reform alone, but a new way of life, the freedom and dignity of the individual . . . We shall continue to love and trust him as one of the Americans who best understood Japan's position.

The Emperor was astounded. As his biographer Kawahara points out:

> It was as if the sky had fallen. The Japanese, who are brought up to be submissive to authority, had eventually come to respect the supreme commander of their former enemies. When Hirohito was first informed of the news at a little past 4 P.M. on April 11, 1951, he simply sat and stared into space for a long time. Later, when he had received more details from Grand Chamberlain Mitani, he seemed genuinely surprised again, saying, "So it's really true . . ."

The Emperor paid tribute to MacArthur by calling on him one last time, as servant to master, although he no longer held an official position, after MacArthur ungraciously refused his own invitation. On the previous occasion they had discussed the "peace problem." Hirohito had then gone behind MacArthur's back through finance minister Hayato Ikeda to the shogun's arche-enemy Joseph Dodge, the Conservative banker seeking to tie MacArthur's hands. According to one account Hirohito's message was "to the effect that [the Yoshida] Government desires the earliest possible treaty. As such a treaty probably would require the maintenance of U.S. forces [on Japanese soil] . . . if the U.S. Government hesitates to make these conditions, the Japanese Government [itself] will try to find a way to offer them."

When Dulles had gone out in June 1950 as Washington's emissary shortly before the Korean War broke out he found Yoshida, who had no wish to encourage the remilitarization of Japan and also feared his nation being sucked into the Korean War, generally uncooperative toward his proposed defense of South Korea. The Emperor had promptly sent a message putting down both MacArthur and Yoshida, which showed his own preference for the Japanese and American hardliners.

After MacArthur's dismissal, not only had Hirohito called generously on him but he sent his grand chamberlain Mitani to see him off on June 16, 1951. Yoshida was also in attendance. At least 200,000 Japanese came to see MacArthur depart, many of them openly crying. This was an astonishing popular outpouring for a man who had ruled as the only *"gaijin* oppressor" in Japan's history. There was a nineteen-gun salute and a warm embrace from General Matthew Ridgway, his easygoing, capable successor, which was broadcast live. Yoshida expressed his "shock and sorrow beyond words." The melody of "Auld Lang Syne" was played in the background.

The Mainichi wrote that day:

> Oh, General MacArthur—General, General, who saved Japan from confusion and starvation. Did you see from your window the green wheat stirring in the wind? The harvest will be rich this year. That is the fruit of the general's five years and eight months—and the symbol of the Japanese people's gratitude.

Kawahara's tribute is more measured and more impressive:

> Thus ended the "reign" of the man the Japanese called "the Emperor outside the moat." But if we look impartially at him as an administrator,

his accomplishments were impressive: He solved the food shortages; he prevented a Communist revolution; he rebuilt the Japanese economy; and he maintained the imperial institution. If for nothing else Japan owes him an enormous debt of gratitude for averting the creation of "two Japans" by resisting Soviet pressure for a Russian occupation of Hokkaido.

But privately Hirohito was vastly relieved: with MacArthur's departure, the Mikado was free to resume his rightful place as supreme authority in Japan. The Emperor no longer had to endure MacArthur's lectures and attempts to contain Japan's military reconstruction. The Korean War provided the large kickstart of capital needed to create Japan's economic miracle of the 1950s, 1960s and 1970s. It also permitted Japan to re-emerge as a significant military power. Hirohito now ended his popular tours, once again returning "above the clouds" to become a remote authoritarian figure.

What of MacArthur's other main sparring partner? Harry S Truman had been a very different kind of president to his predecessor. A small-town lawyer from Missouri, he had been despised by MacArthur who had been in some awe of the patrician Roosevelt, as being on a lower rung of the hidden American class ladder. The feeling was amply reciprocated: to Truman MacArthur was the epitome of an arrogant, stuffed shirt American officer from a bygone age. Truman labeled him a "counterfeit" and a "common coward" for leaving Corregidor in 1942 under direct presidential order—an example of the President's almost incredible meanness of spirit on occasion. He once showed a picture of MacArthur to a visitor, saying, "Well you know who that is, that's God." He described MacArthur as a "four-flusher and no two ways about it," and his valedictory speech as "a hundred percent bullshit," criticizing the congressmen present as "damn fool" for "crying like a bunch of women."

Yet it is impossible to dismiss criticism from such a source as trivial, as MacArthur did. Truman was an extraordinarily shrewd politician who presided over an administration that set up the architecture of postwar security that more or less maintained global peace until the end of the Cold War. Although of limited stature educationally and perhaps intellectually, he made so many tough decisions that he had almost acquired the mantle of presidential greatness.

His decision to drop the bombs on Hiroshima and Nagasaki, although highly controversial and indeed privately opposed by MacArthur, was nothing if not bold and decisive—although it also suggested that he was held in thrall by the techno-military elite at least at the outset of his presidency. He approved the Marshall plan which helped to reconstruct Europe after the end of the Second World War.

He espoused the Kennan doctrine of containment, not confrontation or appeasement, of Stalin's Russia. He quietly reversed Roosevelt's overconciliatory attitude toward the Russian dictator, presided over the founding of NATO, the (some would say blameworthy) loss of China to Mao's Communists and most of the Korean War, for whose conduct he can be severely faulted, as can MacArthur. Nevertheless there was a touch of statesmanship about this plucky, determined man of humble origins. He was a politician to his fingertips where MacArthur was a soldier and proconsul.

Was there substance in Truman's contempt for MacArthur? There were many who believed the general was a charlatan and poseur, merely carrying out orders from Washington while attempting to take the credit for himself. Yet that view is at odds with Truman's other main gripe about MacArthur—that he refused to obey orders and campaigned against presidential directives.

Moreover Truman, whose qualities were initially underrated and who left such a lasting stamp on American postwar policy, was certainly possessed of character defects every bit as serious as those of MacArthur. His pettiness, both in his behavior toward MacArthur, who after all was one of America's greatest generals long before Truman emerged to prominence, and his prickliness toward criticism, to which MacArthur drew attention, were deeply unpresidential. It was on the issue of Korea, however, that the clash of personalities became one of earnestly debated national policies and that both men were to emerge as furious opponents. The argument rages to this day.

PART VIII
THE EMPEROR'S NEW CLOTHES

39 : RETURN OF THE SAMURAI

TWO IMMEDIATE CONSEQUENCES FLOWED FROM THE WAR AND FROM THE manner of MacArthur's dismissal. The Americans began to consider as a matter of priority how to wind up the occupation; and Japanese politics, which had already lurched sharply to the right in 1948, were now confirmed in their drift toward anti-Communist conservatism. Up to now, the occupation had been prolonged largely because of the country's dire economic straits and because MacArthur's powerful enemies in Washington were determined to undo his work. The supreme commander, although in charge, had indeed sought an end to the occupation as far back as 1947, so that there would be no chance to undo his reforms.

There is some evidence to suggest that the delay in Japan's economic recovery until the change of direction the following year was at least substantially caused by the direct refusal of the *zaibatsu* to invest and engage in economic activity until the threat posed to their interests by MacArthur and the SCAP reformists was removed. In 1948 the anti-*zaibatsu* reforms were abandoned, and Japan's bosses, in alliance with their friends in Washington, emerged victorious.

Economic recovery got under way, sharply accelerated by the Korean War. In 1949 a prices and wages policy imposed by SCAP helped to stabilize the economy. By the following year, many companies were at least partially solvent. By 1951 industrial production had returned to its level of the early 1930s. Almost certainly recovery could have occurred three years earlier if the *zaibatsu* had not been determined to pursue their interests against MacArthur and, in effect, to engage in an investment and production strike (as they did unpatriotically against militarist attempts to take them over during the war).

With MacArthur's removal, there was no longer any need to prevaricate: the Americans could safely negotiate a peace treaty with the Japanese and end the occupation. There remained one problem. America's Far Eastern allies, given so limited a role throughout the occupation, were not disposed to end it unconditionally, as they continued to regard Japan with deep suspicion. The British pressed for economic restrictions on Japan's growth; the Chinese were deeply hostile; Australia and New Zealand would only consent if the United States signed a formal security treaty with them; the Philippines required a similar defense agreement; and the Soviet Union flatly opposed any end to the occupation.

The chief American negotiator of the peace treaty with Japan was John Foster Dulles, an arcane but senior Republican serving a Democratic administration and thereby ensuring a bipartisan policy. Dulles got on famously with Hirohito as well as the Japanese government. He toyed with three chief options. The first was a direct American guarantee of Japan's security, and agreement by the Japanese not to rearm. A second option was the militarization of Japan so as to ensure that the country could defend itself. A third was a formal guarantee by America, Russia, Britain and China to respect Japan's neutrality provided the country did not rearm at all. The Russians and the Chinese naturally favored the latter. The Communist countries joined America's allies in vigorously opposing the second option, which was favored by the Americans. The first option was adopted as a compromise that failed to satisfy only the Russians, and then not too seriously.

It was also the choice favored by most senior Japanese, giving them the best of all possible worlds. Rearmament would have been cripplingly expensive, in Japan's perilous economic state, and would have aroused the immediate hostility of most of Asia. An American guarantee would enable Japan to concentrate on economic recovery from behind a shield. For the Japanese right it had the advantage of guaranteeing American support in the event of Communist attack; prior to 1948, the Pentagon's strategic thinking was that Japan was unnecessary to the defense of the Pacific, and could be happily left neutral. American strategy in the Pacific was tied to an arc of islands south of Okinawa. For the left, it kept Japan's militarists in check, however ritually they might denounce the presence of American "imperialists" in Japan.

The foundations for Japan's postwar rise to economic superpower status were being laid. Japan would become a "pacifist commercial democracy." The Americans were reasonably happy, but they wanted to enlist Japan as a major ally against the Soviet Union—something that never really happened. The Philippines, Australia and New Zealand were largely satisfied that Japan would remain under some American restraint, as U.S. bases remained there and the country's growing army was held in check. The Japanese carefully sided with neither Nationalist China nor Communist China, which half pleased the latter. Only the Russians were angry, with Andrei Gromyko, the Soviet delegate to the San Francisco Peace

Conference on September 8, 1951, vigorously attacking the agreement. Forty-eight nations signed the treaty. Under its terms, Japan fully accepted the wholesale dissolution of its former empire. Korean independence was restored, while Japanese claims to Formosa, the Pescadores, Southern Sakhalin and the northern Kuriles were renounced. American control of the Ryukyu islands, in particular Okinawa, was recognized by Japan. There were no economic restraints placed upon the country, and its right to self-defense was recognized. In the preamble the United States agreed that "in the interests of peace and security, [it] is . . . willing to maintain certain of its armed forces in and around Japan, in the expectation, however, that Japan will increasingly assume responsibility for its own defense against direct and indirect aggression." On April 28, 1952, the day before the Emperor's birthday, the occupation ended and Hirohito, albeit hedged in by the new Japanese constitution, was formally ruler of his land again.

The peace treaty was enormously satisfactory to the Japanese and in particular to the outstanding leader of the immediate postwar period, Shigeru Yoshida (although it was actually negotiated with the country's sole, and very short-lived, Socialist administration, that of Katayama). Yoshida's views coincided with those of MacArthur, whose closest Japanese confidante he was. His role was to be pivotal both in defining the country's new political coloring after the Americans had gone, and the new pattern of power between the main forces in Japan: the bureaucracy, business and the politicians. After MacArthur's departure he was unquestionably the dominant figure in Japan, and the biggest shaper of postwar Japanese society.

Japanese politics after the occupation seemed on the surface to plunge into a dark age of unending factional squabbles within the Liberal Democrat Party presided over by a succession of shuffling, obscure politicians. The country that underwent one of the most vicious, dramatic and sinister power struggles in the world before the war now seemed a paragon of dullness: a single party ruled throughout the post-occupation period, giving Japan a stability unprecedented in any major industrial democracy. A natural consensus seemed to have evolved around the idea that Japan should be underarmed and pro-American, and should pursue economic growth without looking back.

This political stability underpinned astonishing growth. A prominent architect of the postwar economic boom in Japan quipped to this author years later that the businessmen had been responsible for 70 percent of the Japanese economic miracle, the bureaucracy for 70 percent. That added up to 140 percent, so the politicians were responsible for minus 40 percent. Shigeru Yoshida, the shaper of postwar Japan, was to define his view of commercial reconstruction taking precedence over political power as follows: "Just as the United States was once a colony of Great Britain but is now the stronger of the two, if Japan becomes a colony of the United States it will eventually become the stronger." This view seemed ludicrously far-fetched at a time when Japan was still half-devastated and half-starved, possessing a fraction of the natural resources of the United States. It did not seem so implausible later.

In fact, beneath the surface of Japan's external consensus and tailcoat intrigue, there was a political ferment. The policy of subservience to the United States was by no means quietly accepted by large parts of Japanese opinion. The right saw it as humiliating, the left as immoral. If either had triumphed, the course of Japan's postwar politics would have been very different. Yoshida's policy prevailed for decades because it persuaded most influential Japanese that it was by far the best suited to securing Japan's self-interest. During the postwar years, however, the country twice came perilously close to open insurrection and several times to takeover by the out-and-out right. The balance remains precarious. Japan lives under a volcano, Mount Fuji. It is dormant, not extinct.

America withdrew from Japan in 1952, leaving a country which had agreed, in effect, to act as a stationary aircraft carrier for the projection of American forces in the Far East and which, in return, looked for protection against the Soviet Union to the American umbrella, both conventional and nuclear. The catchphrase used to describe this policy was "pacifist commercial democracy." It squared many circles: it tapped the absolute hatred of many Japanese for war after the shattering experience of the bombs and defeat; it gave the Japanese time and money to concentrate upon their economic reconstruction and regeneration; it allayed the fears of Japan's Asian neighbors, ever suspicious of the country that had launched a war that killed millions; and it placed Japan at the front rank of nations resisting what seemed an irresistible tide of communism flowing through the region.

The creator of Japan's postwar security system, Shigeru Yoshida, was not, however, anything resembling a pacifist himself. MacArthur's closest Japanese collaborator during the occupation, Yoshida was an immensely able right-wing politician who laid the foundations for the country's one-party political domination for the next half century. He was a remarkable personality: although deeply conservative, he had been an outspoken opponent of the Pacific War as early as 1941. As a member of the Yohansei group of conservatives in the armed forces, the business community and the bureaucracy, he was in the minority at the time: he had helped to draft the first memorandum submitted by Prince Konoye advocating an end to the war in early 1945. The memorandum suggested, in the most conspiratorial terms, that Tojo and his supporters were radicals seeking to reshape the Japanese economy and society on the Soviet model. The evidence for this was Tojo's attempt to force big business to accept the domination of the ministry of munitions—something which had automatically taken place in war in such countries as Britain and Germany.

In fact the *zaibatsu* beat off the challenge; at that stage, after years of channelling and benefiting from the direction of Japanese militarism, the big corporations had become increasingly opposed both to Tojo and the militarists. When military defeat came in Saipan, the conservatives and the *zaibatsu* were instrumental in his fall. The *zaibatsu* continued to prosecute the war, because they were not against the fighting as such, but their prime concern was to suppress Tojo's apparently "socialist" tendencies, which seemed to hark back to those of the "Imperial Way" group during the 1936 uprising. Konoye echoed Yoshida's arguments in pointing out to the Emperor that military defeat was as nothing compared to the prospect of "leftist revolution."

There was a lurking fear among intelligent conservatives in Japan that the intensely hierarchical nature of society laid it open to hijack by the Communists, whose ideal structure of society it mirrored. If the Communists secured control, they could slide in at the top more easily than in any country on earth, simply taking advantage of the methodical brainwashed mind-set of Japanese before the war to propagate their own ideas: the people of Japan could have then become the most formidable shock troops of global communism. Konoye and Yoshida insisted that the militarists were door-openers for the Communists. "Wiping out" militarist training and carrying out the reconstruction of the military were "the peculiarities and prerequisites for saving Japan from Communist revolution."

The army replied by having Yoshida arrested in April 1945. He had been entirely acceptable to MacArthur as prime minister after Shidehara in 1946 for a year, and then again after the historic defeat of the moderate left in 1948, winning four more elections before being forced out in November 1954. Yoshida was a tough-minded, cantankerous, even eccentric personality, glorying in representing a straightforward throwback to the half-democratic and capitalist Japan of the 1920s. A former ambassador in London who was aged 67 when he first became prime minister, he wore a pince-nez and wing collar, preferred English tailored tailcoats and suits, puffed cigars and rode in an elderly Rolls-Royce, partly as a way of irritating the Americans.

Known to the Japanese admiringly as "one man," he was happy to refer to the country's trade enemies as "a bunch of bastards," to theorists on MacArthur's staff as "quite peculiar types" or "red subversives," and to form a covert alliance with General Willoughby.

However, his opposition to the power of the armed forces and his insistence that Japan had to rebuild before rearming led him both to support Article Nine of the new constitution and to articulate the theory of the country as a pacifist commercial democracy. Yoshida argued that while Japan regained its economic strength, so too it could forge its political authority. He deeply admired the Meiji leaders for expanding Japan's influence without drifting into war with Britain or America.

He wrote that it was by this means that "a small island nation in the Far East came in half a century to rank among the five great powers of the world." He favored the *zaibatsu*, the aristocracy, the old educational system and the authority of the Emperor. He argued that the Americans were operating on an "erroneous assumption that we are an aggressive people of ultra-militarist tendencies to be refashioned into a peace-loving nation."

Yoshida later openly boasted of how he had outwitted the Americans. The occupation, he said, "was hampered by its lack of knowledge of the people it had come to govern, and even more so, perhaps, by its generally happy ignorance of the amount of requisite knowledge it lacked." He noted that on one occasion SCAP had issued a directive ordering a purge of all "standing directors"—that is, any director—of Japanese firms. The Japanese chose to translate this as "managing director"—a fraction of the total. Thus, said Yoshida, "we were able to save many ordinary directors who might otherwise have been so classified from the purge."

Yoshida's views soon came under fire from both left and right. The left, reinforced by the colossal pacifist sentiment in postwar Japan, argued that Japan should opt for "total neutrality" and abandon its subjugation to the United States, preferring an equality of relations with America, Russia and China. In fact, the left had an ulterior motive in urging closer relations with China: the socialists, suppressed during the inter-war years, felt that Japan's most important relationship should be with the country it had so brutalized.

On the other side, Yoshida was viewed with intense suspicion by many unreconstructed conservative politicians. The militarists had good reason for hating him, but they were no longer so powerful. Yoshida himself came from the most liberal agency of the bureaucracy: the foreign ministry. But he was acute enough—unlike his prewar predecessors—to realize that the bureaucracy itself needed a wider power base from which to dominate

Japanese politics. He did two things to try and secure one: first, he carved out an alliance between the ruling conservative party and the *zaibatsu*. Second, he encouraged senior bureaucrats to run for public office, as a kind of climax to their careers. The old party bosses, themselves largely the creatures of the *zaibatsu*, intensely resented his attempt to infiltrate bureaucratic control into politics. But in the early stages of Yoshida's dominance they had no choice but to rally round him, in the face of the threat from the left.

On May Day, 1952, the annual left-wing demonstrations degenerated into savage violence. Rioters set fire to American cars parked by the palace moat, while fierce battles with the police ensued. It marked the beginning of a major left-wing campaign against the "problem"—the argument that although the American occupation was formally ended, in practice it continued with the presence of thousands of American servicemen and the subordination of Japan's foreign policy. A constant outpouring of press reports alleged excesses by American servicemen, including their supposed penchant for turning the areas around their bases into centers of vice and prostitution.

In 1954 an American hydrogen bomb was set off at Bikini, and a small Japanese fishing boat was caught in the radiation; unfortunately this became apparent only after part of the catch had been sold. There was a widespread panic among this fish-loving people, and for a while seafood virtually disappeared from their tables. The Americans suggested that the boat had violated the warning zone around the test, but this was later found not to be the case. A wave of anti-Americanism swept Japan. Yoshida's brand of pro-Americanism was put on the defensive and his chief rival on the right, Ichiro Hatoyama, put an end to his ascendancy the following year.

Hatoyama was a politician of the old school, which argued that Yoshida had practiced a policy of "subservience" to America: it was decided to put the bureaucrats that Yoshida represented in their place. Moreover, he was determined to revise the constitution. "The present constitution," said Hatoyama, "was imposed on us in English when neither the government nor the people had freedom. It must take a very patient man to be grateful to it. It was drawn up with a view to sapping our strength." He believed in full Japanese rearmament. In addition he wanted the police force centralized and the unions brought to heel even more than they already had been.

Finally he wanted Japan to resume relations with the Soviet Union as a means of ending its dependence on America. Yoshida's attitude to the *zai-*

batsu had been to cooperate, considering them essential to the economic regeneration of Japan after the war, while dominating them: indeed the power of the state was at a zenith immediately after the war, because the *zaibatsu* needed state assistance in reconstruction. Hatoyama's attitude was one of straightforward partnership with big business.

When the divided Socialists came together in 1955, so did the two main conservative parties, in the Liberal Democratic Party. Hatoyama wrote into the party's program the goals of constitutional revision and rearmament. The ruling party was now committed to restoring Japan as a major military power, and one independent of the United States. But it was blocked by the fact that the opposition had more than a third of the seats in parliament: a two-thirds vote was required for revision. Hatoyama's attempt to restore relations with Russia largely failed: there was no peace treaty and no territorial settlement, because the Russians showed no willingness to return the occupied Kuriles. Diplomatic relations were, however, normalized.

Hatoyama's successor was Nobosuke Kishi, the former minister of munitions in Tojo's government, and originally regarded as a war criminal by MacArthur. Kishi was originally a super-bureaucrat whose commitment to economic recovery was second to none; but he was also closely allied to the *zaibatsu*. Kishi understood how to manipulate the power centers of Japan—the bureaucracy, the *zaibatsu*, the militarists and now the new one, the politicians—as did virtually no one else, and represented the first attempt to return Japan fully to its pre-occupation values.

He wanted nothing less than to renegotiate the 1951 security treaty with the United States to give Japan an equal say, as well as constitutional revision to permit full rearmament. This was opposed by the United States, Japan's Asian neighbors, and by the Russians and the Chinese. But what stopped him in his tracks was a massive display of opposition from ordinary Japanese, mobilized by the left-of-center parties. When, in 1960, some 4 million people took to the streets and serious rioting followed, President Eisenhower's visit to Japan had to be cancelled. It was one of the few times in Japanese political history that popular opposition had been massively felt, and had been successful. Kishi managed only to push through a mildly amended security treaty, and resigned in humiliation.

From that moment on the LDP decided to return to its shell and espouse the Yoshida program: alliance with the United States, gentle but steady rearmament, and an all-out effort for economic growth to double the national income. Political controversy was to be eschewed. Japan had moved perilously close to outright confrontation between the elites and the people, and for once the elites had retreated. Defense spending was even reduced as a proportion of gdp—which however was growing fast—from 1.2 percent to 0.8 percent.

Eisaku Sato, a later prime minister and brother of Kishi, even espoused the view that Japan would not possess, manufacture or admit nuclear weapons—which seemed a rebuff aimed at the Americans, whose aircraft carriers regularly carried them into Japanese ports. It was not widely believed that the Americans removed their weapons before docking, even after Sato's pronouncement. Sato also publicly espoused the MacArthur constitution. "The spirit of the constitution has become the flesh and blood of the nation," he declared.

The security equation remained largely unchanged throughout the early 1960s. However, as the United States found itself increasingly trapped in the quagmire of Vietnam, the certainties that bound the Japanese government to its closest ally began to erode. While left-wing Japanese eagerly indulged in ritual criticism of United States imperialism, the right was far from certain that Vietnam was a clear-cut case of America fighting the good fight against Communist insurgents. Gradually many Japanese conservatives began to identify with the small Asian nation fighting, and indeed prevailing, against all the might of the United States. This demonstration of American weakness caused many to question, once again, the whole basis of Japan's security dependence on the United States.

Two further shocks followed: after America's withdrawal from Vietnam, the Americans began to raise doubts about their commitment to Korea and the Philippines. The Japanese feared that they were about to be abandoned, when they had deliberately remained under-armed and dependent upon the United States. In 1971, moreover, President Nixon floated the dollar, which was a decision primarily motivated by the need to reduce the value of the currency against Japan, then flooding America with imports: this was seen, rightly, as a direct slap in the face.

The ruling elite of the Liberal Democrats, however, did not react with a prompt reversion of Kishi's policies. Instead it began a steady return to the old prewar Japanese values, most notable in the increasingly revisionist attitude toward the Pacific War. This was best illustrated in an interview in 1969 with Kakuei Tanaka, whowas to become one of the most powerful postwar prime ministers:

> I don't think World War II was such a simple war in the history of the
> Japanese nation. During the occupation it was simply regarded as a war of

aggression by Japan, and that was that. But it was not that simple . . . At that time, we Japanese had virtually no natural resources. There were some hundred million of us then, and when we tried to obtain cheap imports we were kicked around by the high tariffs. We tried to immigrate elsewhere, and we were slapped with exclusion. Our export goods were discriminated against. Didn't we hit the very bottom in the Depression? Still, we went on to assault Imphal, Guadalcanal and Sydney, and tried to take one-third of the earth. That was aggression. That was going too far. But after the Sino-Japanese war, everything that came thereafter including the days when the Japanese nation was spitting blood—Was that not a war of aggression?—you say in one sentence and demand my answer. That's very difficult.

In the mid-1970s, Takeo Fukuda, a close friend of Kishi's, briefly came to dominate the Liberal Democratic Party. In 1978 Fukuda raised the issue that had been dormant for nearly two decades: that the defense of Japan must be brought to the forefront of political debate. That seemed to lift the lid on a Pandora's box of long-suppressed views. Defense agency officials, as well as Fukuda, argued that although Japan would continue to respect the principles of nuclear disarmament, the country was not constitutionally barred from possessing nuclear weapons, cruise missiles and bacteriological weapons. Only intercontinental ballistic missiles were absolutely aggressive in intent.

Fukuda then paid an official visit to the Yasukuni shrine. Yasuhiro Nakasone, one of Japan's most-tough-minded right-wingers, felt free to address students at Tokyo university about the repeal of Article Nine. The chairman of Japan's joint chiefs of staff, Hiro Omi Kurisu, attacked the concept of "defensive defense" which had ruled Japan for 20 years. He suggested that the position was untenable: officers from the self-defense force might, in any confrontation, be forced to shoot first because of their inherent weakness, which would be constitutionally illegal. This proved too much even for Fukuda, and Kurisu was dismissed.

The underlying trend of Japanese attitudes to defense was patently clear throughout the post-occupation years. Yoshida set the course, from which one prime minister after another has attempted to strike out in a rightward direction—toward less reliance on the Americans and building up Japan's own armed forces. Every time the overwhelming logic for keeping a low defense profile so as to proceed with economic growth and co-operation with the rest of Asia has prevailed. Kishi tried dramatically to break out of the confines of this policy, and failed dismally. Fukuda and Nakasone did so much more slowly—and achieved more as a result. If the LDP hierarchy was straining at the leash on defense issues, it can be imagined how high nationalist feelings ran among the rank-and-file.

By the mid-1980s, Japan's defense budget was the eighth largest in the world. The armed forces' strength was around 240,000 men, with an army the size of Britain's and 650 combat aircraft. It deployed as many ships as the Americans in the East Asian region, and more aircraft. It had pretty good equipment, including F-15 fighters, Chinook helicopters, Hawkeye early warning systems, and Hawk missiles. In addition Japan had a large military aerospace industry and arms manufacturing was growing, particularly of ship-to-ship missiles, micro-electronics, biotechnology and fine ceramics.

During that same period, Japan's peaceful nuclear program was accelerating fast and a debate was under way about the desirability of acquiring "small-size nuclear weapons." In spite of the size of the defense budget, Japan's average spending in the mid-1980s was still below the guideline figure of 1 percent of gdp. If this were tripled it would enable the Japanese to dispense with the American defense umbrella. Japan would be in a position to acquire at least 16 aircraft carriers, 34 attack destroyers, 85 ordinary destroyers, a further 350 fighter aircraft and five to six times as many tanks.

After Kishi's defeat in 1960, Japan resolved for three decades to keep defense spending down, so as not to annoy America and the rest of Asia, on which its trade and protection depended—even though the gut feeling of most leading Japanese politicians was that the country should go its own way and rearm as it pleased. By the mid-1980s, Prime Minister Nakasone was trying to resist the traditional policy of Japan's elders in arguing that Japan's best interests were secured through a policy of manic economic growth and relying on the military protection of others—even though Japan's defenses were far from inconsiderable.

Epilogue

H IROHITO DIED A CONTENTED MAN. THE FIRST QUARTER-CENTURY OF HIS rule, from 1921 until 1945, had ended as a spectacular and appalling disaster for his nation (and many others besides); the next 45 years had been ones of national reconstruction and economic expansion which had left Japan second only to the United States as the most powerful economy on earth: in addition, Japan was militarily powerful and politically respected. It had overcome the trauma of military defeat and foreign occupation with dignity and panache; and it regarded the period as no more than a probably inevitable stage in its historical evolution to national greatness.

After all, its great colonial enemies had been forced out of Asia after 1945, a triumph for Japan's prewar objectives; the Russian and Chinese Communist empires had tried to fill their places, but had largely failed; and Japan's economic primacy in Asia was not in doubt, nor was the extent of its penetration of Asian economies. As for the American shogun, the only foreigner who had dared to tell the Emperor what to do to his face, he was long dead and forgotten.

To a new generation of Japanese and indeed Americans, MacArthur seems from another age, his father a Civil War veteran, with his nineteenth-century sense of style, America's only imperial proconsul with his regal airs and haughty self-importance. History has largely swallowed President Truman's version of events, and a popular image of MacArthur lingers as the half-crazed anti-communist (often confused with his crude and rabid near-namesake Senator McCarthy) who nearly started the Third World War, spurned his President's orders and even contemplated the nuclear bombing of China (he was one of several models for Kubrick's Dr. Strangelove).

The truth, as we have seen, was very different. But Hirohito and the Japanese establishment ruthlessly played their part in seeking to exorcise this extraordinary figure from their national consciousness. During the

Senate hearings following MacArthur's return, he was asked what the difference was between the Japanese and German occupations.

> Well, the German problem is a completely and entirely different one from the Japanese problem. The German people were a mature race.
>
> If the Anglo-Saxon was say 45 years of age in his development, in the sciences, the arts, divinity, culture, the Germans were quite as mature. The Japanese, however, in spite of their antiquity measured by time, were in a very tuitionary condition. Measured by the standards of modern civilization, they would be like a boy of twelve as compared with our development of 45 years.
>
> Like any tuitionary period, they were susceptible to following new models, new ideas. You can implant basic concepts there. They were still close enough to origin to be elastic and acceptable to new concepts.
>
> The German was quite as mature as we were. Whatever the German did in dereliction of the standards of modern morality, the international standards, he did deliberately. He didn't do it because of a lack of knowledge of the world. He didn't do it because he stumbled into it to some extent as the Japanese did. He did it as a considered policy in which he believed in his own military might, in which he believed that its application would be a shortcut to the power and economic domination that he desired.

It was a bad public slip during a long session of questioning, although one which had the ring of truth. But it provided the necessary excuse for the Japanese government to portray him as a clapped-out racist and imperialist. Plans for memorials to MacArthur in Japan were abandoned. When the Peace Treaty in San Francisco was signed in September 1951, Truman in an appalling display of petty-mindedness did not invite the man who had made it all possible—and nor did the Japanese insist he attend: it was *Hamlet* without the prince. It had been necessary to tarnish MacArthur because otherwise his popularity would live on among a people for whom he had been the only liberator in their history—a liberator from the oppression of their own elites.

With the coronation of the new Emperor, Akihito, the final traces of MacArthur's occupation seemed to have been expunged. Even in renouncing his divinity, Hirohito had not renounced his direct descent from the sun goddess—which was itself a major contradiction, nullifying the renunciation, for if he was descended from a god, surely he was still divine? Now divinity had returned with a vengeance to the imperial institution. Indeed anyone observing the imperial coronation of November 1990 might have felt he was not just in another age, but on another planet.

Behind the society moths, the police cordons, the crowds and the bombs, there was a Bunraku puppet show come to life. The marionette-style figure at the center of the enthronement tableau was dressed in a billowing rust-colored dressing gown, while the black forage cap on his head was surmounted by a three-foot-high plume; beside him, his tiny wife resembled a porcelain figure imprisoned in the exquisite symmetry of the five-layered kimono, heavier than her, that cascaded from her shoulders and waist.

The new Emperor of Japan was perched on the Takamikura, an intricately carved purple-and-laqueur stage with a canopy surmounted by a golden phoenix, representing Mount Takachiho where the Sun Goddess, Amaterasu Omikami, is said to have placed her grandson in 600 BC to initiate the dynasty that has spawned 125 emperors in unbroken succession.

Ten days later, as the celebration surrounding the imperial enthronement came to a head, on November 22, 1990, the ritual known as the Daijosai, the "Great Food-offering Ceremony," was staged. The Emperor took a purifying bath, then walked along a carpet that was laid before him and rolled up behind, to symbolize a passage between heaven and earth. Accompanied by two women priests, he entered a bedchamber and offered the first rice of the season to the Sun Goddess; then he ate some himself, accompanied by millet and rice wine. The ceremony was secret, but according to most scholars, the Emperor then lay on the bed and had mock sexual intercourse with the Sun Goddess, being reborn as a living God himself.

This man-become-god emerged in 1990 to preside over a country that was economically second only to the United States, and twice the size of Germany, with private financial assets of $7 trillion—about 14 times the total annual economy of Great Britain—which were growing at the rate of some $800 billion a year. A society which owned the four biggest banks in the world and most of the skyscrapers of Los Angeles. A people at the most innovative and futuristic edge of world technology, with the skills to adapt and mass-market shape-changing titanium alloys to make bra frames and water-absorptive resins to make diapers. An industrial power whose achievement in the fields of car assembly, electronic goods, photographic equipment, memory chips and robotics had turned Canon, Mitsubishi, Hitachi, Fujitsu and Toyota into household names the world over.

The unreality of an ancient pagan animist ceremony more appropriate to anthropological study or a science fiction comic strip than the world's most advanced country, causing the normally bustling streets of central Tokyo to be closed off by some 37,000 police, was striking. The temptation for most observers was to dismiss the enthronement as quaint and irrelevant: opinion polls showed that only 13 percent of Japanese were seriously interested in their first Imperial coronation in 62 years.

Both responses were misguided. The ceremony marked a direct reversal of the enforced renunciation of divine status undertaken by Emperor Hirohito at General MacArthur's behest in 1946. While the new Emperor Akihito became constitutionally no more than a "symbol of the state," rather than Japan's supreme governing authority, and the Prime Minister, Toshiki Kaifu, was accorded equal status at the ceremony, the sacred Shinto rites, in the eyes of most ordinary Japanese, reasserted the throne's former supremacy in a country where obeisance to authority and seniority remain binding forces. Nor was the ancient ceremony at odds with Japan's relentless obsession with progress and innovation: the views of the general public still counted for less than those of the country's perennial governing class to an extent unmatched in the major Western democracies. The consensus within that class was that the time had come to restore the institution of Emperor to its former glory, if not power.

The decision could not have been taken lightly. The imperial institution enshrined, obviously, the continuity of the Japanese nation; but it also symbolized national consensus in a state with a bewildering variety of powers, factions and classes that make strong leadership virtually impossible. The Emperor was a figure that represented a Japan united only in its intense competitive defensiveness toward the outside world and in its elaborately structured system of deference toward authority. As between the major centers of Japanese power—the civil service, banking and industry, the politicians, the armed forces—there was no clear hierarchy. In most constitutional monarchies, the institution was a figurehead at the apex of a system in which the will of the people expressed through democratic elections was sovereign. In Japan, the will of the people counted for little: the formal supremacy of the Emperor was necessary to reconciling the conflicting claims to sovereignty of competing interests. The danger was that the Emperor could become a pawn of one of them—as has often happened throughout Japan's history.

It is unwise to deride the pinnacle of any country's social and political system, however anachronistic it might seem. The reversion to tradition at the enthronement ceremony marked the growing self-confidence of newly rich Japan in its past: a self-confidence that barely recognized the transgressions that caused the Pacific War. Just weeks before the coronation, the ministry of education, which vets history textbooks, censored an eye witness wartime account of how soldiers threw babies in the air and caught them on bayonets. Two years before, Prime Minister Noboru Takeshita suggested that it was not clear who was the aggressor in the Pacific War. Yasuhiro Nakasone, the country's most impressive recent leader, visited the Yasukuni shrine in Tokyo which glorifies the Japanese soldiers in that war. The extremist nationalism so much in evidence in the buildup to the Pacific War had not entirely disappeared, either: in January 1990, the mayor of Nagasaki, Hitoshi Motoshima, was shot in front of his city hall by right-wing fanatics a month after asserting that Emperor Hirohito bore some responsibility for the war.

In recent years visits to the shrine by Japanese Prime Ministers have become almost routine. The shrine contains, along with the remains of the executed war criminals, including Tojo, exhibits that openly glorify their actions, argue that Japan was seeking to free Asia from western imperialism and that the United States forced Japan into war, and glosses over Japanese atrocities such as the Rape of Nanking as though they never happened. Visiting the shrine in October 2005, Japan's increasingly nationalist prime minister, Junichiro Koizumi, remarked insensitively of Chinese and Korean protests, "no foreign government should criticise the way we honor our war dead."

The questions every student of the world's emerging superpower had to answer were whether the events that led to the militarist hurricane in the Far East in the middle of this century were an aberration in Japan's history or a natural development; and whether the Japanese system, as it regained its self-confidence, was reverting to some of the old ways, or had matured beyond them. Japan has shown no sign of carrying out the necessary public self-examination; the nature of Emperor Akihito's enthronement suggest a disturbing regression. The three mainstays of Japan's social cohesion—division at the top, that can only be reconciled through elaborate consensus-building, the rigid hierarchy in social and working life symbolized by a divine Emperor, and intense nationalism and distrust of foreigners—seemed to have survived Hiroshima and Nagasaki.

Hirohito, just after surrendering to the Allies, composed a *waka*, a short, allegorical classic verse:

> Under the heavy snow of winter,
> The pine tree bends,
> But does not break,
> Or change its color.
> People should be like this.

Who won in the end, Little Boy or the Emperor? By the time of Akihito's enthronement ceremony 45 years later, the answer seemed much less clear than on August 5, 1945.

Thus the defeat of the shogun MacArthur in June 1951 amounted to an imperial restoration, no less significant than that nearly a century earlier in which the Meiji Emperor had taken the place of the Tokugawa shogun. Hirohito after 1951 was once again at the apex of a Japanese pyramid which consisted of the bureaucratic class, first and foremost, the great economic combines and a now reduced but still powerful military class. At the bottom remained the elected politicians and the Japanese people, expressing their will through elections but enjoying very little real authority.

It would be wrong, though, to view Japan as unchanged by the MacArthur shogunate. The fightback of Japan's old elites to absolute authority has been long, and is far from complete. The occupation left behind a land reform which has proved impossible to reverse and has created a class of independent-minded farmers in Japan with disproportionate political influence. So far Article Nine has proved impossible to reverse, in spite of the existence of powerful armed forces, because of the popular outcry that would ensue. The armed forces have clawed back most of their power and privileges, but still play second fiddle to the samurai-in-suits, the Japanese salarymen whose success has been a much greater accomplishment than the military adventurism of the 1930s and 1940s—although as the economic miracle has faltered over the past decade this has been tarnished. Above all, Japan shows precious little remorse for its prewar policies and the Emperor has regained his position of primacy. It often seems today as if MacArthur and the occupation had never been.

Yet the shogun sowed a seed, that of popular sovereignty, if not among the elites then among the ordinary people: the strength of its growth will not be tested until the system itself comes under crisis—which may not be all that far away as Japanese politicians become more overtly nationalist and the economy falters. It was the appearance of Commodore Perry's wooden black ships that caused Japan to change irreparably and engage with the world a century before MacArthur's shogunate; it is too soon to write off the transformation that another American so boldly attempted. Perhaps MacArthur's shogunate has grown deeper popular roots than is widely appreciated.

For the moment, the sickly, falsely modest absolute monarch who unexpectedly transformed himself from prospective war criminal to skillful mass-politician after the Second World War appears to have comprehensively outwitted the romantic, vainglorious idealist that was Japan's only foreign ruler in its history. But the struggle between these two opposites, Emperor and shogun, has not yet ended with their deaths; history has a longer perspective.

The last word must go to that perhaps most extraordinary of all twentieth-century Americans, Douglas MacArthur. Winston Churchill and Richard Nixon considered him among the most influential of Americans in world history. In his vanity, arrogance, prickliness, sense of destiny, scorn of politicians, aloofness, impetuousness and ambition, as well as his readiness to violate legal and constitutional norms, there is much to dislike about MacArthur. He was perhaps the American military figure who came closest to staging a Latin American-style pronunciamento in the seat of American government, Washington, D.C.

But this was also the man who all his life risked death in order to be at the front with his men in an age when generals had become bureaucrats issuing distant orders from comfortable headquarters; who launched the basis for modern officer training at West Point; who as chief of staff established the foundations of the modern American army; who staged one of the most spectacularly successful retreats in history, chaperoning two armies safely into the Bataan Peninsula—and then withstood a prolonged siege that caught the imagination of the world; who battled across the Pacific in a series of superbly imaginative actions that minimized casualties to fulfill his pledge to return to the Philippines; who was far-sighted enough to object—uniquely among senior American commanders—to the dropping of the two atomic bombs on Japan; who defied his own vengeful countrymen to show mercy and magnanimity to occupied Japan; who sought to introduce democracy, human rights and social justice to temper one of the most authoritarian societies in the world; who saved South Korea from being overrun and staged one of the most brilliant amphibious operations in military history at Inchon; and who was later to challenge the wisdom of America's Vietnam commitment before the event.

Truly, he bore the stamp of greatness. He was the last American hero.

SELECTED BIBLIOGRAPHY

ONE: THE MEIJI ERA

Abe, Yoshiya. "Religious Freedoms under the Meiji Constitution." *Contemporary Religions in Japan,* December 1969.

Akita, George. *Foundations of Constitutional Government in Modern Japan, 1868-1900.* New Jersey: Princeton UP, Princeton, 1967.

Barr, Pat. *The Coming of the Barbarians.* London: Macmillan, 1967.

____. *The Deer Cry Pavilion.* London: Macmillan, 1968. Both are highly readable.

Beasley, W.G. *The Meiji Restoration.* Stanford, California: Stanford UP, 1972.

Beckman, George M. *The Modern History of Japan.* New York: Praeger, 1963.

____. *The Making of the Meriji Constitutions.* Westport: Green Press, 1957.

Borton, Hugh. *Japan's Modern Century.* New York: Ronald Press, 1955.

Boxer, C.R. *The Christian Century in Japan.* London: Cambridge UP, 1967.

Colcutt, Martin, Jansen, Marius and Kumakura Isao. *Cultural Atlas of Japan.* Oxford: Phaidon, 1988.

Conroy, Hilary. *The Japanese Seizure of Korea.* Philadelphia: Pennsylvania UP, 1960.

Crowley, James. "From Closed Door to Empire," In *Modern Japanese Leadership,* edited by B. Silberman and H.O. Harootunian. Tucson: Arizona UP, 1966.

Gluck, Carol. *Japan's Modern Myths.* Princeton: Princeton UP, 1985.

Hackett, Roger. *Yamagata Aritomo in the Rise of Modern Japan, 1838-1922.* Cambridge, Mass., 1971.

Hardacre, Helen. *Shinto and the State.* Princeton: Princeton UP, 1989.

Havens, Thomas R. *Nishi Amane and Modern Thought.* Princeton: Princeton UP, 1970.

Hirschmeier, Johannes. *The Origins of Entrepreneurship in Meiji Japan.* Cambridge, Mass.: Harvard UP, 1964.

Holtom, Daniel C. *Modern Japan and Shinto Nationalism.* New York: Paragon, 1943.

____. *The National Faith of Japan.* New York: E.P. Dutton, 1938.

Hozumi, Hobushige. *Ancestor Worship and Japanese Law.* Tokyo: Maruzen, 1912.

Ike, Nobutake. *The Beginnings of Political Democracy in Japan.* Baltimore: John Hopkins Press, 1950.

Irokawa Daikichi. *The Culture of the Meiji Period.* Translated by Marius Jansen. Princeton: Princeton UP, 1985.

Ito, Hirobumi. *Commentaries on the Constitution of the Empire of Japan.* Translated by Ito Miyoji. Tokyo: Igirisu Horitsu Gakko, 1889.

Jansen, Marius B. "The Meiji State, 1868-1912." In *Modern East Asia: Essays in Interpretation,* James Crowley (ed.). New York: Harcourt Brace Jovanovich, 1970.

Keene, Donald. *The Sino-Japanese War of 1894-5*. Tokyo: Kodansha, 1971.
____. *Japanese Culture in Landscapes and Portraits*. Tokyo: Kodansha, 1971.
Kennedy, Malcolm. *A History of Japan*. London: Wiedenfeld & Nicolson, 1963.
Kinmouth, Earl. *The Self-Made Man in Meiji Japanese Thought*. Berkeley: California UP, 1981.
Kishimoto, Hideo. *Japanese Religion in the Meiji Era*. Tokyo: Obunsha, 1956.
Lehmann, Jean-Pierre. *The Image of Japan: From Feudal Isolation to World Power, 1850-1950*. London: Allen & Unwin, 1978.
Livingston, Jon, Moore, Joe, and Oldfather, Felicia. *Imperial Japan, 1800-1945*. New York: Random House, 1973.
Lockwood, William. *The Economic Development of Japan*. New Jersey: Princeton UP, Princeton, 1954.
McLaren, Walter. *A Political History of Japan during the Meiji Period*. London: George Allen & Unwin, 1916.
Marshall, Byron K. "Professors and Politics: The Meiji Intellectual Elite." *Journal of Japanese Studies*, winter 1977.
Masao, Muruyama. *Thought and Behavior in Modern Japanese Politics*. Ed. Ivan Morris. London: Oxford UP, 1963.
Mason, R.H.P. *Japan's First General Election, 1890*. Cambridge: Cambridge UP, 1969.
Mayo, Marlene. *The Emergence of Imperial Japan*. Lexington: D.C. Heath, 1970.
Minami, Ryoshin. *The Turning Point in Economic Development: Japan's Experience*. Tokyo: Kinokuniya, 1973.
Morioka, Kinomi. "The Appearance of Ancestor Religion in Modern Japan." *Japanese Journal of Religious Studies*. Tokyo: June-September 1977.
Morris, Ivan. *The World of the Shining Prince*. London: Oxford UP, 1964.
____. *The Nobility of Failure*. London: Oxford UP, 1975.
Murdoch and Yamagata. *A History of Japan*. London: Routledge & Kegan Paul, 1949.
Nobutake, Ike. *The Beginnings of Political Democracy in Japan*. Baltimore: John Hopkins Press, 1950.
Norbeck, Edward. *Religion and Society in Modern Japan*. Houston: Rice University, 1970.
Norman, E.H. *Japan's Emergence as a Modern State*. New York: Institute of Pacific Relations, 1940.
____. *Soldier and Peasant in Japan*. New York: Institute of Pacific Relations, 1943.
Okamoto, Shumpei. *The Japanese Oligarchy and the Russo-Japanese War*. New York: Columbia UP, 1970.
Orchard, John. *Japan's Economic Position*. New York: McGraw-Hill, 1930.
Passin, Herbert. *Society and Education in Japan*. New York: Columbia UP, 1965.
Patrick, Hugh (ed.). *Japanese Industrialisation and Its Social Consequences*. Berkeley: California UP, 1976.
Pittau, Joseph. *Political Thought in Early Meiji Japan, 1868-1889*. Cambridge, Mass.: Harvard UP, 1967.
Pyle, Kenneth. *The New Generation in Meiji Japan*. Berkeley: California UP, 1969.
Reischauer, Edwin. *Japan: The Story of a Nation*. London: Duckworth, 1970. .
____. *Japan: Government and Politics*. New York: Nelson, 1939.
Robertson Scott, J.W. *The Foundations of Japan*. New York: Appleton, 1922.
Sadler, A.L. *The Life of Shogun Tokugawa Ieyasu*. Tokyo: Tuttle, 1978.
Sansom, G.B. *Japan: A Short Cultural History*. New York: Appleton-Century-Crofts, 1943.
____. *A History of Japan*. London: Cresset Press, 1964.

Scalopino, Robert A. *Democracy and the Party Movement in Pre-War Japan.* Berkeley: California UP, 1953.

Scheiner, Irwin. *Christian Converts and Social Protest in Meiji Japan.* Berkeley: California UP, 1970.

Shigenobu, Okuma. *Fifty Years of New Japan.* London: Smith, Elder, 1909.

Shively, Donald. *The Japanisation of the Middle Meiji.* New Jersey: Princeton UP, Princeton, 1971.

Smethurst, Richard J. *A Social Basis for Prewar Japanese Militarism: The Army and the Rural Community.* Berkeley: California UP, 1974.

Smith, T.C. "The Japanese Village in the Seventeenth Century." In John Hall and Marius Jansen, *Studies in the Institutional History of Early Modern Japan.* Princeton: Princeton UP, 1968.

———. *Political Change and Industrial Development in Japan.* Stanford: Stanford UP, 1955.

———. *Agrarian Origins of Modern Japan.* Stanford: Stanford UP, 1959.

Smith, Warren W. *Confucianism in Modern Japan.* Tokyo: Hokuseido Press, 1959.

Spaulding, Robert M. *Imperial Japan's Higher Civil Service Examinations.* Princeton: Princeton UP, 1967.

Statler, Oliver. *Japanese Inn.* New York: Random House, 1961.

Storry, Richard. *A History of Modern Japan.* London: Penguin, 1960.

Takane, Masaaki. *The Political Elite in Japan.* Berkeley: California UP, 1981.

Tiedemann, Arthur E. *An Introduction to Japanese Civilization.* New York: Columbia UP, 1974.

Titus, David. *Palace and Politics in Prewar Japan.* New York: Columbia UP, 1974.

Tokutomi, Kenjiro. *Footprints in the Snow.* Translated by Kenneth Strong. Tokyo: Tuttle, 1971.

Totten, George O. *The Social Democratic Movement in Prewar Japan.* New Haven: Yale UP, 1966.

Wakukawa, Seiyei. *The Japanese Farm Tenancy System in Japan's Prospect.* Cambridge, Mass.: Harvard UP, 1946.

Walworth, Arthur. *Black Ships off Japan.* New York: Alfred Knopf, 1941.

Waswo, Ann. *Japanese Landlords: The Decline of a Rural Elite.* Berkeley: California UP, 1977.

Yanagida, Kunio. *Japanese Manners and Customs in the Meiji Era.* Tokyo: Obunsha, 1957.

Yazaki, Takeo. *Social Change and the City in Japan.* Tokyo: Japan Publications, 1968.

TWO: THE THIRTIES

Agawa, Hiroyuki. *The Reluctant Admiral.* Tokyo: Kodansha, 1982.

Bamba, Nobuya. *Japanese Diplomacy in a Dilemma.* Vancouver, 1972.

Beasley, W.G. *Japanese Imperialism, 1894-1945.* Oxford: Clarendon Press, 1987.

Behr, Edward. *Hirohito.* London: Hamish Hamilton, 1989.

Bergamini, David. *Japan's Imperial Conspiracy.* New York: William Morrow, 1971.

Bisson, T.A. "Increase of Zaibatsu predominance in Wartime Japan." *Pacific Affairs,* March 1945.

———. "The Zaibatsu's Wartime Role." *Pacific Affairs,* December 1945.

Bix Herbert. *Hirohito and the Making of Modern Japan.* London: Duckworth, 2000.

———. "Japanese Imperialism and the Manchurian Economy, 1900-1931." *China Quarterly,* 51.

Borton, Hugh. *Japan since 1931: Its Political and Social Development.* New York, 1940.

Boyle, John. *China and Japan at War, 1937-45.* Standford: Stanford UP, 1972.

Brown, Delmer. *Nationalism in Japan.* Berkeley: California UP, 1955.

Butow, Robert. *Tojo and the Coming of War.* Princeton: Princeton UP, 1961.

Byas, Hugh. *Government by Assassination.* New York: Alfred Knopf, 1942.

Coffey, Thomas. *Imperial Tragedy.* World Publishing Co., 1970.

Cohen, Jerome. *Japan's Economy in War and Reconstruction.* Minneapolis, 1949.

Connors, Lesley. *The Emperor's Adviser, Kinmochi Saionji.* New York: Croom Helm, 1987.

Coo, Alvin, and Conroy, Hilary. *China and Japan: A Search for Balance Since World War I.* Santa Barbara, 1978.

Cowan, C.D., ed. *The Economic Development of China and Japan.* London, 1964.

Craigie, Sir Robert. *Behind the Japanese Mask.* London: Hutchinson, 1945.

Crowley, James. *Japan's Quest for Autonomy.* Princeton: Princeton UP, 1966.

____. *Japan's Military Foreign Policies in Japan's Foreign Policy, 1868-1941.* New York, 1974.

Duus, Peter. *Party Rivalry and Political Change in Taisho Japan.* Cambridge: Harvard UP, 1968.

Feis, Herbert. *The Road to Pearl Harbor.* Princeton: Princeton UP, 1950.

Gayn, Mark. *Japan Diary.* New York: William Sloan, 1948.

Goodman, Grant (ed.). *Imperial Japan and Asia: A Reassessment.* New York, 1967.

Grew, Joseph. *Ten Years in Japan.* London: Hammond, 1945.

Guillain, Robert. *I Saw Tokyo Burning.* London: John Murray, 1981.

Hadley, Eleanor. *Anti-trust in Japan.* Princeton: Princeton UP, 1970.

Halliday, Jon. *A Political History of Japanese Capitalism.* New York, 1975.

Harada, Kumao. *Prince Saionji and the Political Situation.* Tokyo: Iwanami Shoten, 1956.

Hata, Ikuhito. *The Emperor's Five Decisions.* Tokyo: Kodansha, 1984.

Havens, Thomas. *Farm and Nation in Modern Japan.* Princeton: Princeton UP, 1974.

Hewes, Lawrence. *Japan: Land and Men.* Iowa State College Press, 1955.

Hosoya, Chihiro. "Japanese Documents on the Siberian Intervention, 1917-22." *Journal of Law and Politics,* 1960.

Ikei, Asaru. "Japan's Response to the Chinese Revolution of 1911." *Journal of Asian Studies,* 1966.

Inoue, Kiyoshi. *The Formation of Japanese Imperialism.* Tokyo, 1972.

____. *The Emperor's Responsibilities.* Tokyo: Gendai Hyoronsha, 1975.

Iriye, Akira. *Across the Pacific: An Inner History of American-East Asian Relations.* New York, 1967.

____. *After Imperialism: The Search for a New Order in the Far East, 1921-31.* Cambridge, Mass.: Cambridge UP, 1965.

____. *Pacific Estrangement: Japanese and American Expansion, 1897-1911.* Cambridge, Mass.: Cambridge UP, 1972.

____. "The Failure of Military Expansionism." In J.W. Morley, ed., *Dilemmas of Growth in Prewar Japan.* Princeton: Princeton UP, 1971.

Harries, Meirion and Susie. *Soldiers of the Sun.* London: Heinemann, 1991.

Jansen, Marius B. *Japan and China: From War to Peace, 1894-1972.* Chicago, 1975.

____. *The Japanese and Sun Yat-Sen,* London: 1954.

____. "Yawata, Hanyehping and the 21 Demands." *Pacific Historical Review,* 23, 1954.

Jones, F.C. *Japan's New Order in East Asia: Its Rise and Fall, 1937-45.* London, 1954.

____. *Manchuria since 1931.* Cambridge, Mass.: Cambridge UP, 1949.

Kajima, Morinosuke. *The Diplomacy of Japan, 1894-1922.* Tokyo, 1980.

Kanroji, Osanaga. *The Emperor and Poems and Horses.* Tokyo: Shuken Asahi, 1967.

____. *Hirohito, an Intimate Portrait.* Los Angeles: Gateway, 1975.

Kato, Matsuo. *The Lost War.* New York: Alfred Knopf, 1946.

Kawahara, Toshiaki. *Hirohito and His Times.* Tokyo: Kodansha International, 1990.

Kawai, Kazuo. *Japan's American Interlude.* Chicago: Chicago UP, 1960.

Kido, Koichi. *Nikkei.* Tokyo: Daigaku Shuppankai, 1966.

Kim, Eugene. *Education in Korea under Japanese Colonial Rule.* Kalamazoo: Western Michigan UP, 1973.

——. *The Japanese colonial Administration in Korea.* Kalamazoo: Western Michigan UP, 1973.

Lockwood, William. *The Economic Development of Japan.* Princeton: Princeton UP, 1964.

Li, Lincoln. *The Japanese Army in North China, 1937-41.* Tokyo, 1975.

Lowe, Peter. *Great Britain and Japan 1911-15.* London, 1969.

McCormack, Gavan. *Chang Tso-Lin in North-East China, 1911-28.* Stanford: Stanford UP, 1977.

Maruyama, Masao. *Thought and Behavior in Modern Japanese Politics.* London: Oxford UP, 1963.

Maxon, Yale. *Control of Japanese Foreign Policy.* Berkeley: California UP, 1957.

Mayo, Marlene, ed. *The Emergence of Imperial Japan.* Lexington, 1970.

Miller, Fran O. *Minobe Tatsukichi.* Berkeley: California UP, 1965.

Montgomery, Michael. *Imperialist Japan.* London: Christopher Helm, 1988.

Morgan Young, A. *Imperial Japan.* London: Allen & Unwin, 1938.

Morley, James W., ed. *Deterrent Diplomacy: Japan, Germany and the USSR, 1935-40.* New York, 1976.

——., ed. *Japan Erupts.* New York, 1984.

——., ed. *Japan's Foreign Policy, 1868-1941: A Research Guide.* New York, 1974.

——., ed. *The China Quagmire: Japan's Expansion on the Asian Continent, 1933-41.* New York, 1983.

——., ed. *The Fateful Choice: Japan's Advance into South East Asia, 1939-40.* New York, 1976.

Morris, Ivan, ed. *Japan, 1931-45: Militarism, Fascism, Japanism?* Oxford: OUP, 1964.

Mosley, Leonard. *Hirohito, Emperor of Japan.* New York: Prentice Hall, 1967. Still vigorously readable if a trifle dated.

Myers, Ramon and Peattie, Mark, eds. *The Japanese Colonial Empire, 1895-1945.* Princeton: Princeton UP, 1984.

Nahm, Andrew, ed. *Korea under Japanese colonial Rule.* Kalamazoo: Western Michigan UP, 1973.

Nakamura, Takafusa. *Economic Growth in Prewar Japan.* London, 1983.

——. *Alliance in Decline: A Study in Anglo-Japanese Relations, 1908-23.* London, 1972.

Ogata, Sadako. *Defiance in Manchuria.* Berkeley: California UP, 1964.

Oka, Yoshitake. *Konoye Fumimaro: A Political Biography.* Tokyo, 1983.

Pacific War Research Society. *Japan's Longest Day.* Tokyo: Kodansha International, 1968.

Packard, Jerrold M. *Sons of Heaven.* New York: Scribners, 1987.

Peattie, Mark R. *Ishiwara Kanji and Japan's confrontation with the West.* Princeton: Princeton UP, 1974.

Roberts, J.G. *Three Centuries of Japanese Business.* New York, 1973.

Scalopino, Robert A. *The Japanese Communist Movement, 1920-66.* Berkeley: California UP, 1967.

Schumpeter, E.B. (ed.). *The Industrialisation of Japan and Manchukuo, 1930-40.* New York, 1940.

Shillony, Ben-Ami. *Revolt in Japan.* Princeton: Princeton UP, 1973.

Shiroyama, Saburo. *War Criminal: The Life and Death of Koki Hirota.* Tokyo: Kodansha International, 1977.

Silberman, Bernard and Harootunian, H.O., eds. *Japan in Crisis*. Princeton: Princeton UP, 1974.

Steiner, Kurt. *Local Government in Japan*. Stanford: Stanford UP, 1965.

Sugiyama Memorandum. *Hajime Sugiyama*. Tokyo: Hara Shobo, 1967.

Swearingen Roger, and Langer, Paul. *Red Flag in Japan*. Cambridge: Harvard UP, 1952.

Takeuchi, Tatsuji. *War and Diplomacy in the Japanese Empire*. London: Allen & Unwin, 1936.

Terasaki, Gwen. *A Bridge to the Sun*. London: Michael Joseph, 1958.

Toland, John. *The Rising Sun*. New York: Random House, 1970.

Tolischus, Otto. *Tokyo Record*. New York: Reynal & Hitchcock, 1943.

Totten, George, ed. *Democracy in Prewar Japan: Groundwork or Façade?* Boston: D.C. Heath, 1967.

Tsunoda, Ryusaku. *Sources of Japanese Tradition*. New York, 1958.

Wada, Teijun. *American Foreign Policy towards Japan During the Nineteenth Century*. Tokyo, 1928.

Wilson, Dick. *When Tigers Fight*. London: Hutchinson, 1982.

Wilson, George M. *Radical Nationalist in Japan: Kita Ikki, 1883-1937*. Cambridge, Mass.: Harvard UP, 1969.

Young, John W. "The Hara Cabinet and Chang Tso-Lin, 1920-1." *Monumenta Nipponica* 27, 1972.

Yoshida, Shigeru. *Memoirs*. Boston: Houghton Mifflin, 1962.

Yuan Tsing. *The Japanese Intervention in Shantung During World War I in China and Japan*. Santa Barbara, 1978.

THREE: THE PACIFIC WAR AND THE AMERICAN OCCUPATION

Allen, Louis. *Burma, the Longest War*. London: J.M. Dent, 1984. A brilliant account.

Ba, Maw. *Breakthrough in Burma*. New Haven: Yale UP, 1968.

Barbey, Daniel. *MacArthur's Amphibious Navy*. Annapolis: US Naval Institute, 1969.

Beard, Charles A. *President Roosevelt and the Coming of War*. New Haven: Yale UP, 1948.

Belote, James H. *Corregidor: The Saga of a Fortress*. New York: Harper, 1967.

Bennett, Henry Gordon. *Why Singapore Fell*. London: Angus & Robertson, 1944.

Blair, Clay. *MacArthur*. London: Futura, 1977. .

Brooks, Lester. *Behind Japan's Surrender*. New York: McGraw-Hill, 1968.

Burtness, Paul and Ober, Warren, eds. *The Puzzle of Pearl Harbor*. Evanston, Illinois: Row Peterson, 1962.

Busch, Noel. *The Emperor's Sword*. New York: Funk & Wagnalls, 1969.

Butow, R.C.J. *Japan's Decision to Surrender*. London: Oxford UP, 1954.

Byas, Hugh. *Government by Assassination*. Harper, New York, 1958.

Byrnes, James F. *Speaking Frankly*. New York: Harper, 1947.

Bywater, Hector. *The Great Pacific War*. London: Constable, 1925.

Chennault, Claire Lee. *Way of a Fighter*. New York: Putnam, 1949.

Clarke, Hugh and Yamashita, Tokeo. *To Sydney by Stealth*. London: Horowitz, 1966.

Cohen, Jerome. *Japan's Economy in War and Reconstruction*. Minneapolis: University of Minnesota Press, 1949.

Craig, William. *The Fall of Japan*. New York: Dial, 1967.

Davis, Burke. *Get Yamamoto*. New York: Random House, 1969.

Dower, John W. *Embracing Defeat*. New York: Norton, 1999.

Eichelberger, Robert. *Our Jungle Road to Tokyo*. New York: Viking, 1950.

Falk, Stanley. *Bataan: The March of Death*. New York: Norton, 1962.

_____. *Decision at Leyte*. New York: Norton, 1966.

Fuchida, Mitsuo, and Okumiya, Masatake. *Midway: The Battle that Doomed Japan*. Annapolis, Maryland: U.S. Naval Institute, 1955.

Guillain, Robert. *I Saw Tokyo Burning*. London: Murray, 1981.

Havens, Thomas. *Valley of Darkness*. New York: Norton, 1978.

Halsey, William and Bryan. *Admiral Halsey's Story*. New York: McGraw-Hill, 1947.

Hattori, Takushiro. *The Complete History of the Greater East Asia War*. Tokyo: Hara Shobo, 1966.

Hersey, John. *Hiroshima*. New York: Alfred Knopf, 1946.

Higashikuni, Prince Toshihiko. *The War Diary of a Member of the Royal Family*. Nihon, Shuho Sha, 1957.

Holmes, W.J. *Undersea Victory*. New York: Doubleday, 1966.

Homma, Masaharu. *Diary*. Unpublished.

Hull, Cordell. *Memoirs*. New York: Macmillan, 1948.

Hunt, Frazier. *MacArthur and the War Against Japan*. New York: Scribner, 1944.

Ike, Nobutaka. *Japan's Decision for War*. Stanford: Stanford UP, 1967.

Inoguchi, Rikihei, Nakajima, Tadashi, and Pineau, Roger. *The Divine Wind*. Annapolis, Maryland: U.S. Naval Institute, 1958.

Ito, Masanori and Pineau, Roger. *The End of the Imperial Japanese Navy*. New York: Norton, 1962.

Ito, Masashi. *The Emperor's Last Soldiers*. New York: Coward-McCann, 1967.

James, David. *The Rise and Fall of the Japanese Empire*. London: Allen & Unwin, 1951.

Kahn David. *The Code-Breakers*. New York: Macmillan, 1967.

Kase, T. *Journey to the Missouri*. New Haven: Yale UP, 1950.

Kato, Masuo. *The Lost War*. New York: Alfred Knopf, 1946.

Kawai, K. *Japan's American Interlude*. Chicago: University of Chicago UP.

King, Ernest, and Whitehill, Walter, *Fleet Admiral King*. London: Eyre & Spottiswoode, 1953.

Kiyosawa, Kiyoshi. *Diaries in Darkness*. Tokyo: Shuei Sha, 1966.

Kogun. *The Japanese Army in the Pacific War*. Quantico, Virginia: U.S. Marine Corps Association,

Konoye, Fumimaro. *The Konoye Diary*. Tokyo: Kyodo Press, 1968.

____. *My Efforts Rowards Peace*. Tokyo: Nippon Dempo Tsushinsha, 1946.

Lamont, Lansing. *Day of Trinity*. New York: Athenaeum, 1965.

Laurence, William. *Dawn Over Zero*. New York: Alfred Knopf, 1946.

Leahy, William. *I Was There*. New York: Whittesley, 1950.

Lebra, Joyce, ed. *Japan's Geater East Asia Co-Prosperity Sphere in World War II*. London: Oxford UP, 1975.

Lord, Walter. *Day of Infamy*. New York: Holt, Rinehart & Winston, 1957. An unsurpassedly gripping account of Pearl Harbor.

____. *Incredible Victory*. New York: Harper, 1967.

MacArthur, Douglas. *Reminiscences*. New York: McGraw-Hill, 1964.

Moorad, George. *Lost Peace in China*. New York: Button, 1949.

Morison, Samuel Eliot. *Coral Sea, Midway and Submarine Operations*. Boston: Little, Brown & Co., 1949.

Nakasone, Seizen. *Tragedy of Okinawa*. Tokyo: Kacho Shobo, 1951.

Neumann, William. *America Encounters Japan*. Baltimore: John Hopkins Press, 1963.

Nishino, General. *Isle of Death: Guadalcanal*. Tokyo: Masu Shobo, 1956.

Okuyama, Ryoko. *Left Alive on Saipan*. Tokyo: Hara Shobo, 1967.

Omura, Bunji. *The Last Genro*. Philadelphia: Lippincott, 1938.

Peacock, Don. *The Emperor's Guest*. New York: Oleander, 1989.

Perret, Geoffrey. *Old Soldiers Never Die*. London: Andre Deutsch, 1996.

Potter, E.B., and Nimitz, Chester W. *The Great Sea War*. New Jersey: Prentice Hall, 1960.

Rappaport, Armin. *Henry L. Stimson and Japan, 1931-3*. Chicago: Chicago UP, 1963.

Romulo, Carlos. *I Saw the Fall of the Philippines*. New York: Doubleday, 1943.

Roosevelt, Franklin D. *Papers*. New York: Franklin D. Roosevelt Library.

Saeki, S. *The Shadow of Sunrise*. Tokyo: Kodansha International.

Saito, Yoshie. *Deceived History: An Inside Account of Matsuoka and the Tripartite Pact*. Tokyo: Yomiuri Shimbun, 1955.

Shigemitsu, M. *Japan and her Destiny*. New York: Dutton, 1958.

Shillony, Ben-Ami. *Politics and Culture in Wartime Japan*. Oxford: Clarendon Press, 1981.

Shimomura, Kainan. *Notes on the Termination of the War*. Tokyo: Kamakuro Bunko, 1948.

Slim, William J. *Defeat into Victory*. New York: McKay, 1961.

Smith, S.E. *The United States Navy in World War Two*. New York: Morrow, 1966.

Spector, Ronald H. *Eagle Against the Sun*. London: Macmillan, 1980.

____. *The United States Marine Corps In World War Two*. New York: Random House, 1962.

Stewart, Adrian. *The Underrated Enemy*. London: William Kimber, 1987.

Stimson, Henry L. *The Diary of Henry L. Stimson*. New Haven: Yale University Library, 1947.

Storry, Richard. *The Double Patriots*. Boston: Houghton Mifflin, 1957.

Sugano, Shizuko. *The End at Saipan*. Suppan Tokyo: Kyodo Sha, 1959.

Sugiyama, General Hajime. *Notes*. Tokyo: Hara Shobo, 1967.

Takagi, Sokichi. *History of Naval Battles in the Pacific*. Tokyo: Iwanami Shoten, 1949.

Takahashi, Masaye. *The 2/26 Incident*. Pkyo: Chuo Koron Sha, 1965.

Taleja, Thaddeus. *Climax at Midway*. New York: Norton, 1960.

Tanemura, Sako. *Secret Diary of Imperial Headquarters*. Tokyo: Diamond Sha, 1952.

Thorne, Christopher. *Allies of a Kind*. New York, 1978.

Togo, Shigenori. *The Cause of Japan*. New York: Simon & Schuster, 1956.

Toland, John. *But Not in Shame*. New York: Random House, 1961.

____. *The Last 100 Days*. New York: Random House, 1966.

Tolischus, Otto. *Tokyo Record*. New York: Reyna & Hitchcock, 1943.

Tomioka, Sadatoshi. *The Outbreak and Termination of the War*. Tokyo: Mainichi Shimbun, 1968.

Trefousse, Hans Louis. *What Happened at Pearl Harbor?* New York: Twayne, 1958.

Tregaskis, Richard. *Guadalcanal Diary*. New York: Random House, 1943.

Truman, Harry S. *Memoirs*. New York: Doubleday, 1956.

Tsuji, Masanobu. *Guadalcanal*. Nara: Tamba-Shi, 1950.

Wainwright, Jonathan. *General Wainwright's Story*. New York: Doubleday, 1946.

Weller, George. *Singapore Is Silent*. New York: Harcourt, 1943.

Whitney, Courtney. *MacArthur, His Rendezvous with History*. New York: Alfred Knopf, 1956.

Wilcox, Robert. *The Secret War*. New York: Morrow, 1987.

Wilmott, H.P. *Empires in the Balance*. 1982.

Wohlstetter, Roberta. *Pearl Harbor: Warning and Decision*. Stanford: Stanford UP, 1962.

Yabe, Teiji. *Fumimaro Konoye*. Privately printed, 1951-2.

Yamamoto, Jumaichi. *Memoirs of the Greater East Asia War*. Compiled from his papers and privately printed, 1964.

FOUR: HIROSHIMA AND NAGASAKI

Akisuki, Tatsuichiro. *Nagasaki 1945*. Tokyo: Namara Features.

Alperowitz, Gar. *Atomic Diplomacy: Hiroshima and Potsdam*. New York: Simon & Schuster, 1965.

Amrine, Michael, *The Great Decision*. New York: Putnam's, 1959.

Arisue, Seizo. *Memoirs*. Tokyo: Fuyo Shobo, 1974.

Batchelder, Robert. *The Irreversible Decision*. Boston: Houghton Mifflin, 1962.

Bateson, Charles. *The War with Japan*. Sydney: Ure Smith, 1968.

Blackett, P.M.S. *Fear, War and the Bomb*. New York: Whittlesey House, 1948.

Brackman, Arnold C. *The Other Nuremberg*. New York: William Morrow, 1987.

Butow, Robert. *Japan's Decision to Surrender*. Stanford: Stanford UP, 1954.

——. *Tojo and the Coming of the War*. Princeton: Princeton UP, 1961.

Byrnes, James F. *Speaking Frankly*. New York: Harper, 1947.

Campbell, J.W. *The Atomic Story*. New York: Henry Holt, 1947.

Churchill, Sir Winston. *The Second World War*, vol.6. London: Cassell, 1954.

Craig, William. *The Fall of Japan*. London: Weidenfeld & Nicholson, 1968.

Feis, Herbert. *Japan Subdued*. Princeton: Princeton UP, 1961.

——. *The Atomic Bomb and the End of World War II*. Princeton: Princeton UP, 1966.

Giovannitti and Freed. eds. *The Decision to Drop the Bomb*. New York: Coward-McCann, 1965.

Gow, Ian. *Okinawa 1945*. London: Grub Street, 1986.

Groueff, Stephane. *The Manhattan Project*. London: Collins, 1967.

Groves, Leslie R. *Now It Can Be Told*. London: André Deutsch, 1963.

Hachiya, Michihiko. *Hiroshima Diary*. Translated by W. Wells. Chapel Hill: North Carolina UP, 1955.

Hall, J.W. and Jansen, M.B., eds. *Studies in the Institutional History of Early Southern Japan*. Princeton: Princeton UP, 1968.

Hirshfeld, Burt. *A Cloud over Hiroshima*. Folkestone: Bailey Bros & Swinfen, 1974.

Hull, Cordell. *The Memoirs of Cordell Hull*, vol.2. New York: Macmillan, 1948.

Ibuse, Masuki. *Black Rain*. Tokyo: Kodansha International, 1969.

Jungk, Robert. *Brighter than 1000 Suns*. London: Gollancz, 1958.

LeMay, Curtis E. *Mission with LeMay*. New York: Doubleday, 1965.

MacArthur, Douglas. *Reminiscences*. New York: McGraw-Hill, 1964.

Major, John. *The Oppenheimer Hearing*. New York: Stein & Day, 1971.

Miller and Spitzer. *We Dropped the A-Bomb*. New York: Cromwell, 1946.

Nagasaki, City of. *The Records of the Atomic Bombing in Nagasaki*, 1975.

Nagasaki Association. *Report from Nagasaki*. 1980.

Ooghterson, A.W. and Warren, S. *Medical Effects of the Atomic Bomb in Japan*. New York: McGraw-Hill, 1956.

Osada, Arata. *Children of Hiroshima*. New York: Harper & Row, 1980.

Osako, Ichiro. *Hiroshima 1945*. Tokyo: Chuko Shinsho, 1975.

Ota, Y. *Town of Corpses*. Tokyo: Kawade Shobo, 1955.

Takayama, Hitoshi (ed.). *Hiroshima in Memoriam and Today*. Hiroshima Peace Culture Center, 1973.

Thomas, Gordon, and Morgan-Witts, Max. *Ruin from the Air*. London: Hamish Hamilton, 1977.

Togo, Shigenori. *The Cause of Japan*. New York: Simon & Schuster, 1956.

Truman, Harry S. *Year of Decisions: 1945*. Garden City, New York: Doubleday, 1955.

Trumbull, Robert. *Nine Who Survived Hiroshima and Nagasaki*. New York: Dutton, 1957.

FIVE: POST-WAR JAPAN

Abegglen, James C. "The Economic Growth of Japan." *Scientific American*, March 1970.

Abegglen, James and Stalk, George. *Kaisha: the Japanese Corporation*. Tokyo: Tuttle, 1985.

Abegglen, James C. et al. *U.S. Japan Economic Relations*. Berkeley: California UP, 1980.

Adams, T.F.M. and Iwao. *A Financial History of the New Japan*. Tokyo: Kodansha, 1972.

Barnet and Mueller. *Global Reach*. New York: Simon & Schuster.

Beasley, W.G. *The Modern History of Japan*. New York: Tuttle, 1990.

Bisson, T.A. *Japan's War Economy*. New York: Institute of Pacific Relations, 1945.

____. *Prospects for Democracy in Japan*. New York, 1949.

____. *Zaibatsu Dissolution in Japan*. Berkeley: California UP, 1954.

Boltho, Andrea. *Japan: An Economic Survey, 1953-73*. London: Oxford UP, 1975.

Broadbridge, Seymour. *Industrial Dualism in Japan*. Chicago: Aldine, 1966.

Bronte, Stephen. *Japanese Finance*. London: Euromoney Publications, 1982.

Buckley, Roger. *Japan Today*. Cambridge: Cambridge UP, 1990.

Burstein, Daniel. *Yen! Japan's New Financial Empire and Its Threat to America*. New York: Simon & Schuster, 1988.

Buruma, Ian. *A Japanese Mirror*. London: Jonathan Cape, 1984.

Chen, Edward. *Hyper-Growth in Asian Economies*. London: Macmillan, 1979.

Chikushi, Tetsuya. "Young People as a New Human Race." *Japan Quarterly*, summer 1986.

Clark, Rodney. *The Japanese Company*. New Haven: Yale UP, 1979.

Cohen, Jerome. *Japan's Economy in War and Reconstruction*. Minneapolis: Minnesota UP, 1949.

Consider Japan. *The Economist*, London: Duckworth, 1963.

Cortazzi, Hugh. *The Japanese Achievement*. London: Sidgwick & Jackson, 1990. A splendid book.

Craig, Albert (ed.). *Japan: A Comparative View*. Princeton: Princeton UP, 1979.

Crichton, Michael. *Rising Sun*. New York: Alfred Knopf, 1992.

Curtis, Gerald. *The Japanese Way of Politics*. New York: Columbia UP, 1988.

Cusumano, Michael. *The Japanese Automobile Industry*. Cambridge: Harvard UP, 1985.

Dale, Peter. *The Myth of Japanese Uniqueness*. New York: Croom Helm, 1986.

Destler, I.M. *The Textile Wrangle*. Ithaca, New York: Cornell UP, 1979.

Doi, Teruo and Shattuck, Warren (eds.). *Patent and Know-How Licensing in Japan and the United States*. Washington UP, 1977.

Doi, Takeo. *The Anatomy of Dependence*. Tokyo: Kodansha International, 1973.

Dore, Ronald. *British Factory, Japanese Factory*. Berkeley: California UP, 1973.

____. *Taking Japan Seriously*. London: Athlone Press, 1987.

Dunn, Frederick. *Peace-Making and the Settlement with Japan*. Princeton: Princeton UP, 1979.

Emmott, Bill. *The Sun Also Sets*. London: Simon & Schuster, 1989. Well-written and thought-provoking.

____. *Japan's Global Reach*. London: Century Business, 1992.

Fukutake, Tadashi. *Japanese Society Today*. Tokyo: Tokyo UP, 1981.

Gayn, Mark. *Japan Diary*. New York: William Sloane Associates, 1948.

Hadley, Eleanor. *Anti-Trust in Japan*. Princeton: Princeton UP, 1974.

Haitani, Kanji. *The Japanese Economic System*. Lexington: D.C. Heath, 1976.

Halberstam, David. *The Reckoning*. Tokyo: Yohan, 1987.

Hale, David. *Britain and Japan as the Financial Bogeymen of U.S. Politics*. Chicago, 1987.

Halloran, Richard. *Japan: Images and Realities*. Tokyo: Tuttle, 1970.

Harari, Ehud. *The Politics of Labor Legislation in Japan*. Berkeley: California UP, 1973.

Hasegawa, Nyozekan. *Japanese National Character*. Tokyo: Board of Tourist Industry, 1942.

Hata, Ikuhiko. "Japan under the Occupation." *Japan Interpreter,* winter 1976.

Harries, Meirion and Susie. *Sheathing the Sword*. London: Heinemann. A masterly study.

Havens, Thomas. *Farm and Nation in Modern Japan*. Princeton: Princeton UP, 1974.

Henderson, Dan. *Foreign Enterprise in Japan*. Tokyo: Tuttle, 1975.

Hewins, Ralph. *The Japanese Miracle Men*. London: Secker & Warburg, 1967.

Hiraishi, Nagahisa. *Social Security*. Japanese Industrial Relations Series No.5.

Ho, Alfred. *Japan's Trade Liberalisation in the 1960s*. New York: International Arts and Sciences Press, 1973.

Hollerman, Leon. *Japan's Dependency on the World Economy*. Princeton: Princeton UP, 1967.

Horsley, William and Buckley, Roger. Nippon: *New Superpower*. London: BBC Books, 1990.

Imai, Masaaki. *Kaizen, the Key to Japan's Competitive Success*. New York: Random House, 1986.

____. *Never Take Yes for an Answer*. Tokyo: Simul Press, 1975.

____. *Sixteen Ways to Avoid Saying No*. Tokyo: Nihon Keizai Shinbun, 1981.

Inoguchi, Takashi and Okimoto (eds.). *The Political Economy of Japan*. Stanford: Stanford UP, 1988.

Ito, Mitsuharu. "Munitions Unlimited: The Controlled Economy." *Japan Interpreter,* summer 1972.

Itoh, Hirochi. *Japanese Politics: An Inside View*. Ithaca, New York: Cornell UP, 1973.

James, Clayton. *The Years of MacArthur*. Boston, 1985.

Johnson, Chalmers, "Japan: Who Governs?" *Journal of Japanese Studies,* autumn 1975.

____. *Japan's Public Policy Companies*. Washington: American Enterprise Institute, 1978.

____. "Miti and Japanese International Economic Policy." In Robert Scalopino (ed.). *The Foreign Policy of Modern Japan*. Berkeley: California UP, 1977.

____. *MITI and the Japanese Miracle*. Tokyo: Tuttle, 1986.

Kamata, Satoshi. *Japan in the Passing Lane*. London: Unwin, 1984.

Kaplan, Eugene. *Japan: The Government-Business Relationship*. Washington: U.S. Department of Commerce, 1972.

Kearns, Robert. *Zaibatsu America*. New York: Free Press, 1992.

Kennan, George. *Memoirs, 1925-50*. Boston, 1967.

Kosaka, Masataka. *A History of Postwar Japan,* Tokyo: Kodansha, 1972.

Kubota, Akira. *Higher Civil Servants in Postwar Japan*. Princeton: Princeton UP, 1969.

Kuriyama, Takakazu. *New Directions for Japanese Policy in the Changing World of the 1990s*. Tokyo: Ministry of Foreign Affairs, 1990.

Kurzman, Dan. *Kishi and Japan*. New York: Obolensky, 1960.

Lebra, Takie. *Japanese Patterns of Behaviour*. Honolulu: Hawaii UP, 1976.

Lee O-Young. *Small Is Better*. Tokyo: Kodansha, 1984.

Lincoln, Edward. *Japan's Industrial Policies*. Washington: Japan Economic Institute of America, 1984.

____. *Japan: Facing Economic Maturity*. Washington: Brookings, 1988.

Livingston, Jon and Oldfather, Felicia. *Postwar Japan*. New York: Random House, 1973.

Lynn, Leonard. *How Japan Innovates*. Colorado: Westview Press, 1982.

MacArthur, Douglas. *Reminiscences*. New York: McGraw-Hill, 1964.

Magaziner, Ira and Hout, Thomas. *Japanese Industrial Policy*. Berkeley: California University Institute of International Studies, 1981.

Manchester, William. *American Caesar, Douglas MacArthur, 1880-1964*. London: Hutchinson, 1978.

Maruyama, Masao. *Thought and Behavior in Modern Japanese Politics*. London: Oxford UP, 1969.

Matsumura, Yutaka. *Japan's Economic Growth, 1945-60*. Tokyo: Tokyo News Service, 1961.

Moore, Charles. *The Japanese Mind*. Tokyo: Tuttle, 1973.

Munday, Max. *Japanese Manufacturing Investment in Wales*. Cardiff: Wales UP, 1990.

Nakane, Chie. *Japanese Society*. Berkeley: California UP, 1976.

Noda, Nobuo. *How Japan Absorbed American Management Methods*. Manila: Asian Productivity Organisation, 1970.

Ogawa, Terutomo. *Multinationalism, Japanese Style*. Princeton: Princeton UP, 1982.

Ohkawa, Kazushi and Rosovsky, Henry. *Japanese Economic Growth*. Stanford: California, Stanford UP, 1973.

Ohmae, Kenichi. *Beyond National Borders*. Tokyo: Kodansha International.

____. *The Borderless World*. New York: Harper Business, 1990.

____. *The Mind of the Strategist*. New York: McGraw-Hill, 1982.

Passin, Herbert (ed.). *The United States and Japan*. Washington: Columbia Books, 1975.

Patrick, Hugh, and Rosovsky, Henry (eds.). *Asia's New Giant*. Washington: Brookings, 1976.

Peattie, Mark. *Ishiwara Kanji and Japan's Confrontation with the West*. Princeton: Princeton UP, 1975.

Pempel, T.J. (ed.). *Policymaking in Contemporary Japan*. Ithaca, New York: Cornell UP, 1977.

Prestowitz, Clyde. *Trading Places: How We Allowed Japan to Take the Lead*. New York: Basic Books, 1988.

Prindl, Andreas. *Japanese Finance*. New York: Wiley, 1981.

Roberts, John. *Mitsui*. Tokyo: Weatherhill, 1973.

Schaller, Michael. *Douglas MacArthur*. London: Oxford UP, 1989.

____. *The American Occupation of Japan*. London: Oxford UP, 1985.

Seidensticker, Edward. *Tokyo Rising*. New York: Alfred Knopf, 1990.

Shiba, Kimpei and Nozue, Kenzo. *What Makes Japan Tick?* Tokyo: Asahi Evening News Co., 1976.

Shingo, Shigeo. *Study of Toyota Production Systems*. Tokyo: Japan Management Association, 1981.

Shirai, Taishiro, ed. *Contemporary Industrial Relations in Japan*. University of Wisconsin Press, 1983.

Steven, Rob. *Class in Contemporary Japan*. Cambridge: Cambridge UP, 1984.

Stone, P.B. *Japan Surges Ahead*. New York: Praeger, 1969.

Supreme Commander for the Allied Powers. *History of the Non-military Activities of the Occupation of Japan 1945-51*. Washington: National Archives, 1951.

Suzuki, Yoshio (ed.). *The Japanese Financial System*. London: Oxford UP, 1988.

Takana, Kakuei. *Building a New Nation*. Tokyo: Simul Press, 1973.

Thayer, Nathaniel. *How the Conservatives Rule Japan*. Princeton: Princeton UP, 1969.

Thomsen, Harry, et al. *The Evolution of Japanese Direct Investment in Europe*. Brighton: Harvester, 1991.

Tonata, Seiichi. ed. *The Modernisation of Japan*. Tokyo: Institute of Asian Economic Affairs, 1966.

Trevor et al. *Manufacturers and Suppliers in Britain and Japan*. London: Policy Studies Institute, 1991.

Truman, Harry S. *Memoirs*. New York: Doubleday, 1956.

Tsurumi. *A Cultural History of Postwar Japan*. Tokyo: Iwanami Shoten, 1984.

Viner, Aron. *Inside Japan's Financial Markets*. London: Economist Publications, 1987.

Vogel, Ezra. *Japan as Number One*. Tokyo: Tuttle, 1980.

Weinstein, Martin. *Japan's Postwar Defense Policy, 1947-68*. New York: Columbia UP, 1971.

Whitney, Courtney. *MacArthur: His Rendezvous with History*. New York, 1956.

Wickens, Peter. *The Road to Nissan*. New York: Macmillan, 1987.

Wildes, Harry. *Typhoon in Tokyo: The Occupation and Its Aftermath*. New York: Macmillan, 1954.

Willoughby, Charles, and Chamberlain, John. *MacArthur, 1941-51*. New York, 1955.

Wilson, James. "The Rise of the Bureaucratic State." *Public Interest*, fall 1975.

Yamamura, Kozo. *Economic Policy in Postwar Japan*. Berkeley: California UP, 1967.

Yoshida, Shigeru. *The Yoshida Memoirs*. Cambridge: Houghton Mifflin, 1962.

Yoshino, M.Y. *The Japanese Marketing System*. Cambridge, Mass.: MIT Press, 1971.

Zengage, Thomas and Ratcliffe, C. *The Japanese Century: Challenge and Response*. London: Longman, 1988.

SIX: JAPANESE CULTURE

Anderson, Ronald. *Education in Japan: A Century of Modern Development*. Washington: U.S. Dept of Health Education and Welfare, 1975.

Aso, Makoto. *Education and Japan's Modernisation*. Tokyo: Ministry of Foreign Affairs, 1972.

Benedict, Ruth. *The Chrysanthemum and the Sword*. Tokyo: Tuttle, 1954.

Bornoff, Nicholas. *Pink Samurai*. London: Grafton Books, 1991.

Cogan, John. "Should the U.S. Mimic Japanese Education?" *Phi Delta Kappa*, March 1984.

Horio, Teruhisa. *Educational Thought and Ideology in Modern Japan*. Tokyo: Tokyo UP, 1988.

Imai, Masaaki. *Sixteen Ways to Avoid Saying No*. Tokyo: Nihon Keizai, Shinbun, 1981.

Ishihara, Shintaro. *The Japan That Can Say No*. London: Simon & Schuster, 1991.

Joseph, J. *The Japanese*. London: Viking, 1993.

Kenrick, Douglas Moore. *Where Communism Works*. Tokyo: Tuttle, 1988.

Kobayashi, Kaoru. *Japan. The Most Misunderstood Country*. Tokyo: Japan Times, 1984. Perceptive and full of insights.

Martineau, Lisa. *Caught in a Mirror*. London: Macmillan, 1992. .

Murakami, Yoshiol. "Bullying in the Classroom." *Japan Quarterly*, 32.

Nathan, John. *Mishima: A Biography*. Tokyo: Tuttle, 1974.

Nishimura, Hidetoshi. "Educational Reform." *Japan Quarterly*, 37.

Oppenheim, Philip. *New Masters*. London, 1982. Thought-provoking.

Reischaeur, Edwin. *The Japanese Today*. Tokyo: Tuttle, 1988. Highly readable.

Rohlen, Thomas. *Japan's High Schools*. Berkeley: California UP, 1983.

Schooland, Ken. *Shogun's Ghost*. New York: Bergin & Garvey, 1990.

Tasker, Peter. *Inside Japan*. London: Penguin, 1987.

Viner, P. *The Emerging Power of Japanese Money*. Illinois: Dow Jones-Irwin, 1988.

Vining, Elizabeth Gray. *Windows for the Crown Prince*. Tokyo: Tuttle, 1989.

Wolferen, Karel van. *The Enigma of Japanese Power*. New York: Vintage Books, 1989.

Index